Fodor's 3rd Edition

Vietnam

The Guide
for All Budgets

Completely
Updated

Where to Stay, Eat,
and Explore

On and Off
the Beaten Path

When to Go,
What to Pack

Maps, Travel Tips,
and Web Sites

Fodor's Travel Publications • New York, Toronto, London, Sydney, Auckland
www.fodors.com

Fodor's Vietnam

EDITOR: Deborah Kaufman

Editorial Contributors: Van Anh, Lisa Bjorksten, Carissa Bluestone, David Dudenhoefer, Satu Hummasti, David Joiner, William Richardson, Craig Thomas, George Vaughton

Maps: David Lindroth, *cartographer*; Rebecca Baer and Bob Blake, *map editors*

Design: Fabrizio La Rocca, *creative director*; Guido Caroti, *art director*; Jolie Novak, *senior picture editor*; Melanie Marin, *photo editor*

Cover Design: Pentagram

Production/Manufacturing: Yexenia M. Markland

Cover Photo (Thien Mu Pagoda, Hue): Owen Franken

Copyright

Important Tip

Although all prices, opening times, and other details in this book are based on information supplied to us at press time, changes occur all the time in the travel world, and Fodor's cannot accept responsibility for facts that become outdated or for inadvertent errors or omissions. So **always confirm information when it matters,** especially if you're making a detour to visit a specific place.

Special Sales

Fodor's Travel Publications are available at special discounts for bulk purchases for sales promotions or premiums. Special editions, including personalized covers, excerpts of existing guides, and corporate imprints, can be created in large quantities for special needs. For more information, contact your local bookseller or write to Special Markets, Fodor's Travel Publications, 1745 Broadway, New York, NY 10019. Inquiries from Canada should be directed to your local Canadian bookseller or sent to Random House of Canada, Ltd., Marketing Department, 2775 Matheson Boulevard East, Mississauga, Ontario L4W 4P7. Inquiries from the United Kingdom should be sent to Fodor's Travel Publications, 20 Vauxhall Bridge Road, London SW1V 2SA, England.

PRINTED IN THE UNITED STATES OF AMERICA

10 9 8 7 6 5 4 3 2 1

CONTENTS

Maps

ON THE ROAD WITH FODOR'S

A trip takes you out of yourself. Concerns of life at home completely disappear, driven away by more immediate thoughts—about, say, what marvels will beguile the next day, or where you'll have dinner. That's where Fodor's comes in. We make sure that you know all your options, so that you don't miss something that's around the next bend just because you didn't know it was there. Mindful that the best memories of your trip might have nothing to do with what you came to Vietnam to see, we guide you to sights large and small all over the country. You might set out to sail among the jagged limestone islands of Halong Bay, but back at home you find yourself unable to forget sipping coffee and people-watching at sidewalk cafés on the vibrant streets of Ho Chi Minh City. With Fodor's at your side, serendipitous discoveries are never far away.

About Our Writers

Our success in showing you every corner of Vietnam is a credit to our extraordinary writers. Although there's no substitute for travel advice from a good friend who knows your style, our contributors are the next best thing—the kind of people you would poll for travel advice if you knew them.

Lisa Bjorksten, who updated the South-Central Coast and Highlands and Mekong Delta chapters, has a passion for adventure. After graduating from college with a communications degree, Lisa worked as a journalist in Sydney, Australia, for the *Sydney Morning Herald* and *News Limited.* But the travel bug just kept biting, and after several travel forays into the West, Lisa found herself living and working in Ho Chi Minh City. After extensive travel through Southeast Asia, Lisa is now back in Sydney, publishing her articles internationally.

The first time **David Dudenhoefer** visited Southeast Asia, he hitchhiked most of the way from Bangkok to Singapore. This time around he relied more on the local airlines to update the Side Trips to Cambodia chapter. He has contributed to six Fodor's guides during his decade and a half as a freelance journalist, during which time he has worked in 20 countries, writing and taking photos for dozens of newspapers and magazines.

David Joiner, who contributed to the Hanoi chapter, has lived and worked in Vietnam on three separate occasions, twice as a volunteer teacher and once, most recently, as a freelance writer and editor for several travel and cultural publications. Originally from Ohio, he is these days drawn to interesting people and experiences in Asian countries. He often spends his free time in local *bia hoi* (watery draft beer) establishments, worrying over (and not working on) the novel he's told too many people he's writing. He has an MFA in Creative Writing from the University of Arizona.

William Richardson updated Smart Travel Tips, parts of the Hanoi chapter, and the Background and Essentials chapter. An environmental scientist by profession and a businessman by necessity, William has been living in Hanoi since 1994. He has worked as a consultant on small business investments and on environmental conservation in Vietnam. But he prefers to risk life and limb while touring the back roads of Vietnam on a Minsk motorcycle.

Craig Thomas, a recovering lawyer, is a freelance journalist based in Ho Chi Minh City. Craig, who writes for a number of regional newspapers and magazines, updated the Central Coast and Ho Chi Minh City chapters. Committed to one day speaking fluent Vietnamese, he spends his spare time pestering his Vietnamese friends to teach him new and obscure words.

George Vaughton updated the North chapter. A former freelance journalist who wrote articles about Hong Kong and Beijing, where he lived for several years, George is now back home in the United Kingdom studying law.

You can rest assured that you're in good hands—and that no property mentioned in the book has paid to be included. Each has been selected strictly on its merits, as the best of its type in its price range.

How to Use This Book

Up front is Smart Travel Tips A to Z, arranged alphabetically by topic and loaded with tips, Web sites, and contact information. Destination: Vietnam helps get you in the mood for your trip. Subsequent chapters in Vietnam are arranged regionally. All city chapters begin with exploring information, with a section for each neighborhood (each recommending a good tour and listing sights alphabetically). All regional chapters are divided geographically; within each area, towns are covered in logical geographical order, and attractive stretches of road between them are indicated by the designation En Route. To help you decide what you'll have time to visit, all chapters begin with our writers' favorite itineraries. (Mix itineraries from several chapters, and you can put together a really exceptional trip.) The A to Z sections in the chapters list additional resources. At the end of the book you'll find Background and Essentials, including a chronology of Vietnamese history, essays about Vietnam, a Books and Movies section, and a Vietnamese vocabulary and menu guide.

Icons and Symbols

★ Our special recommendations
✕ Restaurant
🏠 Lodging establishment
✕🏠 Lodging establishment whose restaurant warrants a special trip
🐤 Good for kids (rubber duck)
☞ Sends you to another section of the guide for more information
✉ Address
☏ Telephone number
🕐 Opening and closing times
🎟 Admission prices (those we give apply to adults; reduced fees are sometimes available for children, students, and senior citizens)

Numbers in white and black circles ③ ❸ that appear on the maps, in the margins, and within the tours correspond to one another.

For hotels, you can assume that all rooms have private baths, phones, TVs, and air-conditioning unless otherwise noted and that all hotels operate on the European Plan (with no meals) if we don't specify another meal plan. We always list a property's facilities but not whether you'll be charged extra to use them, so when pricing accommodations, do ask what's included. For restaurants, it's always a good idea to book ahead; we mention reservations only when they're essential or are not accepted. All restaurants we list are open daily for lunch and dinner unless stated otherwise; dress is mentioned only when men are required to wear a jacket or a jacket and tie. Look for an overview of local dining-out habits in Smart Travel Tips A to Z and in the Pleasures and Pastimes section that follows each chapter introduction.

Don't Forget to Write

Your experiences—positive and negative—matter to us. If we have missed or misstated something, we want to hear about it. We follow up on all suggestions. Contact the Vietnam editor at editors@fodors.com or c/o Fodor's at 1745 Broadway, New York, NY 10019. And have a fabulous trip!

Karen Cure

Karen Cure
Editorial Director

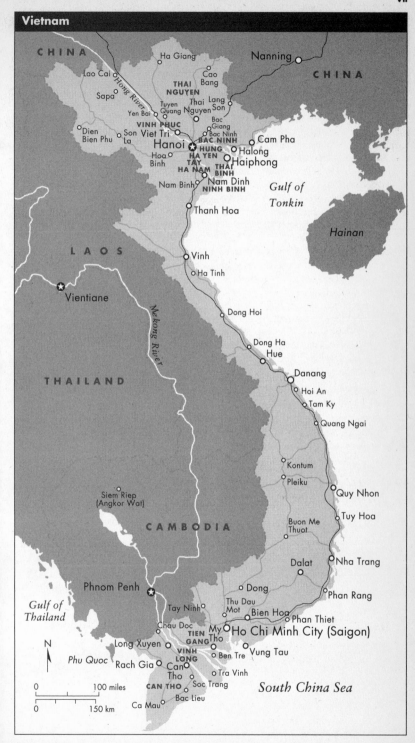

Southeast Asia

CHINA

Guangzhou
Macau
HONG KON

Mandalay
Hanoi
Haiphong

BURMA
(MYANMAR)
LAOS
Luang
Prabang
HAINAN

Pegu
Chiang
Mai
Vientiane

Rangoon
(Yangon)
Hue
Danang

THAILAND
Korat

Bangkok
VIETNAM

Andaman
Sea
Siem Riep

CAMBODIA

Isthmus of
Kra
Phnom Penh
Ho Chi Minh City
(Saigon)

Gulf of
Thailand

PA

Phuket
South China
Sea

Songkhla
Kota
Kinabalu

George Town
WEST
MALAYSIA
MALAYSIA
BRUNEI
SABA

Medan
Kuala Lumpur
SARAWAK

Kuching
BORNEO

SINGAPORE

SUMATRA
KALIMANTAN

KEPULAUAN
Jambi
INDONESIA

Palembang
Banjarmasin

INDIAN OCEAN
GREATER
SUNDA
IS

Jakarta
Java Sea

Bandung
Surabaya

Yogyakarta
JAVA
LE

BALI

LOMBOK

0   500 miles

0   750 km

N

Taipei

TAIWAN

PACIFIC OCEAN

Laoag
LUZON
Baguio

Manila

PHILIPPINES

MINDORO

PALAU

VISAYAS   *SAMAR*

Iloilo City
PANAY

Cebu City

NAN   *NEGROS*

MINDANAO

Sulu Sea

Davao

Celebes Sea

HALMAHERA

BIAK

**PAPUA-
NEW GUINEA**

Makassar Strait

SULAWESI
(The Celebes)

M O L U C C A S

SERAM

IRIAN JAYA

BURU

N D S

Ujung
Pandang

Banda Sea

KEPULAUAN
ARU

Flores Sea

E R   S U N D A   I S L A N D S

KEPULAUAN
TANIMBAR

FLORES   TIMOR

Timor Sea

SUMBA

AUSTRALIA

World Time Zones

Numbers below vertical bands relate each zone to Greenwich Mean Time (0 hrs.).
Local times frequently differ from these general indications,
as indicated by light-face numbers on map.

Algiers, **29**

Anchorage, **3**

Athens, **41**

Auckland, **1**

Baghdad, **46**

Bangkok, **50**

Beijing, **54**

Berlin, **34**

Bogotá, **19**

Budapest, **37**

Buenos Aires, **24**

Caracas, **22**

Chicago, **9**

Copenhagen, **33**

Dallas, **10**

Delhi, **48**

Denver, **8**

Dublin, **26**

Edmonton, **7**

Hong Kong, **56**

Honolulu, **2**

Istanbul, **40**

Jakarta, **53**

Jerusalem, **42**

Johannesburg, **44**

Lima, **20**

Lisbon, **28**

London
(Greenwich), **27**

Los Angeles, **6**

Madrid, **38**

Manila, **57**

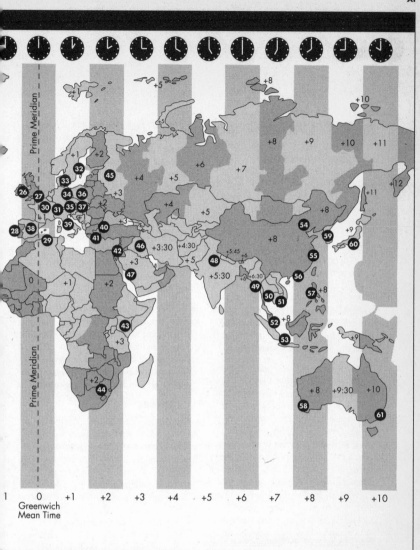

Mecca, **47**
Mexico City, **12**
Miami, **18**
Montréal, **15**
Moscow, **45**
Nairobi, **43**
New Orleans, **11**
New York City, **16**

Ottawa, **14**
Paris, **30**
Perth, **58**
Reykjavík, **25**
Rio de Janeiro, **23**
Rome, **39**
Saigon (Ho Chi Minh City), **51**

San Francisco, **5**
Santiago, **21**
Seoul, **59**
Shanghai, **55**
Singapore, **52**
Stockholm, **32**
Sydney, **61**
Tokyo, **60**

Toronto, **13**
Vancouver, **4**
Vienna, **35**
Warsaw, **36**
Washington, D.C., **17**
Yangon, **49**
Zürich, **31**

ESSENTIAL INFORMATION

ADDRESSES

To find addresses in Vietnam it helps to know a few local practices. You may see addresses with numbers separated by a slash, such as "361/8 Nguyen Dinh Chieu St." This means you should head for No. 361 on Nguyen Dinh Chieu Street and then look for an alley next to the building; you want No. 8 in this alley. When you see addresses with a number followed by a letter, such as "97A," this means there is more than one No. 97 on the street and you need to find the one numbered specifically with an "A." If you see "54bis," look for a building adjacent to No. 54; this is a leftover from the French that means 54½.

The English word *street* (abbreviated St.) is used throughout the book rather than the Vietnamese words *pho* and *duong*. This was done to make sure street names are clear; in Vietnamese, the words pho and duong come before the names of the streets, which can prove very confusing when trying to find your way around. In addition, many Vietnamese refer to streets only by name (without adding pho or duong), so you may only see these words on street signs and maps.

AIR TRAVEL

International flights into Vietnam typically connect through hubs such as Bangkok, Singapore, Manila, Hong Kong, Kuala Lumpur, Phnom Penh, Beijing, Seoul, Osaka, Tokyo, Dubai, Melbourne, Sydney, and Taipei and fly into Ho Chi Minh City and Hanoi. It's also possible to fly into the international airport in Danang, in central Vietnam, via Bangkok. Although negotiations to offer direct U.S.–Vietnam service are ongoing, at press time there were no direct flights between Vietnam and North America. There are also no direct flights to Vietnam from the United Kingdom.

Note that two airlines may jointly operate a connecting flight from an Asian hub, so **ask if your airline operates every segment of your flight**—you may find that your preferred carrier flies only part of the way. For instance, if you purchased a ticket through an international carrier such as Air France, Cathay Pacific, or Thai International Airways but are not flying directly to Hanoi or Ho Chi Minh City, it is possible that your connecting flight into Vietnam will be on Vietnam Airlines.

Some airlines' layovers are short; others, particularly those offering discounted fares, require an overnight stay in a connecting city. Before buying your ticket, **check to see who covers the cost of the hotel—you or the airline—if you have to stay overnight.**

CARRIERS

From the United States, Continental, Delta, Northwest, and United Airlines have flights into Tokyo, Singapore, and Bangkok, which then connect with regional carriers. Although there's no direct service from the United Kingdom, British Airways, Cathay Pacific, and Thai Airways fly to Bangkok and Hong Kong, from which there is at least one daily flight to Ho Chi Minh City and Hanoi. Qantas has direct flights to Ho Chi Minh City from Sydney and Melbourne.

Domestic routes in Vietnam are flown by Vietnam Airlines, which has one of the youngest airplane fleets in the world, and its smaller semiprivate competitor, Pacific Airlines. Despite the appearance of competition, however, ticket prices for both airlines are set by the government.

➤ TO AND FROM THE U.S.: **Continental** (☎ 800/231–0856, WEB www.continental.com). **Delta** (☎ 800/221–1212, WEB www.delta.com). **Northwest** (☎ 800/225–2525, WEB www.

nwa.com). **United Airlines** (☎ 800/241–6522, WEB www.ual.com).

➤ To and from the U.K.: **British Airways** (☎ 08457/733–377, WEB www.britishairways.com). **Cathay Pacific** (☎ 020/8834–8888, WEB www.cathaypacific.com). **Thai Airways** (☎ 020/7491–7953, WEB www.thaiairways.com).

➤ To and from Australia: **Qantas** (☎ 13/1313, WEB www.qantas.com).

➤ Within Vietnam: **Pacific Airlines** (✉ 100 Le Duan St., Dong Da District, Hanoi, ☎ 04/518–1503 or 04/733–2162; ✉ 177 Vo Thi Sau St., District 3, Ho Chi Minh City, ☎ 08/932–5978; WEB www.pacificairlines.com.vn). **Vietnam Airlines** (✉ 25 Trang Tien St., Hoan Kiem District, Hanoi, ☎ 04/832–0320, 04/934–9660, or 04/934–9620; ✉ 116 Nguyen Hue St., District 1, Ho Chi Minh City, ☎ 08/823–0695, 08/823–0696, or 08/829–2118; WEB www.vietnamair.com.vn).

CHECK-IN AND BOARDING

Always **ask your carrier about its check-in policy.** Plan to arrive at the airport about 2 hours before your scheduled departure time for domestic flights and 2½ to 3 hours before international flights. Assuming that not everyone with a ticket will show up, airlines routinely overbook planes. When everyone does, airlines ask for volunteers to give up their seats. In return, these volunteers usually get a certificate for a free flight and are rebooked on the next flight out. If there are not enough volunteers, the airline must choose who will be denied boarding. The first to get bumped are passengers who checked in late and those flying on discounted tickets, so **get to the gate and check in as early as possible,** especially during peak periods.

Vietnam Airlines closes its check-in counters 40 minutes before boarding, so **check in early.** Even if other passengers have yet to clear customs, it's still nearly impossible to get on the flight if you show up at the counter less than 40 minutes before your flight. And since most of the flights are overbooked, you are probably looking at a long, dreary wait if you miss your flight.

Always **bring a government-issued photo ID to the airport;** even when it's not required, a passport is best.

CUTTING COSTS

The least expensive airfares to Vietnam are priced for round-trip travel and must usually be purchased in advance. Airlines generally allow you to change your return date for a fee; most low-fare tickets, however, are nonrefundable. It's smart to **call a number of airlines,** and when you are quoted a good price, **book it on the spot**—the same fare may not be available the next day. Always **check different routings** and look into using alternate airports. Also, price off-peak flights, which may be significantly less expensive than others. Travel agents, especially low-fare specialists (☞ Discounts and Deals, *below*), are helpful.

Consolidators are another good source. They buy tickets for scheduled international flights at reduced rates from the airlines, then sell them at prices that beat the best fare available directly from the airlines. Sometimes you can even get your money back if you need to return the ticket. Carefully read the fine print detailing penalties for changes and cancellations, purchase the ticket with a credit card, and **confirm your consolidator reservation with the airline.**

When you **fly as a courier,** you trade your checked-luggage space for a ticket deeply subsidized by a courier service. There are restrictions on when you can book and how long you can stay. Some courier companies list with membership organizations, such as the International Association of Air Travel Couriers; these require you to become a member before you can book a flight.

Many airlines, singly or in collaboration, offer discount air passes that allow foreigners to travel economically in a particular country or region. Vietnam Airline's Indochina Ticket, for example, can route you through either Hanoi or Ho Chi Minh City to Phnom Penh and Vientiane and back to your point of origin for around $190. These visitor passes usually must be reserved and purchased before you leave home.

Information about passes can be difficult to track down on airline Web sites, which tend to be geared to travelers departing from a given carrier's country rather than to those intending to visit that country. Try typing the name of the pass into a search engine, or search for "pass" within the carrier's Web site.

➤ CONSOLIDATORS: **Cheap Tickets** (☎ 800/377–1000 or 888/922–8849, WEB www.cheaptickets.com). **Discount Airline Ticket Service** (☎ 800/576–1600). **Unitravel** (☎ 800/325–2222, WEB www.unitravel.com). **Up & Away Travel** (☎ 212/889–2345, WEB www.upandaway.com). **World Travel Network** (☎ 800/409–6753).

➤ COURIER RESOURCES: **International Association of Air Travel Couriers** (☎ 352/475–1584, WEB www.courier.org). **Now Voyager Travel** (☎ 212/431–1616).

ENJOYING THE FLIGHT

During rainy season within Vietnam (December through February in north and central Vietnam, May through November in the south), **avoid flying in late afternoon and early evening,** when storms generally occur.

State your seat preference when purchasing your ticket, and then repeat it when you confirm and when you check in. For more legroom, you can request one of the few emergency-aisle seats at check-in, if you are capable of lifting at least 50 pounds—a Federal Aviation Administration requirement of passengers in these seats. Seats behind a bulkhead also offer more legroom, but they don't have under-seat storage. Don't sit in the row in front of the emergency aisle or in front of a bulkhead, where seats may not recline.

Ask the airline whether a snack or meal is served on the flight. If you have dietary concerns, **request special meals when booking.** These can be vegetarian, low-cholesterol, or kosher, for example. It's a good idea to pack some healthy snacks and a small (plastic) bottle of water in your carry-on bag. On long flights, try to maintain a normal routine to help fight jet lag. At night, **get some sleep.** By day, **eat light meals, drink water** (not alcohol), and **move around the cabin**

to stretch your legs. For additional jet-lag tips consult *Fodor's FYI: Travel Fit & Healthy* (available at bookstores everywhere).

Smoking policies vary from carrier to carrier. Many airlines prohibit smoking on all of their international flights; others allow smoking only on certain routes or certain departures. Ask your carrier about its policy. Vietnam Airlines does not permit smoking on its flights.

Bear in mind that Vietnam Airlines does not screen in-flight movies on all of its flights. Bring a book or some other means of keeping yourself occupied.

FLYING TIMES

Flying time from Los Angeles to the Southeast Asian hub of Bangkok is approximately 18 hours, Chicago to Bangkok is 20 hours, New York to Bangkok is 22 hours, and London to Bangkok is 11 hours. Bangkok to Ho Chi Minh City takes one hour. The flight from Sydney to Ho Chi Minh City takes about nine hours.

HOW TO COMPLAIN

If your baggage goes astray or your flight goes awry, complain right away. Most carriers require that you **file a claim immediately.** The Aviation Consumer Protection Division of the Department of Transportation publishes *Fly-Rights,* which discusses airlines and consumer issues and is available on-line. At PassengerRights.com, a Web site, you can compose a letter of complaint and distribute it electronically.

➤ AIRLINE COMPLAINTS: **Aviation Consumer Protection Division** (✉ U.S. Department of Transportation, Room 4107, C-75, Washington, DC 20590, ☎ 202/366–2220, WEB www.dot.gov/airconsumer). **Federal Aviation Administration Consumer Hotline** (☎ 800/322–7873).

RECONFIRMING

Check the status of your flight before you leave for the airport. You can do this on your carrier's Web site, by linking to a flight-status checker (many Web booking services offer these), or by calling your carrier or travel agent. Always confirm international flights at least 72 hours ahead of the scheduled departure time. It's a good idea to **confirm both domestic flights within Vietnam and flights out of Vietnam two days in advance.** Flights are occasionally delayed or canceled altogether.

AIRPORTS

The major gateways to Vietnam are Hanoi's Noi Bai Airport, Ho Chi Minh City's Tan Son Nhat Airport, and to a lesser extent Danang Airport. As the main gateway for thousands of *Viet Kieu,* returning overseas Vietnamese who still raise suspicion among the country's government workers, Ho Chi Minh City's airport has procedures that can involve more in-depth immigration checks and baggage searches—if customs (☞ Customs and Duties, *below*) has any cause for suspicion. Still, in general at all three airports you are more than likely to get through immigration, pick up your waiting bags, and breeze in and out of customs before you break a sweat.

For domestic air travel, major transportation hubs are Ho Chi Minh City, Hanoi, and Danang, but there is also service to Ban Me Thuot, Dalat, Dien Bien Phu, Haiphong, Hue, Nha Trang, Phu Quoc Island, Pleiku, Qui Nhon, Son La, and Vinh.

➤ AIRPORT INFORMATION: **Danang Airport** (✉ 3 km [2 mi] southwest of Danang, ☎ 0511/830–339). **Noi Bai International Airport** (✉ 35 km [22 mi] north of Hanoi, ☎ 04/886–5060). **Tan Son Nhat Airport** (✉ Hoang Van Thu Blvd., Tan Binh District, 7 km [4 mi] from central Ho Chi Minh City, ☎ 08/844–3179).

AIRPORT TRANSFERS

Figuring out how to get into Hanoi or Ho Chi Minh City from the airport can be a little overwhelming when you first arrive. There are a few options: either have your hotel or tour company arrange to pick you up, or take a taxi or shuttle bus into the city center. *See* Chapters 2 and 6 for more information about traveling between the airport and the city center.

DUTY-FREE SHOPPING

There is a limited selection of alcohol, cigarettes, snack foods, and souvenirs in both Tan Son Nhat and Noi Bai airports. High prices and second-rate goods mean that you're better off not leaving your gift shopping to the last minute.

BIKE TRAVEL

In scenic cities such as Hanoi and Hue, biking can be an ideal way to get around town, see the sights, and, in the case of Hoi An and Nha Trang, head to the beach. However, you should **avoid bicycling in Ho Chi Minh City** because of the smog and heavy traffic; also, the city is much more spread out than others in Vietnam.

You can usually rent Vietnamese-made bicycles or the sturdier Phoenix bicycles made in China for 25,000d to 35,000d per day from most tourist cafés and some hotels and tourist agencies. Make sure the bike has an attached wheel lock, or borrow a lock from the owner. The Memory Café in Hanoi rents bicycles and motorcycles, and many reputable bicycle rentals can be found on Hang Bac Street.

Hardy travelers have been known to bring their own mountain bikes and cycle the length of the country. Bikes can be placed on ferries, buses, and trains at an added cost, which varies by destination. A few tour operators organize bike trips across the country (☞ Tours and Packages, *below*).

➤ BIKE RENTALS: **Memory Café** (✉ 33bis Tran Hung Dao St., Hoan Kiem District, ☎ 04/943–5854).

BIKES IN FLIGHT

Most airlines accommodate bikes as luggage, provided they are dismantled and boxed; check with individual airlines about packing requirements. Airlines sell bike boxes, which are often free at bike shops, for about $15 (bike bags start at $100). International travelers often can substitute a bike for a piece of checked luggage at no charge; otherwise, the cost is about $100. Domestic and Canadian airlines charge $40–$80 each way.

BOAT AND FERRY TRAVEL

For many riverside or seaside towns in Vietnam, boat rides are a natural attraction, sometimes the only way to get around, and a great way to get a view of life on, in, or near the water.

In northern Vietnam and in the Mekong Delta, ferries are often the only way to get to destinations where bridges have not yet been built or have been destroyed, or to get to islands such as Cat Ba. Bicycles, cars, and motorbikes can usually be brought on board for a fee.

Even if you do not go through a travel agency or tourist office, cheap boats for hire will certainly find you—probably before you even get to the water's edge. With a bit of bargaining you can negotiate a deal, and apart from paying more than the locals for the same trip, you can count on being delivered safely back to your starting point. Just make sure you **agree on a price before you set off.**

FARES AND SCHEDULES

See individual chapters for travel agencies and other tourist cafés that provide information on boat routes, fares, and schedules.

BORDER CROSSINGS

Air travel is the recommended way to go between Vietnam and other points in Asia. You must **obtain a visa to visit most countries near Vietnam**—Laos, Cambodia, and China—which can be difficult; it's best to make visa arrangements before you go to Vietnam. Cambodia and Laos currently provide visas on arrival at international airports (with a photo), but this is subject to change; inquire at these countries' embassies for the most up-to-date policies. In general, Thailand automatically grants short-term-stay visas to most Western visitors. Note also that tourist visas can be arranged quickly for most Asian countries from their respective embassies in Bangkok.

Going overland from Vietnam to other points is neither easy nor comfortable, though it is possible. Again, it's important that you prearrange visas before making the journey overland. Vietnam–China border crossings include Mong Cai, Huu Nghi, and Lao Cai (near Sapa). Two trains per week run from Hanoi to Beijing, crossing at Dong Dang. The trip takes 55 hours. Traveling overland into Laos today is easier than in previous years, when rebel activity

and banditry made the trip hazardous; many travelers make the journey via the Lao Bao border crossing, located 85 km (53 mi) from Dong Ha in central Vietnam, or opt to cross the border at Cau Treo, near Vinh, also in central Vietnam. Entering Cambodia on the Mekong River has become commonplace at Vinh Xuong, 30 km (19 mi) north of Chau Doc. Travelers also make the trip into Cambodia by bus through Moc Bai, northwest of Ho Chi Minh City, from which it takes about eight hours to reach Phnom Penh.

➤ VISA OFFICES: **Chinese Embassy Visa Section** (✉ 520 12th Ave., New York, NY 10036, ☎ 212/868–2078; ✉ 46 Hoang Dieu St., Ba Dinh District, Hanoi, ☎ 04/845–3736, FAX 04/823–2826). **Embassy of Laos** (✉ 2222 S St. NW, Washington, DC 20008, ☎ 202/332–6416; ✉ 22 Tran Binh Trong St., Hoan Kiem District, Hanoi, ☎ 04/942–4576, FAX 04/822–8414). **Royal Embassy of Cambodia** (✉ 4500 16th St. NW, Washington, DC 20011, ☎ 202/726–7742; ✉ 71A Tran Hung Dao St., Hoan Kiem District, Hanoi, ☎ 04/942–4788, FAX 04/826–5225).

BUS TRAVEL

Although an extensive and dirt-cheap public bus system services every nook and cranny of the country, these buses are the most uncomfortable way to travel in Vietnam. Buses are often cramped, unbearably hot, packed with chain-smokers, and notoriously loud. Roads can be rough. Buses also break down like clockwork and operate under arbitrary schedules. Departure times depend on when they fill up, and arrival times depend on how many times they stop to pick up passengers—who are sometimes carrying pigs, chickens, snakes, goats, or fish—by the roadside.

Air-conditioned minibuses are a better alternative and are only slightly more expensive than regular buses; these are often available at or near most bus stations. Tourist minibuses between Hanoi and Ho Chi Minh City depart daily, usually in the early morning. An even better option is to take the more convenient, reliable, and infinitely more comfortable privately run tour buses organized by travel agencies, tourist offices, and travel cafés to most destinations. Even the most budget-conscious backpackers opt for the minivans or the reasonable tourist buses.

See individual chapters for information on travel agencies and other tourist cafés that organize bus trips around the country; you can also find information on state-run bus companies and their services.

CUTTING COSTS

Sinh Café Travel, based in Ho Chi Minh City, has created a niche market with its privately run, open tour bus schedules. For $38 heading north and $33 going south, you can purchase an open-ended ticket on the Sinh Café bus that enables you to break your journey at several points—Nha Trang, Dalat, Hoi An, Hue, and Ninh Binh—en route to Hanoi or Ho Chi Minh City. You can stay for as much time as you can spare at each stop on this tour itinerary; the Sinh Café's 45-seat air-conditioned bus leaves daily from these stops. Service is run in partnership with several smaller agencies that have their own buses. Since the service is not a tour but a private means of transportation, you have the flexibility to stay (or not) in any of the stops for any number of days before hooking up with the next available seat arranged by the Sinh Café office at each of these points. The buses also stop at various sights along the way. Note, however, that Sinh Café does tend to pack these buses quite full.

PAYING

Tour companies that run bus services accept dollars and dong. Public buses require dong.

RESERVATIONS

Although it's usually possible to get a seat a day before departure, you should **book your tickets as early as possible** to be on the safe side.

➤ BUS INFORMATION: **Sinh Café Travel** (✉ 246–248 De Tham St., District 1, Ho Chi Minh City, ☎ 08/836–7338, 08/835–5601, or 08/836–9420, WEB www.sinhcafevn.com).

BUSINESS GROUPS
AND COMMERCE OFFICES

Many international business groups and chambers of commerce have offices in Hanoi and Ho Chi Minh City to serve the growing community of foreigners living in Vietnam and doing business here. You're usually welcome at monthly meetings, forums, and business lunches put on by these organizations. There may be a fee for certain functions, especially if a meal is involved.

➤ CONTACTS: **American Chamber of Commerce** (✉ 59A Ly Thai To St., 5th floor, Hoan Kiem District, Hanoi, ☎ 04/934–2790, FAX 04/934–2787, amchamhn@pressclub.netnam.vn; ✉ New World Hotel, 76 Le Lai St., Room 323, District 1, Ho Chi Minh City, ☎ 08/824–3563, FAX 08/824–3572, amcham@hcm.vnn.vn). **Australian Business Group of Vietnam** (✉ Dao Tan St., Ba Dinh District, Hanoi, ☎ 04/831–7733, FAX 04/831–7757, abgvhan@fpt.vn; ✉ 17/21 Ly Tu Trong St., District 1, Ho Chi Minh City, ☎ 08/822–7360, FAX 08/822–7408, abgv@hcm.fpt.vn). **British Business Group** (✉ British Embassy, 31 Hai Ba Trung St., Hoan Kiem District, Hanoi, ☎ 04/826–6306, FAX 04/934–4196, bbgvhn@fpt.vn; ✉ 25 Le Duan St., District 1, Ho Chi Minh City, ☎ 08/829–8433, FAX 08/822–1971, bbgv.hcmc@hcm.fpt.vn). **Canadian Vietnam Business Association** (✉ 14 Mac Dinh Chi St., Ba Dinh District, Hanoi, ☎ FAX 04/716–1301, cvbahanoi@fpt.vn; ✉ IMAC, 103 Pasteur St., District 1, Ho Chi Minh City, ☎ 08/822–9632, FAX 08/822–9633, cvba@hcm.vnn.vn). **EUROCHAM** (✉ No. 504-1, 15 Ngo Quyen St., Hoan Kiem District, Hanoi, ☎ 04/825–1958, FAX 04/825–7919, glnhn@hn.vnn.vn; ✉ 17 Le Duan Blvd., 3rd floor, District 1, Ho Chi Minh City, ☎ 08/823–5505, FAX 08/823–5504, eurocham@hcm.vnn.vn). **United States Foreign Commercial Office** (✉ 6 Ngoc Khanh St., Ba Dinh District, Hanoi, ☎ 04/824–2422, FAX 04/831–4540, WEB usatrade.gov).

BUSINESS HOURS

Vietnam has a tradition of afternoon siestas (especially in the countryside), which means that all activities except eating tend to stop during lunch, between 11:30 and 2. Urban life is changing rapidly in Vietnam, however, and as free-market economics affect Ho Chi Minh City and Hanoi, more and more businesses are staying open during lunchtime to accommodate the increasing number of tourists and office-bound Vietnamese who use their midday break as a time to catch up on shopping or doing chores.

Cafés and restaurants are open all day, almost every day. Most sidewalk stalls serving breakfast and lunch finish by 2 and don't reopen for dinner until 4. By 10 PM in Hanoi and 11 PM in Ho Chi Minh City, activity starts slowing down; smaller cities die down even earlier. In bigger cities more popular venues stay open much later. You can always find late-night noodle stands. Bars and nightclubs usually close at about 1 AM or whenever the last customer leaves.

BANKS AND OFFICES

Vietnam for the most part has a five-day workweek. Whereas some offices remain open on Saturday mornings, many do not. Most government agencies and foreign-invested companies take the weekend off.

Banks are only open on weekdays, usually from 8 AM to 4:30 PM. Post offices are open seven days a week.

GAS STATIONS

Vendors sell gas at many intersections in the cities, although you will have trouble finding gas after 10 PM. If you cannot find a gas station, look for a bottle on the street curb.

MUSEUMS AND SIGHTS

Most museums in Vietnam are closed on Sunday and Monday. Some are also closed on Saturday or are only open Saturday morning. Museums in more rural areas may close for a few hours at lunchtime. Pagodas are generally open from dawn to dusk and later if it's the 1st or 15th day of the lunar month.

SHOPS

Small family-run shops seem to stay open indefinitely, primarily because living and working quarters are often one and the same. Larger stores, such as supermarket chains and department stores, can stay open as late as 10 PM in major cities.

CAMERAS
AND PHOTOGRAPHY

For photographers, the best time of year to visit Vietnam is from September to November, when the skies in the north are blue and the light has a wonderful golden quality. In the winter months, the central and northern regions of Vietnam are gray, while the spring and summer months bring heavy rains. If you plan to photograph the northern mountains, visit in the late spring just before the first rice is harvested. The *Kodak Guide to Shooting Great Travel Pictures* (available at bookstores everywhere) is loaded with tips.

➤ PHOTO HELP: **Kodak Information Center** (☎ 800/242–2424, WEB www. kodak.com).

EQUIPMENT PRECAUTIONS

Don't pack film and equipment in checked luggage, where it is much more susceptible to damage. X-ray machines used to view checked luggage are becoming much more powerful and therefore are much more likely to ruin your film. Try to **ask for hand inspection of film,** which becomes clouded after repeated exposure to airport X-ray machines, and **keep videotapes and computer disks away from metal detectors.** Always **keep film, tape, and computer disks out of the sun.** Carry an extra supply of batteries, and **be prepared to turn on your camera, camcorder, or laptop** to prove to airport security personnel that the device is real.

FILM AND DEVELOPING

Print film is widely available in Vietnam, but be sure to **check the expiration dates** before you buy it. Slide film is hard to find. Getting film developed in Vietnam is cheap; each 4-inch by 6-inch print costs about 1,800d. Although many places do a fine job on prints, having slide film developed in Vietnam is a risky undertaking.

CAR RENTAL

At present, you (as a tourist) are not permitted to drive a car yourself, although you can rent motorbikes and scooters in major cities (☞ Transportation Around Vietnam, *below*). The only foreigners allowed to drive are those with business or diplomatic visas who have registered with the Ministry of Transportation and obtained a Vietnamese driver's license (exceptions are made for Laotian and Chinese nationals). These cumbersome procedures—and the hectic state of the country's traffic—assure that very few foreigners find themselves behind the wheel. American car-rental companies have been negotiating with authorities to set up car-rental agencies in Hanoi and Ho Chi Minh City, but no licenses have been signed. Even if a deal is inked, the first step is likely to be only chauffeur-driven rental cars.

A rented car automatically comes with a driver who will, hopefully, speak some English. Cars and minivans with drivers are readily available from private and state-run travel agencies, tourist offices, and through most hotels in bigger cities such as Ho Chi Minh City, Hanoi, Hue, Danang, Nha Trang, and Vung Tau. You are charged either by the kilometer or by the day, or both. A daily rate runs anywhere from $30 to $60 per day, depending on the city in which you rent the vehicle, whether the vehicle has air-conditioning, the make of the car, and your bargaining skills. The agreed-on price should include gas and tolls (but clarify all this before you set off). Travel agencies can also arrange for English-speaking guides to accompany you and the driver. For overnight trips you're generally responsible for the driver's lodging costs as well, which may or may not be included in the price quoted to you; make sure to clarify this up up front.

The most common type of vehicles for rent are Japanese-made sedans and minivans and Korean-made Kias. Four-wheel-drive vehicles such as Toyota Land Cruisers and Mitsubishi Pajeros are ideal for major forays into river deltas, highlands, or mountains, but there aren't many of these available for rent, and they are often twice the price of a sedan. Note that most rental cars lack seat belts. You should **negotiate a price in advance and check out the vehicle before you rent it.** Note that the name "Land Cruiser" is overused in Vietnam, especially in Hanoi. Too many people consider a Land Cruiser—made only by Toyota—to be any four-wheel-drive vehicle that's not a Russian jeep.

CAR AND MOTORBIKE TRAVEL

As a tourist you are currently not allowed to drive cars yourself, although many foreigners do drive motorbikes. For more information on renting a car with a driver, *see* Car Rental, *above*.

You can rent motorbikes and scooters in major cities at most tourist cafés and some hotels and guest houses for about 45,000d to 80,000d a day. A deposit is usually required along with a passport or a photocopy of one (it's best to leave a copy). Although automobile driving is off-limits for tourists, motorbike riding by tourists is generally accepted by the police; it is technically illegal, but few Vietnamese police seem to enforce this rule. Temporary insurance for tourists is basically nonexistent, and your own auto insurance generally does not apply. It's a good idea, however, to **make sure your medical insurance covers you in case of a motorbike accident,** even if you are only a passenger. Be sure to **wear a helmet,** though not all agencies rent them.

EMERGENCY SERVICES

If you have hired a car and driver for the day or longer and the car breaks down, you should not be held responsible for the cost of repairs. Make sure everyone is clear about this before you take off on a long journey. Your exemption from financial responsibility may be little consolation when your vehicle does break down, however. Mechanical and engine problems with Japanese-made sedans, Toyota Land Cruisers, or Mitsubishi Pajeros are rare. But expect breakdowns in Russian-made jeeps and cars. Most mechanical problems can be fixed, and there are mechanics on virtually every block in the cities.

As for motorbikes, the Japanese-made ones are quite dependable. Repair shops for these are also ubiquitous throughout the cities. In the country-side old East German Simsons and Soviet-era Minsk motorcycles are the standards. They break down regularly, but everyone claims to know how to fix them (although it's not always true), and parts—at least for the Minsks—are readily available.

In case of a traffic accident, remember that the foreigner is always at fault. So, in minor accidents, even if you've done nothing wrong it's a good idea to stay in the car and let your driver do the talking or to try to get out of the situation as quickly as possible without involving the police. Even if the case seems crystal clear, you'll likely be fighting a losing battle and will probably be asked to pay damages immediately even if you are not to blame. Many of Vietnam's civil laws provide for the underprivileged, and as a foreigner you are automatically considered privileged.

In general, Vietnam's traffic police—easily recognizable by their peach-color jumpsuits—are best avoided.

GASOLINE

Unleaded gasoline is sold by the liter in Vietnam. (There are about 4 liters to the gallon.) Gas stations sell at a government-regulated price of about 6,000d per liter. Minsks and some other makes of motorcycle take a 2%–4% oil-gas mixture; oil is added after you purchase your gasoline. Make sure you are getting the right gas for your vehicle: most fuel pumps are clearly marked with octane content. If communication proves impossible, find people with similar vehicles and watch what they pump into their gas tanks. Gas sold by vendors on the street is a good option when stations are closed. The prices are slightly higher, however, and it's not unheard of for watered-down gas of the lowest octane to be sold on the street.

PARKING

Any traveling by car you do will be with a hired driver, so he (drivers are rarely women) will be the one responsible for finding adequate parking. On many streets in Ho Chi Minh City and Hanoi it is illegal to leave an unattended car; the streets are simply too narrow or crowded. Instead, cars—and motorbikes and bicycles—are often parked in guarded lots, driveways, even on roped-off pieces of sidewalk. A few streets have marked automobile parking, and some of the newer high-rises in Ho Chi Minh City and Hanoi have underground or elevated garages.

ROAD CONDITIONS

Highways are the main transport route for cars, public buses, transport trucks, tractors, motorbikes, bicycles, pedestrians, oxcarts, and a host of farm animals. For example, Highway 1, or, as its French builders called it, La Route des Mandarins, is the primary north–south commercial route; this is the backbone of Vietnam's road system. Formerly a narrow, crumbling road, the highway has been upgraded along its entire length, which extends from near the Chinese border, north of Hanoi, through Ho Chi Minh City and to the heart of the Mekong Delta in the south. Other major roadways include Highway 5 from Hanoi to Haiphong; Highway 6 from Hoa Binh to Dien Bien Phu; Route 70, which bisects the northwest; Highway 7, the Nghe An Province route into Laos; Route 14 through the central highlands; Route 22, west out of Ho Chi Minh City toward Tay Ninh and the Cambodian capital of Phnom Penh; and Route 80, through the upper Mekong Delta. Construction on a second north–south route, the Truong Son Highway, follows the famed wartime supply route known as the Ho Chi Minh Trail; this ambitious project, which was partially complete at press time, cuts through Vietnam's western mountains and extends from the northern province of Ha Tay to Ho Chi Minh City.

Vietnam's major roads are for the most part paved, and the entire country's road network is continually being upgraded with extensive soft loans from the World Bank and the Asian Development Bank. Road conditions in the north are far worse than in the south, where the U.S. war effort built or paved many of the roads. Thoroughfares labeled national roads cover only 12,000 km

(7,500 mi) of Vietnam's transportation system; only 60% of these roads are paved. The lowest category of roads, called provincial or district roads, account for 40,000 km (25,000 mi) of the system. Only 8% of these are paved. Most dirt roads turn to mud during the rainy season and become impassable.

When driving around the country, try to **travel during the day.** Driving at night can be hazardous because many vehicles either don't have lights or drive with their high beams on at all times, and it is difficult to see bad spots in the road.

ROAD MAPS

City maps and maps of Vietnam and Southeast Asia can be purchased from sidewalk vendors, hotel gift shops, bookstores, tourist cafés, and the ubiquitous postcard sellers who roam the city streets seeking out visitors. Detailed road atlases and topography maps of rural regions are, however, rare; with the exception of the most recent editions, they're also notoriously inaccurate.

RULES OF THE ROAD

Considering that Vietnam's streets are a frenzy of motorists, bicyclists, motorcyclists, and pedestrians, it's no surprise that the country's traffic fatalities per capita are among the highest in the world. There seems to be a vague understanding among riders, drivers, and pedestrians that they're all in it together. But this doesn't make the streets much safer. Traffic police are treated with contempt, pedestrians seem oblivious to the flow—and danger—of vehicles, late-night construction workers play cards in the intersections, and children have been known to dart into streets without warning.

Though traffic lights are all over Hanoi and Ho Chi Minh City, you shouldn't put too much faith in them; red lights are often ignored, especially at night and especially in Hanoi. Right turns on red are forbidden, although you'd never realize this by watching an intersection. One-way streets are also dangerous, as there is usually a trickle of traffic flowing the wrong way. And although the Vietnamese

technically drive on the right side of the road, the concept of lanes has yet to catch on.

Driving a motorbike in Hanoi is easier than doing so in hectic Ho Chi Minh City, but traffic skills remain poor throughout the country. When riding a motorbike or bicycle, **use your skills of predicting, timing and weaving.** It is imperative that you **use the horn,** since most drivers rarely glance around before changing lanes. Unfortunately, since everyone uses the horn at every opportunity, it has become less of a warning and more of an announcement of one's status as a motorcycle rider.

Always **give trucks, army jeeps, and buses the right-of-way.** It's not that they won't necessarily *want* to stop for you—they just might not have any brakes. The best way to get through traffic on foot is to **walk at a steady pace across the street and, of course, watch out;** the oncoming vehicles will have a better chance of avoiding you if the drivers can get a sense of where you will be going next. If you stop suddenly, it's harder for drivers to judge where you are in relation to them.

CHILDREN IN VIETNAM

Traveling with very young children to Vietnam is not recommended, largely because of health considerations: young children's immune systems are not as developed as those of adults, and Vietnam doesn't have emergency children's medical care up to international standards. One hospital that does treat children, however, is the Hanoi Family Medical Practice in the Van Phuc Diplomatic Compound, in Hanoi (☞ Hanoi A to Z *in* Chapter 2).

If you do travel to Vietnam with young ones, brace yourself—and your child—for an interesting trip. Foreign youngsters, particularly Caucasians and especially blonds, are the center of attention almost everywhere they go in Vietnam, even in the major cities. People may want to hold your baby and may even take him or her across the street to show a friend—often without asking. Toddlers get pinched, poked, hugged, squeezed, and even grabbed between the legs or, worse, have their pants pulled down to see if they're "cut from the same cloth" as Vietnamese children. Of particular annoyance is the regularity with which complete strangers touch Western babies, especially on the face and mouth. Intestinal parasites can be transmitted by hands, so be sure people's fingers are clean before they start poking and prodding. No malice is intended by any of this, but it can be stressful.

FLYING

If your children are two or older, **ask about children's airfares.** As a general rule, infants under two not occupying a seat fly at greatly reduced fares or even for free. When booking, **confirm carry-on allowances** if you're traveling with infants. In general, for babies charged 10% of the adult fare you are allowed one carry-on bag and a collapsible stroller; if the flight is full, the stroller may have to be checked or you may be limited to less.

Experts agree that it's a good idea to use safety seats aloft for children weighing less than 40 pounds. Airlines set their own policies: U.S. carriers usually require that the child be ticketed, even if he or she is young enough to ride free, since the seats must be strapped into regular seats. Do **check your airline's policy about using safety seats during takeoff and landing.** Safety seats are not allowed everywhere in the plane, so get your seat assignments as early as possible.

When reserving, **request children's meals or a freestanding bassinet** (not available at all airlines) if you need them. But note that bulkhead seats, where you must sit to use the bassinet, may lack an overhead bin or storage space on the floor.

LODGING

Hotels, particularly those of international standard, are usually happy to add a cot or small bed to your room to accommodate children. Some hotels offer this service free for children under 12 and at only 10%–20% of the room rate for those older than 12 years. Separate rooms for children are likely to be cheaper; when making reservations ask if you can get a discount for your children and what the cutoff age is for these.

PRECAUTIONS

Food hygiene is the most pressing concern when traveling with children. Be especially cautious with fruit shakes or juices, which may be made with contaminated ice. Limp salads and greens are risky if they have been sitting at room temperature and are served raw. Root vegetables, such as potatoes and carrots, should be skinned and well cooked. For more information on food safety, *see* Precautions *in* Dining, *below.*

Transportation is another issue. Most taxis, rental cars, and buses in Vietnam don't have seat belts—let alone car seats for infants. And although trains are a safer option, the toilets are usually filthy and without running water.

SIGHTS AND ATTRACTIONS

Places that are especially appealing to children are indicated by a rubber-duckie icon (☺) in the margin.

SUPPLIES AND EQUIPMENT

Few restaurants have high chairs, although diapers, baby bottles, and canned milk are available at minimarkets. Vietnam is also a great place to buy embroidered baby clothes and linens.

COMPUTERS ON THE ROAD

If you're bringing a laptop, check to see whether your computer's adapter can take 220 volts, the electrical voltage used in Vietnam. It is also advisable to **use an electrical surge protector,** because power surges can cause permanent damage to your computer. Internal modems are particularly susceptible to power surges, especially when electricity returns after a power cut. Also, be sure to unplug your equipment after use. For longer stays, consider investing in a voltage stabilizer.

CONSUMER PROTECTION

Whether you're shopping for gifts or purchasing travel services, **pay with a major credit card** whenever possible, so you can cancel payment or get reimbursed if there's a problem (and you can provide documentation). If you're doing business with a particular company for the first time, **contact your local Better Business Bureau and the attorney general's offices** in your state and (for U.S. businesses) the company's home state as well. Have any complaints been filed? Finally, if you're buying a package or tour, always **consider travel insurance** that includes default coverage (☞ Insurance, *below*).

➤ BBBs: **Council of Better Business Bureaus** (✉ 4200 Wilson Blvd., Suite 800, Arlington, VA 22203, ☎ 703/276–0100, FAX 703/525–8277, WEB www.bbb.org).

CRUISE TRAVEL

Several cruise lines touch down in Vietnam at Danang, Haiphong, Halong Bay, Ho Chi Minh City, and Nha Trang. Choices range from a traditional ocean liner to a clipper-type tall ship to a luxury yacht. To get the best deal, **book with a cruise-only travel agency.**

To learn how to plan, choose, and book a cruise-ship voyage, consult *Fodor's FYI: Plan & Enjoy Your Cruise* (available in bookstores everywhere).

➤ CRUISE LINES: **Orient Lines** (✉ 1510 S.E. 17th St., Suite 400, Fort Lauderdale, FL 33316, ☎ 305/527–6660 or 800/333–7300). **Princess Cruises** (✉ 10100 Santa Monica Blvd., Los Angeles, CA 90067, ☎ 310/553–1770). **Radisson Seven Seas Cruises** (✉ 600 Corporate Dr., Suite 410, Fort Lauderdale, FL 33334, ☎ 800/333–3333). **Seabourn Cruise Line** (✉ 55 Francisco St., San Francisco, CA 94133, ☎ 415/391–7444 or 800/929–9595). **Silversea Cruises** (✉ 110 E. Broward Blvd., Fort Lauderdale, FL 33301, ☎ 305/522–4477 or 800/722–9955).

CUSTOMS AND DUTIES

When shopping abroad, **keep receipts** for all purchases. Upon reentering the country, **be ready to show customs officials what you've bought.** If you feel a duty is incorrect, appeal the assessment. If you object to the way your clearance was handled, note the inspector's badge number. In either case, first ask to see a supervisor. If the problem isn't resolved, write to the appropriate authorities, beginning with the port director at your point of entry.

Keep in mind that it is illegal to export antiques unless you get special permission to do so (☞ Shopping, *below*). If you purchase an item that looks like an antique, be sure to get a note from the store owner stating that it is not.

IN AUSTRALIA

Australian residents who are 18 or older may bring home A$400 worth of souvenirs and gifts (including jewelry), 250 cigarettes or 250 grams of tobacco, and 1,125 ml of alcohol (including wine, beer, and spirits). Residents under 18 may bring back A$200 worth of goods. Prohibited items include meat products. Seeds, plants, and fruits need to be declared upon arrival.

➤ INFORMATION: **Australian Customs Service** (Regional Director, ✉ Box 8, Sydney, NSW 2001; ☎ 02/9213–2000 or 1300/363263; 1800/020504 quarantine-inquiry line; FAX 02/9213–4043; WEB www.customs.gov.au).

IN CANADA

Canadian residents who have been out of Canada for at least seven days may bring in C$750 worth of goods duty-free. If you've been away fewer than seven days but more than 48 hours, the duty-free allowance drops to C$200; if your trip lasts 24 to 48 hours, the allowance is C$50. You may not pool allowances with family members. Goods claimed under the C$750 exemption may follow you by mail; those claimed under the lesser exemptions must accompany you. Alcohol and tobacco products may be included in the seven-day and 48-hour exemptions but not in the 24-hour exemption. If you meet the age requirements of the province or territory through which you reenter Canada, you may bring in, duty-free, 1.5 liters of wine *or* 1.14 liters (40 imperial ounces) of liquor *or* 24 12-ounce cans or bottles of beer or ale. If you are 19 or older you may bring in, duty-free, 200 cigarettes and 50 cigars. Check ahead of time with the Canada Customs and Revenue Agency or the Department of Agriculture for policies regarding meat products, seeds, plants, and fruits.

You may send an unlimited number of gifts (only one gift per recipient, however) worth up to C$60 each duty-free to Canada. Label the package UNSOLICITED GIFT—VALUE UNDER $60. Alcohol and tobacco are excluded.

➤ INFORMATION: **Canada Customs and Revenue Agency** (✉ 2265 St. Laurent Blvd. S, Ottawa, Ontario K1G 4K3, ☎ 204/983–3500, 506/636–5064, or 800/461–9999, WEB www.ccra-adrc.gc.ca/).

IN NEW ZEALAND

All homeward-bound residents may bring back NZ$700 worth of souvenirs and gifts; passengers may not pool their allowances, and children can claim only the concession on goods intended for their own use. For those 17 or older, the duty-free allowance also includes 4.5 liters of wine or beer; one 1,125-ml bottle of spirits; and either 200 cigarettes, 250 grams of tobacco, 50 cigars, *or* a combination of the three up to 250 grams. Meat products, seeds, plants, and fruits must be declared upon arrival to the Agricultural Services Department.

➤ INFORMATION: **New Zealand Customs** (Head office: ✉ The Customhouse, 17–21 Whitmore St. [Box 2218, Wellington], ☎ 09/300–5399 or 0800/428–786, WEB www.customs.govt.nz).

IN THE U.K.

From countries outside the European Union, including Vietnam, you may bring home, duty-free, 200 cigarettes or 50 cigars; 1 liter of spirits or 2 liters of fortified or sparkling wine or liqueurs; 2 liters of still table wine; 60 ml of perfume; 250 ml of toilet water; plus £145 worth of other goods, including gifts and souvenirs. Prohibited items include meat products, seeds, plants, and fruits.

➤ INFORMATION: **HM Customs and Excise** (✉ Portcullis House, 21 Cowbridge Rd. E, Cardiff CF11 9SS, ☎ 029/2038–6423 or 0845/010–9000, WEB www.hmce.gov.uk).

IN THE U.S.

U.S. residents who have been out of the country for at least 48 hours may bring home, for personal use, $800 worth of foreign goods duty-free, as long as they haven't used the $800 allowance or any part of it in the past 30 days. This exemption may include 1 liter of alcohol (for travelers 21 and older), 200 cigarettes, and 100 non-Cuban cigars. Family members from the same household who are traveling together may pool their $800 personal exemptions. For fewer than 48 hours, the duty-free allowance drops to $200, which may include 50 cigarettes, 10 non-Cuban cigars, and 150 ml of alcohol (or perfume containing alcohol). The $200 allowance cannot be combined with other individuals' exemptions, and if you exceed it, the full value of all the goods will be taxed. Antiques, which the U.S. Customs Service defines as objects more than 100 years old, enter duty-free, as do original works of art done entirely by hand, including paintings, drawings, and sculptures.

You may also send packages home duty-free, with a limit of one parcel per addressee per day (except alcohol or tobacco products or perfume worth more than $5). You can mail up to $200 worth of goods for personal use; label the package PERSONAL USE and attach a list of its contents and their retail value. If the package contains your used personal belongings, mark it PERSONAL GOODS RETURNED to avoid paying duties. You may send up to $100 worth of goods as a gift; mark the package UNSOLICITED GIFT. Mailed items do not affect your duty-free allowance on your return.

➤ INFORMATION: **U.S. Customs Service** (for inquiries, ✉ 1300 Pennsylvania Ave. NW, Washington, DC 20229, WEB www.customs.gov, ☎ 202/354–1000; for complaints, ✉ Customer Satisfaction Unit, 1300 Pennsylvania Ave. NW, Room 5.5A, Washington, DC 20229; for registration of equipment, ✉ Office of Passenger Programs, 1300 Pennsylvania Ave. NW, Room 5.4D, Washington, DC 20229, ☎ 202/927–0530).

IN VIETNAM

When you enter Vietnam you will be given a yellow customs declaration slip and a blue departure slip. You need these to get out of the country, so **do not lose your customs forms** (if you do, a customs search, a fine, and a long delay are likely when you try to leave the country). Do not attempt to bring any weapons, pornographic materials, or anything that could be considered subversive (such as political or religious materials) into Vietnam, as you may receive a hefty fine, be detained, or, in extreme cases, jailed. It is a good idea to **declare cameras, camcorders, laptop computers, and any other expensive electronics** that you want to take out of the country again, although it's not required. Contact the Embassy of Vietnam for more information on customs requirements.

➤ INFORMATION: **Embassy of Vietnam** (✉ 1233 20th St. NW, Suite 400, Washington, DC 20036, ☎ 202/861–0737, ℻ 202/861–0917, 🕸 www.vietnamembassy-usa.org).

DINING

The restaurants we list are the cream of the crop in each price category. Properties indicated by an ✕🏠 are lodging establishments whose restaurant warrants a special trip. Vietnam has a variety of eateries: small, basic Western-style restaurants serving Vietnamese food; stalls or stands on the street, surrounded by small plastic stools, serving very cheap and often quite good rice and noodle dishes; upscale Western-style restaurants (including hotel restaurants), which can be elegant and hip, serving Vietnamese, Chinese, Japanese, French, American, Italian, or other international cuisines; tourist cafés, which cater primarily to budget travelers, serving mediocre Western and Vietnamese dishes; and peddlers selling food and drinks from their handcarts or shoulder poles.

Keep in mind that Vietnam's best eating isn't found only in elegant restaurants or hotel dining rooms but also at stalls on every street corner and in every marketplace. To taste Vietnamese favorites, you need only step out of your hotel and onto the streets. These soup, rice, noodle, and seafood kitchens are usually run by several generations of a single family, and sitting down on the low plastic chairs at one of these self-contained sidewalk operations for a bowl of *bun cha* (chopped grilled meat over vermicelli-style rice noodles) feels like joining in a family gathering.

If you stick to local restaurants, food will constitute a minor part of your travel costs. Smaller restaurants—even those serving international cuisines—are surprisingly cheap. Expect to pay international prices at hotel restaurants.

MEALS AND SPECIALTIES

The first thing you should know about Vietnamese food is that it is not "Chinese food without the spices." Sophisticated cuisine, distinct from what is north of its border, has evolved in Vietnam over the last few thousand years. Soy sauce is not as common in Vietnam as in China, for instance; instead, the nearly universal seasoning of choice in the country is *nuoc mam*—inadequately translated as fish sauce—a clear amber liquid pressed out of large barrels of anchovies and salt. This exquisitely complex condiment submerges itself in the flavors of other ingredients— it's truly a remarkable concoction. Don't be put off by the smell of this potent liquid; skeptical foreigners have been known to become converts after a couple of experiences. But do take care not to overdo it, as a little bit goes a long way.

Com, the Vietnamese word for "food," is also the word for "rice." Plan to eat a lot of it in Vietnam, either steamed, fried, or made into rice paper or noodles. The most famous Vietnamese dish, especially in the north, is *pho,* a clear broth containing chicken or beef and soft rice noodles. Very popular at breakfast, pho is also served day and night. Spring rolls, known as *cha gio* in the south and *nem* in the north, are another Vietnamese classic. Stuffed with pork, shrimp, or crab, these rice paper rolls are deep-fried until golden. The central city of Hue is said to have the best food in Vietnam. Here you can try a local delicacy, *banh khoai,* a thin, crispy yellow pancake stuffed with shrimp, pork, and bean sprouts and served with peanut sauce and slices of star fruit, green banana, and mint.

Seafood is delicious, abundant, and cheap all over Vietnam, but particularly in coastal towns such as Nha Trang, Danang, and Halong Bay, where large crabs and prawns are grilled to perfection. Beef and pork are also generally of high quality, but chicken tends to be somewhat tough in Vietnam. Dog meat isn't as inexpensive or plentiful as you might think, and the chance of encountering it shouldn't deter you from exploring Vietnam's back-alley food scene; just watch out for dishes that contain *thit cho.* Be sure to wander the markets in search of the dozens of incredible indigenous fruits, including rambutans, longans, lychees, mangosteens, jackfruit, mangoes, kumquats, papayas, pineapples, star fruit, and the spiky olfactory overload known as durian.

Upscale international restaurants to suit nearly every palate can be found in Ho Chi Minh City and Hanoi. The nation's top hotels have won over an expatriate clientele with their superb cuisine. French, Italian, Indian, Chinese, Korean, Mexican, Middle Eastern, Thai, Californian, and, yes, certain configurations of fast food are all represented in the northern and southern hubs. And if *onigiri* are your favorite, you're in luck; Ho Chi Minh City alone has more than 30 Japanese restaurants. As soon as you venture outside Hanoi and Ho Chi Minh City, finding top-notch Western food is difficult. However, family-run restaurants and cafés with fresh seafood offerings, delicious meats, and tasty *an chay* (vegetarian dishes) are nearly everywhere.

Good, strong coffee and Vietnamese tea are served with breakfast, after dinner, and any time of day at local cafés.

MEALTIMES

Breakfast is served beginning at 6 at most sidewalk stalls and 7 at most restaurants; lunch is served anywhere between 11:30 and 2; and dinner is available any time after 5 and usually before 8. Restaurants are generally open daily (except major holidays), and although the Vietnamese eat dinner fairly early, most restaurants remain open well into the night, even after they are supposed to close. Unless otherwise noted, the restaurants listed in this guide are open daily for lunch and dinner.

PAYING

As a rule the only restaurants that accept credit cards and perhaps traveler's checks are the more upscale places. However, if you do pay with plastic, these places normally add a 5% service charge to your bill.

PRECAUTIONS

It's important to **be careful of what you eat and drink** in Vietnam. Fresh, leafy vegetables are known to carry parasites, so avoid those of dubious origin or those likely to have been washed in tap water. Also, try to eat only fruit that you peel yourself. If you don't want some ingredient to be included, just ask (or gesture) for it not to be added.

That said, dining at street-side food stands can be as safe as or safer than eating in restaurants, especially in cities. The stands often serve fresher food than many restaurants because they have a faster turnover; they also prepare the food in front of you. Be more careful of food stalls once you are out of urban areas. Most of all, use common sense when choosing where to eat: pick a food stand, restaurant, or café that looks clean, is crowded, and has fresh food.

It is imperative that you **avoid drinking tap water as well as beverages with ice,** which is often made from local water. Most decent restaurants either make their own ice using boiled water or buy ice in bulk from huge freezer warehouses. Your best bet is to **drink bottled water,** particularly the La Vie and Evian brands; be sure to check the spelling on the container as there are many knockoffs, some quite amusing.

Keep in mind that monosodium glutamate (MSG) is used in many dishes in Vietnam, particularly in the ubiquitous pho. If you don't want MSG in your food, ask—the cooks may not have already added it to the dish. Many people are unfamiliar with the term MSG, so try referring to it by a popular brand name, Ajinomoto, or in Vietnamese, *mi chinh.*

RESERVATIONS AND DRESS

Reservations are always a good idea; we mention them only when they're essential or not accepted. Book as far ahead as you can, and reconfirm as soon as you arrive. (Large parties should always call ahead to check the reservations policy.) We mention dress only when men are required to wear a jacket or a jacket and tie.

WINE, BEER, AND SPIRITS

You'll find Heineken, Carlsberg, Foster's, and San Miguel, along with local beers such as Saigon Beer, Tiger, Ba Ba Ba (333), and Halida. *Bia tuoi* (also known as *bia hoi* in Hanoi), a watery draft beer, is available on many city street corners; look for low plastic stools occupied by jovial, red-faced men. The popular rice wine (*ruou* or *deo*), which is similar to sake, is highly inebriating. You may want to skip the snake rice wine (with a cobra in the bottle) made "especially for men." Imported French, Italian, Australian, Spanish, Californian, and even Chilean wines are available in Ho Chi Minh City and Hanoi. Brave souls may want to pop open a bottle of Russian, Bulgarian, or Vietnamese bubbly—one of the latter bears the label "Product of the Thanh Ha Fertilizer Company."

DISABILITIES
AND ACCESSIBILITY

Very few places in Vietnam, including hotels, restaurants, sights, and office buildings, are geared toward people who use wheelchairs. In many hotels makeshift ramps provide sufficient access into the building, but service areas such as restaurants, business centers, and rest rooms are up or down flights of stairs not serviced by elevators.

Health-care issues for travelers with disabilities should be considered before coming to Vietnam. Equipment of international-standard quality is for the most part unavailable, and hygiene is a concern.

➤ LOCAL RESOURCES: **Bright Futures for People with Disabilities** (✉ 190 Lo Duc St., Hai Ba Trung District, Hanoi, ☎ 04/971–2894). **Vietnam Blind Association** (✉ 139 Nguyen Thai Hoc St., Ba Dinh District, Hanoi, ☎ 04/845–2060, FAX 04/845–2682). **Vietnam Sports Association for the Disabled** (✉ 1B Le Hong Phong St., Ba Dinh District, Hanoi, ☎ 04/823–2287, FAX 04/825–3172).

LODGING

Most elevators in larger hotels can accommodate wheelchairs, but very few guest rooms are equipped with large enough bathrooms or sufficient grab bars. Vietnam's newer hotels are the ones most likely to conform somewhat to international standards regarding wheelchair access and services for guests with disabilities.

RESERVATIONS

When discussing accessibility with an operator or reservations agent, **ask hard questions.** Are there any stairs, inside *or* out? Are there grab bars next to the toilet *and* in the shower/tub? How wide is the doorway to the room? To the bathroom? For the most extensive facilities meeting the latest legal specifications, **opt for newer accommodations.** If you reserve through a toll-free number, consider also calling the hotel's local number to confirm the information from the central reservations office. Get confirmation in writing when you can.

SIGHTS AND ATTRACTIONS

Many of Vietnam's most famous sights are all but inaccessible to people with mobility problems. Pagodas often have stairs or narrow entrances, and ramps are unheard of.

TRANSPORTATION

City planning has largely ignored the requirements of people who use wheelchairs: there are virtually no curb cuts or permanent ramps, public transportation is inaccessible, and most office buildings have no elevators or escalators (some new office buildings, where many expatriates conduct business, have large elevators and temporary ramps). Taxi drivers often help passengers get from chair to backseat and back again. Cyclo drivers can also be helpful.

Vietnam Airlines claims it has the facilities and equipment to handle passengers using wheelchairs. The reality sometimes proves otherwise, however. When flying Vietnam

Airlines, call ahead to be sure the appropriate equipment will be available at your departure and arrival points.

➤ COMPLAINTS: **Aviation Consumer Protection Division** (☞ Air Travel, *above*) for airline-related problems. **Departmental Office of Civil Rights** (for general inquiries, ✉ U.S. Department of Transportation, S-30, 400 7th St. SW, Room 10215, Washington, DC 20590, ☎ 202/366–4648, FAX 202/366–3571, WEB www.dot.gov/ost/docr/index.htm). **Disability Rights Section** (✉ NYAV, U.S. Department of Justice, Civil Rights Division, 950 Pennsylvania Ave. NW, Washington, DC 20530; ☎ ADA information line 202/514–0301, 800/514–0301, 202/514–0383 TTY, 800/514–0383 TTY, WEB www.usdoj.gov/crt/ada/adahom1.htm).

TRAVEL AGENCIES

In the United States, the Americans with Disabilities Act requires that travel firms serve the needs of all travelers. Some agencies specialize in working with people with disabilities.

➤ TRAVELERS WITH MOBILITY PROBLEMS: **Access Adventures** (✉ 206 Chestnut Ridge Rd., Scottsville, NY 14624, ☎ 716/889–9096, dltravel@prodigy.net), run by a former physical-rehabilitation counselor. **Flying Wheels Travel** (✉ 143 W. Bridge St. [Box 382, Owatonna, MN 55060], ☎ 507/451–5005, FAX 507/451–1685, WEB www.flyingwheelstravel.com).

DISCOUNTS AND DEALS

Be a smart shopper and **compare all your options** before making decisions. A plane ticket bought with a promotional coupon from travel clubs, coupon books, and direct-mail offers or purchased on the Internet may not be cheaper than the least expensive fare from a discount ticket agency. And always keep in mind that what you get is just as important as what you save.

DISCOUNT RESERVATIONS

To save money, **look into discount reservations services** with Web sites and toll-free numbers, which use their buying power to get a better price on hotels, airline tickets, even car rentals.

When booking a room, always **call the hotel's local toll-free number** (if one is available) rather than the central reservations number—you'll often get a better price. Always ask about special packages or corporate rates.

When shopping for the best deal on hotels, **look for guaranteed exchange rates,** which protect you against a falling dollar. With your rate locked in, you won't pay more, even if the price goes up in the local currency.

➤ AIRLINE TICKETS: ☎ 800/AIR–4LESS.

➤ HOTEL ROOMS: **Steigenberger Reservation Service** (☎ 800/223–5652, WEB www.srs-worldhotels.com). **Travel Interlink** (☎ 800/888–5898, WEB www.travelinterlink.com). **Turbotrip.com** (☎ 800/473–7829, WEB www.turbotrip.com). **VacationLand** (☎ 800/245–0050, WEB www.vacation-land.com).

PACKAGE DEALS

Don't confuse packages and guided tours. When you buy a package, you travel on your own, just as though you had planned the trip yourself.

ECOTOURISM

Although a few nongovernmental organizations have been set up to recycle waste (one Hanoi project turns corks from wine bottles into place mats), most recycling is done on an ad hoc basis. This being said, not much in Vietnam goes to waste. The moment you set down a water bottle or soda can, someone will collect it for resale.

ELECTRICITY

To use electric-powered equipment purchased in the United States or Canada, **bring a converter and adapter.** The electrical current in Vietnam is 220 volts, 50 cycles alternating current (AC). In the north and other parts of the country, wall outlets take the Continental-type plugs, with two round prongs; they use the flat-pin plugs in much of the south. Many of the international hotels can provide you with converters and adapters.

If your appliances are dual-voltage, you'll need only an adapter. Don't use

110-volt outlets marked FOR SHAVERS ONLY for high-wattage appliances such as blow-dryers. Most laptops operate equally well on 110 and 220 volts and so require only an adapter and a surge protector (☞ Computers on the Road, *above*).

Blackouts sometimes occur, especially in summer, when everyone uses fans and air conditioners. Upscale hotels usually have generators, but you may want to keep a flashlight handy if you're staying in a minihotel.

E-MAIL AND THE INTERNET

Although Vietnam has five Internet service providers, all of them rent lines from the same Internet access provider, the Vietnam Data Corporation (VDC), and the limited bandwidth is often overwhelmed. Note that you may have difficulty e-mailing large files. FPT Vietnam sells Internet access cards that can be used from any phone jack using a code number.

Some of the business centers in larger international hotels provide Internet access, and there are numerous Internet cafés in Hanoi, Ho Chi Minh City, and some of the smaller tourist destinations such as Hoi An, Nha Trang, and even Sapa.

➤ INTERNET HOOKUP: **Corporation for Financing and Promoting Technology, FPT** (⊠ 75 Tran Hung Dao St., Hoan Kiem District, Hanoi, ☎ 04/822–3100; ⊠ 75 Le Thi Hong Gam St., District 1, Ho Chi Minh City, ☎ 08/821–4160).

➤ INTERNET CAFÉS: **A–Z Queen Café II** (⊠ 50 Hang Be St., Hoan Kiem District, Hanoi, ☎ 04/934–3728). **Emotion Cybernet Cafe** (⊠ 52 Ly Thuong Kiet St., Hoan Kiem District, Hanoi, ☎ 04/934–1066). **Sinh Café Internet** (⊠ 246 De Tham St., District 1, Ho Chi Minh City, ☎ 08/836–7338).

EMBASSIES AND CONSULATES

If your passport is stolen or lost or you are in need of any other kind of emergency assistance, contact your country's embassy or consulate. Embassies are in Hanoi and consulates in Ho Chi Minh City.

➤ AUSTRALIA: **Consulate** (⊠ 5B Ton Duc Thang St., District 1, Ho Chi Minh City, ☎ 08/829–6035).

Embassy (⊠ 8 Dao Tan St., Van Phuc Quarter, Ba Dinh District, Hanoi, ☎ 04/831–7755). **Web site** (WEB www.ausinvn.com).

➤ CANADA: **Consulate** (⊠ 235 Dong Khoi St., District 1, Ho Chi Minh City, ☎ 08/824–5025). **Embassy** (⊠ 31 Hung Vuong St., Ba Dinh District, Hanoi, ☎ 04/823–5500).

➤ NEW ZEALAND: **Consulate** (⊠ 41 Nguyen Thi Minh Khai St., 15th floor, District 1, Ho Chi Minh City, ☎ 08/822–6907). **Embassy** (⊠ 63 Ly Thai To St., Hoan Kiem District, Hanoi, ☎ 04/824–1481).

➤ UNITED KINGDOM: **Consulate** (⊠ 25 Le Duan Blvd., District 1, Ho Chi Minh City, ☎ 08/823–2604, FAX 08/822–1971). **Embassy** (⊠ 31 Hai Ba Trung St., Hoan Kiem District, Hanoi, ☎ 04/825–2510). **Web site** (WEB www.uk-vietnam.org).

➤ UNITED STATES: **Consulate** (⊠ 4 Le Duan Blvd., District 1, Ho Chi Minh City, ☎ 08/822–9433, FAX 08/822–9434). **Embassy** (⊠ 7 Lang Ha St., Ba Dinh District, Hanoi, ☎ 04/843–1500). **Web site** (WEB www.uscongenhcmc.org).

EMERGENCIES

If something has been stolen from you, contact the police or your embassy, especially regarding more costly items such as expensive jewelry or laptop computers. Also contact your embassy if your passport has been stolen or lost. For medical emergencies, seek assistance from local hospitals or clinics or from your hotel in more rural areas; *see* Health, *below, and* Emergencies *in* the A to Z sections of individual chapters.

➤ CONTACTS: **Ambulance** (☎ 115). **Fire** (☎ 114). **Police** (☎ 113).

ENGLISH-LANGUAGE MEDIA

To get a clear idea of what's happening in Vietnam, you're better off skipping local media in favor of regional publications such as the *Bangkok Post, South China Morning Post,* or the *Far Eastern Economic Review.*

BOOKS

Hotel gift shops and bookstores in Hanoi and Ho Chi Minh City carry a nice selection of coffee-table photo books on Vietnam. For books dealing with Vietnam's history or politics, or for English-language translations of Vietnamese fiction, you'll find more choices abroad. For more information on books about Vietnam, *see* Books and Videos *in* Chapter 8.

➤ BOOKSTORES: **Bookazine** (✉ 28 Dong Khoi St., District 1, Ho Chi Minh City, ☎ 08/829–7455). **The Bookworm** (✉ 15A Ngo Van So St., Hoan Kiem District, Hanoi, ☎ 04/ 943–7226). **The Cat** (✉ 243 De Tham St., District 1, Ho Chi Minh City, ☎ 08/836–0016). **Foreign Language Bookshop** (✉ 61 Trang Tien St., Hoan Kiem District, Hanoi, ☎ 04/824–8914 or 04/825–3423). **Xunhasaba** (✉ 32 Hai Ba Trung St., Hoan Kiem District, Hanoi, ☎ 04/ 825–4068; ✉ 76E Le Thanh Ton St., District 1, Ho Chi Minh City, ☎ 08/ 824–2491).

NEWSPAPERS AND MAGAZINES

Vietnam News, the state-owned English-language daily, contains a mind-numbing mix of investment features and calls for foreign aid. You may find it most useful for the movie and art exhibitions listings.

Timeout, with restaurant and entertainment listings, is a local-information supplement to the weekly *Vietnam Investment Review,* the English-language mouthpiece of the Ministry of Planning and Investment; the *Investment Review* is available at newsstands. The monthly *Vietnam Economic Times,* also available at newsstands, is both better written and more entertaining than *Vietnam Investment Review,* with some enlightening in-depth features. It's also accessible via the Internet, at www.vneconomy.com.vn. The *Guide,* a supplement to the *Vietnam Economic Times,* is packed with tips about Vietnamese culture as well as news briefs about upcoming cultural events. *Vietnam Discovery,* published by the Vietnam National Administration of Tourism, comes with a very useful pull-out map with listings section; it's readily available at restaurants, hotels, travel agencies, and newsstands. Passengers flying on Vietnam Airlines should take a look at *Heritage,* the glossy in-flight magazine filled with features about Vietnamese culture and tourist destinations.

RADIO AND TELEVISION

Most hotels and minihotels in Vietnam have satellite TV. CNN, CNBC Asia, Star TV, and MTV Asia are standard; some hotels also have the BBC, Discovery Channel, and French and German channels.

ETIQUETTE AND BEHAVIOR

Vietnamese people rarely say "no." Usually they answer in the positive to avoid confrontational situations. If a situation is unpleasant, most people simply stay quiet and ignore it until it passes. Anger is generally viewed as a sign of weakness, and its display in public is considered ill-mannered. It is better to **remain calm and good-natured while trying to work out a disagreement** with someone.

Keep in mind that pointing at people and beckoning to them with your hand facing up is thought to be the height of rudeness. So remember to **call people's attention with your hand facing down.** Crossing your fingers for good luck is also a sure way to embarrass yourself in Vietnam. Patting children on the head is considered a bad omen and is best avoided. In many pagodas you are required to remove your shoes before entering.

When hosting Vietnamese guests, be sure to offer drinks and food as soon as they arrive. It's considered impolite simply to ask if they would like anything. Also, Vietnamese women seldom drink beer or coffee, so have some green tea or soft drinks on hand. Don't be surprised if a social event ends quickly; they usually don't drag on too long in Vietnam unless you have gone out drinking or are doing business.

Giving gifts to Vietnamese can be an unfulfilling affair for someone from the West. Often the recipient simply acknowledges the gift and carries on as before. But this is not a sign of disrespect; any gift is always highly appreciated.

Public displays of affection are frowned upon in Vietnam. It's fine to put your arm around someone of the same sex, but refrain from touching people of the opposite sex—beyond a handshake in a business setting. Respect for elders is a key value in

Vietnam; invite older people to sit down before you do so.

When visiting hill-tribe and ethnic-minority homes and villages, be respectful: only enter a home if invited, and ask before you photograph someone.

BUSINESS ETIQUETTE

No matter what your line of work, there is one thing that no businessperson in Vietnam can do without: name cards. If you don't have business cards already, printers in any bigger town can whip them up overnight for pennies apiece. After the initial pleasantries of your business meeting, offer the most senior person present your business card with both hands and a slight bow. Accept the host's name card with both hands as well, and be sure to have enough cards for everyone else present. It is particularly offensive to place a business card in your pants pocket, especially a rear pocket.

Following this exchange, sit down and be prepared to drink several cups of tea and talk about personal matters like family, country, and your impressions of Vietnam. In Vietnam, business meetings often start slowly, with both parties exchanging chitchat. Don't rush in and expect to get down to business right away.

When using an interpreter, address the person with whom you are talking, not the interpreter. If you can, it's a good idea to take along your own interpreter. Note that nodding is not necessarily agreement. And laughter, which might be seen as inappropriate by you, can be used to dispel the nervousness of a situation, particularly a very serious situation for which you might expect a much more somber reaction.

Finally, don't be surprised to find alcohol a part of a business function. Alcohol provides the means to see how a potential business partner behaves under the influence. You could find yourself faced with having to drink or decline any number of strange alcoholic concoctions, such as rice wine with snake's blood. Opting for the alcoholic mixture of medicinal herbs, almost always additionally on offer, is a graceful way out of a possibly embarrassing situation. Another thing to remember is that an empty cup will almost always be refilled; just leave the cup full if you have had enough.

GAY AND LESBIAN TRAVEL

Homosexuality is tolerated in Vietnam, though it's technically illegal. It is not uncommon for people of the same sex to hold hands or link arms in Vietnam.

➤ GAY- AND LESBIAN-FRIENDLY TRAVEL AGENCIES: **Different Roads Travel** (✉ 8383 Wilshire Blvd., Suite 902, Beverly Hills, CA 90211, ☎ 323/651–5557 or 800/429–8747, FAX 323/651–3678, lgernert@tzell.com). **Kennedy Travel** (✉ 314 Jericho Turnpike, Floral Park, NY 11001, ☎ 516/352–4888 or 800/237–7433, FAX 516/354–8849, WEB www.kennedytravel.com). **Now, Voyager** (✉ 4406 18th St., San Francisco, CA 94114, ☎ 415/626–1169 or 800/255–6951, FAX 415/626–8626, WEB www.nowvoyager.com). **Skylink Travel and Tour** (✉ 1006 Mendocino Ave., Santa Rosa, CA 95401, ☎ 707/546–9888 or 800/225–5759, FAX 707/546–9891, WEB www.skylinktravel.com), serving lesbian travelers.

GUIDEBOOKS

Plan well and you won't be sorry. Guidebooks are excellent tools—and you can take them with you. You may want to check out the color-photo-illustrated *Fodor's Exploring Vietnam*, thorough on culture and history.

HEALTH

As with any trip to a developing country, you should **check with the Centers for Disease Control and Prevention and your physician** about current health risks in Vietnam and recommended vaccinations before you go.

A first-aid kit with antacids, antidiarrheal, cold medicine, Band-Aids, antiseptics, aspirin, and other items you may need is a good idea. Also, know your blood type and **bring enough medication to last the entire trip;** you may be able to get common prescription drugs in Vietnam, but don't count on their availability or their quality. Just in case, however, have your doctor write you a prescription using the drug's generic name, because brand names vary from country to country.

FOOD AND DRINK

The major health risk in Vietnam is traveler's diarrhea, caused by eating contaminated fruit or vegetables or drinking contaminated water. So **watch what you eat.** Avoid ice, uncooked food, and unpasteurized milk and milk products, and **drink only bottled water,** such as Evian or La Vie, or water that has been boiled for several minutes, even when brushing your teeth. It's recommended you **avoid eating unpeeled fruit and uncooked vegetables or those you suspect have been washed in unboiled water.** Mild cases may respond to Imodium (known generically as loperamide) or Pepto-Bismol, both of which can be purchased over the counter. Drink plenty of purified water or tea—chamomile (*ka-moe-mie*) is a good folk remedy. In severe cases, rehydrate yourself with a salt-sugar solution (½ teaspoon salt [*muoi*] and 4 tablespoons sugar [*duong*] per quart of water); **if symptoms persist or worsen, seek medical assistance.**

MEDICAL CARE

Vietnam's medical infrastructure is not up to international standards. Hospitals and pharmacies are often undersupplied and out-of-date. Only a handful of Vietnamese doctors have top-quality Western training. Foreign insurance is very rarely accepted, so you should **expect to pay immediately in cash on completion of treatment.** The larger hospitals in Hanoi and Ho Chi Minh City have experience treating foreigners (mainly due to motor-cycle accidents, the biggest cause of injury or death of Westerners in Vietnam), and there are medical facilities with full-time Western physicians on staff (☞ Emergencies *in* A to Z sections of Chapters 2 and 6). Blood supply is a serious problem in Vietnam: the nation's blood banks are small and, say Western doctors, insufficiently screened.

Foreign-run medical clinics provide basic treatment and 24-hour on-call services; foreign-run local hospitals can perform some serious operations. Both can arrange for emergency medical evacuation to better hospitals in other countries in the region— Medevac planes dedicated to Vietnam are on standby in Singapore. Embassies have duty officers on call who can assist with logistics. If you get sick outside Hanoi or Ho Chi Minh City, get yourself to those cities as soon as possible. For more information on medical care, *see* individual chapters.

MEDICAL PLANS

No one plans to get sick while traveling, but it happens, so **consider signing up with a medical-assistance company.** Members get doctor referrals, emergency evacuation or repatriation, hot lines for medical consultation, cash for emergencies, and other assistance.

➤ MEDICAL-ASSISTANCE COMPANIES: **International SOS Assistance** (WEB www.internationalsos.com; ✉ 8 Neshaminy Interplex, Suite 207, Trevose, PA 19053, ☎ 215/245–4707 or 800/523–6586, FAX 215/244–9617; ✉ 12 Chemin Riantbosson, 1217 Meyrin 1, Geneva, Switzerland, ☎ 22/785–6464, FAX 22/785–6424; ✉ 331 N. Bridge Rd., 17-00, Odeon Towers, Singapore 188720, ☎ 338–7800, FAX 338–7611).

OVER-THE-COUNTER REMEDIES

Pharmacies are almost as common as tea stalls in Vietnam, and many pharmacists in major cities speak English. Look for a shop with a green sign that reads *Nha Thuoc*. These usually stock painkillers (such as Panadol); eye, nose, and ear drops (such as Polydexa); cold remedies (such as Tiffy); and various antibiotics—for which no prescription is needed in Vietnam. Remember to check the expiration date when buying any sort of medication.

PESTS AND OTHER HAZARDS

Malaria- and dengue-bearing mosquitoes bite at dusk and at night. No matter where you go, it's a good idea to protect yourself from mosquito-borne illnesses with a good insect repellent containing DEET, and if you're in susceptible regions, use aerosol insecticides indoors, wear clothing that covers the body, and bring mosquito nets.

SHOTS AND MEDICATIONS

Tetanus-diphtheria and polio vaccinations should be up-to-date—if you haven't been immunized since childhood, **consider bolstering your tetanus and polio vaccinations.** If you have never contracted measles, mumps, or rubella, you should also be immunized against them. Also note: **immunizations for hepatitis A and typhoid fever are advised.** According to the Centers for Disease Control and Prevention (CDC), there is a risk of contracting malaria only in rural areas of Vietnam, except in the Red River delta and the coastal plain north of Nha Trang, which are safe. The CDC recommends taking mefloquine (brand name Larium) for malaria. Dengue fever occurs in Vietnam, but the risk is small except during periods of epidemic-size transmission; there is no vaccine to prevent it. Therefore, you should **take precautions against mosquito bites.**

If you're staying for a month or more and are traveling to rural areas, you should be vaccinated against Japanese encephalitis; for six months or more, against hepatitis B as well. Some of these vaccinations require staggered treatments, so plan ahead.

➤ HEALTH WARNINGS: **National Centers for Disease Control and Prevention** (CDC; National Center for Infectious Diseases, Division of Quarantine, Traveler's Health Section, ⊠ 1600 Clifton Rd. NE, M/S E-03, Atlanta, GA 30333, ☎ 888/232–3228 general information; 877/394–8747 travelers' health line; 800/311–3435 public inquiries; FAX 888/232–3299, WEB www.cdc.gov).

HOLIDAYS

The traditional lunar new year, known as Tet in Vietnam and celebrated throughout much of Southeast Asia, falls in January or February, depending on the lunar calendar. Note that accommodations are scarce and museums, offices, and shops tend to shut down for days at a time during Tet. Other national holidays include New Year's Day, the anniversary of the founding of the Vietnamese Communist Party (February 3); Liberation Day (April 30), commemorating the day the North Vietnamese army took Saigon; International Workers Day, or May Day (May 1, the date following Liberation Day, which means a two-day holiday); Ho Chi Minh's birthday (May 19); National Day (September 2); and Christmas Day (December 25).

INSURANCE

The most useful travel-insurance plan is a comprehensive policy that includes coverage for trip cancellation and interruption, default, trip delay, and medical expenses (with a waiver for pre-existing conditions).

Without insurance you will lose all or most of your money if you cancel your trip, regardless of the reason. Default insurance covers you if your tour operator, airline, or cruise line goes out of business. Trip-delay covers expenses that arise because of bad weather or mechanical delays. Study the fine print when comparing policies.

If you're traveling internationally, a key component of travel insurance is coverage for medical bills incurred if you get sick on the road. Such expenses are not generally covered by Medicare or private policies. U.K. residents can buy a travel-insurance policy valid for most vacations taken during the year in which it's purchased (but check preexisting-condition coverage). British and Australian citizens need extra medical coverage when traveling overseas.

Always **buy travel policies directly from the insurance company**; if you buy them from a cruise line, airline, or tour operator that goes out of business you probably will not be covered for the agency or operator's default, a major risk. Before making any purchase, **review your existing health and home-owner's policies** to find what they cover away from home.

➤ TRAVEL INSURERS: In the United States: **Access America** (⊠ 6600 W. Broad St., Richmond, VA 23230, ☎ 800/284–8300, FAX 804/673–1491 or 800/346–9265, WEB www. accessamerica.com). **Travel Guard**

International (⊠ 1145 Clark St., Stevens Point, WI 54481, ☎ 715/345–0505 or 800/826–1300, FAX 800/955–8785, WEB www.travelguard.com).

➤ INSURANCE INFORMATION: In the United Kingdom: **Association of British Insurers** (⊠ 51 Gresham St., London EC2V 7HQ, ☎ 020/7600–3333, FAX 020/7696–8999, WEB www.abi.org.uk). In Canada: **RBC Travel Insurance** (⊠ 6880 Financial Dr., Mississauga, Ontario L5N 7Y5, ☎ 905/791–8700 or 800/668–4342, FAX 905/813–4704, WEB www.rbcinsurance.com). In Australia: **Insurance Council of Australia** (⊠ Level 3, 56 Pitt St., Sydney, NSW 2000, ☎ 02/9253–5100, FAX 02/9253–5111, WEB www.ica.com.au). In New Zealand: **Insurance Council of New Zealand** (⊠ Level 7, 111–115 Customhouse Quay, [Box 474, Wellington], ☎ 04/472–5230, FAX 04/473–3011, WEB www.icnz.org.nz).

LANGUAGE

Vietnamese, or *kinh,* is written in a Roman-based script, called *quoc ngu,* created by a French Jesuit scholar in the 17th century. Before that the Vietnamese created their own system, called *nom,* which drew on the Chinese system of characters. Although letters may look familiar, the language is tonally based and therefore quite foreign to Western ears. Barring a few exceptions in tones and words, written Vietnamese is homogeneous throughout the country. However, accents differ dramatically, particularly between north and south. *See* the Vocabulary and Menu Guide at the end of this book for more information.

It's best to **use a phrase book as a point-and-show device,** although a little Vietnamese goes a long way. With a few Vietnamese words, you may find daily interchange—such as bargaining with cyclo drivers—much easier, so **attempt to learn at least numbers and some important pronouns and verbs.** (Some helpful phrases and words are listed in the Vocabulary and Menu Guide.) In large cities English is practically a second language; in the countryside, particu-

larly outside tourist spots, communicating can be difficult if you don't speak any Vietnamese. French is still spoken among an elite but shrinking crowd of older Vietnamese. A surprisingly large number of Hanoians can speak Russian, although there is hardly any opportunity to use it. English is by far the most widely used language in Vietnam's tourist trade.

LODGING

The lodgings we list are the cream of the crop in each price category. We always list the facilities that are available, but we don't specify whether they cost extra; when pricing accommodations, always ask what's included and what costs extra. Properties are assigned price categories based on the range from their least-expensive standard double room at high season (excluding holidays) to the most expensive. Properties marked ✗☷ are lodging establishments whose restaurants warrant a special trip. Unless otherwise indicated, assume that all rooms have private baths (which may have a shower instead of a tub.)

Graham Greene did much to romanticize hotel life in Vietnam in his book *The Quiet American.* But aside from the Continental Hotel in Ho Chi Minh City, immortalized in Greene's book, and a handful of other older institutions including the Metropole Hotel Sofitel in Hanoi, hotels in Vietnam have little old-world charm. The focus today is on newness; the vast majority of joint-venture, international-standard hotels in the nation are less than 10 years old. And many of the older hotels that have survived the wrecking ball have fared poorly from years of neglect, bad management, and lack of funds. State-run properties tend to be run-down and sterile.

Although hotel staffers are generally enthusiastic and some have received training abroad, really good service is still a rarity. A few hotels, however, are as luxurious and have as high standard of service as any international establishment in the world. Beach and mountain resorts are rapidly being developed; particular standouts include the Ana Mandara in Nha Trang, the Furama Resort in China Beach, the Sofitel Dalat Palace in Dalat, and the Victoria Sapa Hotel in Sapa.

In major cities and tourist destinations, the hotel industry continues to grow, with more and more international and smaller-size hotels opening. Many of the larger, international hotels often aren't fully booked and may give you a better room rate than what's listed; when calling to make reservations, **ask if you can get a deal on the price of a room.**

Vietnam has a selection of other mid-size, mid-level hotels and guest houses, generally state run and usually perfectly acceptable for a night's sleep, especially in cities and popular tourist areas. Yet another option is minihotels.

In smaller towns or rural areas expect much more basic accommodations. Phones, televisions, and fax machines are the norm at most hotels outside the major cities, even the smaller ones, but don't expect luxury in anything but the country's most popular destinations. If you are going to very off-the-beaten-path places, you may not have much choice in the kind of place in which you stay—the one or two guest houses in town, which may not be up to your usual standard, may be your only lodging option.

Assume that hotels operate on the **European Plan** (EP, with no meals) unless we specify that they use the **Continental Plan** (CP, with a Continental breakfast), **Breakfast Plan** (BP, with a full breakfast), **Modified American Plan** (MAP, with breakfast and dinner), or the **Full American Plan** (FAP, with all meals).

Reservations are recommended during July and August and during Tet, the lunar new year (January or February); prices sometimes fluctuate at that time.

APARTMENT RENTALS

If you want a home base that's roomy enough for a family and comes with cooking facilities **consider a furnished rental.** These can save you money, especially if you're traveling with a group. Home-exchange directories sometimes list rentals as well as exchanges.

Hanoi and Ho Chi Minh City have a number of international-standard serviced apartments. Most of these are underused, and agents are only too happy to cut deals with short-term occupants.

➤ SERVICED APARTMENTS: **Landmark Building** (⊠ 5B Ton Duc Thang St., District 1, Ho Chi Minh City, ☎ 04/822–2098). **Oriental Park** (⊠ 33 Quang An St., Tay Ho District, Hanoi, ☎ 04/829–1200). **Somerset Grand Hanoi** (⊠ 49 Hai Ba Trung St., Hoan Kiem District, Hanoi, ☎ 04/934–2342).

HOSTELS

No matter what your age, you can **save on lodging costs by staying at hostels.** In some 4,500 locations in more than 70 countries around the world, Hostelling International (HI), the umbrella group for a number of national youth-hostel associations, offers single-sex, dorm-style beds and, at many hostels, rooms for couples and family accommodations. Membership in any HI national hostel association, open to travelers of all ages, allows you to stay in HI-affiliated hostels at member rates; one-year membership is about $25 for adults (C$35 for a two-year minimum membership in Canada, £13 in the United Kingdom, A$52 in Australia, and NZ$40 in New Zealand); hostels run about $10–$30 per night. Members have priority if the hostel is full; they're also eligible for discounts around the world, even on rail and bus travel in some countries.

➤ ORGANIZATIONS: **Hostelling International—American Youth Hostels** (⊠ 733 15th St. NW, Suite 840, Washington, DC 20005, ☎ 202/783–6161, FAX 202/783–6171, WEB www.hiayh.org). **Hostelling International—Canada** (⊠ 400–205 Catherine St., Ottawa, Ontario K2P 1C3, ☎ 613/237–7884 or 800/663–5777, FAX 613/237–7868, WEB www.hihostels.ca). **Youth Hostel Association Australia** (⊠ 10 Mallett St., Camperdown, NSW 2050, ☎ 02/9565–1699, FAX 02/9565–1325, WEB www.yha.com.au). **Youth Hostel Association of England**

and Wales (✉ Trevelyan House, Dimple Rd., Matlock, Derbyshire DE4 3YH, U.K., ☎ 0870/870–8808, FAX 0169/592–702, WEB www.yha.org. uk). **Youth Hostels Association of New Zealand** (✉ Level 3, 193 Cashel St. [Box 436, Christchurch], ☎ 03/379–9970, FAX 03/365–4476, WEB www.yha.org.nz).

HOTELS

All hotels listed in this book have private bath or shower unless otherwise noted. Most hotels listed, and especially those in major tourist centers, have air-conditioning or fans, satellite TV, and international direct-dial (IDD) phones, which you need to make international calls.

The Vietnam National Administration of Tourism has instituted its own rating system, which vaguely conforms to international standards of quality. Yet hotels billed as five star in Vietnam are often more like three- or four-star hotels in the United States.

➤ TOLL-FREE NUMBERS: **Best Western** (☎ 800/528–1234, WEB www.bestwestern.com). **Choice** (☎ 800/424–6423, WEB www.choicehotels.com). **Hilton** (☎ 800/445–8667, WEB www.hilton.com). **Holiday Inn** (☎ 800/465–4329, WEB www.basshotels.com). **Nikko Hotels International** (☎ 800/645–5687, WEB www.nikkohotels.com).

MINIHOTELS

Unique to Vietnam, these privately owned, often family-run operations range from the utilitarian to the plush; they usually provide friendly service, spotless if basic rooms, and a homey environment. Although such facilities as swimming pools and exercise facilities are rare at these minihotels and their restaurants are often bland and lifeless, guest rooms generally have air-conditioning and usually include satellite TV, IDD telephones, refrigerators, and bathtubs. They may also include lots of street noise.

MAIL AND SHIPPING

When mailing packages into and out of Vietnam, be aware that your parcels will probably be scrutinized at the post office. Note that videotapes,

books, and compact discs are especially sensitive items to ship or mail to and from Vietnam. It should take about two weeks, sometimes longer, for mail to arrive in the West from Vietnam.

Note that Vietnam does not use postal codes.

OVERNIGHT SERVICES

The U.S. Postal Service, DHL, FedEx, and UPS all have express mail services to Vietnam. Unfortunately, the service isn't always that fast: it can take from four to seven days, depending on how long the package sits in customs.

➤ MAJOR SERVICES: **DHL** (✉ 778 Lang Rd., Dong Da District, Hanoi, ☎ 04/775–3999; ✉ 4 Phan Thuc Duyen St., Tan Binh District, Ho Chi Minh City, ☎ 08/844–6203, WEB www.dhl.com). **FedEx** (✉ 6B Dinh Le St., Hoan Kiem District, Hanoi, ☎ 04/826–4952; ✉ 141 Nguyen Hue Blvd., No. 286, District 1, Ho Chi Minh City, ☎ 08/823–4326 or 08/823–4399, WEB www.fedex.com). **UPS** (✉ 77 Lang Ha St., Ba Dinh District, Hanoi, ☎ 04/514–2888; ✉ 1 Tien Giang St., Tan Binh District, Ho Chi Minh City, ☎ 08/848–8488; WEB www.ups.com).

POSTAL RATES

Postage is based on weight. On average, a postcard or letter to the United States costs about 16,000đ; one to Europe costs about 13,000đ. Stamps are sold at post office (*buu dien*) branches, which are generally open daily 6 AM–8 PM, and at many hotels and shops. Usually the postal clerk will cancel the stamps on your letter and give it back to you to put into the mail slot. This policy exists in part to eliminate any possibility of stamps being peeled off your letter for resale and your letter being thrown away.

RECEIVING MAIL

Don't be surprised if you receive an already opened parcel—just be grateful it arrived at all. Most parcels are opened as a matter of course, and sometimes the recipient in Vietnam is charged for the "service" of checking the parcel. In lieu of the parcel, you may receive a note providing information on where to collect a particular piece of mail. Sending items such as videos, books, compact discs, and cassettes through the mail is risky. Packages make many stops along the way, and opportunities abound for theft or loss. If these items do arrive, they're sometimes confiscated or checked for subversive material. Such "quarantines" for videos sometimes provide opportunity for replication by unscrupulous postal clerks or customs officials before they're handed over to you. Most letters and postcards will arrive within about two weeks of being mailed from abroad.

The main post offices in Hanoi and Ho Chi Minh City (☞ individual chapters for addresses) have *poste restante*, where you can have mail sent to you from abroad.

SHIPPING PARCELS

To ship your treasures home, take unwrapped items to the post office between 8 AM and 4:30 PM. You can buy packing boxes and large envelopes there. Customs employees at the post office will check all items being sent out of the country.

It is not unheard of for parcels to go missing. **Tape boxes securely** to discourage prying fingers. Finally, cultivate patience; it can take up to three months for parcels from Vietnam to reach North America. Your package is more likely to reach its destination safely if you use DHL, FedEx, or UPS, though the cost will be much higher.

MONEY MATTERS

Although Vietnam is not as much of a bargain as other Southeast Asian countries, it is still a relatively inexpensive destination. However, some upscale international hotels in Ho Chi Minh City and Hanoi command prices exceeding $200 per night. But this is far from average. Reasonably priced minihotels and guest houses are abundant and can run less than $20 per night in Hanoi or Ho Chi Minh City. Elsewhere they're even cheaper.

Food can be a steal. If you eat at small local restaurants, street-side cafés, food stalls, or markets, you'll pay between $1 and $5 and save hundreds

over your hotel-restaurant-bound counterparts. A meal at an upscale restaurant, including wine, costs an average of $15–$20.

Sample costs: a cup of coffee in a street café will cost you 2,500d (16¢); a cyclo ride will generally cost from 5,000d to 10,000d (from 33¢ to 66¢) per kilometer; a liter of *bia hoi* (fresh draft beer) is 2,500d (16¢); bottled beer goes for between 12,000d and 25,000d (about 79¢–$1.65); and a bowl of noodles from a food stall is 5,000d (33¢).

Be aware that Vietnam has an official dual-pricing system, so foreigners often are expected to pay more than double what locals do for trains, buses, flights, and other goods and services. In 1999 an official decree banned dual pricing at temples and tourist sites; despite this rule, higher entrance fees for foreigners remain the norm. Prices throughout this guide are given for adults. For information on taxes, *see* Taxes, *below.*

ATMS

Although ATMs are rare, you can find a few at major banks in Hanoi and Ho Chi Minh City. Outside of these cities, ATMs are virtually nonexistent. For information about specific bank and ATM locations, *see* individual chapters.

CREDIT CARDS

Credit cards have yet to catch on as a form of payment by the Vietnamese, but they are accepted at most large international hotels, upscale restaurants, better shops, large tour operators, and airline agencies. Restaurants, hotels, and shops sometimes insist on a service charge of up to 5% if you pay by credit card, however. MasterCard and Visa are the most widely accepted cards. Some locations also accept American Express and Diners Club.

Throughout this guide, the following abbreviations are used: **AE,** American Express; **DC,** Diners Club; **MC,** MasterCard; and **V,** Visa.

Keep a record of the contact phone number on the back of your cards, the issuing bank's name and address, and your credit card number in a safe place, separate from your cards. Should you lose your credit cards in Vietnam and be unable to reach the issuing bank, contact ANZ Bank in Hanoi or Ho Chi Minh City for help.

➤ REPORTING LOST CARDS: **ANZ Bank** (✉ 14 Le Thai To St., Hoan Kiem District, Hanoi, ☎ 04/825–8190, FAX 04/825–8188; ✉ 11 Me Linh Sq., District 1, Ho Chi Minh City, ☎ 08/829–9319).

CURRENCY

The Vietnamese unit of currency is the dong (abbreviated as *d* throughout this guide), which comes in 100d, 200d, 500d, 1,000d, 2,000d, 5,000d, 10,000d, 20,000d, 50,000d, and 100,000d notes. Since a 50,000d note is worth about $3.30, you have to lug around quite a few notes. It's a good idea to **keep plenty of 5,000d, 10,000d, and 20,000d notes handy for cyclos, cabs, and snacks.** Pulling out 100,000d for a bowl of noodles that costs 5,000d is viewed by many Vietnamese like paying with gold bullion. Familiarize yourself with the 5,000d and 20,000d notes, as they are both blue. The many zeros on bills sometimes make it difficult to see the difference between 5,000d and 50,000d notes, as does the appearance of Ho Chi Minh's countenance on every banknote.

CURRENCY EXCHANGE

Technically it is illegal for many smaller establishments to receive payments in anything but Vietnamese dong, but such rules are widely ignored. U.S. dollars are accepted at almost every private business, but many state enterprises—including trains—only accept dong. Note that prices in this book are listed in dong for establishments that accept only local currency, such as museums, and dollars for tour operators and other establishments that accept U.S. dollars (working with dollar figures can be more convenient than trying to wrestle with equivalent prices in the millions of dong).

It's recommended that you **carry both dong and dollars** with you at all times. Twenty- and fifty-dollar bills are good for exchanging money and for paying hotel bills, although you will get a

lower exchange rate on these bills than you would for hundred-dollar bills.

The official exchange rate at press time was 15,390d to the U.S. dollar, 9,934d to the Canadian dollar, 24,562d to the British pound, and 15,796d to the euro. The Vietnamese dong has been stable for the past few years, but you should still **keep tabs on the exchange rate.**

Although traveler's checks are accepted for exchange at many places, cash—in the form of U.S. dollars or dong—is much more widely accepted. It's best to **bring at least a few hundred dollars in cash** or as much as you feel comfortable carrying. A money belt is a good idea.

For the most favorable rates, **change money through banks.** The Bank for Foreign Trade of Vietnam, or Vietcom Bank, has numerous branches all over the country and gives the official government rate. International banks have a presence in Vietnam and provide extensive banking services, including currency exchange, cash transfers, and cash advances on credit cards. Although they don't often have the best exchange rates, hotels are convenient places to change money. You can usually get the highest exchange rates in gold or jewelry shops, which are eager to convert their business profits into dollars. Using the services of black-market money changers is a high-risk option. Not only do they often fail to give you the best rate, some of these freelance money changers are out to cheat customers. Note that at many places you may get a better exchange rate using higher-denomination bills (i.e., a $50 instead of a $10).

It's a good idea to **get a bit of local currency before you leave home.**

➤ EXCHANGE SERVICES: **International Currency Express** (☎ 888/278–6628 orders). **Thomas Cook Currency Services** (☎ 800/287–7362 orders and retail locations; WEB www.us. thomascook.com).

TRAVELER'S CHECKS

Traveler's checks are accepted in Vietnam but not by every place and especially not in rural areas and small towns. You should **ascertain from an individual establishment whether it accepts traveler's checks,** particularly the type you are carrying, before assuming you can use them. (Banks that issue traveler's checks will tell you every place should take them, which may be correct but isn't always true.) Banks in Vietnam charge a fee, usually 1%–2%, for cashing traveler's checks into dollars. The fee is lower if you cash the checks for dong. Lost or stolen checks can usually be replaced within 24 hours. To ensure a speedy refund, buy your own traveler's checks—don't let someone else pay for them: irregularities like this can cause delays. The person who bought the checks should make the call to request a refund.

OUTDOORS AND SPORTS

Sports such as badminton, martial arts, and Ping-Pong remain popular pastimes in Vietnam. In line with the old Soviet imperative of athletic prowess, Vietnamese schools stress gymnastics. The uneven parallel bars don't pack in the crowds, however, like Vietnam's new sport to watch: soccer. A national semiprofessional league fills stadiums during its autumn-to-spring season. There is a local team in almost every city and town in the nation. Vietnam considers the Southeast Asian Games, held every two years, to be a gauge of their success and competitiveness in the international sports arena.

With the influx of international businesspeople and tourists, golf courses have been opening—or re-opening, as the case may be—after a long period of "antibourgeois" dormancy. These days most fairways are in the south. There are three 18-hole golf courses outside Saigon, for example. Another delightful course is in Phan Thiet, 200 km (125 mi) east of Saigon. In the north, there is one golf course 40 km (25 mi) from Hanoi. One of the nicest, and oldest, courses in the country—dating from the 1920s—is in Dalat, in central Vietnam.

Hanoi and Ho Chi Minh City have plenty of tennis courts, although none of them are free. Swimming pools can be found at many luxury hotels;

inquire about one-day memberships. Some sports clubs in the cities also have pools, but they are not always clean or adequately treated—or even full of water.

Tourist cafés in Hanoi and Ho Chi Minh City organize trekking tours. Mountain biking has a bright future as an adventure activity, but in-country orchestration has proven difficult so far. A few companies in Hanoi also organize kayaking tours of Halong Bay. Contact tour organizations for more information (☞ Travel Agencies, *below*).

The coast has good spots for surfing, particularly Danang. Outside of China Beach, Nha Trang and Vung Tau, you need to bring your own surfboarding, snorkeling, and scuba-diving gear. Jet-skiing and paragliding clubs have opened in the resort towns of Vung Tau and Nha Trang, which also have a few scuba-diving schools.

For information on outdoor activities and sports in particular cities and regions, *see* individual chapters.

PACKING

Since you never know where you will have to lug your bags, it is always a good idea to **pack light.** Bring luggage that is easy to carry and makes the most sense for your travel plans, whether that means a backpack (especially one that doubles as a bag), rolling suitcase, or duffle bag. Be sure to leave room in your suitcase or bring expandable totes for all your bargain purchases. A lock for your suitcase can come in handy, as can a cable lock to secure your bag if you are planning to travel by train.

For warm weather, bring cotton, linen, and any other natural-fiber clothing that allows your skin to breathe and is easy to wash. You can get your laundry done very inexpensively at most hotels, although you may not want to give them your delicate items—they've been known to get ruined. Avoid synthetic or other hard-to-clean fabrics, as you may have difficulty getting them laundered. Pack a light raincoat or umbrella during the rainy season and warmer clothing in winter and early spring. Dress in Vietnam is generally informal, except during meetings. Shorts are acceptable for both men and women, although women may feel more comfortable in longer shorts or skirts.

Sandals, nylon or canvas sneakers, and walking shoes are fine for the cities and more developed parts of the country. Hiking boots are recommended if you're going to head into the hills or onto trails or if you are traveling during the rainy season. Keep in mind that you must remove your shoes when entering most temples, so you may want to bring ones that are hassle-free. A hat and sunblock are always good ideas.

In your carry-on luggage, **pack an extra pair of eyeglasses or contact lenses and enough of any medication** you take to last a few days longer than the entire trip. You may also ask your doctor to write a spare prescription using the drug's generic name, since brand names may vary from country to country. In luggage to be checked, **never pack prescription drugs or valuables.** And don't forget to carry with you the addresses of offices that handle refunds of lost traveler's checks. Check *Fodor's How to Pack* (available in bookstores everywhere) for more tips.

To avoid customs and security delays, carry medications in their original packaging. Don't pack any sharp objects in your carry-on luggage, including knives of any size or material, scissors, manicure tools, and corkscrews, or anything else that might arouse suspicion.

And **don't forget mosquito repellent and a first-aid kit** (with, perhaps, antacids, antidiarrheal, cold medicine, Band-Aids, and antiseptics). Other items to consider are a Swiss-army knife, prophylactics, feminine hygiene products, packs of tissues (toilet paper is not always supplied in public places), moist towelettes, and your favorite toilet articles (in plastic containers, to avoid breakage and reduce the weight of luggage).

CHECKING LUGGAGE

You are allowed one carry-on bag and one personal article, such as a purse or a laptop computer. Make sure that everything you carry aboard will fit under your seat or in the overhead bin. Get to the gate early, so you can board as soon as possible, before the overhead bins fill up.

If you are flying internationally, note that baggage allowances may be determined not by piece but by weight—generally 88 pounds (40 kilograms) in first class, 66 pounds (30 kilograms) in business class, and 44 pounds (20 kilograms) in economy.

Airline liability for baggage is limited to $2,500 per person on flights within the United States. On international flights it amounts to $9.07 per pound or $20 per kilogram for checked baggage (roughly $640 per 70-pound bag) and $400 per passenger for unchecked baggage. You can buy additional coverage at check-in for about $10 per $1,000 of coverage, but it excludes a rather extensive list of items, shown on your airline ticket.

Before departure, **itemize your bags' contents** and their worth, and label the bags with your name, address, and phone number. (If you use your home address, cover it so potential thieves can't see it readily.) Inside each bag, **pack a copy of your itinerary.** At check-in, **make sure that each bag is correctly tagged** with the destination airport's three-letter code. If your bags arrive damaged or fail to arrive at all, file a written report with the airline before leaving the airport.

PASSPORTS AND VISAS

Make two photocopies of the data page of your passport (one for someone at home and another for you, carried separately from your passport). If you lose your passport, promptly call the nearest embassy or consulate and the local police.

U.S. passport applications for children under age 14 require consent from both parents or legal guardians; both parents must appear together to sign the application. If only one parent appears, he or she must submit a written statement from the other parent authorizing passport issuance for the child. A parent with sole authority must present evidence of it when applying; acceptable documentation includes the child's certified birth certificate listing only the applying parent, a court order specifically permitting this parent's travel with the child, or a death certificate for the non-applying parent. Application forms and instructions are available on the Web site of the U.S. State Department's Bureau of Consular Affairs (www.travel.state.gov).

ENTERING VIETNAM

American, Australian, British, and Canadian citizens are required to have a passport and a visa to enter Vietnam. You can obtain a visa from the Vietnamese embassy. The standard processing fee is $65 for a two-week turnaround and $80 for a four- or five-day rush turnaround. Although officially the embassy is only supposed to grant 30-day visas (that you may be able to extend once you're in Vietnam), persistent callers have been known to receive two-month visas.

➤ VISA INFORMATION: **Embassy of Vietnam** (⊠ 1233 20th St. NW, Suite 400, Washington, DC 20036, ☎ 202/861–0737, FAX 202/861–0917, WEB www.vietnamembassy-usa.org).

PASSPORT OFFICES

The best time to apply for a passport or to renew is in fall and winter. Before any trip, check your passport's expiration date, and, if necessary, renew it as soon as possible.

➤ AUSTRALIAN CITIZENS: **Australian State Passport Office** (☎ 131–232, WEB www.passports.gov.au).

➤ CANADIAN CITIZENS: **Passport Office** (to mail in applications: ⊠ Department of Foreign Affairs and International Trade, Ottawa, Ontario K1A 0G3; ☎ 800/567–6868 toll-free in Canada or 819/994–3500, WEB www.dfait-maeci.gc.ca/passport).

➤ NEW ZEALAND CITIZENS: **New Zealand Passport Office** (☎ 0800/22–5050 or 04/474–8100, WEB www.passports.govt.nz).

➤ U.K. CITIZENS: **London Passport Office** (☎ 0870/521–0410, WEB www.passport.gov.uk).

➤ U.S. CITIZENS: **National Passport Information Center** (☎ 900/225–5674, 35¢ per minute for automated service or $1.05 per minute for operator service, WEB www.travel.state.gov).

REST ROOMS

Hotels, guest houses, and restaurants that cater to tourists usually have Western-style toilets, at least in bigger towns. In bus and train stations, on trains themselves, and in restaurants in the countryside, you are more likely to find squat toilets. Most of these do not flush; use the plastic ladle to splash water around. Many public toilets charge a 500d entry fee, which entitles you to a scrap of toilet paper, usually kept in a basket near the front door. Unless you are really desperate, avoid the public toilets in parks and on street corners.

In remote areas the "bathroom" may actually be a small room with a sloped cement floor or a rickety platform perched over a pond.

SAFETY

Although it is widely accepted that Vietnam is safe for tourists, pickpocketing and bag snatching are becoming serious problems in Ho Chi Minh City, and even Hanoi is beginning to see more petty crime. You may want to **remove any jewelry that stands out.** The rest of Vietnam's cities are safer—the biggest hassles are being stared at and being overcharged for purchases. You should take standard precautions, however.

In the big cities **do not walk with your bag or purse on your street-side shoulder or leave it at your feet in a cyclo,** as the snatch-and-ride stealing method (on a motorbike or bicycle) is common. Put your wallet in your front pocket or in a zipped-up bag or purse, and be extra alert when you enter busy markets or crowds. Also, watch out for children or elderly people who may be acting as decoys or pickpocketing you themselves. When sitting in a street café or in a cyclo, make sure you **either hold your bag in your lap with your hands through the straps or put the straps around your neck;** if you do put it at your feet, wrap its handles around your ankles so no one can grab it. If someone does steal your bag, don't pursue the thief—assailants often carry knives. As for cyclos, be sure to negotiate a price before you get in, don't go with a driver you don't feel comfortable with, and don't travel by cyclo after dark, especially in cities. You should also avoid parks at night in large cities.

You should **avoid leaving passports, cameras, laptop computers, and other valuables in your hotel room,** unless the room has a safe. If it doesn't, consider leaving your valuables in the hotel's safe or with the front desk. It is advised that you leave your passport in your hotel safe and carry only a photocopy with you while out exploring. A lock for your luggage can come in handy—even one for other purposes such as for added protection on doors and windows.

Minihotels in popular tourist areas such as Halong Bay seem to be thief magnets, so **always be sure your doors and windows are locked.** If you've hired a boat for a tour of the bay, have someone trustworthy watch your things if you take a dip in the water. And be extra cautious if you decide to spend the night on the boat.

Dozens of Vietnamese are killed every year by unexploded war ordnances. However, it is very unlikely you will visit any area where there are still unexploded ordnances. If you are going someplace where you believe you may be in danger, be sure to travel with a very experienced guide.

LOCAL SCAMS

When changing money, always count the received bills carefully. If you choose to change money on the street, count the Vietnamese dong before handing over your American money. Some black-market money changers try to shortchange customers. For instance, if the total should be 1,390,000d they will give you 1,300,009d.

WOMEN IN VIETNAM

Vietnam is a relatively safe place for women travelers. Since Vietnamese women, especially in rural areas, do not wear shorts or sleeveless tops, you may feel more comfortable following suit. Female travelers seem to encounter more hassles—such as grabbing and heckling—in central Vietnam than in other areas. Women who drink and smoke are frowned upon,

and these activities may provoke criticism in rural areas. Walking alone or taking a solo cyclo ride at night is best avoided; if you're taking a taxi alone at night, sit in the back seat. Finally, don't venture too far down deserted beaches alone, and as you would anywhere, use your common sense.

Don't wear a money belt or a waist pack, both of which peg you as a tourist. If you carry a purse, choose one with a zipper and a thick strap that you can drape across your body; adjust the length so that the purse sits in front of you at or above hip level. Store only enough money in the purse to cover casual spending. Distribute the rest of your cash and any valuables between a deep front pocket, an inside jacket or vest pocket, and a hidden money pouch. Do not reach for the money pouch once in public.

SENIOR-CITIZEN TRAVEL

To qualify for age-related discounts, **mention your senior-citizen status up front** when booking hotel reservations (not when checking out) and before you're seated in restaurants (not when paying the bill). Be sure to have identification in hand.

➤ EDUCATIONAL PROGRAMS: **Elderhostel** (⌧ 11 Ave. de Lafayette, Boston, MA 02111-1746, ☎ 877/426–8056, FAX 877/426–2166, WEB www.elderhostel.org). **Interhostel** (⌧ University of New Hampshire, 6 Garrison Ave., Durham, NH 03824, ☎ 603/862–1147 or 800/733–9753, FAX 603/862–1113, WEB www.learn.unh.edu). **Folkways Institute** (⌧ 14600 S.E. Aldridge Rd., Portland, OR 97236-6518, ☎ 503/658–6600 or 800/225–4666, FAX 503/658–8672, WEB www.folkwaysinstitute.org).

SHOPPING

Bone up on your bargaining skills before your trip. The fixed-price standard of America and Western Europe doesn't apply in Vietnam, where paying the asking price on the street is just not done. Major exceptions include state department stores, restaurants, post offices, and transportation tickets—basically, the government-run businesses. Also, plenty of Western-style shops have opened, such as minimarts and even small supermarkets, and prices in these are usually marked and non-negotiable. However, in other shops and markets and in minihotels, motorbike rental agencies, and some art galleries, bargaining is almost always expected; when dealing with anybody selling goods on the street (postcard and coconut sellers, boys who want to shine your shoes, cyclo drivers, and such), it's positively de rigueur.

It's important to **keep the bargaining process good-natured;** shopkeepers generally don't respond kindly to aggressive haggling. If you have time, comparison-shop for similar items in several stores to get a feel for prices. The final price will depend on your bargaining skill and the shopkeeper's mood but generally will range from 10% to 40% off the original price. If you don't have much time or really like an item, don't hesitate to buy it—you may not see it again (or you may see it for half the price). Also, **don't assume that all tourist-oriented shops are a rip-off**—some actually sell very nice items, but you need to use your judgment about whether a shop seems good.

Knowing numbers in the Vietnamese language puts you in a better position than if you go in armed with nothing but English and cash; most shopkeepers will respect your attempt at learning the language, and they'll think you've been in Vietnam for more than 20 minutes. One expression that's good to know if you're going on a buying spree is *dat qua!* It means "too expensive," and it's a good opening to negotiations if someone's quoted you a steep price. Step 2: shake your head and feign disinterest. Step 3: express interest in *another* shop or person selling the same item. If that doesn't get the price down, start walking away. If they've gone as low as they can, you won't hear from them; if they haven't, they'll call you back. One trick the Vietnamese are not fond of is "testing" the price: seeing how low the merchants will lower their price but then not buying. If you name a price, be prepared to honor it if or when they agree to sell.

It's very important to **make sure an item can be legally taken out of the country before you buy it.** If you are interested in buying antiques, be aware that many items of historic or cultural value to Vietnam may not be exported, though this policy is unevenly enforced. The laws allow the export of antiques of a certain age. If you do buy antiques, you will need approval from the Ministry of Culture to take any pieces out of the country; this can sometimes be arranged by the merchant for a fee. For the most up-to-date policy, contact the Embassy of Vietnam before your trip.

Check on customs and shipping fees to make sure your bargain doesn't turn costly. With any purchase **make sure to get a receipt** for the amount paid, both for potential returns and for customs. If you are purchasing an item that looks like it could be an antique, be especially sure to get a receipt stating when it was made. Many lacquer and stone statues are designed to resemble antiques but are relatively new. The best of these replicas should have a Ministry of Culture label affixed to them that states they are not antiques; or get a note and bill from the shop stating the same thing. Note that some of the Vietnam War memorabilia for sale in Ho Chi Minh City is real, but much of it is mass-produced in Vietnam or China. There are very few antiques in Vietnam's tourist shops.

KEY DESTINATIONS

The best place to shop in Vietnam is in Ho Chi Minh City, where souvenirs from throughout the country are sold at very competitive prices. You'll find wonderful embroidered linens, beaded shoes and bags, and stylish ready-to-wear clothes. Southern tailors are also reputed to be the most skilled cutters in the country, so you may want to have a suit or a traditional Vietnamese *ao dai* (a straight-cut silk gown worn over flowing pants) made here.

Hanoi has Vietnam's best selection of silks and velvets. Hang Gai Street in the Old Quarter is the place to have a padded velvet jacket made to measure. Other Hanoi specialties are blue-and-white pottery from nearby

Bat Trang village and lacquer vases, bowls, and plates.

In the northern mountain town of Sapa, you can buy cloth and clothing embroidered by women of the Dao and H'mong ethnic-minority groups. Or you can ask them to add embroidered designs to your favorite jeans or jacket.

Hoi An is famous for its hundreds of tailor shops. The selection of fabrics is limited, but these tailors can't be beat for speed or price. It's possible to have a whole new wardrobe made for less than the price of a single brand-name shirt. Just be sure to double-check the quality of the stitching.

Hue is known for its conical "poem hats," or *non bai tho*. Made of palm fronds, these hats have cut-out designs, only visible when held up to the light, or an inner rim embroidered with flowers and symbols.

SMART SOUVENIRS

If T-shirts bearing Vietnam's flag or printed with "Good Morning, Vietnam!" don't appeal, there are plenty of other unique souvenir options. On Hang Quat Street in Hanoi's Old Quarter, several shops carve wonderful wood-block stamps. For a few dollars you can have these customized with images and words of your choosing. Also in Hanoi, on Hang Gai Street, many shops sell thin silk sleeping bags for between $10 and $15. They won't keep the chill away but they do make luxurious liners for padded sleeping bags.

In Hoi An many of the houses have a pair of "eyes" over their doors—reputedly to keep ghosts and evil spirits away. Each eye is actually a circle of wood with a yin-yang symbol in the center, surrounded by carved petals. A pair costs about $2. Hoi An is also the place to buy colorful silk lanterns. Ranging from $2 to $15, these lanterns have light wooden frames that are collapsible for easy packing.

WATCH OUT

What seemed like a bargain in the shop might prove otherwise. When buying custom-made clothes, always **check that the seams are double-stitched and without raw edges.** Vietnamese color silks often run, as do the indigo-dyed fabrics made by some of the ethnic-minority groups. Unless you live somewhere with cheap dry cleaners and no rain, **don't go overboard when buying silk.** And be aware that much of what gets called "silk" in Vietnam contains a high percentage of synthetic fibers.

You're better off without some things. Bear in mind that the counterfeit CDs and DVDs that are sold throughout the cities may be confiscated by customs when you get home. Souvenirs made from tortoiseshell or bits and pieces from other endangered creatures should also be shunned, unless you *want* bad karma for adding to the plight of Vietnam's beleaguered wildlife.

SIGHTSEEING GUIDES

In Hanoi and Ho Chi Minh City, travel agencies can provide English-speaking guides for about $15 a day. You may also be approached on the street by former interpreters or by cyclo drivers who want to make 50,000d for a full day's work guiding you around the city. Although this is just as viable an option as any, make sure you understand their English by conducting an informal interview before you agree on an amount.

At places like Marble Mountain, near Danang, you may encounter children who will attach themselves to you as unofficial—and often unwanted—guides. Some of them are charming and informative; others are plain annoying. Your best defense is to tell them up front how much you will—or won't—tip them.

STUDENTS IN VIETNAM

Student discounts for sights and transportation are not common for foreigners in Vietnam. Vietnam's small population of university students is not as well organized as in America or Europe. But the average student group is very interested in learning English or studying abroad. The result is a community of intelligent young locals who for the most part are thrilled to practice their English with you.

➤ IDs AND SERVICES: **STA Travel**
(☏ 212/627–3111 or 800/781–4040,
FAX 212/627–3387, WEB www.sta.com).
Travel Cuts (✉ 187 College St.,
Toronto, Ontario M5T 1P7, Canada,
☏ 416/979–2406 or 888/838–
2887, FAX 416/979–8167, WEB www.
travelcuts.com).

TAXES

AIRPORT TAX

Every time you fly into or out of an
airport in Vietnam, whether on a
domestic or international flight, you
must pay an airport tax. The domestic airport tax ranges from 10,000d to
25,000d, depending on the airports;
the international departure tax is
about $12 in Ho Chi Minh City and
$14 in Hanoi. You must get your
boarding pass and airport tax receipt
before going through the security
check.

VALUE-ADDED TAX

Vietnam's VAT tax is 20% on luxury
items such as alcohol, cigarettes, and
cars; 10% for hotels, bars, and nightclubs; and 5% for most other goods
and services. Larger hotels, especially
state-owned and joint-venture operations, often add another 5% service
tax. **Ask about added taxes before
checking in or ordering.**

TAXIS

Metered taxis are common in Hanoi
and Ho Chi Minh City and are becoming more common in Vietnam's
smaller cities. Simply wave down a
cab on the street, or ask the hotel or
restaurant staff to call you a cab. In
Hanoi and Ho Chi Minh City, the
moment you step into a cab the meter
reads between 3,500d and 14,000d;
after that the rate runs about 6,000d
or 7,000d per kilometer. Fares are
always quoted in dong, and many
drivers will complain if you try to pay
with $1 bills. Although tipping is not
required, some cabbies have developed a habit of "not having change"
in the hope you'll tell them to keep it.

Although many cabbies act like reckless kings of the road, taxis are the
safest way to get around Vietnam's
cities. For information about specific
cab companies, *see* individual chapters. A faster but less safe option is

motorbike taxis (☞ Transportation
Around Vietnam, *below*).

TELEPHONES

Although phone booths are rare and
can only be operated with phone
cards, public phones are common in
shops and even people's homes.

Long-distance calls can be made from
most hotels and guest houses, as well
as from post offices. You cannot place
collect calls from Vietnam.

AREA AND COUNTRY CODES

The country code for Vietnam is 84.
When dialing a Vietnamese number
from abroad, drop the initial "0"
from the local area code. Some city
codes follow:

Dalat, 063; Danang, 0511;
Haiphong, 031; Halong Bay, 033;
Hanoi, 04; Ho Chi Minh City, 08;
Hoi An, 0510; Hue, 054; Nha Trang,
058; Phan Thiet, 062; Vung Tau, 064.

CELL PHONES

Cell phones in Vietnam operate on
the GSM900 system. Cell-phone users
from Europe, Australia, and Asia can
receive and place roaming calls in
Vietnam. Another option is to buy a
prepaid phone card that allows you
to use your cell phone here. It's also
possible to rent cell phones from
VMS Mobifone.

➤ CELL-PHONE RENTAL AND SERVICES:
VMS Mobifone (✉ 54 Lang Ha St.,
Ba Dinh District, Hanoi, ☏ 04/833–
4448; ✉ 123 Hai Ba Trung St.,
District 1, Ho Chi Minh City,
☏ 08/822–8171).

DIRECTORY AND OPERATOR ASSISTANCE

Vietnam has an incredibly efficient
operator service. Call **116** for local
directory assistance. Calling **1080** will
put you in touch with an information
service staffed partly by English
speakers who can tell you everything
from the current time to what percentage of Vietnam's population is
under the age of 20. If they don't
know the answer offhand, they will
take your number and call you back.

INTERNATIONAL CALLS

To call overseas from Vietnam, dial
00 + the country code (1 for the

United States and Canada, 61 for Australia, 64 for New Zealand, and 44 for the United Kingdom) + the area code + the number. Remember when calling that Vietnam is 7 hours ahead of Greenwich Mean Time, 12 hours ahead of Eastern Standard Time, and 15 hours ahead of Pacific Standard Time.

International phone calls from Vietnam cost a small fortune. Most hotels have international direct-dial (IDD), which they advertise as a selling point and which you need in order to call overseas. The connection can be surprisingly clear. The hotel will charge you for your call when you check out.

LOCAL CALLS

You can make local calls for free from most hotels. Even if your hotel room doesn't have a phone, you can usually make calls from the reception desk. Once in a while you will be charged around 1,000d–2,000d to make a call.

LONG-DISTANCE CALLS

To make an intercity or interregional telephone call, dial the city's area code + the number. For instance, to call Danang from Hanoi, dial 0511 + the number. When making a local call, omit the area code.

LONG-DISTANCE SERVICES

As of press time, access numbers for reaching U.S. long-distance operators did not work in Vietnam, although the phone companies claim otherwise. It's worth a try, but don't count on being successful. The hope is that this situation will change in the near future.

PHONE CARDS

You can purchase phone cards at the telephone companies that are usually in or near post offices. These phone cards can be used on special phones inside the phone company offices or in hotel lobbies. Cards are available in the following denominations: 30,000d, 60,000d, 150,000d, and 300,000d. Card calls to the United States, Europe, and Canada cost about 60,000d ($4) for the first minute and about $3 (45,000d) for each additional minute.

➤ PHONE-CARD SALES: **Mobicard Sales** (✉ 32 Lang Ha St., Ba Dinh District, Hanoi, ☎ 04/835–3850; ✉ 123 Hai Ba Trung St., District 1, Ho Chi Minh City, ☎ 08/822–8171).

PUBLIC PHONES

Most public phones, which accept only phone cards and no coins, are in people's shops or homes. Look for a blue sign that reads DIEN THOAI CONG CONG. Local calls cost 1,000d–2,000d.

TIME

Vietnam is 7 hours ahead of Greenwich Mean Time. Vietnam is 15 hours ahead of Los Angeles, 12 hours ahead of New York, 7 hours ahead of London, and 3 hours behind Sydney. Daylight saving time is not observed.

TIPPING

Tipping at restaurants is not common in Vietnam, although many upscale places add a service charge and/or 10% gratuity to bills. If this hasn't been done and the service is good, you might consider leaving 5%–10%. You might also consider tipping other people in the service industry a few thousand dong, including bellhops and cyclo drivers, as they are learning to appreciate gratuities. Although it's not necessarily expected, tour guides are more than happy to receive a tip if you enjoyed their services.

A common ploy among taxi drivers is to claim they don't have the 2,000d or 5,000d note you're expecting as change. Whether you challenge them on this scheme is up to you. Many cyclo drivers will request in English a "souvenir" after you've paid the agreed amount, to which you might feel compelled to answer, "But *I'm* the tourist." Of course, they're really requesting a tip.

TOURS AND PACKAGES

Because everything is prearranged on a prepackaged tour or independent vacation, you spend less time planning—and often get it all at a good price.

BOOKING WITH AN AGENT

Travel agents are excellent resources. But it's a good idea to collect brochures from several agencies, as some agents' suggestions may be influenced by relationships with tour and package firms that reward them for volume sales. If you have a special interest, **find an agent with expertise in that area**; the American Society of Travel Agents (ASTA; ☞ Travel Agencies, *below*) has a database of specialists worldwide.

Make sure your travel agent knows the accommodations and other services of the place being recommended. Ask about the hotel's location, room size, beds, and whether it has a pool, room service, or programs for children, if you care about these. Has your agent been there in person or sent others whom you can contact?

Do some homework on your own, too: local tourism boards can provide information about lesser-known and small-niche operators, some of which may sell only direct.

BUYER BEWARE

Each year consumers are stranded or lose their money when tour operators—even large ones with excellent reputations—go out of business. So **check out the operator.** Ask several travel agents about its reputation, and try to **book with a company that has a consumer-protection program.** (Look for information in the company's brochure.) In the United States, members of the National Tour Association and the United States Tour Operators Association are required to set aside funds to cover your payments and travel arrangements in the event that the company defaults. It's also a good idea to choose a company that participates in the American Society of Travel Agents' Tour Operator Program (TOP); ASTA will act as mediator in any disputes between you and your tour operator.

Remember that the more your package or tour includes the better you can predict the ultimate cost of your vacation. Make sure you know exactly what is covered, and **beware of hidden costs.** Are taxes, tips, and transfers included? Entertainment and excursions? These can add up.

➤ TOUR-OPERATOR RECOMMENDATIONS: **American Society of Travel Agents** (☞ Travel Agencies, *below*).

National Tour Association (NTA; ✉ 546 E. Main St., Lexington, KY 40508, ☎ 859/226–4444 or 800/682–8886, WEB www.ntaonline.com). **United States Tour Operators Association** (USTOA; ✉ 275 Madison Ave., Suite 2014, New York, NY 10016, ☎ 212/599–6599 or 800/468–7862, FAX 212/599–6744, WEB www.ustoa.com).

GROUP TOURS

Among companies that sell tours to Vietnam, the following are nationally known, have a proven reputation, and offer plenty of options. The classifications that follow represent different price categories, and you'll probably encounter these terms when talking to a travel agent or tour operator. The key difference is usually in accommodations, which run from budget to better, and better-yet to best.

➤ SUPER-DELUXE: **Abercrombie & Kent** (✉ 1520 Kensington Rd., Oak Brook, IL 60521-2141, ☎ 630/954–2944 or 800/323–7308). **Absolute Asia** (✉ 180 Varick St., New York, NY 10014, ☎ 212/627–1950 or 800/736–8187). **Travcoa** (✉ 2350 S.E. Bristol St. [Box 2630, Newport Beach, CA 92660], ☎ 714/476–2800 or 800/992–2003).

➤ FIRST-CLASS: **Global Spectrum** (✉ 5683 Columbia Pike, Suite 101, Falls Church, VA 22041, ☎ 800/419–4446 or 703/671–9619). **Mountain Travel-Sobek** (✉ 6420 Fairmount Ave., El Cerrito, CA 94530, ☎ 510/527–8100 or 800/227–2384). **Orient Flexi-Pax Tours** (✉ 630 3rd Ave., New York, NY 10017, ☎ 212/692–9550 or 800/545–5540). **Pacific Bestour** (✉ 228 Rivervale Rd., River Vale, NJ 07675, ☎ 201/664–8778 or 800/688–3288). **Pacific Delight Tours** (✉ 132 Madison Ave., New York, NY 10016, ☎ 212/684–7707 or 800/221–7179).

LOCAL OPERATORS

Most state- and privately run travel agencies in Vietnam organize tours of the whole country, both from overseas or once you arrive. Privately run companies are more likely to be able to customize trips, have better English-speaking guides, and offer you a wider range of restaurant and hotel choices. The state-run operators are generally much less flexible and provide fewer options. The main drawback to organizing your trip through tour operators in Vietnam is that you generally don't have the same recourse to consumer protection as you do with many larger, American-based companies. *See* Travel Agencies, *below,* and individual chapters for more information on local tour operators and travel agencies.

PACKAGES

Like group tours, independent vacation packages are available from major tour operators and airlines. The companies listed below arrange vacation packages in a broad price range.

➤ AIR/HOTEL: **Absolute Asia**(☞ Group Tours, *above*). **Orient Flexi-Pax Tours** (☞ Group Tours, *above*). **Pacific Bestour** (☞ Group Tours, *above*). **Pacific Delight Tours** (☞ Group Tours, *above*). **United Vacations** (☎ 800/328–6877).

➤ FROM THE U.K.: **Abercrombie & Kent** (✉ Sloane Square House, Holbein Pl., London SW1W 8NS, ☎ 0845/0700610). **Kuoni Travel** (✉ Kuoni House, Dorking, Surrey RH5 4AZ, U.K., ☎ 01306/740500).

THEME TRIPS

➤ ADVENTURE: **Asian Pacific Adventures** (✉ 826 S. Sierra Bonita Ave., Los Angeles, CA 90036, ☎ 323/935–3156 or 800/825–1680). **Green Bamboo Café** (✉ 80 Tran Nhat Duat St., Hoan Kiem District, ☎ 04/928–3008, WEB www.vietnamonline.com/greenbamboo). **Himalayan Travel** (✉ 110 Prospect St., Stamford, CT 06901, ☎ 203/359–3711 or 800/225–2380). **Intrepid Small Group Adventures** (✉ 1311 63rd St., Suite 200, Emeryville, CA 94608, ☎ 510/654–1879 or 800/227–8747).

➤ BICYCLING: **Backroads** (✉ 801 Cedar St., Berkeley, CA 94710-1800, ☎ 510/527–1555 or 800/462–2848). **Butterfield & Robinson** (✉ 70 Bond St., Toronto, Ontario M5B IX3, Canada, ☎ 416/864–1354 or 800/678–1147). **Global Spectrum** (☞ Group Tours, *above*). **Green Bamboo Café** (☞ Adventure, *above*).

➤ CUSTOMIZED PACKAGES: **Absolute Asia** (☞ Group Tours, *above*). **Gecko Travel** (✉ 94 Old Manor Way, Portsmouth P06 2NL, U.K., ☎ 023/9237–6799). **Global Spectrum** (☞ Group Tours, *above*). **Green Bamboo Café** (☞ Adventure, *above*). **Pacific Experience** (✉ 63 Mill St., Newport, RI 02840, ☎ 401/849–6258 or 800/279–3639).

➤ LEARNING VACATIONS: **Earthwatch** (✉ Box 9104, 680 Mount Auburn St., Watertown, MA 02272, ☎ 617/926–8200 or 800/776–0188). **Myths and Mountains** (✉ 976 Tee Ct., Incline Village, NV 89541-9004, ☎ 800/670–6984). **Smithsonian Study Tours and Seminars** (✉ 1100 Jefferson Dr. SW, Room 3045, MRC 702, Washington, DC 20560, ☎ 202/357–4700).

➤ VIETNAM VETERANS: **Global Spectrum** (☞ Group Tours, *above*). **Vietnam Veterans of America Foundation** (✉ 8605 Cameron St., Suite 400, Silver Spring, MD 20910, ☎ 301/585–4000).

TRAIN TRAVEL

The 2,600-km (1,612-mi) rail system, built by the French, runs north–south, servicing coastal towns between Hanoi and Ho Chi Minh City. The main drawback of train service is that it's slow. The quickest train from Ho Chi Minh City to Hanoi, the Reunification Express, takes about 30–41 hours, depending on how many stops it makes. Train travel is better for the shorter hops between Hanoi and Hue; Hanoi and Lao Cai, which gets you to Sapa; or Ho Chi Minh City and Nha Trang.

Train travel through Vietnam can be an enjoyable experience, not to mention a time saver if you take overnight trips, provided you can get a soft sleeper or at least a soft chair. Bear in mind, however, that Vietnam's trains are not luxurious. Regardless of what class ticket you hold, the bathrooms are often dirty. Noise is another problem; day and night, when the train stops, vendors may pop into your compartment to try to sell you soda, beer, and cigarettes. Smoking is permitted in all compartments.

Security is another concern. At all times **keep the metal grille over the window shut,** as kids sometimes throw rocks and debris at passing trains. Do not place any valuables near the windows: when the train stops, people may try to grab items through the windows.

Finally, you probably want to **bring food and water with you,** although you can sometimes get some on the trains or from vendors in stations.

CLASSES

There are several seating and sleeping options on the train: the best are soft-berth sleepers, which generally have comfortable, 4-inch-thick mattresses and contain only four bunks; next are the mid-range soft sleepers, which also have only four bunks but with 2-inch-thick mattresses; then come hard-berth sleepers, which have reed mats instead of mattresses and six bunks (the top ones are cheapest); after that are soft seats, which are wooden seats with a soft cushion but no space to lie down; and finally, hard seats, which are just what they sound like. Don't skimp: **when traveling long distances by train, always reserve the soft-berth sleeper.**

The Victoria Sapa Hotel in the mountain town of Sapa sells a train-hotel package that includes luxurious train service, complete with plush carriages, for those traveling between Hanoi and Lao Cai and staying at the hotel. If you want to travel in style and can spare the cash, this is the way to go.

FARES AND SCHEDULES

Fares vary based on the length of trip and the class of travel. You can purchase tickets at train stations; travel agencies can also help you book tickets.

Train service runs daily between Hanoi and Ho Chi Minh City (30–41 hours, $50 for soft sleeper with air-conditioning), daily between Hanoi and Hue (12–14 hours, $20 for a soft sleeper), daily between Hanoi and Lao Cai (9–11 hours, $8 for soft sleeper), and daily between Ho Chi Minh City and Nha Trang (15–22 hours, $25–$35). It's also possible to take a train from Hanoi to Beijing (twice weekly on Thursday and Friday, 55 hours, $100). The northeastern border crossing is at Dong Dang, just north of Lang Son.

The Victoria Sapa's deluxe train carriages leave Hanoi on Monday, Wednesday, and Friday evenings. They depart from Lao Cai on Tuesday and Thursday mornings and on Sunday evenings. Acquiring a berth on this carriage requires that you stay at the hotel for at least one night. A four-berth compartment costs $50 on Mondays, Wednesdays, and Thursdays; a two-berth compartment costs $80. On weekends, tickets for the four-berth and two-berth sleepers cost $70 and $120, respectively.

➤ TRAIN INFORMATION: **Hanoi Railway Station** (Ga Hanoi; ✉ Le Duan St. at Tran Hung Dao St., Hoan Kiem District, ☎ 04/801–1033 recorded information; 04/747–0308 information; 04/942–3697 ticketing). **Saigon Railway Station** (Ga Saigon; ✉ 1 Nguyen Thong St., District 3, Ho Chi Minh City, ☎ 08/846–8704). **Victoria Sapa Hotel** (✉ Sapa District, Lao Cai Province, ☎ 020/871–522, FAX 020/871–539).

PAYING

Train tickets must be paid for in dong, unless you book through a tour company. Foreigners are charged higher fares than Vietnamese nationals. Once you disembark you may need to show your ticket again, so **don't throw away your ticket stub.** If you discard your ticket on the train you may face a major hassle when trying to leave the station and may even be forced to pay again.

RESERVATIONS

It's a good idea to **book ahead,** especially for overnight travel, although for some trips you can only reserve a few days in advance. Tickets can either be booked at the train station or through a local tour company.

TRANSPORTATION
AROUND VIETNAM

There are no subways in Vietnam, nor is there much of a mass transit system to speak of. Public bus service is spotty and unreliable, and the buses are generally unsafe and overcrowded. They do go almost everywhere, however. Nonetheless, you are better off taking one of the private tour buses run by travel agencies and tourist cafés (☞ Bus Travel, *above*). The train is a better option as a mode of public transportation for getting across the country, or at least from north to south. But the easiest way to get around the country is on tourist buses, minivans, or in a car with a driver.

Cyclos (pedicabs), the bicycle-drawn buggies that are unfortunately on the verge of becoming outlawed, provide the most entertaining and cheapest means of transportation in Vietnam. In Ho Chi Minh City the cyclos are too narrow to seat two healthy Westerners; in Hanoi the cyclos are wider and may be able to accommodate more than one person. Although cyclo drivers are supposed to charge 2,000d per kilometer, they definitely deserve more since many double as informed English-speaking tour guides. Plan to pay 10,000d–25,000d per hour. Bargaining is advised, but it's worth giving the guys a break (and a tip). Many streets are cyclo-restricted; if your cyclo driver seems to be taking a circuitous path, it's probably because he's following the law.

One of the quickest ways to get around Vietnam's major cities is to ride on the back of a motorbike taxi, known as a *xe om*. This service usually costs about 20,000d. Motorbike drivers are often ex-cyclo drivers who have saved up enough money for a bike. They'll drive up alongside you and ask where you're going and whether you're interested in a ride. It's relatively safe to travel on motorbikes; unfortunately, the same can't be said for the roads, especially at rush hour.

You can also rent motorbikes and scooters in major cities (☞ Car and Motorbike Travel, *above*).

TRAVEL AGENCIES

A good travel agent puts your needs first. Look for an agency that has been in business at least five years, emphasizes customer service, and has someone on staff who specializes in your destination. In addition, **make sure the agency belongs to a professional trade organization.** The American Society of Travel Agents (ASTA)—the largest and most influential in the field with more than 24,000 members in

some 140 countries—maintains and enforces a strict code of ethics and will step in to help mediate any agent-client disputes involving ASTA members if necessary. ASTA (whose motto is "Without a travel agent, you're on your own") also maintains a Web site that includes a directory of agents. (If a travel agency is also acting as your tour operator, *see* Buyer Beware *in* Tours and Packages, *above*.)

➤ LOCAL AGENT REFERRALS: **American Society of Travel Agents** (ASTA; ✉ 1101 King St., Suite 200, Alexandria, VA 22314, ☎ 800/965–2782 24-hr hot line, FAX 703/739–3268, WEB www.astanet.com). **Association of British Travel Agents** (✉ 68–71 Newman St., London W1T 3AH, ☎ 020/7637–2444, FAX 020/7637–0713, WEB www.abtanet.com). **Association of Canadian Travel Agents** (✉ 130 Albert St., Suite 1705, Ottawa, Ontario K1P 5G4, ☎ 613/237–3657, FAX 613/237–7052, WEB www.acta.ca). **Australian Federation of Travel Agents** (✉ Level 3, 309 Pitt St., Sydney, NSW 2000, ☎ 02/9264–3299, FAX 02/9264–1085, WEB www.afta.com.au). **Travel Agents' Association of New Zealand** (✉ Level 5, Tourism and Travel House, 79 Boulcott St. [Box 1888, Wellington 6001], ☎ 04/499–0104, FAX 04/499–0827, WEB www.taanz.org.nz).

TRAVEL AGENCIES IN VIETNAM

Almost every city and province has a state-run tourist agency that does everything from book trains, planes, and automobiles to arrange guided tours and extend visas. These state-run agencies are often pricey, slow, and not that helpful, but in some smaller provinces they're the only game in town. Hotels, big and small, are frequently affiliated with a state-run or private agency, or they have their own travel services that can organize excursions for you.

The larger firms (Vietnam Tourism, Saigon Tourist, Hanoi Tourism) are huge state-owned agencies with fingers in many pies. If you book a tour outright through, for example, Saigon Tourist, expect to be shuttled every step of the way from the Saigon Tourist hotel to the Saigon Tourist

FESTIVALS AND SEASONAL EVENTS

There are nearly 400 major festivals throughout the country and countless smaller celebrations. Every festival is dedicated to something: a legendary event, a supernatural being, or quite often a famous ancestor. Each region has its own festivals, and festivals common to the entire country are celebrated differently wherever you go. A 4,000-year dependence on the rice harvest has generated an abundance of harvest festivals. Each region celebrates differently, so you may want to ask your tour guide or operator about specific harvest festivals.

The dates of most festivals are based on the lunar calendar, as are weddings, funerals, and other important occasions. The biggest festival, Tet, the lunar new year, falls in January or February, depending on the lunar calendar. Although it is a very picturesque and lively time of year in Vietnam, accommodations are scarce; museums, offices, and shops tend to close for days at a time; and the weather in the north can be cold and drizzly.

The following are some of the most important festivals:

➤ EARLY–MID-JAN.: **Ong Tao,** the Festival of the Kitchen God, falls on the 23rd day of the 12th and last month of the lunar year, right before Tet. During this festival, every family buys a carp for the kitchen god, who watches over the house throughout the year, so he can ride to heaven on it. For a bon voyage to Ong Tao, houses are cleaned and gifts offered. When the kitchen god returns home, New Year celebrations begin.

➤ MID-JAN.–MID-FEB.: **Tet,** Vietnam's largest and most important festival, is a celebration of the lunar new year; it usually takes place over the course of a week between mid-January and mid-February. The themes of this holiday are renewal, spiritual growth, ancestral reverence, and family ties. In many cases entire communities shut down. Many museums, markets, restaurants, shops, and offices close for a four- or five-day weekend.

➤ MAR.–APR.: Early spring, in the middle of the second lunar month, is

the time of the Buddhist **pilgrimage to the Perfume Pagoda** near Hanoi. The crowds at this time can clog the winding river with rowboats and make ascending the slippery stairs to the mountaintop a bit of a traffic nightmare, but you'll be welcomed with open arms by the thousands of pilgrims.

➤ APR.: **Thanh Minh** is celebrated on the fifth day of the third lunar month and is a day of ancestor worship; ceremonies usually involve burning incense over the graves of deceased loved ones.

The **H'mong Spring Festival** is celebrated in the northwest mountain town of Sapa on the fifth day of the third lunar month.

➤ APR.–MAY: The biannual **Hue Festival,** next scheduled to be held in April and May of 2004, is a cultural celebration exhibiting the arts and music of Vietnam and other countries in the region.

➤ LATE MAY–EARLY JUNE: A three-day celebration in the fourth lunar month brings some colorful and oversize mythology to the village of **Phu Dong,** just across the Red River from Hanoi. The event commemorates the legendary exploits of the genie Thanh Giong, an ancient warrior born in Phu Dong who helped ward off Chinese invaders. Two hundred men hoist a massive centuries-old likeness of the local hero—he was said to have been gargantuan—in a spectacular procession on the final day, when a Giong-led victory over the Chinese is reenacted.

Tet Doan Ngu, the celebration of the summer solstice, falls on the fifth day of the fifth month. Historically the festival takes place during the hottest time of the year, when fevers and malaria are most common. Fruit, rice, cakes, and liquor are served to ward off these diseases, and effigies are burned to satisfy the god of death.

➤ AUG.–SEPT.: **Tet Trung Nguyen or Vu Lan,** the second most important festival after Tet, takes place on the 14th or 15th day of the seventh lunar month. It is a time to give thanks and praise to parents and ancestors. But its most important function is to help lost souls by pardoning and looking after them. These homeless spirits, Buddhists believe, include those who died unnatural deaths: soldiers killed in war, murder victims, and ancestors whose graves are not properly tended by the living.

On **Ram Thang Bay,** the 15th day of the seventh lunar month, the portals of hell are allegedly thrown open, and its souls ascend to the material world for a day, where offerings of fruit, sticky-rice cakes, flowers, and sweetened rice cookies are intended to ease their transition to heaven. Captured animals, in particular birds and fish, are released to signify the liberation of lost souls, and it is not uncommon to see a Vietnamese throw a cupped bird skyward or let a carp slither out of his or her hands into a lake or stream. Burning paper models of material objects, called *hang ma,* is also common, and although this tradition has ancient origins, modern times are providing a curious twist— paper models of motorcycles, mobile phones, luxury cars, and even new homes are set ablaze in the hope of providing comfort for the damned. This festival is a favorite for parents, who bring children to the pagodas to teach them about gratefulness, piety, and respect. On the night before Vu Lan, big pagodas in Hanoi and Saigon are packed.

➤ SEPT.: Ten thousand screaming, chanting, gambling Vietnamese gather in the northern town of Do Son in the eighth lunar month for the **Do Son Buffalo Fighting Festival.** Hordes attend for the deep reverberating thud of 2,000-pound beasts racing toward each other from a distance of 250 yards and, perhaps more than anything, for the glory that comes with a victory. The hometown of the winning buffalo and its trainers earns bragging rights for an entire year. A buffalo-meat feast follows the competition.

➤ SEPT.–OCT.: **Trung Thu, or the Mid-Autumn Festival** (also known as the Moon-Watching Festival), one of the larger and more important festivals in Vietnam, is especially for children. Families shop for toys and masks for youngsters and throw parties for their children and friends. Trung Thu cakes are for sale a full two months before the festival begins. Parading around with gongs and drums and doing dragon dances is the order of the day, as is eating fruits and cakes. The festival takes place on the 14th or 15th day of the eighth lunar month.

➤ NOV.–DEC.: **Trung Thap,** which falls on the 10th day of the 10th lunar month, is a festival surrounding the traditional harvesting of herbal plants.

1 DESTINATION: VIETNAM

Vietnam Today: Motorbikes and Water Buffaloes

What's Where

Pleasures and Pastimes

Fodor's Choice

Great Itineraries

VIETNAM TODAY: MOTORBIKES AND WATER BUFFALOES

Vietnam is a country on the move. The introduction of economic reforms, known as *doi moi,* in the mid-1980s acted as a catalyst, releasing the energies of the nation left behind after decades of war and isolation. Now wherever you travel in Vietnam—in the towns, the cities, and the countryside—you will see people on the go.

From the rows of *pho* (noodle soup) stalls lining the sidewalks to the numerous vendors selling postcards to the huge neon signs advertising Western chic, it is apparent that this drive to make it in the new era cuts across social boundaries. Flashing billboards hawk everything from Lifebuoy soap to Heineken beer to the newest luxury apartments, and they tower above streets jammed with motorbikes, bicycles, and more and more cars.

It seems as if once the sun rises, the entire population is up within an hour rushing headlong into another day. The roads are often gridlocked with motorbikes by 6:30 AM, making you wonder just where so many people are going so early in the morning. The answer is in frantic pursuit of advancement, which ends each day only when everyone is too exhausted to continue. Most Vietnamese are in bed by 10 PM. All this goes on despite the continued presence of the old Communist Party cadres, who have by no means completely embraced the gung-ho, American-style capitalism that they themselves initiated.

It is especially in the main cities—Hanoi, Haiphong, Danang, and most of all Ho Chi Minh City (Saigon)—that you see this rush to make money. But travel just 50 km (30 mi) from the heart of downtown Ho Chi Minh City or Hanoi and you still see farmers sowing rice seeds with water buffalos, and duck herders wooing their flocks across roads. These scenes are no less exhilarating than those in the booming cities.

Vietnam is a country of stunning beauty, with a pristine coastline of golden beaches stretching 3,226 km (2,000 mi) from tip to tail along the South China Sea. To the

north, Vietnam borders China along the rugged Hoang Lien mountain chain, a breathtaking landscape of deep valleys and tall, mysterious peaks shrouded in mist. Down the country's enormous arched spine are forest-covered highlands, which can be as deliciously cool as a European spring. These mountains, as well as those in the north, are home to Vietnam's ethnic-minority groups—the Black Thai, Flower H'mong, Ede, and Muong—whose traditional way of life has been basically preserved despite the passing centuries and the ravages of war. The majority of Vietnamese, however, live along the coast, and in the country's two major deltas—the Red River delta in the north and the Mekong Delta in the south. Here the land fans out into patchworks of wet vivid-green rice paddies, fruit orchards, and fishing hamlets inhabited by a thousand generations of farmers and fisherfolk.

In the midst of this beautiful country, stark reminders of the high price paid by the Vietnamese people for their independence are never far away. Although few visible signs of the damage sustained by Vietnam remain, every town has its monument to war, be it a captured American jet fighter or a victorious North Vietnamese tank. And dotting the cities and countryside are huge Soviet-style memorials recording the millions who died in the country's most recent struggle against outside forces.

For 2,000 years the country has been fending off foreign invaders, most notably the Chinese, French, Japanese, and Americans. The Chinese were the first to invade, and by the time they were driven out by Ngo Quyen in AD 938, they had ruled the country for 1,000 years. During the following centuries the Vietnamese migrated south in ever-increasing numbers, battling with the kingdoms of Champa and Angkor as they went. These expansionist ambitions led to conflicts between competing Vietnamese lords—the Nguyen and the Trinh—vying for control of the country.

The French initially entered the scene at the beginning of the 19th century by invitation from the Nguyen lords, who sought assistance in crushing a rebellion against them. But by the mid-19th century, the French had taken over by force, annexing large parts of Vietnam to create the colony of Cochin China. The Japanese occupation during World War II interrupted the French monopoly, briefly. With Japan's surrender, the French returned to rule Vietnam, but not without conflict: by 1946 anti-French sentiments had developed into the French-Indochina War.

The French were defeated at Dien Bien Phu in 1954, and the country was split into two under the Geneva Accords that same year. Cold-war concerns drew the American military into Vietnam, which led to full-scale U.S. involvement in the Vietnam War. But American firepower only reinforced the conviction among many Vietnamese that they would not be defeated. And the 1968 Tet Offensive was the turning point. By 1973 most U.S. troops had left the country, and the Saigon regime fell in 1975.

But strife did not end there for the Vietnamese. Following Khmer Rouge border incursions in 1978, Vietnam became involved in armed conflict with Cambodia until 1989, effectively ending the "killing fields" of Pol Pot. In response to Vietnam's involvement in Cambodia, the Chinese invaded northern Vietnam in 1979, devastating much of the countryside and many towns and villages. But the Vietnamese army repulsed the Chinese, who had advanced to the outskirts of Hanoi. For the first time in decades, the Vietnamese people lived in relative peace. They were not, however, without a new set of visitors: the Soviets, who contributed aid, advisers, and the concrete-block buildings still standing today in Hanoi and Ho Chi Minh City.

Since the departure of the Soviets in the early 1990s, what has become evident is the Vietnamese people's amazing resilience after so many thousands of years of conflict. From each of their foreign rulers they have taken what appealed to them and melded the most dissonant elements of foreign cultures into a way of life uniquely their own. When you visit Vietnam you can't help but marvel at the Vietnamese people's endurance. Waiflike, silk-clad women bear yokes hung with baskets of rice weighing twice their own weight. Or they build roads, protected only by a conical hat and a perfectly white handkerchief tied over nose and mouth. You also can't help but admire their panache: don't be surprised to encounter a pair of bareheaded men careening on a motorbike through city traffic at the height of a midday downpour, the driver tooting his horn with a soggy cigarette in his mouth, his companion, arms outstretched, balancing a large pane of glass on his knees. That mixture of practicality and bravado is in some ways the essence of Vietnam, and it is what's taking the country into the future.

WHAT'S WHERE

The geographical organization of the following paragraphs mirrors the organization of the book. Beginning with Hanoi, the coverage starts in the north of the country, moves south to the Mekong Delta, and ends with a chapter on Cambodia

Hanoi

Quieter and more reserved than brash, bustling Ho Chi Minh City, the northern city of Hanoi is the self-appointed capital of Vietnamese culture. This city of majestic lakes, wide tree-lined boulevards, and hauntingly familiar French colonial architecture is one of the most charming cities in Southeast Asia. Hanoi oozes history and legend: Ho Chi Minh declared Vietnamese independence here in 1945 in Ba Dinh Square; the Old Quarter, a dense 15th-century collection of the original 36 Streets, beckons you into its maze; the Lake of the Restored Sword is the physical, emotional, and legendary heart of the capital; and the many makeshift sidewalk cafés invite you to sip green tea or coffee and share your tales of the city. Hanoi is the home base for touring parts of the north; use it as a jumping-off point to other sites in the area, such as the Perfume Pagoda or Halong Bay, and destinations farther afield, such as Sapa or Dien Bien Phu.

The North

A world away from Hanoi, the rest of northern Vietnam is home to more than 50 ethnic minorities, most of whom live in the fiercely beautiful highlands of the Truong Son Mountains, formerly the Tonkinese Alps. An overnight train will take you to the enchanting trading outpost of Sapa, where you can spend a long weekend in Montagnard country, trekking to the remote villages of the Dao, the H'mong, and the Thai. Jump into a jeep for a bumpy weeklong circuit through the idyllic valley village of Mai Chau and out to Dien Bien Phu, site of the doomed French garrison that surrendered to the Vietminh in 1954. To the east lies the grandeur of Halong Bay, a dramatic region of limestone islets and secluded coves that has earned official World Heritage status. Northeast of Hanoi up Highway 1 is Lang Son, a frontier town where Vietnamese and Chinese residents have put aside the animosity generated by a brief but fierce border war in 1979 in order to proceed with the business of doing business. Here is where people gather to buy and sell everything from monkeys to Mercedes-Benzes.

The Central Coast

Two of Vietnam's finest cities, Hue and Hoi An, are in the central coast region, both providing a fascinating glimpse of Vietnam's past. Hoi An is an ancient trading and fishing town with a heavy Chinese influence. Ancient homes, temples, and meeting houses remain as they were 200 years ago. Hue, the former capital of Vietnam, was once the home of the country's emperors. Although much of Hue was destroyed during the Vietnam War, its Imperial City and palatial royal tombs are still impressive reminders of Vietnam's regal past. In between Hue and Hoi An is Danang, the region's major transportation hub and site of the splendid Cham Museum.

The South-Central Coast and Highlands

If you want to take time out to relax, make sure to visit the south-central coast and highlands. Here you'll find Vietnam's two main resort towns—ocean-side Nha Trang and the cool mountain town of Dalat. On the South China Sea, Nha Trang has a glorious palm-lined boulevard running the length of its beach, flanked by hotels and ocean-side restaurants. Although not as developed as other beach resorts in Southeast Asia, it is a nice place to spend a couple of days. If it's mountains and lakes you're after, head to temperate Dalat, the country's number one destination for Vietnamese newlyweds.

In Dalat the pace is slow, and activities include strolling along the lake, visiting waterfalls, paddleboating on the lake, playing a round of golf, touring Emperor Bao Dai's summer palace, and sipping the local specialty—artichoke tea. Also in the region are the somewhat isolated highland towns of Pleiku and Kontum—good jumping-off points for treks into Vietnam's remaining forests and for visits to the villages of the country's hill tribes.

Ho Chi Minh City (Saigon)

Ho Chi Minh City, still called Saigon by most, is a lively—some might say hectic—city with French colonial architecture, broad boulevards, and a busy waterfront on the Saigon River. High-rises have transformed the skyline of this southern city, and an ever-increasing number of cars compete for space on the streets with a sea of motorbikes and bicycles. The city is filled with history—from the French-built Notre Dame Cathedral to the War Remnants Museum and the Reunification Palace. And its streets are alive with activity. For a good view of it all, head up to the rooftop bar at the Caravelle Hotel or Hotel Majestic. The city also makes a good base for daylong excursions to the northernmost part of the Mekong Delta and the infamous Cu Chi Tunnels.

Mekong Delta

The Mekong Delta is a patchwork of waterways, tropical fruit orchards, mangrove swamps, and brilliant green rice paddies that run their way south of Ho Chi Minh City into the emerald-color South China Sea. It's a land touched by ancient and modern cultures, from the Funanese to the Khmer, Cham, and Vietnamese, all living side by side today after centuries of strife. Running through the upper delta is the Mekong River, dotted with small fertile islands where fruit grows in abundance. In the lower delta are crocodile-infested swamps and cajeput forests teeming with monkeys and wild pigs. The farther south you go, the more untamed the delta becomes. If you're looking for wild frontiers, take time to explore the farthest reaches of the Mekong Delta—it doesn't get much more isolated than this.

Cambodia

With its spectacular Angkor Temple Complex, colonial buildings, and Khmer cities, Cambodia is well worth a trip. It's not difficult to visit Cambodia from Vietnam, particularly if you're heading over from Ho Chi Minh City or the Mekong Delta. The capital city of Phnom Penh is in the southern part of the country, roughly parallel with Ho Chi Minh City. The country is bordered by Vietnam to the east and south; Thailand and Laos share its northern border.

PLEASURES AND PASTIMES

Architecture

The diverse architecture of Vietnam reveals much of the country's history: each invading or vanquished civilization left its mark here in the form of its buildings. Cham temples, such as the Po Klong Garai and Po Re Me Cham Towers on the central coast, are the oldest buildings in the country, dating back hundreds of years. Temples and pagodas throughout Vietnam, particularly in Hoi An and the Cholon district of Ho Chi Minh City, reflect the influence of the Chinese. French architecture has probably had the most pervasive foreign influence on Vietnamese building. Some of the finest examples of classic French colonial architecture, such as the Opera House, still stand in Hanoi. And American-style urban planning and Soviet-era bunker-style architecture are also prominent throughout the country.

Art

Whether you are a seasoned collector or just like pretty pictures, you can appreciate the explosion of Vietnamese art splashed onto canvases throughout the country. Much of the work is derivative (copies of French masters, for instance) or clichéd, but some is truly unique and impressive. A handful of painters, including members of the loosely knit but hiply and cleverly named Gang of Five (Ha Tri Hieu, Hong Viet Dung, Dang Xuan Hoa, Pham Quang Vinh, and Tran Luong), are treated as conquering heroes by expatriates, collectors, and international artists. The undisputed art capital is Hanoi, where dozens of galleries line their walls with the latest by Vietnam's rising stars. An afternoon meandering through the galleries is a must. Lacquerware and stone and wood

sculptures are for sale everywhere. Many pieces are painstaking replicas of ancient figures or statues, whereas others are chintzy knockoffs. If you're in the country to make major art purchases, it is crucial you work with a respected dealer—fakes of the more famous artists are sprouting like weeds.

Beaches

Unlike in Thailand and other Southeast Asian countries, Vietnam's beach culture is still largely undeveloped. The country's endless stretch of pristine coast is still a working shoreline, with thousands of fishing families who row daily into the surf in tiny, oval-shape boats woven from reed and rattan. Some towns along the coast, however—such as Nha Trang, China Beach, and Phan Thiet—are actively seeking to develop tourism. Resorts in these towns are often new enough that they still retain an air of glorious isolation, but they're starting to draw an international crowd. For now, for the most part, there are few restaurants or bars along the waterfront, no boutiques selling designer surf wear, and no lifeguards. And although the coral reefs and sea life are incredible and the surf is excellent, particularly in Danang, very few places rent gear or give lessons. Check with your hotel or bring your own snorkeling, scuba-diving, boating, or surfing equipment. Jet-skiing, paragliding, and scuba-diving clubs have opened in Vung Tau, Nha Trang, and China Beach. For some of the most beautiful, untouched beaches in Vietnam, you'll need to head north to Halong Bay or south to Phu Quoc Island.

Dining

Although it may not look it at first glance, Vietnam is a nation obsessed with its culinary traditions. The cuisines in south, central, and north Vietnam differ subtly. Southern Vietnamese cooking uses a wide selection of greens, fruits, meats, and seafood. The French, ever the gourmands, left their mark on the region in the form of elaborate vegetable dishes (French transplants such as asparagus are still grown in the southern highlands). The Indian influence is also apparent in the south, judging by the number of curries. Central Vietnam is known almost as much for its culinary presentation—exquisitely displayed dishes are small but varied and numerous—as for its use of spices. Here the seafood and fresh fish are adorned with plenty of chili. Shrimp sauce is also a favorite, as are different forms of *banh,* rice pancakes with all kinds of fillings. In the more temperate latitudes of the north, dishes are traditionally lighter and consist of fewer ingredients. Stir-fry is more popular in the north than elsewhere—understandable given China's proximity. But the dish that reigns supreme in Hanoi and the north (although also commonly found in the south) is *pho,* the ubiquitous noodle soup that can safely be called Vietnam's national dish. Served at all hours but especially at breakfast, this chicken (or beef or pork or shrimp) soup for the soul is a work of art that perfectly balances texture and taste.

Shopping

There is plenty to buy at good prices in Vietnam, although perhaps not of as high quality as elsewhere in Asia: custom-made clothing in silks and linens, delicate blue-and-white ceramics, elegant black-and-red lacquerware, colorful textiles made by ethnic-minority groups, and intricate wood carvings of Buddhas and animals. Local markets sell all sorts of items, from aluminum kitchenware, straw baskets, and lacquer chopsticks to plastic barrettes, velvet slip-on shoes, conical hats, and baseball caps. In addition, Vietnam—particularly Hanoi—has a booming contemporary arts scene, although paintings can get pricey. The asking price might be as little as $30, but don't be surprised if it's more than $1,000. In general, Hanoi is less expensive than Ho Chi Minh City and is a better place to find silks and have clothes tailor-made. Ho Chi Minh City, however, has better markets and choicer shops filled with more contemporary-looking goods appealing to expatriates and Vietnam's growing moneyed class. In the rest of the country, shopping is more tourist oriented and is centered on the major sights in the towns. One exception is the colorful market in Sapa, in northern Vietnam. Here hill tribes from around the area convene to sell and exchange their beautifully embroidered, indigo-dyed clothing, as well as other handicrafts and food staples.

FODOR'S CHOICE

Even with so many special places in Vietnam, Fodor's writers and editors have their favorites. Here are a few that stand out.

Cultural Landmarks

Angkor Temple Complex, Cambodia. This architectural marvel consists of more than 300 Khmer structures, scattered across the jungle.

Central Post Office, Ho Chi Minh City. Completed in 1891, this classic colonial building, with a huge map of old Indochina inside, is one of the best examples of the French architectural presence in Vietnam.

Cham Museum, Danang. Savor the glories of the ancient kingdom of Champa at the impressive Cham Museum.

Emperor's Tombs, Hue. Vietnam's emperors were laid to rest in these elaborately constructed, extraordinarily beautiful, and peaceful tombs.

Hotel Continental, Ho Chi Minh City. The setting for Graham Greene's *The Quiet American* and the meeting place for journalists and diplomats during the Vietnam War, the Continental is one of most historic hotels in town.

Temple of Literature, Hanoi. The country's first university is a fine example of 11th-century Vietnamese architecture and an oasis in the middle of Hanoi.

Old Quarter, Hanoi. The streets here in the heart of old Hanoi, which take their name from the crafts and trades practiced by guilds hundreds of years ago, pulse with life at the many shops, eateries, markets, and residences.

Old Town, Hoi An. Eighteenth-century pagodas, houses, and assembly halls built by the early Chinese communities living in Hoi An have been preserved in pristine condition in this delightful historic district.

Dining

Café des Amis, Hoi An. Five ambrosial courses of seafood or vegetarian fare are served nightly; come again the next night, as the unwritten menu changes daily but is always French-influenced Vietnamese cuisine. *$$$*

Le Camargue, Ho Chi Minh City. An elegant open-air villa is the perfect spot to enjoy unique Eurasian cuisine. $$$

Restaurant Bobby Chinn, Hanoi. The friendly, eccentric chef-owner whips up impressive contemporary cuisine drawing on Californian, Mediterranean, and Asian influences. $$–$$$

Lemongrass, Ho Chi Minh City. Excellent Vietnamese food and a tasteful Franco-Viet dining room make this an expat favorite. $$

Emperor Restaurant, Hanoi. You can dine on fine Vietnamese food, including seafood and Hue specialties, in one of two romantic settings: a renovated French villa or a Hue-temple-style dining room. $–$$

Ngoc Suong, Nha Trang. Try some of the world's freshest and finest seafood while dining in a delightful garden. $

KOTO, Hanoi. This Continental restaurant overlooking the Temple of Literature is dedicated to training children in need of assistance with the finer points of food and service. ¢–$

Lodging

Sofitel Dalat Palace, Dalat. On the cool slopes of rolling green hills, this perfectly restored French château–like resort is an ideal retreat, especially for golfers. $$$$

Pan Sea Angkor, Cambodia. Elegant rooms with Khmer art and one of the best restaurants in town make this hotel the perfect base from which to explore the Angkor Temple Complex. $$$$

Caravelle Hotel, Ho Chi Minh City. The most popular hotel in the city has the best location and luxurious rooms with great city views. $$$–$$$$

Metropole Hotel Sofitel, Hanoi. Its beautifully renovated French colonial architecture and central location make this one of the most popular hotels in Hanoi. $$$–$$$$

Hoi An Riverside Resort, Hoi An. On a stretch of the Thu Bon River, this friendly resort has one of the most peaceful, idyllic settings. $$$

Hotel Majestic, Ho Chi Minh City. One of Vietnam's great colonial hotels conjures colonial Saigon in its heyday. $$$

Auberge Hotel, Sapa. This delightful hotel has hardwood floors, grand mountain views, and great prices. ¢–$

Stilt house, ethnic-minority villages. A night in a traditional stilt house—such as those in Mai Chau or outside Sapa—a world away from fax machines and honking Honda Dreams may be your most relaxing downtime in Vietnam. ¢

The Natural World

Hai Van Pass, north of Danang. This stretch of Highway 1, perched on top of the Truong Son mountain range, takes in an unforgettable panorama of the startlingly limpid South China Sea.

Halong Bay, northern Vietnam. Jutting dramatically out of the South China Sea, Halong Bay's limestone archipelago is a water-bound sculpture garden.

Mekong Delta, southern Vietnam. Traveling along Mekong River tributaries on a boat to a tropical fruit orchard may be one of your most memorable excursions in Vietnam.

Phu Quoc Island, southern Vietnam. Catch this beautiful relatively unspoiled island with white-sand beaches and swaying palms before it becomes overdeveloped.

Sapa, northern Vietnam. Hill-tribe cultures thrive in the magnificent verdant highlands shadowed by Vietnam's tallest mountain, Fansipan.

Shrines and Places of Worship

Caodai Holy See, Tay Ninh. This colorfully decorated temple south of Ho Chi Minh City is devoted to Caodaism, a religion based on an amalgamation of Eastern and Western thought.

Emperor Jade Pagoda, Ho Chi Minh City. A Vietnamese "It's a Small World," this pagoda is lined with carnival-like sculptures and reliefs of gods and mythical figures.

Marble Mountains, south of Danang. Remarkable cave temples house dozens of statues of the Buddha, some said to have magical powers.

Perfume Pagoda, near Hanoi. Every spring, thousands make the pilgrimage to the Buddhist shrines carved into the limestone of the Huong Tich Mountains.

Shopping

Daily market, Sapa. Hill tribes from around Sapa convene at this colorful market to sell and exchange their beautiful handicrafts and food staples.

Hoi An. The whole town, a perfectly preserved ancient port, is dedicated to seamstress boutiques and to souvenir shops that sell pottery and paintings by local artists.

Tax Department Store, Ho Chi Minh City. Some of the city's best bargains—from designer clothes to handmade bags to custom-made clothes—can be found at this huge store.

GREAT ITINERARIES

Highlights of Vietnam

1 to 2 Weeks

If you have one to two weeks in Vietnam, divide your time between the country's two major urban centers, Hanoi and Ho Chi Minh City, and take short trips to the surrounding areas. For instance, from Ho Chi Minh City you could make a daylong foray into the Mekong Delta or to the Cu Chi Tunnels and the Caodai Holy See in Tay Ninh. From Hanoi you could take a day trip to the Perfume Pagoda, Hoa Lu, or Phat Diem or make an overnight excursion to beautiful Halong Bay.

With two weeks you can probably also fit in a visit to one or maybe two destinations in the middle of the country—Hoi An, Hue, Danang, Dalat, or Nha Trang, for instance. You might begin in Ho Chi Minh City; fly to Danang and visit nearby Hoi An; take a train, bus, or car to Hue; and from there fly to Hanoi. Or fly directly to Hue for a night and then fly on to Hanoi. Another option is to stay in Danang and organize day trips to China Beach, Hoi An, and to more distant Hue. This itinerary doesn't give you much time to explore each region, but it does give you a chance to see more of the country.

TRANSPORTATION

Air travel to Ho Chi Minh City, Danang or Hue, and Hanoi is the best way to make use of limited time. Note that not all routes are flown every day and that Vietnam Airlines does not have service between every city (for instance, there is no service between Dalat and Nha Trang, between Danang and Hue, or between Hanoi and Haiphong). Check with your travel agent and confirm the availability of flights with Vietnam Airlines as soon as you are in the country. Once at your destination, rent a car and driver to get to places that are close enough to be easily reached by road.

3 Weeks or More

If you have three weeks or longer, you can travel the length of the country; plan on spending even more time in Vietnam if you want to get to more off-the-beaten-path spots. Seeing the whole country will give you a sense of its diversity—from the Mekong Delta's floating markets to the beaches of central Vietnam, from the former imperial capital of Hue to northern Vietnam's rugged highlands. Start either in Hanoi or in Ho Chi Minh City—and spend a couple of days exploring. Then use the city as a base for making one- to three-day excursions to points nearby: to the Mekong Delta in the south, for instance, or to Halong Bay in the north. After seeing the region, head north or south, depending on the city you began in; along the way, stop in such places as Dalat, Nha Trang, Hoi An, and Hue. Two or three days in each destination should be sufficient to see the sights, but who knows: you may find a delightful hotel on a secluded beach and decide to stay much longer.

TRANSPORTATION

If you're set on seeing as much as possible in the shortest amount of time, it makes the most sense to fly between major cities and towns—just be prepared to either backtrack a bit or skip a city or two since Vietnam Airlines doesn't fly between every destination in the country. A series of flights from town to town up the coast from Ho Chi Minh City to Hanoi doesn't take much longer than a direct flight between the two. Only two destinations in the northwest—Dien Bien Phu and Son La—are serviced by Vietnam Airlines; the rest you'll have to cover by land. To get to more inaccessible areas like the central highlands and the DMZ (Demilitarized Zone), be prepared to brave the roads with a jeep and driver or minibus tour.

A slower and less comfortable but perhaps more romantic way to get across the country is by train. The Reunification Express (☞ Train Travel *in* Smart Travel Tips A to Z) travels the length of the country from Ho Chi Minh City to Hanoi (and vice versa), stopping at most major towns along the coast. The scenery is often spectacular, sometimes drab, but the experience itself is never boring. Depending on how long you wish to stay in each place, this trip could even be managed on a two-week visit. You can also quite easily combine air travel with your train journey. For example, from Ho Chi Minh City you could fly to Nha Trang, then to Danang, and from there take a train or bus or hired car to Hue. From Hue fly to Hanoi, and from there explore northern Vietnam.

A third option is to hire a car or minibus with a driver to drive you the length of the country from Ho Chi Minh City to Hanoi, or vice versa. Keep in mind that when driving around Vietnam you should set aside more time than you think to get from place to place. A distance of 100 km (62 mi) can take from 90 minutes to two hours, depending on road conditions.

2   HANOI

Ancient lore and postmodern kitsch collide in Vietnam's capital. Experience both in the sensory feast of Hanoi's Old Quarter, where traditional guilds are juxtaposed with modern glitter. Wander around the city's lakes and along its wide, tree-lined boulevards, where French colonial architecture and age-old temples meet. Explore its lively art and café scenes, and breeze through its quirky museums. Then head out of town on excursions to some of northern Vietnam's highlights.

By Michael
Mathes, Elka
Ray, and
Felicity Wood

Updated by
David Joiner
and William
Jeff Richardson

ANOI, THE SELF-APPOINTED STRONGHOLD of "true" Vietnamese, anti-imperialist culture, has learned to covet satellite TV and blue jeans. The country's leaders let in a flood of overseas investment from China, Malaysia, Singapore, Taiwan, and even the United States, Europe, and Australia, and now the capital of the Socialist Republic of Vietnam relishes its newfound economic liberalization despite itself. And yet while Western fashions, music, and food have managed to elbow their way into the once-impenetrable north, Hanoi is appealing because it retains its ancient culture, French colonial architecture, broad tree-lined boulevards, and beautiful lakes.

The city dates to the 7th century, when Chinese Sui dynasty settlers occupied the area and set up a capital called Tong Binh. In 1010 King Ly Thai To is said to have seen a golden dragon ascending from Hoan Kiem Lake. The dragon is a traditional Chinese symbol of royal power, and the king took the omen literally: he relocated his capital to the shores of the lake, the site of present-day Hanoi, and named his new city Thang Long, or "City of the Ascending Dragon." During the 11th century the old citadel was built, and 36 villages, each with its own specialized vocation, sprang up to service the royal court. This is the origin of the 36 streets that define the city's Old Quarter.

In 1428 King Le Loi is said to have driven Vietnam's Chinese overlords from the country with the help of a magic sword from heaven. Celebrating his success after the war with a boating excursion on a lake, Le Loi was confronted by a gigantic golden tortoise that retrieved the sword for its heavenly owner. Thus the lake became known as the Lake of the Restored Sword, or Ho Hoan Kiem. In 1789 the Chinese reconquered Hanoi, but not for long. Nguyen Hue, leader of a rebellion in Tay Son (in the south), drove the Manchu invaders out of the country and crowned himself Emperor Quang Trung. By then, however, the country was officially led by the Nguyen dynasty, which moved the capital to Hue under the rule of Gia Long in 1802. This chapter in northern Vietnam's history was in part orchestrated by the French, who began to play a stronger role in the political and commercial fabric of the country.

The French usurped more and more control, setting up the protectorate of Annam in 1883–84, which meant the Hue royalty held the reins but only under the auspices of French rule. In the following years the French set up its administration and used Hanoi as the Eastern Capital, or Dong Kinh (the origin of *Tonkin*), of French Indochina. The French filled in canals between Hanoi's many lakes and created a plain on which to remake the capital in its own mold, thereby eliminating much of the Chinese character of the city. They constructed the large villas and administrative buildings that cluster in the streets around the present-day Presidential Palace and the Ho Chi Minh Mausoleum and that continue to give the city a somewhat dilapidated but still striking colonial-era feel.

In 1954 the French were defeated by the Vietminh at Dien Bien Phu, and France, Britain, the United States, and the Soviet Union decided at the Geneva Accords to divide the country at the 17th parallel. From 1954 until 1975, Hanoi served as the capital of the Democratic Republic of Vietnam, or North Vietnam, from which Ho Chi Minh initiated his struggle to reunify the country. Despite American attempts to smash the Communist administration by bombing it from the air, the city survived the war with most of its grandeur remarkably intact. The post-1975 socialist order sought to seal off the city and, after the war with China in 1979, expelled ethnic Chinese from Vietnam, although many of these predominantly mercantile families had lived in Vietnam for generations.

In the decades after 1975, relations with the Soviet Union were strengthened. Tens of thousands of Russian advisers came to live in Hanoi and other parts of the country, leaving their mark in such buildings as the Cultural Friendship Palace (formerly known as the Viet Xo Cultural Palace). But the '80s were a tough time for Hanoians and everyone else. Natural disasters and international isolation led to near mass starvation. Then in 1986 the government proclaimed *doi moi*, the move to a market economy. Foreign investors started preliminary explorations, and the Soviet Union dissolved, taking with it foreign assistance to Vietnam. But more and more foreign investment started coming, especially after the American embargo was lifted in 1994.

More than a decade of economic reforms has changed the attitudes of the ruling party members considerably, and reformist city leaders are learning the ways of capitalism quickly. The sanctimonious concept known as market socialism is intended to strike a delicate balance between socialist ideals and economic prosperity, but although most young Hanoians are familiar with the former, it is the latter they crave.

Few can argue that the last decade of change in Hanoi has been anything short of a godsend. Hanoi in the 1990s welcomed billions of dollars of foreign investment and the many international visitors eager to see this city (and nation) in the midst of renewal. Since the late 1990s, however, the economy has slowed its overheated pace, in part due to lingering effects of the Asian financial crisis that rocked Vietnam's regional neighbors and prompted a conservative rethink by the powers that be, and in part because Vietnam has proven at times to be an unsupportive environment for investment. The country has seen more and more foreign investors pack their capital and technology and leave, while international aid has also fallen off—along with local employment. But despite continued grumbling by foreign investors, the economy slowly continues to open. General secretary of the Communist Party Nong Duc Manh is regarded as a reform-minded leader, and he has tacitly acknowledged Vietnam's need to implement economic change. And the two most important issues in the 2002 National Assembly election dealt with corruption and the ability of Vietnam to become more widely integrated in the global economy. One clear boon for Vietnam has been the normalization of trade relations with the United States in 2001 after years of negotiation. The agreement, which requires stronger government efforts to protect intellectual property rights on Vietnam's part, is expected to benefit Vietnam's exports by sharp tariff reductions. This agreement may also be a stepping stone to gaining membership in the World Trade Organization in the near future.

Hanoians have increasing amounts of disposable income, and the city is rapidly modernizing: less than a decade ago the predominant sound at an intersection was the delicate ring of bicycle bells; today motorcycles and cars are taxing the city's antiquated road system. Life for a pedestrian is, in short, dangerous. But the chaos has its own attraction. Dust hangs heavy in the air as a side effect of the construction boom, and you can see changes that took years to happen in the West occurring literally before your eyes. Where the prison commonly referred to by U.S. soldiers as the Hanoi Hilton once stood is now a 20-story office building. Where once a small lake sat is now a gas station.

Nonetheless, Hanoi remains a city of academics, artists, diplomats—and contradictions. Although you will see people carrying their new TVs on the back of their Honda Dream motorbikes, you will also see people carrying hundreds of pounds of rice on bicycles. People may zoom around all day doing business, but they also take time out for discussions over a cup of coffee in a café.

Pleasures and Pastimes

Art Galleries

Hanoi is Vietnam's undisputed fine arts capital, with dozens of art galleries happily partaking in an artistic renaissance. At least half a dozen are serious venues and not just wall space for souvenir art. A tour of the finer galleries—showing the works of young painters like Dinh Y Nhi, Truong Tan, and Le Thiet Cuong—affords a glimpse into the modern Vietnamese psyche. Exhibits at government-sponsored galleries show Vietnam's awkward transformation from communism to "free-market socialism." Here, idyllic portraits of village life hang next to political propaganda posters. Extraordinary watercolors on rice paper, the multifarious weavings of the ethnic minority groups, the burnished inlay of lacquer, a Chinese creation embraced by Vietnam as its own—all have emerged from hibernation to create a national oeuvre palatable to Western sensibilities (perhaps too palatable, say critics, who have voiced their disdain for the wall candy that says little about the strains or surges in Vietnamese society). With the burgeoning reputation of Vietnamese art in both domestic and international circles, however—and perhaps due to tourists' predilection for wall candy—prices have risen remarkably in the past decade.

Cafés

More than any other city in Vietnam, Hanoi has a flourishing café society, a legacy of French colonial days. Historic haunts compete with trendy cafés serving coffee to the sounds of jazz and MTV. At the humbler end of the spectrum, myriad sidewalk spots—often consisting of just a few tiny stools and tables—play host to students, artists, Communist Party cadres, and philosophical types who sip *ca fe den,* or black coffee, sometimes with a whipped egg on top.

Dining

Hanoi's cuisine holds plenty of excitement if you're an adventurous diner. What it doesn't have in color or spice it makes up for in unusual offerings—from eight-course meals of dog meat (*thit cho*) to barbecued songbirds and snake-penis wine. (In the outlying snake village of Le Mat, your dinner is skinned alive and its blood mixed with rice wine for a 100-proof shot of virility.)

If you're looking for a dinner a bit less provocative, you're in luck: Hanoi is also home to Vietnam's most famous dish—*pho* (rice noodles in chicken or beef broth). This and other northern specialties are best enjoyed at the bustling sidewalk food stalls lining many streets. Hanoi also has a wide selection of good international restaurants, and new ones open all the time. They also close frequently, so some listings may be gone by the time you get to Hanoi; check in advance before setting out.

International cuisine options run the gamut from Vietnamese, Thai, and Japanese to Indian, French, Spanish, and Italian. Prices range from the incredibly cheap to the just plain inexpensive—even in more upscale restaurants you'll pay less than in other big cities around the world (except perhaps at the big international hotels). In Hanoi, restaurants usually close by 10 PM. Sidewalk eateries stop serving breakfast and lunch by 2 and usually reopen for dinner around 4. You can always find a late-night noodle stand.

The capital is also a city for beer drinkers. Pints of *bia hoi* (fresh but weak draft beer) are enjoyed from late morning, with snack foods like boiled peanuts, dried squid, and pork rolls. Hundreds of bia hoi sites dot the city, providing ample opportunity for you to experience this quintessential Hanoi pastime.

Lakes

Hanoi's network of lakes is perhaps its most romantic asset. In the evenings groups of Vietnamese of all ages line the shores of Hanoi's biggest lake, West Lake (Ho Tay), and central Hoan Kiem Lake to soak up the calming breeze off the water. With such an abundance of water, it's surprising that boating is not really part of Hanoi life. Apart from the canoes used by fisherfolk and a few low-budget paddleboats popular with courting couples, the lakes are free of nautical traffic. You can, however, hire cruise boats on West Lake for large parties. And the private, upscale Hanoi Club on the lake's southeast fringe has introduced some speedboats, Jet Skis, and catamarans.

Lodging

In the last decade, many luxurious joint-venture international hotels have opened in Hanoi—too many, it appears, and the resulting price war means good news for visitors. It's possible to negotiate cheaper room rates at upscale hotels, particularly off-season. Some of these hotels are in the early years of their existence, which is reflected in the sometimes haphazard service. Patience may be required. Minihotels, which are reasonably priced and generally have such amenities as cable TV, IDD telephones, and air-conditioning, are another good option. These smaller properties are often a better choice than the huge state-run hotels, many of which were built in the '60s and haven't been properly maintained or renovated since.

Most hotels are in the historic, crowded, and central Hoan Kiem District, which includes the bustling Old Quarter, or in the Ba Dinh District, around Ho Chi Minh Mausoleum and on West Lake. Although hotels in the Ba Dinh District may seem a little far away—you may need to take a taxi to get into the center of town—they are out of the hustle and bustle of downtown and closer to most of the embassies and some corporate offices.

Unless otherwise noted, all hotels have IDD phones and private bathrooms.

Shopping

It is often said that the average working Hanoi woman spends more than 50% of her salary on clothing. And judging by the activity around the vendors selling both bolts of cloth and ready-to-wear fashions, it's more than just an urban myth. The Vietnamese—both men and women—are generally sharp dressers (if they can afford to be), mixing classic European style and retro '70s items. You can easily get clothing—in silk, linen, or any other fabric—tailor-made in a day or two. Hanoi has some of Vietnam's best selections of silver jewelry, pottery, hand-woven textiles, embroidery, and art, as well as traditional prints, bright wooden water puppets, pottery, and baskets from nearby villages. Finding quality gifts may take some hunting, however, as standards of work vary greatly. Unlike those in many other Asian cities, Hanoi's larger markets are generally better for sightseeing than for purchasing souvenirs, so smaller stores are your best bet.

EXPLORING HANOI

Hanoi is divided into four main districts, or *quan*. The **Hoan Kiem District**, named after the lake at its center, stretches from the railway tracks to the Red River, north of Nguyen Du Street, and is the hub of all local and tourist activity. Just north of the lake is the Old Quarter, a charming cluster of ancient streets. South of the lake you'll find the modern city center, once the French Quarter, which houses grand colonial-style villas that have been converted into hotels and offices; the best examples of French-era architecture are around Dien Bien Phu Street and Le Hong Phong Street, where embassies line the road.

The **Ba Dinh District** includes the zoo, the Ho Chi Minh Mausoleum, and areas around West Lake. Stately buildings, fine hotels, and open spaces define the area. North of both Ba Dinh and Hoan Kiem is picturesque West Lake. The **Hai Ba Trung District,** which covers the southeast part of Hanoi, is a calm, elegant residential area; the primary attraction here is Lenin Park, in the northwest corner of the district. The **Dong Da District,** to the southwest, is where the Temple of Literature can be found (along its northern edge).

Unlike Ho Chi Minh City, Hanoi does have a few places where you can take a pleasant stroll, particularly around the edges of its many lakes. The escalating traffic congestion along its narrow streets, where the footpaths are already crowded with sidewalk vendors, often forces you back out into the melee, however.

Getting around Hanoi on foot can be tiring, so if you intend to stick within the Old Quarter or elsewhere in Hoan Kiem District, break up your walks with a cyclo (pedicab) ride or two. Otherwise consider taking taxis, or if the weather is good and you're feeling a little more adventurous, hop on the back of a *xe om* (motorcycle taxi). Although the traffic may look a little daunting, once you learn to trust your driver, you will (perhaps) realize there actually is a knack for navigating what seems like streams of vehicular anarchy. If you're feeling really brave, consider renting a bicycle for a day and pedaling yourself around. However you choose to travel, keep in mind that many streets in Hanoi— and throughout Vietnam—bear different names in different sections.

Once you have seen the sights in Hanoi, it's time to jump off into the "real" Vietnam—the countryside. Less than an hour out of Hanoi in any direction brings you to stretches of rice paddies interrupted only by villages and jagged rocky outcrops, which makes taking day trips, with the capital as a base, a very viable option.

Great Itineraries

IF YOU HAVE 2 DAYS

If you'll just be passing through, your time would be best spent exploring the Old Quarter and visiting the Ho Chi Minh Mausoleum and the adjacent museum. On your second day head to the Temple of Literature, browse through the city's many art galleries, and take in an evening show at the water-puppet theater.

IF YOU HAVE 5 DAYS

Spend two days wandering the Old Quarter and exploring the Ba Dinh District, where you'll find such interesting sights as the Ho Chi Minh Mausoleum, One-Pillar Pagoda, and the Temple of Literature. Then devote your remaining time to side trips from the city: to Halong Bay (☞ Chapter 3), where you can easily spend two days exploring the limestone grottoes by boat; a one-day trip to the Perfume Pagoda (☞ Side Trips from Hanoi, *below*); or an overnight stay in a Thai minority family's stilt house in Mai Chau Valley (☞ Chapter 3).

IF YOU HAVE 10 DAYS

Spend a few days seeing the major sights described above while making arrangements to travel to Sapa (☞ Chapter 3) by car or train (allow a day or an overnight for traveling either way). Sapa's mountain trails

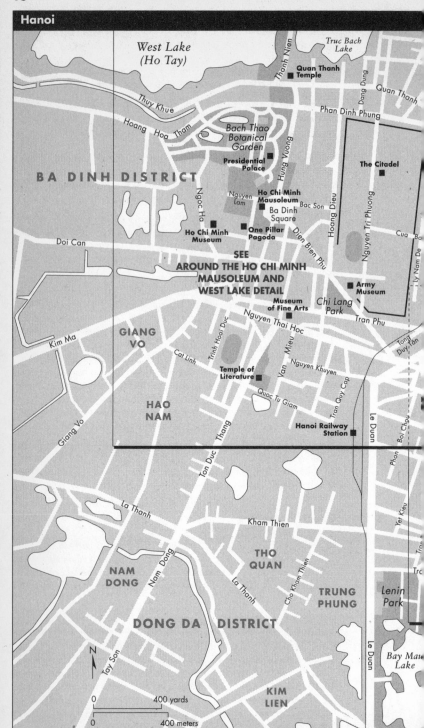

West Lake
(Ho Tay)

Truc Bach
Lake

Quan Thanh
Temple

Thanh Nien

Dang Dung

Quan Thanh

Thuy Khue

Phan Dinh Phung

Hoang Hoa Tham

Bach Thao
Botanical
Garden

Hung Vuong

The Citadel

BA DINH DISTRICT

Presidential
Palace

Ngoc Ha

Nguyen
Lam

Ho Chi Minh
Mausoleum

Bac Son

Ho Chi Minh
Museum

Ba Dinh
Square

One Pillar
Pagoda

Dien Bien Phu

Hoang Dieu

Nguyen Tri Phuong

Cua

Ly Nam De

Doi Can

**SEE
AROUND THE HO CHI MINH
MAUSOLEUM AND
WEST LAKE DETAIL**

Army
Museum

Chi Lang
Park

Kim Ma

Museum
of Fine Arts

Nguyen Thai Hoc

Tran Phu

Tong
Duy Tan

**GIANG
VO**

Cat Linh

Trinh Hoai Duc

Van Mieu

Nguyen Khuyen

Giang Vo

**HAO
NAM**

Temple of
Literature

Quoc Tu Giam

Tran Quy Cap

Le Duan

Phan Boi Chau

Hanoi Railway
Station

Ton Duc Thang

La Thanh

Kham Thien

**THO
QUAN**

Yet Kieu

Nam Dong

Cho Kham Thien

**NAM
DONG**

La Thanh

**TRUNG
PHUNG**

**Lenin
Park**

DONG DA DISTRICT

N

Tay Son

Le Duan

**KIM
LIEN**

Bay Mau
Lake

0   400 yards

0   400 meters

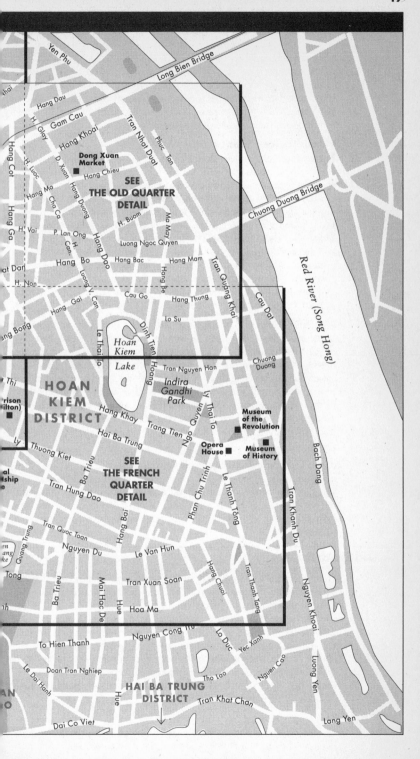

Yen Phu

Long Bien Bridge

Hang Dau

H. Giay Gam Cau

Hang Khoai

Tran Nhat Duat

Phuc Tan

Chuong Duong Bridge

Red River (Song Hong)

D. Xuan **Dong Xuan Market**

Hang Chieu

SEE THE OLD QUARTER DETAIL

Hang Co

Hang Ma Cho Ca

Hang Duong

H. Buom

Ma May

H. Luoc

Hang Ga

H. Vai P. Lan Ong

H. Can

Luong Ngoc Quyen

Hang Dao

Hang Bac

Hang Mam

Tran Quang Khai

Cau Dat

at Dar

Hang Bo

Hang Be

H. Non

Luong V. Can

Cau Go

Hang Thung

g Bong

Hang Gai

Le Thai To

Lo Su

Hoan Kiem Lake

Dinh Tien Hoang

Chuong Duong

Thi

HOAN KIEM DISTRICT

Tran Nguyen Han

(rison (ilton)

Hang Khay

Indira Gandhi Park

Ly Thai To

Quyen

Museum of the Revolution

Trang Tien

Ly

Hai Ba Trung

Opera House

Museum of History

Thuong Kiet

SEE THE FRENCH QUARTER DETAIL

Ba Trieu

al nship e

Tran Hung Dao

Hang Bai

Phan Chu Trinh

Le Thanh Tong

Tran Khanh Du

Bach Dang

Tran Quoc Toan

Nguyen Du

Le Van Hun

en ang ke

Quang Trung

Hang Chuoi

Tran Thanh Tong

Nguyen Khoai

Tong

Ba Trieu

Mai Hac De

Tran Xuan Soan

Hoa Ma

h

Hue

Nguyen Cong Tru

Lo Duc

Yec Xanh

Nguen Cao

Luong Yen

To Hien Thanh

Tho Lao

Le Dai Hanh

Doan Tran Nghiep

AN O

Hue

HAI BA TRUNG DISTRICT

Tran Khat Chan

Lang Yen

Dai Co Viet

and ethnic minority villages will occupy you for at least two full days. Upon your return to Hanoi, take in the sights you may have missed, such as Lenin Park or the Opera House and the nearby Museum of History and Museum of the Revolution. Your next excursion could be to the mist-covered islets of Halong Bay or a shorter trip to the Perfume Pagoda or the ancient Vietnamese capital of Hoa Lu. If you have time, make your way to the nearby professional crafts villages such as Bat Trang, the source of most ceramics sold in Hanoi, just 12 km (7 mi) away on the east side of the Red River.

When to Tour Hanoi

In terms of weather, the ideal time to visit Hanoi is between October (with temperatures averaging 80°F) and mid-December (with temperatures ranging from the upper 60s to mid-70s), when the heat and humidity are not so oppressive. But be prepared for cold snaps and chilly nights. The brief spring from March to April is also a pleasant time. From January to March a layer of clammy mist—the infamous *mua phun*—hovers over Hanoi. The city begins its summer swelter in May and sweats through August, when the monsoons bring heavy downpours and sudden flooding. This continues until late September, so if you choose to brave the elements at this time, bring rubber footwear and rain pants or buy them in Hanoi—because you could be in it up to your knees. Temperatures range from the mid-70s to the high 90s.

Late January to early February is a good time to visit if you want to breathe in the excitement of Tet, the lunar new year, a movable date based on the Chinese lunar calendar. In preparation for Vietnam's largest festival, the Old Quarter comes alive with floor-to-ceiling displays of moon cakes, red banners, joss sticks, and red envelopes for giving lucky money (*mung tuoi*) to children. Beware: when Tet does arrive, many shops and restaurants close for up to a week—although some restaurants have discovered the financial benefits of staying open. If you're planning to conduct any business, this is definitely not the time to do it.

February and March are the months to join the mass Buddhist pilgrimage to the Perfume Pagoda, but be prepared to deal with serious crowds—many thousands each day—if you make the trip during this peak season. Smaller religious festivals take place at Hanoi's temples and outlying villages in March and April. Because all Vietnamese festivals follow the lunar calendar, check with your tour operator or travel agency for exact dates.

The Old Quarter

Hoan Kiem Lake, Long Bien Bridge, a former city rampart, and a citadel wall surround the oldest part of Hanoi. The area was unified under Chinese rule, when ramparts were built to encircle the city. When Vietnam gained its independence from China in the 11th century, King Ly Thai To built his palace here, and the area developed as a crafts center. Artisans were attracted from all over the northern part of the country and formed cooperative living and working situations based on specialized trades and village affiliation. In the 13th century the various crafts—silversmiths, metalworkers, potters, carpenters, and so on—organized themselves into official guilds.

This area is referred to as the 36 Streets (Pho Co)—actually there are nearly 70. To this day the streets are still named after the crafts practiced by the original guilds, and they maintain their individual character despite the encroachment of more modern lifestyles. Note the slim buildings called tunnel or tube houses—with narrow frontage but deceiving depth—that combine workshops and living quarters. They were built this way because each business was taxed according to the width of its storefront. In addition to the specialty shops you'll still find here, each street has religious structures reflecting the beliefs of the village from which its original guilds came. Some are temples dedicated to the patron saint of a particular craft. Hang Bong and Hang Dao, for example, each have five of these pagodas and small temples. Many are open to the public and provide welcome relief from the intensity of the streets.

Numbers in the text correspond to numbers in the margin and on the Old Quarter map.

A Good Walk

Begin your walking tour of the Old Quarter in the northern section of the Hoan Kiem District, at the **Dong Xuan Market** ① on Hang Chieu Street. From here you can dive right into the bustle of the ancient streets—but be careful in the traffic. These streets are narrow, and the main roadways are clogged with motorbikes, street sweepers, endless mercantile activity, and more. Also be aware that many streets in Hanoi bear different names in different sections. The main artery north through the Old Quarter, for example, is 1½ km (1 mi) long and changes its name six times. This is the street on which you'll start.

From the intersection of Hang Chieu and Dong Xuan streets, head south on Dong Xuan, which immediately turns into Hang Duong (Sugar) Street and then into Hang Ngang Street. Spare a moment for 48 Hang Ngang Street, where President Ho Chi Minh wrote his country's Declaration of Independence in 1945. Continue south to **Hang Dao Street** ②, which divides the Old Quarter and serves as a convenient corridor from which to venture down any of the appealing side streets. Once you come to busy **Hang Bac Street** ③, turn left and continue to Ma May Street, where you should make another left and walk about 100 yards to No. 87, the graceful **Antique House** ④.

From here, backtrack to Hang Bac, turn left, and walk half a block to Hang Be Street, part of the historic boatbuilding district. Bamboo rafts, called *cai mang,* were once designed on this street for the shallow rivers, lakes, and swamps of the city. From Hang Be Street make a right on Cau Go Street, the southeast border of the Old Quarter. This neighborhood was known for its flower market in colonial times, a vestige of which can be found before the intersection with Hang Dao Street. Just beyond this flower mart and to the left is the northern tip of **Hoan Kiem Lake** ⑤, the focal point for legends surrounding King Le Loi's encounter with the Ho Guom tortoise. On the left (east), a distinctive red footbridge leads to **Ngoc Son Temple** ⑥, a good spot to rest and enjoy the lake.

Walk back to Cau Go Street and through the chaotic intersection here. To the west of this roundabout, Cau Go Street becomes **Hang Gai Street** ⑦, where you can wander through art galleries or shop for embroidery, silk, and other souvenirs. From here turn north onto Hang Hom Street, which leads to **Hang Quat Street** ⑧. This area has a few of the oldest musical instrument shops still standing in the Old Quarter. A quick jog to the left on Hang Non Street will bring you to Hang Thiec Street, where utilitarian tin chests and utensils dangle from every doorway. Farther north, this street turns into Thuoc Bac Street, which eventually intersects with **Hang Ma Street** ⑨. This street takes its name from the paper goods and fake money made for burning to appease and comfort ancestral spirits. Walking east on Hang Ma Street leads you back to Hang Chieu Street and the Dong Xuan Market. At the

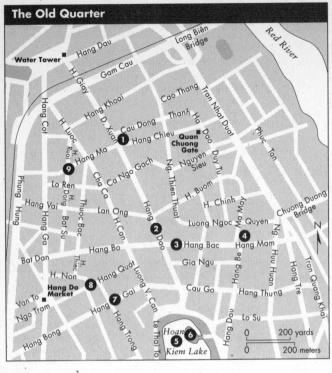

The Old Quarter

end of Hang Chieu is the run-down O Quan Chuong, the last remaining of the five gates of ancient Hanoi.

TIMING

One walk will not be enough to acquaint you with the various specialties of the mazelike Old Quarter. Be prepared to get distracted by the activity, honked at by motorbikers, approached by beggars, hounded by cyclo drivers, confounded by the food stalls selling all kinds of dishes, and accept that you will lose your way at least twice—no matter what time of day. Because the Old Quarter is filled with shops, this is the kind of walk that could take 2 hours or 10, depending on how much of a browser you are. If you use a landmark such as Dong Xuan Market or Hang Da Market, or the northern edge of Hoan Kiem Lake, you could complete a circuit in two to three hours.

Sights to See

4 Antique House (Ngoi Nha). On the southern edge of the Old Quarter's Rattan Street stands a Chinese-style house built at the end of the 19th century. A rich darkwood facade fronts a sparsely decorated interior. Exquisitely carved chairs, bureaus, and tea tables decorate the second floor, where a balcony overlooks a courtyard festooned with Chinese lanterns. A Chinese family that sold traditional medicines on the ground floor originally occupied this house until they resettled in 1954 in southern Vietnam, along with many other Chinese living in the Old Quarter. It's hard to imagine that from 1954 until 1999, when a cooperative venture between the local government and a group of architects from Toulouse, France, turned the house into a museum, five families shared this small space. These five families, incidentally, now live 50 yards away on Hang Bac Street, where they continue to share new, but still cramped, living quarters. ⊠ 87 Ma May St., Hoan Kiem District, ☎ 04/926–0585. ☞ 5,000d. ☺ Mon.–Sat. 9–noon and 1:30–5.

❶ Dong Xuan Market. Once conveniently accessible by riverboat, this market, the oldest and largest in the city, has seen trading with the whole of Southeast Asia. The huge structure, to which the French added a number of features including a new facade, was destroyed by a massive fire in 1994—ironically enough on July 14, Bastille Day. The fire displaced 3,000 workers, caused millions of dollars in damage and losses, and took five human lives, not to mention the lives of thousands of exotic and endangered animals. The market reopened in December 1996 with a bit of a stir: hundreds of women, livid over unfair stall allocations, took to the streets in anger, inducing the prime minister's office to intercede. Today the market looks more like a concrete shopping mall but continues to sell all manner of local and foreign goods. ⊠ *Dong Xuan and Hang Chieu Sts., Hoan Kiem District,* ☎ *no phone.* ☉ *Daily 6–6.*

❸ Hang Bac Street. Silversmiths and money changers once dominated this street, which still has a wide selection of jewelry shops. The Dong Cac jewelers' guild was established here in 1428, and it later erected a temple (now gone) in tribute to three 6th-century brothers whose jewelry skills, learned from the Chinese, made them the patron saints of Vietnamese jewelry.

❷ Hang Dao Street. Since the 15th century, when it was one of the original silk-trading centers, Hang Dao Street has been known for its textiles. It first specialized in lovely pink silk, always in particular demand because the color symbolizes the Vietnamese lunar new year. By the 18th century the street had branched out into a whole spectrum of colors. When the French colonized Vietnam, Hang Dao Street became the center for all traffic in silk, with massive biweekly trade fairs. Indians who settled here at the turn of the 20th century introduced textiles from the West, and today shops on this street sell ready-made clothing in addition to bolts of silk.

★ ❼ Hang Gai Street. The Street of Hemp now sells a variety of goods, including ready-made silk, lovely embroidery, and silver products. With plenty of art galleries, crafts stores, and souvenirs, this is a popular spot for tourists.

❾ Hang Ma Street. Here you can find delicate *ma,* paper replicas of material possessions made to be burned in tribute to one's ancestors. These faux luxury villas and Honda Dream motorbikes are sold alongside merchandise such as imported party decorations.

★ ❽ Hang Quat Street. The Street of Fans now sells a stunning selection of religious paraphernalia, including beautiful funeral and festival flags, porcelain Buddhas, and lacquered Chinese poem boards. Giant plane trees shade the street, which is bookended by Strawberry Temple (Den Dau) and a traditional wooden house honoring Vietnamese soldiers (Nha Tuong Niem Liet Si). Shooting off the street is **Tich To,** an alley bursting with bright, lacquered water puppets, rattan and bamboo baskets, and porcelain and ceramics. If you can pull your attention away from all the eye-grabbing street-level sights, you'll discover the time-worn facades of several French colonial teahouses.

★ ❺ Hoan Kiem Lake (Ho Hoan Kiem or Ho Guom). The spiritual, legendary, and social heart of Hanoi, Hoan Kiem Lake, the Lake of the Restored Sword, is one of the most enchanting spots in the city. In the early morning mist locals come to the lakeshore to swing their arms and legs in exercise, play badminton, and practice tai chi. The lake serves as a gathering point and performance venue during major festivals such as Tet and for holidays like National Day, but it's also a relaxing lunchtime escape or evening rendezvous for friends and lovers. Vietnamese of all ages delight in recounting the legend of how the Lake of the Restored Sword got its name: 15th-century war hero Le Loi used a magic golden sword from heaven to vanquish Chinese invaders. While Le Loi was boating on the lake in celebration of his successful martial exploits, a gigantic tortoise rose from the depths and seized the blade, restoring it to its heavenly owner. The legend may owe some of its universal popularity to the real turtles still living in the lake. The apparently unique species, known as *Rafetus swimhoei,* are a city favorite—some estimate they're the largest freshwater turtles on earth, but no one knows for sure. Huge crowds gather at the water's edge whenever one of these near-mythical creatures comes up for air, which herpetologists (yes, they're the reptile experts) say is happening with increasing frequency as the lake becomes more polluted.

❻ **Ngoc Son Temple** (Den Ngoc Son). On an island in Hoan Kiem Lake, this quiet 18th-century shrine, whose name means "jade mountain," is one of Hanoi's most picturesque temples. This shrine is dedicated to 13th-century military hero Tran Hung Dao, the scholar Van Xuong, and to Nguyen Van Sieu, a Confucian master who assumed responsibility for repairs made to the temple and the surrounding areas in 1864. He helped build both Pen Tower (Thap But), a 30-ft stone structure whose tip resembles a brush, and the nearby rock hollowed in the shape of a peach, known as the Writing Pad (Dai Nghien). To get to the temple, walk through Three-Passage Gate (Tam Quan) and across the Flood of Morning Sunlight Bridge (The Huc). The island temple opens onto a small courtyard where old men, oblivious to visitors, are engrossed in spirited games of *danh co tuong,* or Chinese chess. In the pagoda's anteroom is a 6-ft-long stuffed tortoise that locals pulled from Hoan Kiem Lake in 1968. ✉ *Dinh Tien Hoang St., Hoan Kiem District,* ☎ *no phone.* 🎫 *12,000d.* ☉ *Daily 8–8, later for festivals and 1st and 15th days of every lunar month.*

The French Quarter

To the French must go the credit of thoroughly transforming this once-swampy southern suburb of Hanoi. In order to reflect the grandeur and aesthetic befitting the capital of their protectorate (the French called it Tonkin, from the Vietnamese *Dong Kinh,* or Eastern Capital), French developers rebuilt much of southern Hanoi from the ground up. The wide tree-lined boulevards combine with the majesty of Parisian-style villas and the shuttered elegance of government buildings to form a handsome seat of colonial power. The French are long gone, of course, and for decades Hanoians lacked the affluence to renovate or further build on the architectural contributions of the colonialists. Villas fell into disrepair, and only those buildings appropriated for state offices were even moderately maintained. This part of the city was caught in a 1920s- and '30s-style time warp.

Although much of the French Quarter's appeal lies in its grand but aging architecture, the area is fast becoming a leading diplomatic and commercial section of the city. As you walk through this airy, surprisingly green district, note the considerable international presence here: more than a dozen embassies occupy renovated villas or compounds in the grid of avenues south of Hoan Kiem Lake, and 20-story office buildings have begun to shadow the streets of this lovely part of town.

Numbers in the text correspond to numbers in the margin and on the French Quarter map.

A Good Walk

This 3- to 4-km (2- to 2½-mi) walk, beginning southeast of Hoan Kiem Lake, ends on the west side of the lake. If you've arranged for a driver to pick you up afterward, tell him to meet you in front of the Nha Tho Lon, the Grand Cathedral, also known as St. Joseph's.

Start on the steps of the downtown area's grandest building, the restored **Opera House** ⑩. In front of you is Trang Tien Street, which leads straight out to the southern edge of Hoan Kiem Lake. The area behind and to the south of the Opera House is Nhuong Dia, site of the original Thang Long naval base, which protected the city from enemies attacking via the Red River. By 1875 the French had filled this area with their own military barracks and hospitals. From the Opera House steps turn sharply to the right and follow Trang Tien Street east to its end. Here, at No. 1, is the **Museum of History** ⑪, which houses some of Vietnam's dearest artifacts. This often empty landmark stands in a tranquil garden whose only fault is its proximity to the honking, smoke-belching trucks on Tran Quang Khai Boulevard. Just up Trang Tien Street, at 25 Tong Dan Street, is the **Museum of the Revolution** ⑫.

Return to the huge intersection in front of the Opera House. From here head south on Phan Chu Trinh Street—that's the second road on the left if you're looking west from the Opera House steps. As you walk down this street, you'll pass buildings housing the Algerian embassy (⌂ 12 Phan Chu Trinh St.) and its stately ambassador's residence, the Union of Vietnamese Youth, and the Vietnam Students Association.

Turn right onto **Tran Hung Dao Street** ⑬. A leisurely 1-km (½-mi) walk will bring you past an embassy row of sorts to Quan Su Street. Turn right at Ba Trieu Street and stroll along the tree-shaded sidewalk to Ly Thuong Kiet Street. Cross the intersection and turn right again. Walk about 100 yards until you reach the **Museum of Vietnamese Women** ⑭, on your left, in a modern, three-story structure at the end of a wide courtyard. Retrace your steps to Tran Hung Dao Street and turn right, continuing to Quan Su Street.

At the intersection of Tran Hung Dao and Quan Su streets, on your right-hand side very close to the police headquarters, is a large shuttered building that houses the Ministry of Transportation and Communication. To the left is the **Cultural Friendship Palace** ⑮, the Soviet Union's most striking architectural contribution to this district of the city. Opposite the west side of the Cultural Friendship Palace, at 17 Yet Kieu Street, is the Fine Arts College. Founded by the French as an Indochina-wide arts academy in 1924, the college today trains many of Vietnam's best young artists. Next door to the college is the Alliance Française, a popular center for learning French and a vibrant Western cultural hub.

Now travel north on Quan Su Street to the nearby **Ambassador's Pagoda** ⑯. At Ly Thuong Kiet Street turn right, then left about 100 yards later at Hoa Lo Street. This is the site of what's left of the infamous **Hoa Lo Prison** ⑰, the late-19th-century "fiery furnace" that the French euphemistically called La Maison Centrale and that American prisoners of war sardonically nicknamed the Hanoi Hilton.

From Hoa Lo continue east on Ly Thuong Kiet Street for another block and a half. On the left is the entrance to a bustling market with CHO 19–12 (19–12 Market or December 19 Market) on rusting iron gates. Some of Hanoi's most intense street commerce goes on in here, especially in the early morning. (If you want to skip the market, continue east on Ly Thuong Kiet Street and take a left on Quang Trung Street.) The market spills out onto Hai Ba Trung Street, named after the re-

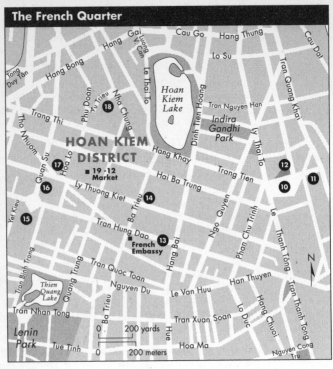

bellious and heroic Trung sisters, who led a short-lived revolt against the Chinese in AD 40. Turn right on this street and then left on Quang Trung Street. Beyond Trang Thi Street, the road merges with Nha Chung Street. Heading north on Nha Chung brings you to the Hoan Kiem District Culture Center (Nha Van Quan Hoan Kiem), a Soviet-style culture and sports complex. Another 215 yards or so and you've reached **St. Joseph's Cathedral** ⑱, a proud but tired-looking stone-and-cement edifice that fronts a small square. From here it's just a two-block walk east to Hoan Kiem Lake or two blocks north to busy Hang Gai Street in the Old Quarter.

TIMING

This is a full-morning walk that could extend into the afternoon if you're keen on Vietnamese history or would like to comb through the many photographs and other exhibits outlining Vietnam's modern-day revolutions. The museums, including the one at Hoa Lo Prison, are closed on Monday and at lunchtime. If you wish to see all three museums on this walk and you have other afternoon plans, then start early; both the Museum of History and the Museum of the Revolution open at 8. You can also save time by hopping in a cyclo or taxi on Phan Chu Trinh Street, at the Opera House, and going straight to the Cultural Friendship Palace.

The 19–12 Market slows down in mid-afternoon, but by 5 it's lively again with an after-work crowd. Rush hour is not the loveliest of times to roam the city, however, as the mass of motorbikes in narrow arteries like Nha Chung Street turns pedestrians into second-class citizens.

If you're in Hanoi on a Sunday night, you may want to wind up at the cathedral by 7 or 7:30, when Mass lets out and throngs of churchgoers, particularly elderly Vietnamese women in traditional outfits, throng the streets and the square in front.

Sights to See

16 **Ambassador's Pagoda** (Chua Quan Su). This stately prayer house once served the many ambassadors who called on the Le kings. A hall named Quan Su was built in the 15th century to receive these guests, mostly Buddhists, and a pagoda was built for them in which they could comfortably worship. The hall burned to the ground, but the pagoda was saved. The Ambassador's Pagoda escaped destruction a second time, as it was the only pagoda not burned or ransacked in the final chaotic days of the Le dynasty. This pagoda sees more action than most in town, as it serves as headquarters for the Vietnam Buddhist Association. Government elites often make official visits to the pagoda, and people commonly hold "send-off" ceremonies here for the souls of family members who have recently died. The pagoda is also in part dedicated to a monk who is said to have saved King Ly Than Tong from his deathbed, so many older women come here to pray for good health. Dozens of young monks reside on the south side of the complex and study in the classrooms directly behind the pagoda. ⊠ *73 Quan Su St., Hoan Kiem District,* ☎ *04/825–2427.* ▭ *Free.* ◷ *Daily 7:30–11:30 and 1:30–5:30.*

15 **Cultural Friendship Palace** (Cung Van Hoa Huu Nghi). Never one to downplay its influence, the Soviet Union assisted with the design and construction of this "workers' cultural palace," formerly known as the Vietnam Xo Cultural Palace. Inaugurated September 1, 1985, the rigid 120-room white colossus stretches from Yet Kieu Street to Tran Binh Trong Road. The palace actually consists of three structures: the performance building houses a 1,200-seat concert hall, and the study and technology buildings contain a library, conference hall, and observatory. At the various clubs hosted here, Hanoians gather to share ideas on everything from biochemistry and chess to billboard usage in the Old Quarter. The Vietnam Trade Union headquarters is just across the street, next to the Ministry of Transportation and Communication. The broad open space here known as May 1 Square is conducive to commemorating the past and present glories of the Communist Party, and you'll invariably see propaganda posters and waves of dangling street lights consisting of blinking yellow stars and red hammers and sickles. On the square's northeast corner is a beautiful Chinese-style meeting hall, the courtyard of which serves as a gathering place for former high-ranking Communist officials who now spend their afternoons playing Ping-Pong and chess or just sitting around drinking tea. ⊠ *91 Tran Hung Dao St., Hoan Kiem District,* ☎ *04/825–3787. Closed to the public except for performances.*

OFF THE BEATEN PATH

DAU PAGODA – This 11th-century pagoda from the Ly dynasty houses Vietnam's two most famous mummies. (Admittedly, there's not a lot of competition.) In 1639 the Buddhist monks Vu Khac Minh and Vu Khac Truong locked themselves in a private room to meditate, instructing their disciples not to disturb them for 100 days. On the 100th day, their disciples entered the room to find both monks seated in a lotus position, perfectly preserved in death. The monks' bodies were covered in a thin but durable red lacquer. What makes these mummies unique is that they still have all their bones and organs.

Dau Pagoda contains several other noteworthy artifacts, including a giant bronze bell built in 1801, a bronze book detailing the pagoda's construction, several stone stelae dating to the 17th century, and six altars for the worship of 18 *arhats* (enlightened monks). The pagoda, which was partially destroyed by French forces in 1947, consists of five halls, an accessible (just barely) bell tower, and a small walking garden full of jackfruit and longan trees, birds of paradise, and a temple dedicated to local deities. Rice fields and ponds surround the pagoda, and you'll pass duck farmers and lotus vendors near the grove-shaded road that leads to the entrance.

The pagoda is less than an hour's ride south of Hanoi. Take a taxi or hire a private car to get here, and keep an eye peeled for a sign directing you to turn right off Highway 6 toward the pagoda. ⊠ *Hwy. 6, Gia Phuc hamlet, Ha Tay Province, 24 km (15 mi) south of Hanoi,* ☎ *no phone.* 🎫 *Free.* ⊙ *Daily dawn–dusk.*

⑰ **Hoa Lo Prison.** There's not much left of the infamous "Hanoi Hilton," the prison that once housed captured American servicemen during the Vietnam War, including U.S. Air Force pilot Douglas "Pete" Peterson, the first U.S. ambassador to Hanoi. What does remain, however, is a small section of the old prison, which is now a museum, and the tree under which Do Muoi, the aging former general secretary of the Communist Party, used to sit while writing on the backs of leaves during his imprisonment by the French in the years of Vietminh resistance.

Hoa Lo Prison Museum is a blunt reminder of the horrors of colonialism and wartime imprisonment. Here, through the front gates of the old French Maison Centrale (Central House, or Prison), built in 1896, you can get a handle on what life was like for Vietnamese prisoners held during France's occupation of Vietnam. (The number of prisoners under the French grew from 615 in 1913 to 2,000 in 1953.) In the southern hall, beyond the grisly guillotine and body basket, are cells where death row prisoners, including Hoang Van Thu, Tran Dan Ninh, and Nguyen Van Cu (who escaped and became a powerful early leader of modern Vietnam), were held. These cells are dank, dark, and anything but welcoming.

On exhibit upstairs are Vietnamese propaganda photos of American POWs, including Senator John McCain and former Ambassador Peterson, cheerily shooting pool, cooking, and writing letters. You won't be able to see the building where the American pilots were kept since it has been torn down, as has the cell from which Do Muoi and 100 other prisoners escaped in 1945 through the maze of sewers that ran under the prison, parts of which are on display in the courtyard.

If you're looking for historical detail about the prison, you may be disappointed by the museum's guidebooks, which are far more inclined to talk about the size of the cells than reveal any nuggets about what took place behind the musty yellow walls. Note, too, that there's little information in English at the museum. ⊠ *1 Hoa Lo St., Hoan Kiem District,* ☎ *04/824–6358.* 🎫 *10,000d.* ⊙ *Tues.–Sun. 8:30–11:30 and 1:30–4:30.*

⑪ **Museum of History** (Bao Tang Lich Su). Opened in 1932 as the museum of the École Française d'Extrême Orient, this building has served in its present capacity since 1958, when the French turned it over to Hanoi authorities. The ground floor houses treasures from early history, particularly Vietnam's Bronze Age. Of special interest are the Ngoc Lu bronze drums, vestiges of this period some 3,000 years ago that have become enduring national Vietnamese symbols. Tools from the Paleolithic Age are on display, as are ceramics from the Ly and Tran dynasties. Painstakingly elaborate but somewhat corny dioramas depict various Vietnamese victories over hostile invaders. Upstairs, exhibits focus on more modern Vietnamese culture. Standouts include 18th- to 20th-century bronze bells and *khanh* gongs (crescent-shape, decorative gongs); Nguyen-dynasty lacquered thrones, altars, and "parallel sentence" boards (Chinese calligraphy on lacquered wood carved into shapes of cucumbers, melons, and banana leaves); and an entire wing devoted to 7th- to 13th-century Champa stone carvings.

As you explore the museum, be sure to consult the English-language brochure you are given with the purchase of your entrance ticket, as the information it contains about the exhibits is nearly the only information on hand. Displays provide little explanatory text, even in Vietnamese, and English-language translation is lacking. It's possible to arrange in advance for one of four English-speaking museum guides. English- and French-speaking historians can also be arranged for large guided tours. ⊠ *1 Trang Tien St., Hoan Kiem District,* ☎ *04/825–3518.* ⌨ *15,000d.* ☺ *Tues.–Sun. 8–11:30 and 1:30–4:30.*

⑫ **Museum of the Revolution** (Bao Tang Cach Mang). Built in 1926 to house the French tax office, this cavernous museum opened its doors in 1959 and now has 29 halls, individual rooms that focus on specific events or periods in Vietnam's arduous road to independence. The focus naturally lands on the country's efforts against French colonialism, Japanese fascism, and American imperialism. The photographs from the August 1945 Revolution are particularly interesting. History buffs may do better here than at the Museum of History, just across the street: just about all the exhibits here have English and French commentary, so a few hours of exploration can be a great learning experience. On the other hand, it may be difficult to swallow some of the museum section titles, such as "The Peaceful Struggle for National Reunification, 1954–1957." English-language guided tours must be arranged in advance. ⊠ *25 Tong Dan St., Hoan Kiem District,* ☎ *04/825–4151.* ⌨ *10,000d.* ☺ *Sat. 8–11:30, Tues.–Fri. and Sun. 8–11:30 and 1–4.*

⑭ **Museum of Vietnamese Women** (Bao Tang Phu Nu Vietnam). From revolutionary leaders to Olympic medalists, this museum highlights the achievements and traditional roles of Vietnamese women. Historical photographs and various display areas portray Vietnamese heroines from wars against invading countries. The top floor has an exhibit of traditional clothing worn by women from Vietnam's 54 ethnic minority groups. ⊠ *36 Ly Thuong Kiet St., Hoan Kiem District,* ☎ *04/825–9937.* ⌨ *10,000d.* ☺ *Tues.–Sun. 8–4.*

⑩ **Opera House** (Nha Hat Lon). The centerpiece of French architecture in Hanoi and one of the grandest buildings in the city, the Hanoi Opera House is a small-scale version of the Paris Opéra designed by Charles Garnier and completed in 1875. The Hanoi structure, finished in 1911, incorporates the same grand elements of Napoleonic architectural style. Perhaps because of the theater's French history, its steps were the site of frequent denunciations against colonial rule. Immediately following World War II, in August 1945, Vietminh troops commandeered the Opera House and announced from its balcony the triumph of the August Revolution.

Complete with an enhanced orchestra pit for 60 musicians and a movable stage, the 400-seat, three-tier theater hosts national celebrations, ballet, symphonies, pop and rock concerts, and opera. Seeing a show may be the only way to get into the Opera House, as its doors are usually closed. ⊠ *1 Trang Tien St., Hoan Kiem District,* ☎ *04/824–8029.*

⑱ **St. Joseph's Cathedral** (Nha Tho Lon). The imposing square towers of this cathedral rise up from a small square near Hoan Kiem Lake on the edge of the Old Quarter. French missionaries built the cathedral in the late 19th century and celebrated the first Mass here on Christmas Day 1886. It feels as though nothing has changed since then—the liturgy has not been modernized since the cathedral was built. The small but beautiful panes of stained glass were created in Paris in 1906. Also of note is the ornate altar, with its high gilded side walls. The government closed down the cathedral in 1975, but when it reopened 10 years later the number of returning devotees was substantial.

Sunday Mass is a popular event, and the pews—men and women are separated—are often full. On major holidays like Christmas and Easter it can be positively chaotic, with 5,000 people either trying to cram their way in or trying to follow along with the service from the front steps. The creaky wooden front doors open for Mass, but if you're visiting at midday, you'll have to walk through the iron gates to the left of the main entrance and enter through the side door, which is up the steps near the back of the structure. ⊠ *Nha Tho St., Hoan Kiem District,* ☎ *04/828–5967.* ☼ *Mon.–Sat. 5 AM–7 PM, Sun. 4 AM–7 PM.*

NEED A
BREAK?
Café Moca (⊠ 14–16 Nha Tho St., Hoan Kiem District, ☎ 04/825–6334), opposite St. Joseph's Cathedral, sells excellent international coffees at reasonable prices. The striking two-story brick interior—those wrought-iron chandeliers were custom made—could belong to a student coffeehouse in Cambridge or Berkeley. Note that the staff has been known to shoo out individual customers to make room for tour groups.

---

⑬ Tran Hung Dao Street. Once called rue Gambetta, Tran Hung Dao Street is now named after the revered Vietnamese warrior who repulsed Kublai Khan's Mongol hordes three times between 1257 and 1288. This long, tree-lined boulevard is the southern border of the French Quarter and a marked example of the stateliness with which the French imbued these east–west streets. Several diplomatic missions line the boulevard; among them, fittingly, is the massive **French embassy** (No. 57), which takes up an entire city block. Also here are the Indonesian embassy at the corner of Ngo Quyen Street (taking a right here brings you to the Metropole Hotel Sofitel and the Government Guest House, the former Palace of the Governor of Tonkin) and the Finnish and German ambassadors' residences. The embassy of Cambodia stands at 71A Tran Hung Dao Street; India at Nos. 58–60; Iraq at No. 66; and the Philippines at No. 27B.

Around the Ho Chi Minh Mausoleum

This once-forested area west of the citadel—which is still a military base—is an expansive and refreshingly tranquil district, where stalwart buildings and monuments seem to revel in the glories of Ho Chi Minh and the Communist cause. As you travel northwest on Dien Bien Phu Street, you'll leave the tightly woven fabric of the Old Quarter behind and find yourself surrounded by sweeping French-era villas and massive ocher-color government buildings, most of which are protected from the sun by a phalanx of tall tamarind trees. Many of these villas house the embassies of socialist (or once-socialist) nations that have stood fast by Vietnam during the last few decades. Scattered among these gems are occasional anomalies of Soviet-era architecture.

Several important sights, including the final resting place of Ho Chi Minh and his former home, are close to Ba Dinh Square, where the beloved leader read his Declaration of Independence in 1945. The One-Pillar Pagoda, the underrated Fine Arts Museum, the Army Museum, and the famed Temple of Literature are within easy walking distance of the square.

If you're coming here from the French Quarter, ask a cyclo or taxi driver to take you from Hoan Kiem Lake to the Ho Chi Minh Mausoleum, in Ba Dinh District.

*Numbers in the text correspond to numbers in the margin and on the
Around the Ho Chi Minh Mausoleum and West Lake map.*

A Good Walk

Start at **Ba Dinh Square** ⑲ and the **Ho Chi Minh Mausoleum** ⑳, in the
heart of the Ba Dinh District. Once you have passed by the unflinch-
ing guards and through the mausoleum itself, you'll be directed through
large iron gates toward **Ho Chi Minh's Residence** ㉑ in the tranquil wooded
compound of the **Presidential Palace** ㉒. Although visitors are welcome
to Ho's house, the palace itself is off-limits, as is much of the surrounding
parkland. Behind the Presidential Palace, however, are the large **Botanical Gardens** ㉓, which are open to the public, although the entrance
is a bit far away, on Hoang Hoa Tham Street. A short pathway leads
from Ho Chi Minh's house to the **One-Pillar Pagoda** ㉔, the reconstructed
Buddhist tower in the center of a small square pond. To the left is Dien
Huu Pagoda; this charming but seldom-visited temple sits in the shadow
of the architecturally disorienting **Ho Chi Minh Museum** ㉕.

From the museum walk out the front doors and down the steps toward
Ba Dinh Square. Turn right on Hung Vuong Street, the road in front
of the mausoleum, then left on Le Hong Phong Street. This wide,
shaded boulevard leads back to Dien Bien Phu Street, where you should
bear right. Walk about 200 yards until you reach shady Chi Lang Park,
once a small lake bordering the southern edge of the citadel but later
filled in by the French. Here, set back behind a wide square of polished marble, is a sight you are not likely to find elsewhere in the world:
a statue of Vladimir Ilyich Lenin. Although long discredited in his home
country, Lenin still looms large in Vietnam, and Hanoi's aging party
cadres continue to place flowers here in celebration of Lenin's October Revolution.

Lenin appears to be leaning resolutely toward the **Army Museum** ㉖,
just across Dien Bien Phu Street. To the left of the museum entrance
is the 100-ft tower known as the Flag Pillar, the surviving remnant of
the Nguyen-dynasty citadel, which has become a historic symbol of
the city. From the Army Museum, retrace your steps to the intersection of Le Hong Phong, Dien Bien Phu, and Hoang Dieu streets. Turn
left on Hoang Dieu Street and continue south, going past the Chinese
embassy on your right, until you reach very busy Nguyen Thai Hoc
Street. One block to the right is the **Fine Arts Museum** ㉗, set back in
a courtyard. From here the **Temple of Literature** ㉘ is just across the street,
secluded behind a low stone wall. To get to the entrance, proceed south
down Van Mieu Street, opposite the art museum, and turn right on
Quoc Tu Giam Street. You can't miss the entrance, on the right.

TIMING
Taking in all these sights within a comfortable time frame depends on
your preferences and how long you want to spend traversing through
museums or gazing at architectural anomalies. Three hours should be
enough to get from the Ho Chi Minh Mausoleum to the Fine Arts Museum, provided you don't venture over to the Botanical Gardens. Leave
at least another 30 to 40 minutes for the Temple of Literature. Or con-
versely, you could start at the Temple of Literature—it opens in the summer at 7:30, in winter at 8—and make your way up to the Botanical
Gardens or to West Lake, taking in the sights along the way. Generally speaking, this walk is more pleasant during the week, but so long
as there's no special holiday, weekends are quite fine, too. The only
real delay is lining up to view "Uncle Ho"; keep in mind, too, that his
mausoleum is closed in the afternoon. If you are an early riser, consider catching the dawn patrol of people doing calisthenics and tai chi
in front of the mausoleum in Ba Dinh Square.

Around the Ho Chi Minh Mausoleum and West Lake

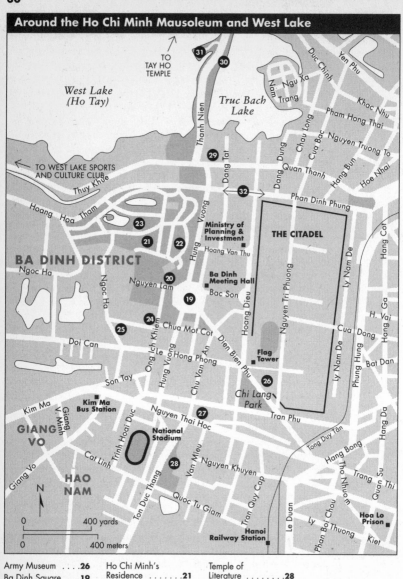

West Lake (Ho Tay)

TO TAY HO TEMPLE

Truc Bach Lake

TO WEST LAKE SPORTS AND CULTURE CLUB

Thuy Khue

Hoang Hoa Tham

BA DINH DISTRICT

Ngoc Ha

Ngoc Ha

Doi Can

Son Tay

Kim Ma Bus Station

Kim Ma

GIANG VO

Giang V. Minh

HAO NAM

Giang Vo

Cat Linh

Trinh Hoai Duc

Ton Duc Thang

Nguyen Thai Hoc

National Stadium

Quoc Tu Giam

Van Mieu

Nguyen Khuyen

Tran Quy Cap

N

0   400 yards
0   400 meters

Hanoi Railway Station

Le Duan

Phan Boi Chau

Ly Thuong

Kiet

Hoa Lo Prison

Quan Su

Trang Thi

Hang Da

Tho Nhuom

Hang Bong

Tong Duy Tan

Tran Phu

Chi Lang Park

Flag Tower

THE CITADEL

Hoang Dieu

Nguyen Tri Phuong

Ly Nam De

Ly Nam De

Phung Hung

Cua Dong

Bat Dan

Hang Ga

H. Vai

Hang Cot

Phan Dinh Phung

Hang Bun

Hoe Nhai

Nguyen Truong To

Cua Bac

Quan Thanh

Chau Long

Dang Dung

Pham Hong Thai

Khac Nhu

Duc Chinh

Yen Phu

Nam Trang

Ngu Xa

Dang Tat

Thanh Nien

Hung Vuong

Nguyen Lam

Hoang Van Thu

Ministry of Planning & Investment

Ba Dinh Meeting Hall

Bac Son

Chua Mot Cot

Dien Bien Phu

Hong Phong

Chu Van An

Le Hong Phong

Hung Vuong

Ong Ich Khiem

Army Museum **26**	Ho Chi Minh's Residence **21**
Ba Dinh Square . . . **19**	One-Pillar Pagoda **24**
Botanical Gardens **23**	Phan Dinh Phung Street **32**
Fine Arts Museum **27**	Presidential Palace **22**
Ho Chi Minh Mausoleum **20**	Quan Thanh Temple **29**
Ho Chi Minh Museum **25**	Temple of Literature **28**
	Tran Quoc Pagoda **31**
	War memorial **30**

Sights to See

26 **Army Museum** (Bao Tang Quan Doi). Although not as provocative as its Ho Chi Minh City counterpart, the Army Museum is nonetheless an intriguing example of Vietnam's continuing obsession with publicizing its past military exploits. At the southern edge of what was once the Thang Long citadel, which housed the imperial city, the museum buildings were once used as French military barracks. In the courtyard of the museum, Chinese- and Soviet-made weaponry—including MiG fighters, antiaircraft guns, and what is said to be the tank that smashed through the gates of the Presidential Palace in Saigon on April 30, 1975—surround the wreckage of an American B-52 and F-4 fighter jet shot down over Hanoi. Other, far-less-arresting displays include depictions of the Trung sisters' revolt against Chinese overlords in AD 40, sound-and-light shows highlighting battles and troop movements during the wars against the French and Americans, bicycles known as steel horses that were used on the Ho Chi Minh Trail, captured French and American firearms and uniforms, field maps and tables of major attacks, and the dreaded pungee sticks.

Adjacent to the museum is the **Hanoi Flag Pillar,** a 100-ft tapered hexagonal guard tower atop a three-tier square base. Built in 1812, the pillar escaped destruction by the French when they leveled much of the citadel; instead they used the tower as an observation and communication station—much like the Vietnamese military before them. The intricate fan- and flower-shape holes allow light into the tower, which has a crisp red-and-yellow Vietnamese flag fluttering from its flagpole. ⊠ *28 Dien Bien Phu St., Ba Dinh District,* ☎ *04/823–4264.* ⊠ *10,000d.* ⊙ *Tues.–Sun. 8–11:30 and 1–4:30.*

19 **Ba Dinh Square.** Dien Bien Phu Street comes to an end at the minimally landscaped Ba Dinh Square, in the center of which flutters Hanoi's largest Vietnamese flag. You can almost hear the echoes of Ho Chi Minh's voice ringing out over loudspeakers to the half million northern Vietnamese who gathered to hear Uncle Ho's Declaration of Independence on September 2, 1945. A quarter century later, six days after Ho's death in 1969 (also on September 2), another 100,000 Hanoians gathered here to pay homage to their late president. On the west side of the square is the mausoleum itself, a cold and squat cubicle that's nonetheless arresting in its simplicity and grandeur.

Across the square from the mausoleum and slightly to the left is the Ba Dinh Meeting Hall, the four-story headquarters of the Communist Party and the site where the National Assembly convenes. Across the square and to the right, where Dien Bien Phu Street meets the square, stands the huge and graceful Ministry of Foreign Affairs. Directly opposite the mausoleum and at the end of short Bac Son Road is the monument to Vietnam's revolutionary martyrs. A palm- and willow-shaded mansion to the right of the monument is the home of former minister of defense General Vo Nguyen Giap, who orchestrated the brilliant siege at Dien Bien Phu in 1954.

23 **Botanical Gardens** (Vuon Bach Thao). This 50-acre park behind the Presidential Palace was designed by French landscape engineers in 1890. After defeating the French in Hanoi in late 1954, the state rebuilt the gardens and opened the grounds and its extensive network of trails to the public. Athletes in search of exercise congregate here for pickup soccer games, badminton, tai chi, and jogging. Lovers looking for seclusion head to the sculpture garden on the east side of the park, or cross the bridge to an island in the middle of the tree-shaded, preternaturally green lake. Between dusk and closing time, this island

retreat is definitely rated R. ✉ *Entrance on Hoang Hoa Tham Rd.,
Ba Dinh District,* ☎ *no phone.* 🎫 *1,000d.* ☉ *Daily 7:30 AM–10 PM.*

★ ㉗ **Fine Arts Museum** (Bao Tang My Thuat). The evolution of Vietnamese
art is sparingly chronicled in this musty three-story museum, which
opened in 1966 after serving as a boardinghouse for French girls living in Indochina. The architecture, sculpture, drawing, and fine arts
of Vietnam are displayed in a series of exhibits, mainly organized
chronologically, starting with an impressive collection of Stone Age and
Bronze Age artifacts on the third floor. Also here are examples of lacquer and wood sculpture, including a fantastical bodhisattva with
1,000 eyes and arms, a 16th-century statue from the Hoi Ha Pagoda.

Several stone statues and wooden sculptures lining the open-air hall-
ways reflect the wide range of artistic styles incorporated into Vietnamese
art. Note the intrusion of the Soviet aesthetic on mid-20th-century sculpture: the martial, even superhuman, forms are a far cry from the elegance and lightheartedness of the Dong Ho village folk art or the
centuries-old evocative lacquered-wood depictions of arhats from the
Tay Phuong Pagoda. On the lower floors are oil and watercolor paintings by such Vietnamese masters as Nguyen Tu Nghiem, Bui Xuan Phai,
and To Ngoc Van. The central exhibition rooms on the first floor contain some of Vietnam's most stunning lacquer painting, much of it excellent examples of socialist realism and so-called combat art.

Conspicuously absent are the most recent works of art from Vietnam's bold young painters. The unfortunate reality is that these artists
are busy showing their works in stylish Hanoi and Ho Chi Minh City
galleries and selling to eager collectors, while the Ministry of Culture,
which is ultimately responsible for the art museum, doesn't have the
financial resources to buy their works. Note that many of the exhibits
are in a state of perpetual rearrangement and may be closed at any time.
✉ *66 Nguyen Thai Hoc St., Ba Dinh District,* ☎ *04/823–3084.* 🎫
10,000d. ☉ *Tues.–Sun. 9:15–5.*

★ ⑳ **Ho Chi Minh Mausoleum** (Lang Chu Tich Ho Chi Minh). It's hard to
overstate Ho Chi Minh's heroic stature among the Vietnamese and how
significant his mausoleum and the surrounding area are in Vietnam's
ideological consciousness. Respected as a determined revolutionary pa-
triot and loved as a public figure who empathized with the people, particularly of the North, Ho Chi Minh has reached icon status in the minds
of most Vietnamese. Perhaps it's because schools throughout the country focus almost exclusively on the man's positive exploits, deferring
any responsibility for failed economic policies or mismanagement onto
Ho's successors, that the youth of Vietnam, although often frustrated
by the limitations of the rigid Communist system, continue to admire
and venerate the man. Many of the faithful who visit the tomb are, in
fact, school children on field trips; some of them walk past Ho's reclining body with tears in their eyes, others suppress giggles, but mostly
they appear mystified at the pinkish-yellow glow that seems to emanate
from the frail, wispy-bearded corpse. Thousands of Vietnamese still
visit the revered site—and ☞ **Ba Dinh Square,** where independence was
declared in 1945—to pay homage to Uncle Ho. During the country's
major national holidays, Vietnam's power troika—the general secretary of the Communist Party, the prime minister, and the president—
line up in front of the mausoleum with other national leaders to review
columns of parading ethnic minorities, rolling tanks, and goose-step-
ping soldiers. In the days leading up to Vietnam National Day (September 2) and Ho Chi Minh's birthday (May 19), thousands of curious
citizens and loyal party members come to pay their respects to the pa-
triarch, preserved for eternity behind bullet-proof glass.

Had officials followed the president's wishes, this structure would never have been built, as Ho Chi Minh had expressed in his will his desire to be cremated. But the preservation of the Vietnamese leader and his memory has gone the way of such other Communist figureheads as Lenin, Stalin, and Mao. Ho's embalmed body, touched up now and again in Russia, is virtually the only thing inside the mausoleum. The structure itself is a squat, cold, gray cubicle ringed by columns and topped by a flat, square frieze adorned with the words "Chu Tich (President) Ho Chi Minh" in red plum marble. It was built using materials native to Vietnam, such as marble from Marble Mountain outside Danang.

When you enter the mausoleum, be aware of the strict propriety expected of visitors. Although you will see Vietnamese pilgrims moving in a solemn single-file procession, you must sign in at an office at No. 8 Hung Vuong Street, south of the mausoleum, then leave your possessions at another checkpoint closer to the actual tomb, where uninformative brochures are for sale. Your purchase of them amounts to your entrance donation. No cameras, hats, or bags of any kind may be brought in the building, and you are expected to behave respectfully; don't wear shorts or tank tops or put your hands in your pockets while inside. Talking is also forbidden, and once inside the chilly room containing Ho's corpse you are discouraged from lingering for more than a few moments in front of the glass. ⊠ *Enter at corner of Hung Vuong and Le Hong Phong Sts., Ba Dinh District,* ☎ *04/845–5128.* 🖃 *4,000d donation.* ☉ *Tues.–Thurs. and weekends 8–11; usually closed Oct. and/or Nov., when Ho's body is moved to Russia for maintenance.*

㉕ **Ho Chi Minh Museum** (Bao Tang Ho Chi Minh). With English commentary on the sometimes bizarre exhibits, this museum is a must-see—if only for 15 minutes—on the Uncle Ho circuit. A collection of manifestos, military orders, correspondence, and photographs from the Communist Party's early days to the present are mixed with historical exhibits covering the October and August revolutions, the fight against fascism, Ho's revolutionary world movement, and Vietnam's struggle against imperialism.

You're encouraged to start at the top and wind your way down. The centerpiece on the top floor is a gargantuan gold lotus flower that itself contains smaller exhibits about Ho's revolutionary activities. Labyrinthine murals and installations lead from the section called "Past" into the "Future," where you'll find everything from space-age conceptual representations of peace to models of automobiles symbolizing America's military failure. A red "volcano" surrounded by national totems symbolizes the various national liberation movements. Under the banner "Ho Chi Minh and Young People," huge plastic fruit sits atop a slanting table framed by a backdrop black-and-white photo of nuclear reactors, a display that would look more at home on the set of *Dr. Strangelove*. The few Vietnamese who wander the floors seem less interested in the exhibits and more curious about the specifics of the overwrought Soviet architecture. Note that you must leave your cameras and bags at the reception area. ⊠ *3 Ngoc Ha St., Ba Dinh District (also accessible from Chua Mot Cot St.),* ☎ *04/846–3752.* 🖃 *5,000d.* ☉ *Tues.–Thurs. and weekends 8–11 and 1:30–4.*

OFF THE
BEATEN PATH

HO CHI MINH TRAIL MUSEUM – The elaborate network of paths of the Ho Chi Minh Trail was used by North Vietnam to transport supplies to Vietcong strongholds in South Vietnam during the Vietnam War. The Ho Chi Minh Trail Museum (Bao Tang Duong Mon Ho Chi Minh) provides color

MEET UNCLE HO

Ho Chi Minh (literally, "bringer of light") is the final and most memorable pseudonym in a series of more than 50 that Vietnam's intrepid leader, originally named Nguyen Sinh Cung, acquired during the course of his remarkable life. Born in 1890 in the central Vietnamese province of Nghe An, Ho received traditional French schooling and became a teacher. However, he inherited from his father (who abandoned the family early on) a wanderlust that became fueled by a lifelong obsession with Vietnamese independence.

In 1911 Ho signed on to the crew of a French freighter; two years later a stint aboard another French ship took him to the United States, where he settled for a year in Brooklyn, New York, and found work as a laborer. Ho then left for London, where he became an assistant pastry chef. He mastered several languages—among them English, French, German, Russian, Cantonese, and Japanese. He moved to Paris for six years and became increasingly active in Socialist, Communist, and Nationalist movements. After helping to found the French Communist Party, Ho left for Moscow in 1924. It soon became clear that to foment a successful workers' revolution in Vietnam, he would have to dedicate himself to organizing his countrymen.

By the end of the 1920s, several poorly organized revolts had incited aggressive French retaliation, which was only compounded by economic depression. In 1930, while based in Hong Kong, Ho consolidated a number of rebellious factions under the umbrella of the Indochinese Communist Party. However, it was not until 1941—after escaping arrest in Hong Kong, forging documentation "proving" his death, shuttling between China and the Soviet Union, and disguising himself as a Chinese journalist—that he was able to sneak back into Vietnam.

Shortly thereafter Ho founded the Vietminh Independence League. In July 1945, U.S. OSS officers met with Ho; impressed with Ho's operation, they agreed to supply him with arms. In August, Ho called for a general uprising, known as the August Revolution. Ho proclaimed himself president of the Democratic Republic of Vietnam in the north. The following year, Ho, in order to rid northern Vietnam of Chinese troops, agreed to an accord with the French: Vietnam would be a "free state" within the French Union and 25,000 French troops would be stationed there. Tensions between the Vietminh and the French escalated, however, and soon led to the French-Indochina War.

By 1950 the United States was supplying military aid to the French, and Ho's government was recognized by the Soviet Union and China. The French-Indochina War ended in 1954 with the Vietminh's defeat of the French at Dien Bien Phu. American involvement in Vietnam escalated rapidly.

Ho died of natural causes in September 1969 at the age of 79. After his death the fighting continued, although in 1970 Henry Kissinger began secret talks with the North Vietnamese. By 1975 the Vietnam War had ended, and the country was reunited.

Ho never married—he asserted that the Vietnamese people were his family—thus he preferred the familiar "Uncle Ho." Although he died more than 30 years ago, Uncle Ho is still very much present in Vietnam, from his embalmed body in the Ho Chi Minh Mausoleum to his portrait on Vietnamese currency.

on the trail, one of the war's most riveting symbols of dedication and perseverance. This museum lies some distance outside of Hanoi and can be hard to find, so it's best if you hire a taxi or car and driver. ⊠ *Hwy. 6, 20 km (12 mi) south of Hanoi, Ha Tay Province,* ☎ *034/820–889.* ✆ *10,000d.* ☉ *Tues.–Sun. 7:30–11 and 1:30–4:30.*

㉑ **Ho Chi Minh's Residence** (Nha Bac Ho). After 1954 Ho Chi Minh had the run of the Presidential Palace, but the ostentation was too much for the ascetic president, who openly shunned luxury and preferred the humble former home of the palace's electrician, where he lived for four years. Then, the story goes, in 1958 Ho Chi Minh moved to this simple but tasteful wooden house on stilts, which served as his living quarters and work space until his death in 1969. An elegant but spare study—some books, his small typewriter, a few newspapers, and an electric fan presented to him by a group of Japanese Communists are visible—adjoins his equally spare bedroom. Downstairs he received his guests: foreign dignitaries, Politburo members, army cadres, and schoolchildren. Surrounding the house are well-tended gardens with flame trees, willows, mango trees, and aromatic frangipani. Cyprus trees thrive on the edge of the pond, which Ho had stocked with carp. A crisp clap of the hands apparently still brings the fish to the surface.

Regardless of Ho Chi Minh's faith in the accuracy of the city's anti-aircraft gunners, some doubt must be thrown on the claim that Ho Chi Minh spent so much time in this open-air sanctum, with only the trees, his wooden house, and a trusty old war helmet as protection. American bombers targeted Hanoi during the war, and they surely would have emptied their loads on Ba Dinh District had they known their arch-enemy was feeding fish and conferring with his generals in the unprotected confines of his stilt house. Indeed, Ho's Politburo ordered the construction of a nearby bomb shelter, later dubbed House No. 67. Legend holds that Uncle Ho refused to use the shelter as a home, preferring to confer with the Politburo in this fortified bunker but to sleep in his stilt house.

Before visiting Ho's residence, wait for the rest of the group that accompanied you through the mausoleum to go on ahead; it's much more enjoyable to walk through the jasmine-scented compound unhurried and without the inevitable chatter of other tourists. You'll exit this area via a pebbled pathway to the south of the mausoleum. As if they were themselves sights on the tour, older Vietnamese intellectuals wearing bifocals and striped cotton pajamas sit on park benches and read the Communist Party mouthpiece, *Nhan Dan (The People)*, or sip green tea and smoke cigarettes. ⊠ *Hung Vuong St., Ba Dinh District,* ☎ *no phone.* ✆ *3,000d.* ☉ *Daily 7:30–11 and 1:30–4.*

OFF THE BEATEN PATH

THE MUSEUM OF ETHNOLOGY – This impressive museum (Bao Tang Dan Toc Hoc Vietnam) with more than 15,000 artifacts examines the history, culture, and traditions of Vietnam's 54 ethnic minority groups as well as the majority Kinh (Viet) people. Ha Duc Linh, a Tay minority architect, designed the museum's two-story exhibition building, which was inspired by the bronze drum that symbolizes Vietnamese culture.

The museum's ground floor presents a time line of Vietnamese civilization, as well as explanations of the various language families to which Vietnam's ethnic minority groups belong. An interior courtyard houses rotating exhibits. The second floor contains a "Shared Traditions" exhibit linking ethnic groups in Vietnam with those found in other Asian countries. Included in this exhibit are examples of ceremonial objects, Thai ritual trees, shamanic masks, traditional batik designs, H'mong hemp weaving, and a Black Thai stilt house with items used in daily life. A "Religious Life" exhibit displays funerary statues, religious architecture, Cham ritual objects and handicrafts, Khmer silk dyeing, embroidery, and jewelry displays. Behind the museum is a walking garden that highlights a few types of houses built by different ethnic minority groups in Vietnam. The museum also serves as a research center.

English-speaking guides can be arranged upon entry for individuals and small groups; larger group tours should be arranged in advance. You'll need to hire a taxi to get to the museum, which is about 8 km (5 mi) west of the city center. ⊠ *Nguyen Van Huyen St., Cau Giay District,* ☎ *04/756-2193.* ☞ *10,000d.* ☉ *Tues.–Sun. 8:30–5:30.*

㉔ **One-Pillar Pagoda** (Chua Mot Cot). The French destroyed this temple on their way out in 1954. It was reconstructed by the new government and still commemorates the legend of Emperor Ly Thai Tong. It is said that the childless emperor dreamed that Quan Am, the Buddhist goddess of mercy and compassion, seated on a lotus flower, handed him a baby boy. Sure enough, he soon met and married a peasant woman who bore him a male heir, and in 1049 he constructed this monument in appreciation. The distinctive single pillar is meant to represent the stalk of the lotus flower, a sacred Vietnamese symbol of purity. The pillar was originally a single large tree trunk; today it's made of more durable cement. An ornate curved roof covers the tiny 10-square-ft pagoda, which rises out of a square pond. Steps leading to the pagoda from the south side of the pond are usually blocked off, but if there aren't too many people around, a monk may invite you into this miniature prayer room.

Just a few yards from the One-Pillar Pagoda is **Dien Huu Pagoda**, a delightful but often-overlooked temple enclosing a bonsai-filled courtyard. A tall and colorful gate opens out onto the path leading to the Ho Chi Minh Museum, but the entrance is opposite the steps to the One-Pillar Pagoda. ⊠ *Ong Ich Kiem St., Ba Dinh District,* ☎ *no phone.* ☞ *Free.* ☉ *Daily 6 AM–6 PM; 6 AM–9 PM on the 1st and 15th of every lunar month.*

㉒ **Presidential Palace** (Phu Chu Tich). This imposing three-story palace just north of the Ho Chi Minh Mausoleum testifies to France's dedication to architectural elegance in Indochina. Constructed from 1900 to 1906, the bright, mustard-yellow building served as the living and working quarters of Indochina's governors-general. When Ho Chi Minh returned to Hanoi after the defeat of the French in 1954, he refused to live in the palace itself but chose the more modest quarters of the palace electrician. He did, however, offer use of the palace to distinguished guests during their visits to the capital. Today the building is used for formal international receptions and other important government meetings. You can view the structure from the outside but cannot enter the palace. Surrounding the building are extensive gardens and orchards, as well as the famed Mango Alley, the 300-ft pathway from the palace to Ho Chi Minh's stilt house. ⊠ *Hung Vuong St. and Hoang Van Thu St., Ba Dinh District,* ☎ *no phone.*

★ ㉘ **Temple of Literature** (Van Mieu–Quoc Tu Giam). An unusually well preserved example of Vietnamese architecture, this monument to Confucius, built in 1070 by Emperor Ly Thanh Tong, is widely considered the most important historic site in Dong Da District. In 1076 it became the site of Vietnam's first university, Quoc Tu Giam, which specialized in training students—many of them sons and daughters of emperors and other high-ranking dignitaries—to pass the rigorous examinations for government and civil service posts. The achievements of several centuries of the university's 1307 doctoral recipients are recorded on 82 stelae (stone slabs), which rest on stone tortoises. The oldest of these, the Dai Bao Stela, dates to 1442. It wasn't until 1802 that Emperor Gia Long moved his capital and the national university to Hue. The French later used the building as, appropriately, their school of civil administration, dubbing it the Temple of the Crows because of the birds that tended to gather here.

The complex has five courtyards. The first two, now bare of buildings, used to house the wooden hostels and dormitories for students. A central walkway once reserved for the king runs down the center of these open sections between two square lotus-flower ponds. Separating these courtyards from the middle section of the compound is an elaborate two-story gate, the second floor of which is called the Poet's Balcony. University examinations eventually came to include poetry competitions, introduced by Emperor Le Loi, and poetry readings still take place from this balcony on special occasions—as do concerts of traditional and classical music. The gate opens onto a large square fishpond, which is bracketed on either side with the stone stelae. Through an ancient wooden doorway is the fourth area, containing the temple dedicated to Confucius and his disciples. On the far side of this temple is the site of what was the Van Mieu Library, destroyed by bombing raids in 1954. The fifth and final courtyard includes two restored former libraries, one of which now contains a small museum; a pair of drum and bell towers; and a forecourt area in which folk music is performed daily. At press time, restoration work was under way for Hau Duong Hall, a two-story building that holds a gypsum stone statue of Chu Van An, a revered teacher and former advisor to the emperor. ⊠ *Quoc Tu Giam St., Ba Dinh District,* ☎ *04/845–2917 or 04/823–5601.* ☜ *12,000d, English-speaking guide 20,000d.* ☉ *Mid-Apr.–mid-Oct., daily 7:30–6; mid-Oct.–mid-Apr., daily 8–5.·*

West Lake

About 3 km (2 mi) northwest of Hoan Kiem Lake is West Lake (Ho Tay), a body of water that's steeped in legend. It is said that a giant golden calf from China followed the peals of a monk's bronze bell to this spot. When the ringing stopped, the calf lost its direction and kept walking in circles, creating the basin of West Lake. Like Hoan Kiem's tortoise, the calf is said still to dwell in the lake. If so, it likely feeds on the snails that are considered a local delicacy.

West Lake's wealth of history takes a more tangible form in the temples and war memorials that line its shores. Development is changing the face of the shore, however, as luxury hotels and high-rent villas eat away at the land of traditional flower villages like Nghi Tam, where wealthy expatriates seclude themselves behind walls of bougainvillea.

The lake itself is a weekend boating spot for Vietnamese families, which paddle around the murky waters in boats shaped like ducks and dragons, or in rubber dinghies for rent on Thanh Nien Street. Afterward they stop in one of the floating restaurants for snails boiled in lemon leaves or *banh tom* (deep-fried shrimp cakes). You can also rent boat houses made of bamboo for an afternoon of fishing (although eating what you catch is not recommended).

Numbers in the text correspond to numbers in the margin and on the Around the Ho Chi Minh Mausoleum and West Lake map.

A Good Walk

Start your walk at the beginning of the wide causeway of Thanh Nien Street that divides West Lake from the smaller Truc Bach Lake, which was created in the 17th century when fishermen built a dike that closed off the southeast section of West Lake. The dike was later turned into a dirt path, and during the Vietnam War young volunteers—Thanh Nien means "youth"—helped expand the path into a causeway. Note the floating seafood restaurants and the neon signs of the times along this road—billboards for beer, gas, and computers. At the very beginning of Thanh Nien duck into the ornate **Quan Thanh Temple** ㉙. Sidewalk vendors in front will offer you incense and flowers. This is a marvelous spot to take a rest and soak up the atmosphere; try to ignore the street noise beyond the walls.

Staying on the same side of the street, walk for about five minutes to where the road bends to the right. Here you will find a small, unnamed **war memorial** ㉚ to antiaircraft gunners, stationed on the roof of a nearby factory, who shot down 10 American planes in 1967. Walk about 215 yards north; then cross the street to Hanoi's oldest pagoda, the delightful **Tran Quoc Pagoda** ㉛, on an islet jutting into West Lake. The West Lake side of the causeway is often crowded with picnicking students, many of whom may attempt to communicate in English with you. (The Truc Bach Lake side is more of a lovers' lane in the evenings, with couples nuzzling on motorbikes or benches.) From the pagoda it's a 10- to 15-minute walk back to the beginning of Thanh Nien Street, where you will find a small flower garden (*vuon hoa*) bearing the name of Ly Tu Trong, a revolutionary martyr from the Vietnam War whose white-plaster statue faces the Presidential Palace to the south. Older women gather here to exercise and perform tai chi, while the busy park across the street plays host to badminton games.

If you're up for walking back into the center of town, or at least want to walk part of the way before getting a cyclo or taxi, then head east along the beautiful and shaded **Phan Dinh Phung Street** ㉜. The street ends just over 1 km (½ mi) from the edge of West Lake, near a rectangular park and Hanoi's own version of the Leaning Tower of Pisa: the old water tower and critical military fortification built by the French. This is the northern edge of the Old Quarter, and cyclos are everywhere. Some taxis should be waiting near the Galaxy Hotel, to the right of the park.

TIMING

The causeway can be traversed in about 20 minutes, but allow for an hour or more if you want to peek around the temples. Allow even more time if you want to rent a paddleboat from the quay on the Truc Bach side. The walk along Phan Dinh Phung Street to the water tower is another 15 to 25 minutes.

Sights to See

㉜ **Phan Dinh Phung Street.** This beautiful shaded avenue leads past sprawling French villas and Chinese mandarin mansions (many occupied by long-serving party members) as well as the gracious but seldom-used **Gothic North Door Cathedral** (Cua Bac), at the corner of Phan Dinh Phung and Nguyen Bieu streets. The large wheel of stained glass at the cathedral is reminiscent of Renaissance-era artwork in Europe and is enchanting from the inside; try the large front doors or ask around for a caretaker to let you in. Another option is to come on Sunday at 10 AM for an English-language service. On the right side of the street stand the tall ramparts of the **citadel,** the military compound that once protected the Imperial Palace of Thang Long. In a surprising move, army officials in 1999 opened to the public Nguyen Tri Phuong Street, which runs straight through this once secretive space.

㉙ **Quan Thanh Temple** (Chua Quan Thanh or Tran Vu Quan). A 3½-ton, 13-ft-tall black bronze statue of the Taoist god Tran Vu is housed here, protected on either side by wooden statues of civil and military mandarins. Built by King Ly Thai To in the 11th century, this much-made-over temple was once known as the Temple of the Grand Buddha; its present name translates into "Holy Mandarin Temple." An important collection of 17th-century poems can be seen in the shrine room. On the right side of this room is an altar dedicated to Trum Trong, the master bronze caster who oversaw the construction of Tran Vu's statue. Note the red, gold-stitched boots in the center of the shrine room; although such boots customarily appear in temples with figures of civil and military mandarins, Emperor Thanh Thai presented them in a vein of humor to Tran Vu's shoeless statue. Above the ornamented main gate is a 1677 replica of the bronze bell that supposedly lured the West Lake's legendary golden calf from China. Huge mango and longan trees drape over the courtyard, keeping the temple and its environs cool and somewhat dark, even in midday. Two mounted stone elephants, symbols of loyalty, flank the entrance here. ⊠ *Quan Thanh and Thanh Nien Sts., Ba Dinh District,* ☎ *04/823–4378.* ⌨ *5,000d donation.* ◷ *Daily 8–4:30.*

OFF THE
BEATEN PATH

TAY HO TEMPLE – Phu Tay Ho, a temple dedicated to a 17th-century princess named Lieu Hanh, more popularly known here as Thanh Mau (Mother of the Nation), is attractive for its gigantic banyan trees and the view from across West Lake's eastern shore. In the middle chamber of the main prayer hall is a sub-altar containing the statue of a holy tiger that protects Lieu Hanh, who is visible through the wooden slats of a locked separating wall inside the back chamber. In a second worship hall, women come to pray to another national mother figure, Nhi Thuong Ngan, for happiness and luck in motherhood and marriage. Two prayer stupas in the shady courtyard are dedicated to the guardian spirits of young boys and girls, Lau Cau and Lau Co, respectively. In spring and summer, you can sometimes catch locals treading water as far as 200 yards from the lakeside wall of the temple, fully clothed and with their conical hats glinting in the sun as they manipulate long pole-nets to collect snails from the bottom of the lake. A taxi is the easiest way to reach Phu Tay Ho. ⊠ *At the end of Pho Phu Tay Ho St., directly off Dang Thai Mai St., Tay Ho District,* ☎ *no phone.* ⌨ *Free.* ◷ *Daily.*

㉛ **Tran Quoc Pagoda** (Chua Tran Quoc). Hanoi's oldest temple dates from the 6th century, when King Ly Nam De had a pagoda, named Khai Quoc, built on the bank of the Red River. More than a thousand years later excessive erosion of the riverbank caused King Le Kinh Tong to move the pagoda to Goldfish Islet (Ca Vang) on West Lake and rename it Tran Quoc. This modest temple is noted for its stela dating from 1639, which recounts the history of the pagoda and its move from the Red River, and the lovely brick stupas adjacent to the main temple. Tran Quoc is an active monastery where resident monks in brown robes hold daily services. Architecturally distinct from other Hanoi pagodas, Tran Quoc maintains a visitor's hall in front and various statues, including a gilded wooden depiction of Shakyamuni Buddha. In the main courtyard is a giant pink-and-green planter holding a bodhi tree, purportedly a cutting from the original bodhi tree beneath which the Buddha reached his enlightenment. The bodhi was a gift from former Indian president Razendia Prasat, who visited the pagoda in 1959. ⊠ *Thanh Nien St., Tay Ho District,* ☎ *no phone.* ⌨ *5,000d donation.* ◷ *Daily 8–4:30.*

③⓪ **War memorial.** If you're interested in Vietnam War history, head for this small memorial between West Lake and Truc Bach Lake; it marks the capture of one of the war's most famous POWs. On October 26, 1967, Navy lieutenant commander John McCain's jet fighter was shot down, sending him parachuting into Truc Bach Lake. Suffering from badly broken bones and severe beatings, he was imprisoned in the "Hanoi Hilton" and other North Vietnamese prisons for more than five years. He went on to become an Arizona senator and a vocal advocate of reconciliation between the United States and his former captors. In 1997 he traveled to Hanoi to meet the old man who allegedly plucked him from the lake and near-certain death. McCain's bid for the Republican nomination in the 2000 presidential race sparked renewed interest in the man among Hanoi's intelligentsia, not to mention a flurry of activity at the lake itself when McCain made a return visit in April 2000, just ahead of the 25th anniversary of the end of the Vietnam War. The underwhelming red-sandstone memorial features a bound and suspended prisoner with his head hanging low and the letters U.S.A.F. (the memorial is incorrectly labeled, as McCain belonged to the navy and not the air force). ⊠ *Thanh Nien St., Ba Dinh District.*

🕭 **West Lake Sports and Culture Club.** Kitsch doesn't keep people from flocking to this popular pool and amusement complex, which consists of three sections. The Water Park has several pools, giant slides, and wading pools with dinosaurs and submerged pachyderms, as well as plenty of lifeguards on staff. A Ferris wheel dominates Lunar Park, which also has a roller coaster, rubber paddleboats, and other rides. The third section is a members-only sports and culture club. Hire a taxi to get here. ⊠ *614 Lac Long Quan St., Tay Ho District,* ☎ *04/718–4193.* 🎫 *Water Park weekdays 40,000d, weekends 50,000d; Lunar Park an additional 3,000d plus extra for rides and games.* ⊙ *Mid-Apr.–mid-Oct., daily 9–6.*

DINING

Most of Hanoi's international restaurants and many places serving Vietnamese cuisine are in the Hoan Kiem District. Local specialties, such as *banh cuon* (a thin rice crepe with savory stuffing) and *mi xao* (Chinese egg noodles), can be found on Ngo Cam Chi Street (off Hang Bong Street) in the Old Quarter. Goat meat is the specialty of Lang Ha Street, south of the U.S. embassy, and dog meat (for really adventurous eaters) is served in restaurants on Nghi Tam Road between West Lake and the Red River.

Tong Duy Tan Street, where the king's food was cooked in ancient times, is busy with noodle shops serving seafood dishes and *ga tan*, a chicken soup cooked with eight Chinese herbs, including lotus seed; it is considered especially good for women's health. For men there's *pin tan*, the same soup made with bull parts, instead, for the same effect. Toasted bread soaked in honey is served with the soup—you are charged by the slice. Make sure to avoid dishes with "scallops"; they are actually tough, bitter periwinkles. Eat upstairs at the restaurants in this area for a better view of the street.

Another excellent food street, known as Xoi Alley, tees off Tong Duy Tan Street toward Trang Thi Street. *Xoi,* or sticky rice, is a glutinous grain served with sausage, boiled egg, dried shredded pork, or cucumbers and fish sauce. Here you can find sticky rice, fried noodles, or pho any time of day and late into the night. The "fast food" advertised in café windows actually means cheap rice, omelets, and noodle dishes.

Hanoi's dining scene is in constant flux. Although the establishments listed below have staying power, it is recommended that you call before heading out to a particular restaurant, as places may close as suddenly as they open. In addition, it's not uncommon for owners and managers to change, transforming the whole restaurant for better or worse.

CATEGORY	COST*
$$$$	over 270,000 dong
$$$	170,000 dong–270,000 dong
$$	70,000 dong–170,000 dong
$	30,000 dong–70,000 dong
¢	under 30,000 dong

per person for a main course at dinner, including 10% tax and 5% service

Hoan Kiem District

Cafés

$–$$ ✕ **Au Lac Café.** On a sunny day this outdoor café across the street from the Metropole Hotel is a great spot for lunch or breakfast. Cappuccinos, pastas, tasty salads, and even bagels are served on an outdoor terrace. Don't confuse it with the look-alike next door, Diva Café. ✉ *57 Ly Thai To St., Hoan Kiem District,* ☎ *04/825–7807. No credit cards.*

¢ ✕ **Café 252.** This is the famous breakfast spot frequented by Catherine Deneuve while she was in Vietnam filming *Indochine.* It's strictly no-frills but serves good pastries, real café au lait, and the best yogurt in town. ✉ *252 Hang Bong St., Hoan Kiem District,* ☎ *04/825–0216. No credit cards.*

¢ ✕ **Che Thap Cam Cu.** This hole-in-the-wall serves only one thing, *che*— a sweet green bean concoction that is part drink, part pudding. Especially popular with Vietnamese women, che is a typical treat on sultry summer afternoons. A number of imitators have sprung up following the success of this old Hanoi institution. Walk to the end of the alley and look for the shop on your left. ✉ *72G Tran Hung Dao St., Hoan Kiem District,* ☎ *04/824–5642. No credit cards.*

Chinese

$$–$$$ ✕ **First Restaurant.** Diners come to this Chinese restaurant, complete with straight-back chairs and a preponderance of red, for its well-prepared Shanghai specialties and warm service. Shanghai-style Chinese food can be a bit on the oily side and spicier than other eastern Chinese dishes, but if you've never had the authentic item, you're in for a treat. The Shanghai cold duck is a house specialty. Standard Chinese fare includes lemon chicken, chili prawns, and fried noodle and rice dishes. ✉ *12 Trang Thi St., 3rd floor, Hoan Kiem District,* ☎ *04/824–0060. MC, V.*

Contemporary

$$–$$$ ✕ **Restaurant Bobby Chinn.** Hanoi's most gregarious chef, American
★ Bobby Chinn, dishes up contemporary cuisine drawing on Californian, Vietnamese, Mediterranean, and other Asian influences. His menu, which changes monthly, emphasizes the freshest organic produce and ingredients. Favorites include panfried tuna with wasabi mashed potatoes, Vietnamese tapas, and an à la carte tasting menu. Artwork by Hanoi's up-and-coming artists, a broad selection of wines, excellent cocktails, and a view overlooking Hoan Kiem Lake make this restaurant-bar popular with the city's expat crowd. Reservations are recommended. ✉ *1 Ba Trieu St., Hoan Kiem District,* ☎ *04/934–8577 or 04/934–8578,* WEB *www.bobbychinn.com. AE, MC, V.*

42

Hanoi Dining and Lodging

West Lake
(Hoy Tay)

③ - ⑥

Thuy Khue

Hoang   Hoa Tham

Phan Dinh Phung   ②

Quan Thanh

Dang Dung

Hung Vuong

Bach Thao
Botanical
Garden

**BA DINH
DISTRICT**

Ngoc Ha

Nguyen
Lam

**Presidential
Palace**

THE CITADEL

**Ho Chi Minh
Mausoleum**

Ba Dinh
Square

Nguyen
Lam

Hoang Dieu

Nguyen Tri Phuong

Cua

**Ho Chi Minh's
Museum**

**One Pillar
Pagoda**

Dien Bien Phu

Le Hong Phong

**Army
Museum**

Kim Ma   ❶
          ①

②

Cat Linh

**The Restaurant,
Hanoi Press Club**

③
**Museum
of Fine Arts**

Chi Lang
Park

Tran Phu

❺

Tong
Duy Tan

**GIANG
VO**

**HAO
NAM**

Trinh Hoai Duc

**Temple of
Literature**

Van Mieu

Nguyen Thai Hoc

Nguyen Khuyen

④

Quoc Tu Giam

Tran Quy Cap

❻

**Hanoi
Railway
Station**

Le Duan

Phan Boi Chau

**Cultu
Friends
Pala**

Ton Duc Thang

La Thanh

Kham Thien

Yet Kieu

Nam Dong

**THO
QUAN**

Cho Kham Thien

La Thanh

**TRUNG
PHUNG**

❼ ⑦

Tr

**DONG DA
DISTRICT**

Le
P

Le Duan

Bay N
Lak

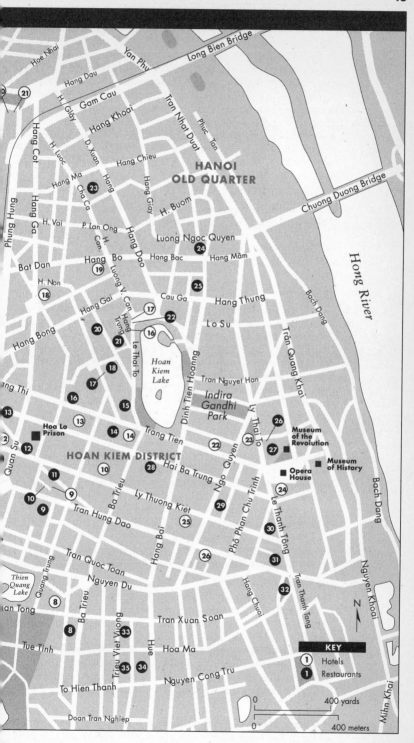

Hoe Nhai
Yan Phu
Long Bien Bridge
Hang Dau
H. Giay
Gam Cau
Hang Khoai
Tran Nhat Duat
Phuc Tan
Chuong Duong Bridge
Hang Cot
D. Xuan
Hang Chieu
Hang Ma
Cha Ca
Hang Giay
HANOI OLD QUARTER
Hang Ga
H. Vai
P. Lan Ong
H. Buom
Phung Hung
Cam
Luong Ngoc Quyen
Hang Bo
Hang Bac
Hang Mâm
Bat Dan
Hang Dao
Luong V. Can
Hong River
H. Non
Hang Gai
Cau Ga
Hang Thung
Hang Bong
Le Thai To
Lo Su
Bach Dang
Hoan Kiem Lake
Dinh Tien Hoang
Tran Nguyet Han
Indira Gandhi Park
Tran Quang Khai
ng Thi
Hoa Lo Prison
Ly Thai To
Museum of the Revolution
Quan Su
HOAN KIEM DISTRICT
Trang Tien
Museum of History
Hai Ba Trung
Ngo Quyen
Le Thanh Tong
Opera House
Ba Trieu
Ly Thuong Kiet
Pho Phan Chu Trinh
Tran Hung Dao
Hang Bai
Bach Dang
Tran Quoc Toan
Nguyen Du
Hang Chuoi
Nguyen Khoai
Thien Quang Lake
Quang Trung
Ba Trieu
Tran Xuan Soan
Tran Thanh Tong
an Tong
Hue
Hoa Ma
Tue Tinh
Trieu Viet Vuong
To Hien Thanh
Nguyen Cong Tru
Doan Tran Nghiep
Minh Khai

KEY
① Hotels
● Restaurants

0   400 yards
0   400 meters

Continental

$$$–$$$$ ✕ **The Restaurant, Hanoi Press Club.** An exceptional assortment of fine wines, cigars, and single-malt scotch complements chef Donald Berger's international cuisine at this semiformal restaurant where Hanoi's movers and shakers gather. The former Ritz-Carlton chef prepares the finest ingredients with French technique. The oysters with caviar, salmon, and champagne are blissful. The seared Magret duck breast with pineapple and mango, and osso buco with chilled capellini are also good. An outside deck area is more casual, and Deli on the ground floor serves lunches, sandwiches, pies, and salads. ⊠ *Hanoi Press Club, 59A Ly Thai To St., 3rd floor, Hoan Kiem District, ☎ 04/934–0888,* WEB *www.hanoi-pressclub.com. Reservations essential. AE, DC, MC, V.*

Eclectic

$$ ✕ **Al Fresco.** Casual open-air dining and jumbo portions of ribs, pasta, T-bone steak, Mexican salad, and pizza make this colorful restaurant-bar a popular dining spot. The Mexican rolls, filled with avocado and chicken, are highly recommended. Al Fresco is a block south of Hoan Kiem Lake. ⊠ *23L Hai Ba Trung St., Hoan Kiem District, ☎ 04/826–7782. MC, V.*

French

$$–$$$ ✕ **Café des Arts de Hanoi.** Run by an amiable Frenchman, this cozy
★   restaurant is popular with Hanoi's French expatriates. Terra-cotta floors, wooden tables, and changing exhibits of paintings by local artists give the place a homey feel. At night the long wooden bar is a fine place to stop for a drink. The menu lists such typical French fare as *croque monsieur* (ham and cheese sandwich dipped in egg and sautéed in butter), beefsteak with fries, and a delicious pastis-flavored shrimp dish. The eggplant Parmesan is a good vegetarian option. ⊠ *11B Bao Khanh La., Hoan Kiem District, ☎ 04/828–7207. AE, MC, V.*

$–$$ ✕ **Hoa Sua.** More than a restaurant, Hoa Sua is a humanitarian proj-
★   ect: young people in need of assistance are trained as waiters and cooks. The latter project seems to have turned out better than the former, as service can be erratic. But the food—both French and Vietnamese—is decent and inexpensive. Try the goat cheese on toast, the avocado salad, or the vegetable terrine (skip the chicken); save room for the fruit crumble or chocolate mousse. Reserve a table for lunch on the terra-cotta terrace, shaded by umbrellas and palms, or head into the air-conditioned interior. The adjoining pastry shop sells a mouthwatering selection of breads, cakes, and pastries for takeout. ⊠ *81 Tho Nhuom St., Hoan Kiem District, ☎ 04/942–4448. No credit cards.*

Ice Cream

¢ ✕ **Fanny's Ice Cream.** This French-managed café across the street from Hoan Kiem Lake dishes up the best ice cream in town. The offerings, all made with natural ingredients and no preservatives, include unique local flavors like young rice or tamarind, along with old favorites such as coffee, rum raisin, and coconut. Try the refreshing lemon or, if you're determined to sin, a double scoop of raspberry and dark, wickedly rich chocolate. ⊠ *48 Le Thai To St., Hoan Kiem District, ☎ 04/828–5656. No credit cards.*

Indian

$–$$ ✕ **Tandoor.** This small Indian restaurant in the Thuy Loi minihotel makes up for its lackluster setting with a wonderful yet inexpensive menu. Food is prepared fresh, with hand-ground spices. You can't go wrong with anything here, but fluffy garlic nan bread, tender chicken *masala*, and eggplant curry are particularly good. The fish *tikka* in red sauce and the chicken kebab marinated in yogurt are also sensational. Service is very friendly, although it can become chaotic at dinnertime. The restaurant delivers. ✉ *24 Hang Be St., Hoan Kiem District,* ☎ *04/824–2252. MC, V.*

¢–$ ✕ **Dakshin.** Dashkin focuses on vegetarian Indian food and is the only
★ restaurant in Hanoi serving southern Indian delicacies. Specialties include paper *masala dosa,* a crispy thin pancake of rice and lentils, and *appan with stu* (a rich vegetable stew), a specialty from the Kerala region that in itself merits a visit. Documentaries on Indian culture and history are screened here. You can also use e-mail free—a unique extra in Hanoi. The staff members are friendly and helpful, and several speak English. ✉ *94 Hang Trong St., 3rd floor, Hoan Kiem District,* ☎ *04/928–6872 or 04/928–6873. AE, MC, V.*

Italian

$–$$ ✕ **Mediterraneo.** Delicious, reasonably priced Italian food is served in the bright, California-like atmosphere of this central eatery. Along with the best *bruschetta* (toasted bread with olive oil and various toppings) in town and homemade pastas, the Italian hosts serve excellent cappuccinos, Napoli-style thin-crust pizzas cooked in a wood-burning oven, and interesting homemade grappas—try licorice or peach. ✉ *23 Nha Tho St., Hoan Kiem District,* ☎ *04/826–6288. MC, V.*

Japanese

$$–$$$ ✕ **Saigon Sakura.** This take-off-your-shoes Japanese restaurant has clean Zen decor and good-value fixed-price lunches, and it's popular with expats. Try the excellent calamari with vinegar marinade or the unbeatable $15 sushi deal. Service is enthusiastic—staff members yell a traditional Japanese greeting as you walk in the door. The sushi bar is a nice option if you're dining alone. ✉ *17 Trang Thi St., Hoan Kiem District,* ☎ *04/825–7565. AE, MC, V.*

Spanish

$$–$$$ ✕ **La Salsa Tapas Bar and Restaurant.** You can nibble on small servings of ceviche, zesty meatballs, and marinated mushrooms or choose an entrée of warm duck salad, panfried salmon, or lamb tenderloin. If you're not in the mood to see and be seen, avoid the cozy downstairs bar and hide out in the quieter upstairs dining room. To wash down your meal, try some of La Salsa's Spanish wines or the house sangria, which is made according to a secret family recipe. ✉ *25 Nha Tho St., Hoan Kiem District,* ☎ *04/828–9052. MC, V.*

Thai

$$ ✕ **Bangkok-Hanoi.** The Bangkok-Hanoi feels authentic: the chef is from Thailand, Thai decorations and music fill the little eatery, and there's even ice-cold Singha beer. The spicy salads are excellent. For dessert try a dish of sweet taro or pumpkin in coconut milk. The 40,000d set lunches make this a popular afternoon-dining spot. ✉ *52A Ly Thuong Kiet St., Hoan Kiem District,* ☎ *04/934–5598. No credit cards.*

$ ✕ **Van Anh Thai Food.** This small, plain restaurant, run by a Thai man, Wijit Lekkhumpoon, and his Vietnamese wife, Van Anh, has gained a cult following among Hanoi's expats. Among the incredibly cheap Thai delights are spicy seafood soup, leaf-wrapped chicken, fried fish cakes, and spicy papaya salad. It's very clean and, thanks to all the fluorescent lights, very bright. ✉ *5A Tong Duy Tan St., Hoan Kiem District,* ☎ *04/928–5163. No credit cards.*

Vegetarian

$–$$ ✕ **Vegetarian Restaurant Com Chay Nang Tam.** Unusual vegetarian dishes, many prepared to resemble meat, are served in a dimly lighted villa. The warm corn squares are a pleasing starter, and the "ginger fish," made of tofu, is a good main course. The restaurant has limited seating, so reservations are recommended, especially for larger parties. ✉ *79A Tran Hung Dao St., Hoan Kiem District,* ☎ *04/826–6140. No credit cards.*

$ ✕ **Tamarind Cafe.** Two women run this restaurant serving creative, international vegetarian fare such as Zen pasta (pasta and stir-fried vegetables in a sweet soy sauce) and Taiwanese *popiah,* sweet crepes with various fillings. The fresh fruit juices and blends—particularly the "Sapa spice tickler" (pineapple, carrot, ginger, and lemon juice)—are refreshing. The modern Chinese dining room is suitable for Ma May Street, one of Hanoi's ancient Chinese trading areas. Weekday evenings the Tamarind hosts live entertainment such as salsa-dancing lessons and jazz. The restaurant is run in tandem with TF Handspan Tourism, which has a tour desk on the premises. ✉ *80 Ma May St., Hoan Kiem District,* ☎ *04/926–0580. No credit cards.*

Vietnamese

$$ ✕ **Nam Phuong.** Aimed more at tourists than at a local clientele, this restaurant in a nicely renovated French villa provides a good introduction to Vietnamese cuisine. Just bear in mind that portions of the tasty and beautifully presented dishes, such as beef in coconut milk, are disappointingly small. But the experience of dining here is lovely, with musicians playing traditional Vietnamese instruments and waitstaff dressed in traditional outfits. ✉ *19 Phan Chu Trinh St., Hoan Kiem District,* ☎ *04/824–0926. AE, MC, V.*

$–$$ ✕ **Emperor Restaurant.** In a renovated French villa, the Emperor has
★ what is arguably the most-beautiful and romantic setting in all of Hanoi. A climb up the curved wooden staircase takes you into the elegant, high-ceiling Hue-temple-style dining room; downstairs the resident jazz band plays in the Emperor Pub. Among the beautifully presented dishes are seafood and Hue specialties, including delectable Hue spring rolls and banana-leaf-wrapped fish. ✉ *18B Le Thanh Tong St., Hoan Kiem District,* ☎ *04/826–8801 or 04/826–8802. AE, MC, V.*

$ ✕ **Cha Ca La Vong.** Right in the thick of the Old Quarter is Hanoi's most famous purveyor of *cha ca*—grilled boneless fish cubes marinated in dill and served with rice noodles and peanuts. Watch out: you cook cha ca at your table on a brazier that can send hot grease flying. On a warm evening, you may feel as though you're being grilled along with the fish. Portions are small, but that doesn't seem to dissuade the tourists who pack the upstairs restaurant. Fewer people sit downstairs. The grease-covered walls add to the authentic, pungent experience. ✉ *14 Cha Ca St., Hoan Kiem District,* ☎ *no phone. No credit cards.*

¢–$ ✕ **Hue Restaurant.** Come here for imperial Hue cuisine and other tra-
★ ditional Vietnamese fare in a rustic outdoor-indoor setting. Each dish comes with a specific sauce—some sauces include a strong-smelling fermented shrimp paste, but if this bothers you, no one will mind if you just use the sauces you prefer. "Pork pie" is a poor translation for culinary nirvana— *banh xeo,* a some-assembly-required platter of sugar-cane-wrapped ground pork that you roll with greens and vegetables in rice paper and dip into a delicious peanut sauce. For those who wince at this carnivorous frenzy, vegetarian delights are plentiful. Note that the chefs use MSG liberally. ✉ *6 Ly Thuong Kiet St., Hoan Kiem District,* ☎ *04/826–4062. No credit cards.*

¢ ✕ **Dac Kim Bun Cha.** After shopping on Hang Bac Street, consider lunch-
★ ing at this Old Quarter institution. The tiny first floor is used for food preparation, but staff members will lead you up the winding tiled stairs until enough empty plastic stools can be found for your party. You may be planted cozily among other customers. Ordering should-n't be hard: the restaurant serves only two delicious dishes: *bun cha* (grilled pork patties with rice noodles) come with heaping plates of herbs

and lettuce; as a side, try the huge pork- and crab-filled spring rolls. Wash both down with *bia lanh* (cold beer) or *che da* (iced Vietnamese tea). ⊠ *1 Hang Manh St., Hoan Kiem District,* ☎ *no phone. No credit cards. No dinner.*

Around Lenin Park

Cafés

¢ ✕ **129 Mai Hac De.** Locals and visitors flock to this closet-size café to perch on knee-high stools and sip smooth, creamy fruit shakes. The basic café menu lists pastries, baked potatoes, some rather mediocre rice and noodle dishes, and a selection of excellent grilled sandwiches. This is a fine place to stop for a snack and some perhaps much-needed caffeine after a tour of Lenin Park. ⊠ *129 Mai Hac De St., Hai Ba Trung District,* ☎ *no phone. No credit cards.*

Italian

$$–$$$ ✕ **Il Grillo.** The espresso and cappuccino and tasty pasta and antipasti keep diners coming back to this pleasant, intimate Italian eatery where the busy interior could be almost anywhere in Italy. The wine list includes an extensive selection of Italian wines; other occasional imports are buffalo mozzarella, pickled sardines, and cured meats. ⊠ *116 Ba Trieu St., Hai Ba Trung District,* ☎ *04/822–7720. AE, MC, V.*

$–$$ ✕ **La Terraza.** One of the original Italian restaurants of Hanoi, La Terraza serves Australian- and American-style pizzas, simple pastas, sandwiches, and salads. If you're looking for lots of toppings and thick-crust pizzas—a rarity in Hanoi, where most of the pizza has thin crust—this is the place. The owners and staff are pleasant and accommodating, and the interior is very simple. The restaurant is on one of Hanoi's interesting café rows that is rarely visited by tourists. ⊠ *125 Trieu Viet Vuong St., Hai Ba Trung District,* ☎ *04/978–0622. AE, MC, V.*

Japanese

$$$–$$$$ ✕ **Restaurant Benkay.** High prices match the high standards at this elegant hotel restaurant. The traditional Japanese interior is as delicately understated as the service, and the food will transport you straight to Tokyo. Set lunches, such as breaded pork or chicken, start at just $7, although once here it's all too tempting to go for the five-course $88 *kaiseki* menu of seafood specialties or the divine $60 sushi dinner. Be forewarned that portions are small. ⊠ *Hotel Nikko Hanoi, 84 Tran Nhan Tong St., Hai Ba Trung District,* ☎ *04/822–3535. AE, DC, MC, V.*

$$–$$$ ✕ **Ky Y.** The Japanese equivalent of your friendly neighborhood diner, this cozy restaurant is always packed with Japanese businesspeople and expats in the know. Astonishingly low prices encourage overindulgence in sushi or sashimi; the lunch specials are a steal at less than $6. Seating is at low, take-your-shoes-off tables in small private rooms or at a long polished bar on the ground floor. ⊠ *166 Trieu Viet Vuong St., Hai Ba Trung District,* ☎ *04/978–4677. AE, MC, V.*

Vietnamese

¢ ✕ **Cafe Que Huong.** Locals and foreigners alike drop by this relaxed restaurant for its typical Vietnamese fare served in a villa with an attached courtyard. On warm summer nights sit at an outside table beneath a roof of thatched palm and order the excellent, tender fried squid; wash it down with a cold beer. Other good bets include the tofu with tomato sauce and the fried greens with garlic—guaranteed to keep Dracula away. ⊠ *42 Tang Bat Ho St., Hai Ba Trung District,* ☎ *04/971–1444. No credit cards.*

Around the Ho Chi Minh Mausoleum

Continental

¢–$ ✕ **KOTO.** The name is an acronym for "Know One, Teach One," the
★   restaurant's founding principle. Australian-Vietnamese Jimmy Pham
established KOTO in order to train young people in need of assistance
in a caring environment. The largely Continental menu is as inspira-
tional as its objectives: breads are fresh, and exotic fruit shakes and
desserts are delicious. The restaurant makes a good stop for lunch after
a morning visit to the Temple of Literature, which it overlooks. ⊠ *61
Van Mieu, Dong Da District,* ☎ *04/747–0338. MC, V. No dinner.*

Italian

$–$$ ✕ **Luna D'Autunno.** Dining at this friendly Italian eatery is inside, on
an outdoor terra-cotta terrace with a pizza oven, or at an adjoining
wine bar called Vino da Gino. Gino Benelli, the proprietor, is an amiable Italian expat, and his wife Bui The Thu Hang a great hostess. Try
one of the well-stuffed sandwiches, the platter of marinated vegetables
with feta cheese, or a four-cheese pizza. Delivery is free. ⊠ *11B Dien
Bien Phu St., Ba Dinh District,* ☎ *04/823–7338. AE, MC, V.*

Japanese

$–$$ ✕ **Edo.** Edo, in the Hanoi Daewoo Hotel, is one of Hanoi's better restau-
rants. The grilled salmon and *teppanyaki* (grilled meat) dishes are especially good, and, come noon, the $11 sushi lunch buffet lures in hordes
of hungry businesspeople. ⊠ *Hanoi Daewoo Hotel, 360 Kim Ma St.,
Ba Dinh District,* ☎ *04/831–5000. AE, MC, V.*

Vietnamese

$$ ✕ **Brother's Cafe.** Entering this beautiful restaurant is like stepping back
in time. The front room, decorated with carved wooden beams and
Buddha statues, is an old, tile-roof pagoda that backs onto a quiet court-
yard. Outside, tables are shaded by potted palms and cooled by an-
tique brass fans. At night the courtyard is lighted by candles. With no
à la carte menu, you help yourself to a large buffet of hot and cold dishes,
including seafood, pork, and chicken, plus five kinds of Vietnamese
salads. ⊠ *26 Nguyen Thai Hoc St., Ba Dinh District,* ☎ *04/733–3866.
MC, V. No lunch Sun.*

Around West Lake

Vietnamese

$–$$ ✕ **Seasons of Hanoi.** French elegance meets Vietnamese charm in a beau-
★   tifully restored villa dating from 1902 and filled with antiques from In-
dochina. The coconut and lemongrass chicken curry is a rich choice,
and the fish baked in a clay pot is tasty but salty. Also recommended is
the divine eggplant cooked in a clay pot. Sunday brunch is popular. ⊠
95B Quan Thanh St., Ba Dinh District, ☎ *04/835–5444. AE, MC, V.*

LODGING

Hotels in Hanoi range from charming and idiosyncratic to some of the
most luxurious in the region (although even the swankiest properties
tend to have spotty service; managers are working hard to develop more
professional staffs, but for the time being, it's a good idea to cultivate
patience). The general character of hotels varies somewhat by district:
Ba Dinh District and the shores of West Lake have larger and more
upscale facilities. The central Hoan Kiem District has it all, with stylish
new business hotels, old state-run places, and hundreds of minihotels.
With the opening of several upscale, international joint-venture hotels
in the past decade, increased competition has led to across-the-board

price cuts. Not only can you get terrific deals at these high-end hotels, but even minihotels have been forced to renovate and slash prices. Many hotels suffer from low occupancy rates, so be sure to ask about discounts.

CATEGORY	COST*
$$$$	over 2.5 million dong
$$$	1 million dong–2.5 million dong
$$	750,000 dong–1 million dong
$	400,000 dong–750,000 dong
¢	under 400,000 dong

All prices are for a standard double room, including 10% tax and 5% service.

Hoan Kiem District

$$$–$$$$ **Metropole Hotel Sofitel.** The exquisite Metropole, built by the French
★ in the early 1900s, combines old-fashioned European grandeur with modern convenience. And you can't beat the central location in the heart of Hanoi. The impeccably decorated rooms with French-style shuttered windows are luxurious, if not incredibly spacious. The bar-side pool is a nice option on a sunny day or warm evening, and the lobby bar is a good bet any day of the week. The Le Beaulieu restaurant sometimes serves a wonderful seasonal-seafood buffet with imported French oysters and crabs. ⊠ *15 Ngo Quyen St., Hoan Kiem District,* ☎ *04/826–6919,* FAX *04/826–6920,* WEB *www.sofitel-hanoi-vietnam.com. 244 rooms. 2 restaurants, room service, in-room safes, minibars, cable TV, pool, health club, 2 bars, dry cleaning, laundry service, concierge, Internet, business services, meeting rooms, airport shuttle, car rental, travel services. AE, DC, MC, V. CP.*

$$$ **Hilton Hanoi Opera.** What really makes this hotel stand out is its location. Where else can you relax in the swimming pool and look out at the Opera House? So convincingly does the design of this hotel complement that of the nearby Opera House that many newcomers take it for an original French building. Sadly, this elegance gives way to an ostentatious lobby inside. The rooms, on the other hand, are both tasteful and comfortable. Within the hotel are a bakery, a fancy Chinese restaurant, and a French bistro that serves a massive if somewhat uninspired Sunday brunch. ⊠ *1 Le Thanh Tong St., Hoan Kiem District,* ☎ *04/933–0500,* FAX *04/933–0530,* WEB *www.hilton.com. 269 rooms. 3 restaurants, room service, in-room data ports, in-room safes, minibars, cable TV, pool, health club, 2 bars, dry cleaning, laundry service, concierge, business services, meeting rooms. AE, D, MC, V. CP.*

$$–$$$ **Dan Chu Hotel.** The location of this colonial-era hotel, not far from Hoan Kiem Lake, is great, and an airy, verdant backyard commands a certain serene elegance. The rooms are spacious and have high ceilings but are somewhat drab—some lack windows and all have frightful synthetic bedspreads. ⊠ *29 Trang Tien St., Hoan Kiem District,* ☎ *04/825–4937,* FAX *04/826–6786. 56 rooms. Restaurant, room service, in-room data ports, minibars, cable TV, bar, dry cleaning, laundry service, concierge, business services, car rental, travel services. AE, DC, MC, V. CP.*

$$–$$$ **De Syloia Hotel.** Hanoi's only true boutique hotel, the French colonial–style De Syloia is small but fashionable and stands in the French Quarter. Wooden furniture, large beds, and cream-color linens fill the well-appointed and well-maintained rooms. The staff is friendly, attentive, and helpful. The restaurant serves mainly Vietnamese food with some Western dishes. Because the hotel is often fully booked you should make reservations well in advance. ⊠ *17A Trang Hung Dao*

St., Hoan Kiem District, ☎ 04/824–5346, FAX 04/824–1083, WEB www. desyloia.com. 33 rooms. Restaurant, room service, in-room data ports, minibars, cable TV, bar, dry cleaning, laundry service, concierge, business services. AE, DC, MC, V. CP.

$$–$$$ 🏨 **Guoman Hotel.** This well-run central hotel is popular with business travelers. The rooms are pleasant, and the service is efficient. The main restaurant, Café Paradise, has an American chef who turns out good and reasonably priced international fare. An outdoor café hosts nightly barbecues. ✉ 83A Ly Thuong Kiet St., Hoan Kiem District, ☎ 04/822–2800, FAX 04/822–2822. 149 rooms. 3 restaurants, room service, in-room safes, minibars, cable TV, health club, bar, laundry services, Internet. AE, DC, MC, V. CP.

$$–$$$ 🏨 **Hoa Binh Hotel.** In a grand old building, the Hoa Binh is poised to accommodate an upscale crowd but seems to be lacking an experienced staff. The spacious rooms are clean and have high ceilings, but they betray sloppy renovations. However, the hotel is efficient and well-maintained and wins points for nostalgic charm. It also has a decent French restaurant and a massage service (with staff trained at the Institute of Traditional Medicine) that is one of the best deals in town, at just 50,000d per hour. Ask about discount room rates for longer stays. ✉ 27 Ly Thuong Kiet St., Hoan Kiem District, ☎ 04/825–3315, FAX 04/826–9818. 88 rooms. Restaurant, in-room data ports, minibars, cable TV, massage, sauna, bar, dry cleaning, laundry service, business services, car rental. AE, MC, V. CP

$$–$$$ 🏨 **Melia Hanoi.** What the Melia lacks in charm it makes up for in price, keeping this glitzy 23-story hotel tower consistently busy. After discounts, which you should bargain for when you make your reservation, you receive top-notch facilities and service at minihotel prices. One restaurant serves international cuisine; the other specializes in Chinese and Thai food and hosts a daily lunch buffet and a popular nightly Thai dinner buffet. ✉ 44B Ly Thuong Kiet St., Hoan Kiem District, ☎ 04/934–3343, FAX 04/934–3344, WEB www.solmelia.com. 308 rooms. 2 restaurants, room service, in-room data ports, in-room safes, minibars, cable TV, pool, health club, dry cleaning, laundry service, concierge, business services, meeting rooms. AE, MC, V. CP.

$$ 🏨 **Saigon Hotel.** This property has friendly service and, despite the concrete '60s architecture, is quite pleasant. Rooms are small and plain, but the beds are comfortable. The rooftop garden is a terrific place for an evening drink; from here you can see the Hanoi Towers office complex, on the site of the former "Hanoi Hilton" prison. The hotel is not far from the train station, opposite the United Nations Vietnam headquarters, and near the Fansland Cinema, which sometimes shows movies in English and has a sidewalk Thai restaurant. The restaurant serves Vietnamese, French, and American food. ✉ 80 Ly Thuong Kiet St., Hoan Kiem District, ☎ 04/942–4499, FAX 04/942–2631, WEB www. saigon-tourist.com. 44 rooms. Restaurant, room service, in-room data ports, in-room safes, minibars, cable TV, massage, sauna, 2 bars, dry cleaning, laundry service, business services, meeting rooms, car rental, travel services. AE, DC, MC, V. CP.

$–$$ 🏨 **Chains First Eden Hotel.** In the Old Quarter, this hotel is an excellent point of departure for walking tours. You can start by checking out the chaos on the streets from the hotel's top-floor restaurant, which serves Vietnamese and Western fare. The rooms themselves have all the amenities but also have darkly oppressive furniture and curtains that may induce flashbacks to the 1970s. Deluxe rooms contain individual fax machines. All in all, the hotel feels a bit faded. ✉ 3A Phan Dinh Phung St., Hoan Kiem District, ☎ 04/828–3896, FAX 04/828–4066. 42 rooms. Restaurant, some in-room faxes, minibars, cable TV, laundry service, travel services. AE, MC, V. CP.

$–$$ ⬛ **Galaxy Hotel.** Built in 1918, this granite-face hotel has been fully
★ renovated to accommodate business travelers and seems wholly modern. The comfortable rooms have typical hotel furnishings and are quieter than you might expect given the hotel's proximity to the bustling
Old Quarter; some have garden views. ✉ *1 Phan Dinh Phung St., Hoan
Kiem District,* ☎ *04/828–2888,* 𝐅𝐀𝐗 *04/828–2466. 60 rooms. 2 restaurants, room service, in-room safes, minibars, cable TV, bar, laundry
service, dry cleaning, concierge, business services, meeting rooms, car
rental, travel services. AE, DC, MC, V. CP.*

$–$$ ⬛ **Thuy Nga Hotel.** This upscale minihotel just a stone's throw from
central Hoan Kiem Lake is a gem. Service is efficient and friendly, and
the rooms are tasteful with wooden furniture and plush carpeting. Some
of the standard rooms lack windows, so be sure to ask about this before you reserve. It's worth splurging on the top-floor VIP suite (about
$75), which has a large terrace with a stunning view over the lake. ✉
4 Ba Trieu St., Hoan Kiem District, ☎ *04/934–1256,* 𝐅𝐀𝐗 *04/934–
1262. 20 rooms. Restaurant, in-room data ports, in-room safes, minibars, cable TV, laundry service. AE, DC, MC, V. CP.*

$ ⬛ **Eden Hotel.** The Eden is a top-rate minihotel in a decent location near
Thuyen Quang Lake. Bright rooms with carved-wood furniture have
all of the conveniences—carpeted floors, big baths, and 10 television
channels. Happily absent are the neon and nylon of some other minihotels. In the lobby, birds sing over a tremendous fish tank, and an altar
is stacked with fake gold, oranges, beer, and Cokes for the ancestors.
✉ *78 Tho Nhuom St., Hoan Kiem District,* ☎ *04/942–3273,* 𝐅𝐀𝐗 *04/
942–4619. 25 rooms. Restaurant, minibars, cable TV, dry cleaning, laundry service, concierge, car rental, travel services. AE, MC, V. CP.*

¢–$ ⬛ **Win Hotel.** The Win is immaculate and homey all at once. On a quiet
★ street just off Le Thai To Street, it's also just a short skip from Hoan
Kiem Lake. Floor-to-ceiling one-way windows let Hanoi in, or you can
keep the light out with lace and red-velvet curtains. Carved hardwood
furniture, tastefully arranged artificial flowers, high ceilings, clean
baths, and a fluffy dog in the lobby make you feel at home. An added
bonus is its location next to Café Nhan, which is the size of a mansion and is famous for its avocado shakes and rocket-fuel coffee. ✉
34 Hang Hanh St., Hoan Kiem District, ☎ *04/828–7371 or 04/828–
7150,* 𝐅𝐀𝐗 *04/824–7448. 8 rooms. Fans, in-room data ports, minibars,
cable TV, laundry service, car rental, travel services. AE, MC, V. CP.*

¢ ⬛ **Camellia II Hotel.** This well-run, well-maintained minihotel, located
near Hang Da Market in the thick of the Old Quarter, has clean,
bright rooms and a friendly staff. There's a glossy feel to everything
here—shiny bathrooms, lots of glazed wood, and an abundance of satin.
Although the hotel is not exactly tasteful, given the price, it's hard to
quibble, and the location is great for its street life. The $25 rooms are
slightly larger but offer no real advantage over the cheaper rooms. ✉
31 Hoang Dieu St., Hoan Kiem District, ☎ *04/828–5704,* 𝐅𝐀𝐗 *04/
828–5777. 12 rooms. Fans, in-room data ports, minibars, cable TV,
laundry service. MC, V. CP.*

¢ ⬛ **Lavender Hotel.** It's hard to find fault with this cheery minihotel just
around the corner from Xoi Alley—a street lined with noodle and rice
shops that stay open late. The friendly manager, Mr. Thang, speaks great
English and runs a tight ship: the rooms are clean and bright with big
windows and sparkling bathtubs. Rooms in the front have balconies.
Guests have access to the hotel e-mail account. ✉ *3D Tong Duy Tan
St., Hoan Kiem District,* ☎ *04/828–6723,* 𝐅𝐀𝐗 *04/828–6474. 12 rooms.
Fans, in-room data ports, minibars, cable TV. AE, MC, V. CP.*

¢ ⬛ **Phan Thai Hotel.** Modern minihotel conveniences, inoffensive decor,
balconies, and a friendly staff make this a very decent accommodation.
Conveniently located in the Old Quarter, it's near Hoan Kiem Lake

on a candy-selling street. The top floors provide a fabulous view of Old Quarter roofs and the Long Binh train and bicycle bridge. Also upstairs is a family altar, with tiled dragons and a many-armed goddess. ✉ *44 Hang Giay St., Hoan Kiem District,* ☎ *04/824–3667,* 🖷 *04/826–6677,* 🖳 *www.camellia-hotels.com. 16 rooms. Restaurant, minibars, cable TV, laundry service, Internet, business services, car rental, travel services. AE, DC, MC, V. CP.*

¢ 🏨 **Prince Hotel** (Hoang Tu). This posh minihotel has comfortable and elegant rooms, nice bathrooms with tubs, and a very enthusiastic English-speaking staff. Balconies afford views that range from a peek at the beautiful Hai Ba Trung Pagoda to the havoc of nearby apartments to the Somerset Grand Hanoi. Convenient to the train station, the Prince is also not too far from the city center. ✉ *96A Hai Ba Trung St., Hoan Kiem District,* ☎ *04/824–8314,* 🖷 *04/824–8323. 20 rooms. Fans, in-room data ports, minibars, cable TV, bar, dry cleaning, laundry service, car rental. No credit cards. CP.*

¢ 🏨 **Vinh Quang Hotel.** This hotel stands on Hang Quat, or Fan Street, one of the most charming and lively streets in the Old Quarter. Now, instead of selling fans, stores here specialize in red-velvet banners with messages like GOOD LUCK IN YOUR NEXT LIFE. Aside from the cheap East-West fusion furnishings, the Vinh Quang has neat, efficient rooms and a great central location. Front rooms have balconies overlooking the color and activity of Hang Quat Street. Some of the smaller back rooms are windowless. ✉ *24 Hang Quat St., Hoan Kiem District,* ☎ *04/824–3423,* 🖷 *04/825–1519. 25 rooms. Restaurant, fans, minibars, cable TV, bar, laundry service, travel services. MC, V. CP.*

Around Lenin Park

$$$ 🏨 **Hotel Nikko Hanoi.** With its sleek and airy lobby affording a peek into a tiny Japanese garden, this 15-story hotel is a shining example of understated Japanese elegance. The rooms are both simple and luxurious, with light, understated wooden furniture and large closets. The corner suites have spacious bathrooms that overlook Lenin Park across the street. Superior and executive rooms are the same size, but the latter have more windows. Three restaurants serve Japanese, Chinese, or French food: the Chinese dining room does an excellent Sunday dim sum, and Restaurant Benkay has the most authentic—and most expensive—Japanese food in town. ✉ *84 Tran Nhan Tong St., Hai Ba Trung District,* ☎ *04/822–3535,* 🖷 *04/822–3555,* 🖳 *www.hotelnikkohanoi.com.vn. 260 rooms. 3 restaurants, room service, in-room data ports, in-room safes, minibars, cable TV, pool, sauna, health club, bar, dry cleaning, laundry service, concierge, business services, meeting rooms. AE, MC, V. CP.*

$$–$$$ 🏨 **Green Park Hotel.** Ignore the exterior, painted a terrifying shade of
★ green, and you'll discover a charming hotel, where the marble-floor lobby is always full of fresh flowers and staff members go out of their way to make you feel at home. The rooms—some of which look toward nearby Lenin Park—are spacious, quiet, and, given the hotel's exterior, surprisingly tasteful. Front rooms have larger windows and are slightly bigger than back ones, but all are pleasant. The corner suites are especially wonderful, with lots of sunlight and luxurious bathrooms. The top-floor restaurant serves Asian and Western food and has a lovely view over Lenin Park and Thuyen Quang Lake. ✉ *48 Tran Nhan Tong St., Hai Ba Trung District,* ☎ *04/822–7725,* 🖷 *04/822–5977,* 🖳 *www. hanoi-greenpark-hotel.com. 40 rooms. Restaurant, room service, in-room data ports, in-room safes, minibars, cable TV, massage, dry cleaning, laundry service, concierge, business services, meeting room, travel services. AE, DC, MC, V. CP.*

Around the Ho Chi Minh Mausoleum

$$$ ⊞ **Hanoi Daewoo Hotel.** The pool here—the longest in Southeast
★ Asia—is just one example of how over the top this hotel is. Even its
impressive collection of more than 1,000 paintings by contemporary
Vietnamese artists, hanging in public spaces and guest rooms, is wor-
thy of a book. Space is abundant—from the open marble lobby that
spills into a large two-story lounge overlooking the pool to the four
restaurants. Rooms are big and lavishly decorated; some overlook the
zoo, West Lake, or downtown Hanoi. The main drawback is that you
need to take a taxi to get downtown; there is shuttle service, but it's
infrequent. ⊠ *360 Kim Ma St., Ba Dinh District,* ☎ *04/831–5000,* FAX
04/831–5500, WEB *www.lhw.com. 411 rooms. 4 restaurants, room ser-
vice, in-room data ports, in-room safes, minibars, cable TV, pool, aer-
obics, gym, hot tub, sauna, 2 bars, dance club, dry cleaning, laundry
service, concierge, business services, meeting rooms, car rental, travel
services. AE, DC, MC, V.*

$$$ ⊞ **Hanoi Horison Hotel.** An impressive green glass–fronted facade has
earned the Horison the nickname "Emerald City." Rooms are luxuri-
ous, if not overly large, and are done in soothing pastels. In the spacious lobby, which has a marble floor and Indonesian artwork, there
is a bakery that serves good pastries. There's also an international restaurant, and the Chimney Pub occasionally hosts live music. ⊠ *40 Cat
Linh St., Ba Dinh District,* ☎ *04/733–0808,* FAX *04/733–0888,* WEB *www.
swiss-belhotel. 350 rooms. Restaurant, room service, in-room data ports,
in-room safes, minibars, cable TV, tennis court, pool, gym, bar, lobby
lounge, laundry service, business services, meeting rooms, travel services. AE, DC, MC, V. CP.*

Around West Lake

$$$ ⊞ **Hanoi Club.** Well-appointed rooms at this swank private sports club
afford spectacular sunset views over West Lake and include the use of
the club's plush facilities. The only drawback? With two tennis courts,
squash courts, a huge gym, a driving range, an outdoor pool, and sail-
boats to keep you busy, you'll have trouble finding time to sightsee.
Moreover, the hotel has Western, Chinese, and Japanese restaurants,
so you won't even need to go out for food. ⊠ *76 Yen Phu St., Tay Ho
District,* ☎ *04/823–8115,* FAX *04/823–8390. 12 rooms. 3 restaurants,
room service, in-room safes, minibars, cable TV, driving range, 2 ten-
nis courts, pool, massage, health club, boating, squash, bar, dry clean-
ing, laundry service, Internet, business services, meeting rooms. AE,
MC, V. CP.*

$$$ ⊞ **Sofitel Plaza Hotel.** Stunning views of Truc Bach and West lakes and
a central location are two of the highlights of this luxury hotel. Cen-
tral Hanoi is only a few minutes' drive away, plus it's a short hop to
the Ho Chi Minh Mausoleum and diplomatic district. The rooms are
both comfortable and tasteful, but what makes this hotel stand out is
its fourth-floor swimming pool with a view over the neighboring lakes
and a retractable roof for year-round swimming. Two restaurants serve
Chinese and Western food, and a top-floor bar affords a great view of
the city. ⊠ *1 Thanh Nien St., Ba Dinh District,* ☎ *04/823–8888,* FAX
04/829–3888, WEB *www.sofitel.com. 322 rooms. 2 restaurants, room
service, in-room data ports, in-room safes, minibars, cable TV, pool,
health club, massage, bar, dry cleaning, laundry service, concierge, business services, meeting rooms, travel services. AE, DC, MC, V.*

$$–$$$ ⊞ **Ho Tay Villas.** For complete silence try these villas, 5 km (3 mi) out-
side Hanoi on West Lake: peaceful accommodations that feel like a cross
between an elegant estate and a socialist summer camp. The grounds

are gorgeous, with lots of flowering trees, wild birds, and excellent separate swimming pool facilities open to the public. Rooms are clean, with all the amenities, although perhaps a little musty from age and proximity to the lake. You can even stay in a suite that has its own meeting room. ⊠ *Dang Thai Mai St., Quan Tay Ho,* ☎ *04/0804–7772,* ℻ *04/823–2126. 75 rooms. Restaurant, fans, in-room data ports, minibars, cable TV, tennis court, pool, bar, laundry service, meeting rooms, travel services. MC, V. CP.*

$ 🎏 **Dragon Hotel.** It's hard to imagine Mother Teresa, who stayed here in 1996, surrounded by so much extravagance—a many-armed statue of the Goddess of Mercy, carp-filled pools, gold dragon statues—and that's before you get into the room. With ornately carved wooden furniture, institutional carpeting, and mirrors beside the beds, the rooms are a tribute to tackiness. It's not all in bad taste, however; the staff is friendly, and the rooms overlook a leafy canal. There's also a lovely terra-cotta patio strung with birdcages. ⊠ *9 Tay Ho Rd., Ba Dinh District,* ☎ *04/829–2954,* ℻ *04/829–4745. 23 rooms. In-room data ports, in-room safes, cable TV, laundry service, travel services. V. BP.*

NIGHTLIFE AND THE ARTS

The Arts

The arrival of television has dealt a serious blow to Hanoi's once vibrant performing-arts scene, and it is unclear whether or not it will ever recover. Throughout the city, formerly thriving movie houses have gone dark as Hanoians tune in to Vietnam Television and satellite TV, and VCRs and DVD players fly off the shelves, further jeopardizing the fate of film and performing arts in Vietnam.

Nonetheless, some Hanoians remain firm in their belief that nothing beats a live performance. With the multimillion-dollar restoration of the Opera House in the late 1990s, Hanoi's performing-arts scene has begun slowly to reemerge. The imposing French-built arts palace hosts Vietnam's top traditional musicians and pop stars as well as the occasional Western performer. Elsewhere in the city, you can catch a performance of Vietnamese folk opera, traditional music, or enchanting water puppetry. If you want a peek at the results of years of Eastern European physical training, head to the circus at the northern edge of Lenin Park for Vietnam's version of the Cirque du Soleil.

To find out about upcoming cultural events, pick up a copy of *The Guide,* a useful arts and entertainment monthly available at many hotels, including the Metropole.

Circus

Vietnam Central Circus (Rap Xiec; ⊠ Tran Nhan Tong and Tran Binh Tong Sts., at north end of Lenin Park, Hoan Kiem District, ☎ 04/822–0277) was founded in the 1950s in the mountains, along with the Communist Party. The troupe's jovial director, Nguyen Quang Vinh, has spent time in Las Vegas with Ringling Brothers and Barnum & Bailey Circus, with which the Vietnam Circus has an exchange program. Besides an evening of guaranteed entertainment—the elephants and monkeys are accompanied by the antics of 160 human performers—the circus arena itself is also a significant bit of architecture, with its distinctive 1,500-seat, round-top building. In winter, bring a jacket. The two-hour shows take place weekends: Sunday-morning shows cost 15,000d and start at 9 AM; evening shows on Saturday and Sunday cost 30,000d and start at 8 PM.

Film

Alliance Française (⊠ 42 Yet Kieu St., Hoan Kiem District, ☎ 04/942–2970) sponsors weekly viewings of French films, as well as art exhibits.
August Cinema (⊠ 45 Hang Bai St., Hai Ba Trung District, ☎ 04/825–5611) often screens non-Vietnamese movies; check the listings outside the theater for English-language films.
Fansland Cinema (⊠ 84 Ly Thuong Kiet St., Hoan Kiem District, ☎ 04/942–4484) occasionally shows non-Vietnamese films; check the listings outside the theater to see if an English-language movie is playing. Screenings are usually at 5:30 and 8.

Theater and Opera

Hanoi's performing-arts legacy is impressive. As in Europe, the emperors often kept acting guilds and musicians in or around the Imperial Palace. Roving drama and musical troupes entertained citizens in the countryside. The arrival of the French and the 20th century saw an explosion of theater culture in the capital, the lingering remnants of which can be experienced at a handful of small drama houses that host troupes performing traditional folk arts.

Tuong is a classical art form developed in central Vietnam. It uses very few stage props, and the actors must conform to age-old rules of behavior concerning their specific characters. Content usually focuses on Vietnamese legends, and music is minimal. The northern folk art known as *cheo* is more of a "people's opera," incorporating both comic and tragic elements. Music and singing are prominent, as cheo developed into a loud and lively art form in order to outdo the noise and distractions of the marketplace, where it was originally performed. *Cai luong,* the "renovated opera" that emerged in the early 20th century, is more similar to Western dramas and operas than the other styles. Music and singing are an important feature of these performances. Although cai luong is a southern creation, the form has endeared itself to Hanoians. The Hanoi theaters listed below stage productions; none prints schedules in English, so call or drop by the theater to see if there's something on for an evening when you're in town.

Hanoi Cai Luong Theater (⊠ 72 Hang Bac St., Hoan Kiem District, ☎ 04/825–7823) hosts performances of cai luong- and tuong-style shows on Saturday evening.
Hanoi Traditional Opera (⊠ 15 Nguyen Dinh Chieu St., Ba Dinh District, ☎ 04/943–7361), a tiny, simple drama house, seats 50 people. Cheo operas and traditional music concerts are usually staged on Friday and Saturday evenings at 8 PM, but call or stop by to confirm. This theater will arrange special performances for groups of 10 or more. Tickets cost 50,000d.
Opera House (Nha Hat Lon; ⊠ 1 Trang Tien St., Hoan Kiem District, ☎ 04/993–0113), whose Vietnamese name translates into "House Sing Big," is worth a visit no matter what happens to be showing. This beautifully restored French building hosts regular classical music concerts, ballets, and Western and Vietnamese operas, plus a variety of singers. The nearby Hilton Hanoi Opera hotel often has information on upcoming performances, or check *The Guide* or *Vietnam News.* Tickets usually cost between 80,000d and 150,000d.
Vietnam Opera and Ballet Theater (⊠ 18 Nui Truc St., Ba Dinh District, ☎ 04/846–1292) is where Vietnam's up-and-coming opera singers and ballerinas train to learn the skills they will need to perform at the Hanoi Opera House and even with foreign troupes. Performances take place only four times a month and are usually held the last two weekends of the month at 8 PM. Tickets range from 40,000d to 50,000d.

Youth Theater (Nha Hat Tuoi Tre; ✉ 11 Ngo Thi Nham St., Hoan Kiem District, ☎ 04/943–4673), a 650-seat facility, is one of the larger theaters in the city and focuses mainly on contemporary drama, although music and dance are sometimes performed. About a dozen foreign theater groups perform here annually. Shows take place on Friday, Saturday, and Sunday at 8 at a ticket cost of 40,000d. Thursday through Sunday the theater hosts comedy acts aimed at children, for which tickets cost 30,000d.

Traditional Music

As many of Vietnam's dramatic performances are closely linked with the strains of Vietnamese music, there are very few concerts of exclusively traditional music in the city. Your best bet is to see a water-puppet performance or go to the theater to watch cheo, tuong, or cai luong.

If you happen across an old man or woman on the street who's playing a one-stringed instrument in an impromptu fashion, consider yourself extremely lucky. *Xam*, a type of melancholy folk music, is a dying art in Vietnam—and not because it's the music played at funerals, although xam artists are often invited to perform at such functions. Xam artists are simply dying off, and no one's replacing them. Four professional xam musicians were on hand throughout the day and evening at Hoan Kiem Lake in Hanoi—one at each corner—in the xam heyday of the early 1940s. A half century later there's not a single true xam master plying his or her trade on the streets of the capital. One aging xam professional, the unflagging Hoang Thi Cau of Ninh Binh Province, has done much to save her art from extinction by teaching xam to some cheo performing groups in and around Hanoi and by recording her performances for future generations. But the prospects for this ancient art are bleak; cheo artists are understandably concerned with preserving their own beloved art, and experts say that true xam music cannot be performed by anyone but a bona fide xam master.

Water Puppetry

The thousand-year-old art of *roi nuoc,* or water puppetry, is unique to northern Vietnam and easily ranks as one of Southeast Asia's most beautiful and complex art forms. Long considered an art of the common people, water puppetry gained acceptance at royal celebrations and was often performed for reigning emperors and kings. Water puppetry is performed on—and under, in particular—a small pond whose surface conceals the flurry of activity beneath it. Through the near-magical use of bamboo rods and a system of pulleys and levers, master puppeteers stand waist deep at the back of the pond (usually behind a curtain) and make their lacquered marionettes literally walk on water. Shows usually depict scenes from rural life and Vietnamese legend, and the experience is positively delightful.

National Puppet Theater (✉ 361 Truong Chinh St., Dong Da District, ☎ 04/853–4545) holds water-puppet shows that are more in the vein of village performances, harking back to the days when water puppets were used as political commentary right under the noses of bad kings or provincial French rulers. Traveling water-puppet theaters traditionally relayed information from village to village. You may find that you are as much of the show as the puppets. Performances take place Saturday at 8, and tickets cost 30,000d.

Thang Long Municipal Water Puppet Theater (✉ 57 Dinh Tien Hoang St., on northeast shore of Hoan Kiem Lake, Hoan Kiem District, ☎ 04/824–9494) is the best place to see water puppetry performed in Hanoi. Seven or eight puppeteers pull the strings from behind elaborate stage sets while half a dozen musicians play soothing traditional folk music. The resident Thang Long Water Puppet Troupe is the only troupe that has toured Europe and North and South America in the past. If you're in Hanoi on a package tour, it's highly likely you're already scheduled for a show here. If not, get your tickets early, as performances sell out quickly. Tickets cost 40,000d, including a cassette of the music, or 20,000d without. The curtain goes up at 8 every night but Monday, and there's a 9:45 AM matinee on Sunday. Occasionally there are 6 PM shows as well. There's a 10,000d fee to use your camera; videotaping costs 50,000d. Souvenir puppets are available to buy.

Nightlife

Hanoi has enough bars and clubs to keep you busy. They range from the low-key Met Pub to the eclectic R&R Tavern to the popular Apocalypse Now dance club. Because many ventures are short-lived—Hanoi's nightclubs are curiously prone to electrical fires and other mysterious disasters—it's wise to call ahead when possible.

Bars and Pubs

Da Gino (⊠ 11B Dien Bien Phu St., Ba Dinh District, ☎ 04/747–0081), an Italian wine bar adjacent to Luna d'Autunno restaurant, has an Italian-language library and rotating exhibitions by artists and photographers. The bar is laid-back and casual and attracts an expat crowd.

Emotion Cybernet Cafe (⊠ 52 Ly Thuong Kiet St., Hoan Kiem District, ☎ 04/934–1066) has Internet access, cheap food and drinks, and a large-screen TV that's regularly tuned in to soccer matches.

Emperor Pub (⊠ 18B Le Thanh Tong St., Hoan Kiem District, ☎ 04/826–8801) is where Hanoi's expat yuppies gather to be seen, thanks to its classy villa setting, cushy couches, pool table, and resident jazz band.

Funky Monkey (⊠ 15B Hang Hanh St., Hoan Kiem District, ☎ 04/938–6113), a hip little nightspot popular with expats and tourists, is a nice alternative to the throngs at Hanoi's discos, though you won't get away from the smoke. There's a pool table.

Highway 4 (⊠ 5 Hang Tre St., Hoan Kiem District, ☎ 04/926–0639) is a fine place to go for a drink, a snack, and some travel advice. This stylish bar specializes in Vietnamese *deo* (rice wine), which is used in traditional medicines. Deo is quite strong, so you should avoid drinking it on an empty stomach. The menu is in English, and the place is easy to find thanks to the number of Russian Minsk motorcycles parked out front—this is the official headquarters of Hanoi's Minsk motorcycle club.

Library Bar, Press Club (⊠ 59A Ly Thai To St., Hoan Kiem District, ☎ 04/934–0888) has plush couches, an unobtrusive staff, and a menu of fancy (and expensive) cocktails and Cuban cigars. On Friday evening the attached terrace hosts an after-work happy hour popular with Hanoi's expats; a live jazz band plays Friday night.

Met Pub (⊠ 15 Ngo Quyen St., Hoan Kiem District, ☎ 04/826–6919), on the Ly Thai To Street side of the Metropole Hotel, is where high-rolling businesspeople watch satellite TV at the wood-panel bar and middle-aged expats drink martinis and listen to live jazz. An after-work crowd comes for the lively happy hour, despite the rather pricey snack foods and drinks. Nightly dinner buffets have changing themes.

Minh's Jazz Club (⊠ 31 Luong Van Can St., Hoan Kiem District, ☎ 04/828–7890) is owned by one of Hanoi's best-known jazz musicians, Quyen Van Minh. Live jazz and rock, performed by both foreign and local musicians, including Minh's son, are the big draws here.

Polite Pub (⊠ 5 Ngo Bao Khanh St., Hoan Kiem District, ☎ 04/825–0959) is the hangout of choice for Hanoi's young expats, who lounge at the bar listening to rock or alternative tunes or challenge each other to games of Foosball and pool. On weekends, the place is often packed from 9 PM to midnight, before the dance club Apocalypse Now goes into full swing.

R&R Tavern (⊠ 38A Cua Dong St., Hoan Kiem District), run by a mellow American and his Vietnamese wife, is a Hanoi institution. The pub has an all-American menu of nachos and burgers, draft beer, darts, and Grateful Dead classics.

Spotted Cow (⊠ 23C Hai Ba Trung St., Hoan Kiem District, ☎ 04/824–1028) is the bar of choice for committed frat-brother types. Cheap draft beer, darts, and plenty of rowdy fun can be found at this small, Australian-run joint.

Vertigo (⊠ Restaurant Bobby Chinn, 1 Ba Trieu St., Hoan Kiem District, ☎ 04/934–8577 or 04/934–8578) has laid-back music and soft lighting, plush couches and floor pillows on Persian carpets, and water pipes with various flavored tobaccos. The wines and cocktails are excellent, and you can choose food from the tapas menu or a California-style sushi bar. Mellow businesspeople and sophisticated locals gather here, and the place stays open as late as it has customers.

Dance Clubs

Apocalypse Now (⊠ 5C Hoa Ma St., Hai Ba Trung District, ☎ 04/971–2783) trades on the mystique of the Francis Ford Coppola movie with Vietnam War props—fake blood dripping from the lamps, a helicopter coming out of one wall, and helmets used as light shades. Black paint and no windows add to the bomb-shelter atmosphere, where expatriates hunker down for drinking and dancing until almost dawn. Until 11 PM you'll be blasted with rock oldies, which give way to dance hits and techno as the night wears on. Despite—or because of—its sweaty, meat-market feel, this club is very popular on weekends after 11 PM. On weeknights you can play a game on the free pool tables.

Club Q (⊠ Daewoo Hotel, 360 Kim Ma St., Ba Dinh District, ☎ 04/831–5000) has high-tech sound and lighting, plus live music nightly. Sing in English in one of the five very private karaoke rooms. The club could do with some more clientele to fill up the dance floor, however.

New Century (⊠ 10 Trang Thi St., Hoan Kiem District, ☎ 04/928–5285) is Hanoi's hippest nightspot, thanks to slick industrial decor, dry ice, lasers, and the best light show in town. The latest dance hits plus techno keep the mainly local crowd bopping on the dance floor. On weekends, getting a table here—especially one with a view over the dance floor—can be tough.

Spark Club (⊠ 88 Lo Duc St., Hai Ba Trung District, ☎ 04/978–1410) hosts live music every night, with young up-and-coming or wanna-be Vietnamese singers, and fashion shows on Thursday and Sunday evenings. Lights and stools surround a central dance floor.

OUTDOOR ACTIVITIES AND SPORTS

Participant Sports

Basketball

U.S. citizens in Hanoi hoop it up on the half court of the **American Club** (⊠ 19–21 Hai Ba Trung St., Hoan Kiem District, ☎ 04/824–1850) on Wednesday evenings around 7. The club has a membership policy, but Americans passing through town are more than welcome.

Somewhat serious full-court action can be found at the **Hanoi Sports Center** (Trung Tam The Duc The Thao Hanoi; ⊠ 115 Quang Thanh St., at southeast corner of West Lake, Ba Dinh District, ☎ 04/845–5193) most days, particularly weekends, from 2 to 4. You might end up being paired with someone from the Vietnam women's team, which practices here regularly. As referees are used, small monetary contributions are expected.

Biking

Memory Café (✉ 33bis Tran Hung Dao St., Hoan Kiem District, ☎ 04/943–5854) rents bicycles. Ms. CoCo will show you on a map where to go. One of the best trips is simply to head south along the river. Another more ambitious trip takes you over the Long Bien Bridge into the countryside. Go south from the bridge, under the car bridge, and continue south along the river. After two hours you should reach Bat Trang, a village where pottery is sold.

Boating

Paddleboating and sculling are the en vogue forms of boating in Hanoi. You can rent dragon-shape paddleboats on **Truc Bach Lake** at a few spots, one on the southwest corner of the lake and another on the causeway. Thien Quang Lake, just north of Lenin Park, also has paddleboats for rent. Go to the **Student Culture Center** (Nha Van Hoa Hoc Sinh Sinh Vien) on the small island that is connected by bridge to Tran Nhan Tong Street. Boats are from 6,000d to 10,000d per half hour. The newer plastic boats are more expensive than the rusting metal hulks.

A **boat house** on the southern edge of Bay Mau Lake, in the middle of Lenin Park, rents old racing sculls for 12,000d per hour. There are also swan-shape paddleboats that cost 8,000d per hour. Access is via Dai Co Viet Road.

In Hanoi, sailing—and water- and jet-skiing—are, for the most part, reserved for members of the elite **Hanoi Club** (✉ 76 Yen Phu St., Tay Ho District, ☎ 04/823–8115). If you're not a member or the guest of a member, the only way you'll be able to use the club's catamarans and other goodies (including tennis, racquetball, squash, and exercise facilities and a swimming pool) is if you stay at the hotel or apartment facilities managed by the club.

Bowling

Bowling is a popular activity for Vietnam's trendy young urbanites. If your image of bowling includes folks in matching shirts, you're in for a surprise: pumping music, lights, and attached bars add a little extra excitement to this wholesome pursuit. Call ahead to reserve a lane.

Cosmos Bowling Centre (✉ 8B Ngoc Khanh St., Ba Dinh District, ☎ 04/831–8668) is a hopping spot that charges 10,000d per game on Sunday; 15,000d on Monday, Wednesday, and Friday; and 30,000d on Tuesday, Thursday, and Saturday.

Hanoi Starbowl Centre (✉ 2 Pham Ngoc Thach St., Dong Da District, ☎ 04/574–1614), housed in a trendy shopping mall, has 30 lanes of high-tech fun for 15,000d per game during the day, 25,000d from 4 to 7 PM, and 40,000d from 7 PM on.

Hanoi Superbowl (✉ Fortuna Hotel, 6B Lang Ha St., Ba Dinh District, ☎ 04/831–3333) has 24 lanes. Games cost 10,000d on weekday mornings and 25,000d at other times.

Golf

King's Island Golf & Country Club (✉ Dong Mo, Son Tay town, Ha Tay Province, about 45 km [28 mi] west of Hanoi, ☎ 034/834–666) is a gorgeous 18-hole lakeside course surrounded by the beautiful Tan Vien Mountain. Greens fees are $50 for guests on weekdays and $80 on weekends. Caddy fees add an extra $8, and renting clubs will set you back another $20. You reach the club via a scenic boat trip across a reservoir.

Health Clubs

A few major hotels in Hanoi allow you to purchase one-day memberships to their exercise facilities, even if you aren't staying at the hotel.

Clark Hatch Fitness Center (✉ Metropole Hotel Sofitel, 15 Ngo Quyen St., Hoan Kiem District, ☎ 04/826–6919 ext. 8881) has all your basic workout equipment—weights, a few machines, treadmills, and stationary bicycles—which you can use while watching the activity on the street below. It also has the best $17.

Daewoo Hotel Fitness Center (✉ Hanoi Daewoo Hotel, 360 Kim Ma St., Ba Dinh District, ☎ 04/831–5000 ext. 3309) has treadmills, stationary bikes, and machines, plus yoga and aerobics classes. You can also use the 50-meter pool and the saunas, all for $20 a day.

Guoman Hotel Fitness Center (✉ 83A Ly Thuong Kiet St., Hoan Kiem District, ☎ 04/822–2800) has treadmills, stationary bikes, a stair climber, and some machines. The $8 fee includes use of the sauna.

Jogging

If you're an early riser, you may want to join the throngs of runners that pack the city streets at 5 AM. It is understood by everyone that runners are off the roads by 6:30 AM, however. Jogging is definitely not recommended in the traffic-heavy streets of Hanoi during the day or evening, even though you may see some expatriates huffing and puffing through the center of town.

The best place to run in the city is around spacious **Lenin Park** (✉ main entrance on Trạn Nhan Tong St., Hai Ba Trung District), a favorite sports and exercise locale for Vietnamese and expats tired of the exhibitionist nature of a Hoan Kiem Lake workout (although that's not a bad place for a run, too).

Many people run on the trails at the **Botanical Gardens** (✉ entrance on Hoang Hoa Tham Rd., Ba Dinh District).

The **Hash House Harriers** (ask at the Metropole Hotel Sofitel or the Spotted Cow bar for locations and times) run every Saturday afternoon around 2 PM. The throngs of expatriates running through the capital's suburbs always garner lots of attention.

Swimming

Army Hotel pool (✉ 33A Pham Ngu Lao St., Hoan Kiem District, ☎ 04/826–5540) is a clean and well-run saltwater pool that charges $4 for a day pass.

Hanoi Daewoo Hotel pool (✉ 360 Kim Ma St., Ba Dinh District, ☎ 04/831–5000), an arched 80-meter affair, costs $20 for a day pass, including use of the gym, sauna, and whirlpool.

Sofitel Plaza Hotel pool (✉ Sofitel Plaza Hotel, 1 Thanh Nien St., Ba Dinh District, ☎ 04/823–8888) has the best pool in town, with a retractable roof and breathtaking views over West Lake. A day pass costs $15 and includes use of the hotel's well-equipped gym, Jacuzzi, and sauna.

Thang Loi Hotel pool (✉ Yen Phu St., Ba Dinh District, ☎ 04/829–4211), near West Lake, is an inviting place to swim; Fidel Castro stays at the hotel when he visits. Entrance to the pool, open from 6 AM to 10 PM, costs less than $2.

Tennis

Hanoi Daewoo Hotel (✉ 360 Kim Ma St., Ba Dinh District, ☎ 04/766–0912) has two courts that are open to visitors. The cost is $6 per hour before 4 PM and $10 in the evenings.

Hanoi Horison Hotel (✉ 40 Cat Lin St., Dong Da District, ☎ 04/733–0808) charges $4 per hour until 4 PM and $6 per hour thereafter.

Thang Loi Hotel (✉ Yen Phu St., Ba Dinh District, ☎ 04/829–4211 ext. 391) has two courts out on West Lake that you can rent for $2–$5 per hour, depending on the time of day (evening is the most expensive due to the lights). Hours of operation are 6 AM–10 PM.

Ultimate Frisbee

The **Hanoi Ultimate Club** (HUC) plays every Thursday night from 7 to 9 at the Van Phuc/United Nations International Schoolfield (UNIS; ✉ Pho Van Bao St., large pitch near tennis courts) and every Sunday afternoon, from 4 until sundown at the Hanoi International Trade Center (HITC; ✉ 239 Xuan Thuy, grass field on west side of building). The fee is 10,000d. You must bring a white and dark-color T-shirt.

Spectator Sports

Sports have been an integral and institutionalized part of the Hanoi educational system for years. Competition on an international level, however, has only recently taken off, although financial strains severely limit the number of meets or tournaments in which Vietnam can participate. Many resources are still committed to the study and improvement of martial arts such as tae kwon do and *wushu*, two disciplines in which Vietnam is world renowned. Ping-Pong and badminton are also determinedly pursued.

The Hanoi Sports Department and the Vietnam Sports Center can provide information on sporting events in the city, including dates of charity races, major tournaments, and so on. **Hanoi Sports Department** (✉ 10 Trinh Hoai Duc St., Ba Dinh District, ☎ 04/846–2145). **Vietnam Sports Center** (✉ 36 Tran Phu St., Ba Dinh District, ☎ 04/845–3272).

Soccer

No sport captures the attention and hearts of the Vietnamese quite like soccer. The game's biggest crowds are down in Ho Chi Minh City, but the religiously followed semiprofessional national league packs them in at the 20,000-seat capacity **National Stadium** (✉ corner of Nguyen Thai Hoc and Trinh Hoai Duc Sts., Ba Dinh District, ☎ 04/843–7649). The season runs roughly from October to May, and when the Hanoi Police face off against the Ho Chi Minh City Police in the capital, you can bet the stadium is rocking. Smaller matches are held at the Army Stadium, in the southern portion of the citadel, with access from Hoang Dieu Street. Nearly every Vietnamese bar in town has a soccer schedule, and with a bit of gesturing and pointing you should be able to figure out whether or not a huge match is going to be played while you're in town.

SHOPPING

Hanoi has plenty of shopping options: the area north of Hoan Kiem Lake bustles with tiny shops carrying everything from shoes to clothes to antique timepieces. Hanoi is Vietnam's fine arts capital, as well, and running along the southern part of Hoan Kiem Lake, where Hang Khay Street turns into Trang Tien Street, are arts-and-crafts galleries and antiques shops. You can find paintings and watercolors, as well as crafts such as lacquerware and puppets, on Trang Tien and Hang Khay streets in Hoan Kiem District. Any number of shops along Hang Gai and Duc Loi streets, not far from Hoan Kiem Lake, can custom-design clothes inexpensively. Hang Gai, which turns into Hang Bong Street, is also good for souvenirs, antiques, elegant hand-embroidered linens, and inexpensive silk linens that make nice liners for padded sleeping bags. Nha Tho Street is lined with shops selling custom-designed clothes, antiques, and items for the home. Most souvenir and silk shops in the tourist area of the Old Quarter are open to about 10 PM on weekends.

Markets

Hang Be Market (✉ Gia Ngu St., Hoan Kiem District, ☎ no phone) is also known as the flower market. Flower sellers concentrate on the Cau Go Street end of the market, but inside is a tunnel of bustling traders selling every imaginable item.

Hang Da Market (✉ Hang Da St., Hoan Kiem District, ☎ no phone) is a sprawling two-story market. The outer stalls sell imported liquor and foodstuffs; flower vendors are on the south side. Also to the south, several inside stalls sell blue-and-white pottery at very reasonable prices. On the northern edge of this market is a colorful bird market.

Hom Market (Cho Hom; ✉ Pho Hue and Tran Xuan Soan Sts., Hai Ba Trung District, ☎ no phone) is one of the biggest and most crowded markets in town. Upstairs is a Western-style market with air-conditioning, and downstairs is a Vietnamese-style open market. If you need plastic tubs, candles, or padded bras, this is the place to go.

Long Bien Market (✉ Hang Dau St. at Yen Phu St., near Long Bien Bridge, Hoan Kiem District, ☎ no phone) really kicks off at around 3 to 4 AM and is well worth seeing after a late night on the town. All of the produce from north of Hanoi lands here before being distributed throughout the city. Just follow the crowds on the streets adjacent to the bridge ramp to witness the intense buying and selling of the freshest produce in town.

19–12 Market (Cho 19–12; ✉ Ly Thuong Kiet St. between Hoa Lo and Quang Trung Sts., Hoan Kiem District, ☎ no phone), the December 19 Market, sells items for everyday use: vegetables, meat (even dog meat), poultry, clothes, pots and pans, toilet paper, and so on.

Specialty Shops

Art

When buying art in Vietnam, be careful of fakes. Paintings by Vietnam's most famous painters—Bui Xuan Phai, Nguyen Tu Nghiem, and Le Thiet Cuong—are the most widely copied. Serious art collectors should consult the well-respected high-end galleries. To really appreciate Hanoi's art scene, consider contacting the well-respected fine arts consultant **Suzanne Lecht** (☎ 04/862–3184, FAX 04/862–3185), who can lead you on studio tours and advise you on major purchases.

Apricot Gallery (✉ 40B Hang Bong St., Hoan Kiem District, ☎ 04/828–8965) displays works by the country's most famous contemporary artists. Even if you have no intention of shelling out thousands of dollars for a painting, this beautiful gallery is still worth visiting and will give you a great introduction to modern Vietnamese art.

Co Xanh (Green Palm Gallery; ✉ 51 Hang Gai St., Hoan Kiem District, ☎ 04/826–7116) is the top end of souvenir art galleries, with a good selection of paintings by graduates of the Hanoi Fine Arts College. Prices are determined by the stature of the painter and size of the piece but can easily run into the hundreds of dollars. Mr. Ha, the easygoing owner, is very reputable and speaks excellent English.

Hanoi Studio (✉ 13 Trang Tien St., Hoan Kiem District, ☎ 04/934–4433) houses works by many of Vietnam's well-known and up-and-coming contemporary artists. The manager, Ms. Hang, speaks good English and is very informative.

Mai Gallery (✉ 3B Phan Huy Chu St., Hoan Kiem District, ☎ 04/825–1225), which is down an alley, is run by the daughter of Vietnam's leading art critic, Duong Tuong. It is largely a showcase for Hanoi painters and is very popular with serious collectors.

Red River Gallery (✉ 71A Nguyen Du St., Hai Ba Trung District, ☎ 04/822–9064) is the gallery that put the Gang of Five painters—Ha Tri Hieu, Hong Viet Dung, Dang Xuan Hoa, Pham Quang Vinh, and Tran Luong—on the map. Red River exhibits the most established Vietnamese artists and is a must-see for serious art collectors willing to shell out thousands of dollars.

Salon Natasha (✉ 30 Hang Bong St., Hoan Kiem District, ☎ 04/826–1387), the avant-garde hub of Hanoi's art scene, is run by a Russian expatriate and her husband, artist Vu Dan Tan. It exhibits and sells some of the most provocative art in Vietnam today. Natasha, a respected and trusted art dealer, sells painted vases and unframed oil paintings by well-known artists at reasonable prices.

Trang An Gallery (✉ 15 Hang Buom St., Hoan Kiem District, ☎ 04/826–9480), housed in a gorgeous colonial-era structure, is an impressive, well-designed gallery with three rooms and a courtyard. The gallery hosts regular exhibits of the latest paintings and avant-garde installations of Vietnam's internationally recognized young artists.

Van Gallery (✉ 25–27 Trang Tien St., Hoan Kiem District, ☎ 04/825–1532), near the Opera House, carries a good selection of high-end souvenir art, plus some works by Hanoi's big-name painters.

Clothing and Accessories

It's possible to have clothes made to order with enough time—one day to three weeks, depending on what you want made and the tailor's schedule. You may also need to return a couple of times to have the clothes fitted.

La Boutique and The Silk (✉ 10F Dinh Liet St., Hoan Kiem District, ☎ 04/934–323; ✉ 6 Nha Tho St., Hoan Kiem District, ☎ 04/928–5368) carries a colorful selection of woven silk scarves imported from Laos, as well as shirts, jackets, and trousers made from embroidered and woven ethnic-minority fabrics. The shop also sells some silver jewelry made by various ethnic-minority groups.

Cao Minh (✉ 47 Tran Hung Dao St., Hoan Kiem District, ☎ 04/824–2727) is a good but expensive tailor from Ho Chi Minh City, where tailors are generally considered to be more talented.

Co (✉ 18 Nha Tho St., Hoan Kiem District, ☎ 04/828–9925) stocks some ready-to-wear linen clothing and provides quality custom-made garments. Owing to this store's popularity, it may take more than a week to have clothes made, and the tailoring may be outsourced if the shop is very busy

Duc Loi Silk–Queen Silk (✉ 76 Hang Gai St., Hoan Kiem District, ☎ 04/826–8758) has a colorful selection of ready-made silk shirts and scarves. This shop has a wide choice of printed silk fabrics and can make clothes quickly.

Ipa-Nima (✉ 59G Hai Ba Trung St., Hoan Kiem District, ☎ 04/942–1872, 🌐 www.ipanima.com) is the place to get beautifully designed, funky, and fashionable handbags made of rattan, brocade, crochet, beads, and all kinds of other materials. It also sells very original jewelry and accessories such as cuff links.

Jade Collection (✉ 17A Phan Boi Chau St., Hoan Kiem District, ☎ 04/822–2228) is managed by a French-Vietnamese woman trained in fashion design. Choose from ready-to-wear pieces or have them copied in your size.

Kenly Silk (✉ 108 Hang Gai St., Hoan Kiem District, ☎ 04/826–7236) can cut to order, has good and relatively inexpensive silk and linen clothing, and fill orders in a timely manner.

Khai Silk (⊠ 121 Nguyen Thai Hoc St., Ba Dinh District, ☎ 04/823–3508; ⊠ 96 Hang Gai St., Hoan Kiem District, ☎ 04/825–4237) is where the Princess of Thailand shops for fine silk blouses, sweaters, scarves, lingerie, sheets, and more. Linen is also available, as are men's clothes.

Le Minh Silk (⊠ 79–111 Hang Gai St., Hoan Kiem District, ☎ 04/828–8723) offers the usual Hang Gai Street selection of ready-made silk shirts, ties, and padded velvet jackets. Upstairs is the best selection of locally made and imported silk fabrics in Hanoi, including crepes and taffetas.

Phuong Anh (⊠ 56 Hang Hom St., Hoan Kiem District, ☎ 04/826–1556) is a small, crowded shop where you can get a dress and other clothes made for you in three days (even faster if you are really pressed for time and beg).

Song (⊠ 5 and 7 Nha Tho St., Hoan Kiem District, ☎ 04/828–6965 or 04/828–9650) is a beautiful boutique stocked with women's clothing in silk, cotton, and linen. The French designer exports her clothes and has a second shop in Melbourne.

Thanh Ha (⊠ 114 Hang Gai St., Hoan Kiem District, ☎ no phone) does a nice job on women's suits. The store also stocks some pretty beaded handbags and satin slippers.

Embroidery

Tan My (⊠ 66 Hang Gai St., Hoan Kiem District, ☎ 04/825–1579) is the most famous embroidery shop in Hanoi. Employees from Thuong Tin Province, which is known for its rich embroidery tradition, adorn tablecloths, silk clothing, and wall hangings with intricate designs. Ready-made work depicts everything from traditional Vietnamese floral patterns and dragon designs to scenes from Western fairy tales, or you can custom-order.

Tuyet Lan Hand Embroidery (⊠ 65 Hang Gai St., Hoan Kiem District, ☎ 04/825–7967; ⊠ 182 Hang Bong St., Hoan Kiem District, ☎ 04/928–5428) does beautiful embroidery, especially children's bed sheets.

Handicrafts

Co Xanh (Green Palm Gallery; ⊠ 51 Hang Gai St., Hoan Kiem District, ☎ 04/826–7116) sells boxes and figurines made of silver. The owner, Tran Thanh Ha, speaks English and is very reputable.

Craft Link (⊠ 43 Van Mieu St., Ba Dinh District, ☎ 04/843–7710) is a terrific place to buy local handicrafts. Proceeds go to the ethnic-minority women who make these crafts.

Craft Window (⊠ 99 Nguyen Thai Hoc St., Ba Dinh District, ☎ 04/733–5286) has an excellent selection of crockery, ethnic-minority crafts, beaded handbags, and beautiful embroidered greeting cards.

KAF (⊠ 31B Ba Trieu St., Hoan Kiem District, ☎ 04/934–9022) carries quality reproductions of antique Buddha statues and lacquerware.

Quang's Ceramics (⊠ 22 Hang Luoc St., Hoan Kiem District, ☎ 04/828–3440), a huge shop in the Old Quarter, sells colorful crockery and ceramic lamps made in the nearby pottery village of Bat Trang.

Housewares and Furnishings

Delta Deco (⊠ 12 Nha Tho St., Hoan Kiem District, ☎ 04/828–9616) is a small boutique filled with stylish, Italian-designed and locally made housewares, including beautiful wooden bowls and trays, mirrors, ceramics, candlesticks, and boxes.

DOME (⊠ 10 Yen The St., Ba Dinh District, ☎ 04/843–6036) stocks well-designed, modern home furnishings—linens, furniture, lamps, candles, and more. Simple, curved designs in wrought iron are a signature style, one you'll see in restaurants and hotels throughout town.

Mosaique (⊠ 22 Nha Tho St., Hoan Kiem District, ☎ 04/933–1699) custom-designs Japanese paper lamps, place settings, aromatherapy items, bedding, and some jewelry and clothing.

Nguyen Freres (⊠ 5 Hai Ba Trung St., Hoan Kiem District, ☎ 04/928–6181) sells a selection of more upscale Vietnamese designs, including mirrors, tapestries, carpets, and fine woodwork.

Nha Dep (⊠ 29 Trang Tien St., Hoan Kiem District, ☎ 04/934–5607) is a large showroom filled with high-quality wooden furniture, plush sofas, modern office furniture and supplies, and glassware.

Musical Instruments

Hanoi Music Center (⊠ 42 Nha Chung St., Hoan Kiem District, ☎ 04/824–3058) sells guitars, metronomes, keyboards, and pianos.

Pham Bich Huong (⊠ 11 Hang Non St., Hoan Kiem District, ☎ no phone) carries a great selection of traditional Vietnamese instruments; the proprietor, however, speaks almost no English.

SIDE TRIPS FROM HANOI

Although Hanoi is the cultural and historic centerpiece of northern Vietnam, much of the city's history and many of its legends and traditions are rooted in the region surrounding the capital. Citadels, temples, art guilds, and festival focal points ring the city, and a few hours' drive in any direction will bring you to points of interest ranging from pagodas to idyllic valleys and national parks. Hanoi serves as a base for day trips or short excursions to the Perfume Pagoda, the Thay Pagoda, the ancient capital of Hoa Lu, Phat Diem Cathedral, and the primeval beauty of Cuc Phuong National Park.

Tours organized by Hanoi's tourist cafés and travel agencies cover all of the sights and are the most time-efficient way to see this region. Tourist café tours are less expensive than those run by travel agencies: a group trip to Perfume Pagoda or Hoa Lu through a tourist café costs about $20 per person, including entrance tickets and meals. If a daily group tour isn't available to the site you want, these companies can arrange a private car and driver for the day. A good example is the "Suburbs of Hanoi" tour: this full-day trip goes to the silk-making village of Ha Dong, the Bat Trang pottery village, a snake farm in Gia Lam across the Red River, and the village of Dong Ho, where the ancient folk art of wood-block printing is still practiced. The trip averages $35 for an air-conditioned car and driver for the whole day. An English-speaking guide costs from $10 to $20 per day.

For history, religion, and a bit of hiking, head west to the Thay and Tay Phuong pagodas. Combine a trip here with Co Loa Citadel, and you've got a full day of exploring. Go with a group tour or rent a private car with a driver for between $30 and $50 for the trip.

Co Loa Citadel

❶ *15 km (9 mi) north of Hanoi.*

Less than 30 minutes north of Hanoi is a series of large earthen ramparts that used to protect one of the country's earliest capitals from Chinese invaders. Co Loa, or "snail," so named for the spiral-shape protective walls and moats that resembled the design of a nautilus, was built by An Duong Vuong more than 2,000 years ago and remains one of northern Vietnam's important historical relics.

At the end of the Bronze Age, in the 3rd century BC, King Vuong decided to move the power seat of the Lac Viets—a sophisticated society of indigenous northern Vietnamese, considered by many Vietnamese

Hanoi Side Trips

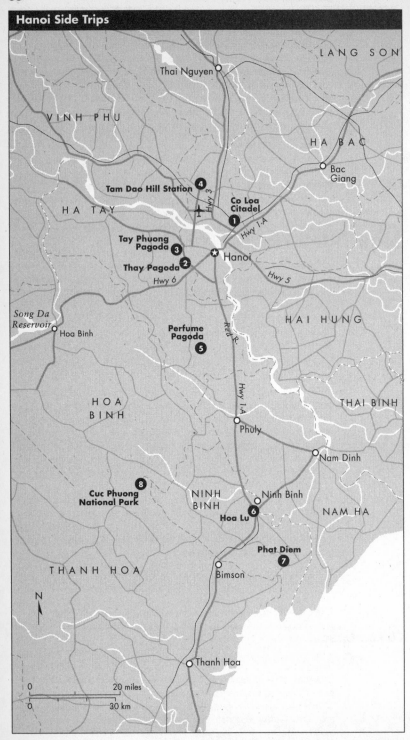

to be their direct ancestors, who eventually were incorporated into the Chinese empire. They relocated north of the Red River Delta to a fortress designed to be the ultimate protection from the invading Chinese. Nine large earthen ramparts guarded the inner palace of Co Loa. Carefully designed gates were built at angles to each other, and defense mounds created further obstacles for attackers. A series of moats fed by tributaries of the Red River lent an air of medieval invincibility to the place.

According to one of Vietnam's oldest legends, certain forces conspired against King Vuong and his well-protected citadel. After decades of failed attempts to defeat King Vuong's armies, Chinese general Trieu Da ordered his own son, Trong Thuy, to surrender to King Vuong and then propose marriage to King Vuong's daughter, My Chau. Against the advice of his ministers, the king accepted. Trong Thuy lived harmoniously in his new home for three years, eventually coercing his wife into revealing defense secrets and helping him steal a magic crossbow— a gift to King Vuong from the gods that held all the military secrets to the citadel. With their newfound knowledge, Trieu Da and his troops immediately invaded Co Loa and conquered the Lac Viets. King Vuong had his daughter beheaded. Trong Thuy realized his betrayal and drowned himself in Ngoc Pond.

Only three of the earthen ramparts are extant today. The rectangular inner wall has a perimeter of 1½ km (1 mi), a middle rampart is in the shape of a polygon with a perimeter of 6½ km (4 mi), and the outer wall is 8 km (5 mi) long. You can explore the site of the ancient imperial palace. Nearby, under an old banyan tree, is Ba Chua, a temple dedicated to Princess My Chau. Inside, there is a headless stone statue of the princess. A temple to An Duong Vuong has also been built on the site of the inner palace. In front of this temple is Ngoc Pond, where Trong Thuy is said to have killed himself.

A large and colorful festival on the sixth day of Tet, the lunar new year, celebrates King An Vuong Duong, now considered the guardian spirit of Co Loa. Communists banned this and other festivals after taking power in 1954, proclaiming that such rituals had no place in the new socialist order. But by the late 1980s Hanoi was no longer so eager to squelch such celebrations, and the Co Loa Festival and others like it have enjoyed a revival of sorts.

Co Loa is a popular destination for school groups, too, which can sometimes transform the normally serene temples into playgrounds reverberating with the laughter and chatting of hundreds of children. Don't be surprised, either, if the kindly priests and caretakers in each building you visit persistently request extra money from you.

Arriving and Departing

You should be able to hire a car with driver for about $50 to go from Hanoi to Co Loa Citadel as well as the Thay and Tay Phuong pagodas. A round-trip and a visit to Co Loa alone takes about two hours. Tourist cafés and travel agencies can arrange minivan tours to the three sites if there is enough interest. This trip takes about two-thirds of a day, depending on how long you linger at the sites.

Thay Pagoda and Tay Phuong Pagoda

40 km (25 mi) southwest of Hanoi in Hay Tay Province.

Two lovely pagodas can be combined with the Co Loa Citadel to make an enjoyable day trip from Hanoi. The **Thay Pagoda,** or Master's Pagoda, is named in honor of Tu Dao Hanh, a 12th-century monk. The grounds of the four main sanctuaries here ring shrill with the chirping of cicadas and are lush with fruit trees and a giant frangipani said to be 700 years old. In the upper pagoda (Chua Thuong) a statue of Master Hanh sits in the foreground of a large central altar that supports the statues of 18 arhats, monks who have reached enlightenment. The altar to the left of this holds Ly Nhan Tong, a king who was the supposed reincarnation of Tu Dao Hanh. Stone steps adjacent to the pagoda lead farther up the mountain to various shrines and temples and lovely vista points. The Thay Pagoda is the site of one of two ancient water-puppetry stages remaining in Vietnam. Constructed during the 15th century, this small stage sits on stilts in the middle of a pond and was used during elaborate pagoda ceremonies and royal visits. Water-puppetry shows still take place here, particularly on the annual festival of the pagoda, which is from the fifth through the seventh days of the third lunar month. Admission to the pagoda is 2,000d.

Numerous caves provide opportunities for exploration around the hillsides near Thay Pagoda. A few hiking trails also crisscross the landscape. Twenty kilometers (12 mi) to the northwest of the pagoda is **Ba Vi Mountain,** a 4,250-ft peak that affords spectacular views of the Red River valley and the mountains to the west. Four guest houses offer lodging in this surprisingly relaxing and remote nature preserve, which also has tennis courts, a swimming pool, and various lakes and forests to explore; you can reserve rooms through travel agencies and tourist cafés in Hanoi.

❸ The **Tay Phuong Pagoda,** or Western Pagoda, comprises three sanctuaries built into Cau Lau Mountain and surrounded by a square enclosure. Each ancient wooden structure is separated by a small pool of water that reflects an eerie soothing light into the temples. Begun in the 3rd century, the pagoda was rebuilt in the 9th century and expanded to its present size under the Tay Son dynasty in 1794. The centuries-old curved rooftops are particularly noteworthy, as are the masterpieces of wood sculpture: more than six dozen figures carved from jackfruit wood. The pagoda's rafters are elaborately carved with bas-reliefs of dragons and lotuses, and ceramic animal statues grace the rooftops. Admission to the pagoda is 10,000d.

Arriving and Departing
Trips organized by tourist cafés and travel agencies usually cover the admission fees for these sites. It's easy to combine a trip to these two pagodas with a visit to Co Loa Citadel, north of Hanoi.

Tam Dao Hill Station

❹ *85 km (53 mi) northwest of Hanoi in Vinh Phuc Province.*

Up in the clouds, at an elevation of 3,050 ft, the damp hill station of Tam Dao feels like the mountain town that time forgot—almost. In 1907 French developers scaled the rugged 4,590-ft peaks (there are three of them) north of Hanoi and decided the cool weather of a nearby mountain retreat could serve the French well. The result was a graceful town of elegant villas surrounded by lush vegetation and sweeping views of the valley below. Since the French left in 1954, however, little grace has been bestowed on Tam Dao, whose chalet charm took a decided turn for the worse when Soviet-era architecture announced itself in the form of a monstrously square 40-room hotel. Most villas—and the town church—have fallen into disrepair, although a few developers remain confident that Tam Dao could be resuscitated as a tourist resort; they've bought up some crumbling lodges and have begun to build. Tam Dao's main attraction lies in its elevation and subsequent cool temperatures: it's a nice way to beat the heat of Hanoi, and the hiking is fair.

Few people, even locals, realize that Tam Dao and the surrounding peaks are in a national park, which may be one reason why logging and poaching remain a problem for the area (most of the restaurants here list supposedly protected animals on their menus). But for the most part, a hike up to the radio transmitter above the town is a walk into dense jungle. Small Buddhist temples line the concrete steps up to the tower, and a spring bubbles up from beneath the underbrush and splays out into a small waterfall. If you're spending the night up in these mountains, bring a sweater and some rain gear.

People have been known to ride mountain bikes up to Tam Dao and spend the night, but the climb is extreme (a 10% gradient over long stretches). Less-active riders put their bikes in minivans on the way up and then career down the extremely winding and dangerous—but ultimately exhilarating—route to the base of the mountain.

Dining and Lodging

$–$$ ✕ 🏨 **Mela Hotel.** Some rooms at this semi-luxurious minihotel-villa on the town's outskirts have views of the valley. The excellent restaurant, which serves Asian and Western food, seems to be the only one in Tam Dao that doesn't have endangered (or soon-to-be endangered) animals on the menu. For just 50,000d, the hotel can arrange bird-watching guides. ✉ *Near path to Tam Dao waterfall, Tam Dao District,* ☎ *211/ 824–321,* 🖷 *211/824–352,* 🖳 *www.melahotel.com. 25 rooms. Restaurant, pool, meeting room; no a/c. MC, V.*

¢ 🏨 **Green World Hotel.** Rooms at this hotel just down the street from Tam Dao's "karaoke row" either overlook the lush valley or an unkempt badminton court. Guest quarters may be bland, but the hotel makes up for this with bizarre, giant portraits of the owner's son on the lobby walls. You can hire forest guides through the hotel front desk for 100,000d per day. ✉ *Tam Dao District,* ☎ *211/824–315,* 🖷 *211/824– 276. 30 rooms. Restaurant, meeting room; no a/c. No credit cards.*

Arriving and Departing

There are no organized group tours to Tam Dao, but you can easily arrange a trip here on your own through a travel agency or tourist café.

Perfume Pagoda

★ ❺ *60 km (37 mi) south of Hanoi.*

Considered Vietnam's most important Buddhist site, the Perfume Pagoda (Chua Huong) is the largest of a cluster of shrines carved into the limestone of the Huong Tich Mountains. In late spring the trails leading up to the shrines are clogged with thousands making their pilgrimage to pray to Quan Am, the goddess of mercy and compassion.

According to a Vietnamized version of the Chinese legend, Quan Am was a young wife falsely accused of trying to kill her newlywed husband. Thrown out of her mother-in-law's house, she took refuge in a monastery, posing as a monk. A reckless girl one day blamed her pregnancy on the monk, not knowing he was a she. Without a word of self-defense, the vilified monk took the child in and raised him. Only after Quan Am died did villagers discover her silent sacrifice. In the past, pilgrims came to the grottoes to pray for Quan Am's help in bearing sons and in fighting unjust accusations.

From the shores of the Yen River, you are ferried to the site, 4 km (2½ mi) away, on sampans that seem to be made of flimsy aluminum. It's a spectacular ride through the flooded valley, past boats laden with fruit and farmers at work in their fields. You'll be let off at Chua Tien Chu. From there, follow a stone path uphill to the various pagodas and shrines. Three kilometers (2 miles) later you'll reach the Perfume Pagoda. A steep set of stairs takes you inside the impressive cavern, where gilded Buddhas and bodhisattvas sit nestled in rocky recesses. The air is misty from incense and the cooking fires of the Buddhist monks who tend the shrines.

In early spring, from just after Tet to the middle of the second lunar month, thousands of Buddhists make their pilgrimage to the Perfume Pagoda. This is an intense—and sometimes stressful—time to visit, as the crowds of Vietnamese faithful clog the Yen River with extra boats and make navigating the slippery stairs more of an exercise in caution than a journey of discovery. The atmosphere at this time of year is positively electric with thousands of Buddhists crowding into the cavern to leave offerings, catch a droplet of water from a holy stalactite, or buy Buddhist trinkets and mementos from the dozens of stall owners. Note that the climb up to the pagoda can be rough going, especially when it's muddy, and that local operators sometimes lead the climb at a very fast pace. Admission is 33,000d.

Arriving and Departing

Day trips from Hanoi to the Perfume Pagoda, leaving at about 6:30 AM, are available from any number of travel agencies, such as Vietnam Tourism and Vinatour, as well as from tourist cafés, such as the Real Darling Café (☞ Travel Agencies *in* Hanoi A to Z, *below*). These tours run as low as $10 per person, including all transport and entrance fees. You can also rent a car for about $30, and a guide for $10; you'll still have to pay the 33,000d per person entrance fee to get into the pagoda itself.

Hoa Lu

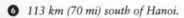 ⑥ *113 km (70 mi) south of Hanoi.*

Hoa Lu, the first capital of independent Vietnam, is known as "Halong Bay without the water." Both the stunning natural surroundings of limestone outcrops and meandering streams and Hoa Lu's status as a former seat of power make for an interesting excursion.

After three decades of internal strife following the expulsion of the Chinese by Ngo Quyen in 938, Dinh Bo Linh (also known as Dinh Tien Hoang) unified the country. (A colorful festival on the 12th day of the third lunar month commemorates this successful reunification.) The new king moved the capital to Hoa Lu, in a valley whose maze of narrow streams and inhospitable limestone outcroppings served as natural protection for the fledgling nation; he had numerous fortifications built around his citadel in order to avert another Chinese invasion, and word quickly spread of his ruthless treatment of prisoners. (The king reportedly fed enemies to tigers and then boiled their bones in ceremonial urns.) Despite such tactics, the Dinh dynasty was short-lived; Dinh Tien Hoang was assassinated by bodyguards in 979. The killers were discovered and put to death, and General Le Dai Hanh ascended to the throne, establishing the Early Le dynasty. Upon Le Dai Hanh's death in 1009, Ly Thai To became the first king of the Ly dynasty and moved the capital to Thang Long, the site of present-day Hanoi.

Much of the ancient capital of Hoa Lu has been destroyed or has succumbed to the forces of nature, but the two sanctuaries that do survive hint at the tastes of the king and his court. The first temple honors Dinh Tien Hoang. The musty, dimly lighted back chamber here houses statues of the king and his three sons. The main hall has been heavily

restored, and much of the wood construction visible today is from renovations done in the 17th century. In the temple courtyard stands a 3-
ft-high sculpture made of stone. The dragon lying atop it is meant to
symbolize the king sleeping, while Vietnamese unicorns stand guard
on each side to protect him. To the left of the temple is a small structure containing three stone stelae inscribed with the king's blessings
as well as details about various restorations. In 1696, the entire temple compound was shifted from its original northward orientation—
the direction of evil, according to Taoist belief—to face the more
auspicious east. In 1898, Emperor Nguyen Thanh Thai had the temple raised 2 ft as a gesture of respect to Dinh Tien Hoang. The entire
walled-in compound was designed in the shape of the Chinese character meaning "country."

The second temple is named after Le Dai Hanh, the general who became the first emperor of the Le dynasty in 980. The back chamber
here houses ornate wooden statues of Le Dai Hanh, his son Le Tri Trung,
and one of his five wives, Duong Van Nga, arguably the most interesting of the three figures. Upon the emperor's death, Duong Van Nga
beseeched the head military mandarin of the time to prevent Chinese
invaders from entering the country. She promised that she'd take away
the rule of her six-year-old son and put it in the mandarin's hands, mar-
rying him if he succeeded. When the mandarin repelled the Chinese,
she made good on both promises. Her lifetime saw her become the wife
of two kings, as well as the mother of two kings—the only woman with
such a distinction in Vietnamese history. Depending on the angle from
which you view her statue, her face will appear to reflect one of three
feelings: seriousness over her daily affairs, sadness for the death of her
husbands, and a half smile of satisfaction after the military mandarin
defeated the invading Chinese forces and reinstalled her as queen.

A short bus or car ride away from Hoa Lu—drivers and tour-group
operators know exactly where to go—is a **trio of caves** accessible by
a traditional boat ride down the Hoang Long River, a peaceful stream
that winds through rice paddies after cutting its path through the steep
limestone cliffs around Hoa Lu. Village women row you the 2 km (1
mi) through Tam Coc, a series of three caves, one of which has a cement plaque on its far side commemorating Nguyen Cong Cay, a Vietnamese weapons maker who lived in Hoa Lu from 1947 to 1950 and
plotted with other resisters against the French. At the far end of the
boat ride, other women in similar boats are waiting to sell you soft
drinks, bananas, even embroidery. It's a hard sell and somewhat ruins
the idyllic moment. Another cave, Bich Dong, is also reachable by boat;
you can disembark to visit the 17th-century pagoda here.

Lodging

Most people treat Hoa Lu as part of a day trip and return to Hanoi
by nightfall, but a growing number of adventure travelers are picking
up on the charms of the region and are choosing to spend the night in
the provincial capital of Ninh Binh. If you're going to visit Hoa Lu or
Phat Diem Cathedral, and don't mind a night away from the big city,
consider staying here. Accommodations are nothing to write home about,
but this is a good jumping-off point for the area. Contact travel agencies in Hanoi to book a room at one of the area minihotels.

¢–$ 🏨 **Hoa Lu Hotel.** The largest hotel in Ninh Binh is a huge, rather drab
affair. The rooms are adequate, and there's a restaurant downstairs.
The hotel can arrange local tours. ⊠ *Tran Hung Dao St., Ninh Binh,*
☎ *030/871–217,* FAX *030/874–126,* WEB *www.vietnamtourism.*
com/vietnamopentour. 58 rooms. Restaurant, meeting rooms, travel
services. No credit cards.

¢   🖃 **Trang An Hotel.** This government-owned property sparkles on the outside but is a bit shoddy on the inside. Longan trees festooned with colorful lights dot the courtyard in front, which also has a water fountain. The rooms are reasonably priced and have high windows that open to let in breezes and lots of sunshine. Deluxe and standard rooms are available, and though there's a slight difference in price, the rooms are virtually the same. The hotel can arrange local tours. ⊠ *Le Hong Phong St., Ninh Binh,* ☎ *030/874–742,* 𝔽𝔸𝕏 *030/874–743. 30 rooms. Restaurant, meeting room, travel services. No credit cards.*

Arriving and Departing

Tourist cafés and travel agencies run minibus tours to Hoa Lu for about $20 per person, which includes entry tickets, boat ride, and lunch. You can also rent a car. It makes sense to combine an excursion to Hoa Lu with a trip to nearby Phat Diem, an enclave of Catholic churches. This trip takes the good part of a day.

Phat Diem

❼ *121 km (75 mi) southeast of Hanoi.*

On your way back to Hanoi from Hoa Lu, take a 25-km (16-mi) detour to Phat Diem. You know you're headed in the right direction when you pass one stone church after another. Although tensions between organized religions and the Vietnamese central government still exist, relations have improved considerably between officials and Vietnam's Catholic order since former secretary-general Do Muoi made a conciliatory visit to Phat Diem in 1993. Many of these structures have been built in the last several years with financial assistance from American organizations.

All churches in the area pale in comparison to the massive complex known as **Phat Diem Cathedral,** built in 1891 in Kim Son village, one of the first landfalls of Portuguese missionaries in the 16th century. The cathedral, a hulking edifice made of stone and hardwood, was designed by a Vietnamese priest named Father Sau, who died the same year the cathedral was completed. He is now interred in the narrow courtyard behind the bell tower, which was immortalized by Graham Greene in a description of a battle that took place here between French and Vietnamese forces in *The Quiet American.* The third floor of this tower supports a 2-ton bronze bell that purportedly can be heard from 10 km (6 mi) away. The cathedral is flanked on both sides by four small chapels, all built in the late 19th century and dedicated to various saints. The prayer hall is a wooden marvel; almost the entire interior is made of Vietnamese (and surely Laotian) ironwood, with 48 massive pillars supporting arched ceiling beams in what is truly an artist's loving creation. The curved eaves are a nod to Sino-Vietnamese architecture, but the crosses and saints (all sitting in the lotus position) reflect the fervor of the 150,000-strong congregation. Many of Phat Diem's Catholics fled south in 1954, when Vietnam was divided into north and south. A great deal of restoration work has been done on the complex, which was bombed heavily by U.S. B-52s in 1972.

Catholicism has experienced a comeback in these parts, and because a more liberal tone has been adopted toward religion by Hanoi, **Sunday Mass** is now extremely popular. Services are held at 5 and 9 AM; by 10 everyone's already out in the fields. On holidays such as Christmas and Easter, expect crowds of 10,000 or more.

The church is said to help provide shelter for the faithful who visit Phat Diem and wish to stay in charming Kim Son village, but there are no genuine accommodations for tourists. Consider Ninh Binh (☞ Lodging *in* Hoa Lu, *above*) for a nearby stay.

Arriving and Departing

Some tours that go to Hoa Lu do not stop at Phat Diem, so ask ahead. If you can't find one that stops on the day you wish to go, consider hiring a car and driver—although finding one who will get you there for 5 AM Mass might be tough. It shouldn't run more than $50 round-trip.

Cuc Phuong National Park

❽ *130 km (81 mi) southwest of Hanoi. The park entrance is in Ninh Binh Province, 40 km (25 mi) from Ninh Binh town.*

Outside the general loop of tourist traffic in the north is secluded and prehistoric-looking Cuc Phuong, one of Vietnam's most important protected areas. Established in 1962 by President Ho Chi Minh as Vietnam's first national park, Cuc Phuong consists of 54,320 acres (about 85 square mi) of heavily forested subtropical lowlands sheltering 97 mammal species, including nine species of civet, a kind of barking deer called the muntjac, and the extremely rare Delacour's langur. Approximately 300 bird species and 53 types of reptiles and amphibians live here as well, along with nearly 2,000 species of flora.

The low-key Endangered Primate Rescue Center, which can be visited with staff accompaniment, focuses its rescue efforts on channels of illegal trade, then tries to establish populations in captivity. Although Cuc Phuong's habitat would seem to be the perfect place to see Vietnam's wildlife in full splendor, mammal- and bird-watching are sadly not particularly successful pastimes in the park. Despite Cuc Phuong's status as a protected preserve, the primary forest habitat has been heavily denuded during the past few decades, and officials believe the park's wildlife numbers are dwindling due to increased hunting and high tourism pressures, which have led to the creation of in-park facilities, hiking trails, and paved roads. The conditions will worsen when the huge Ho Chi Minh Highway, already under construction, splits the park in two in violation of Vietnam's own environmental-protection laws. Rerouting of the highway has been under discussion for several years but at press time seemed unlikely.

Despite the misfortunes of northern Vietnam's animals, Cuc Phuong is quite beautiful. April is especially lovely, with its swarms of butterflies. Dozens of miles of trails lead to such highlights as cascading Giao Thuy waterfall, a 1,000-year-old tree, and Con Moong Cave, the "cave of early man," where evidence of prehistoric humans has been discovered. Longer hikes lead to some Muong villages. Many trails are well marked, but exploring this thick forest would be foolish without a guide. Be sure to bring lots of mosquito repellent, especially if you plan to stay the night. ☎ *030/848–006 park headquarters.* ☞ *40,000d.*

Lodging

You can overnight in one of two areas: the park headquarters, just beyond the main gates, or Bong, a tiny village 20 km (12 mi) into the park. If you plan on staying overnight, you may wish to consider going on a weekday, as Cuc Phuong's proximity to Hanoi makes it a favorite weekend retreat among Vietnamese student groups. Bong, secluded as it is, occasionally fills with a boisterous crowd of 100 to 200 students. Tour operators usually guide people to the facilities at **park headquarters** (☎ 030/848–006), which has 32 rooms. Air-conditioned bungalows here are reasonable at $20 per night. Call the park headquarters for information and reservations. The staff is quite helpful.

In **Bong,** two stand-alone bungalows beside a large, algae-green pool are available for $25. Nine simple rooms in a guest house here cost about $15. There are only four hours of electricity per night in Bong, and guest house bathrooms are shared. Reservations, which can be made through travel agencies in Hanoi, are recommended for either location.

Arriving and Departing

Cuc Phuong is a three-hour drive down Highway 1 from Hanoi and can be visited as a day trip if you leave early in the morning. If you've rented a car, it's possible to drive with a guide into the center of the park and hike out to the road to the west of the park, where your driver will meet you. You then drop your guide off at the headquarters on your way back to Hanoi. Tour operators in Hanoi are loath to recommend this outright, claiming that the road is too dangerous and it would be difficult to find you should you get lost or injured, so you'll have to arrange it once at Cuc Phuong. Cars to Cuc Phuong can be arranged for around 760,000d, including meals and entrance fees, for a day trip. For an overnight trip, expect the cost of a car to increase by 300,000d to 455,000d.

HANOI A TO Z

To research prices, get advice from other travelers, and book travel arrangements, visit www.fodors.com.

AIR TRAVEL

Many international airlines fly into Hanoi; for more information *see* Air Travel *in* Smart Travel Tips A to Z. At press time Hanoi and Washington were discussing opening direct flight paths between the United States and Vietnam through U.S. airlines in conjunction with airline partners.

Vietnam Airlines has nonstop international flights between Hanoi and Bangkok, Beijing, Hong Kong, Kuala Lumpur, Paris, Phnom Penh, Seoul, Taipei, Tokyo, and Vientiane, among other cities. Domestic destinations served from Hanoi include Danang, Dien Bien Phu, Ho Chi Minh City, Hue, Nha Trang, and Son La. Flight schedules are often different each day of the week. Pacific Airlines is Vietnam's smaller carrier, mostly serving domestic routes but also offering occasional flights to Hong Kong and Taiwan; ticket prices are comparable to those of Vietnam Airlines.

➤ CARRIERS: **British Airways** (⊠ 25 Ly Thuong Kiet St., Hoan Kiem District, ☎ 04/934–7239, WEB www.britishairways.com). **Cathay Pacific** (⊠ Hanoi Tower, 49 Hai Ba Trung St., Hoan Kiem District, ☎ 04/826–7298, WEB www.cathaypacific.com). **Pacific Airlines** (⊠ 100 Le Duan St., Dong Da District, ☎ 04/733–2162, WEB www.pacificairlines.com.vn). **Thai Airways** (⊠ 25 Ly Thoung Kiet St., Hoan Kiem District, ☎ 04/826–7921 or 04/826–7923, WEB www.thaiairways.com). **Vietnam Airlines** (⊠ 1 Quang Trung St., Hoan Kiem District, ☎ 04/832–0320, 04/934–9660, or 04/934–9620, WEB www.vietnamair.com.vn).

AIRPORT

Noi Bai International Airport lies about 35 km (22 mi) north of the city. After several years of delays a flashy new international terminal opened here in 2001, and further expansion of the airport is expected to last until 2005. For international flights you must pay an airport departure tax of 220,000d, or about $14 (you can pay in dong or dollars).

➤ AIRPORT INFORMATION: **Noi Bai International Airport** (☎ 04/886–5060).

TRANSFERS

Vietnam Airlines runs a bus service into Hanoi; tickets cost 30,000d per person, and it takes about 40 minutes. Buses leave when full, which can sometimes mean a wait. The bus will usually drop you off at your hotel if it's not too far from the center of town. Buses to the airport depart from the Vietnam Airlines office; book a seat in advance.

The official Airport Taxi fare into town is $10. Pick up a voucher at the stand inside or outside the terminal, pay in advance, and you'll be escorted to your cab. Many unofficial taxi drivers also hover at the terminal's exit and will tug at your sleeve or luggage cart in order to get your business. They'll get you into town for less than the official taxis if you bargain well, but they don't offer receipts and often drive clunking, steering-challenged Russian Volgas. They'll also try to get you to pay for the tolls into town.

To get out to the airport, hire an official taxi for $10; they congregate in front of the Vietnam Airlines office and cruise about the city. You can also call for a taxi. Travelers looking to share taxis congregate in front of the Vietnam Airlines office, as do enterprising private drivers. Be prepared to bargain hard—it's tough to beat the official rate.
➤ TAXIS AND SHUTTLES: **Airport Taxi** (☎ 04/873–0333). **Vietnam Airlines bus** (☎ 04/825–0872).

BIKE TRAVEL

Bikes can be rented at hotels and cafés in the center of town for around 10,000d per day. Make sure the bike you get has a lock. You can get the tires pumped up at just about any street corner for 300d to 500d per tire.

BUS TRAVEL

Try to take minibuses instead of buses, as full-size buses are cramped, hot, and notoriously loud, uncomfortable, and unsafe. Make arrangements for travel by minibus—either independently or with group tours—through travel agencies, tourist cafés, and hotels.

If you must travel by regular bus, note that schedules are quite arbitrary, and few station attendants speak any English or French. Buses leave when full, and arrival times depend on how often a bus stops along the road to cool off its overheated engine or pick up more passengers. Contact the state-owned Hanoi Bus Company for information.

The BIC Bus Company, a Korean joint venture that has made inroads in northern Vietnam, provides service to and from Haiphong, Lang Son, Ninh Binh, and other points south out of Hanoi's Kim Ma Bus Station. The privately owned Hoang Long (Golden Dragon) Bus Company enjoys a large share of the interprovince market, including routes between Hanoi and Haiphong. The high-quality air-conditioned buses haul passengers in and out of Kim Ma Bus Station and from the foot of the Long Bien Bridge. Pseudo-independent minibus service, particularly to Haiphong, is available from the alleyway called Hang Trung, adjacent to the Royal Hotel. These buses are more expensive than their hulking counterparts, yet they're usually just as crowded.
➤ BUS INFORMATION: **BIC Bus Company** (✉ 2 Hoang Van Thu St., Haiphong, ☎ 031/820–800). **Hanoi Bus Company** (✉ 32 Nguyen Cong Tru St., Hai Ba Trung District, ☎ 04/971–4590). **Hoang Long Bus Company** (✉ 62 Yen Phu St., Ba Dinh District, ☎ 04/927–2231). **Minibus service** (Royal Hotel; ✉ 20 Hang Tre St., Hoan Kiem District, ☎ no phone).

BUS STATIONS

Three major bus stations—none of which are in the center of town—serve the capital, in addition to a few express minibus services.

Giai Bat Bus Station (Ben Xe Giai Bat) serves most southern routes, including Vinh, Hue, and ultimately Ho Chi Minh City. It's 7 km (4 mi) south of the Hanoi Railway Station, on Giai Phong Street, opposite the Giap Rat Railway Station. Gia Lam Bus Station (Ben Xe Gia Lam) provides service in the north, to destinations such as Lang Son and Haiphong. It's best to buy your ticket ahead of time. The station is across the Red River and just beyond the tollbooth, 100 yards off Nguyen Van Cu Street on Ben Xe Street. Kim Ma Bus Station (Ben Xe Kim Ma), the closest station to downtown, serves most routes to the northwest, including Dien Bien Phu.

➤ Bus Stations: **Giai Bat Bus Station** (✉ Giai Phong St., Hai Ba Trung District, ☏ 04/864–1467). **Gia Lam Bus Station** (✉ Ben Xe St., Gia Lam District, ☏ 04/827–1529). **Kim Ma Bus Station** (✉ Nguyen Thai Hoc and Giang Vo Sts., Ba Dinh District, ☏ 04/845–2846).

CAMERAS AND PHOTOGRAPHY

For the best film developing, try the storefronts at 1 Trang Thi Street and 19 Ba Trieu Street. Cameras can be fixed at any of the many camera repair shops on Trang Thi Street, on the south side of Hoan Kiem Lake, but for serious repairs, you're better off buying a point-and-shoot camera in Hanoi and fixing your camera when you get home.

CAR AND MOTORBIKE RENTAL

To hire a car and driver, contact any hotel, a large operator such as Vietnam Tourism, one of the tourist cafés, or any other travel agency (as foreigners cannot drive cars in Vietnam, you must hire a driver when you rent a car). If you don't rent from a large hotel you can count on paying around $30 per day in the city for an air-conditioned sedan and a driver. Expect to pay $40 or more per day for a minivan.

You can almost certainly arrange for a pickup at your hotel, although a deposit—usually 50% of the fare and some form of identification, such as a photocopy of your passport—is often expected. There is no need for you to leave your passport with the agency renting you the car. The general time frame for day rentals is from 8 AM until dusk. If you keep the car beyond 5:30 or 6, the rates will rise. Before you rent the car, make sure it is clear *exactly* how much the rate will rise if you keep the car longer.

If you decide to rent a motorbike yourself and drive around the city, keep in mind that the traffic *is* busy, loud, and crazy. Although the streets may be less intimidating in Hanoi than in Ho Chi Minh City, the consensus is that drivers are worse. And visitors are paying the price: Vietnam's number one cause of injuries and death among foreigners is accidents involving a motorcycle. You can purchase helmets on Pho Hue and Lo Duc streets for between $10 and $60. Don't become a Vietnam traffic statistic—wear one.

That said, many hotels and tourist cafés rent motorbikes, with more and more of them throwing a helmet in with the cost. Prices start at less than $5 per day. A deposit is usually required, as is a passport or a photocopy, and you sign a short-term contract (be sure you're aware of the stipulated value of the bike in the contract). And speaking of contracts, you would be wise to consult your insurance policy; many companies refuse to cover motorcycle drivers or riders.

CAR TRAVEL

As Hanoi is the largest city and tourist center in northern Vietnam and a major international gateway, few Western visitors actually arrive here by car. Those who do are usually coming from Ho Chi Minh City via Highway 1 or from Danang or Hue after flying there from Ho Chi Minh City. A much more common method is to tour the south by land, say, by car or train from Ho Chi Minh City to Hue and then fly from there to Hanoi.

It's quite easy to arrange leaving Hanoi by car for side trips. Only a few road tolls are charged, and the cost is minimal—about 5,000d per car.

CYCLO TRAVEL

Cyclo (pedicab) drivers in Hanoi are less likely to speak English than their Saigon counterparts, so definitely bring a map and be prepared to gesture. On the upside, cyclos here are wider than anywhere else in Vietnam, so two medium-size Westerners can squeeze into one; the fare is usually from 5,000d to 10,000d, depending on the distance. A cyclo driver will be more than happy to take you around for the whole day for as little as 40,000d to 50,000d. Make sure you're both on the same wavelength when you're talking money: unsuspecting travelers have been known to agree to a fare of 10,000d, only to have the cyclo driver later claim the agreed-upon figure was $10.

EMBASSIES

If you have passport problems while in Hanoi, have had something very expensive stolen, or are extremely ill, contact your embassy.

➤ CONTACTS: **Australia** (⌗ 8 Dao Tan St., Van Phuc Quarter, Ba Dinh District, ☎ 04/831–7755, FAX 04/831–7711, WEB www.ausinvn.com). **Canada** (⌗ 31 Hung Vuong St., Ba Dinh District, ☎ 04/823–5500, FAX 04/823–5333). **New Zealand** (⌗ 63 Ly Thai To St., Hoan Kiem District, ☎ 04/824–1481, FAX 04/824–1480). **United Kingdom** (⌗ 31 Hai Ba Trung St., Hoan Kiem District, ☎ 04/825–2510, FAX 04/826–5762, WEB www.uk-vietnam.org). **United States** (⌗ 7 Lang Ha St., Ba Dinh District, ☎ 04/772–1500, FAX 04/772–1510, WEB www.uscongenhcmc.org).

EMERGENCIES

Medical facilities in Hanoi are generally not up to international standards, though the quality of care and service is steadily improving. A few foreign-run medical clinics provide basic treatment—usually at Western prices—and can arrange for emergency medical evacuation in the region. Basic treatment and services, such as x-rays, ultrasound, blood screening, and inoculations—not to mention round-the-clock pharmacies—can be found at most of the facilities listed below.

Emergency Viet Duc Hospital (Benh Vien Viet Duc) is open 24 hours for emergency surgery; the staff speaks English, French, and German. Hanoi Family Medical Practice is the creation of Israeli doctor Rafi Kot, who has one of the busiest practices in Hanoi. An expert staff of foreign doctors includes dentists, gynecologists, pediatricians, physiotherapists, psychoanalysts, and speech therapists.

Hanoi French Hospital has excellent French and other internationally trained local medical staff. Gynecology, dentistry, and accident and emergency treatment are among the services provided here; English-speaking doctors are available. International SOS, opened 24 hours for emergencies, provides routine health care and dentistry. The staff can also arrange emergency medical assistance, with referrals or evacuations.

The National Institute of Traditional Medicine specializes in herbal treatments, acupuncture, cupping, and massage, as well as the diagnosis and treatment of illness. Staff members speak English and French. Training classes can be arranged for foreigners. Vietnam-Korea Friendship Clinic is a non-profit facility run by Dr. Jung-Hwan Oh and his volunteer staff. Although the clinic specializes in internal medicine, its services are extensive. It's also inexpensive, which may explain why it's always so busy. The clinic's profits go toward various medical projects that aid Vietnam's rural poor.

Eyewear services, including emergency repair, prescription contacts, sunglasses, and single and multifocal eyeglasses, can be found at Kinh Au Euro Vision. Most major services can be completed here within 20 minutes. Another option is Kinh Thuoc–Kinh Thoi Trang, which can provide most of these services in the same amount of time. For all purchases over 500,000d, Kinh Thuoc–Kinh Thoi Trang arranges a 10% discount.

➤ DOCTORS, DENTISTS, AND HOSPITALS: **Emergency Viet Duc Hospital** (✉ 40 Trang Thi St., Hoan Kiem District, ☎ 04/825–5956). **Hanoi Family Medical Practice** (✉ A-1 Bldg., Van Phuc Diplomatic Compound, Suite 109–112, Kim Ma Rd., Ba Dinh District, ☎ 04/843–0748; 09/ 0340–1919 24-hr emergency mobile phone; WEB www.doctorkot.com). **Hanoi French Hospital** (✉ 1 Phuong Mai St., next to Bach Mai Hospital, Dong Da District, ☎ 04/574–0740; 04/574–1111 24-hr emergency care). **International SOS** (✉ 31 Hai Ba Trung St., Hoan Kiem District, ☎ 04/934–0666; 04/934–0555 24-hr emergency care). **National Institute of Traditional Medicine** (✉ 26 Nguyen Binh Khiem St., Hoan Kiem District, ☎ 04/943–1018). **Vietnam-Korea Friendship Clinic** (✉ 12 Chu Van An St., Hoan Kiem District, ☎ 04/843–7231; 09/1300–4130 24-hr emergency service).

➤ EMERGENCY SERVICES: **Ambulance** (☎ 15). **Fire** (☎ 14). **Police** (☎ 13).

➤ EYEWEAR SERVICES: **Kinh Au Euro Vision** (✉ 34 Le Thai To St., Hoan Kiem District, ☎ 04/826–4487). **Kinh Thuoc—Kinh Thoi Trang** (✉ 35 Trang Thien St., Hoan Kiem District, ☎ 04/826–4391).

ENGLISH-LANGUAGE MEDIA

The selection of English-language reading material is slowly improving in Hanoi. Although nearly all bookstores are state-run and censorship is heavy, some stores carry a good selection of international newspapers and magazines (provided none have infuriated Xunhasaba, the state-owned book distributor that occasionally yanks an issue off the shelves if a story portrays Vietnam too harshly).

The small but cozy Bookworm stocks new and used fiction, nonfiction, and children's literature—the best classic and contemporary English-language reading material you'll find anywhere in Hanoi. A reading room has newspapers, magazines, and coffee and tea service. It's open Thursday–Sunday 10–7.

The Foreign Language Bookshop is squeezed into an alleyway between Trang Tien shopping plaza and Thang Long bookstore on the southeastern side of Hoan Kiem Lake. The Gioi Publishers Bookshop has a small but varied selection of books on Vietnamese history, culture, law, and military exploits.

The National Library of Vietnam is in a lovely compound. There are books in English, but you're not allowed to comb through the stacks; locate the book you want on one of the few computers on offer (you're allotted five minutes), and an assistant will bring it to you. You may not take the book out of the building, and you must show your passport to enter.

The Press Club has a small selection of best-sellers, children's literature, cookbooks, international magazines, and newspapers. Savina sells a wide selection of newspapers and magazines, as well as plenty of books about Vietnam.

Xunhasaba, or the State Enterprise for the Import and Export of Books and Periodicals, carries a wide selection of technical titles, photography books, mystery and romance novels, and 19th-century American and European literature.

➤ BOOKSTORES AND NEWSSTANDS: **The Bookworm** (✉ 15A Ngo Van So St., Hoan Kiem District, ☎ 04/943–7226). **Foreign Language Bookshop** (✉ 61 Trang Tien St., Hoan Kiem District, ☎ 04/825–3423). **Gioi Publishers Bookshop** (✉ 46 Tran Hung Dao St., Hoan Kiem District, ☎ 04/825–3841). **National Library of Vietnam** (✉ 52 Hai Ba Trung St., Hoan Kiem District, ☎ 04/825–3040). **The Press Club** (✉ 59A Ly Thai To St., Hoan Kiem District, ☎ 04/934–0888). **Savina** (✉ 44 Trang Tien St., Hoan Kiem District, ☎ 04/826–0313). **Xunhasaba** (✉ 32 Hai Ba Trung St., Hoan Kiem District, ☎ 04/825–4068).

MAIL AND SHIPPING

The General Post Office (Buu Dien Trung Vong) occupies most of a city block across from Hoan Kiem Lake. Phone, fax, and telex services are available, as is express-mail service from companies such as Federal Express, DHL, and UPS. It's open daily 6:30 AM–8 PM. Dozens of other small post-office branches dot the city.

➤ POST OFFICE: **General Post Office** (✉ 75 Dinh Tien Hoang St., Hoan Kiem District, ☎ 04/825–5948).

MONEY MATTERS

The dollar has proven almighty, even in the capital of Communist Vietnam, and exchanging greenbacks for Vietnamese dong is easy. Many of Hanoi's shops and upscale restaurants will accept both dollars and dong. Some shops, such as art galleries, list all their prices in U.S. dollars.

Most major international banks in Hanoi have a currency exchange and other financial services such as money transfers, credit-card cash advances, and the cashing of traveler's checks. Vietnamese banks, such as Vietcom Bank (Bank for Foreign Trade of Vietnam) and VID Public Bank, also have such services. The rates of exchange at the international banks are controlled by the State Bank of Vietnam, so you'll likely find one is as good as the other. Hotels and many gold and jewelry shops can also change money. Avoid the black-market money changers who gather around the General Post Office; they are illegal (though such rules are rarely enforced) and try to cheat customers.

➤ MAJOR BANKS: **ANZ Bank** (✉ 14 Le Thai To St., Hoan Kiem District, ☎ 04/825–8190, ℻ 04/825–8188). **Bangkok Bank PCL** (✉ 41B Ly Thai To St., Hoan Kiem District, ☎ 04/824–9094, ℻ 04/826–7397). **Chinfon Commercial Bank** (✉ 55 Quang Trung St., Hoan Kiem District, ☎ 04/943–9555, ℻ 04/943–8566). **Citibank** (✉ 17 Ngo Quyen St., Hoan Kiem District, ☎ 04/825–1950, ℻ 04/824–3960). **VID Public Bank** (✉ 2 Ngo Quyen St., Hoan Kiem District, ☎ 04/826–6953, ℻ 04/826–8228). **Vietcom Bank** (✉ 198 Tran Quang Khai St., Hoan Kiem District, ☎ 04/825–9859, ℻ 04/826–9067). **Vietcombank** (✉ 10 Le Lai St., Hoan Kiem District, ☎ 04/824–9041, ℻ 04/257–308).

SIGHTSEEING TOURS

See Travel Agencies, *below.*

TAXIS AND MOTORBIKE TAXIS

Although Hanoi's cabbies act like reckless kings of the road, taxis are still the safest way to get around town. The moment you step into a cab, the meter (all cabs in Hanoi should be metered) reads 14,000d;

after that rates run about 6,000d per kilometer (half mile). A trip across town will cost you about 25,000d.

Taxis tend to congregate at the northwest corner of Hoan Kiem Lake, on Trieu Viet Vuong Street, and outside most major hotels. You can also call for a cab, as all taxi dispatchers speak English. Competition is intense; a cab will probably be at your doorstep in less than three minutes if you're somewhere downtown. And don't be surprised if the cab that shows up is from a different company than the one you called; it means they've intercepted your request.

Motorbike taxis, known as xe om or *Honda om,* are one way to get around the city—if you're brave. Although the traffic may look a little daunting, drivers know (hopefully) how to navigate the traffic.
➤ TAXI COMPANIES: **Airport Taxi** (☎ 04/873–3333). **Hanoi Taxi** (☎ 04/853–5252). **Mai Linh Taxi** (☎ 04/861–6161 nine-seat minibus). **Red Taxi** (☎ 04/856–8686). **Taxi 25** (☎ 04/825–2525).

TRAIN TRAVEL
The ticket office at the main Hanoi train station, Ga Hanoi, is open 7:30–11:30 and 1:30–3:30. You'll find a special counter where foreigners buy tickets, and some of the schedules are even in English. Another, smaller train station, up the tracks from the main one, services northern routes; the foreign booking agents at the main station will direct you.

Trains leave four times daily for Ho Chi Minh City (soft berth $93–$101, 41 hours),but only one is an express (32 hours). The express makes stops at most major cities, including Vinh, Hue, Danang, and Nha Trang. Purchase a day in advance if you want to ensure a seat. Other destinations include Lang Son ($4, twice daily, 6 hours), Lao Cai (hard berth $16, soft sleeper $28; three times daily; 10 hours), and Haiphong ($3, seven times daily, 2 hours).

INTERNATIONAL TRAVEL
Trains connect Beijing with Hanoi twice weekly; the trip takes about 52 hours. The northeastern border crossing is at Dong Dang, just north of Lang Son in the northeast. The closest Chinese city to the Vietnamese border crossing is Nanning, the capital of Guangxi Province. A second international route leads from Hanoi through the border town of Lao Cai, to the northwest, and on to the Chinese provincial capital of Qunming. This train departs every Tuesday and Friday at 6:50 PM and is the same sleeper train many tourists take to Sapa. Standard tourist visas to China allow entry into the country from any port but Nepal. On the Vietnamese side, you'll have to have the appropriate overland exit permit stamped into your visa, which can be obtained at Ga Hanoi. It's sometimes possible to have your visa amended after you've arrived, but it's best to arrange this in advance.
➤ TRAIN STATION: **Ga Hanoi** (✉ Opposite 115 Le Duan St., at west end of Tran Hung Dao St., Hoan Kiem District, ☎ 04/801–1033 recorded information; 04/747–0308 information; 04/942–3697 ticketing).

TRAVEL AGENCIES
The following travel agencies operate in Hanoi—some in many other parts of the country as well. They provide visitor information, transportation and hotel bookings, car and bus rentals, guided tours, private tour guides, and visa extensions. If you've signed on to a package tour from the United States, Europe, or Australia, it is highly likely you'll be cared for by one of these companies. *See* Tours and Packages *and* Travel Agencies *in* Smart Travel Tips A to Z for a further discussion of your options.

Buffalo Tours focuses on "cultural tourism," which includes domestic and regional tour programs with professors and scholars who specialize in culture and history. The company is also quite handy with smaller and more quirky tours and services, such as dinner cruises on West Lake or kayaking trips. Exotissimo Travel is one of the biggest foreign names in Hanoi's tourism business. An international wholesale inbound tour operator for more upscale trips, Exotissimo offers retail and walk-in services as well.

Hanoi Toserco, a large state-run office, arranges inbound and outbound travel services, books hotels, finds housing, and coordinates package tours. Hanoi Tourism is one of the city's biggest state-run travel agencies, catering to high- and low-end travelers with customized and package tours. Saigon Tourist, the largest tour agency in Vietnam, is based in Saigon but has an office in the capital. Service is sometimes impersonal, but the outfit can arrange everything. TF Handspan Travel is a small but reliable outfit specializing in the quirky and adventurous, from mountain-biking trips through Vietnam's northernmost provinces to kayaking trips on the Da River. It has three offices in Hanoi, all of which provide a broad range of services.

Vidotour, one of the largest private tour agencies in Vietnam, can provide many travel services, especially in the south. Vietnam Tourism, one of the country's large state-run travel agencies, has on-line booking services. Vinatour is a midsize state-run agency that provides domestic travel services and can arrange tours to Hong Kong, Malaysia, Singapore, and Thailand.

➤ CONTACTS: **Buffalo Tours** (✉ 11 Hang Muoi St., Hoan Kiem District, ☎ 04/828–0702, FAX 04/826–9370, WEB www.buffalotours.com). **Exotissimo Travel** (✉ 26 Tran Nhat Duat St., Hoan Kiem District, ☎ 04/828–2150, FAX 04/828–2146, WEB www.exotissimo.com). **Hanoi Toserco** (✉ 98 Hang Trong St., Hoan Kiem District, ☎ 04/828–7552, FAX 04/822–6055, WEB vietnamtourism.com/vietnamopentour). **Hanoi Tourism** (✉ 18 Ly Thuong Kiet St., Hoan Kiem District, ☎ 04/824–3011, FAX 04/824–3012). **Saigon Tourist** (✉ 55B Phan Chu Trinh St., Hoan Kiem District, ☎ 04/825–0923, FAX 04/825–1174 tours, WEB www.saigon-tourist.com). **TF Handspan Travel** (✉ 80 Ma May St., Hoan Kiem District, ☎ 04/926–0581, FAX 04/926–0445, WEB www.handspan.com). **Vidotour** (✉ 308 Ba Trieu St., Hai Ba Trung District, ☎ 04/821–5682, FAX 04/974–1444, WEB www.vidotourtravel.com). **Vietnam Tourism** (✉ 30A Ly Thuong Kiet St., Hoan Kiem District, ☎ 04/826–4154, FAX 04/825–7583, WEB www.vn-tourism.com). **Vinatour** (✉ 54 Nguyen Du St., Hoan Kiem District, ☎ 04/942–3963, FAX 04/942–3009).

TOURIST CAFÉS

These (mainly) private companies offer many of the services of large travel agencies but usually at lower prices. Many double as hotels and restaurants, and some have computers where you can check e-mail or surf the Internet. If you don't see a sign for bicycle and motorbike rentals, in most cases they can still be arranged. Most tourist cafés are not equipped to handle tour bookings from overseas; it's mainly a walk-in business.

In terms of price, the tourist cafés' group tours can't be beat. For instance, a full-day guided tour to the Perfume Pagoda, including transportation, entrance fees, and boat rides, costs as little as $10 per person. To Halong Bay it's an even better deal (from less than $15 per person for two boat rides, a guide, lunch, and an overnight stay), but the accommodations are usually in average minihotels.

A friendly couple runs tiny Coco's Memory Café. Green Bamboo Café's tour services are hard to beat. Hanoi's Old Quarter Café specializes in small group trips to remote islands in Ha Long Bay. They rarely publish tour prices by design; bargaining is the name of the game here, and the staff's straightforwardness makes it easier than you might think.

Kim Café Travel is a good draw both for its travel services and its vegetarian restaurant. The owners pride themselves on the quality of their regional tours. Meeting Café is good for arranging small tours.

Backpackers stream in and out of the somewhat run-down Queen Café; if you feel like a number in here, it's because you *are* a number in here. Service, however, is among the best in town. Real Darling Café, a family-owned business, has been firming up its reputation for a decade. It offers more tours than could be taken in a year, including a butterfly tour of Ba Vi and Cuc Phuong national parks.

Sinh Café is affiliated with the Saigon heavy hitter of the same name as well as state-owned Hanoi Toserco. There are around 10 different branches of this café, whose specialty is the Sinh Café Open Tour, a daily bus service that runs the length of the country (☞ Bus Travel *in* Smart Travel Tips A to Z). The Trekking Café gets good business as a tour organizer, cozy restaurant, and book exchange. Friendly employees will help you find the kayaking or trekking adventure—and just about anything else—that you're looking for.

➤ CONTACTS: **Coco's Memory Café** (✉ 33bis Tran Hung Dao St., Hoan Kiem District, ☎ 04/826–5854). **Green Bamboo Café** (✉ 80 Tran Nhat Duat St., Hoan Kiem District, ☎ 04/928–3008, WEB www.vietnamonline. com/greenbamboo). **Hanoi's Old Quarter Café** (✉ 22 Hang Be St., Hoan Kiem District, ☎ 04/926–0313, FAX 04/923–1054). **Kim Café Travel** (✉ 79 Hang Bac St., Hoan Kiem District, ☎ 04/824–2468, FAX 04/824–9049). **Meeting Café** (✉ 59 Ba Trieu St., Hoan Kiem District, ☎ 04/943–8813). **Queen Café** (✉ 50 Hang Be St., Hoan Kiem District, ☎ 04/934–3728, WEB www.queencafe.com.vn). **Real Darling Café** (✉ 33 Hang Quat St., Hoan Kiem District, ☎ 04/826–9386, FAX 04/825–6562). **Sinh Café** (✉ 16 Hang Be St., Hoan Kiem District, ☎ 04/926–0621, WEB www.sinhcafevn.com). **The Trekking Café** (✉ 108 Hang Bac St., Hoan Kiem District, ☎ 04/926–0572, FAX 04/926–0617).

VISITOR INFORMATION

There are no government-run tourism information offices in Hanoi, but you can pick up information from travel agencies, tourist cafés, and your hotel.

3 THE NORTH

HALONG BAY, SAPA, DIEN BIEN PHU

Northern Vietnam's stark beauty lies in its mist-shrouded islets and rice-terraced mountains. Fishing boats ply the magnificent waters of Halong Bay, while diligent farmers harvest crops on the steep slopes of the Tonkinese Alps and fluttering rice stalks whisper the rhythm of Mai Chau Valley. In the shadow of Fansipan, the country's tallest peak, are the villages of northern Vietnam's ethnic-minority groups. This region of imposing mountains bore witness to French ignominy at Dien Bien Phu—and at the same time nurtured Ho Chi Minh's revolution.

By Michael
Mathes

Updated by
George
Vaughton

THE SPECTACULAR TOPOGRAPHY OF THE NORTH includes the Hoang Lien Mountains—or Tonkinese Alps, as they are commonly called—the sprawling Red River delta, and Halong Bay's limestone islets jutting out of the South China Sea. Even though the region has borne the brunt of centuries of war—first the Chinese invaders, then the French colonialists, the Americans, and once again the Chinese—and bomb craters still pockmark the Red River delta, much of northern Vietnam has maintained its austere beauty.

The Red River delta is the most densely populated area of Vietnam, with more than 1,000 people per square mile, compared with approximately 400 per square mile in the Mekong Delta. Many of these inhabitants of the Red River delta, and those in the mountains to the north and west, are very poor. Extreme weather patterns—too much rain and too many damaging storms in the wet season, too little rain in the dry season—make living off the land more difficult than in the south. Years of postcolonial isolation, xenophobia, and ruinous collectivization programs also drove the north to the brink of disaster. Although forced collectivization and other such socialist land schemes have been confined to the dustbins of history, there are new threats and concerns for the indigenous people of northern Vietnam.

In the remote highlands and valleys north and west of Hanoi, ethnic-minority populations continue to live as they have for centuries—despite the government's attempts at cultural integration. The history of these unique ethnic minorities is still the subject of some dispute, but many anthropologists now believe the largest of these groups, the Muong, as well as smaller groups like the Kho-mu, the Khang, the Mang, and the La Ha, have been living in the Hoang Lien Mountains and the northern foothills for thousands of years, preceding even the arrival of the Kinh—the ethnic Vietnamese who now make up 87% of the country's population.

Most other groups migrated from China or Laos—some as late as the 19th century—as a result of war or lack of land. (Communities of a number of these ethnic minorities can still be found in the countries from which they came, including China, Laos, Thailand, Cambodia, and Burma; migration across national borders is common.) Living in the highest elevations, near the climatic limits of hill rice cultivation, are the H'mong and Dao (pronounced zow). The clothing and jewelry of these two groups, particularly the women, are among the most colorful and elaborate in the north. The Muong and Thai (with distinct Black Thai and White Thai subgroups) are two of the larger minorities, each numbering about a million. They practice wetlands cultivation on the middle and lower slopes and generally live in airy, comfortable stilt houses in village clusters ranging from a handful of houses to several dozen.

Slash-and-burn agriculture, the traditional mainstay of ethnic-minority economies, was for centuries an ideal form of natural resource management. Over the last decade or more, however, as the land available for such cultivation shrinks, this method has begun to generate heated controversy in Vietnam and has been blamed for just about every natural calamity that has befallen the north. Indeed, northern Vietnam is the most deforested region of Indochina, with as much as 90% of its primary forests lost to human encroachment. Acres of trees are cut down every day for use as fuel or for wood for construction. A migration of Kinh Vietnamese from the Red River delta farther inland and into the distant valleys is also displacing many nomadic farmers as land privatization plans take hold.

Vietnam's growing energy needs are also wreaking havoc on minority life. The Hoa Binh Dam, Vietnam's first hydroelectric power project, 70 km (43 mi) southwest of Hanoi, displaced 60,000 people from the Da River valley. Most were ethnic minorities who were pushed into higher elevations, geography in which they had little farming experience or expertise. Another, larger hydroelectric project, farther up the Da River in Son La Province, has already been approved. Feasibility studies estimate that 440 square km (170 square mi) of forest and farming area will be sacrificed and anywhere from 110,000 to 143,000 people displaced.

From the mid-19th century until their departure in 1954 after their defeat at Dien Bien Phu, French colonialists had varied and extensive contact with these ethnic-minority groups, all of whom they referred to as Montagnards ("mountain people"). Some of these groups sided with the French against the Kinh Vietnamese; others helped foment rebellion against the French.

Today, tourists in large numbers come to visit ethnic-minority villages in northern Vietnam. For the villagers it has been a mixed blessing. A booming business of selling handicrafts, clothing, and textiles to tourists has sprung up in many communities and around Sapa in particular. Increased contact between these ethnic minorities and tourists has created a flurry of interest in their cultures and lives but has also cost them some privacy. One unfortunate casualty, for instance, has been the near disappearance of Saturday-night "love markets," where young Red Dao men and women in search of a spouse or lover would pair off for an evening of socializing and possible romance. In Sapa there is no sign of this market, which was once the highlight of the trip for visitors. Too many flashbulbs and curious foreign faces have driven the love market out of the spotlight and into more remote areas of the north.

Pleasures and Pastimes

Dining

Except for in Hanoi and the coastal regions, dining in the north is more of a necessity than a delight. Seafood dishes in Haiphong, Cat Ba, Halong Bay, and farther up the coast are delicious. The mountains provide little gratification for gourmands, however. Rice is a staple as well as corn, cassava, and green vegetables. Pond stocking ensures an ample fish supply. Although beef is now readily available in mountain towns, pork is the more common meat. Chicken, pork, and beef are usually tough, however, and little of the animals goes to waste. In the homes of poorer villagers especially, keep an eye out for meat dishes; they're usually accompanied by offal, and your hosts may not realize that most people from the West steer clear of such fare. By the same token, understand that meats are still a delicacy in many poor communities; as foreign visitors are still extremely rare in some areas, your hosts may splurge and butcher a pig or a few chickens in your honor. Deciding what to eat and what to pass up is an issue to treat with some sensitivity.

One "pleasure" that you most likely will be unable to avoid while traveling through the highlands is rice wine, or *ruou* (pronounced *zee*-oo). Distilled locally, ruou is everywhere and is used as a welcoming drink. It is also drunk at lunch; before, during, and after dinner; while gathering with friends; when meeting with officials; at small and large celebrations; and as a good-luck send-off. Refusing it outright is difficult, stopping once you've started is nearly impossible, and getting sick from drinking too much is easy.

A communal twist on the ruou standard is *ruou can* (straw-rice wine), which is consumed by up to a dozen people at the same time through bamboo straws stuck into an earthenware jar. First half-filled with manioc and rice husks, the jar is sealed tight and left to ferment for 17 days. On the day of consumption, a water-sugar mixture is added. The sweet, slightly fetid alcohol is downed at weddings and other major celebrations—such as a couple of foreigners stepping into a remote village. It's beneficial that ruou can is more diluted than its bottled brother, which can be anywhere from 60 to 110 proof.

CATEGORY	COST*
$$$$	over 250,000 dong
$$$	150,000 dong–250,000 dong
$$	60,000 dong–150,000 dong
$	15,000 dong–60,000 dong
¢	under 15,000 dong

per person for a main course at dinner, including 10% tax and 5% service

Hiking

One of the best ways to experience northern Vietnam is by tackling the trails that lead out of the towns and into more remote areas of the highlands. Whether you're stepping into a national park (Cuc Phuong [☞ Chapter 2], Ba Be, and Cat Ba Island national parks all have spectacular hiking) or onto a Montagnard trail, these footpaths lead through more pristine terrain than you would be able to see from the backseat of a bouncing jeep. Wildlife sightings are more likely, though still rare, the farther you are from busy roads and towns. Villages throughout the mountains are connected by trails, and it may not be long before someone produces a publication documenting and mapping a network of the best hiking trails in the north. Until then, however, your best bet is to pick up local maps when you arrive at a destination. Dozens of trails lead out of the hillside town of Sapa, for instance, and into H'mong villages. Minority peoples have a vast knowledge of local routes, but communication may be a problem. You may want to bring a guide along, especially if you intend on trekking to the foot—or if you've got three or four days, to the top—of Mt. Fansipan, Vietnam's highest peak.

The tourist cafés in Hanoi (☞ Hanoi A to Z *in* Chapter 2) organize tours that combine four-wheel-drive transportation and serious hiking. It won't exactly be a one-on-one experience with nature, but the tour operators have researched the hikes with knowledgeable locals and are pretty familiar with the needs and desires of Western travelers.

If you want to hike but are concerned about land mines and unexploded ordnance in the north, keep in mind that there is little to fear if you stay on marked trails or on clear footpaths. However, unless you're with an experienced guide, you should not hike along Vietnam's border region with China, specifically in the area around Lang Son and Mong Cai. Mine laying was common during the 1979 border war, and it's best to skip unmarked hillside exploring.

Jeep Trips

Adventure awaits on the roads of the north. Mud slides, breakdowns, and teeth-rattling stretches of "highway" compete for your attention with spectacular scenery, revolutionary history, and ethnic-minority culture. Only in a rented Russian jeep—or in a far more civilized Toyota Land Cruiser or Mitsubishi Pajero—are you in complete control of where and when you stop. The no-nonsense drivers speak little English, but they're also quite familiar with the terrain and can lead you to sights left alone by the big tour companies.

Lodging

Except in the major cities such as Hanoi and Haiphong and established tourist destinations such as Halong Bay and Sapa, accommodations in the north lack many basic amenities. If you're looking for comfort, stick close to Hanoi. In other small cities and towns such as Dien Bien Phu, Lang Son, or Lao Cai, expect hot running water in your hotel room, but don't count on having IDD phones, heaters, or bathtubs. In more remote areas, such as ethnic-minority villages near Yen Phu or small coastal communities in the far northeast, you may have to share a mat or roll-away mattress in the living room of a host family—with a bathroom that's a curtained shack next to a well where you draw your own water. Don't write off such an experience, however; many of the stilt houses in ethnic-minority villages are exquisitely built, cool, and comfortable, and you may find the owners to be your most gracious hosts.

CATEGORY	COST*
$$$$	over 1.5 million dong
$$$	900,000 dong–1.5 million dong
$$	600,000–900,000 dong
$	300,000 dong–600,000 dong
¢	under 300,000 dong

All prices are for a standard double room, including 10% tax and 5% service.

Shopping

The region's ethnic-minority communities, particularly the women, have developed sophisticated trading networks, not just among themselves but for tourists as well. And what's trading hands is positively beautiful: richly dyed textiles; hand-loomed silk scarves, headdresses, and broadcloth; brocaded vests and dresses; woven bamboo baskets of all shapes and sizes; and traditional silver jewelry. The "industry" has even internationalized, and savvy distributors in Hanoi and Ho Chi Minh City are scrambling to send Vietnam's ethnic-minority styles to overseas markets.

Exploring the North

A trip to the north is difficult to rush because traveling around often takes a long time and changing weather can make some roads quite dangerous—even impassable. Roads for the most part are in bad shape. The major highways of the lowlands—Highway 5 to Haiphong, Highway 1 to Lang Son, Highway 6 to Hoa Binh—are being continuously upgraded, and the construction itself slows down traffic flow. In the mountains of the north and northwest, heavily traveled routes are paved but are still in poor condition. Routes to distant villages like Muong Te or remote destinations like Ha Giang town are rutted dirt roads that wash out with the first heavy rain. Traveling them can be physically exhausting.

With this in mind, there are two ways to travel through the north. The most challenging is to cover the region by car, from Hanoi to Son La to Dien Bien Phu to Lai Chau to Sapa and back to Hanoi. This route is adventurous and allows for some great exploring, but it's a challenge: five or more days on rutted mountain roads is not for everyone. Make a run to the Chinese border near Lang Son, or stop at Ba Be Lake on the way back to Hanoi for a leisurely few days in this stunningly remote nature preserve. You'll have to have some idea of your itinerary before leaving Hanoi, however; your driver will want to know how long he'll be away from home.

The easiest way to see the north is to base yourself in Hanoi or Haiphong, from which you can take two- or three-day trips. Using this method is highly recommended because it gives you a way to appreciate northern Vietnam without the discomforts of one endless, grueling road trip. You can either arrange these trips yourself or sign up with tour operators. Some destinations are too far for day trips, but you can easily hire a car or jeep to head there and back, or to get to Sapa, you can hop on the relatively comfortable overnight train from Hanoi.

Tours organized by Hanoi's tourist cafés cover the more popular destinations and are the most inexpensive and time-efficient way to see this region. Large travel agencies in Hanoi such as Vietnam Tourism, Saigon Tourist, and Exotissimo Travel (☞ Hanoi A to Z *in* Chapter 2) arrange tours that are more expensive and, perhaps, more comfortable. Lodging, transportation, entrance fees to sites, and most meals are usually included. If you don't want to be stuck with a group of strangers (tourist cafés usually fill up a minivan or larger—from 6 to 20 people; international tour companies and the large tour operators inside the country try to fill up coach buses—from 15 to 40 people), you're better off renting a car with a driver from your hotel or a tour agency. If you'd like to be in control of every single aspect of the trip, including driving, your best bet is to rent a motorbike.

Numbers in the text correspond to numbers in the margin and on The North map.

Great Itineraries

Destinations in the north can be grouped into two geographic categories: the lowland areas in and around the Red River delta, and the Hoang Lien Mountains, or Tonkinese Alps. If you have more than four days, it's quite easy to venture into both regions. You can reach the delightful scenery on the coast, specifically Halong Bay and Cat Ba, from Hanoi in as little as four hours. Travel in the mountains is usually slower and requires more patience, but you'll soon discover that heading up into the northern highlands brings you into another world: a world of rugged and austere beauty, fascinating cultures, and timeless traditions.

IF YOU HAVE 3 DAYS

If you don't have much time in the north, start with ⛰ **Halong Bay** ③. From Hanoi you can easily get to this jewel in northern Vietnam's topographical crown. Hire a car from the capital or go with an organized trip and head east to Halong City, where you can hop on one of dozens of tour boats that shuttle you around the thousands of limestone islands. Stay in one of the many hotels in town, or if adventure is your modus operandi, spend the night on the boat. From here catch a ferry to **Cat Ba Island** ④, the largest in the Halong Bay region and site of one of Vietnam's most beautiful national parks. Either return to your car in Halong City or take the high-speed ferry back to Haiphong, where you can catch the train or a minibus back to Hanoi.

IF YOU HAVE 6 DAYS

Travel from Hanoi to ⛰ **Sapa** ⑫ and spend three days exploring the mountain trails that lead to ethnic-minority villages. Head to the popular market, where members of ethnic groups such as the Red Dao and the H'mong gather to buy provisions and sell fabrics and clothing. You can see Sapa in a day's travel to and from Hanoi—or book a soft sleeper on the night train from the capital. If you've hired a four-wheel-drive vehicle to Sapa, consider an overnight side trip to the remote but incredibly beautiful ⛰ **Ba Be Lakes** ⑦.

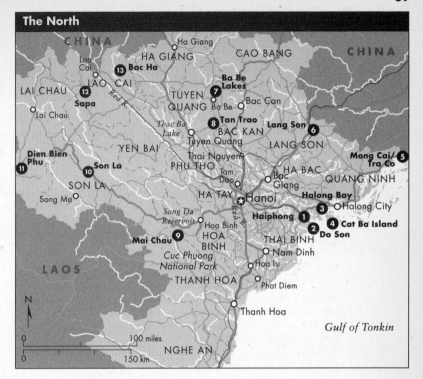

IF YOU HAVE 9 DAYS

If you have more than a week and can stand being in a car for many hours on rough roads, traveling through the farthest reaches of the north can be a true adventure. Hire a four-wheel-drive vehicle and driver, and do a circuit of this dramatic highland region. From Hanoi head for ⊞ **Mai Chau** ⑨; you'll pass the impressive Hoa Binh Hydroelectric Power Dam on the way. Stay overnight in the lovely minority villages near Mai Chau or push on to ⊞ **Son La** ⑩. From here head through spectacular valleys to infamous ⊞ **Dien Bien Phu** ⑪, near the Laotian border, to explore the ruins of the French garrison. Wind your way over the bumpy roads past scenic and laid-back Lai Chau to ⊞ **Sapa** ⑫ and **Bac Ha** ⑬, and then take a full day's drive back to Hanoi. Or break up the journey back by stopping at the ⊞ **Ba Be Lakes** ⑦. An alternative itinerary is to take the return train from Hanoi to Sapa, take a two-day jaunt to Mai Chau from the capital, and fly from Hanoi to Dien Bien Phu. For the last few days head to the crystal-clear waters of ⊞ **Halong Bay** ③.

When to Tour the North

The best time to tour the northern highlands is from late October to mid-December, after the August–October monsoons have abated and any mud slides are likely to have been cleared. As for Halong Bay, the season runs from early summer to mid-autumn. From July to September beware of tropical typhoons; flooding in Haiphong and Hanoi is common during these storms. The capital is hot and extremely humid in summer, which makes it a popular time for residents to head for the hills or the coast.

Beach season—which occurs mainly south of Haiphong at Do Son— is mid-summer, when hotels are filled with vacationing Hanoians who for some reason seem to love the extremely narrow and dirty beaches.

The season culminates with the Do Son buffalo fights. By late October the place is virtually deserted. If you want the beach resort entirely to yourself, go to Do Son in November.

Northern Vietnam has a clearly defined winter, with a cold and clammy mist settling in for a few months starting in January. January and February are quite cold in the mountains, and Mt. Fansipan, Vietnam's highest peak, is occasionally dusted with snow. If you're heading into the highlands in winter and intend to do some trekking, come prepared: a light sweater, a waterproof jacket, a wool hat, long johns, and some insulated hiking boots should keep you warm.

During Tet, the lunar new year, you'll find northern Vietnam cold and drizzly but extremely festive. If you're coming during this time, make plane and hotel reservations very early. Also understand that many tour operations, such as trips to Halong Bay, are severely limited or suspended during this period.

THE NORTHEAST

Natural beauty and nationalized industry share the spotlight in Vietnam's northeast. Take Quang Ninh Province as an example. Halong Bay and the rest of coastal Quang Ninh are battling with the province's expanding coal-mining industry over precious natural resources. A UNESCO World Heritage Site, Halong Bay is a breathtaking collection of limestone islands and secluded coves that captured the imagination and the fancy of millions who saw the movie *Indochine,* starring Catherine Deneuve.

What was once a poor, struggling fishing village catering primarily to Communist Party officials has become the premier vacation spot in the north. Horsepower has long since replaced wind as the means of transport through the bay, and hotels have sprouted like weeds in Halong City, but the emerald waters and mysterious caves of this natural wonder continue to enchant. Just north of Halong Bay lies the gritty, soot-coated town of Cam Pha, the center of Vietnam's coal industry and a threat to the fragile ecosystem of the coast.

Similar destinies and dilemmas face Haiphong. Once the sleepy second cousin to the booming port of Saigon, Haiphong is emerging as more than just Vietnam's second-largest port. The city is awakening to the prospect of both tourism and the rapid development of import-export channels. Tree-lined boulevards, expansive green parks, and impressive if crumbling French colonial architecture fill the downtown. To the north of the city center, 10,000-ton freighters unload containers bound for Hanoi and load up with Vietnamese exports. A new deep-sea port, farther downstream from Haiphong, is scheduled to be fully operational by 2005.

International trade of a slightly different sort dominates the Wild West atmosphere of Lang Son and Mong Cai, two boomtowns on the Chinese border northeast of Hanoi. Nearly abandoned after retreating Chinese troops leveled them during a brief border war in 1979, the towns have risen again. Little animosity seems to remain between the two nations, which have normalized relations and opened border crossings, and cross-border trade—much of it illicit—is bustling. East of Mong Cai is Tra Co, northern Vietnam's most pristine stretch of beach.

Haiphong

❶ *103 km (64 mi) east of Hanoi on Hwy. 5.*

Haiphong, today Vietnam's third-largest city, with a population of more than 1.6 million, has been a hub of the north's industrial activity for the last century and one of its most significant seaports since the Tran dynasty ruled (1225–1400). Because of its strategic location, this port city has seen the coming and going of many foreign invaders. The Bach Dang River, on the outskirts of present-day Haiphong, was the site of one of Vietnam's greatest victories over forces from China: Kublai Khan's 300,000-man army and navy were soundly trumped by Vietnamese under the command of Tran Hung Dao in 1288. Six hundred years later the French settled into Haiphong and began turning it into a major industrial and shipping center. Following the German occupation of France in World War II, the Japanese muscled into Haiphong and began directing valuable Vietnamese exports back to Japan. Once again in control of the port city after the war, the French bombed Haiphong over a bizarre customs dispute, killing up to 1,000 Vietnamese civilians and precipitating the eight-year war between the Vietminh and the French.

Haiphong figured prominently in the war against the Americans as well. Because of its strategic location on the northeast coast, the city was often bombed during the Vietnam War and suffered particularly devastating attacks during the 1972 holiday season that became known as the Christmas bombings. President Richard Nixon ordered the mining of Haiphong Harbor in May 1972. The U.S. Navy was asked to help clear the mines as part of the agreement between the U.S. government and Vietnam in the Paris peace talks of 1973.

In 1979, following conflicts between Vietnam and China, as many as 100,000 ethnic Chinese who had lived for generations in the Haiphong area piled into barely seaworthy boats and fled from what they expected to be deadly reprisals by their Vietnamese neighbors. Few acts of retribution took place, but the damage had been done. Haiphong has struggled to gain back much of its economic power lost because the large section of the merchant class that was Chinese left the city.

Now there is little visible evidence of Haiphong's troubled past, except perhaps the French architecture—much of it delightful—that can be spotted throughout the city center. The city's powerful People's Committee is too busy finding funding for its new deep-sea port and other massive projects to linger over past sentiments.

Haiphong's reputation as a dingy industrial port is not entirely justified. This is indeed the largest and busiest port in the north, and container trucks rumble through town on the way to Highway 5 and Hanoi. But the port itself is on the northern edge of the city and hugs the Cam River, away from the heart of the city. As you cross the Lac Long Bridge into the city center, you leave the dusty and bustling outskirts (where most of the industry with its factories is based) and slip into a quaint, clean downtown. Here huge banyan trees and blossoming magnolias line wide boulevards, and Vietnamese play badminton in the stately Central Square (Quang Truong). Walking through the city center feels like stepping into a time warp: portraits of revolutionary heroes, especially Ho Chi Minh, hang elegantly from the eaves of buildings; socialist realist propaganda posters announce the latest health-awareness campaign; and swarms of bicycles fill the streets.

Today you are most likely to use Haiphong as a transfer point to destinations like Cat Ba, Do Son (both actually part of greater Haiphong), and Halong Bay. Here you can catch a cyclo to the port, and take the first boat out. If you have time, however, settle into an enjoyable two-day stay in Haiphong before moving farther afield. Some say it is what Hanoi was like not too long ago: a sleepy northern city with less traffic and less nightlife, but bursting with potential. Even if you're in town for a half day, make the best of your time by picking up the excellent Haiphong Tourist Map at one of the major hotels and then walking around downtown. Or head to Vietnam Tourism (☞ The Northeast A to Z, *below*), a somewhat helpful operation that can find you a hotel, hire a car and driver, and answer questions about ferry and train schedules.

Exploring Haiphong

It's very easy to navigate central Haiphong. Sidewalks on the main boulevards are wide, and the parks and gardens provide ample room to roam. If you've come to Haiphong by car and plan to spend a leisurely day sightseeing, have the driver park at a hotel and then go for a long walk.

Shady, green **An Bien Park,** framed by Tran Phu and Tran Hung Dao streets, is the site of early morning tai chi classes. At night strolling couples compete with roller skaters, and locals sit at sidewalk stalls drinking fruit shakes and eating sweets. Near the southwestern edge stands a massive statue of local heroine Le Chan, and a colorful **Flower Market** blooms daily. Kids enjoy the playground and amusement rides in the attached **Children's Park**.

At the intersection of Hoang Van Thu and Tran Hung Dao streets ★ stands one of the most beautiful buildings in Haiphong: the **City Theater** (Nha Hat Thanh Pho). Built by the French in 1907, this theater has all the exterior designs of a classic, except for its coat of splendidly pink paint. Once the site of lavish French and Vietnamese productions, the 400-seat theater was taken over by the Vietminh following World War II. President Ho Chi Minh addressed the world's youth in a June 1946 speech from the steps. A huge likeness of Ho now hangs above the wooden front doors—the painting is visible from hundreds of yards away and feels eerily like the focal point of the city. In a way it is; the Haiphong People's Committee now holds its major meetings and assemblies here. Stage productions and concerts do take place, but they're rare. If you're not attending a show, you need written permission from the Department of Culture and Information (☎ 031/745–763) to step inside. ✉ *Between Hoang Van Thu St. and Dinh Tien Hoang St.* ⏲ *Not open to public except for performances or with special permission.*

In the heart of the city, a huge shuttered French villa with creaky wooden staircases, musty corners, and occasionally rotating ceiling fans houses the **Haiphong Museum** (Bao Tang Thanh Pho Hai Phong)—an underrated gem of a building that rivals the City Theater in "pinkness." Although it attempts to cover all of the history, geography, archaeology, agriculture, and wildlife of the region (the stuffed owl with a rodent in its claws is rather macabre), the museum focuses on Vietnam's struggle for independence from various forces. Little is in English, so bring a good guide or be prepared to do some guesswork. ✉ *66 Dien Bien Phu St.,* ☎ *no phone.* 🎫 *2,000d.* ⏲ *Tues. and Thurs. 8 AM–10:30 AM, Wed. and Sun. 8 PM–9:30 PM. Museum will open at other times for groups who call in advance.*

As might be expected of a city whose name means "sea defense," much of Haiphong's more intriguing history is documented in the **Naval Museum.** Here you can see the Bach Dang stakes—the sharp wooden poles driven into the riverbed that impaled Kublai Khan's boats in 1288. A room dedicated to the Vietnam War houses a (presumably deactivated) MK-52 mine pulled from the waters of Haiphong Harbor in 1973, the lighthouse lantern that warned of impending bombing raids, and the antiaircraft gun that brought down a dozen U.S. planes. ⊠ *38 Dien Bien Phu St.,* ☎ *031/822–788.* ⊡ *Free.* ☉ *Tues., Thurs., and Sat. 8 AM–11 AM.*

Haiphong's pagodas are tucked into the city's alleyways or off in the suburbs; no major religious structures except the **Large Cathedral** (Nha Tho Lon) stand out in the middle of town. The cathedral was built in 1880 by Catholic missionaries from Spain; a regular mass is still held. ⊠ *46 Hoang Van Thu St.,* ☎ *no phone.* ⊡ *Free.* ☉ *Daily 7:30 AM– 10:30 PM.*

★ Some beautiful pagodas stand in the southern and eastern districts of the city. The most impressive and moving of these is the **Du Hang Pagoda.** This 300-year-old temple is a good example of traditional Vietnamese architecture. A gate and three buildings surround a stone courtyard crowded with flowers, statues, and bonsai plants. In front and to the right of the compound is a round pond with lotus flowers encircled by white statues of the Buddha and scholars. One of the 10 monks who live here may be chanting his daily prayers and tapping on a round wooden drum in the richly gilded main sanctuary. Occasionally in the afternoons, the senior monk holds one-on-one healing sessions with the sick. Hundreds of Buddhists fill the courtyard on Buddhist holy days, the 1st and 15th of every lunar month. To get here follow Cat Cut Street south until you hit Chua Hang Street. After a few alleyways you'll see the pagoda set back on the left. ⊠ *Off Chua Hang St.,* ☎ *no phone.* ⊡ *Free.* ☉ *Daily 5 AM–11:30 AM and 1:30 PM–9:30 PM.*

Quiet **Nghe Temple** (Den Nghe) is dedicated to Le Chan, a heroic peasant woman who helped organize the popular revolt against the Chinese that was led by the two Trung sisters in AD 40 (☞ Vietnam at a Glance: A Chronology *in* Chapter 9). Later Le Chan helped lay the foundation for the city of Haiphong. Ceramic reliefs at the top of the front wall depict the Trung sisters in royal carriages. Two huge red-and-gold wooden carriages (built in 1916), similar to those used by the Trung sisters and by royalty, are on display. Ancestral altars and chapels are to the right, through the courtyard. ⊠ *Corner of Me Linh and Le Chan Sts.,* ☎ *no phone.* ⊡ *Free.* ☉ *Daily 7–11:30 and 1–10.*

Before repulsing invaders in AD 938, Emperor Ngo Quyen allegedly gathered his armies at the **Drawing Pagoda** (Chua Ve). Similarly, General Tran Hung Dao spied on enemy Chinese troops from a perch on the pagoda grounds and then drew the battle maps that would help him orchestrate a commanding victory in 1288 against Kublai Khan— hence the pagoda's name. Eight Buddhist nuns currently reside here. ⊠ *Behind Holiday Mansion Hotel on Danang St.,* ☎ *no phone.* ⊡ *Free.* ☉ *Daily 7–11:30 and 1–6.*

Dining and Lodging

For a city of 1.6 million people, Haiphong doesn't have many upscale restaurants. Local seafood is excellent and cheap, however, and available at any number of small, nondescript, family-run establishments. A few of the better-known ones are listed here, as are the handful of international restaurants on Dien Bien Phu Street. Restaurants specializing in fish cluster around the north end of Rau Bridge (Cau Rau), a few miles from the city center on the road south to Do Son. Most restaurants close by 10 PM.

Haiphong has little of the style or variety of accommodations available in Hanoi and Ho Chi Minh City—yet. A few international hotels have opened up, but a relative lack of choice makes it easy to decide where to stay (on Dien Bien Phu Street, most likely). It also increases the likelihood that your first choice may be booked. Call ahead if you know your travel dates. If you're shopping around for hotels in person, *definitely* ask to see the room before you hand over your cash; a peculiarly arbitrary pricing system seems to have taken hold in Haiphong, and smaller $20 rooms are often much more pleasant than larger $35 rooms in the same hotel. And keep in mind that almost none of the rates are written in stone—meaning you may be able to make a deal.

$$–$$$$ ✕ **Trung Hoa Restaurant.** This hotel restaurant serves the best Peking duck in town. Other offerings from the Chinese menu include stir-fried meat, vegetable and tofu dishes, seafood, and soup. The dining room is rather dingy and uninspired, but that doesn't seem to dissuade the many Chinese tour groups who dine here. ⊠ *Hoa Binh Hotel, 104 Luong Khanh Thien St.,* ☎ *031/846–909. No credit cards.*

$–$$$ ✕ **Chie Japanese Restaurant.** English and pictures on the menu make ordering the best Japanese food in the city simple, and the staff won't hesitate to suggest a favorite. Recessed tables and red Japanese lanterns make the place seem a little closer to Tokyo than northern Vietnam. Take your shoes off and relax for a while. ⊠ *64 Dien Bien Phu St.,* ☎ *031/821–018. No credit cards.*

$–$$ ✕ **Lucky Restaurant.** The menu at this simple but popular restaurant is eclectic, with dishes ranging from fresh seafood and Vietnamese-style stewed bear in ginseng to French soups and Central European classics. The owner, who lived in East Germany for 11 years, speaks fluent English and German. ⊠ *22 B2 Minh Khai St.,* ☎ *031/842–009. No credit cards.*

$$$$ 🏨 **Harbour View Hotel.** With its French colonial architecture—there's even an antique Citroën in the driveway—this hotel is Haiphong's one-and-only luxury lodging choice. Rooms here are spacious and tastefully decorated, with plenty of delicate touches and welcome amenities such as IDD phones. The hotel can arrange tours of city sights and Halong Bay, as well as bicycle and trekking trips through the surrounding countryside. ⊠ *4 Tran Phu St.,* ☎ *031/827–827,* 𝔽𝔸𝕏 *031/827–828,* 𝖶𝖤𝖡 *www.harbourviewvietnam.com. 127 rooms. 2 restaurants, in-room data ports, in-room safes, minibars, cable TV, gym, massage, bicycles, bar, shop, laundry service, concierge, business services, meeting rooms, travel services. AE, DC, MC, V. CP.*

$$$–$$$$ 🏨 **Tray Hotel.** With clean and spacious rooms, a rooftop restaurant and pool, and a glorious light-filled atrium stretching the entire length of the building, this is clearly the best locally run hotel in Haiphong. Rooms at the back have pleasant views over a park and lake, and all come equipped with IDD phones and satellite TVs. ⊠ *47 Lach Tray St.,* ☎ *031/828–555 or 031/828–222,* 𝔽𝔸𝕏 *031/828–666. 78 rooms. Restaurant, in-room safes, minibars, cable TV, pool, gym, hair salon, massage, sauna, bar, laundry service, business services, meeting rooms. AE, MC, V.*

$ 🏨 **Haiphong Hotel.** Sparkling new but poorly located to the southeast of the city center, this hotel charges reasonable rates for clean and bright rooms with tile floors, wooden furniture, and IDD phones. The staff is friendly but speaks only very basic English. ⊠ *123 Nguyen Binh Khiem St.,* ☎ *031/731–444,* 𝔽𝔸𝕏 *031/731–456,* 𝖶𝖤𝖡 *www.vietnamtourism. com/haiphonghotel. 50 rooms. Restaurant, minibars, cable TV, gym, hair salon, massage, sauna, billiards, bar, laundry service, Internet, car rental, travel services. MC, V.*

$ 🏨 **Navy Guest House.** The rooms in this guest house and the affiliated La Villa Blanche are clean, if unexciting and overpriced. There's little distinction between the standard and superior rooms, so you may want to take the less expensive option. Breakfast is included in the price, and rooms have IDD phones. The restaurant serves Vietnamese, European, and Chinese food. ⊠ *27C Dien Bien Phu St.,* ☎ *031/842–856*

Navy Guest House; 031/842–863 La Villa Blanche; FAX *031/842–278. 100 rooms. Restaurant, refrigerators, tennis court, bar, laundry service, business services. MC, V. CP.*

¢–$ ☎ **Bach Dang Hotel.** Noise pollution from the street and nearby karaoke parlors aside, the rooms here are pleasant, if simple, with pale colors, blue bathrooms, and IDD phones. Try to get one in the back for a bit more quiet. The hotel and its adjacent restaurant are popular with Chinese tour groups. ⊠ *42 Dien Bien Phu St.,* ☎ *031/842–444,* FAX *031/ 841–625. 34 rooms. Restaurant, cable TV, massage, sauna, bar, laundry service, business center. No credit cards.*

Nightlife

If you've got a good set of lungs, you'll be the hit of Haiphong. Every block has its requisite half dozen karaoke clubs, and many hotels are blessed with them as well. The island on Quan Ngua Lake, behind the Tray Hotel, is currently nightlife central, with a dozen or so discos, rhumba and tango clubs, pool halls, bars, and cafés.

Do Son Casino (⊠ Zone 3, Do Son, ☎ 031/861–888) is close enough that you may want to make the trip (☞ Do Son, *below*). The dark **Haiphong Club** (⊠ 17 Tran Quang Khai St., ☎ 031/822–603) hosts live rock music. **Maxim's Bar** (⊠ 51B Dien Bien Phu St., ☎ 031/822– 934) is a café by day and bar by night, with live pop and rock music from 9 PM each evening. The **Saigon Café** (⊠ 107 Dien Bien Phu St., ☎ 031/822–195), Haiphong's version of the corner pub, is popular with locals, expats, and travelers.

Haiphong A to Z

For information on arriving and departing from Haiphong, *see* The Northeast A to Z, *below.*

BICYCLE TRAVEL

Seeing downtown Haiphong by bike is almost idyllic. Unfortunately there are few places to rent them. Harbour View Hotel rents bicycles for $5 a day. Ask your hotel staff if they can recommend other places that rent bicycles.

CYCLO TRAVEL

Haiphong cyclos are often large enough for two Westerners, and you can find them just about anywhere you go. They're great during the calm of midday or later in the evening when the streets are empty; riding one in the hectic and slow evening rush hour is not advised. Cyclo riders will be happy to cart you around this flat city for an entire day for about 30,000d.

MOTORBIKE TAXIS

If you're here without wheels and want to see some pagodas outside the city center, a lift on the back of a motorbike (*xe om*) may be your best option—especially if you're pressed for time. Prices are comparable to fees for cyclos, and you can find them all over town. You'll arrive more quickly than in a three-wheeler but probably more frazzled.

TAXIS

You probably won't need to take a taxi except to get from the train station to your hotel or to the ferry landing. Taxi companies have figured this out, and plenty wait outside the Haiphong Railway Station and at the ferry landing. Try Mai Link or Taxi 84 Company to arrange a ride by phone.

➤ CONTACT: **Mai Link** (☎ 031/833–666). **Taxi 84 Company** (☎ 031/ 848–484).

Do Son

❷ *21 km (13 mi) southeast of Haiphong, 124 km (77 mi) southeast of Hanoi.*

This rapidly overbuilt seaside resort was but a quaint fishing village in the mid-1990s. Today the oceanfront is packed with dozens of hotels. Vietnamese, particularly Hanoians, flock here in midsummer to escape the sweltering heat. Many come to soak up some sun, meander on the promenade, and feast on fresh seafood. Others come for what is euphemistically called "Thai massage," a growing industry in Do Son that has yet to be clamped down. And still others come to swim in the murky waters. The ocean here isn't so much polluted as it is discolored by river silt wash making its way down the coast from Haiphong. But it doesn't make for great beach bathing. Nevertheless, in June, July, and August rooms can be hard to come by. Nearly the entire town is booked up for one week in September during the Do Son Buffalo Fighting Festival. By late autumn beachgoers have completely vacated the place.

The promontory that rises above the finger of land on which Do Son sits provides wonderful views of the fishing harbor on the inland side and of the village itself to the north. The major presence atop the hillside is the **Do Son Casino** (⌧ Zone 3, ☎ 031/861–888), the only casino in a country where gambling is technically illegal. The way around this rule is to limit entry to only those with a foreign passport. Slot machines fill the first of two rooms. In the back hall, roulette, blackjack, baccarat, and *tai siiu* (big and small) are offered. There are few people playing; the staff usually outnumbers the guests.

The beautiful French colonial **Palace of Emperor Bao Dai** has been restored to its original condition, including antique furnishings and household objects. English-language signs in this villa describe the history and use of each room. Bao Dai, who ascended the Vietnamese throne in 1925 at the age of 12, ruled under French colonial control. ⌧ *Atop promontory overlooking Zone 2,* ☎ *031/862–303 or 031/862–304.* 🖃 *20,000d.* ⊙ *Daily 7 AM–8 PM.*

You can spend a few pleasant hours exploring the tiny Buddhist temples and wooded slopes of **Dau Island,** a 10-minute boat ride from Do Son beach. A short walk up to the lighthouse on the highest point lets you take in views of the coast and casino, and on the way you may even be rewarded with glimpses of wild monkeys among the trees. To get here charter a boat from any of the beaches around Do Son for around $20 round-trip. 🖃 *Hill climb 3,000d.*

Each year the village gears up for its famous **Do Son Buffalo Fighting Festival,** a semireligious festival honoring local patron saint Diem Tuoc Dai Vuong, also known as the Great Footprint King. The one-day event, obviously not for animal lovers, takes place on the ninth day of the lunar month, usually in about mid-September. Legend has it that on that date in the 1400s, two old men sat playing chess on nearby Nghe Mountain while two buffalos fought below. One of the men turned out to be a saint who left his birdlike footprint on an altar tray, thus identifying himself as the Great Footprint King. This tale may not have much to do with buffalos, but it was enough to start a tradition that draws thousands of people to Hai Phong and Do Son to gamble on the fights.

On the day of the fight, the buffalos are led into the stadium in a procession with gongs and drums. Two buffalos face off against each other, thundering toward each other from a distance of 650 ft. The fights last anywhere from 10 seconds (sometimes the hit from a first charge is deadly) to 15 minutes. This continues all day until only two bulls remain. The thousands of spectators place their own secret bets. Others are not so clandestine; entire villages, which come to see bulls groomed by their neighbors, may put communal bets of up to $10,000 on the line. After the final battle all the participating buffalos are slaughtered for a victory feast, and the winner's head is paraded around the town.

Lodging

The fresh seafood in Do Son is superb. Most family restaurants lining the beach road in Zones 1 and 2 serve the day's fresh catch. Prices and quality are fairly consistent, so pick a place with an English menu and start ordering. The same cannot be said for the hotels, which for the most part serve mediocre food. Most of the hotels were built quickly in the mid-'90s to accommodate growing numbers of visitors.

$$ 🏨 **The Garden Resort & Hotel.** Gambling may never be so easy in Vietnam once—or if—this hotel is completed. This flashy spot, owned by the developers of Do Son Casino, is just down the hill from gambling central. Under construction for several years, the hotel was scheduled for completion by mid-2003. Plans originally called for a 350-room megacomplex, but the project has been toned down to a 100-room affair. Call the casino (☎ 031/861–888) for inquiries. ✉ *Zone 3, Do Son. 100 rooms. Pool, tennis court, massage, dance club.*

¢–$ 🏨 **Hai Au Hotel.** This uninspired structure is where the Do Son Casino currently shuttles its patrons after an evening of vice (where people can continue their wicked ways at the hotel by taking advantage of free karaoke). Rooms are musty, and it's never a good sign when the porter looks down and scans the floor the moment he turns on the lights. One plus: it's only 150 yards from the beach. ✉ *Zone 2,* ☎ *031/861–222,* FAX *031/861–186. 50 rooms. Restaurant. AE, DC, MC, V. CP.*

Halong Bay

★ ❸ *175 km (109 mi) east of Hanoi, 55 km (34 mi) northeast of Haiphong.*

Halong Bay's 3,000 islands of dolomite and limestone cover a 1,500-square-km (580-square-mi) area extending across the Gulf of Tonkin nearly to the Chinese border. According to legend this breathtaking land-and seascape was formed by a giant dragon that came barreling out of the mountains toward the ocean—hence the name Halong, which translates into "descent of the dragon." Geologists are more likely to attribute the formations to sedimentary limestone that formed here between 300 and 500 million years ago, in the Paleozoic Era. Over millions of years water receded and exposed the limestone to winds, rain, and tidal erosion.

Today the limestone formations are exposed to hordes of tourists—but don't let that discourage you. Hundreds of fishing trawlers and tour boats share space on these crystal waters, yet there seems to be room for everyone. The eons of erosion have left countless nooks and crannies to explore: secluded half-moon beaches lie at the base of steep untouched forest canopies, and grottoes of all shapes and sizes—some well trampled, others virtually unknown—are open jaws of stalactites and stalagmites. One of the largest and most visited is the **Grotto of the Wooden Stakes** (Hang Dau Go), claimed to be the 13th-century storage spot for the stakes that General Tran Hung Dao planted in the Bach Dang River in order to repel the invasion of Kublai Khan. This cavernous grotto has three distinct chambers and is reached by climbing 90 steps. Another quite popular destination in the bay is the **Grotto** of **Bewilderment** (Sung Sot), a stalagmite cave, estimated to be 1 million years old, with 29 chambers inside.

Most people use the main population center, **Halong City,** as a base from which to venture into the bay. Although it's now officially one municipality, Halong City was until 1996 two separate towns: Bai Chay is now Halong City West, where Halong Road winds its way around the coast and past the lifeless central beach; Hon Gai is the grimier Halong City East, where a coal transportation station dominates the center of town and covers nearby roads and buildings with a sooty film. Locals still refer to the towns by their old names. A five-minute ferry ride (500d per person, 7,000d per car) across the mouth of a large inlet links the two communities. Plans for a bridge have been tossed around, but construction has yet to begin.

If you think the mouth of this inlet is a busy place now, just wait a few years, when construction is likely to move full speed ahead on massive Cai Lan, a deep-water port to be built inside Bai Chay Bay. Millions of tons of coal will be delivered on barges through the straits of Bai Chay to a nearby thermal-power plant. It all sounds like an environmental nightmare, and there has been discussion about UNESCO's possibly revoking Halong Bay's status as a World Heritage Site.

Boat trips through Halong Bay are the main attraction. Little of the majesty of this region can be found in the city, so head out onto the water and start exploring. Numerous 10- and 30-ft fishing boats have been converted into Halong Bay's tourist-boat fleet. Hotels or travel agencies in Halong Bay or Hanoi can arrange boat trips for you (often they are part of organized tours from Hanoi), or you can go down to the wharf and bargain yourself onto a boat for the day—although this is becoming more and more difficult. Boats can be had for anywhere from $4 to $20 per hour; if you're going to be out on the bay all day, see if the boat owner will knock 20% off the hourly rate. Unfortunately, if you are making arrangements yourself you may find it's not that simple. An organized ring of boat masters does its best to guide you onto their boats of choice and charge you what they want—even if the creaky dinosaur looks like it's already seen its last three-hour tour. Self-sufficient travelers have fallen victim to the old bait-and-switch: they've arranged a next-day boat tour with local fishermen, only to be told in no uncertain terms the following morning that they could not board their chosen boat, but they could take a different one for quite a bit more money. You may have no choice in the end. Usually travel agencies, however, have their tried-and-true favorites.

Dining and Lodging

Halong is drowning in superb seafood. Specialties include boiled or grilled shrimp, sweet-and-sour fish, and fried squid, washed down with beer. Crabs, sautéed beef with vegetables, and chicken dishes are also readily available. Halong Road and the center of town are crowded with eateries—just look for the sidewalk fish tanks.

Most visitors overnight in Halong City West. The larger hotels, some of which are listed below, are slightly less tacky than the average downtown minihotel, which can be had for $20 or less. The posh hotels offer a 50% discount in summer. Sleeping on a fishing boat in Halong Bay is au courant among today's adventure travelers and can be arranged by most tour agencies; note, however, that the boats are moored close to land, so there's always a risk of bandits.

$-$$ ✕ **Lavender.** With its open front and fish tanks on display, Lavender (Thuy Hien) resembles many other nearby restaurants. But inside, the bamboo-covered walls and green tablecloths make this restaurant more pleasant than its competitors. As you might expect, seafood dominates the menu, but the imaginative owner has added a few of his own creations to the standard fried fish and squid, such as the subtly flavored shrimp steamed in a split coconut. ✉ *99 Halong Rd.,* ☎ *033/846–185. No credit cards.*

$$$$ 🏨 **Halong Plaza Hotel.** A glass-fronted entryway looks out onto the bay from the spacious front lobby at this modern luxury hotel close to the ferry landing. Most of the rooms also have views of the bay, although some face the more industrial back side. All are comfortable and clean, with wood-trimmed beige walls and floral linens. Bathrooms in deluxe rooms have a sunken bath, Jacuzzi, and glorious sea-views—surely the most opulent bathing in town. ✉ *8 Halong Rd.,* ☎ *033/845–810,* ℻ *033/846–867. 105 rooms. Restaurant, minibars, cable TV, pool, gym, massage, bar, laundry service, meeting rooms. AE, MC, V.*

$$$$ 🏨 **Heritage Halong.** This eight-floor glitzy international hotel fronting a nondescript stretch of beach soaks up much of the package-tour business in Halong Bay. Rooms are clean and have IDD phones; those on the top floors in front have lovely views of the distant islands. ✉ *88 Halong Rd.,* ☎ *033/846–888,* ℻ *033/846–999,* 🌐 *heritagehotel.halong. net.vn. 101 rooms. Restaurant, café, in-room safes, minibars, cable TV, pool, massage, sauna, laundry service, meeting rooms. AE, MC, V.*

$–$$ 🏨 **Halong I Hotel.** A French colonial restoration with a circular drive-
★ way and arched open-air passageways leading to the reception area, this grande dame of Halong properties evokes a more sublime era. The whole place is peaceful, and the front verandas are great for sipping tea and playing cards after dinner. Book the Catherine Deneuve Room if you can. The room that the French überstar stayed in while filming *Indochine* tops the price list, but it has an in-room fax and two toilets. Nearby are the affiliated Halong II and Halong III hotels, with less charm and lower prices; the three hotels share booking and reception. ✉ *Halong Rd.,* ☎ *033/846–320 or 033/846–321,* ℻ *033/846–318. Halong I, 23 rooms; Halong II, 38 rooms; Halong III, 56 rooms. 2 restaurants, minibars, cable TV, tennis court, pool, bar, laundry service, travel services. AE, MC, V.*

$ 🏨 **Vuon Dao Hotel.** Ask for one of the top-floor rooms with a view of the sea at this three-story hotel run by Halong Tourist Company, the state-run travel agency. Rooms have IDD phones, and breakfast is included in the room rate. ✉ *Halong Rd.,* ☎ *033/846–427,* ℻ *033/846–287,* 🌐 *www.vietnamhotelinfo.com. 77 rooms. Restaurant, cable TV, laundry service. MC, V. CP.*

Cat Ba Island

❹ *At southern end of Halong Bay, 30 km (19 mi) east of Haiphong by boat.*

One of Halong Bay's most remarkable formations is Cat Ba Island, 420 square km (162 square mi) of wildly steep spines of mountains, narrow valleys and waterfalls, lush wetlands, golden beaches, and one of Vietnam's most beautiful national parks, which protects about two-thirds of the island. The sea life in much of the surrounding inshore waters is also protected. Included in these ecosystems are tropical evergreen forests, 15 kinds of mammals (including wild boars and hedgehogs), 200 species of fish, 21 species of birds, and 640 species of plants. Don't expect to see many wild mammals, such as the endangered monkeys that supposedly swing from the trees.

In 1938 a French archaeologist found traces of an ancient fishing culture on the island dating from the end of the Neolithic Era. Human bones alleged to be 6,000 years old were also found. More recently, during the

Vietnam War, American bombers targeted the military and naval station here, causing numerous casualties and forcing hospitals to set up in nearby caves on the island to avoid the bombings. An ethnic Chinese community numbering about 10,000 settled on Cat Ba over the years, only to leave en masse in 1979 after Chinese troops invaded Vietnam in the brief but bloody border war of that year. The ethnic Chinese, or Hoa, sailed in dinghies to Hong Kong and other Asian ports, many dying along the way. Few ethnic Chinese have returned to Cat Ba.

Today the population of more than 12,000 continues to subsist on fishing and rice and fruit cultivation, but tourism is quickly becoming Cat Ba's primary cash crop. The beaches, particularly the lovely curved stretch of sand just over the hillside from the southeast corner of the wharf, are infinitely nicer than Do Son's. Walk off your seafood dinner by heading to the nearest beach, where you can sip iced coffee and watch the shooting stars. Splendid caves, just off the road to the national park, are great for exploring. One such spot is **Trung Tang cave,** a strategic haven for the North Vietnamese Army in the Vietnam War.

Hiking through Cat Ba can be strenuous: the mountain ridges are steep, trails are poorly marked, and roads are narrow, making blind crests somewhat dangerous. Talk to your hotel manager or one of the many local tour operators about the best hiking trails for your level. A hike through the park—through the tropical forest to a rocky peak overlooking much of the island—is best done with a guide. The park is also a favorite spot for Vietnamese tourists, many of whom seem to be able to scale the slippery rocks in stiletto heels.

Ferries and hydrofoils connect Haiphong to the island, and minihotels have sprouted in the town of Cat Ba, the island's main commercial center, to accommodate the growing numbers of tourists. They're all relatively clean and incredibly cheap. New bars blare teenybopper music and serve chilled margaritas.

Just about any of the hotels can arrange for car or minibus tours of the island and rides to the national park. You can also get to the park on your own (rent a Soviet-era Minsk, or take a motorbike taxi if you're really adventurous) and hire a guide there. But it's much easier to go along on one of the tours, where the park and guide fees are prepaid and a hike is mapped out. Tour packages usually include minibus transportation to the national park, where a guide leads a hike through it, down to a nearby village in a lovely cove, and over to a bay where a boat is waiting to bring you back to town. This runs about $10 per person, with lunch included. Or you can head down to the wharf and arrange for a boat yourself—just make sure they know what you're asking and you know what they're offering. Rates are not set in stone, so be sure to bargain.

Dining and Lodging

The explosion of dining and lodging facilities in Cat Ba means one thing: cheap prices. The seafood here is simply prepared but incredibly fresh. Most restaurants and hotels are right in the middle of town and are easy to find. You may want to try one of the many minihotels in town; they are all about the same. You may be tempted to sleep with the room's windows open to allow in the cool ocean breezes. Be careful, though—you could also allow in some uninvited two-legged guests.

$–$$ ✕ **Huu Dong Restaurant.** Seafood, usually grilled or stir-fried, dominates the menu at this tiki house on stilts, which is hard to miss thanks to a huge soft-drink sign on the roof. Set back from the sea, it's more secluded than its competitors, but thumping beats from nearby discos take the shine from what would otherwise be a romantic spot. ⊠ *Le Thanh Tong St.,* ☎ *033/888–407. No credit cards.*

$–$$ ✕ **Restaurant Gaulois.** Like so many of the restaurants on Cat Ba, Gaulois serves fresh seafood—crab, shrimp, squid, and the day's catch. If you're suffering from shrimp overdose, sample the pancakes or other Western treats on the menu. Beware: Gaulois keeps its own strange time schedule. ⊠ *Le Thanh Tong St.,* ☎ *033/888–482. No credit cards.*

$–$$ ✕ **Tien Dat Restaurant.** Fresh seafood and friendly service are the hallmarks of Tien Dat. In a row of similar restaurants, this brightly lit room opening onto the street may not be much to look at, but more effort goes into the cooking than into the design. The grilled prawns and fried squid, dipped in fish sauce or drizzled with lime juice, are delicious. ⊠ *Zone IV,* ☎ *033/888–962. No credit cards.*

¢–$ 🏨 **Sunflower Hotel.** Just up the hill from the ferry landing, the Sunflower is popular with tour groups arriving from Hanoi. Rooms are simple, with bare white walls, wooden furniture, and tile floors, but those in the back are quiet at least. The top-floor bar has enviable views of the boat-filled bay. ⊠ *Nui Ngoc Rd.,* ☎ *031/888–429,* FAX *031/888–451. 30 rooms. Restaurant, minibars, refrigerators, billiards, bar, laundry service, travel services. MC, V.*

¢ 🏨 **Princes Hotel.** This is the most upscale accommodation in town, although the competition is far from fierce in that respect. It's new, with decent facilities such as cable TV. The clean rooms have tile floors, basic wooden furniture, and IDD phones. ⊠ *Nui Ngoc Rd.,* ☎ *031/888–892,* FAX *031/888–899. 50 rooms. Restaurant, minibars, refrigerators, cable TV, billiards, 3 bars, laundry service, travel services. MC, V.*

Mong Cai and Tra Co

❺ *310 km (192 mi) northeast of Hanoi, 128 km (79 mi) northeast of Halong City.*

The main reason to make the trip into these far reaches of Quang Ninh Province is to experience the pleasant beach at Tra Co. To get here you'll have to first pass through Mong Cai (sometimes called Hai Ninh). The relatively subdued coastal province of Quang Ninh explodes in a flurry of trade and cross-border activity at this boomtown on the Chinese border that has literally risen from the ashes. There is little in this city that speaks of the Chinese invasion in 1979 that left Mong Cai a smoldering, mine-strewn wasteland. Today it's a dusty but bustling city of 50,000, with a population that nearly doubles every day as Chinese cross the border to do business with their southern neighbors.

Much of the activity in town centers on the customs quay on the Ka Long River, where porters heave boxes and bulging sacks onto small wooden boats bound for China on the opposite bank. The boats return with goods destined for Hanoi and ports south. A footbridge links Vietnam with the Chinese city of Dongxing; the Vietnamese border patrol has set up a checkpoint a few hundred yards south of the bridge. The Chinese flash their identity cards and are waved into Vietnam, but the officials are reluctant to let Westerners past the guard station—even if it's just to look—without the appropriate exit permit or a valid visa into China. Vietnamese dong and Chinese renminbi are used interchangeably. Vietnam's antismuggling police units are very active here.

Just 9 km (6 mi) east of Mong Cai, on an island separated from the mainland by a sea channel, is Tra Co, a tiny fishing village on a largely uninhabited 16-km (10-mi) stretch of golden sand. You could conceivably walk up the beach into China; a few military guardhouses face the South China Sea just north of the fishing village, but the military personnel are often snoozing in hammocks strung between the knobby evergreens that come down to the beach. During the day most of the village is deserted; the men are offshore fishing in their boats, and the women and children are hauling in the catch from lengthy nets strung up along the coastline.

If you spend the night in Tra Co, wake up before sunrise and walk down to the water's edge to watch the fisherfolk slip into their boats. On the main north–south road is a once-resplendent Catholic church. A tacky red-tin roof replaced the one bombed out by the Chinese in 1979. A few miles farther south is Mui Ngoc, a beautiful spit of a beach known locally as a smuggler's haven.

Dining and Lodging

Hotels are cheap and basic in Mong Cai; the ones listed below have rooms with private bathrooms. The seedy Tra Co Hotel is right on the sand, while a few other guest houses line the north–south road. Some family homes double as restaurants on this stretch of asphalt. Many restaurants serve authentic southern Chinese dishes as well as fresh seafood. In the breezy evenings young couples and friends gather by the roadside at the Mong Cai Bridge to have fruit shakes, sticky-rice ice cream, or coffee.

¢–$ ✕ **Le Huy Restaurant.** This restaurant, one of the few places in town with full-size furniture and a permanent roof, serves mainly seafood and beer. There is no menu; just point at the food on the counter and the kitchen staff will prepare your selection. Make sure you get the prices in writing when you order. ⌧ *2 Hung Vuong St.,* ☎ *033/881–725. No credit cards.*

$$$–$$$$ ⌆ **Mong Cai Li Lai Hotel.** Not yet open at press time, the Li Lai is shaping up to be the finest hotel in Mong Cai. Scenic gardens surround the property, on the banks of the Kalong River. In addition to amenities like tennis courts and karaoke, the hotel will have Chinese and Western restaurants. *On the Kalong River,* ☎ *033/887–005,* 🕾 *033/881–298. 180 rooms. 2 restaurants, tennis court, pool, massage, sauna, meeting rooms.*

$ ⌆ **Tuan Thanh Hotel.** Traditional Chinese furniture and a cozy lobby that doubles as a coffee shop lend this otherwise standard minihotel a sliver more atmosphere than most. Rooms, which include IDD phones, are a delightful shade of lavender. ⌧ *4 Nguyen Du St.,* ☎ *033/881–481. 10 rooms. No credit cards.*

¢–$ ⌆ **Dong A Hotel.** The rooms at this no-frills hotel have tile floors, pinewood beds, and upholstered chairs; bathrooms are clean but lack bathtubs. The staff speaks minimal English. The Dong A is central, near the spot where the hydrofoil bus arrives and departs. ⌧ *1 Hung Vuong Rd.,* ☎ *033/881–151. 13 rooms. No credit cards.*

Lang Son

❻ *150 km (93 mi) northeast of Hanoi.*

North of Hanoi and the Red River Delta, Highway 1 weaves and wends its way through narrow valleys and past jagged cliffs into the mountains of Lang Son Province. Vietnam's major north–south artery officially ends at the provincial capital of Lang Son, another booming trade outpost near the Chinese border. Like Mong Cai, Lang Son was nearly destroyed by retreating Chinese troops in 1979, but the town has quickly regrown. Blinking neon lights advertise the central post office, minihotels and trading companies abound, and Chinese can be heard in the markets.

Although there is little of beauty in Lang Son, the atmosphere is electric. Traders and smugglers convene in corner cafés and hammer out deals with everyone from local shop owners to border guards. Foot porters hustle down the dusty streets bound for rendezvous points farther south. Market stalls in the winding streets of central Lang Son burst with cheap Chinese goods, mostly plastic toys and appliances. And many ethnic minorities live in Lang Son Province, including the Nung and the Tay, who often come into town to load up on provisions.

Of the many picturesque temples dotting Lang Son, the most pleasant is **Cua Dong Temple.** Wedged between the river and the central square, it sits entirely in the shade of two enormous trees. The cramped interior is packed with gold statuary and offerings of food made by the monks and visitors. ⊠ *Hung Vuong St.,* ☎ *no phone.* 🎫 *Free.* ☉ *Daily dawn–dusk.*

Ky Cung Temple is small but interesting, with low ceilings, air thick with incense, and intricately carved golden Buddhas. Perched on the steep riverbank, the temple affords views over the water from its dusty back courtyard. ⊠ *Trang Dang Ninh St.,* ☎ *no phone.* 🎫 *Free.* ☉ *Daily dawn–dusk.*

A crumbling stretch of the 18th-century **city wall,** including a restored stone gateway, stands at the southern edge of town. An abandoned piece of artillery rusts nearby.

Nineteen kilometers (12 miles) north of Lang Son is the border village of Dong Dang, the site of the **Friendship Gate.** Despite the name, there were sporadic exchanges of gunfire here between Vietnam and China until 1992. Relations are friendlier today, but smuggling is a major concern in this province (a vast network of foot trails makes monitoring border crossings extremely difficult), and the border guards here are serious and often surly. However, visiting the border at Friendship Gate is possible. You may have to leave your passport at the guardhouse on the Vietnamese side before you walk the few hundred yards to the border. Chinese and Vietnamese guards are separated by a 600-yard no-man's-land of sorts.

Numerous caves and grottoes a few miles from Lang Son are worth exploring. The most beautiful are the **Tam Thanh and Nhi Thanh Caves,** which are overlooked by Waiting Woman Mountain. Legend says a woman waited here so long for her husband to return from battle that she turned to stone. The caves contain Buddhist shrines and are tourist-friendly with concrete walkways and multicolor lights. ⊠ *On Western edge of town,* ☎ *no phone.* 🎫 *5,000d each.* ☉ *Daily 7–5.*

The Northeast A to Z

To research prices, get advice from other travelers, and book travel arrangements, visit www.fodors.com.

AIR TRAVEL
Vietnam Airlines flies to Haiphong from Ho Chi Minh City daily and from Danang three times a week.
➤ AIRLINE: **Vietnam Airlines** (⊠ 30 Tran Phu St., ☎ 031/921–242).

BOAT AND FERRY TRAVEL
There is no boat service from Hanoi to Haiphong, but ferries and hydrofoils link all the coastal destinations. Three ferries leave Haiphong for Halong City East at 6 AM, 11 AM, and 4 PM daily. Return times are the same. Faster and more comfortable are the hydrofoils, run by the private company Khach Thuy, that depart from Haiphong at 9:30 and 2:30 and from Halong at 8 and 1. From Halong City East, catch the ferry across the inlet to Halong City West; it's only a five-minute ride

(ferries depart every 10 minutes or so in the morning and early evening and less frequently at other times).

Unless you're a guest of the Vietnamese military, the only way on and off Cat Ba Island is by boat. There is a ferry service from Halong City to Cat Ba, but the more common route is from Haiphong. Ferries leave Haiphong's Binh Station (Ben Binh) for Cat Ba town daily at 6:30 AM and 1:30 PM. The trip takes three hours and includes a brief stopover in Cat Hai. The fare is 70,000d. Don't take the 11 AM ferry, as it stops at Cat Hai and does not continue on to Cat Ba town; you'll be stuck at Cat Hai until the 1:30 ferry arrives a few hours later. Two hydro-foils, run by Thong Nhat, also run this route, leaving Haiphong at 9 AM and 9:30 AM and departing Cat Ba at 4 PM and 4:15 PM. The one-way cost is 90,000d. If you're coming from Hanoi, you could take the 6 AM train to Haiphong, catch a cyclo or taxi from the train station to the ferry landing, and take the 9 AM express to Cat Ba. This has be-come a popular alternative to the slow ferries, so you'll need a reser-vation. A warning: the hydrofoils are often overbooked, and some passengers holding tickets for the one air-conditioned cabin may be shifted back to the engine room.

Greenlines runs hydrofoil service from Haiphong to Mong Cai at 7:30 AM daily. The return trip departs at 12:30 PM. The journey costs 230,000d and takes four hours. The Mui Ngoc Company runs hydrofoils between Halong City and Mong Cai, departing from Halong at 8 AM and 1 PM, and from Mong Cai at 9 AM and 2 PM. The cost is 180,000d for the three-hour trip. These boats are an excellent way to reach Mong Cai, but be warned: you must be capable of hopping from the hydrofoil into a small motorboat for the run up to Mong Cai beach. Buses then drive the last 14 km (9 mi) into town.
➤ CONTACTS: **Greenlines** (✉ 43 Tran Phu St., Mong Cai, ☎ 033/881–214). **Khach Thuy** (✉ 1 Binh Station Ferry Landing, Haiphong, ☎ 031/842–927). **Mui Ngoc Company** (✉ 1 Tran Phu St., Mong Cai, ☎ 033/883–988). **Thong Nhat** (✉ 3 Binh Station Ferry Landing, Haiphong, ☎ 031/838–050 in Haiphong; 031/841–050 in Cat Ba; 04/971–6922 in Hanoi).

BUS TRAVEL
State-run public buses travel from Hanoi to Haiphong, Mong Cai, and other points in the area, but they are ancient, unsafe, and usually packed to the gills—basically, not worth your trouble. The coaches of the privately owned BIC Bus Company make the two-hour trip to Haiphong and back to Hanoi 10 times per day. No reservations are required, and tickets cost 25,000d each way; buses depart from Kim Ma Bus Station in the Ba Dinh District of Hanoi. Beware: rival com-panies run the same route from the same station at the same cost but have less-comfortable coaches. BIC also runs services to Lang Son, de-parting daily at 6 AM and 2 PM, for 50,000d.

You can also hitch a ride on a minivan that shuttles tourists to and from Haiphong on their way to Cat Ba Island or Halong Bay. Reserve your seat at one of the many tourist cafés in Hanoi.
➤ BUS INFORMATION: **BIC Bus Company** (✉ 2 Hoang Van Thu St., Haiphong, ☎ 031/820–800).

CAR TRAVEL
Hiring a car and driver from one of the many travel agencies and tourist cafés in Hanoi or going with an organized tour on a minivan are the easiest ways to get around the northeast. These aren't always the most pleasant means, however, as many of the roads are in bad condition.

To get to Haiphong from Hanoi, for instance, you must take Highway 5, one of the most hectic stretches of road in the north. The asphalt is just fine, but traffic is congested, and road rules get tossed out the window. Riding to Haiphong by motorbike is not recommended. Renting an air-conditioned car with a driver for a day's drive to Haiphong and back to Hanoi will run from $50 to $70 and will take about two hours. Of note on your way are the half dozen pagodas set back in the rice fields along Highway 5. Cars or minivans traveling on to Halong Bay from Haiphong must cross the Cam River by ferry at Binh Station (Ben Binh), at the north end of Cu Chinh Lan Street. Access is easiest from Ben Binh Street, one block east. Ferries leave every 10 or 15 minutes. Passenger tickets cost 5,000d, more for cars.

Halong Bay is a 3½-hour drive from Hanoi. There are two routes, but your driver will most likely head east on Highway 5. Halfway to Haiphong, just before the city of Hai Duong, you'll turn left onto Highway 18. Much of this road is relatively new or repaved and feels like the autobahn compared to the rest of the country's roads. Renting an air-conditioned car with driver from Hanoi costs between $112 and $150 for a two-day, one-night trip to Halong, including all car and driver expenses. A travel agency such as Vietnam Tourism may charge more. If it's not the weekend or if it's in the dead of winter or heat of summer, bargain hard—you can usually get a better deal.

To get to Mong Cai by car take the highway east from Halong City. The road winds up the coast 40 km (25 mi) to Cam Pha, a dingy coal-mining town. Beyond Cam Pha the road traverses gorgeous valleys and provides some majestic ocean views. About 60 km (37 mi) past Cam Pha, the road to Mong Cai turns to the right in the quiet trading post of Tien Yen. It's another 97 km (60 mi) or so to Mong Cai.

Lang Son is a relatively painless four or so hours from Hanoi. Road improvements on Highway 1 allow for easy access by car, although a four-wheel-drive vehicle is necessary if you're going beyond Lang Son, such as on a longer loop into Cao Bang Province or east to Quang Ninh Province.

EMERGENCIES
There are no medical facilities of international standard in the region. In case of a major medical emergency, try to get to Hanoi or Ho Chi Minh City as quickly as possible. For immediate attention in Haiphong, try the Vietnam-Czech Friendship Hospital (Benh Vien Viet-Thiep).
➤ CONTACT: **Vietnam-Czech Friendship Hospital** (✉ 2 Nha Thuong St., Haiphong, ☎ 031/700–436).

HELICOPTER TRAVEL
If you want to be the first on your block to say you've flown in a Russian helicopter and lived to tell the tale, see Halong Bay in style on the MI70, the 20-seat chopper owned by state-run Northern Service Flight Company. The Hanoi–Halong Bay trip takes 50 minutes, and you get 10 minutes of bliss circling the emerald waters before the pilot touches down and ushers you onto a boat that cruises the bay. Seats on the bird run $175 each—with $20 extra for the boat, food, and an English-speaking guide. Departure is at 8 AM Saturday from Hanoi; you'll be back in Hanoi by tea time. You can also rent the helicopter outright for $3,695, boat trip included. Inquire at the Metropole Hotel Sofitel in Hanoi or from the Northern Service Flight Company office about reservations.
➤ CONTACTS: **Metropole Hotel Sofitel** (✉ 15 Ngo Quyen St., ☎ 04/826–6919, FAX 04/826–6920, WEB www.sofitel-hanoi-vietnam.com). **Northern Service Flight Company** (✉ 173 Truong Chinh Rd., Hanoi, ☎ 04/852–3451, FAX 04/827–2780).

MAIL AND SHIPPING

Stamps can be bought at most hotels. In Haiphong the brightly painted main Post Office, on the corner of Nguyen Tri Phuong and Dinh Tien Hoang streets, has IDD phones and mail, fax, and Internet services.

MINIBUS TRAVEL

Air-conditioned minibuses travel from Haiphong to Halong City. These line up at the Binh Car and Bus Station (Ben O To Binh), which is just on the north side of the Cam River in Haiphong. (The ferry from the Haiphong port to the north bank is 5,000d and runs every 10 or 15 minutes.) The minibuses cost about 55,000d per person and leave when full (and they can get very full). Other buses go on to Mong Cai, stopping at Halong en route. Ask the ticket agent about minibuses back to Hanoi from Halong Bay, if that's where you're headed.

MONEY MATTERS

Money can be exchanged at most hotels in larger towns in the area. If you're going to smaller towns, however, it's a good idea to exchange money before you go.

Major banks, such as VID Public and Vietcom, can exchange your dollars into dong, cash traveler's checks, and give cash advances on credit cards. Asia Commercial Bank can exchange money but cannot cash traveler's checks.

➤ MAJOR BANKS: **Asia Commercial Bank** (✉ 69 Dien Bien Phu St., Haiphong, ☎ 031/823–389). **VID Public Bank** (✉ 56 Dien Bien Phu St., Haiphong, ☎ 031/823–999). **Vietcom Bank** (✉ 11 Hoang Dieu St., Haiphong, ☎ 031/842–658).

TOURS AND PACKAGES

The easiest way to see northeast Vietnam is to arrange trips at a travel agency or tourist café in Hanoi (☞ Hanoi A to Z *in* Chapter 2). The trips generally include transport in a tour bus or minivan, accommodation (double occupancy; standard depends on price of tour), and an English-speaking guide. Tours to Halong Bay usually include a five-hour (or longer) boat trip and lunch on the boat. Tour packages to Cat Ba Island often include guided tours of the national park, a stop at a nearby village in a lovely cove, and a boat trip back to town.

TRAIN TRAVEL

Five trains per day (from 6 AM to early evening) leave Hanoi bound for Haiphong from one of two stations: Hanoi Railway Station (Ga Hanoi) and Long Bien Station. Tickets for all trains can be purchased at the Hanoi Railway Station, but you must ask at the ticket booth whether your train leaves from there or from Long Bien Station. The cost is 63,000d. The unspectacular trip takes just over two hours. There are two stations in Haiphong. The first, Thuong Li Railway Station, is west of the city. You should detrain at the Haiphong Railway Station, which is the end of the line on the Hanoi route. In the Reception Room for Tourists, the attendant can book ferry tickets, explain the schedules to Cat Ba and Halong Bay and train times back to Hanoi, and even recommend a hotel or restaurant. There's also a left-luggage service.

One train per day departs from Hanoi for Lang Son. The picturesque ride takes six hours and costs 29,000d one-way. Two trains per week continue on to the Dong Dang border crossing and then into China. They pass through Pinxiang, 20 minutes north of the border, and terminate in Nanning, the capital of China's Guangxi Province. To take advantage of this you must have a visa to China.

➤ TRAIN STATION: **Haiphong Railway Station** (✉ 75 Luong Khanh Thien St., ☎ 031/921–333).

TRANSPORTATION AROUND THE NORTHEAST

Most likely you will be traveling around this area with an organized tour or with your own car and driver. Getting from place to place in this region by other means is not easy.

Note that Haiphong serves as a departure point to places such as Cat Ba, Do Son, and Halong Bay, so you may end up traveling first to the city on your way to other destinations. Halong Bay can also be reached via Halong City.

TRAVEL AGENCIES

See Hanoi A to Z *in* Chapter 2 for information about travel agencies and tourist cafés in Hanoi.

Haiphong Toserco and Vietnam Tourism Haiphong can provide a local English-speaking guide, hire a car, find you a hotel room, and arrange trips to Halong Bay, Cat Ba Island, and other points.

Halong Tourist Company and Quang Ninh Tourism Company are both government-owned, and although they have experience setting up boat trips in the bay, and guiding package tours to the hotels owned by their companies, they're not experts at dealing with actual people. They can provide an English-speaking guide for about $10 per hour; call ahead. ➤ CONTACTS: **Haiphong Toserco** (✉ 40 Tran Quang Khai St., Haiphong, ☎ 031/841–415, FAX 031/745–977). **Halong Tourist Company** (✉ 1 Halong Rd., Halong City, ☎ 033/846–272, FAX 033/846–284, WEB www.halongtour.com). **Quang Ninh Tourism Company** (✉ 7 Halong Rd., Halong City, ☎ 033/846–350 or 033/846–319). **Vietnam Tourism Haiphong** (✉ 60A Dien Bien Phu St., Haiphong, ☎ 031/829–957, FAX 031/823–651).

THE FAR NORTH

Ethnic-minority villages and natural splendor abound in Vietnam's northernmost region. Cao Bang Province is home to the Dao and Tay groups; Ha Giang Province, the country's farthest north, is populated by the H'mong, the small but distinct group called the Bo Y, and the even smaller Pu Peo group. The terrain in this northernmost area is rugged, and it is one of Vietnam's poorest regions. In the remote districts near the Chinese border, the illiteracy rate surpasses 90%. The rocky, inhospitable mountains leave little room for rice cultivation. Corn and fruit are more common crops here, and honey production is on the rise. Ha Giang Province is extremely beautiful, but there are few facilities for tourists. But if you're an adventurous traveler who delights in finding your own way—even if it means hitching a ride on an ox cart for eight hours—then Vietnam's far north is for you.

The provincial capital of Cao Bang is linked to Lang Son, 120 km (74 mi) to the east, by windy and rutted Highway 4. The road, which essentially follows the Chinese border from the coast westward, was the site of numerous skirmishes in the late 1940s between French colonial troops and Vietminh guerrilla forces. The French tried to maintain garrisons at Lang Son and Cao Bang, but by 1950 the Vietnamese had ousted them from the area.

Ba Be Lakes

★ ❼ *240 km (149 mi) north of Hanoi.*

The idyllic Ba Be Lakes region, in Bac Can Province, has one of Vietnam's oldest national parks. The lake environs are beautiful and peaceful; occasionally you can even hear monkeys as you float down the lake in a wooden longboat. It's quite possible you'll find no other visitors here, which leaves you to explore the breathtaking mountains and caves, El Capitan–like limestone cliffs, gurgling streams, and rushing waterfalls all on your own.

The 9-km (6-mi) fjordlike lake is too big to explore in its entirety in one day, but you can see as much of it as possible if you start out early in the morning, before the mist has burned off, on a rented motorized wooden longboat. Foreigners are rare (for now, so the boatman may see dollar signs in his eyes). But you should be able to hire a boat for about 30,000d per hour. Pack a lunch and have the boatman head to the **Dau Dang Waterfall,** a lovely spot for a picnic. Toward the far end of the lake (a good three hours by boat) is the remarkable Puong Cave, where the Nang River has carved a 300-ft grotto out of the hillside. Bats and swallows swoop through the darkness. At the far end of the lake are the rustic villages of the Tay ethnic minority, where you can overnight. Otherwise try the state-owned guest house.

Lodging

¢–$ 🏨 **Ba Be Guest House.** In the Park Center (the park headquarters), this state-owned guest house stands beneath forested hills near the water's edge. Choose between accommodations in the main hotel building or brick houses, but avoid the musty wooden stilt houses. ✉ *Ask for directions in town,* ☎ *0281/894–014,* 📠 *0281/894–026. 50 rooms. Restaurant, some refrigerators, boating, bar, travel services; no a/c in some rooms, no phones in some rooms, no TV in some rooms. No credit cards.*

¢ 🏨 **Ba Be Hotel.** About 30 minutes away from Ba Be Lakes in Ba Be townlet is this hotel, where cheery manager Nguyen Quynh will set you up with a clean room with a private bathroom. Rooms at the back are serene and have views out over the paddy fields and hills. There is an IDD phone in the lobby. ✉ *Ba Be town,* ☎ *0281/876–115. 8 rooms. Travel services; no room phones. No credit cards.*

¢ 🏨 **Pac Ngoi Village.** For the adventurous, a night in a Tay minority stilt hut is an unforgettable experience. Share a meal cooked on the kitchen's open hearth with your hosts, and then let the sounds of cicadas and waves lapping against the lake's edge lull you to sleep. Beds are arranged in a large central room, so privacy is not a strong point. Ask at the Park Center (or Ba Be Guest House) for booking and transportation. ✉ *Southern end of Ba Be Lake,* ☎ *no phone. Boating; no a/c, no room phones, no room TVs. No credit cards.*

Tan Trao

❽ *130 km (81 mi) north of Hanoi.*

The region's isolated mountains and once-lush jungles provided Ho Chi Minh and his forces with sufficient cover from the French and Japanese. In early 1945 Ho Chi Minh set up headquarters for the Communist Party in the remote village of Tan Trao, high in the mountains west of Thai Nguyen town. Tan Trao was also the birthplace in 1945 of what became known as the August Revolution, when General Vo Nguyen Giap led Vietminh troops eastward to attack a garrison occupied by the Japanese at Thai Nguyen. General Giap's attack inspired similar uprisings throughout the country. Nine years later he would lead the Vietminh to glory at Dien Bien Phu.

Currently no organized tours visit Tan Trao. But there are a few sights here worth seeing: a museum dedicated to Ho Chi Minh, a giant banyan tree where General Giap rallied his troops, Ho Chi Minh's simple jungle hut (*nha lua*), and the Tay minority communal house (*dinh*) where the first National Congress met. If you have hired a jeep or car to Ba Be Lakes and have a day to spare, consider an excursion to Tan Trao. There is no accommodation in the town, so you'll have to stay in a minihotel in the provincial capital of Thai Nguyen, 60 km (37 mi) back toward Hanoi; any tourist café or travel agency in Hanoi can help you arrange accommodations.

The Far North A to Z

CAR TRAVEL

The drive from Hanoi to Ba Be Lakes and Tan Trao runs along paved roads and past green-tea plantations, stunning mountain vistas, and ethnic-minority stilt houses. You should be able to hire a car and driver from travel agencies in Hanoi; the cost, including two nights' lodging for the driver, is about $180.

TOURS

Numerous Hanoi tourist cafés, such as Rainbow Tours, arrange trips to north-central Vietnam, with Ba Be Lakes as the centerpiece. Several run five-day, four-night tours, with stops in Lang Son, Cao Bang city, and the Ba Be Lakes region. The cost, which includes accommodation, meals, transportation, a guide, and any entry fees, can be as high as $450 for one person or as low as $140 per head with four people. However, due to the relatively small number of people heading to the far north, tours are not regular, and it's often not possible to join up for a group tour.

➤ RAINBOW TOURS: (✉ 80 Tran Nhat Duat St., Hoan Kiem District, Hanoi, ☎ 04/928–3008 or 04/928–3154).

THE NORTHWEST

Vietnam's staggering beauty and ethnic diversity are perhaps most evident in the northwest, where dozens of ethnic-minority groups as well as the Kinh, the ethnic majority, inhabit the imposing highlands. Physically and culturally removed from Hanoi, many communities in the remote far west exist today as they have for generations, harvesting terraced rice fields or practicing slash-and-burn agriculture on the rocky hillsides.

Here, babbling mountain streams wind their way through deep, extended valleys. Many of these streams join up with the Song Da, the once-rushing Da River that has been tamed by Hoa Binh Dam, Vietnam's first hydroelectric power project, about 74 km (46 mi) southwest of Hanoi. In the shadow of this Soviet-built hydroelectric marvel, some farmers still live without electricity. The winding, hilly roads beyond Hoa Binh afford panoramic views. Dusty crossroads towns like Man Duc leave little to smile about, but there are exquisite nearby caves and brick homes built right into the limestone rock at the base of towering cliffs. Make sure your driver stops at the picturesque first view of Mai Chau. Here the valley spreads out before you in its remarkable greenness, and the tap-tap-tapping of carpentry signals the building frenzy currently enveloping the district.

Rising majestically above the region is Mt. Fansipan, Vietnam's tallest peak. In its shadow lies the sleepy hill town of Sapa, the tourist center of the northwest, where Dao and H'mong women converge at the local market to buy, sell, and trade.

The northwest lends itself to adventurous four-wheel-drive tours. The Hanoi–Mai Chau–Son La–Dien Bien Phu–Lai Chau–Sapa–Hanoi loop is the most interesting of all, and it's the one followed by most tour operators. It's equally popular with small groups that have rented jeeps or Land Cruisers on their own and want a multiple-day excursion. If you're comfortable with the thought of a four- to seven-day jeep trek, you'll want to spend plenty of time here. If not, there are still some wonderful options to consider. Idyllic Mai Chau is only four or five hours by car from Hanoi; you could push off early one morning and be back the next evening. Sapa is accessible by a fairly comfortable overnight train ride from Hanoi; you may wish to head here for a weekend to see various ethnic-minority groups. You can also fly to Dien Bien Phu and Son La.

Mai Chau

❾ *170 km (105 mi) southwest of Hanoi, south of Hwy. 6, in Hoa Binh Province.*

The Brigadoon of Vietnam, Mai Chau nestles in a serene valley that has been called one of the most beautiful spots in the country. Like the fictitious town that rises every 100 years, Mai Chau appears out of the mist as if in a dream. The town itself is inhabited mainly by the majority Kinh Vietnamese. White Thai villages dot the paddy-rich valley, however, and this is where you're likely to spend most of your time. To visit these villages you must purchase a 5,000d ticket, at the barrier, to pass beyond Mai Chau.

The White (and later the Black) Thai migrated to Vietnam from what is now Thailand about 2,000 years ago. Today they incorporate elements of both cultures. The Mai Chau Valley has a number of Thai villages whose hospitality is genuine and memorable. If you overnight in a stilt house, expect your host family to offer you a roll-up mattress and mosquito net, unlimited use of a tobacco bong (*thuoc lao*), and giant vats of rice wine.

The Mai Chau market teems with villagers selling everything from hand-carved opium pipes to flayed pigs. Except for some women, most villagers have given up wearing traditional garb. Although many villagers still farm, tourism and panning for gold have become the most lucrative industries. A tourist alley of sorts has sprung up in the village, accessible from the dirt road just beyond the Mai Chau Guest House. The de facto mayor of the Thai villages lives on this road, and his house is frequented by visitors and villagers. Baskets, old crossbows, and lovely weavings are laid out on tables in front of the stilt houses. Many other silk scarves and textiles hang from the windows. And they're all for sale.

Buy some bottled water in town before heading out on a long hike through the green (or golden, depending on when you go) rice fields and into the nearby hills. Countless footpaths head off into the mountains from the main valley routes and are used by Montagnards (usually women) who gather wood for cooking fires or for construction. Their baskets are usually extremely heavy, and it takes great skill to balance more than 200 pounds using only shoulder straps or a head brace.

The mountainsides have been largely denuded of their primary forest cover, forcing the villagers to hike more than a day to reach the larger trees needed for building stilt houses. The White Thai villagers here are very friendly and will often invite you into their homes to watch TV together or to share some homemade rice wine or even lunch. Local children will often call out to passing hikers in Thai, "Pai la la?" (Hello, where are you going?) Your response: "Pa in!" (Just walking through!).

Lodging

¢ 🏠 **Mai Chau Guest House.** Just beyond the center of town is this large brick-and-tile stilt house. One room is as sterile as the next; ask for one with a private bathroom. Although the place tries to create some atmosphere by hanging fabrics made by ethnic minorities (for sale, of course) throughout the lobby, it feels forced. ⊠ *Ask for directions in town,* ☎ *018/867–262. 14 rooms, 6 with bath. No a/c, no room phones, no room TVs. No credit cards.*

¢ 🏠 **White Thai Villages.** Many people enjoy staying in one of the White
★ Thai villages behind the guest house, where any of 60 households will put you up. Immaculately clean and surprisingly airy and comfortable, the traditional Thai longhouse sits on stilts about 7 ft up—with barely a nail used in the construction. The split-bamboo floor is soft, smooth, and springy under foot. The going rate is 50,000d per person per night. Your hosts would accept less, but a hefty portion of the money goes to district coffers. ⊠ *Ask for directions in village,* ☎ *018/867–255. No credit cards.*

En Route Northwest of Mai Chau in southern Son La Province, the road rises to a sheltered plateau. As the road sweeps downward, it passes one of the few remaining primary forests in northern Vietnam. The old trees are huge, a sign of how the entire northern highlands once looked when tigers, leopards, and elephants reigned. This forest stretches for only a few hundred yards, and the drive through is eerie. Farther up Highway 6 are the rolling tea plantations and steep escarpments of the Moc Chau district in Son La Province. This area is famed for its tea as well as for the productive dairy industry, supported in part by UN assistance. But locals don't ever seem to enjoy the two together. Beyond Moc Chau the road sweeps down vast valleys and past Black Thai villages, through the town of Yen Chau and eventually to the town of Son La.

Son La

❿ *320 km (198 mi) west of Hanoi on Hwy. 6, 160 km (99 mi) northwest of Mai Chau.*

Son La is a convenient overnight stop on the journey to Dien Bien Phu. Even if you're not overnighting in Son La, take some time to explore the immediate environs. Many hill tribes reside in the area, which until 1980 was considered part of the Tay Bac Autonomous Region. The Tay Bac's support of the French during the French-Indochina War led to repressive government measures against them.

For a commanding view of the town and the surrounding area, climb the stone steps behind the Trade Union Hotel on 26-8 Street to the lookout tower known as **Cot V3.** You can visit a former **French penal colony,** destroyed by American bombers but partially rebuilt. The tiny underground cells and dank corridors leave a strong impression of life in captivity. The ticket includes entry to the **Son La Museum,** housed in a moldy colonial mansion overlooking the prison. Downstairs, the museum displays pictures of life in Son La, past and present; upstairs is a model of a Thai village and an exhibition of ethnic minority clothing. ⊠ *On the hill in the center of town, next to the People's Committee building,* ☎ *no phone.* 🎟 *10,000d.* ☉ *Daily 7:30–11 and 1:30–5.*

If you feel like soaking your tired bones for a while, have your driver or a motorbike taxi take you to the **hot springs,** in beautiful Suoi Nuoc Nong village, a few miles south of the main road. ☎ *No phone.* 🎟 *5,000d.* ☉ *Daily 7–6.*

Dining and Lodging

$ ✕ **Thit De Restaurant.** Goat meat—*thit de*—is the local delicacy here, so why not try some goat kebabs or, if you're really an adventurous eater, *tiet canh* (goat's-blood curd soup)? Goat-free dishes, such as pork and beef, are also available. The flock of goats tethered in the courtyard makes this place easy to spot. ⊠ *Dien Bien Rd.,* ☎ *022/852–394. No credit cards.*

¢ 🏨 **Phong Lan Hotel.** The new wing of this hotel is the most comfortable accommodation in town. Simple pine furniture and green tiles decorate the clean rooms, and bathrooms are pink. Avoid rooms in the older building. ⊠ *Opposite central market,* ☎ *022/853–515,* FAX *022/ 852–318. 50 rooms. No credit cards.*

¢ 🏨 **Trade Union Hotel.** The rooms at this state-owned hotel may be basic, but the location is central, the staff speaks reasonable English, and there are ethnic-minority dance performances in the restaurant each evening. Rooms have bare walls, white-tile floors, and spartan bathrooms. At press time the hotel was planning to add a pool in 2003. ⊠ *26-8 St.,* ☎ *022/852–804,* FAX *022/855–312. 50 rooms. 2 restaurants; no a/c in some rooms. No credit cards.*

Dien Bien Phu

⓫ *470 km (291 mi) west of Hanoi, 150 km (93 mi) west of Son La, 16 km (10 mi) east of Laos.*

The dream of reestablishing colonial rule throughout Indochina turned into an all-too-vivid nightmare for the French at Dien Bien Phu. History has documented General Vo Nguyen Giap's stunning victory over Colonel Christian de Castries and his 13,000 French and Vietnamese troops (as well as Foreign Legion volunteers) as one of the greatest military achievements of the modern era: a surprise 57-day siege culminating in the surrender of the French garrison on May 7, 1954. The Vietminh army had been on the offensive for much of 1953, and General Henri Navarre, commander of French forces in Indochina, was intent on regaining the initiative throughout the region by building up a series of bases from which his troops could mount offensive action. One of these bases, in the far northwest of Vietnam near the Laotian border, had been overrun by the Vietminh in 1952, but Navarre had ordered its recapture (the French took it back in 1953). The ethnic Thai minority called this centuries-old trading post on the Burma–China–Vietnam road Muong Thanh; the Vietnamese named it Dien Bien Phu.

Such a remote garrison ringed by inhospitable mountains would make it unlikely, thought the French, that General Giap would infiltrate the valley with ground troops. The French clearly controlled the skies and used two landing strips in the valley to shuttle in supplies, reinforcements, and batteries of howitzers and other field guns. But by late 1953 Giap had encircled the French garrison with 50,000 men and had accomplished a feat of near-impossible logistics: dragging into offensive position dozens of 105-millimeter artillery cannon and antiaircraft guns up steep and densely forested slopes, all under the nose of French surveillance planes and scout missions.

The surprise assault began on March 13. Two weeks later the airstrips were within Vietminh artillery range, cutting off the base from vital troop reinforcements and forcing the French to turn to parachute drops for resupplying the base. While the French were waiting, the Vietminh were digging. An elaborate tunnel system crisscrossed the valley and gave Giap's soldiers the necessary element of surprise over the French. The French solicited assistance from their longtime allies the Americans and the British, but to no avail. The defenders were steadily dwindling, and the injured began piling up in the French underground hospital. Morale collapsed, and on May 7, after a series of attacks by the Vietminh, the white flag was raised over the command bunker.

Coincidentally, the next day an international conference—whose initial purpose one month earlier was the completion of a peace treaty for the Korean conflict—opened in Geneva. The result was a declaration temporarily partitioning Vietnam along the 17th parallel until national elections could be held to determine a single government (they were never held). Tellingly, the agreement was never signed, partly because of the refusal by the United States to actively participate due to the presence of the Communist Chinese at the convention.

Dien Bien Phu (population 29,000), in the immense Muong Thanh Valley, has served since 1995 as the remote capital of westernmost Lai Chau Province. The shift in provincial power anticipated the erection of a second massive hydroelectric project on the Da River, which, if it ever gets built, will leave the former provincial seat of Lai Chau, 110 km (68 mi) north of Dien Bien Phu, at the bottom of an 800-ft deep reservoir. But Lai Chau is no stranger to water woes. Deforestation in the surrounding ring of mountains has caused catastrophic flooding of the Da River. This has meant major construction in Dien Bien Phu, a district whose primary attraction for tourists is history. The gaudiest example of these newer buildings is the ostentatiously ornate provincial party headquarters.

The informative **Dien Bien Phu Museum** has been built on the site of the battle with the French. There is a section dedicated to the region's ethnic-minority communities, but French ignominy and Vietnamese glory are the main topics here. The main hall recounts the events of the siege and the battle itself, with blinking maps and legends synchronized with a recorded loop outlining the battle's chronology. Outside is a collection of weapons used in and around the garrison: the Vietnamese tanks and guns look as if they were polished yesterday afternoon, the rusting French jeeps are riddled with bullet holes, and the remains of a French plane lie in a twisted heap. ⊠ *7-5 St.,* ☎ *023/826–298.* ▣ *5,000d.* ☽ *Daily 7–11 and 1:30–5.*

The **memorial cemetery,** across the street from the Dien Bien Phu Museum, is the final resting place for many unknown Vietminh soldiers. Here in bas-reliefs are scenes of the battle depicted in larger-than-life-size socialist realism. One of the most emotional aspects of Dien Bien Phu is here: the names of all the Vietminh casualties from the historic battle at Dien Bien Phu are carved on the back side of the front wall of the cemetery. ☎ *No phone.* ▣ *Free.* ☽ *Daily 7–11 and 1:30–5.*

The **command bunker** of Colonel de Castries, in walking distance of the Dien Bien Phu Museum, has been remade with makeshift sandbags filled with concrete. Overhead is a reproduction of the corrugated roof from which a lone Vietminh soldier waved a victory flag—the image, re-created several hours after the fact for a documentary film, became Vietnam's enduring symbol of victory over colonial oppression. ☎ *No phone.* ▣ *5,000d.* ☽ *Daily 7–11 and 1:30–5.*

French veterans organized the construction of the small, rather forlorn-looking **French War Memorial,** which stands across the road from the command bunker. ☎ *No phone.* ▣ *Free.* ☽ *Daily 7–11 and 1:30–5.*

Some of the battle's most intense combat took place at Hill A1, a position labeled **Eliane** by the French. A decrepit French tank and a monument to Vietminh troops now stand here. ☎ *No phone.* ▣ *5,000d.* ☽ *Daily 7–11 and 1:30–5.*

Dining and Lodging

More minihotels are opening in Dien Bien Phu; ask at travel agencies in Hanoi for the most up-to-date information.

$$–$$$$ ✕ **Lien Tuoi Restaurant.** Catering mostly to foreign tourists, this large restaurant serves a wide selection of Western dishes. The most popular item is chicken stewed with mushrooms. Menus are available in English and French. Be prepared to sit on plastic stools. It's only a short walk away from Hill A1. ⊠ *Hoang Van Thai St.,* ☎ *023/824–919. No credit cards.*

¢–$ 🏨 **Muong Thanh Hotel.** This snazzy hotel complex has cornered the market in Dien Bien Phu. Rooms in the main building or Thai stilt houses are clean, and service is friendly. The grounds include a tourist office, a fitness room of sorts, karaoke, a sauna, and even a large pool out back. Breakfast is included in the room rate. Some rooms have IDD phones, and there is one in the lobby. ⊠ *25 Phuong Him Lam St.,* ☎ *023/826–719,* 🗏 *023/826–720. 50 rooms. Restaurant, some refrigerators, pool, gym, massage, sauna, badminton, travel services; no phones in some rooms. No credit cards.*

Sapa

★ ⑫ *35 km (22 mi) south of Lao Cai town, 170 km (105 mi) northeast of Dien Bien Phu, 350 km (217 mi) northwest of Hanoi.*

Ringed by Vietnam's tallest peaks, Sapa is an enchanting hill-tribe village that has become the de facto tourist capital of the northwest. A pilgrimage to Sapa, which is part of Lao Cai Province and is a 90-minute drive from the provincial capital (also known as Lao Cai), affords a glimpse of some of the country's most breathtaking mountain scenery as well as its ethnic-minority cultures. The hill tribes cultivate rice and ginger and hunt wild game by traditional methods; they continue as they always have to worship the soul of rice, their ancestors, and the spirits of earth, wind, fire, rivers, and mountains. To see them in their traditional style of dress—elaborate headdresses, silver adornments, and layers of indigo-dyed, brilliantly embroidered cotton—is to feel yourself caught in a time warp.

The French dubbed the area around Sapa the Tonkinese Alps. In 1922 colonial authorities displaced the minority residents and began building villas for themselves in the town, turning it into a kind of health resort and a retreat from the oppressive heat of Hanoi as well as having it serve a nearby ore mine. Between the end of French colonial rule in 1954 and national reunification 21 years later, the North Vietnamese government made weak attempts to grant the ethnic minorities political representation and the same constitutional rights as the majority Kinh population—provided they took up the struggle against the U.S.-backed Saigon regime. Since 1975 the government has pursued "integration" programs in which the state provides limited education and health care for free. At the core of these programs are settlement and resettlement strategies. Since the late 1980s Sapa has been one of the regions where the government is encouraging relocation.

The protection of Sapa's cultural diversity and the environment seems to have little place on the state agenda, however. Tourism may corrupt the integrity of the local populace and upset the area's fragile ecology. Some of the minority groups practice slash-and-burn agriculture, and along with the depredations of two centuries of outside interests, this has already reduced the virgin forest to a mere 12 square km (5 square mi). Further destruction would be tragic, considering the area's remarkable natural gifts.

The local population is made up of the H'mong, the Dao, the Tay, the Giay, the Muong, the Thai, the Hoa (ethnic Chinese), and the Xa Pho and is divided into 18 local communes with populations of between 970 and 4,500 inhabitants. These hill tribes, known as Montagnards by the French, convene every day in Sapa to exchange everything from staples and handicrafts to live snakes. Be sure to plan your trip to Sapa so that it coincides with this colorful weekend market.

Be prepared to be relentlessly pursued and targeted as a walking dollar sign. Women and children hawkers will be in your face from the moment you come into town. And it's not just in Sapa proper; children along the valley road long ago learned how desperate foreigners are to take cuddly snapshots of ethnic-minority children. You may hear them say "No money, no photo."

The town of Sapa is charming, but economic development has already put a strain on the small but growing community. Before 1954 there were 248 luxury villas throughout town and in the surrounding hillsides. The vast majority of these buildings have disappeared—they were either destroyed by invading Chinese troops during the 1979 border war (fires spread to the surrounding mountains, wreaking environmental havoc) or by the wrecking balls that are making way for new minihotels and marketplaces. The lovely stone church has been spared, however, and services are still held here on Sunday morning and on Christian holidays.

The center of town is a street below the muddy soccer field, but here ★ you'll find the pulse of the community. The **Sapa Market** convenes daily on the slippery stone stairway that crosses this narrow, bitumen-flecked street. Much of the buying and selling takes place under the roof of the drab but roomy marketplace-on-stilts. The market expands on Saturdays when tourists from Hanoi flood into Sapa; you may actually find it quieter and more pleasant weekdays. H'mong and Red Dao women come into town with the rising sun. Most walk in from surrounding villages, while a few catch rides on the backs of motorcycles. They are often dressed in their finest traditional garb: richly embroidered vests and dresses, aqua-and-black cotton shirts, finely detailed silver necklaces and bracelets, and elaborate headdresses that tinkle with every movement. Many of these women have picked up a few French and English words or phrases. Part of the fun is bargaining with them, but don't express too much initial interest, or you may be labeled a sucker. Hold out for as long as you can, and then ask to see the good stuff. Invariably an elderly Dao woman will understand what you're looking for, dig deep into her bamboo basket, and produce fabric of quality superior to what she'd been showing you only moments before.

Sapa is part of the **Nui Hoang Lien Nature Reserve** (☎ 020/871–433), a mountainous 7,400-acre landscape covered by temperate and subtemperate forests. The reserve provides a habitat for 56 species of mammals—including tigers, leopards, monkeys, and bears—17 of which are considered endangered (the Asiatic black bear, for example). An impressive 150 species of birds, including the red-vented barbet and the collared finch bill, can be found only in these mountains. Among the area's geological resources are minerals from sediments deposited in the Mesozoic and Paleozoic periods. From the Muong Hoa River to the peak of Mt. Fansipan, the eastern boundary of the reserve is formed by a ridge of marble and calcium carbonate. Also found in this region is kaolinite, or China clay, used in the making of porcelain.

Guided walking tours of the nature reserve are recommended and are easily arranged through hotels and guest houses in town. Minsk or jeep drivers will be happy to take you down the rutted road from Sapa past the Auberge Hotel for a full day of hiking, swimming in waterfall pools, and visiting H'mong and Thai villages. Hoteliers and tour companies can also make arrangements for you.

A **30-minute hike** from the center of town to the radio tower above Sapa gives you a spectacular panoramic view. Climb the stone steps from the main road. Next to the Ham Rong Hotel is a guard house where you may or may not have to pay 5,000d to hike to the top; it depends on the watchman's mood. The steps lead up past well-manicured gardens and through rocky fields. A path breaks off to the right and winds around boulders to the tower. The town of Sapa is laid out below, and across the valley is Mt. Fansipan.

Hiking **Mt. Fansipan**, Southeast Asia's tallest peak, at 10,372 ft, requires little technical expertise. What it does take is three or four days, as you must depart from Sapa and hike *down* into the valley, then back up the other side. It's recommended that you bring an experienced guide to help you navigate the wet, chilly mountainside and suggest the best route and places to camp. If you're serious about hiking Mt. Fansipan, contact Topas Travel Company (☞ The Northwest A to Z, *below*), which organizes treks to the peak. Or ask for more details at the Auberge Hotel or the Green Bamboo Hotel. It can get very cold in Sapa and even colder on the mountain, so you need to dress accordingly.

Dining and Lodging

It seems like two-thirds of Sapa's buildings are hotels, which clearly compromises the town's rugged charm but also results in a wider selection of options. You can find rooms here for as little as 45,000d per night, although you may want to opt for something a bit more upscale. But even most of the dirt-cheap minihotels have private bathrooms with hot water. Note that power cuts can sometimes be a problem at hotels; you may want to keep a flashlight handy just in case.

$$ ✕ **Delta Italian Restaurant.** Tourists gather at Sapa's only Italian restaurant for large portions of pasta and pizzas cooked in a genuine Italian pizza oven. There's also an extensive international wine list. For lighter fare, try the exquisite crepes. Amiable owner-chef Mr. Tung spent six months studying in Milan before opening the restaurant. Upstairs is a pool table for customers. During peak season, about October–mid-December, it's best to make reservations for weekend dining. ⊠ *Near the market,* ☎ *020/871–799. No credit cards.*

$$ ✕ **La Petite Bouffe.** Classic French and Vietnamese dishes vie for supremacy on the menu at this hotel restaurant. The grilled goose breast is a local legend. Ethnic minority–crafted tablecloths and silver-ended chopsticks subtly complement clay-tile floors and elegant wooden furniture. Also here is an attached bar, the Gecko. It's a good idea to reserve ahead for weekend dining during peak season, about October–mid-December. ⊠ *Post Office Pl., Ham Rong St.,* ☎ *020/871–504,* WEB *www.geckohotel.com. DC, MC, V.*

$ ✕ **Camellia Restaurant.** This family-run operation does a brisk business with visitors to Sapa. Deer is on the menu here, as well as chicken, beef, and Vietnamese spring rolls. Steer clear of the pizzas, but do sample the outstanding coffee. ⊠ *Phansipan St.,* ☎ *020/871–455. No credit cards.*

$$$–$$$$ ✕🏨 **Victoria Sapa Hotel.** The premier hotel in Sapa, the Victoria caters to the luxurious fancy of its guests. The hotel, a French-designed pleasure palace on a hilltop overlooking town, has spacious, clean, and tastefully decorated rooms with inviting bathtubs and heaps of amenities. If all that isn't enough, the hotel also sells a tour package in which you stay in private luxury sleeper and dining cars on the train to and from Hanoi. ⊠ *Overlooking town,* ☎ *020/871–522,* FAX *020/871–539,* WEB *www.victoriahotels-asia.com. 77 rooms. Restaurant, room service, in-room safes, minibars, cable TV, tennis court, pool, sauna, bar, shop, laundry service, Internet, travel services; no a/c. AE, DC, MC, V.*

$-$$ ▥ **Chau Long Hotel.** This mock-chateau construction has open-air staircases and verandas; rich, dark woodwork; and stunning views of the hills. Cream-color bed linens and open fireplaces make the deluxe rooms a cozy retreat after a cold day in Sapa. ⊠ *33 Cau May St.,* ☎ *020/871–245,* FAX *020/871–844,* WEB *www.chaulonghotel.com. 22 rooms. Restaurant, cable TV, bar, laundry service, Internet, car rental, travel services; no a/c. MC, V.*

¢–$ ✕▥ **Auberge Hotel.** Owner Dang Trung, a Hanoi transplant, has the
★ best thing going in Sapa: a lovely, popular hotel with exquisite views of the mountains. Rooms, particularly on the third floor, are cozy and clean and have functioning fireplaces. Competition for these rooms is fierce, so reservations are a must. ⊠ *Cau May St.,* ☎ *020/871–243,* FAX *020/871–666,* WEB *www.sapadiscovery.com. 20 rooms. Restaurant, laundry service, Internet, car rental, travel services; no a/c. No credit cards.*

¢–$ ▥ **The Green Bamboo Hotel.** The small, sunny rooms here are decked out with televisions and private bathrooms. If you're looking for a quiet getaway, stay elsewhere on the weekends. The Green Bamboo sends its backpacker tour groups here, and the bar downstairs is popular. Reservations, which are suggested, should be made at the **Green Bamboo Café** in Hanoi (⊠ 80 Tran Nhat Duat St., Hoan Kiem District, ☎ 04/928–3008). ⊠ *Cau May Rd.,* ☎ *020/871–411,* FAX *020/871–214,* WEB *www.vietnamonline.com/greenbamboo. 28 rooms. Café, refrigerators, bar, laundry service, travel services; no a/c. No credit cards.*

¢–$ ▥ **Royal Hotel.** Perched beneath the road on the very edge of Sapa Valley, this hotel has stolen a chunk of the view, and borrowed a few ideas on room design, from the Auberge. Rooms have pine floors, fireplaces, and wicker furniture and are linked by pleasant, airy corridors. Every room has a balcony, and most have IDD phones. ⊠ *Cau May St.,* ☎ FAX *020/871–313 or 020/871–684. 29 rooms. Restaurant, cable TV, dance club, bar, Internet, laundry service, travel services; no a/c, no phones in some rooms. AE, MC, V.*

Bac Ha

⓭ *100 km (62 mi) northeast of Sapa, 350 km (217 mi) northwest of Hanoi.*

The main reason for venturing to Bac Ha, a small town built on a desolate highland plain northeast of Lao Cai, is the century-old **Sunday-morning market,** one of the largest in the northwest. Ethnic-minority villagers such as the Dao and the Flower H'mong (related to the H'mong but wearing brighter and more elaborate clothing) come from miles around to buy, sell, and trade everything from horses and dogs to medicinal herbs and beautiful handmade tapestries. Tourists are definitely in the background at this market; you'll be tolerated and respected but rarely approached by sellers. One thankful deviation from this function-over-form mentality is the lovely, high-pitched songs performed by Flower H'mong singers. If the market manager hasn't been able to arrange singers for that day, he plays a cassette of their songs over the public address system. The market gets going at about 9 AM, but early birds can be seen setting up their stalls and sipping *pho* (noodle soup) for breakfast as the sun comes up. A 3- to 6-km (2- to 4-mi) walk up the road past the Sao Mai Hotel (turn left at the fork) brings you to some ethnic-minority villages that will be more than happy to see you.

Many minihotels in Sapa arrange day trips to Bac Ha, which leave at about 6 AM. The going rate is $10 per person in a Russian jeep. The road is bumpy, and the trip takes three hours each way. If you're heading back to Hanoi, you may want to travel to Bac Ha on a Sunday morning and then get dropped off at the Lao Cai train station in the afternoon so that you can take the train that evening.

Dining and Lodging

$ ✕ **Cong Fu Restaurant.** This hole-in-the-wall does a brisk business with lunching tourists. Very basic Vietnamese fare, such as pho, and noodle, meat, and chicken dishes, is served. Service can be painfully slow—simple orders like a cold beer sometimes take more than five minutes to arrive. ⊠ *Off main road, about 200 yards from entrance to market,* ☎ *020/880–254. No credit cards.*

¢ 🏨 **Sao Mai Hotel.** The Sao Mai is the ritziest accommodation in town—compared to local homes, that is—which isn't saying much. Rooms are in stilt houses or in an annex with extensive wood paneling. ⊠ *On same road as market but on other side of highway,* ☎ *020/880–288. 25 rooms. No credit cards.*

The Northwest A to Z

To research prices, get advice from other travelers, and book travel arrangements, visit www.fodors.com.

AIR TRAVEL
A 12:30 PM Vietnam Airlines flight connects Hanoi to Dien Bien Phu five times a week; the one-way fare is $43. Flights to Son La's Na San Airport leave Hanoi at 9:30 AM on Monday, Tuesday, Friday, and Sunday; the fare costs $36.

Consider flying to Dien Bien Phu or Son La and returning to Hanoi via some form of ground transportation, either down Highway 6 or up to Sapa and down Route 70 and Highway 2. Talk with one of the travel agencies or tourist cafés in Hanoi to see if they have contacts who can book you a one-way trip back to the capital. They may insist, however, that you pay for the mileage for the driver's return to Dien Bien Phu or Son La.

BICYCLING
If you've got the legs, lungs, and equipment, mountain biking is a formidable but fantastic way to experience the steep mountain ranges of Hoa Binh Province. Most people who do the Hoa Binh–Mai Chau route find alternative transportation to the provincial capital of Hoa Binh, such as an early morning public bus. From there it's about 100 km (62 mi) up and down two major sets of mountains. Hardy bikers reach Mai Chau by evening, exhausted. Slower riders spend the night in a home in one of many roadside villages.

CAR TRAVEL
A sedan is a perfectly viable way to get around much of the northwest if you're traveling in the dry season. Cars, however, are not recommended for the remote and difficult stretches of road; you'll need a jeep or four-wheel-drive vehicle to get you through the trouble spots. You can rent cars in dozens of spots in Hanoi, and you'll be able to book a two-day, one-night car trip to Sapa for about $80, all driver's expenses included. A longer excursion in a four-wheel-drive vehicle is more expensive: the going rate for the popular six-day, five-night excursion through the northwest (Hanoi–Mai Chau–Son La–Dien Bien Phu–Sapa–Hanoi) in a Russian jeep is $200. A Toyota Land Cruiser can be rented for about $530 from the Green Bamboo Café in Hanoi and $600 from Vidotour (☞ Hanoi A to Z *in* Chapter 2) in Hanoi for the same

tour. The price is a bit steep, but the more modern four-wheel-drive vehicles are safer and nicer.

The trip to Mai Chau from Hanoi can be treacherous in the rain, especially beyond Hoa Binh city, where the road rises into the steep mountains and sharp curves give way to long cliff drop-offs. However, the condition of the road is decent enough to manage without a four-wheel-drive vehicle.

Set aside at least five days to visit Dien Bien Phu from Hanoi: two days traveling each way and one full day to see what you came for—although the remarkable scenery makes the trip as interesting as the history of the place. If you're coming from Mai Chau and Son La, the natural next step is to continue clockwise: through the charming high lonesome of Lai Chau, on to Sapa, and then back to Hanoi. The Dien Bien Phu–Sapa road is in worse condition than the Hanoi–Dien Bien Phu road, so a high-clearance four-wheel-drive vehicle is necessary. The journey from Dien Bien Phu to Sapa is a hard day's trip on narrow, rutted roads through beautiful scenery. This round-trip route adds a day or two to your journey but is much more interesting than following the same route back and forth.

The 35-km (22-mi) stretch of road from Sapa north to the border town of Lao Cai is in better condition than the Dien Bien Phu–Sapa route. You may prefer to go directly to Sapa, bypassing Dien Bien Phu, Son La, and Mai Chau, and heading up and down Highway 2 and Route 70.

Cars with drivers can be hired from travel agencies and tourist cafés in Hanoi.

EMERGENCIES
In case of medical emergency, try to get to the larger towns in the region. If you are really ill, get to Hanoi as quickly as possible.

MONEY MATTERS
It's best to exchange money in Hanoi before your trip; however, if you need to, you can usually exchange money (generally cash, not traveler's checks) at your hotel.

MOTORCYCLE TRAVEL
The Hanoi–Dien Bien Phu–Sapa route is only for adventurous motorcyclists. These roads are very remote, and adequate emergency care is virtually nonexistent. Wear a helmet, take a sheet of important words and phrases (such as the Vietnamese expressions for "My clutch is broken"), and go with someone else. You'll need high clearance and maneuverability, however, so doubling up on bikes is not recommended. The route requires a 150-cc engine or larger, and you should have some knowledge of engine mechanics, although locals are adept at fixing ailing Russian Minsks. Also, be prepared to get wet in mud puddles. At some larger washout spots, however, enterprising locals set up ferry services on small boats for motorcycles.

If you drive a motorbike from Hanoi to Mai Chau, pay extra attention on the mountain roads: the trucks that run this route are notoriously stingy when it comes to giving adequate room to two-wheelers. For more information on renting motorbikes, *see* Hanoi A to Z *in* Chapter 2.

SAFETY
Make sure you hire a good driver whom you can trust, as roads can be bad. Don't drink tap water or eat raw vegetables, and make sure meat is well cooked. Bring the right clothing; it gets chilly in the mountains—even in spring and autumn—and downright cold in winter.

TOURS

Most travel agencies and tourist cafés in Hanoi (☞ Hanoi A to Z *in* Chapter 2) organize two kinds of trips to the northwest: an overnight to Mai Chau, and a six-day, five-night excursion loop by jeep. On the very popular Mai Chau tour, you travel either on a 12-seat minibus or in a 30-seat tour bus, and you generally stay at the White Thai village behind the guest house. This tour costs about $20 per person, lodging included. The six-day loop tour, which is also popular, costs about $80 per person, with a minimum of four people. That makes it pretty crowded in a Russian jeep. Lodging is not included on this tour, but you don't have to find it yourself. The driver does that for you; you just need to pay for it. Note that these tourist cafés often insist on full prepayment; don't let that go without a fight, as up-front payment may give the driver little incentive to perform ideally. If you're taking a jeep tour, remember to take the name and telephone number of the manager at the Hanoi agency where you arranged your trip.

The Topas Travel Company (also known as Phu Thinh) conducts one- to seven-day hiking trips to Mt. Fansipan and other areas around Sapa. The Fansipan trip costs $220 for one person, less per person for a group trip, which includes food, tents, and tours of remote mountain villages. The company will also custom-design trekking, horseback-riding, and mountain-biking tours according to your interests.

➤ CONTACT: **Topas Travel Company** (✉ 20 Cau May St., Sapa, ☎ 020/871–331, ℻ 020/871–596, WEB www.topas.dk/vietnam).

TRAIN TRAVEL

If you don't want to lose a whole day driving to Sapa, take the overnight train from Hanoi to Lao Cai. The most comfortable trip is on Friday night, when you get a soft sleeper in a four-person compartment on the "luxury" train. The one-way ticket costs about $25. The train leaves the Hanoi railway station at 8:15 PM and takes 11 hours. The easiest way to buy tickets is through a Hanoi travel agency.

Don't lose your ticket after boarding the train. You need to present it to the station guards in Lao Cai when arriving at the station and again when departing the station upon returning to Hanoi. You can purchase your return ticket in Sapa (and check train and bus schedules) at the small post office in the center of town. Hotels in Sapa can book a return trip in a private soft-sleeper carriage.

Minibuses waiting at the Lao Cai train station can take you the 35 km (22 mi) to Sapa for 25,000d. The buses leave when full and usually drop you off in front of the Auberge Hotel. From Sapa buses return to the Lao Cai train station twice daily, at 6:30 AM and 2 PM, but you can join with other travelers and share a bus or jeep that will leave at the time you want. If you'd like to combine a one-way train to Sapa with a return to Hanoi by jeep or car, you can arrange that in Sapa at the Auberge Hotel or at one of the tour agencies dotting the main roads.

4 THE CENTRAL COAST

HUE, HOI AN, DANANG

In Hue, explore the majestic tombs of emperors and the partially restored Imperial City, and absorb the almost eerie quiet of the long-gone ruling families' weighty presence. Perfectly preserved Hoi An lets you see how ordinary Vietnamese traders and fisherfolk lived in centuries past. In Danang, learn about the history and culture of the Cham people. Then take a trip to famous China Beach and to the ruins of the ancient Cham city at My Son. At all times, enjoy the unique and delicious cuisine for which this region is famous.

By Sherrie
Nachman

Updated by
Craig Thomas

VIETNAM'S LOVELY CENTRAL COAST extends from the 17th parallel, which once divided the country, to the former Imperial City of Hue and south to the historically rich port town of Hoi An. As you drive along National Highway 1—which, like most other roads in Vietnam, is in rough shape but is slowly being upgraded—expect to catch glimpses of the emerald-green South China Sea and scenes of traditional Vietnamese rural life as they have appeared for centuries. The age-old rhythm of planting and harvesting continues undisturbed, and families dry their rice in their front yards only inches from the road against a stunning backdrop: the dramatic peaks of the Truong Son Mountains cascading into the sea. Beach lovers come here for the numerous long, sandy beaches, while cultures vulture comb through ancient Cham ruins and visit tombs and pagodas. The highlights of the region are Hue and Hoi An, two of Vietnam's most interesting and hospitable cities. While Hanoi and Ho Chi Minh City may give you a taste of contemporary Vietnam and its recent history, Hue and Hoi An, with their UNESCO World Heritage Sites, put you in a seemingly mythical Vietnam of centuries past.

Once the capital of Vietnam and the home of its emperors, Hue today is largely in ruins, the consequence of both French attacks in the late 19th century and American bombings during the Vietnam War. Only during the past decade have efforts been made to restore Hue's imperial architecture. Despite the ruins, the Imperial City, as Hue is known, continues to evoke the grandeur of its royal past. In contrast, the much smaller city of Hoi An, originally a Chinese trading village on the sea, is incredibly well preserved. Families live in 200-year-old homes— amazing landmarks incorporating architectural elements from traditional Chinese, Vietnamese, and Japanese styles, reflecting those who populated Hoi An over the centuries.

The third major city in this region is Danang, which may be familiar to you as an important U.S. Air Force base during the Vietnam War. Today it is a port town that has little in the way of sights except for its fabulous museum of Cham culture. The ancient Kingdom of Champa existed from the 2nd to the 17th century around present-day Danang, Nha Trang, and Phan Rang, although its power was significantly weakened by the Viet and the Khmer in the 15th century. The city also has the region's largest airport, which makes it a convenient jumping-off point for visiting Hue (which itself has a small airport), Hoi An, and other points of interest in the region.

In between Danang and Hoi An are the Marble Mountains, where temples have been built in the caves, and China Beach, made famous by the television show of the same name. As you drive between Hue and Danang on National Highway 1, be sure to stop at Lang Co Beach and the dramatic Hai Van Pass, which runs across the Truong Son Mountain range and overlooks the South China Sea below.

Pleasures and Pastimes

Art and Architecture

Because this area served as the seat of the Kingdom of Champa from the 2nd to the 15th century, it has the greatest concentration of Cham art and architecture in the country. You can savor the glories of Champa at the excellent Cham Museum in Danang. Exploring the grand remnants of the Imperial City of Hue and the magnificent Imperial Tombs will introduce you to the history of Vietnam's emperors. In Hoi An, the well-preserved houses and pagodas have hardly changed in the last

200 years, giving you a sense of 17th- and 18th-century Vietnamese life. Hoi An's streets are also lined with art galleries, small shops selling all kinds of artifacts, and small cafés.

Dining

The central coast is known for its outstanding cuisine. Hoi An's specialties include "white roses," delicious and beautiful shrimp dumplings that resemble roses (if you squint a little), and the simple *com ga* (spicy rice and chicken). Imperial Hue's cuisine, distinguished by the elegant radial symmetry of its presentation, is said to be the most sophisticated in Vietnam. One specialty of Hue is *banh khoai,* a rice pancake filled with shrimp and pork and topped with sprouts, fresh mint, and spicy star fruit. Be sure to try the peanut dipping sauce that accompanies this dish. Another popular regional dish, served in both Hue and Hoi An, is *bun bo Hue,* a dish of rice noodles and broth topped with pork, beef, and pork rinds. There aren't many formal restaurants in this area, but there are plenty of small, pleasant family-run places serving outstanding food. Imagine the Vietnamese version of a really good diner—nothing fancy, but decent portions of good, cheap food.

Almost all hotels and many restaurants post costs in dollars and accept both dollars and dong. Roadside cafés and smaller restaurants post prices in dong, but they also accept dollars. More and more establishments in this area are accepting credit cards—although a "service charge" of 3%–4% is generally added—and traveler's checks.

CATEGORY	COST*
$$$$	over 225,000 dong
$$$	105,000 dong–225,000 dong
$$	45,000 dong–105,000 dong
$	15,000 dong–45,000 dong
¢	under 15,000 dong

per person for a main course at dinner, including 10% tax and 5% service

Lodging

You won't find many luxury hotels in this region, but there is a growing number of clean, comfortable accommodations, including some with tennis courts or swimming pools. Most have private bathrooms, unless otherwise noted. Hotel choices, especially in Hue and Hoi An, are numerous, and new minihotels pop up regularly. Almost all hotels post costs in dollars and accept either dollars or dong.

CATEGORY	COST*
$$$$	over 2.5 million dong
$$$	1 million dong–2.5 million dong
$$	750,000 dong–1 million dong
$	400,000 dong–750,000 dong
¢	under 400,000 dong

All prices are for a standard double room, including 10% tax and 5% service.

Outdoor Activities

The entire region is excellent for bicycling and motorcycling because the traffic hysteria that reigns in Ho Chi Minh City does not exist here. There aren't many cars in Hoi An and there are relatively few in Hue; Danang is much more of a city with the concomitant traffic. The beaches in Hoi An, like everything else about the town, are exceedingly pleasant places in which to relax. Close to Danang is the famous China Beach, which is nice but doesn't quite live up to its acclaimed glory from the eponymous television program.

Exploring the Central Coast

It's relatively easy to travel around the fascinating and culturally rich central coast region. Hue and Hoi An are only about three hours from each other by car; Hoi An is less than an hour south of Danang, and Hue is about two hours north. The best plan is probably to fly into Danang, travel to Hoi An, and leave from Hue. Trips to My Son and China Beach usually originate or end in Danang or Hoi An.

Numbers in the text correspond to numbers in the margin and on the Central Coast, Hue, Danang, and Hoi An maps.

Great Itineraries

IF YOU HAVE 3 DAYS

Fly from Hanoi, Ho Chi Minh City, or Nha Trang to Danang, but bypass the city itself. Instead head straight for ⊞ **Hoi An** ㉔–㊲ and spend a day to a day and a half seeing the city and/or relaxing at nearby Cua Dai Beach. Have dinner overlooking the river at Café des Amis, and stay in the Hoi An Riverside Resort, the city's friendliest and most picturesque. From Hoi An it is a quick three-hour drive to ⊞ **Hue** ①–⑯; spend your remaining time exploring the Imperial City and the tombs and pagodas that line the banks of the Perfume River (Song Huong).

IF YOU HAVE 5 DAYS

Spend a half day in **Danang** ㉑ exploring the treasures of the Cham Museum. That same day head out to the **Marble Mountains** ㉒ and then continue on to ⊞ **Hoi An** ㉔–㊲ for a couple of nights. See Hoi An's historical and architectural treasures at a leisurely pace, but make sure to fit in a visit to Cua Dai Beach and to the Cham temples at My Son. You'll probably have time to have a shirt, dress, pants, or just about anything else you desire made in the silk shops that line Tran Phu and Le Loi streets; any clothing item can be made in less than 24 hours. Spend your last two days in **Hue** ①–⑯.

When to Tour the Central Coast

The central coast is plagued by some of Vietnam's worst and most unpredictable weather. Rain can strike at any moment, especially in Hue. The official rainy season begins in November and ends in March, so the best time to go is from April to October (although it still may be rainy or overcast). Like the rest of the country, the area comes alive during Tet, the celebration of the lunar new year, which takes place in January or February.

HUE

Hue (pronounced hway), bisected by the Perfume River and 13 km (8 mi) inland from the South China Sea in the foothills of the Annamite Mountains (Truong Son Mountains), stands as a reminder of Vietnam's imperial past. The seat of 13 Nguyen-dynasty emperors between 1802 and 1945, Hue was once Vietnam's splendid Imperial City. Although it was devastated by the French in the 19th century and again by fighting between the Vietnamese Communists and the Americans in the 20th, the monument-speckled former capital has a war-ravaged beauty. One can still imagine its former splendor, despite gaping holes in its silhouette. Hue is a UNESCO World Heritage Site, and the city's gems are slowly being restored.

As early as the 2nd century BC, Hue was home to rulers: this was the seat of command for the Chinese Han army and was called Tay Quyen. By the 2nd century AD, local chieftains had captured Hue and renamed it K'ui Sou. Between the 10th and 14th centuries, the Cham and the Vietnamese fought over control of the city. By the 15th century, the

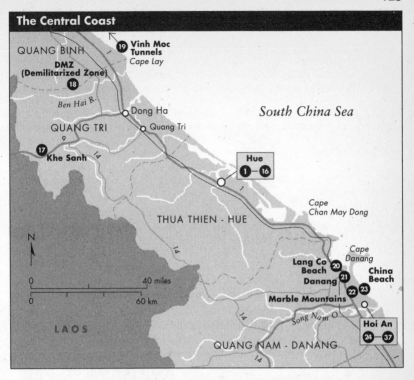

The Central Coast

QUANG BINH

19 Vinh Moc Tunnels
Cape Lay

DMZ (Demilitarized Zone)
18

Ben Hai R.

Dong Ha

QUANG TRI

Quang Tri

South China Sea

17
Khe Sanh

14

Hue
1 — 16

THUA THIEN - HUE

Cape Chan May Dong

N

Cape Danang

Lang Co Beach 20
21
Danang

China Beach

0   40 miles
0   60 km

Marble Mountains
22 23

Song Nam O

Hoi An
24 — 37

LAOS

QUANG NAM - DANANG

14

14

Vietnamese had successfully captured the city from the Cham and renamed it Phu Xuan. In 1558 the city became the capital of a region ruled by Lord Nguyen Hoang, which established control of South Vietnam by the Nguyen lords. (During this time, two warring factions—the Nguyen lords, who controlled South Vietnam, and the Trinh lords, who controlled North Vietnam—were fighting for control of the whole country.)

With the Tay Son Rebellion in the 18th century, the Nguyen lords were temporarily defeated. Led by the sons of a wealthy merchant, the Tay Son rebels were acting on a general sentiment of discontent with both Nguyen and Trinh rule. The Tay Son emperor, Quang Trung, was installed in Hue from 1786 to 1802, until the ousted Lord Nguyen Anh returned, with French backing. At the same time, Nguyen Anh captured Hanoi from the Tay Son rebels, who had defeated the Trinh and the Chinese-backed Ly dynasty based in the northern capital. In 1802, Nguyen Anh anointed himself Emperor Gia Long and made Hue the capital of a newly united Vietnam. Twelve Nguyen-dynasty emperors followed him to the throne until 1945, and their impressive tombs, Imperial City, and pagodas are reminders of the important role the city once played.

It was under Emperor Gia Long's rule that the city's architectural identity was established—and the prospect of French colonial rule in Vietnam initiated. With guidance, ironically, from the French architect Olivier de Puymanel, Gia Long designed and built the city's surrounding fortress in the style of the Forbidden City in Beijing. The result is a fairly modern structure that looks centuries old. Enclosed within the thick walls of the Chinese-style citadel is the Imperial City (Hoang Thanh), where all matters of state took place and which was off limits to all but mandarins and the royal family. Within the Imperial City was the Forbidden Purple City (Tu Cam Thanh), where the emperor and his family lived; very little of it remains today.

In the 1830s, voices of dissent arose against the French presence in Vietnam. The French responded by attacking Hue in 1833 (they had been looking for an excuse to assert their claims to the country in exchange for assisting Gia Long to the throne) and making the country—particularly Tonkin and Annam—into a protectorate. During this time, a Western-style city was established across the river from the citadel to accommodate the French forces; some of these old French colonial buildings still stand. In 1885, after repeated disagreements between the French and the emperors of Hue, the French pillaged the Royal Court, burned the Royal Library, and replaced Emperor Ham Nghi with the more docile Emperor Dong Khanh.

It was the Tet Offensive of 1968, however, that really destroyed large parts of the Imperial City. During one of the fiercest battles of the Vietnam War, the North Vietnamese army occupied the city for 25 days, flying its flag in defiance and massacring thousands of supposed South Vietnamese sympathizers. The South Vietnamese and the Americans moved in to recapture the city with a massive land and air attack and in doing so further destroyed many of Hue's architectural landmarks. Overall, more than 10,000 people died in the fighting, many of them civilians.

Although much of the Imperial City was reduced to rubble, many sections still exist, and Hue's main draw continues to be the remnants of its glorious past. Today tourists keep the city thriving. There are many hotels and numerous cyclo drivers who can give you a tour of the Imperial City for only 50,000d. On top of it all, Hue is known for its outstanding cuisine.

Exploring Hue

Hue itself is quite small, and you can easily get around the Imperial City on foot. Within walking or biking distance, too, are the local market and the Imperial Museum. To visit the sprawling tombs and pagodas on the outskirts of Hue, you will need to hire a car and driver—or a motorbike if you're more adventurous. Several of the tombs and pagodas, most notably Minh Mang Tomb and Thien Mu Pagoda, sit along the banks of the Perfume River and can be reached by boat. Don't feel obligated, however, to take one of those slow-moving boat trips up the Perfume River—you may find the scenery far from spectacular and the pace very slow.

The Citadel

A GOOD WALK

You'll most likely be staying on the east bank of the Perfume River, so it's best to begin your walk at the Phu Xuan Bridge and Le Loi Street. Cross the Phu Xuan Bridge, making sure to notice the French-built Tran Tien Bridge, a symbol of Hue, off to your right. Once you're across the river, a right will take you down Tran Hung Dao Street to the **Central Market** ①. After you visit the market, head back along Tran Hung Dao Street to the Phu Xuan Bridge; the street will turn into Le Duan. Take the first right after the bridge, which will lead you across a moat and through the Ngan Gate (Cua Ngan) into the **Citadel** ②. After entering through the Ngan Gate, you will see four of the Nine Holy Cannons on your right. These bronze cannons depict the four seasons; the other five depict the Chinese elements—water, soil, wood, metal, and fire. Take the first left and make your way along 23 Thang 8 Street (this is the name of the street, not a specific address); on your right

Hue

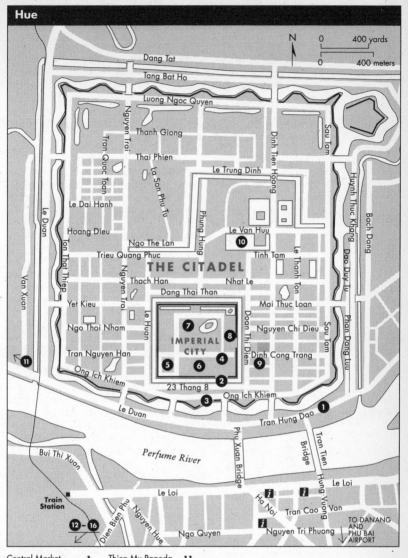

N

0   400 yards

0   400 meters

Dang Tat

Tang Bat Ho

Luong Ngoc Quyen

Nguyen Trai

Thanh Giong

Thai Phien

La Son Phu Tu

Le Trung Dinh

Dinh Tien Hoang

Sau Tam

Huynh Thuc Khang

Bach Dang

Le Duan

Van Xuan

Ton That Thiep

Tran Quoc Toan

Le Dai Hanh

Hoang Dieu

Ngo The Lan

Trieu Quang Phuc

Nguyen Trai

THE CITADEL

Le Van Huu

10

Tinh Tam

Le Thanh Ton

Dao Duy Tu

Thach Han

Nhat Le

Dang Thai Than

Mai Thuc Loan

Phan Dang Luu

Yet Kieu

Le Huan

7

8

IMPERIAL CITY

Doan Thi Diem

Nguyen Chi Dieu

Sau Tam

Ngo Thoi Nham

5

4

Dinh Cong Trang

9

Tran Nguyen Han

6

Ong Ich Khiem

2

23 Thang 8

11

3

Ong Ich Khiem

1

Le Duan

Tran Hung Dao

Tran Tien

Perfume River

Phu Xuan Bridge

Bridge

Hung Vuong

Bui Thi Xuan

Le Loi

Le Loi

Van

Train Station

Dien Bien Phu

Nguyen Hue

Le Loi

Ha Noi

i

i

Tran Cao

TO DANANG AND PHU BAI AIRPORT

12 – 16

Ngo Quyen

i

Nguyen Tri Phuong

you will see the entrance of the Imperial City. Across from the entrance to the Imperial City is the 122-ft **Flag Tower** ③.

The **Imperial City** ④, once a large royal complex, is now mostly in ruins. Enter through the Noontime, or Royal, Gate (Cua Ngo Mon), and take an immediate left toward the **Nine Dynastic Urns** ⑤, which symbolize the formidable Nguyen dynasty. Head back toward the entrance to the Imperial City and turn left across the Golden Water Bridge (Trung Dao Bridge), once used only by the emperor. Straight ahead is one of the few still-intact structures in the Imperial City: the intricately decorated **Palace of Supreme Harmony** ⑥.

Exit the palace through the back of the gift shop. On either side of the path leading to the entrance of the **Forbidden Purple City** ⑦ are the Halls of the Mandarins, where mandarins (court officials) dressed in special attire before paying homage to the emperor. Through the courtyard in front of the halls you can see the vast empty expanse on the threshold of the Forbidden Purple City—a result of the Tet Offensive. To your right, the Royal Theater, or Festival Hall, is largely intact. Behind it is the intimate and partially restored **Royal Library** ⑧.

Heading east from the Royal Theater, exit the Imperial Enclosure through the beautiful and ornate Eastern Gate (Hien Nhan Mon). Make a right on Doan Thi Diem Street and then take the first left on Le Truc Street to get to the **Imperial Museum** ⑨. In a beautifully preserved building that was formerly part of the palace, the museum houses a fine collection of imperial objects. Across the street are the unimpressive Military Museum and Hue's Archaeological Center, once a kind of prep school for male members of the royal court and now closed to the public.

Make a left out of the Imperial Museum and then another left onto Dinh Tien Hoang Street. Follow the street north through what feels like a quiet suburban residential neighborhood for about 1 km (½ mi). At the intersection with Tinh Tam Street is **Tinh Tam Lake** ⑩, overgrown with lotus flowers in spring and summer. On the other side of Dinh Tien Hoang Street, across from the footpath that bisects Tinh Tam Lake, is another lake, Tang Tau, with a small island; once the location of the Royal Library, this is the current home of the small Ngoc Huong Pagoda. It's a very peaceful place to take a break.

TIMING
This walk should take you about four hours at a very leisurely pace. Early morning and late afternoon are the best times to explore Hue because it can get quite warm in the middle of the day, especially from April to October. Also, many tour guides insist they need a two- to three-hour break in the middle of the day.

SIGHTS TO SEE

❶ **Central Market** (Cho Dong Ba). Hue's large indoor Central Market has the usual collection of fresh fruits, dried fish, and motor parts. It's the best place to pick up two local specialties: conical hats, which can be decorated to order, and sesame-seed candy. It's also a good spot to see Hue daily life or to have a delicious and inexpensive meal. ✉ *On citadel side of riverfront, next to Tran Tien Bridge,* ☎ *no phone.* ☉ *Daily 7:30–dusk.*

❷ **The Citadel** (Kinh Thanh). Seeking to secure his empire, Emperor Gia Long built this almost 4-square-km (1½-square-mi) citadel with a 65-ft-wide moat in the heart of Hue in 1805. Gia Long was assisted in the design by the French architect Olivier de Puymanel, and the result is a combination of French military architect Vauban's work and classic Chinese-style architecture. The citadel was initially built of earth and later reinforced by 6-ft-thick brick walls and fortified by 10 gates. Today much of the citadel is given over to residential and even agricultural use. Enclosed in the structure is the ☞ **Imperial City,** where official government activity once took place, and the ☞ **Forbidden Purple City,** which was the private sanctuary of the emperors and their families. 🔁 *Free.*

❸ **Flag Tower** (Cot Co). This 122-ft structure, Vietnam's tallest flagpole, is one of the symbols of Hue. It was originally built in 1809 to serve as the Imperial Palace's central observation post. Like much of Hue, it has a history of being destroyed. The Flag Tower was toppled during a typhoon in 1904. It was rebuilt in 1915, destroyed again in 1947, and rebuilt anew in 1949. When the North Vietnamese occupied the city during the Tet Offensive of 1968, the National Liberation Front flag flew from the Flag Tower. The interior is closed to the public. ✉ *In front of 23 Thang 8 St., facing Ngo Mon Gate.*

❼ **Forbidden Purple City** (Tu Cam Thanh). Built at the beginning of the 19th century, the Forbidden Purple City, inside the ☞ **Imperial City,** was almost entirely destroyed during the Vietnam War; now it's largely a wide-open field. At its threshold is a vast expanse of spotty vegetation and rubble. In its glory days the Forbidden Purple City housed members of the imperial family and the concubines and eunuchs who served them. Anyone else who entered was executed. After the 1968 Tet Offensive, only the **Royal Theater,** on the right-hand side, and the intimate and partially restored Royal Library behind it remained intact. ✉ *In Imperial City,* ☎ *no phone.* 🔁 *55,000d admission to Imperial City includes Forbidden Purple City.* ☉ *Daily 7–5.*

❹ **Imperial City** (Hoang Thanh). The Imperial City, also known as the Imperial Enclosure, was once a complex of palaces and pavilions where civil and religious ceremonies took place. Inside it was the ☞ **Forbidden Purple City,** where the royal family lived. Now the Imperial City betrays disappointingly few remnants of its past glory beneath the sporadic vegetation that has taken over the ruins. Nonetheless, it still conveys a sense of splendor. There are four gateways into the enclosure: the **Gate of Peace** (Cua Hoa Binh), **the Gate of Humanity** (Cua Hien Nhan), the **Gate of Virtue** (Cua Chuong Duc), and the **South Gate** (Ngo Mon). You can only get to the Imperial City after you have entered the citadel. ✉ *Inside citadel,* ☎ *no phone.* 🔁 *55,000d.* ☉ *Daily 7–5.*

❾ **Imperial Museum.** This beautiful wooden structure built in 1845 houses miscellaneous royal knickknacks, such as wooden incense boxes, many inlaid with mother-of-pearl. The museum's walls are inscribed with Vietnamese poetry. There is also a good collection of ceramics, traditional musical instruments, and old weapons. ✉ *Dinh Cong Trang St. at Doan Thi Diem St.,* ☎ *no phone.* 🔁 *22,000d.* ☉ *Daily 7–noon and 1:30–5.*

❺ **Nine Dynastic Urns** (Cuu Dinh O The-Mieu). Each of these urns, weighing approximately 5,000 pounds and cast in 1835, is dedicated to a ruler of the Nguyen dynasty. The central urn, the most elaborately decorated of the nine, features Emperor Gia Long, the founder of this dynasty. Nature motifs cover the urns, including the sun and moon, rivers and mountains, and various landscapes. Many of the designs are Chinese in origin, dating back 4,000 years. ✉ *To left of entrance to Imperial City, when entering through Ngo Mon Gate,* ☎ *no phone.* 🔁 *55,000d admission to Imperial City includes Nine Urns.* ☉ *Daily 7–5.*

❻ **Palace of Supreme Harmony** (Thai Hoa Dien). This richly decorated wooden palace painted gold and red was constructed in 1803. In its imperial glory in the 19th century, it was where the emperor held special events, ceremonies, and festivals for the new moon. This is also where the emperor received dignitaries. Throngs of mandarins paid their respects to his highness while he sat on his elevated throne. Now the palace houses a gift shop where 10,000d will get you an imperial tune from the authentically outfitted minstrels. ✉ *In Imperial City,* ☎ *no phone.* 🎫 *55,000d admission to Imperial City includes Palace of Supreme Harmony.* ☉ *Daily 7–5.*

⑧ Royal Library (Thai Binh Lau). The Royal Library, a wooden structure east of the Forbidden Purple City on a field of grass and rubble, is one of the few largely intact buildings in the Imperial City. The delicately carved architecture has survived, although there are no books or other library-like objects left. ✉ *In Imperial City,* ☎ *no phone.* 🎫 *55,000d admission to Imperial City includes Royal Library.* ☉ *Daily 7–5.*

⑩ Tinh Tam Lake (Ho Tinh Tam). In spring and summer lotus flowers cover this little lake. You can do as the emperors once did and walk across one of the bridges to the island for a brief respite. ✉ *Dinh Tien Hoang and Tinh Tam Sts.*

The Imperial Tombs and the Thien Mu Pagoda

A GOOD BOAT RIDE OR DRIVE

Many of the prearranged boat rides organized through hotels or tourist offices provide you with an all-day tour of the Imperial Tombs as well as of the Thien Mu Pagoda. These boat trips are worth taking if you have the time, although a faster way to visit the tombs is by car. The tombs and pagodas of Hue are beautiful and peaceful and consist of more than just small tombstones: the emperors were laid to rest in elaborate pine forests and gardens with their own islands amid minilakes and pagodas. Boat tours generally stop at any combination of the following places: the Tomb of Tu Duc, the Tomb of Minh Mang, and the Thien Mu Pagoda. The Tomb of Khai Dinh and the Tomb of Duc Duc are more easily accessible by car. You can also get to each of the other tombs by car—or by motorbike or bicycle, if you are more adventurous.

The price of admission for each tomb and pagoda varies; some, such as the Thien Mu Pagoda, are free, whereas others, such as the Tomb of Tu Duc, cost as much as 50,000d. Many boat trips, such as those arranged through Thua Thien–Hue Tourism, DMZ Tour Office, and other government agencies (☞ Travel Agencies *in* Hue A to Z, *below*), are advertised at a cost of $15 or so. But the agencies neglect to inform you of the additional admission fees that you must pay at some stops. Other boats, holding up to 10 people, cost $10–$35, depending on whether you rent the boat yourself for only three or four people or join a pre-existing group. You can arrange both options at the pier opposite the train station or through your hotel. The Huong Giang Tourist Company's tours give you the terrific option of going by boat and returning by car. Another option is to hire a car and driver to take you by land to the tombs.

Many boat tours follow this route down the Perfume River: heading west along the river, you approach the **Thien Mu Pagoda** ⑪ on the right-hand side. After about 6 km (4 mi), you come to the **Tomb of Tu Duc** ⑫. The **Tomb of Dong Khanh** ⑬ is a short walk northeast of the Tomb of Tu Duc. Once back on the boat you proceed another 5 km (3 mi) down the river and then on foot 1 km (½ mi) inland to the **Tomb of Minh Mang** ⑭, on the west side of the river.

To get to the **Tomb of Khai Dinh** ⑮, 1½ km (1 mi) inland on the other (east) side of the river, you're better off going by car on a separate trip, although some boat trips will take you here. The **Tomb of Duc Duc** ⑯, which lies within the city limits on the east bank of the river, is also most easily reached by car.

TIMING

It takes about a day to visit most of the tombs and pagodas by boat. Going by car to all of the tombs will take you about half a day. You may, however, be happy to see just a couple of them; set aside about an hour for each (not including transportation time). Organized tours begin in the morning at about 8 and return at around 3. These trips are available daily throughout the year.

SIGHTS TO SEE

⑪ **Thien Mu Pagoda.** At this Mahayana Buddhist temple is one of Hue's most famous monuments, the seven-story, octagonal Phuoc Nguyen Tower. It was built in 1844 by Emperor Thieu Tri and is a peaceful spot overlooking the Perfume River. Each of the tower's tiers is dedicated to a different human incarnation of Buddha. Across the temple's main entrance is the famed Austin car that in 1963 delivered the Buddhist monk Thich Quang Duc to Saigon, where he set himself on fire in an act of pacifist protest against President Diem's regime. The main sanctuary, behind the tower, houses a splendid, large Laughing Buddha; it's open daily 7–11 and 2–5. The temple is still a training center for monks, so you may see the young novices with their mostly shaved heads going about their daily activities. Behind the temple compound is a large cemetery stretching over the hills. ⊠ *About 2½ km (1½ mi) southwest of citadel on left bank of Perfume River,* ☎ *no phone.* 🎫 *Free.* ⊘ *Daily 7–5.*

⑬ **Tomb of Dong Khanh.** Peace and quiet reign at this small tomb set among rice fields and fruit trees. More modest and less crowded than its grand neighbor, the Tomb of Tu Duc, the Tomb of Dong Khanh has few interesting artifacts but seduces with its pastoral environs. ⊠ *Northeast of Tu Duc on right side of river; follow road that leads to Tomb of Tu Duc about ½ km (⅓ mi) around corner,* ☎ *no phone.* 🎫 *22,000d.* ⊘ *Daily 7–5.*

⑯ **Tomb of Duc Duc.** This partially renovated tomb has a story that beats any soap opera. Be sure to visit with a guide who can explain the family history of exile, untimely death, and heartbreak of Emperors Thanh Tri, Duy Tan, and Duc Duc, as well as their many wives and children. You may even have a chance to meet the grandson of Duc Duc, who still lives on the premises. ⊠ *2 km (1 mi) from Le Loi St. on right bank of river,* ☎ *no phone.* 🎫 *Free.* ⊘ *Daily 7–5.*

⑮ **Tomb of Khai Dinh.** An unbelievable concoction of glitzy elements, the Tomb of Khai Dinh, completed in 1931, is well worth a visit. Khai Dinh became emperor in 1916 at the age of 31 and died in 1925. A climb up the few flights of steps, flanked by dragons, takes you to a surprisingly colorful tomb heavily decorated with tile mosaics. Scenes from the four seasons welcome you into the main building. It's best to visit this tomb by car, since it's not directly on the river. ⊠ *About 16 km (10 mi) south of Hue and about 1½ km (1 mi) inland on right bank of Perfume River,* ☎ *no phone.* 🎫 *50,000d.* ⊘ *Daily 8–5.*

⑭ **Tomb of Minh Mang.** A Hue classic, the Tomb of Minh Mang, emperor from 1791 to 1841, was completed in 1843 by his successor. His tomb is one of the most palatial, with numerous pavilions and courtyards in a beautiful pine forest. The burial site is modeled after the Ming tombs in Beijing. Sculptures of mandarins, elephants, and lions line the route to the burial site. ⊠ *About 11 km (7 mi) south of Hue and 1½ km (1 mi) inland on left bank of Perfume River,* ☎ *no phone.* 🎫 *50,000d.* ⊘ *Daily 8–5.*

★ ⑫ **Tomb of Tu Duc.** The Tomb of Tu Duc, one of Hue's most visited tombs, has its own lake and pine forest. Built in 1867 by thousands of laborers, the tomb was once the second residence of Tu Duc, emperor from 1829 to 1883. Despite having more than 100 wives and numerous concubines, Tu Duc somehow found the time to escape here to relax and write poetry. One of his favorite spots was the Xung Khiem Pavilion on the pond filled with lotus blossoms. It's easy to see why he chose this place as a retreat—you may end up spending an hour just wandering around the grounds. ☒ *About 5 km (3 mi) south of Hue on right bank of Perfume River,* ☏ *no phone.* ☒ *50,000d.* ☉ *Daily 8–5.*

OFF THE BEATEN PATH **TU HIEU PAGODA –** You have to walk through a junglelike path from the road and pass a crescent-shape pool to get to one of Hue's most beautiful and peaceful pagodas. This temple, built in 1843, houses a large gold Buddha flanked by gladiolus. It's a good place for quiet meditation. The monks live in simple rooms off to the side. ☒ *About 3 km (2 mi) south of Hue,* ☏ *no phone.* ☒ *Free.* ☉ *Daily 8–5.*

Dining and Lodging

Most restaurants in Hue tend to be modest in appearance but impressive in terms of the fare. Meals typically consist of a large selection of appetizers and main courses that are shared by a group rather than ordered individually. While this can make it difficult to estimate the cost of an individual meal, it allows you to sample Hue's many unique dishes, including *banh khoa,* a meat-filled rice pancake.

Most of the city's hotels stand on the east bank of the Perfume River. Hue has an excellent selection of lodgings in all price ranges. The larger hotels even have small swimming pools and tennis courts. Most have travel services and can arrange for a car and driver for a customized tour. Hotels of all sizes arrange boat tours to the tombs and pagodas as well as guided tours in and around Hue.

$$–$$$ ★ ✗ **Century Riverside Hotel Restaurant.** Perhaps the most upscale dining establishment in Hue, the Century is decorated in traditional Vietnamese style with many Western touches, such as white-linen tablecloths. Two particularly fine Vietnamese dishes are the grilled fish in banana leaves and the superb spring rolls. Diners here are usually guests of the Century Riverside or the adjacent Huong Giang Hotel. ☒ *49 Le Loi St.,* ☏ *054/823–390. AE, MC, V.*

$$ ✗ **Tropical Garden.** Outstanding Western, Asian, and regional dishes round out the menu at the Tropical Garden. House specialties include grilled shrimp and tropical fried rice, which you can enjoy while local musicians perform live Hue folk songs. There's a large garden area, and the interior is air-conditioned for hot summer months. ☒ *5 Chu Van An St.,* ☏ *054/847–143. AE, MC, V.*

$–$$ ★ ✗ **Club Garden.** One of Hue's most upscale spots, the Club Garden is primarily filled with tourists, who come for the fabulous fixed-price five-course dinner for less than $10. A friendly family of waiters serves outstanding Vietnamese and Chinese food. The seafood and fish dishes are particularly good, as are the pork buns. Outside is a large garden, but the air-conditioned, fly-free interior is nicer. A dimly lighted street leads you to the entrance of this small restaurant, where a string of hanging lights welcomes you. ☒ *8 Vo Thi Sau St.,* ☏ *054/826–327. No credit cards.*

$–$$ ✗ **Huong Giang Hotel Restaurant.** From the windows of this spacious third-floor restaurant you can take in great views of the Perfume River. Large portions of very solid Vietnamese food and Western dishes, such as chicken and french fries, are served. The service is excellent; the only downside is the occasional large tour group that takes over the place. Make a reservation if you want a seat by the window. For a little extra, you can have a "royal meal," for which you dress in court clothes provided by the restaurant and are individually attended to by waitstaff in period costume. ✉ *51 Le Loi St.,* ☎ *054/822–122. AE, MC, V.*

$ ✕ **Am Phu.** A favorite with locals, this restaurant, which has been in operation for more than 80 years, serves excellent Vietnamese cuisine. The nonglamorous dining area keeps the place relatively free of Western tourists. Everyone eats together at large tables covered with red plastic tablecloths. Although there are no prices listed on the menu, most dishes cost less than 40,000d, depending on how large a serving is requested. ✉ *35 Nguyen Thai Hoc St.,* ☎ *054/825–259. No credit cards.*

$ ✕ **Lac Thanh Restaurant.** Packed with tourists and teeming with postcard and cigarette vendors, this dive (and its next-door copycat) serves some of the tastiest and cheapest meals in Hue. Some notable dishes include Asian basics such as shrimp and vegetables over crispy noodles and tofu, or beef and vegetables wrapped in rice paper and dipped in peanut sauce. For dessert, try the delicious coconut ice cream topped with chocolate sauce and peanuts. ✉ *6A Dien Tien Hoang St.,* ☎ *no phone. No credit cards.*

$ ✕ **Ngoc Anh.** This relaxed, open-air restaurant—the Vietnamese version of a sidewalk café—serves high-quality Vietnamese and Chinese food. The sizzling-hot clay-pot seafood special is exceptional. ✉ *29 Nguyen Thai Hoc St.,* ☎ *054/822–617. No credit cards.*

¢ ✕ **Banh Beo Ba Cu.** Don't be put off by the grungy interior of this restaurant. The quality of the decor is in inverse proportion to the quality of the food. This favorite among locals serves only eight dishes, all specialties of the region. The price of 3,000d per dish should allow you to try them all—if you're hungry enough. Particularly memorable is the *banh uot thit nuong* (grilled meat rolled in pastry). ✉ *47 Nguyen Hue St.,* ☎ *no phone. No credit cards.*

¢ ✕ **Banh Khoai.** Come to this two-table, family-run food stall for some of the best banh khoai in town. The meat-filled rice pancake (three for 10,000d) topped with bean sprouts comes to the table piping hot. Break it up with chopsticks into your small rice bowl, add the greens and sauce, and eat. This is a great dining experience if you don't mind eating in what is essentially this family's kitchen. You may have to share your table with the cook, who might need the space to peel shrimp. ✉ *2 Nguyen Tri Phuong St., off Hanoi St.,* ☎ *no phone. No credit cards.*

¢ ✕ **Bun Bo Hue.** This very downscale sidewalk food stall close to the center of Hue serves some of the best bun bo Hue, the Hue noodle specialty made with beef and pork. This is the only dish served, and there is no menu. ✉ *11B Ly Kiet St.,* ☎ *no phone. No credit cards.*

¢ ✕ **Mai Huong.** Although it may not live up to your fantasy of a Parisian patisserie, this small "coffee shop" is still a good place for a slice of coconut or apple cake and a cup of tea. Just keep in mind that the ice cream doesn't even vaguely resemble the Baskin-Robbins variety. ✉ *14 Nguyen Tri Phuong St.,* ☎ *no phone. No credit cards.*

$$–$$$ ⌂ **Century Riverside Inn.** Though not opulent by Western standards, the Century, a large Western-style establishment on the river, is the most luxurious hotel in town, with clean and comfortable rooms. About half the rooms, which are done in light colors, have river views. After a long day of sightseeing, you can relax by the small riverfront swimming pool. ✉ *49 Le Loi St.,* ☎ *054/823–390,* ℻ *054/823–399,* ⓦⓔⓑ *www.centuryhotels. com. 158 rooms. 5 restaurants, room service, minibars, refrigerators, cable TV, 2 tennis courts, pool, bicycles, bar, shop, dry cleaning, laundry service, Internet, meeting rooms, travel services. AE, MC, V.*

$$–$$$ ⌂ **Huong Giang Hotel.** Large rooms decorated in traditional Viet-
★ namese style and the most helpful staff in Hue make the Huong Giang,

on the north end of the east bank, the most pleasant hotel in town. Bamboo furniture fills the rooms, and there is an almost palatial feel to the lobby. Ask for one of the renovated older rooms—they're better than the newer, more hastily built ones surrounding the pool. The hotel also has a very good restaurant and rooftop bar-garden with panoramic views of the river. The travel office in the hotel is exceptional. ⌧ *51 Le Loi St.,* ☎ *054/822–122,* 𝖥𝖠𝖷 *054/845–555,* 𝖶𝖤𝖡 *www. huonggiangtourist.com. 134 rooms. 2 restaurants, café, cable TV, tennis court, pool, 2 bars, dry cleaning, laundry service, Internet, meeting room, travel services. AE, MC, V.*

$–$$ 🏨 **Dong Da Hotel.** This spacious hotel on a quiet street corner falls somewhere between a minihotel and a Western-style accommodation. Rooms are clean and modern and have simple Japanese-style furnishings, including rice-paper room dividers. At press time the Dong Da was undergoing renovation to upgrade and expand the number of rooms by early 2003. ⌧ *15 Ly Thuong Kiet St.,* ☎ *054/823–071,* 𝖥𝖠𝖷 *054/823–204. 40 rooms. 2 restaurants, cable TV, bar, laundry service, Internet, meeting rooms, car rental, travel services. AE, MC, V.*

$ 🏨 **Hoa Hong Hotel II.** Almost as comfortable as its more expensive neighbors, the Century Riverside and the Huong Giang, this hotel has similarly styled semiluxurious rooms. It's one of the tallest buildings in town and has the reassuring air of a Holiday Inn. The rooms are nondescript, but everything is relatively new and tasteful. Although the hotel is not on the water, it's tall enough so that many rooms have excellent views of the river. Traditional music and dance are performed nightly in the hotel's restaurants. ⌧ *1 Pham Ngu Lao St.,* ☎ *054/824–377,* 𝖥𝖠𝖷 *054/826–949. 52 rooms. 2 restaurants, minibars, cable TV, laundry service, meeting room, travel services. MC, V.*

¢–$ 🏨 **Dong Duong (L'Indochina) Hotel.** It's just as clean and pleasant as its hotel counterpart, the Huong Giang Hotel, but the Dong Duong has larger rooms and a more intimate environment. The cozy and sunny rooms are arranged in a horseshoe shape around a small garden. Staying here you sacrifice having access to a restaurant (though there is a dining room that serves breakfast) and recreational facilities, but you get the feel of a small inn and easy access to the center of town. ⌧ *2 Hung Vuong St.,* ☎ *054/823–866,* 𝖥𝖠𝖷 *054/825–910,* 𝖶𝖤𝖡 *www.huonggiangtourist.com. 67 rooms. Fans, minibars, refrigerators, cable TV, laundry service, car rental, travel services. AE, MC, V.*

¢–$ 🏨 **Dong Loi Hotel.** Although this hotel looks slightly worn, it is very reasonably priced and is in the downtown area. The rooms are tidy, no-frills accommodations, with unmatched curtains, bedding, and towels. The staff will arrange city tours and excursions outside Hue for you. An adjoining restaurant serves French and Vietnamese dishes at reasonable prices. ⌧ *19 Pham Ngu Lao St.,* ☎ *054/822–296,* 𝖥𝖠𝖷 *054/826–234. 40 rooms. Restaurant, minibars, refrigerators, cable TV, laundry service, Internet, car rental, travel services. AE, MC, V.*

¢–$ 🏨 **Hoa Hong I.** The smaller and less luxurious of the Hoa Hong family of hotels, this place has comfortable rooms with IDD phones and bathrooms with tubs. You may just have to ignore the fake-flower finishing touches and the overly cutesy pastel decor. ⌧ *46C Le Loi St.,* ☎ *054/824–377,* 𝖥𝖠𝖷 *054/826–949. 10 rooms. Restaurant, minibars, refrigerators, laundry service, travel services. MC, V.*

¢ 🏨 **A Dong Hotel 1.** This pleasant, clean, and airy minihotel is a great budget alternative. There's nothing particularly charming about the place, but it does a great job of providing large, basic, immaculate rooms. And the hotel scores big with fresh fruit and flowers delivered daily to your room. The staff speaks very little English but is eager to please. ⌧ *1 Chu Van An St.,* ☎ *054/824–148,* 𝖥𝖠𝖷 *054/849–419. 10 rooms.*

Restaurant, minibars, refrigerators, bar, laundry service, car rental, travel services. No credit cards.

¢ 🏨 **A Dong Hotel 2.** The cheaper of the A Dong hotels, this one is a fine small, clean, and well-run minihotel. Rooms are plain, but all have a private bathroom. ✉ *21 Doi Cung St.*, ☎ *054/822–765*, 𝔽𝔸𝕏 *054/849–419. 15 rooms. Restaurant, laundry service, car rental, travel services. AE, MC, V. To use credit cards you must pay at the hotel's nearby affiliated restaurant.*

¢ 🏨 **Binh Minh.** Rooms are sunny at this small budget hotel, and some have sliding doors that lead to balconies. The staff is very knowledgeable and speaks English. ✉ *36 Nguyen Tri Phuong St.*, ☎ *054/825–526*, 𝔽𝔸𝕏 *054/828–362. 36 rooms. Restaurant, minibars, refrigerators, cable TV, laundry service, travel services. AE, MC, V.*

¢ 🏨 **Duy Tan Hotel.** Despite its large and semigrand appearance, this hotel functions as a glorified minihotel. Rooms are bright and spacious, although the renovation job is pretty spotty. Note that only some of the rooms have full tubs in the bathrooms. ✉ *12 Hung Vuong St.*, ☎ *054/825–001*, 𝔽𝔸𝕏 *054/826–477. 66 rooms. Restaurant, minibars, refrigerators, cable TV, laundry service, meeting rooms, car rental, travel services. No credit cards.*

¢ 🏨 **Hoan My Hotel.** This bright white minihotel slightly off the beaten path (about a mile from the city center) has modest, clean rooms at great prices. The staff speaks very little English, so you may have to make do with a little sign language. The inexpensive Banh Beo Ba Cu restaurant is nearby. ✉ *44 Dong Da St.*, ☎ *054/821–560*, 𝔽𝔸𝕏 *054/821–561. 20 rooms. Restaurant, fans, minibars, refrigerators, cable TV, laundry service, travel services. No credit cards.*

¢ 🏨 **Hue Hotel.** The adjacent Thua Thien–Hue Tourism runs this property with two types of rooms. The more expensive rooms are clean but sparse and have superb air-conditioning. The cheaper rooms, which have fans only, are not as clean as the pricier ones, although they are still acceptable. Oddly, the cheaper rooms look out over the river, while the more expensive ones are set back closer to Le Loi Street. The staff speaks very little English and is not very helpful. ✉ *15 Le Loi St.*, ☎ *054/823–513*, 𝔽𝔸𝕏 *054/824–806. 11 rooms. Fans; no a/c in some rooms. No credit cards.*

¢ 🏨 **Le Loi Hue Hotel.** A little run-down but passable, this hotel close to the train station has rooms with many amenities, including IDD phones. Le Loi Hue often has vacancies when other places are booked. ✉ *2 Le Loi St.*, ☎ *054/822–153*, 𝔽𝔸𝕏 *054/824–527. 164 rooms. Restaurant, minibars, refrigerators, cable TV, laundry service, Internet, car rental, travel services. AE, MC, V.*

¢ 🏨 **Saigon Hotel.** Don't be put off by the strangely decorated restaurant—note the neon-backlighted cow's head—in this minihotel. Rooms are sunny and squeaky clean, and the bathrooms are in excellent condition and have tubs. ✉ *46 Hung Vuong St.*, ☎ *054/821–007*, 𝔽𝔸𝕏 *054/821–009. 15 rooms. Restaurant, fans, laundry service, car rental, travel services. No credit cards.*

¢ ✕🏨 **Tre Xanh Hotel.** This central minihotel, only came into operation in May 2002, has clean rooms, full tubs in the bathrooms, and an enthusiastic English-speaking staff. Plans were underway at press time to add a restaurant. ✉ *33A Hung Vuong St.*, ☎ *054/828–888*, 𝔽𝔸𝕏 *054/827–777. 18 rooms. Minibars, cable TV. MC, V.*

Nightlife and the Arts

Compared to Ho Chi Minh City and Hanoi, Hue is a sleepy town with little in the way of nightlife. Several bars on Le Loi and Hung Vuong streets, however, cater to the backpacker crowd. One of the most popular places to wet your whistle after a long day of sightseeing is **Rendez Vous** (⊠ 2 Hung Vuong St., ☎ 054/849–175), which serves cheap beer and is favored by backpackers. With Western music and inexpensive beer, **DMZ** (⊠ 44 Le Loi St., ☎ 054/823–414) attracts a backpacking crowd.

A culturally enlightening way to spend an evening in Hue is to take a **night cruise** on the Huong River. Boats with musical groups performing traditional Hue folk songs can be rented through most tourist agencies or directly at the river next to the Floating Restaurant (⊠ off Bach Dang St., near intersection with Nguyen Thai Hoc St.). If you still have the energy after a day of visiting Hue's tombs and pagodas, don't miss this enchanting experience.

Shopping

There aren't many places to shop in Hue, although you can pick up some nice souvenirs—including wood carvings and replicas of antique compasses and teapots—at the stands inside the Imperial City and along Le Loi Street. Although the Central Market isn't filled with spectacular finds, it does have two Hue specialties: conical hats, decorated to order, with poems stitched inside (*non la tho*), and sesame-seed candy.

Side Trip from Hue

Hue is a convenient location from which to visit the former Demilitarized Zone (DMZ), which lies less than 100 km (60 mi) north of the city. A trip here can be combined easily with a visit to the Vinh Moc Tunnels and to the numerous former battlefields of the war that dot the area.

Virtually all the tour agencies in Hue (☞ Travel Agencies *in* Hue A to Z, *below*) can arrange trips to the DMZ, Khe Sanh, and the Vinh Moc Tunnels. Given the scattered locations of these sites, tours generally leave Hue early in the morning and return about 12 hours later.

Khe Sanh
⑰ *145 km (90 mi) northwest of Hue.*

One of the biggest battles of the war—and one of the most significant American losses—took place in 1968 at Khe Sanh, the site of a U.S. Army base. Khe Sanh lies in a highland valley not far from Highway 9, which links Vietnam with southern Laos. General William Westmoreland, the commander of U.S. forces in Vietnam from 1965 to 1968, became convinced in late 1967 that the North Vietnamese were massing troops in the area in preparation for a campaign to seize South Vietnam's northernmost provinces. Relying on an analogy with the French defeat at Dien Bien Phu, he reinforced Khe Sanh with thousands of marines and ordered the dropping of more than 75,000 tons of explosives on the surrounding area. The North Vietnamese suffered horrendous casualties—estimates are that as many as 10,000 North Vietnamese soldiers and hundreds of U.S. Marines lost their lives, a sacrifice that seems senseless given the abandoning of the base by the American forces in June 1968. Although the debate continues, many military experts believe that the battle at Khe Sanh was merely a feint designed to pull American forces away from the population centers of South Vietnam in preparation for a massive assault by the North Vietnamese in the Tet Offensive of early 1968.

Although there is only a small **museum** commemorating the battle at Khe Sanh, a visit to the base provides a sense of how isolated and besieged the U.S. Marines must have felt as they were bombarded from the surrounding mountains. In the museum, which opens whenever tours come through the area, there are a number of interesting pictures of the battle and a book for visitors' comments that reflects the continuing debate about the American presence in Vietnam.

DMZ

⑱ *85 km (53 mi) northeast of Khe Sanh, 90 km (56 mi) northwest of Hue.*

The origins of the DMZ (Demilitarized Zone) date to the Geneva Accords of 1954—really just a cease-fire and interlude in the extensive fighting for control of Vietnam—which divided the country in half at the 17th parallel at the Ben Hai River. The northern half of the country became the Communist-led Democratic Republic of Vietnam, and the south became the Republic of Vietnam (led by Ngo Dinh Diem and supported by the United States). The DMZ, which consisted of an area extending 5 km (3 mi) on either side of the borderline, was supposed to have been a temporary measure, enforced only until the Democratic Republic of Vietnam and the Republic of Vietnam could be reunited following elections in 1956. The elections never took place, and the inaptly named DMZ was only abolished after many years of fighting that culminated in the victory of the North Vietnamese forces in 1975. Almost as soon as it was created, the DMZ was militarized, and by 1965 it had become a key battleground in the fight between north and south. The fighting forced virtually all the inhabitants of the area to flee and rendered the DMZ a wasteland.

The area south and west of the DMZ was the scene of some of the most bitter fighting of the war. Some names that may be familiar from the war are Con Thien, Camp Carroll, the Rockpile, Hamburger Hill, Quang Tri, and Khe Sanh.

Vinh Moc Tunnels

⑲ *20 km (12 mi) north of the DMZ.*

Between 1966 and 1968, local villagers built the 3-km-long (2-mi-long) Vinh Moc Tunnels to escape American bombing. The tunnels were later used by the North Vietnamese army to transport goods to Con Co Island. Less claustrophobic than the tunnels at Cu Chi, the tunnels are a testament to the determination and ingenuity of the Vietnamese people under extreme circumstances. Make sure to be in the front of the line when you descend into the tunnels in order to benefit from the guide's presentation.

Hue A to Z

To research prices, get advice from other travelers, and book travel arrangements, visit www.fodors.com.

AIR TRAVEL

Vietnam Airlines flies to Hue's Phu Bai Airport, 15 km (9 mi) south of the city center, from Ho Chi Minh City (1 hour, $65 one-way, once or twice a day) and Hanoi (50 minutes, $65 one-way, once or twice a day). The Vietnam Airlines office in Hue is open daily 7–11 and 1:30–4:30. The flight schedule changes frequently, so confirm departure times with your hotel travel agent or with the airline a day or two before your flight. Taxis are available at the airport to take you into town; the cost is generally about 80,000d.

➤ CARRIER: **Vietnam Airlines** (✉ 7 Nguyen Tri Phuong St., ☎ 054/824–709).

BICYCLE TRAVEL

One of the easiest ways to get around Hue is by bicycle, which you can rent from the Century Riverside Inn on Le Loi Street or at any number of places on Hung Vuong Street.

BUS TRAVEL

The Sinh Café Bus stops in Hue on both its northbound and southbound routes. The one-way fare from Hanoi to Hue is $12 ($9 March–May), and the trip takes about 12 hours. One-way open tour tickets from Ho Chi Minh City to Hue, with stops in Dalat, Nha Trang, and Hoi An, can be purchased for less than $25 ($20 in low season). For more information *see* Bus Travel *in* Smart Travel Tips A to Z. The Sinh Café bus usually departs, both northbound and southbound, between 7 and 8 AM. Call for details, as the schedule changes.

➤ INFORMATION: **Sinh Café Bus** (✉ At Hung Vuong Hotel, 2 Hung Vuong St., ☎ 054/826–918).

CAR AND MINIBUS TRAVEL

Cars or minibuses with drivers can be rented through hotels, booking offices, and government-run travel agencies for $40 and up per day, depending on the kind of vehicle, its age, and whether or not it has air-conditioning. A guide will cost about $25 a day above and beyond the cost of the car and driver. Keep in mind that some of the hard-to-reach monuments, such as the Tomb of Tu Duc, are more accessible if you hire a car and guide.

It's also possible to rent a car or minibus for travel from Hue to Hoi An, Danang, or other points nearby; the cost is approximately $25–$50 for the trip, depending on the condition of the car.

CYCLO TRAVEL

You can almost always find a cyclo outside hotels or cruising along the right bank. For 20,000d you should be able to get pretty much anywhere, although you will almost always have to negotiate to get down to this price. If you hate to bargain, hire a cyclo at the Century Riverside Inn on Le Loi Street; the inn posts suggested cyclo prices, which the drivers follow.

EMERGENCIES

If you have an illness that is not life threatening, seek assistance through your hotel staff. In case of emergency, contact Hue General Hospital (Benh Vien Trung Uong Hue). It's a good idea to take an interpreter with you, as only some of the staff members and doctors speak English.

For a pharmacy, visit Thuoc Tay. The woman working here speaks better French than English, but she is very helpful, especially if you write down what you need. If she doesn't have what you're looking for, she will recommend someone else who does. The sign claims the pharmacy stays open 7:30 AM–10 PM, but it does close for lunch. On Hung Vuong Street there are several other pharmacies (*nha thuoc*) near this one.

➤ CONTACTS: **Hue General Hospital** (✉ 16 Le Loi St., ☎ 054/822–325). **Thuoc Tay** (✉ 5 Hung Vuong St., ☎ no phone).

MONEY MATTERS

The Thua Thien–Hue branch of Vietcom Bank (ICBV) changes money and gives cash advances on Visa and MasterCard. It's open weekdays 7–11 and 1:30–3:30. You can exchange money at most hotels in Hue.

➤ MAJOR BANK: **Vietcom Bank** (✉ 46 Hung Vuong St., ☎ 054/824–571).

TAXIS

Taxis are metered. Expect to pay less than $5 for trips around town. Call Hue Taxi ATC to arrange a ride, or just hail one on the street, although they are not always easy to find. Taxi drivers will also take you anywhere you want to go for a prearranged price. A one-hour taxi trip should cost about $10.

➤ TAXI COMPANY: **Hue Taxi ATC** (☎ 054/824–500 or 054/833–333).

TOURS

Guided tours can be arranged through travel agencies (☞ Travel Agencies, *below*). Many hotels are affiliated with one of the government-run tourism agencies. The DMZ Tour Office arranges different types of tours: guided city tours for $15 per day include tours of the citadel and Imperial Tombs; excursions to surrounding areas include the DMZ and the Bru or Van Kieu ethnic-minority village.

Many hotels and travel agencies in Hue can arrange dragon-boat rides and boat tours, which shuttle you from one tomb and pagoda to the next along the Perfume River. The boat companies are usually affiliated with the Thua Thien–Hue Tourism, or they are run independently. Most boat tours depart at 8 AM daily and cost 40,000d per person, excluding tomb and pagoda entry fees, which can run as high as 50,000d each.

You can also arrange for your own boat with guide at the pier across from the train station on Le Loi Street; a small boat, seating approximately six people, costs $15 a day. In addition, Lac Thanh Restaurant on Dien Tien Hoang Street has its own mini–tourist company, which rents boats. Make arrangements at the restaurant or at the pier.

TRAIN TRAVEL

Trains from all over Vietnam come into the Hue Railway Station (Ga Hue). The ticket office is open daily 7:30–5. Five trains depart daily for Ho Chi Minh City (24 hours, $35–$55 for a sleeping berth), and five depart daily for Hanoi (15 hours, $35–$40 for a sleeping berth).

➤ TRAIN STATION: **Hue Railway Station** (✉ on right bank at southwest end of Le Loi St.).

TRAVEL AGENCIES

Hue has several private tourist companies, primarily located on Le Loi and Hung Vuong streets. Most of these can arrange visits to Hue's tombs, pagodas, and other sights; they can also help you with bus, train, and air tickets. They all accept credit cards.

DMZ Tour Office arranges minibus and car rentals that include a guide, tours of Hue by car, boat tours along the Perfume River, and trips to the DMZ. It also books train and air tickets. It's open daily 8–7.

Huong Giang Tourist Company is a first-class travel agency that gives excellent tours of Hue (including a boat tour of the tombs from which you return by car) and organizes trips to the DMZ. The agency is affiliated with the Huong Giang Hotel but is in a separate location. It's open daily 7–noon and 1:30–5.

Thua Thien–Hue Tourism (Cong Ty Du Lich Thua Thien–Hue) is a government-run tourism agency providing similar services to those of other agencies in town. It's open daily 8–5.

➤ CONTACTS: **DMZ Tour Office** (✉ 26 Le Loi St., ☎ 054/825–242). **Huong Giang Tourist Company** (✉ 17 Le Loi St., ☎ 054/832–220, FAX 054/821–426). **Thua Thien–Hue Tourism** (✉ 30 Le Loi St., ☎ 054/822–369, 054/822–288, or 054/822–355).

DANANG AND ENVIRONS

Although Danang was once an important port town and a critical U. S. Air Force base during the Vietnam War, today it is a dreary, slightly run-down city with only one tourist attraction: an impressive museum of Cham culture. Because Danang is not a big tourist destination, there are few good hotels or restaurants, except for the Furama Resort in nearby China Beach. Danang has a major regional airport, however, which makes it the arrival point for Hue (which also has a small airport), Hoi An, and other nearby cities.

There's really no reason to spend more than a morning in Danang visiting the Cham Museum. But just south of Danang, en route to Hoi An, are China Beach and the cave-temples of the Marble Mountains. Both China Beach and the Marble Mountains can be seen as part of a single day trip from Danang (or Hoi An) or as stops on your way to Hoi An. A pilgrimage to My Son, Vietnam's most significant Cham ruins, also merits at least a half day, either from Danang or Hoi An.

Lang Co Beach

⑳ *35 km (22 mi) north of Danang, 73 km (45 mi) south of Hue.*

A convenient stopover on the trip from Hue to Danang, Lang Co is an idyllic hamlet on a peninsula jutting out into the South China Sea. Lang Co Beach is a good place to have lunch and spend the day, and for the true sun worshiper, it may be worth a night's stay. Take the turn off Highway 1 at the sign for the Lang Co Beach Resort; this will lead you to the long, sandy beach.

Lodging

$$$ 🏨 **Lang Co Beach Resort.** When the Lang Co Beach Resort opened in March 2002, it brought a much-needed upgrade to this beautiful beach's accommodations scene. Although the resort has a bit of the feel of a state-owned hotel, which it is, the facilities are nonetheless first-rate. The staff is friendly and speaks English well. Rooms are basic but have whirlpool tubs, and most have fantastic ocean views. ⊠ *Off Hwy. 1,* ☎ *054/873–555,* 📠 *054/873–504. 45 rooms. Restaurant, in-room hot tubs, in-room safes, cable TV, tennis court, pool, massage, travel services. AE, MC, V.*

En Route Although the trip from Lang Co to Danang involves a sometimes hair-raising drive on a winding mountain road, it's worth the effort for the spectacular views from the **Hai Van Pass** (Deo Hai Van). The panoramic view of the South China Sea and Truong Son Mountain range is unparalleled in Vietnam. (Unfortunately, the mountains' natural beauty is slightly spoiled by the hordes of postcard vendors who try to sell you packets of coconut cookies and chewing gum.) If you look closely, you can make out the Marble Mountains in the distance beyond Danang.

Danang

㉑ *108 km (67 mi) south of Hue, 30 km (19 mi) north of Hoi An, 972 km (603 mi) north of Ho Chi Minh City.*

Danang became an important port city at the end of the 19th century when silt filling up the Thu Bon River eliminated neighboring Hoi An's access to the sea. The French gained control of Danang (which they called Tourane) in 1888, taking it by force from Emperor Gia Long—he had promised it to them in exchange for their help but had reneged on his agreement. In its heyday, during the first half of the 20th cen-

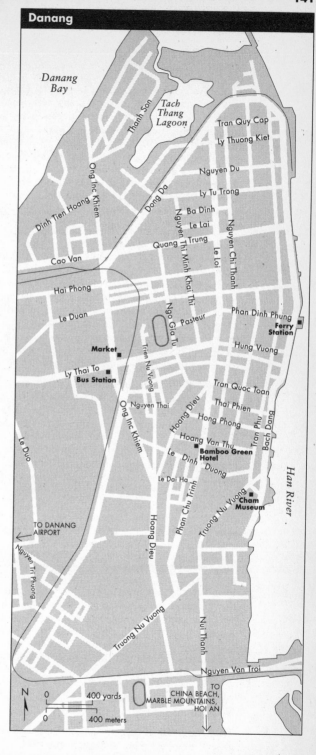

Danang

Danang Bay

Thanh Son

Tach Thang Lagoon

Tran Quy Cap

Ly Thuong Kiet

Nguyen Du

Ong Inc Khiem

Dong Da

Ly Tu Trong

Ba Dinh

Le Lai

Dinh Tien Hoang

Nguyen Thi Minh Khai Thi

Quang Trung

Le Loi

Nguyen Chi Thanh

Cao Van

Hai Phong

Phan Dinh Phung

■ **Ferry Station**

Le Duan

Ngo Gia Tu

Pasteur

Hung Vuong

■ **Market**

Trien Nu Vuong

Ly Thai To ■
Bus Station

Tran Quoc Toan

Nguyen Thai

Thai Phien

Hoang Dieu

Hong Phong

Tran Phu

Bach Dang

Ong Inc Khiem

Hoang Van Thu ■
Bamboo Green Hotel

Le Dinh

Duong

Le Dai Ha

Phan Chu Trinh

Truong Nu Vuong

Cham Museum ■

Han River

Le Duo

TO DANANG AIRPORT

Nguyen Tri Phuong

Hoang Dieu

Truong Nu Vuong

Nui Thanh

Nguyen Van Troi

N

0 — 400 yards

0 — 400 meters

TO
CHINA BEACH,
MARBLE MOUNTAINS,
HOI AN

tury, the city was second only to Saigon as Vietnam's most cosmopolitan center.

During the Vietnam War, Danang played a significant role: it was the first place U.S. Marines landed in March 1965, and it subsequently became home to a large U.S. Air Force base. Only 200 km (124 mi) south of the DMZ, the city was an ideal location for launching bombing missions. The influx of army personnel brought enormous growth, numerous refugees, and all kinds of entertainment, including movie theaters, bars, and prostitution. Soldiers would take time off at the nearby R&R resort of China Beach. By March 1975, Danang was in a state of total chaos as people tried to escape the fast-encroaching North Vietnamese army and had to fight for space on any boat or plane leaving the city. Today there are remnants of the American presence in the city, as well as vestiges of the French in the wide avenues and old villas. But this somewhat run-down city is not a place where you are likely to want to linger after visiting its highlight, the Cham Museum.

★ On display at the **Cham Museum** are artifacts from the Kingdom of Champa, which ruled this region for more than 1,000 years. The museum was founded by the French in 1915 to exhibit Cham sculptures and fragments of temples and towers found by archaeologists. Exhibits are arranged chronologically, reflecting the changing seats of power in the kingdom from Emperor Indrapura to Tra Kieu to My Son to Khuong My. The highly sensual, innovative, and expressive works from Tra Kieu's reign (7th century) and that of My Son (8th–9th centuries) and the abundant sandstone carvings of the god Shiva testify to the prosperity of the Kingdom of Champa.

As you walk through the museum, keep in mind that the Cham religion combines native beliefs with elements of Indian culture and early Hindu thought (the god Shiva is often represented on Cham ruins). The Cham adopted many elements of Indian art and Sanskrit as their sacred language. Note the Cham Buddha depicted on a throne in an imperial pose, with his feet flat on the ground, in contrast to the traditional image of Buddha seated in the lotus position. This subtle difference in Buddha styles reflects the Cham belief in the spiritual continuum between crown and divinity: the nobility were thought to be "higher up" because they were more directly connected to God. The symbol of fertility, Uroja (meaning "woman's breast"), which you will also see throughout the museum, reveals the esteem afforded women in Cham culture.

You'll see the following cast of characters as you look at the Cham sculptures: Vishnu, god of conservation and life; Garuda, the holy bird; Rama, god of creation and birth; Sarasvati, Rama's wife and goddess of sacred language, whose animal counterpart is a swan; Laksmi, Vishnu's wife and goddess of prosperity; Shiva, god of the dead, who is represented in phallic form (*linga*); Skanda, god of war and son of Shiva and Uma, who is often depicted as a peacock; Ganesha, god of peace and the son of Shiva and Uma, whose disobedience prompted Shiva to cut off his head. When Uma prayed to the gods for forgiveness and for a new head for Ganesha, they gave her a consolation prize of the head of the first animal she spotted—hence the omnipresent elephant-head-and-human-body motif.

The central **Tra Kieu Altar** in the Tra Kieu Room—in the middle gallery, opposite the entrance and across the courtyard—illustrates in relief-sculpture part of the Hindu *Ramayana* epic story. This is the museum's best-preserved relief. Beginning on the left panel and working clockwise, the narrative runs as follows: Rama successfully breaks the

THE KINGDOM OF CHAMPA

Despite its nearly 12 centuries of ascendancy over a large swathe of what is present-day Vietnam, very little remains to record the existence of the Kingdom of Champa. The impressive collection of artifacts at the Cham Museum in Danang and the crumbling but still impressive towers and temple complexes that dot the Vietnamese coast from Phan Rang to Danang are among the few vestiges of this once-powerful kingdom.

The Cham, who came to power in the 2nd century AD, settled mainly in coastal areas with a dearth of cultivable land. Their economy was largely based on maritime trade through ports at Hoi An and Qui Nhon and on piracy. Contact with Indian traders in the 4th century had a demonstrably strong influence on the Cham, bringing Hindu religion and art into their culture. The receptive Cham also embraced Mahayana Buddhism in the 9th century, and Islam from the 17th century until the present.

Believed to be of Indonesian origin, the Cham people were (and are) culturally and ethnically distinct from their northern neighbors the Viet (Kinh), and the Khmers to their south. Conflict with these two more populous and powerful kingdoms marked the history of the Kingdom of Champa from its inception until its effective demise in the 15th century.

The first mention of the Kingdom of Champa appears in Chinese historical writing in the year AD 192, by which time King Sri Mara had established a small kingdom in the area of modern-day Quang Tri Province. From its modest beginning, the Kingdom of Champa expanded rapidly and by the 4th century had unified under its control a coastal strip of territory stretching from modern-day Dong Hoi to Phan Thiet. From this base the Cham continued to expand northward, managing for a time to wrest control of the Red River delta and several provinces of southern China from the Chinese Han dynasty, which ruled Vietnam. During the 5th century the Chinese regained control of northern Vietnam and in 446 sacked the Cham capital of Simhapura (located near present-day Danang).

For several centuries China managed to maintain control of northern Vietnam despite ongoing rebellions, until internal turmoil in China in the 10th century gave the Viet an opportunity to throw off Chinese rule for good. Vietnam's independence soon translated into increased pressure on the Cham. Although the Cham managed to repel early Viet incursions, they were also forced to contend with invasions in the southern portion of their kingdom by the Khmers. In retaliation for these raids, the Cham captured and pilfered the Khmer capital of Angkor Wat in the year 1177. Still, it was to be the increasingly powerful Viet who posed the fatal threat to the Kingdom of Champa. From the late 13th century onwards the Viet slowly moved south, claiming Cham territory. The Cham's last great king, Binasuor, managed to halt the slide for three decades in the mid-14th century, but the reversal was only temporary. In 1471 the Viet, led by their king Le Thanh Tong, overran the Cham capital of Vijaya, bringing about Champa's end as an independent kingdom. The nominal existence of a rump Champa was eliminated in 1820 by the Vietnamese king Minh Mang, at which time the last Cham king and many of his subjects fled to Cambodia.

Today there are an estimated 77,000 Cham descendants living in Vietnam, with the majority in the Phan Rang–Phan Thiet region and with significant populations in Ho Chi Minh City and Chau Doc.

sacred bow; Rudra is granted the right to marry King Janak's daughter Princess Sita; the fathers, King Videha and King Dasaratha, interact; and the wedding festivities follow.

English-speaking guides can lead you on tours of the Cham Museum, but make sure you understand what your potential guide is saying and that he or she is truly knowledgeable about the museum's contents before wasting your time and money. ⊠ *Intersection of Tran Phu and Le Dinh Duong Sts.,* ☎ *no phone.* 🎫 *20,000d.* ☉ *Daily 8–6.*

OFF THE
BEATEN PATH

MY SON – About 70 km (43 mi) southwest of Danang, or 45 km (28 mi) due west of Hoi An, are the My Son Cham ruins: former temples and towers dedicated to kings and divinities, particularly Shiva, who was considered the founder of the Kingdom of Champa. Construction first began in the 4th century under the order of the Cham king Bhadresvara and continued until the 13th century. With more than 70 brick structures, of which some 20 remain in recognizable form today, My Son was the most important religious and architectural center of the Kingdom of Champa. Although extensively damaged by American bombing during the war, the My Son complex still retains vestiges of its former glory. Most of the statuary that formerly adorned the temples was taken to the Cham Museum in Danang by the French in the early 20th century. Seeing both the museum and the temples of My Son will enable you to fully appreciate the wonders of Cham culture. Make arrangements for a car and driver through the Danang Tourism Services Company (☞ Car Travel *in* Danang and Environs A to Z, *below*).

Lodging

$–$$ 🏨 **Bamboo Green.** Rooms at Bamboo Green are large and tasteful, with modern conveniences like satellite TVs, IDD phones, and efficient room service. The hotel is just a 10-minute walk from the Cham Museum. ⊠ *158 Phan Chu Trinh St.,* ☎ *0511/822–996,* 🅵🅰🆇 *0511/822–998,* 🆆🅴🅱 *www.vntourism.com/danangtourism. 46 rooms. 2 restaurants, room service, minibars, refrigerators, massage, bar, dry cleaning, laundry service, Internet, business services, meeting rooms, car rental, travel services. AE, MC, V.*

Shopping

Fabric shops and tailors along Hung Vuong Street can make clothes for you cheaply and quickly. Shirts and pants should cost less than $10 apiece.

Marble Mountains

★ ㉒   *11 km (7 mi) southwest of Danang, 19 km (12 mi) north of Hoi An.*

Five beautiful limestone peaks, known as the Marble Mountains, rise above the beach south of Danang and north of Hoi An. Tours from Danang en route to Hoi An generally stop here, and a visit to the mountains can easily be combined with a trip to China Beach. The five Marble Mountains have been equated with the five basic elements of Chinese philosophy: Tho Son (earth), Thuy Son (water), Hoa Son (fire), Moc Son (wood), and Kim So (metal). Over the centuries the *dong* (caves) in the Thuy Son Peak have been turned into temples and shrines. The first to use them were the Cham, who converted them into Hindu shrines. The Buddhists have since taken over, adorned, sanctified, and inhabited them.

The climb up the path leading to the various cave-pagodas is not particularly strenuous, unless attempted in the middle of a hot, sunny day. Polite children in traditional school uniforms (white shirt and blue trousers) may take you by the hand and give you a free guided tour of the various Buddhist cave sanctuaries. Since there is only one path, and there are enough people around, it's usually not a problem to have them accompany you. At the end of these tours, don't be surprised if they offer you the "best price . . . for you only" for marble souvenirs, such as miniature Marble Mountains. You shouldn't feel obliged to buy one, however.

After entering through Ong Chon Gate, the main entrance, you'll see the **Linh Ong Pagoda,** a Buddhist shrine inside a cave, filled with a large collection of Buddhas. The hole at the top of the cave filters in an ethereal sort of natural light. As you continue on the main path, you'll come to another temple, the **Tam Thai Tu Pagoda,** where monks still live. The path then leads to a spectacular view of the mountains and the surrounding countryside. ✉ *Off Hwy. 1.* ✆ *Free, but donation may be requested at pagodas.*

China Beach

➁ *12 km (7 mi) southeast of Danang, 25 km (16 mi) north of Hoi An.*

Yes, the TV show *China Beach* was based on this place, but the China Beach that was an R&R resort spot for U.S. soldiers during the Vietnam War is actually 5 km (3 mi) north of what is now called China Beach (Bac My An). China Beach's pristine and quiet sandy stretches are a welcome change from Danang's portlike atmosphere. Activity here is limited to lazing on the sand and surfing. It's best to come between May and July, when the water is placid. Waves can be very large at other times—in fact, the first international surfing competition in Vietnam was held in China Beach in December 1992.

One of the most beautiful and pleasantly deserted beaches in all of Vietnam is just a short stroll from the China Beach Resort (the 1960s-era concrete hotel at the foot of the Marble Mountains). Walk south down the beach from the resort for about ½ km (⅓ mi) until you arrive at a pristine white-sand beach straight out of a tourist brochure.

Lodging

$$$ 🏨 **Furama Resort.** French Vietnamese–style villas surround an artificial tropical swimming lagoon right on the beach at this resort. Rooms overlook either the lagoon or the ocean. Shuttered windows, cane furniture, ceiling fans, and Vietnamese pieces hark back to the French colonial era. The resort has a shuttle service from Danang's airport and can organize tours for you to Danang, Hue, and Hoi An. ✉ *68 Ho Xuan Huong St., Bac My An,* ✆ *0511/847–333; 08/821–1888 in Ho Chi Minh City;* 𝔽𝔸𝕏 *0511/847–666;* 𝕎𝔼𝔹 *www.furamavietnam.com. 200 rooms. 2 restaurants, room service, in-room safes, minibars, cable TV, driving range, 2 tennis courts, pool, health club, sauna, beach, bicycles, 2 bars, dry cleaning, laundry service, Internet, meeting rooms, airport shuttle, travel services. AE, MC, V.*

Outdoor Activities and Sports

Surfboards, surfing gear, and bicycles can be rented from the Furama Resort and the China Beach Resort.

Danang and Environs A to Z

To research prices, get advice from other travelers, and book travel arrangements, visit www.fodors.com.

AIR TRAVEL

Vietnam Airlines flies to Danang's airport, 3 km (2 mi) southwest of the city, from Ho Chi Minh City (twice daily, $65 one-way), Hanoi (twice daily, $65 one-way), and Nha Trang (once daily, $37 one-way). To make arrangements in Danang, go to the Vietnam Airlines booking office; it's open daily 7–11 and 1:30–4:30. Booking offices in Hoi An, including those in your hotel, can also make plane reservations. A regular taxi to the airport should cost no more than 50,000d; to reserve one, call Airport Taxis, Danang's most reliable taxi company.

➤ CARRIER: **Vietnam Airlines** (✉ 35 Tran Phu St., Danang, ☎ 0511/821–130, FAX 0511/832–759).

➤ TAXI COMPANY: **Airport Taxis** (☎ 0511/825–555).

CAR TRAVEL

You can rent cars and motorbikes for travel within Danang. China Beach and the Marble Mountains are easily accessible by car from Danang, as is Hoi An. You can make arrangements at most hotels and through the Danang Tourism Services Company. Depending on the type of car you rent, the round-trip price to Hoi An with a stop at the Marble Mountains should cost no more than $30.

➤ CONTACT: **Danang Tourism Services Company** (✉ 76 Hung Vuong St., ☎ 0511/823–993 or 0511/825–653, FAX 0511/821–312).

EMERGENCIES

Contact your hotel for medical assistance or if something has been stolen.

MONEY MATTERS

Changing money at your hotel is the easiest option. Vietcom Bank is the only place in Danang that gives credit-card cash advances; it's open weekdays 7:30–11 and 1–4.

➤ MAJOR BANK: **Vietcom Bank** (✉ 140 Le Loi St.).

TAXIS

In Danang, the taxi drivers hanging around the Cham Museum have the cheapest rates in town—about $15 for the day. They also provide transportation to Hoi An for about $10. Taxis are preferable to cyclos since the roads are bad, even in town, and the scenery is grim.

TRAVEL AGENCY

Danang Tourism Services Company is your best bet for travel services in Danang. In addition to travel arrangements and car rentals, the agency can handle visa extensions and can book you into one of its many affiliated hotels.

➤ CONTACT: **Danang Tourism Services Company** (✉ 76 Hung Vuong St., ☎ 0511/823–993 or 0511/825–653, FAX 0511/821–312).

HOI AN

Perhaps the most delightful of all Vietnamese towns, enchanting riverside Hoi An, 30 km (19 mi) south of Danang, defies the insidious pace of modernization. Preserved in pristine condition are its 18th-century houses, pagodas, and assembly halls built by the early Fujian, Canton, Chaozhou, and Hainan—Chinese communities living in Hoi An. The many galleries selling the works of local artists and artisans and the numerous cafés give the town a strong bohemian feel. Hoi An has great cuisine and is probably the most tourist-friendly town in the whole country, with many Internet cafés and with English being widely spoken. The whole town can easily be navigated on foot in an hour, but plan to spend more time in Hoi An than you think you'll need, since it's easy to fall in love with the place. Just outside of town is the pleasant Cua Dai Beach, which you reach by taking a 5-km (3-mi) ride through a picturesque slice of rural Vietnam. Also nearby are the My Son

Cham ruins (☞ Danang and Environs, *above*), which evoke the ancient history of this region.

Hoi An, or Faifo as it was called in previous centuries, is a composite of many foreign influences. From the 2nd to 10th century AD, the city was under the control of the Kingdom of Champa and was an important port town. During the 14th and 15th centuries, the Cham and the Vietnamese fought for control of Hoi An, and as a consequence the city ceased to be a trading center. Peace between the Cham and the Vietnamese in the 16th century once again made possible the accommodation of ships from all over Asia and Europe, bringing merchants in search of silk, porcelain, lacquer, and medicinal herbs. During the Tay Son Rebellion in the 1770s, Hoi An was severely damaged by fighting.

After a speedy reconstruction the town managed to sustain a two-century tenure as a major international port town where Chinese, Japanese, Dutch, and Portuguese merchants came to trade. During the off-season, seafaring merchants set up shop, and foreigners' colonies began to develop along Hoi An's riverfront. To this day, ethnic Chinese, who settled early in Hoi An, make up a significant portion of the population.

The French arrived in the late 1800s and made Hoi An an administrative post. They even built a rail line to Danang (then called Tourane). By this time, the Thu Bon River, which connected Hoi An to the sea, had begun to fill up with silt, making navigation almost impossible. Danang gradually eclipsed Hoi An as the major port town in the area. Fortunately, Hoi An was not destroyed during the Vietnam War, and today the old town combines Vietnamese, Japanese, and Chinese architectural styles.

If at all possible, time your visit to Hoi An to coincide with the 14th day of the month according to the lunar calendar. On this night the streets of the old town are restricted to pedestrian traffic, and paper lanterns replace electric lights. Although the locals complain a bit about the inconvenience, the effect is magical.

Exploring Hoi An

The old town is strictly reserved for pedestrians, bicycles, and the occasional motorbike. With ancient structures on almost every corner, it's the perfect place for a leisurely stroll. You can get a map from your hotel or from the local tourist office at the corner of Nguyen Hue and Phan Chu Trinh streets.

To get tickets to official monuments you must go to the central tourist office at the corner of Nguyen Hue and Phan Chu Trinh streets, rather than to the locations themselves. For 50,000d you get to choose from a "menu" of sights: one of three museums, one of three assembly halls, one of four old houses, and the Japanese Bridge or the Quan Cong Temple. Once you buy your first ticket from the tourist office, you may purchase an additional entry ticket there to any sight for 10,000d (these are also available at most hotels).

A Good Walk

A good place to begin exploring Hoi An is at the tourist office, where you must purchase your ticket for official monuments, on Nguyen Hue Street, close to the corner of Phan Chu Trinh Street. You can hire an English- or French-speaking guide in the office for 50,000d.

After purchasing your ticket, start your walk at the small colonial-era **Museum of History and Culture** ㉔, approximately one block south of the tourist office, at the corner of Tran Phu and Nguyen Hue streets.

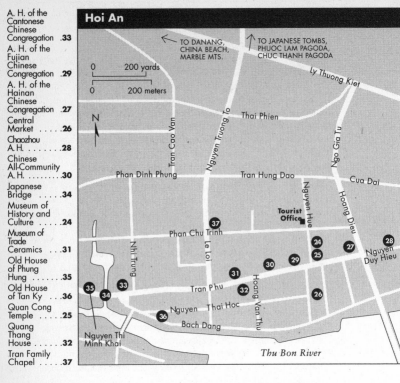

Hoi An

TO DANANG,
CHINA BEACH,
MARBLE MTS.

TO JAPANESE TOMBS,
PHUOC LAM PAGODA,
CHUC THANH PAGODA

Ly Thuong Kiet

0   200 yards
0   200 meters

N

Thai Phien

Tran Cao Van

Nguyen Truong To

Phan Dinh Phung   Tran Hung Dao   Cua Dai

Ngo Gia Tu

Nguyen Hue

Hoang Dieu

Tourist
Office

Phan Chu Trinh   ㉗   ㉘

㉔   Nguyen
㉕   Duy Hieu

Le Loi

Nhi Trung

㉚   ㉙

㉛

Tran Phu   ㉜

Hoang Van Thu

㉖

㉟   ㉝

㉞

Nguyen   Thai Hoc

㉟

Bach Dang

Nguyen Thi
Minh Khai

Thu Bon River

The entrance to the museum brings you to a collection of ancient ceremonial gongs and other religious objects. Walk across the courtyard filled with birdcages to get to **Quan Cong Temple** ㉕, dedicated to a deified Chinese general. Leave through the front entrance and you'll find yourself directly in front of the **Central Market** ㉖, one of Vietnam's most pleasant and easy to navigate. Stay clear of the river unless you want to stumble onto the day's catch.

After exiting the market from where you came in, make a right onto Tran Phu Street and walk to No. 178, just before Hoang Dieu Street, the **Assembly Hall of the Hainan Chinese Congregation** ㉗. Continue east on Tran Phu Street, which turns into Nguyen Duy Hieu Street after it intersects with Hoang Dieu Street. Just past the intersection on the left, at No. 157, is the **Chaozhou Assembly Hall** ㉘, with its fine wood carvings. Turn around and start walking back down Tran Phu Street the way you came. Continue until you get to the corner of Tran Phu and Tran Quy Cap streets; cross over Tran Phu so that you are on the even-number side of the street. Almost immediately on your right, at No. 46, is the colorful **Assembly Hall of the Fujian Chinese Congregation** ㉙, now a temple devoted to Thien Hau, the goddess of the sea. Continue along Tran Phu Street until you come to No. 64, the **Chinese All-Community Assembly Hall** ㉚, on your right; as its name implies, it was used as a meeting place for all the Chinese communities in Hoi An. At No. 80 is the Diep Dong Nguyen House, which has been converted into the **Museum of Trade Ceramics** ㉛. Farther along on your left is the ancient **Quang Thang House** ㉜, at No. 77.

At the intersection of Tran Phu and Chau Thuong Van streets, on the north side, is the **Assembly Hall of the Cantonese Chinese Congregation** ㉝. Farther along Tran Phu Street, past a row of souvenir shops and the intersection with Nhi Trung Street, is the entrance to the red wooden **Japanese Bridge** ㉞. After visiting the bridge, keep going on Tran Phu Street, but note that the street name changes to Nguyen Thi Minh Khai Street. At No. 4 is the **Old House of Phung Hung** ㉟, where eight generations of one family have lived for more than 200 years. Turn around and head back east on Tran Phu Street. Take the small road that forks in front of the Japanese Bridge (Chau Thuong Van Street) to get to Nguyen Thai Hoc Street. At No. 101 is the **Old House of Tan Ky** ㊱. Continue east on Nguyen Thai Hoc Street and then make a left onto Le Loi Street. Cross Phan Chu Trinh Street; on the corner is the **Tran Family Chapel** ㊲, where you can get a tour from members of the Tran Family.

TIMING

At a leisurely pace, this walk will probably take you about three or four hours, perhaps a little longer if you stop to linger at some of the sights. Other sights outside of town will take about an hour each.

Sights to See

㉝ **Assembly Hall of the Cantonese Chinese Congregation.** The main altar of this hall, founded in 1786, is dedicated to Quan Cong, a revered General of the Chinese Han dynasty. ⊠ *176 Tran Phu St., at Nguyen Thai Hoc St.,* ☎ *no phone.* ▦ *Included in 50,000d tourist-office ticket.* ⊙ *Daily 8–5.*

㉙ **Assembly Hall of the Fujian Chinese Congregation.** Built as a meeting place for Chinese residents of Hoi An, this hall later became a temple dedicated to the Fujian goddess of the sea and protector of fishermen, Thien Hau. It's a reminder of how important fishing and trading were to the Chinese community in Hoi An. Thien Hau is represented in the mural near the entrance. Another mural depicts six Fujian families who fled from China to Hoi An in the 17th century. The gate is newer: it was constructed in 1975. ⊠ *Opposite 35 Tran Phu St.,* ☎ *no phone.* ▦ *Included in 50,000d tourist-office ticket.* ⊙ *Daily 8–5.*

㉗ **Assembly Hall of the Hainan Chinese Congregation.** This hall, founded by Chinese from Hainan, was constructed in 1883 in memory of more than 100 merchants who were mistakenly (some say purposefully) killed by a general in Emperor Tu Duc's army because they were thought to be pirates. ⊠ *178 Nguyen Duy Hieu St.,* ☎ *no phone.* ▦ *Included in 50,000d tourist-office ticket.* ⊙ *Daily 8–5.*

㉖ **Central Market.** Hoi An's Central Market is one of the most enjoyable markets in Vietnam. The merchants here are friendly, and a large selection of merchandise is available. The outer aisles of the market are lined with silk shops that can handle custom clothing orders—pants, shirts, dresses, and even suits—all made for you in less than 24 hours. In the center aisles are fresh and dried fruit, flowers, and fresh tobacco. Miscellaneous items, such as batteries, pajamas, and bicycle pumps, pop up in stands throughout. Walk toward the river to find the fish sellers with their daily catch. ⊠ *Intersection of Tran Quy Cap and Tran Phu Sts.,* ☎ *no phone.* ⊙ *Daily 6–dusk.*

㉘ **Chaozhou Assembly Hall** (Trieu Chau). Constructed by the Chaozhou Chinese community in 1776, this assembly hall exemplifies Chinese wood carving of this period at its finest. Note the carved ceiling and the depiction of Chinese women on the doors in the front of the altar. ⊠ *157 Nguyen Duy Hieu St.,* ☎ *no phone.* ▦ *Included in 50,000d tourist-office ticket.* ⊙ *Daily 8–5.*

㉚ **Chinese All-Community Assembly Hall** (Chua Ba). This assembly hall was built in 1773 as a meeting place for Cantonese, Chaozhou, Fujian,

Hainan, and Hakka families living in Hoi An. ⊠ *64 Tran Phu St.,* ☎ *no phone.* 🎫 *Included in 50,000d tourist-office ticket.* ⊙ *Daily 8–5.*

OFF THE
BEATEN PATH

CHUC THANH PAGODA AND PHUOC LAM PAGODA – If you are interested in seeing even more pagodas, head north on Nguyen Truong To Street for approximately 1 km (½ mi) to the end, turn left, and follow the path until you reach the Chuc Thanh Pagoda, the oldest pagoda in Hoi An. Founded in 1454 by Minh Hai, a Chinese Buddhist monk, the pagoda contains several ancient religious objects, including several bells and gongs made of both stone and wood. On the way back stop at the Phuoc Lam Pagoda, built in the mid-17th century. Note the interesting Chinese architecture and the large collection of ceramics on its roof. Both pagodas are open daily 8–5 and are free.

㉞ Japanese Bridge (Cau Nhat, or Lai Vien Kieu). One of the city's landmarks and one of its oldest structures, this red-painted wooden bridge was originally built in 1593 by the Japanese to link their quarter of town to the Chinese quarter. It has been rebuilt a number of times since. At one end of the structure stand statues of two dogs; at the other end are statues of two monkeys—perhaps indicating the years when the bridge's construction was begun and completed. The small temple (Chua Cau) on the northern side of the bridge is dedicated to Tran Vo Bac De (God of the North), revered by sailors because he controls wind and rain. ⊠ *Tran Phu St., west of intersection with Nhi Trung St.,* ☎ *no phone.* 🎫 *Included in 50,000d tourist-office ticket.* ⊙ *Daily 8–5.*

OFF THE
BEATEN PATH

JAPANESE TOMBS – Erected in the 1600s, these are the few remaining tombs of Hoi An's old Japanese community. Although the tombs—tombstones, really—are not nearly as grand as those in Hue, it's worth the trek if only to see the "suburbs" of Hoi An. En route you'll see families sitting in their front yards and field workers harvesting rice. Buried in the first tomb along the dirt path—clearly visible in the front yard of a family home, although there are no signs—is a Japanese merchant named Masai. About another 1,500 ft ahead is the most famous of Hoi An's Japanese tombs, the burial place of a Japanese merchant named Yajirobei, who died in 1647. Perched right in the middle of a working rice field, his tomb has an almost supernatural feel. It's best if you hire a motorbike and driver to take you 3 km (2 mi) north of the city to see the tombs. (Cars are not recommended because the tombs are at the end of a narrow, rugged path, and it's best to hire a driver for the motorbike because the tombs are almost impossible to find on your own.)

㉔ Museum of History and Culture. This small museum—housed in just one large room—provides a great introduction to Hoi An and its culture. On display are ancient bowls, cups, and other ceramics, many of them archaeological artifacts. A collection of traditional Chinese objects includes pagoda bells and the "watchful eyes" placed above doorways for protection. Birdcages fill the pleasant courtyard here. ⊠ *7 Nguyen Hue St.,* ☎ *no phone.* 🎫 *Included in 50,000d tourist-office ticket.* ⊙ *Daily 8–5.*

★ **㉛ Museum of Trade Ceramics.** The ancient Diep Dong Nguyen House has been converted into a terrific small museum dedicated to the history of ceramics in Hoi An. The collection includes ancient wares, some of them recovered from shipwrecks in the surrounding waters, and a large assortment of household objects, such as bowls and vases. There are also detailed architectural drawings of the house, with an explanation of its design and its Chinese, Vietnamese, and Japanese influences. ✉ *80 Tran Phu St.,* ☎ *no phone.* 🎟 *Included in 50,000d tourist-office ticket.* ⊙ *Daily 8–5.*

㉟ Old House of Phung Hung. Ask the owner to explain in French, or his granddaughter to explain in English, the architectural significance of this house built in 1780. Eight generations of the Phung Hung family have lived here since that time. Note the Japanese influences in the roof, the Chinese influences in the balcony, and the Vietnamese architectural style of the walls. On the second floor is a bowl containing dice: if you roll a red one, it is said, your journey will be lucky; if not, you should probably postpone your trip. ✉ *4 Nguyen Thi Minh Khai St.,* ☎ *no phone.* 🎟 *Included in 50,000d tourist-office ticket.* ⊙ *Daily 8–5.*

㊱ Old House of Tan Ky. One of the oldest private houses in Hoi An, this structure has remained largely unchanged in the 200 years since it was built. Seven generations of the Tan Ky family have lived here. The house incorporates both Chinese and Japanese styles. Chinese poetry is engraved in mother-of-pearl on the walls. The back door was constructed to open onto the river so that waterborne goods could be easily transported into the house. ✉ *101 Nguyen Thai Hoc St.,* ☎ *no phone.* 🎟 *Included in 50,000d tourist-office ticket.* ⊙ *Daily 8–5.*

NEED A BREAK? | You can dine in a 200-year-old home at the **Yellow River (Hoang Ha) Restaurant** (✉ 38 Tran Phu St., ☎ 051/861–053), where the owner serves Chinese specialties and will happily tell you about his family.

㉕ Quan Cong Temple. Founded in 1653 by the Chinese community, this temple is dedicated to Quan Cong, a revered general of the Chinese Han dynasty. Quan Cong lends itself to contemplation and meditation, whether you're standing inside the bright-red interior of the temple or watching the small school of fish that happily dart around in the pond out front. The carp, symbolic of patience in Chinese mythology, is displayed throughout. ✉ *168 Tran Phu St.,* ☎ *no phone.* 🎟 *Included in 50,000d tourist-office ticket.* ⊙ *Daily 8–5.*

㉜ Quang Thang House. One of Hoi An's ancient family homes—built about 300 years ago—this house has some beautiful wood carvings on the walls of the rooms that surround the courtyard. ✉ *77 Tran Phu St.,* ☎ *no phone.* 🎟 *Included in 50,000d tourist-office ticket.* ⊙ *Daily 8–5.*

㊲ Tran Family Chapel. This 1802 house is dedicated to the worship of the Tran family's deceased ancestors. The altar in the house faces west, the direction the Vietnamese believe their ancestors face. Behind the altar stands a box with pictures and names of dead relatives. Tours are given in English by members of the Tran family. ✉ *21 Le Loi St.,* ☎ *no phone.* 🎟 *Included in 50,000d tourist-office ticket.* ⊙ *Daily 8–5.*

Dining and Lodging

$$$ ✕ **Café des Amis.** Be warned: visitors who eat here on their first night
★ in Hoi An have a tendency not to try anywhere else. There is no menu at the Café des Amis. Instead, your waiter will ask if you want to eat a seafood or vegetarian meal and then will start bringing you food. Expect five or six excellent courses of French-influenced Vietnamese cuisine. Funky Western background music and a waterfront location make for a great dining experience. ✉ *52 Bach Dang St.,* ☎ *0510/861–616. No credit cards.*

$–$$$ ✕ **Tam Tam Café.** In a tastefully restored former teahouse, this restaurant-cum-bar is the perfect place to unwind after a day of sightseeing. The French proprietor oversees the preparation of steaks, homemade pastas, and traditional French and Italian dishes. The Tam Tam is also a good spot to while away the warmer hours of the day playing pool or reading with a cold drink. ✉ *110 Nguyen Thai Hoc St.,* ☎ *0510/862–212. No credit cards.*

$$ ✕ **Brother's Café.** The typical, good Vietnamese food served here—such as spring rolls and fried rice—may not be spectacular, but the setting is: a beautifully restored colonial villa on the banks of the Thu Bon River. The stylish interior has ceiling beams, tile floors, and classic Chinese-style wooden furniture. In the evenings you can sit and sip a drink in the lovely garden in back as you watch local fisherfolk ply their trade. ✉ *27 Phan Boi Chau St.,* ☎ *0510/914–150. AE, MC, V.*

$$ ✕ **Vinh Hung Restaurant.** This restaurant, a peaceful oasis across the street from the Cantonese Assembly Hall, serves superb seafood and local specialties such as "white roses," the delicious shrimp dumpling said to resemble a rose. Chinese lanterns and lacquered chairs decorate the place, which caters primarily to tourists. The outdoor Chinese high-back wooden chairs are great for people-watching. ✉ *147B Tran Phu St.,* ☎ *0510/862–203. MC, V.*

$–$$ ✕ **Café Can.** The riverfront Café Can serves fantastic meals at absurdly low prices. The seafood here is excellent, particularly the fish served in banana leaves and the steamed crab. The set meal includes five courses and is a good and inexpensive option for those with healthy appetites. If there is anything you want that this restaurant does not have, the eager staff will probably run out and get it. ✉ *74 Bach Dang St.,* ☎ *0510/861–525. No credit cards.*

$–$$ ✕ **Restaurant Thanh.** This restaurant makes a splendid flounder (or whatever whitefish happens to be fresh that day) cooked in banana leaves, as well as a refreshing squid salad prepared with lemon, onion, peanuts, and cucumber. Unfortunately, the open-air, candlelighted riverfront dining is frequently disrupted by persistent postcard vendors. ✉ *76 Bach Dang St.,* ☎ *0510/861–366. No credit cards.*

$ ✕ **Faifoo.** Come here for refreshing fruit shakes, as well as a great multicourse sampler menu of chicken and pork dishes, all for next to nothing. You might want to avoid the Pizza-Spaghetti-Guacamole, however; it's not one of Faifoo's better dishes. ✉ *104 Tran Phu St.,* ☎ *0510/861–548. No credit cards.*

$ ✕ **Ly Cafeteria 22.** Catering mostly to backpackers, Ly Cafeteria 22 is a great place for a cheap lunch; it's also open for dinner. This very friendly spot serves delicious local specialties such as *cao lau* (a noodle dish topped with pork and bean sprouts) and "white roses." ✉ *22 Nguyen Hue St.,* ☎ *0510/861–603. No credit cards.*

$$$ 🏨 **Hoi An Beach Resort.** The Hoi An Beach Resort is a new but somewhat disappointing addition to the list of accommodations in Hoi An. While slightly less pricey than its sister hotel, the Victoria Hoi An Resort, the hotel is not on the beach but a short walk away. The rooms, which have garden or river views, are a bit sterile but do have nice bathtubs. ✉ *Cua Dai Beach,* ☎ *0510/927–011,* FAX *0510/927–019,* WEB *www.hoiantourist.com. 85 rooms. Restaurant, cable TV, 2 pools, bicycles, laundry service, Internet, business services, meeting rooms, car rental, travel services. AE, MC, V.*

$$$ 🏨 **Hoi An Riverside Resort.** Midway between the town of Hoi An and
★ Cua Dai Beach, the Hoi An Riverside Resort may be the most peaceful accommodation in Vietnam. True to its name, the hotel nestles on a beautiful stretch of the Thu Bon River and faces an idyllic picture of rural Vietnamese life. Dark-wood furniture and warm colors decorate the guest rooms, which have comfortable beds and large bathrooms. The staff is charming and engaging. ✉ *On Cua Dai road approximately 3 km (2 mi) from Hoi An Town,* ☎ *0510/864–800,* FAX *0510/864–900,* WEB *www.hoianriverresort.com. 60 rooms. Restaurant, in-room data ports, in-room safes, cable TV, pool, travel services. AE, MC, V.*

$$$ ⊡ **Victoria Hoi An Resort.** On a brilliant stretch of white beach, Hoi An's most upscale resort is the perfect place to pamper yourself. The bright rooms are tasteful, if a bit spartan, with big soft beds and views of the river or sea. If you tire of soaking up rays at the pool or the beach, take a ride on the resort's resident elephant, Darling. ⊠ *Cam An Beach,* ☎ *0510/927–040,* FAX *0510/927–041,* WEB *www.victoriahotel-vietnam. com. 100 rooms. 2 restaurants, in-room data ports, in-room safes, cable TV, 2 tennis courts, pool, gym, spa, bar, library, business services, meeting rooms, travel services. AE, MC, V.*

$ ⊡ **Hoi An Hotel.** The most cheerful staff in all of Vietnam makes up for the lack of luxury in what is just about the only real hotel in Hoi An town (the rest of the lodgings in town are minihotels, and the other hotels and resorts are by the beach). Rooms are comfortable, spotless, and spacious, if basic (though they do have hair dryers). The outstanding Hoi An tourist office is in the lobby; it runs tours of the city and can help you make travel arrangements for your next destination. ⊠ *6 Tran Hung Dao St.,* ☎ *0510/861–445,* FAX *0510/861–636,* WEB *www.hoiantourist.com. 148 rooms. Restaurant, tennis court, pool, bicycles, laundry service, meeting rooms, car rental, travel services. AE, MC, V.*

¢–$ ⊡ **Hai Yen Hotel.** One of several hotels on the road to the beach, the Hai Yen has spacious and inexpensive suites and an almost rural setting, with rice fields just a few steps away. ⊠ *22A Cua Dai St.,* ☎ *0510/ 862–445,* FAX *0510/862–443. 41 rooms. Restaurant, minibars, cable TV, pool, bar, shop, car rental, travel services. AE, MC, V.*

¢–$ ⊡ **Vinh Hung Hotel I.** This Chinese-inspired hotel near the Japanese Bridge has dark wood carvings and a smiling Buddha in the lobby. Rooms are sunny and cheerfully decorated. ⊠ *143 Tran Phu St.,* ☎ *0510/861–621,* FAX *0510/861–893. 12 rooms. Bar, laundry service, travel services. MC, V.*

¢ ⊡ **Cua Dai Hoi An Hotel.** One of the nicest accommodations in town, this plush minihotel has spotless, sunny rooms, many with balconies. It's between the beach and the town center, both of which are just a short bike ride away (you can rent bikes at the hotel). ⊠ *18A Cua Dai St.,* ☎ *0510/862–231,* FAX *0510/862–232. 24 rooms. Restaurant, bicycles, laundry service, travel services. MC, V.*

¢ ⊡ **Huy Hoang Hotel I.** If you plan to stay at this hotel close to the river and the Central Market, be sure to ask for one of the few brightly decorated, basic rooms with balconies overlooking the tree-lined street. Others rooms here don't have windows and aren't nearly as nice. ⊠ *73 Phan Boi Chau St.,* ☎ *0510/861–453,* FAX *0510/863–722. 26 rooms. Fans, bicycles, car rental, travel services. MC, V.*

¢ ⊡ **Thanh Binh I.** This inexpensive central hotel has clean rooms that get plenty of light. Get here early: the hotel often fills up by noon with budget travelers. ⊠ *1 Le Loi St.,* ☎ *0510/861–740,* FAX *0510/864–192. 15 rooms. Cable TV, laundry service, car rental, travel services. MC, V.*

¢ ⊡ **Thanh Binh II (Peace Hotel).** The squeaky-clean rooms of this sister hotel to the original Thanh Binh Hotel are only a few minutes' walk from Hoi An's main attractions. There is also a tailor shop, on the second floor of the hotel. ⊠ *1A Nhi Trung St.,* ☎ *0510/863–715,* FAX *0510/864–192. 32 rooms. Restaurant, minibars, laundry service, car rental. MC, V.*

Outdoor Activities and Sports

Bicycling

For a low-impact, highly scenic workout, rent a bicycle and ride 20 minutes from the center of town to Cua Dai Beach, a splendid place to catch a breeze and relax in the sun. To get to Cua Dai, ride 5 km (3 mi) east of the town center along Tran Hung Dao Street, which turns into Cua Dai Street, all the way to the beach. If you are feeling really energetic, follow the road out to the Victoria Hoi An Resort and continue on it until it dead-ends. You will pass over a dirt road before coming to a small concrete road that passes through a picturesque small village. The cycling is easy, the villagers friendly, and the route well off the tourist track. Bikes can be rented from a number of places in town (☞ Transportation Around Hoi An *in* Hoi An A to Z, *below*).

Boating

Short paddleboat trips along the Thu Bon (Cai River) can be arranged at Hoang Van Thu Street or through young solicitors who hang out at the riverside cafés across from 50 Bach Dang Street. Hoi An Tourism arranges motorized boat trips, including visits to a ceramics factory and a shipyard. Full-day boat trips to Cham and Cam Kim islands and to My Son can also be arranged at the dock across from 62 Bach Dang Street.

Shopping

Because it's a low-key place, Hoi An is perhaps the most pleasant town in all of Vietnam in which to shop for souvenirs and clothes—and the quality of items here is generally pretty high. Numerous shops along Tran Phu Street sell everything from works of art and ceramics to clothing and opium paraphernalia. Although most ceramic objects are billed as antiques, only some are the real thing. Unless you are an antiques expert or do some serious comparative shopping—which usually means being duped into buying an "antique" and then having another shop owner let you know that you were fooled—it is often impossible to tell a phony from a real antique by the price, since they often cost the same (note that antiques can only be taken out of Vietnam with special permission; *see* Shopping *in* Smart Travel Tips A to Z). Bargaining is advisable, as quoted prices are generally largely inflated, especially for fine art.

For cheap, casual clothing and same-day service on custom orders, try any one of the many tailoring shops on Le Loi or Tran Hung Dao Street. These shops overflow with endless yards of Vietnamese, Japanese, and Chinese silks and cottons. Prices depend on the quality of the material you choose. For somewhat elaborate articles of clothing, such as fitted jackets and formal attire, tiny **Phuong Huy II** (⊠ 25B Tran Phu St., ☎ 0510/862–234) does an excellent job and can turn around any order in a day.

Hoi An A to Z

To research prices, get advice from other travelers, and book travel arrangements, visit www.fodors.com.

AIR TRAVEL
The closest airport to Hoi An is the one in Danang, 30 km (19 mi) north. To get to Hoi An, rent a car with a driver in Danang.

CAR TRAVEL
The only way to get to Hoi An from Danang is by minibus or car, which takes about an hour due to poor road conditions, even though it's only a 30-km (19-mi) trip. The trip to Hoi An costs $5–$10, depending on the number of passengers, and is a very scenic drive through small towns and rice paddies. You can rent a car with a driver from Danang Tourism Services Company or from any travel agency in Hoi An.
➤ CONTACT: **Danang Tourism Services Company** (⊠ 76 Hung Vuong St., ☎ 0511/823–993 or 0511/825–653, ⅋ 0511/821–312).

EMERGENCIES

Dr. Phuoc is highly recommended for his medical skills and his English-language ability. Serious illnesses should be referred to Hoi An Hospital.

➤ CONTACTS: **Dr. Phuoc** (✉ 74 Le Loi St., ☎ 0510/861–419). **Hoi An Hospital** (✉ corner of Cua Dai and Hoang Dieu Sts., ☎ 0510/864–750).

MONEY MATTERS

Change money at your hotel or at the Hoi An Bank, which also does cash advances on Visa and MasterCard.

➤ CONTACT: **Hoi An Bank** (✉ 4 Hoang Dieu St., ☎ 0510/861–340).

SAFETY

The streets of Hoi An are very dark at night, but the city is generally safe. Consider bringing a flashlight to help you find your way around.

TRANSPORTATION AROUND HOI AN

The most enjoyable and most convenient means of getting around Hoi An are on foot, by bicycle (for 7,000d per day), and by motorbike (for about 70,000d per day). There are only a few cyclos, but the town is so small that you probably won't need to use one. Hoi An Tourism rents bicycles and motorbikes. You can also rent bikes from many hotels and cafés.

TRAVEL AGENCIES

There are several booking offices along Le Loi and Tran Hung Dao streets handling train and plane reservations, car rentals, hotel arrangements, and excursions from Hoi An to the Marble Mountains and China Beach.

Hoi An Tourism Office, the state-run travel agency operated out of the Hoi An Hotel, organizes tours following several different itineraries of the city, as well as excursions to the Marble Mountains and China Beach. The staff here speaks perfect English and provides excellent service.

➤ CONTACT: **Hoi An Tourism Office** (✉ 6 Tran Hung Dao St., ☎ 0510/861–373 or 0510/861–362, FAX 0510/861–636).

5 THE SOUTH-CENTRAL COAST AND HIGHLANDS

NHA TRANG AND DALAT

Set aside a few days to escape to two of Vietnam's best-known resort towns: seaside Nha Trang and the mountain village of Dalat. Nha Trang's stretches of sandy beach are ideal for strolling or dancing the night away at waterfront clubs. Head to Dalat for long walks, a visit to Emperor Bao Dai's summer palace, and a taste of the unusual side of Vietnamese domestic tourism. With a little more time, you can include a trip to the rugged mountainous area around Kontum and Pleiku and visit the villages of Vietnam's hill tribes.

T HE SPRAWLING BEACHES OF NHA TRANG and the cool mountain refuge of Dalat are two of Vietnam's oldest and most popular resort destinations. Nha Trang, the capital of Khanh Hoa Province, has long been a favorite destination for the Vietnamese, who come to swim in the sea. Dalat has been a popular retreat since the French first started visiting in the early 1900s. A mountain town in the midst of the central highlands, it has an abundance of natural beauty. Come to Dalat to catch a cool hilltop breeze, even in summer when the rest of the country is sweltering; play golf; hike; and visit the waterfalls along with the many Vietnamese who honeymoon here. Don't expect untouched beaches or mountain terrain in either town, however. Both are established resort areas and continue to undergo further development—for better or worse—as domestic travel increases and the destinations gain international popularity. Although there are several attractions to keep you busy in Nha Trang and Dalat, there are few cultural or historic sights of note. Rather, these towns are great spots to relax and experience Vietnam's diverse natural landscapes.

By Sherrie
Nachman,
Pilar Guzman,
and Craig
Thomas

Updated by
Lisa Bjorksten

For those with more time and a willingness to stray from the beaten path, south-central Vietnam has much to offer outside of Nha Trang and Dalat. The highland towns of Pleiku and Kontum are good jumping-off points for treks into Vietnam's remaining forests and for visits to the villages of the country's hill-tribe minorities. Near the coastal town of Quang Ngai lies a sobering reminder of the savage toll war often exacts on the innocent: the Son My Memorial, erected in memory of the victims of the My Lai massacre. Along the length of the coast you'll find spectacular scenery and beautiful beaches without the tourist clutter. With natural sand dunes and the best shores in the south, the fishing villages of Phan Thiet and Mui Ne (☞ Side Trips from Ho Chi Minh City *in* Chapter 6) are well worth a visit.

Pleasures and Pastimes

Beaches

Nha Trang's several miles of narrow, sandy beaches stretch from the center of town to its north end. Pick a spot to lounge on the beach, go swimming, or have a light meal at a waterfront café. Although pleasant, the beaches are not isolated: most of the town's hotels sit along the beach road, a constant reminder that Nha Trang is a resort area. Development has brought its problems, too: shores are not as clean as they once were.

All along the south-central coast from Quang Ngai south to Nha Trang are numerous small towns with inviting beaches, although with little in the way of facilities. If time allows, head outside Nha Trang to the more isolated Dai Lanh and Doc Let beaches, or go farther south to the quiet, lovely sand at Phan Thiet.

Dining

Nha Trang has numerous outstanding and reasonably priced seafood restaurants, including a few along the beachfront. Many serve the catch of the day. Unusual for a town of its size, Nha Trang also has two restaurants serving Western-style food, which means you won't have any trouble finding burgers or spaghetti here. Another good option is to buy fresh seafood from the vendors along the beach. They will prepare it for you in a matter of moments, and the prices are reasonable.

In contrast, the large agricultural center of Dalat has few good restaurants. Local specialties are dried deer meat, strawberry jam, and artichoke tea. Ask for dishes laden with fresh Dalat vegetables.

CATEGORY	COST*
$$$$	over 250,000 dong
$$$	150,000 dong–250,000 dong
$$	60,000 dong–150,000 dong
$	15,000 dong–60,000 dong
¢	under 15,000 dong

per person for a main course at dinner, including 10% tax and 5% service

Lodging

Competition from new, privately owned hotels has encouraged state-owned accommodations in Nha Trang to spruce up their acts, and most hotels in the region are willing to bargain. Dalat has one of Vietnam's only true luxury hotels outside Ho Chi Minh City and Hanoi—the Sofitel Palace, which is reminiscent of a French château and has the added bonus of an adjacent tennis court and golf course. Other hotels in Dalat are clean and cheerful. Accommodations in the central highlands are much more limited and basic than in the coastal areas, but efforts are under way to provide more facilities.

CATEGORY	COST*
$$$$	over 2.5 million dong
$$$	1 million dong–2.5 million dong
$$	750,000 dong–1 million dong
$	400,000 dong–750,000 dong
¢	under 400,000 dong

All prices are for a standard double room, including 10% tax and 5% service.

Nightlife

Nha Trang has quite an exciting nightlife for such a small Vietnamese city, thanks in part to the large backpacking crowds who come here. Many bars and ice cream shops stay open well past midnight. You can play pool until breakfast time at the beachfront Nha Trang Sailing Club and dance until 4 AM at several bars and nightclubs. Dalat, on the other hand, has little nightlife activity other than a bustling night market.

Outdoor Activities and Sports

As resort towns, both Nha Trang and Dalat provide myriad activities. In Nha Trang you can swim, dive, sail, and snorkel. Dalat's mountains and lakes create an ideal setting for long walks or a paddleboat trip. In the central highlands around Pleiku and Kontum, you can arrange hiking treks and elephant rides into some of Vietnam's best forests. Farther down the coast, Mui Ne has gained a reputation for its extreme sports: kite surfing, quadbiking, and paragliding over sand dunes.

Exploring the South-Central Coast and Highlands

The roads connecting Nha Trang and Dalat are winding and narrow and head through several mountain passes. So though Dalat lies only 200 km (124 mi) southwest of Nha Trang, the trip can easily take seven hours or more by car. If you do go by car, you'll pass through lush countryside covered with rice fields and, closer to Dalat, coffee farms and strawberry fields. The easiest way to get to either city is to fly directly from Ho Chi Minh City; there are no direct flights between Nha Trang and Dalat.

Numbers in the text correspond to numbers in the margin and on the South-Central Coast and Highlands, Nha Trang, and Dalat maps.

Great Itineraries

IF YOU HAVE 3 DAYS

Choose either 🖫 **Nha Trang** ⑤–⑦ or 🖫 **Dalat** ⑧–⑳ as your destination; it takes too long and is too difficult to visit both cities in so short

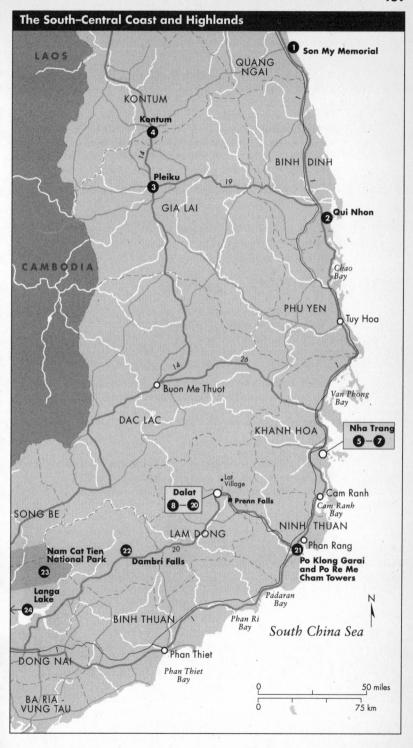

The South-Central Coast and Highlands

LAOS

QUANG NGAI

1 Son My Memorial

KONTUM

Kontum **4**

BINH DINH

Pleiku **3**

GIA LAI

Qui Nhon **2**

CAMBODIA

Chao Bay

PHU YEN

Tuy Hoa

14   26

Buon Me Thuot

Van Phong Bay

DAC LAC

KHANH HOA

Nha Trang **5**—**7**

• Lat Village

Dalat **8**—**20**

■ Prenn Falls

Cam Ranh

Cam Ranh Bay

SONG BE

LAM DONG

NINH THUAN

22   20   **21**   Phan Rang

Nam Cat Tien National Park

Dambri Falls

Po Klong Garai and Po Re Me Cham Towers

23

Padaran Bay

Langa Lake

24

Phan Ri Bay

BINH THUAN

South China Sea

N

DONG NAI

Phan Thiet

Phan Thiet Bay

BA RIA - VUNG TAU

0   50 miles

0   75 km

a time. Spend one day sightseeing and the other days relaxing. With so little time, you should definitely fly here from either Hanoi or Ho Chi Minh City.

IF YOU HAVE 6 DAYS

With six days you could see both ▣ **Nha Trang** ⑤–⑦ and ▣ **Dalat** ⑧–⑳. Spend three days in Nha Trang, being sure to visit as many of the city's restaurants as possible. If you're heading south from Hoi An to Nha Trang, use one of the days to break the journey with a visit to the ▣ **Son My Memorial** ①. On the scenic drive between Nha Trang and Dalat, stop by the **Po Klong Garai and Po Re Me Cham Towers** ㉑, near Phan Rang. Spend two days in Dalat and another day visiting the **southern central highlands,** including hill-tribes villages such as the Ede villages.

When to Tour the South-Central Coast and Highlands

The best time to come to Nha Trang is between April and September, during the dry season. It rains frequently in October, and November and can be chilly. With a temperate climate, Dalat is worth visiting any time of the year but provides the most relief from June through August, when the rest of the country is really hot.

NORTH OF NHA TRANG

The portion of the south-central coast lying between Hoi An and Nha Trang is an area with few tourist attractions but often breathtaking scenery and seemingly endless white-sand beaches. If you're traveling by car between the two cities, don't miss the opportunity to visit the Son My Memorial, built in remembrance of the brutal My Lai massacre.

Farther inland, the central-highland towns of Pleiku and Kontum are good bases from which to explore the villages of the hill tribes.

Son My Memorial

❶ *110 km (68 mi) south of Hoi An.*

My Lai, a sleepy hamlet about 13 km (8 mi) east of the city of Quang Ngai in the Son My district, is a site infamous for the worst atrocity carried out by American forces during the war in Vietnam. On the morning of March 16, 1968, U.S. troops entered the Son My area (including My Lai, Thuan-Yen, and other hamlets) and massacred hundreds of Vietnamese civilians—mostly women and children—in an act that has come to symbolize the often senseless brutality that accompanied the conflict in Vietnam.

Although the full truth concerning the events of My Lai remains shrouded in controversy, what is known is that the area around Son My was considered by the U.S. military to be a stronghold of the Vietcong and that some American soldiers had been killed and wounded in the area in the days preceding March 16, 1968. (A note on the term Vietcong: Vietcong is used throughout this book to refer to the opposition movement in the South because it is the term that is probably the most familiar. However, the history of this term is a complex one; *see* Chronology *in* Chapter 9 for further explanation). In response, three platoons under Charlie Company exacted a terrible revenge that included pillaging, rape, and mass executions of civilians. The killing and destruction, which occurred under the at least tacit approval of higher officers, took place over a number of hours, during which time the soldiers took a break for lunch before resuming their criminal acts.

Hundreds of Vietnamese civilians died; the only reported American casualty was a U.S. soldier who shot himself in the foot in order to avoid participating in the atrocities. Although a cover-up of the events of My Lai was attempted, several participants went public; the resulting scandal contributed to the deterioration of American support for the war in Vietnam. Only one man, Lieutenant William Calley, who led Charlie Company's 1st Platoon—responsible for some of the worst atrocities—was ever convicted for the crimes that took place at My Lai. After serving three years of his sentence, Lieutenant Calley was paroled in 1974.

The Son My Memorial is dedicated to the victims of the massacre at My Lai and lies about 10 km (6 mi) east of National Highway 1A, just north of the town of Quang Ngai. The road leading to the memorial begins next to the My Tra Hotel. The memorial itself sits on the grounds of the former hamlet of Thuan-Yen, where many of the worst crimes occurred. In striking contrast to the terrible events that took place here, the memorial rises against a quiet and pastoral backdrop.

Lodging

$ 🏨 **My Tra Hotel.** This surprisingly modern and efficient hotel is convenient for visits to the Son My Memorial and nearby lovely Bien Khe Beach. The rooms are clean but simple, with watercolors of traditional scenes of rural Vietnamese life. ⊠ *Hwy. 1, north of Quang Ngai across Tra Khuc Bridge,* ☎ *055/842–985,* FAX *055/842–980. 50 rooms. Restaurant, minibars, cable TV, tennis court, massage, bar, Internet. MC, V.*

Qui Nhon

❷ *180 km (112 mi) south of Son My.*

Qui Nhon, which lies 238 km (148 mi) north of Nha Trang and 280 km (174 mi) south of Hoi An, is a good place to break your trip along the coast, although it holds little entertainment or excitement in itself. This is also a good spot from which to begin a trip to the central-highland towns of Pleiku and Kontum. The beaches here are pleasant, although not spectacular and not great for swimming because of pollution and dangerous undertows. There are also interesting **Cham towers** in town (take a right at 906 Tran Hung Dao Street onto Thap Doi Street) and 26 km (16 mi) north of Qui Nhon on Highway 1.

Lodging

¢–$ 🏨 **Hai Au Hotel.** Right on the beach, the Hai Au is the most pleasant hotel in town. Rooms are clean, though basic and somewhat run-down. Half of them overlook the sea. The restaurant, which also overlooks the beach, serves good seafood; the attached circular bar is a popular hangout. Staff members are friendly and helpful. This is a popular spot for tour groups. ⊠ *489 Nguyen Hue St.,* ☎ *056/846–473,* FAX *056/846–926. 56 rooms. Restaurant, cable TV, massage, bar, Internet, business services, meeting room, car rental, travel services. No credit cards.*

En Route If you're making the trip to Pleiku via Highway 19, stop and visit the **Quang Trung Museum,** which is dedicated to Nguyen Hue, later crowned Emperor Quang Trung, one of the leaders of the Tay Son Rebellion. Beginning in 1772 as a peasant uprising, the Tay Son Rebellion was an expression of deep discontent in rural Vietnamese society that eventually led to the temporary overthrow of the Nguyen rulers in Hanoi. The brief Tay Son era was notable for land and tax reform and for a resurgence of indigenous Vietnamese culture. For more information on the rebellion, *see* Vietnam at a Glance: A Chronology *in* Chapter 9. ⊠ *From Hwy. 1 head west 30 km (19 mi) on Hwy. 19; mu-*

seum is 5 km (3 mi) north off Hwy. 19, ☎ *no phone.* 🎟 *15,000d.* ⊙ *Daily 9–noon and 2–5.*

Pleiku and Kontum

Pleiku is 140 km (87 mi) west of Qui Nhon; Kontum is 49 km (30 mi) north of Pleiku.

3 4 The central-highland towns of **Pleiku** and **Kontum** are good bases from which to stage trips to the mountains and forests of the hinterland. Much of the area, particularly around Kontum, is forested and mountainous, and the regions surrounding Pleiku and Kontum were major battlegrounds during the Vietnam War. In the most heavily bombed areas, only now has the vegetation, including coffee trees, begun to recover from the napalm and defoliants rained on this area during the war.

As destinations in themselves, the towns hold little of interest. Pleiku, with its Soviet-style concrete structures, is the larger of the two towns, with about 50,000 residents and more in the way of accommodations and dining options. Sleepy, prettier Kontum has much less bustle and has been likened to Dalat in terms of color, climate, and landscape— but without the flurry of tourist activity found in Dalat.

Traveling to these towns can be fairly rough going because of long driving distances and limited facilities, but they are great places to escape the tourist trail, take in the region's remaining forests, and visit the villages of the many hill tribes that live nearby. The Bahnar and Jarai, two of the largest hill-tribe groups in the area, possess a fascinating culture with traditions that stretch back for centuries. You can join them in drinking the *ruou can* (rice wine) for which this region is famous. Of particular cultural interest are the wood carvings made by the Bahnar tribe (who have villages within walking distance of Kontum) to adorn the graves of their departed. Meant to keep the dead company and to make them laugh, these vary from stern-looking American and French soldiers to amorous couples. The strong animistic beliefs of the Jarai tribe are expressed through traditional musical instruments, such as the wind flute and gongs with which they produce ethereal and entrancing hymns.

Also nearby are Sedang, Rengao, and Kon Ketu Kangeri villages. You can hire a motorbike to reach these villages for about $6–$8 a day or a guide and driver for about $15 through one of the hotel tour agencies (☞ Dining and Lodging, *below*). Note that if you visit any villages in Gia Lai Province, you may have to obtain a travel permit; the hotel tour agencies can assist you with this. Day hikes in the surrounding forests and multiday treks with overnight stays in the homes of hill-tribe villagers can be also be arranged through local hotel tour agencies. It's also possible to join guided tours of the numerous former battlefields from the Vietnam War.

Dining and Lodging

¢–$ ✕🏨 **Dakbla Hotel.** This lime-green hotel lies just over the bridge that leads you into Kontum from Pleiku. The rooms are clean, and the staff speaks English. The hotel restaurant serves good Vietnamese food at reasonable prices. Inside the Dakbla there's a branch of the Kontum Tourist Company, which can arrange treks and visits to the hill-tribe villages in the area. ⊠ *2 Phan Dinh Phung St., Kontum,* ☎ *060/863-333,* 🖷 *060/863-336. 42 rooms. Restaurant, minibars, cable TV, laundry service, Internet, travel services. No credit cards. CP.*

¢   🏨 **Hung Vuong Hotel.** The relatively modern Hung Vuong sits on the main road as you enter Pleiku on Highway 19. The hotel houses the Gia Lai Tourist Company, which can arrange treks and other guided tours of the surrounding area. ⊠ *215 Hung Vuong St., Pleiku,* ☎ *059/ 824–270,* FAX *059/827–170. 31 rooms. Restaurant, minibars, cable TV, Internet, travel services; no a/c in some rooms. No credit cards.*

En Route   The beaches in and around the town of **Dai Lanh,** 83 km (51 mi) north of Nha Trang, are breathtaking and completely devoid of tourists. There are no accommodations in Dai Lanh, but this is a perfect place to spend a few hours on the trip down to Nha Trang.

North of Nha Trang A to Z

To research prices, get advice from other travelers, and book travel arrangements, visit www.fodors.com.

AIR TRAVEL
Vietnam Airlines operates five flights a week from Ho Chi Minh City to Pleiku. There are also daily direct flights from Danang, although none from Hanoi to Pleiku. Kontum is then just a short 49 km (30 mi) drive north from Pleiku on the well-kept and relatively uncrowded Highway 14.
➤ CARRIER: **Vietnam Airlines** (⊠ 55 Quang Trung St., Pleiku, ☎ 059/ 845–9823).

BUS TRAVEL
Local bus services to Pleiku operate from Danang and Nha Trang via smaller coastal towns, but the trip is long and uncomfortable. Your hotel can help you arrange a bus trip.

CAR TRAVEL
Son My and Qui Nhon, right on the coast along Highway 1, are easily accessible. Pleiku and Kontum are easy to get to by car or motorbike, as the roads are in relatively good condition and are uncrowded by local standards. To get to Pleiku, take Highway 19, which begins 10 km (6 mi) north of Qui Nhon. Highway 14 connects Pleiku to Kontum; the highway continues on from Kontum to Danang and other points north, but it's a rough ride.

Reaching the more interesting destinations outside of the towns, such as hill-tribe villages or the remaining old-growth forests of the region, requires some determination and, in certain cases, a four-wheel-drive vehicle or an agreeable elephant. The local travel agencies can make the arrangements.

TRAVEL AGENCIES
To arrange tours to the hill-tribe villages near Pleiku and Kontum, contact the Kontum Tourist Company in the Dakbla Hotel or the Gia Lai Tourist Company in the Hung Vuong Hotel (☞ Pleiku and Kontum, *above*). You don't have to be staying at the hotels to use the travel services.

NHA TRANG

A bustling city with a long stretch of developed beachfront, Nha Trang is not an idyllic, deserted hideaway. Older hotels share the waterfront with an assortment of flashy Western-style joint-venture establishments. And petty crime is on the rise. But the beachfront still retains its charms: swarms of high school students bike to and from classes, and hordes of teenagers play soccer in the few waterfront lots that have not been turned into tourist sights. Recreational attractions include swimming, scuba diving, snorkeling, sailing, and going on boat excursions to neighboring Mieu, Tam, and Monkey islands—lush enclaves with isolated beaches and groves of palm trees.

Exploring Nha Trang

The easiest way to get around town is by bicycle or cyclo. It's also possible to hire a motorbike—with or without a driver—or a car and driver.

⑤ At the beautiful **Long Son Pagoda,** built in the late 19th century and reconstructed a number of times since, a giant, serene white Buddha beckons you up a flight of stairs, at the top of which is a panoramic view of Nha Trang. The entrance to the pagoda itself is down below. The resident monks happily give guided tours, sometimes in English, of the main sanctuary. To reach it from town, follow Yersin Street— on foot, by bike, or by motorbike—inland about 2 km (1 mi) from the coast. When you come to No. 15 on 23 Thang 10 Street (called Thai Nguyen Street as you get closer to the water), make a right (continuing inland) to get to the pagoda. ⊠ *About 550 yards west of railroad station, opposite No. 15 on 23 Thang 10 St.,* ☎ *no phone.* ▭ *Free.* ☉ *Daily 8–noon and 2–4.*

⑥ The **Po Nagar Cham Towers** (Nha Trang Huu Duc), also known as the Mother Goddess or Lady of the City Towers, are some of the best-preserved Cham ruins in Vietnam. This was a site of Hindu worship in the 2nd century; the present buildings were constructed between the 7th and 12th centuries. Today Po Nagar is still an active shrine for Vietnam's remaining Cham community and for Chinese and Vietnamese Buddhists. Of the original eight towers, four remain in various states of preservation. The North Tower (Thap Chinh), built during King Harivarman I's reign in AD 817, originally housed a *linga,* a phallic stone. After the linga was stolen and replaced, the stone statue of the goddess Uma visible today was finally substituted for it. To reach the towers from the center of town, take Quang Trung Street, which turns into 2 Thang 4 Street (the name of the street, not an address); then cross the Cai River twice over the Ha Ra and Xom Bong bridges. Here there are colorful vignettes of postcard-perfect fishing-boat activity. As you cross the second bridge, you'll see the impressive towers jutting up from the hill on the left-hand side. The walk here is not that pleasant, so consider taking a cyclo or a motorbike. Be prepared for swarms of hawkers congregating at the site. ⊠ *On north side of Cai River over Ha Ra and Xom Bong Bridges,* ☎ *no phone.* ▭ *5,000d.* ☉ *Daily 8–5.*

⑦ The **Hon Chong Promontory,** on the same side of the river as the Po Nagar Cham Towers, provides good views of the coastline and the surrounding islands. Climb up the promontory for a view of Tortoise Island (Nha Trang and Hon Rua), both to the northeast. If you look northwest you can see Fairy Mountain (Nui Co Tien), said to resemble a reclining fairy. To get here from the Po Nagar ruins, head north on 2 Thang 4 Street and take a right on Nguyen Dinh Chieu Street. ⊠ *About ¾ km (½ mi) from intersection of Nguyen Dinh Chieu and 2 Thang 4 Sts.,* ☎ *no phone.* ▭ *10,000d.* ☉ *Daily 8–4.*

If your idea of relaxation involves soaking in a mineral mud bath, head to **Thap Ba Hot Spring Center,** on the northern outskirts of Nha Trang. In addition to mud baths there are hot mineral pools and a mineral swimming pool. You can choose to soak solo, with a partner, or in a group. Prices start at 25,000d. A canteen and guest house are available for longer stays, but you're better off visiting from Nha Trang. ⊠ *Cell 25, Ngoc Son, Ngoc Hiep Ward,* ☎ *058/835–335,* ᴡᴇʙ *www. thapbahotspring.com.vn.* ☉ *Mon.–Sat. 8–8, Sun. 7 ᴀᴍ–9 ᴘᴍ.*

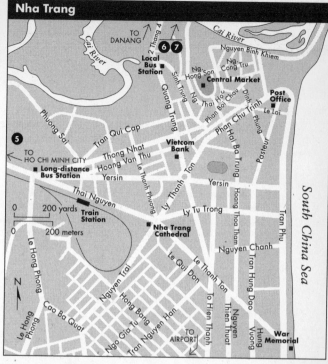

No visit to Nha Trang is complete without a boat trip to the surrounding scenic **islands,** such as Mieu Island (Tri Nguyen Island), Mun Island, and Tam Island. Boat trips can be arranged through local hotels and travel agencies or directly at the port on the south end of town. Both Mieu and Tam islands have bungalows where you can spend a quiet night away from the bustle of Nha Trang.

About 16 km (10 mi) outside of Nha Trang on Highway 1 is Dao Khi, otherwise known as **Monkey Island,** which is popular with tourists during the day but wonderfully deserted at night. There are clean but simple bungalows available for $15 a night and one restaurant that serves good seafood and Vietnamese dishes. To get here, hire a car and driver or take a 15-minute boat ride from the pier in the south part of town.

Forty kilometers (25 miles) north of town is the relatively isolated and largely undeveloped **Doc Let Beach.** The beach here is clean, with white sand and fewer tourists than in Nha Trang. This is a good spot for a day trip, but lodging is available; your best bet is one of the spartan bungalows next to the beach, which go for $6–$10 a night. To get here it's best to hire a car and driver or simply take a cab from Nha Trang.

Dining and Lodging

$–$$$ ✕ **La Louisiane Cafe.** The perfect counterpart to the more adult-oriented Nha Trang Sailing Club, the cheerful Louisiane Cafe is a great place to bring the family. Inside the restaurant are a pool and a dizzying selection of pastries. More substantial fare includes sandwiches, salads, and dishes you might typically find in a French café. The beach chairs outside are free, and there's a bar for something a little stronger than ice cream. ⊠ *29A Tran Phu St., across from airport,* ☎ *058/812-948. No credit cards.*

\$–\$\$\$ ✕ **Nha Trang Sailing Club.** The most hopping of all the seaside café-
★ bars in town, the Sailing Club is popular with expats, locals, and
tourists. It's the place to go if you're looking for something other than
Vietnamese food: burgers, pizza, and sushi are all on the menu for breakfast, lunch, and dinner. This is a great spot to sip cocktails on the beach
on a balmy evening. Diving and sailing trips can be arranged through
the office just behind the restaurant. ⊠ 72–74 Tran Phu St., ☎ 058/
826–528. No credit cards.

\$–\$\$ ✕ **Lac Canh.** Here's your chance to hang out with locals. At each table
in this smoke-filled restaurant is a charcoal grill on which you can make
your own cheap and delicious marinated seafood and meat dishes. Just
be prepared for one odd habit: the diners pile empty beer bottles and
other leftovers on the floor after they're done with them. ⊠ 44 Nguyen
Binh Khum St., ☎ 058/821–391. No credit cards.

\$–\$\$ ✕ **Vietnamese Restaurant.** This family-run Vietnamese restaurant
serves excellent seafood at low prices. Tasty unnamed fried fish is a
specialty. ⊠ 23 Hoang Van Thu St., ☎ 058/822–933. No credit cards.

¢–\$\$ ✕ **Thanh The.** Locals and Vietnamese tourists pack this restaurant specializing in seafood and traditional Vietnamese fare. ⊠ 3 Phan Chu
Trinh St., ☎ 058/821–931. No credit cards.

\$ ✕ **Ngoc Suong.** The best and freshest seafood in town is served at this
★ establishment a block from the beach. It also has a friendly waitstaff.
Fish salad, made from marinated local seafood, is the specialty. The
rather daunting and rambling English-language menu also includes wild-
boar testicles for the more adventurous, but you're better off sticking
with fish. ⊠ 16 Tran Quang Khai St., near Tran Phu St., ☎ 058/954–
516. No credit cards.

¢–\$ ✕ **Banana Split.** This small sidewalk café serves ice cream sundaes as
well as Western-style dishes such as omelets, chicken, and burgers. Open
for breakfast, lunch, and dinner, it's a destination for homesick Western travelers looking to meet other people. Boat trips and other travel
arrangements can also be made here. ⊠ 58 Quang Trung St., ☎ 058/
829–115. No credit cards.

\$\$\$\$ ▨ **Ana Mandara Nha Trang Resort.** This tranquil beachfront resort is
★ the most elegant and most comfortable place to stay in Nha Trang, although the service doesn't quite live up to the setting, style, and architecture. Reminiscent of Balinese- and Thai-style resorts, the hotel
has private thatched cottages, some of which are only footsteps from
the ocean. Local arts and crafts decorate the guest quarters and public spaces. ⊠ 6 Tran Phu St., ☎ 058/829–829, ㎰ 058/829–629, ｗｅｂ
www.six-senses.com/ana-mandara. 68 cottages. Restaurant, room service, in-room safes, minibars, cable TV, pool, bicycles, library, dry cleaning, laundry service, Internet, meeting rooms, travel services, no-smoking
rooms. AE, MC, V.

\$\$\$ ▨ **Yasaka Saigon–Nha Trang Hotel.** Among Nha Trang's hotels, the
Yasaka is second only to Ana Mandara in terms of quality. The tasteful, modern beige rooms are spacious, with sea views, wide-screen televisions, and IDD phones. The large pool is the best in the area. Prices
are high for what you get, so don't be afraid to bargain. ⊠ 18 Tran
Phu St., ☎ 058/820–090, ㎰ 058/820–000. 202 rooms. 2 restaurants,
cable TV, tennis court, pool, gym, dance club, Internet, travel services,
no-smoking rooms. AE, MC, V.

\$\$–\$\$\$ ▨ **Nha Trang Lodge Hotel.** Rooms at this hotel across the street from
the ocean are clean, and some have views of the sea. The lobby may
be tacky and the decor reminiscent of roadside motels across the United
States, but this is still a comfortable place to stay. ⊠ 42 Tran Phu St.,
☎ 058/810–500, ㎰ 058/828–800. 121 rooms. Restaurant, room service, in-room data ports, in-room safes, minibars, cable TV, dry cleaning, laundry service, travel services, no-smoking rooms. AE, MC, V.

¢–$ 🏨 **Hai Yen Hotel.** Although it caters to large cruise ships full of tourists, this big waterfront hotel looks like it hasn't been touched since the '70s. Nonetheless, rooms are passable—meaning they are reasonably clean and have basic amenities such as TVs. ✉ *40 Tran Phu St.,* ☎ *058/822–828,* FAX *058/821–902. 110 rooms. Café, dining room, room service, fans, minibars, pool, hair salon, massage, sauna, 2 bars, lobby lounge, dance club, dry cleaning, laundry service, Internet, meeting rooms, travel services, car rental. MC, V.*

¢–$ 🏨 **Vien Dong Hotel.** A hub of tourist activity, the Vien Dong is popular for its proximity to the beach and its pool. But the hotel is run-down and overpriced, and the staff tends to be excessively impersonal. The travel service is very good, however, and you can use it even if you're not staying at the hotel. ✉ *1 Tran Hung Dao St.,* ☎ *058/821–606,* FAX *058/821–912. 106 rooms. Restaurant, fans, minibars, cable TV, pool, massage, bar, laundry service, travel services, car rental; no a/c in some rooms. AE, MC, V.*

¢ 🏨 **Phuong Hoang Hotel.** The Phuong Hoang sits in the center of town, not too far from the beach. Rooms are clean and nondescript. ✉ *7 Le Thanh Ton St.,* ☎ *058/827–714,* FAX *058/824–991. 26 rooms. Fans, minibars, cable TV, laundry service, Internet, travel services; no a/c in some rooms. No credit cards.*

¢ 🏨 **Sao Mai.** The family that runs this lodging is genuinely nice and eager to please. The rooms are basic, a fact that is reflected in the price, but clean. Rates include a simple Western breakfast. Motorbikes and bicycles are available to rent. ✉ *99 Nguyen Thien Thuat St.,* ☎ *058/827–412. 12 rooms. Fans, bicycles, travel services. No credit cards. BP.*

¢ 🏨 **Seaside Hotel.** A relatively plush minihotel just south of town on the coast, this place has some of the most tastefully decorated rooms in Nha Trang; several even have ocean views. Few services are offered, however, and the staff sleeps in the lobby at night. Nonetheless, it is a great value. ✉ *96B Tran Phu St.,* ☎ *058/821–178,* FAX *058/828–038. 20 rooms. Restaurant, fans, cable TV, laundry service; no a/c. No credit cards.*

¢ 🏨 **Thanh Thanh Hotel.** This efficient, brightly lighted minihotel overlooks the water and is just south of town. Guest rooms incorporate bold red fabrics and have IDD telephones, and some rooms have views of the sea. ✉ *98A Tran Phu St.,* ☎ *058/824–657,* FAX *058/823–031,* WEB *www.vngold.com/nt/thanhthanh. 26 rooms. Restaurant, room service, minibars, cable TV, laundry service, Internet, travel services. MC, V.*

Nightlife and the Arts

People tend to congregate on the beach or at beachfront bar-cafés like the **Rainbow Bar** (✉ Tran Phu St., behind the small amusement park, ☎ no phone). The **Nha Trang Sailing Club** (✉ 72–74 Tran Phu St., ☎ 058/826–528) opens out onto the beach. Its casual atmosphere and notorious cocktails attract homesick travelers and expatriates, who hang out until dawn dancing, drinking, playing pool, and speaking English. The club also serves as a gallery for work by local photographer Long Thanh. The beachside **Huong Duong Center Bar/Discotheque** (✉ Tran Phu St., ☎ 058/823–914), a hangout for Vietnamese teenagers and twentysomethings, is a good place to get away from other travelers.

Outdoor Activities and Sports

Nha Trang has all kinds of water-related activities, including snorkeling, jet skiing, scuba diving, and boating. You can rent equipment through most hotels or operators right on the beach. The **Blue Diving Club** (✉ Coconut Grove Resort, 66 Tran Phu St., ☎ 058/825–390, FAX 058/816–

088), a well-run PADI center, provides beginning instruction in English and arranges guided excursions for all diving levels.

Shopping

Long Thanh (✉ 126 Hoang Van Thu St., ☎ 058/824–875), a friendly and talented photographer, displays his stunning images of Vietnam in his home studio. Prices start at $50.

Nha Trang A to Z

To research prices, get advice from other travelers, and book travel arrangements, visit www.fodors.com.

AIR TRAVEL

The easiest way to get to Nha Trang is by plane. Vietnam Airlines flies between Nha Trang and Ho Chi Minh City (55 minutes, $44) three times daily and once a day to Hanoi (1½ hours, $95) and Danang (70 minutes, $38).

➤ CARRIER: **Vietnam Airlines** (✉ 12B Hoang Hoa Tham St., Nha Trang, ☎ 058/822–135, FAX 058/825–956).

BOAT TRAVEL

Most hotels and travel agencies can organize boat trips to Nha Trang's surrounding isles.

BUS TRAVEL

The Sinh Café bus links Nha Trang with Danang for less than $15 as well as other points north and south of the city. Ha Phuong Tourist Cafe arranges bus trips to points north and south of Nha Trang.

➤ BUS INFORMATION: **Ha Phuong Tourist Cafe** (✉ 22 Tran Hung Dao St., ☎ 058/827–814, FAX 058/829–015). **Sinh Café** (✉ 10 Biet Thu St., ☎ 058/811–981).

CAR TRAVEL

Nha Trang lies 448 km (278 mi) north of Ho Chi Minh City along Highway 1 (nine hours by car) and 1,250 km (775 mi) south of Hanoi. Dalat is 200 km (124 mi) southwest of Nha Trang (seven to eight hours by car). Danang is 541 km (335 mi) north of Nha Trang (11 hours by car). A car and driver can be hired from hotels and from private and state-run travel agencies.

EMERGENCIES

Contact your hotel in case of emergency.

MAIL AND SHIPPING

The main post office branch sells stamps, as do many hotels. It also has a separate office across the road at No. 2 Le Loi Street that provides Internet access. There are several cheap Internet cafés scattered throughout the town. Charges range from 100d to 300d per minute.

➤ POST OFFICE: **Main Branch** (✉ 4 Le Loi St.).

MONEY MATTERS

Vietcom Bank exchanges money, as do many hotels. Cash advances on credit cards can be done at Vietcom Bank or at Sinh Café (☞ Travel Agencies, *below*).

➤ BANK: **Vietcom Bank** (✉ 17 Quang Trung St.).

SAFETY

Crime is on the rise in Nha Trang. Beware of pickpockets and bag snatchers. Be sure to hold your bags close to you, and leave valuables in your hotel safe or in-room safe. Cyclos are generally safe, but try to arrange trips with those waiting outside hotels. Do not walk alone, especially along the beach, at night.

TRAIN TRAVEL

Nha Trang is served three times daily by both express and local trains from Hanoi and Ho Chi Minh City. A soft sleeper to Ho Chi Minh City costs $25–$35; to Hanoi it costs $80–$100, depending on whether you take the express or the local train. The express train (12 hours) between Ho Chi Minh City and Nha Trang is considerably faster than the local train (22 hours); from Hanoi to Nha Trang the express takes 24 hours and the local 32 hours. The ticket office at Nha Trang Railway Station is open daily 6:30 AM–11 AM and 4:30 PM–10 PM.

➤ TRAIN STATION: **Nha Trang Railway Station** (✉ 17 Thai Nguyen St., ☎ 058/822–113).

TRANSPORTATION AROUND NHA TRANG

Bicycles and cyclos provide the best means of getting around Nha Trang. You can rent a bicycle—don't expect anything fancy—at any travel agency and at most hotels for about 15,000d a day. A deposit may be required. Cyclos are available all over town, and drivers will take you anywhere you want around town for about 15,000d. Be sure to bargain to get the best rate.

You can also rent a motorbike, with or without a driver, at any travel agency and at most hotels for about 80,000d a day. A deposit may be required.

Hiring a car and driver is unnecessary unless you want to go to one of the beaches outside of town. You can make arrangements at any of the travel agencies in town.

TRAVEL AGENCIES

Ha Phuong Tourist Cafe and Sinh Café arrange bus trips to points north and south of Nha Trang, boat trips to nearby islands, and visits to the Ede hill-tribe villages in the southern central highlands. The staff at Ha Phuong is particularly friendly and helpful. Sinh Café can also arrange cash advances.

➤ CONTACTS: **Ha Phuong Tourist Cafe** (✉ 22 Tran Hung Dao St., ☎ 058/827–814, FAX 058/829–015). **Sinh Café** (✉ 10 Biet Thu St., ☎ 058/811–981).

THE CENTRAL HIGHLANDS

Part of the southern end of the Truong Son range, Vietnam's central highlands embrace rugged mountains, clear streams, dense forests, and gushing waterfalls spread over the provinces of Lam Dong, Dac Lac, Gia Lai, and Kontum. The area also includes the towns of Pleiku and Kontum (☞ North of Nha Trang, *above*). With the increasing development of coffee plantations and rice farms, the region has become an important agricultural center. Although development and years of warfare have reduced the once large areas of pristine forest and abundant wildlife here, much remains for the determined visitor to enjoy. This is one of the few parts of the country where it is cool enough to wear a sweater, even in summer.

Vietnam's hill tribes have long been the primary inhabitants of the central highlands, but in the last decade the region has seen significant settlement by lowland Vietnamese. A large population of these hill tribes, also known as Montagnards from the French for "mountain people," inhabits the difficult-to-reach western part of the central highlands. Some of the tribes have lived in Vietnam for thousands of years; others came from neighboring Thailand several centuries ago. These tribes of largely nomadic farmers, who live an isolated existence, are culturally and linguistically distinct from each other and from the ethnic Vietnamese who make up the majority of the country's population.

The mountain resort of Dalat is the principal town of the southern central highlands region. It has an abundance of natural beauty—mountains, lakes, and gushing waterfalls—and a good measure of kitsch.

Dalat

308 km (191 mi) north of Ho Chi Minh City, 205 km (127 mi) southwest of Nha Trang.

With its mini–Eiffel Tower and colonial architecture, the mountain resort of Dalat bears a vague resemblance to a small French town. Its temperate climate and cool misty mornings provide a welcome respite from Vietnam's tropical heat. Kitsch is a Dalat specialty, in the form of swan-shape paddleboats, tacky souvenirs, and more. Striking views of majestic mountains and placid lakes are often interrupted by an incongruous Vietnamese dressed as an American cowboy offering a ride and a photo opportunity.

Named for the "River of the Lat Tribe," after the native Lat people, Dalat was "discovered" in 1892 by Dr. Alexandre Yersin (1863–1943), a protégé of scientist Louis Pasteur. It quickly became a vacation spot for Europeans eager to escape the infernal heat of the coastal plains, the big cities, and the Mekong Delta. During the Vietnam War the city, oddly, served as the favorite nonpartisan resting spot for both high-ranking North and South Vietnamese officers, before it capitulated to the North Vietnamese on April 3, 1975.

Dalat today is a favorite of Vietnamese honeymooners, and an effort is under way to transform the town into an international tourist destination. There are several comfortable hotels here, many of them old colonial villas. And an 18-hole golf course originally set up by Emperor Bao Dai is now known as one of the best in the region.

Exploring Dalat

Dalat's prime sight is its market, which ranks among Vietnam's best. Several places outside downtown Dalat also warrant a visit. As these are spread out across hilly ground, it's a good idea to hire a car with a driver and a guide. Decide what you want to see and leave the exact itinerary to your guide.

8 Circumscribed by a path and abutted by a beautiful 18-hole golf course, **Xuan Huong Lake** (Ho Xuan Huong) is a hub of leisurely activity, including paddleboating. Although there's traffic nearby, the lake provides a pleasant place to walk and bike. The dam-generated lake takes its name from a 17th-century Vietnamese poet known for her daring attacks on the hypocrisy of social conventions and the foibles of scholars, monks, mandarins, feudal lords, and kings.

9 Locals come to the picturesque indoor-outdoor **Central Market,** the official center of Dalat, to buy and sell chickens, fruits and vegetables, and specialties such as dried strawberries. The market has a small collection of restaurants and is usually open from dawn until nightfall. ⊠ *Nguyen Thi Minh Khai St.,* ☎ *no phone.*

10 A yellow cement structure built in 1933, **Bao Dai's Summer Palace** (Biet Dien Quoc Truong), on the south side of Xuan Huong Lake, is a wonderfully preserved example of modernist architecture. The palace houses the original 1930s French furnishings of Emperor Bao Dai, the

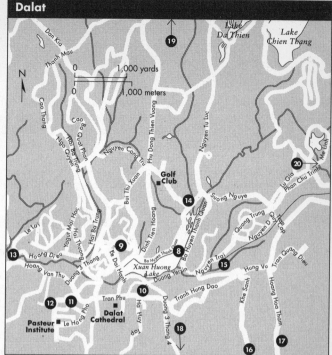

last emperor of the Nguyen dynasty, who ruled from 1926 to 1945 with the support of the French. You can stroll through the rooms and even sit behind the emperor's desk. With its military maps, family portraits, and chairs designated for each family member, the family sitting room has a tactile immediacy, as if it were untouched and suspended in time. Outside, the lovely garden is colorful with plant-covered trellises. ⌧ *Le Hong Phong St., 500 yards southeast of Pasteur Institute,* ☎ *063/ 822–125.* ⌧ *6,000d.* ☉ *Daily 8–5.*

⓫ A visit to the unofficial art gallery at **Hang Nga Guesthouse,** west of Bao Dai's palace, provides an offbeat experience. In a strange building made out of a tree, the hotel and gallery resemble a fairy-tale landscape with life-size wood carvings of animals and fantastical creatures. It looks a bit like Salvador Dalí meets Antoni Gaudí meets the *Swiss Family Robinson.* For reasons that should be obvious when you visit, locals refer to this as the "crazy house." Its owner and designer, Dr. Dang Viet Nga, studied architecture in Russia and has decorated the main dining room with a collection of photos of herself. Each guest room has its own wacky theme. ⌧ *3 Huynh Thuc Khang St.,* ☎ *063/ 822–070.* ⌧ *Free.* ☉ *Daily 7 AM–8 PM.*

⓬ The multitalented, multilingual monk Vien Thuc, known as the Mad Monk of Dalat, resides in the **Lam Ty Ni Pagoda.** An artist, poet, landscape architect, craftsman, and religious scholar, Vien Thuc is a living legend. He will happily escort you through his rooms of watercolor paintings, replete with Zen poetry, and may wrap up a picture even before you've agreed to buy it. Keep in mind that it is very hard to bargain with a monk. ⌧ *2 Thien My St.,* ☎ *no phone.* ⌧ *Free.* ☉ *Daily 9–5.*

⓭ One of Dalat's smaller waterfalls, **Cam Ly Falls** is lovely but crowded with tourists and kids selling gum and dried meat, a local Dalat treat. ⌧ *Hoang Van Thu St.* ⌧ *6,000d.* ☉ *Daily 7–6.*

⓮ For some Dalat color, head to the European-style **Dalat Flower Garden** (Vuon Hoa Dalat), on the northeast side of Xuan Huong Lake. In January and February, around the time of Tet (the lunar new year), its wide variety of *hoa lan* (orchids) are in full bloom. At other times, you'll see all kinds of brilliantly colored flowers, including hydrangeas and fuchsias. ⊠ *2 Phu Dong Thien Vuong St.,* ☎ *063/822–151.* ☒ *5,000d.* ⊙ *Daily 7–5.*

⓯ If you're a train buff or you just want to see what Dalat was like in the first half of the 20th century, visit the **Crémaillère Railway** (Ga Da Lat), to the east of the lake. A movie-set quality pervades this picturesque train station built in the 1920s. From 1928 to 1964 Dalat was linked by train to the small town of Phan Rang–Thap Cham and to then-Saigon. Regular service was suspended in 1964 when Vietcong attacks forced it to shut down. These days the train goes only to **Trai Mat**, a small hill-tribe village 8 km (5 mi) east of Dalat. Along the way the train passes the area's bountiful fields full of strawberries, cabbage, flowers, avocados, and rambutan. The trip, which is falsely advertised as a steam-train ride, is only worth doing if you're with a group: large groups, of up to 20 people, pay as little as $3 per person, but small groups of about 5, or solo travelers, may have to pay $15 for a whole train car. It's a good idea to have a guide negotiate for you in Vietnamese. ⊠ *½ km (¼ mi) east of Xuan Huong Lake,* ☎ *no phone.* ☒ *Station viewing 5,000d.* ⊙ *Daily 8–5; trains leave for Trai Mat daily at 8 AM, 2 PM, and other times.*

⓰ One of Dalat's most famous and popular monuments is the Chinese **Thien Voung Pagoda** (Chua Tao Thien Voung), southeast of town, atop a steep mountain with great views of the surrounding area. Stalls selling candied fruits—a local specialty—and souvenirs line the dirt path leading up to the pagoda. The pagoda itself was built in 1958 by the Chaozhou Chinese congregation. Three large, Hong Kong–made gilded sandalwood sculptures dominate the pagoda in the third of the three buildings. From left to right are Dai The Chi Bo Tat (an assistant of A Di Da, the Buddha of the past), Thich Ca Buddha (Sakyamuni, the historical Buddha), and Quan The Am Bo Tat (Avalokiteçvara, the Goddess of Mercy). Peaceful gardens surround the pagoda. ⊠ *About 3 km (2 mi) southeast of center of town via Khe Sanh St.,* ☎ *no phone.* ☒ *Free.* ⊙ *Daily 9–4.*

⓱ The **Chu Linh Phong Pagoda,** also known as the Su Nu Pagoda, is a serene Buddhist convent built in 1952. Out of respect, avoid visiting during lunchtime, when the nuns (who traditionally shave their heads) sing their prayers. ⊠ *72 Hoang Hoa Tham St.,* ☎ *no phone.* ☒ *Free.* ⊙ *Daily 9–5.*

⓲ **Prenn Falls** (Thac Prenn) is a favorite of Vietnamese honeymooners. In the crowded, touristy park surrounding the falls you can frolic over rope bridges and under the falls themselves. You can also hike up the short path to a sad makeshift zoo, where a few monkeys and birds sit in small cages. Be prepared for persistent hawkers. ⊠ *South of Dalat on Hwy. 20; look for Prenn Restaurant.* ☒ *6,000d.* ⊙ *Daily 8–4:30.*

⓳ The **Valley of Love** (Thung Lung Tinh Yeu) is a popular pilgrimage site for Vietnamese honeymooners. Once named the Valley of Peace by Emperor Bao Dai, the valley now has a name reflecting its transformation from a serene landscape with lovely vistas into a magnet for newlyweds. A walk around the lovely green valley will take you past numerous Vietnamese couples being photographed with locals on horseback dressed as cowboys. Rest on a heart-shape bench, chewing some of the dried deer meat sold everywhere, and you'll fit right in.

✉ *Approximately 3 km (2 mi) north of Xuan Huong Lake, via Phu Dong Thien Vuong St.* ✆ *6,000d.* ⊙ *Daily 7:30–4.*

㉒ The **Lake of Sighs** (Ho Than Tho), northeast of town, takes its name from a tale of two star-crossed lovers, Hoang Tung and Mai Nuong. According to the *Romeo and Juliet*–like legend, Hoang Tung joined the army, but Mai Nuong thought she had been abandoned. Out of despair, she killed herself by jumping into the lake. On discovering her body, her lover did the same. Today the lake draws Vietnamese tourists dressed like cowboys and a slew of paddleboats. ✉ *About 5 km (3 mi) northeast of Dalat, following Phan Chu Trinh St.* ✆ *5,000d.* ⊙ *Daily 8–5.*

Dining and Lodging

$$$–$$$$ ✕ **Le Rabelais.** Imagine visiting a fabulous French country estate complete with chandeliers, period furniture, 3-ft-high floral arrangements, and a portrait gallery—you can almost believe it's true at the beautiful Le Rabelais. Flawless service and an impressive wine list make it worth dining in this restaurant. The French-influenced food, however, doesn't quite live up to the setting. ✉ *Sofitel Dalat Palace, 12 Tran Phu St.,* ✆ *063/825–444. AE, MC, V.*

$ ✕ **Lyla Restaurant.** Serving both Continental and Vietnamese fare, this self-proclaimed family restaurant is one of the better dining choices in Dalat. Try the *xa lat tron thit bo* (mixed salad with beef). Set on a hill, Lyla overlooks the Central Market. ✉ *18A Nguyen Chi Thanh St.,* ✆ *063/834–540. No credit cards.*

$ ✕ **Trong Dong Restaurant.** A local family runs this eatery serving high-quality Vietnamese food. Try the lotus-root salad with house dressing and the clay-pot fish, and round off the meal with a light, delicious caramel flan. Trong Dong is popular with tour groups. ✉ *220 Phan Dinh Phung St.,* ✆ *063/821–889. No credit cards.*

$$$$ 🏨 **Sofitel Dalat Palace.** Reminiscent of a French château, with 15-ft
★ ceilings, ornate fireplaces, and huge public rooms, the Sofitel is one of the most romantic hotels in Vietnam. Spacious rooms with tasteful antique reproductions, old-fashioned claw-foot bathtubs, and original moldings combine happily with unobtrusive modern conveniences and impeccable service. The exquisite Dalat Pines Golf Club, overlooking Xuan Huong Lake, has been renovated to recapture the grandeur and elegance of its original 1922 French design. ✉ *12 Tran Phu St.,* ✆ *063/ 825–444,* 𝐅𝐀𝐗 *063/825–666,* 𝖶𝖤𝖡 *www.sofitel.com. 48 rooms. Restaurant, café, room service, in-room safes, minibars, cable TV, 18-hole golf course, 2 tennis courts, mountain bikes, lounge, piano bar, pub, shops, baby-sitting, dry cleaning, laundry service, concierge, Internet, business services, meeting rooms, airport shuttle, travel services, no-smoking rooms; no a/c. AE, MC, V.*

$–$$ 🏨 **Golf 3 Hotel.** Rooms are spacious and fairly inexpensive, if a bit kitschy, at this hotel right in the center of town. The enormous sunken tubs in the deluxe rooms are reason enough to stay here. If the Golf 3 is full, its sister hotels, the nearby Golf 1 and Golf 2, are other options, though they are less posh. ✉ *4 Nguyen Thi Minh Khai St.,* ✆ *063/ 826–042,* 𝐅𝐀𝐗 *063/830–396. 78 rooms. Restaurant, café, cable TV, massage, bar, dance club, Internet, business services, airport shuttle, travel services, no-smoking rooms; no a/c. AE, MC, V. CP.*

$–$$ 🏨 **Novotel Dalat Vietnam.** A sister hotel of the tonier Sofitel Dalat Palace, the Novotel Dalat has first-class, if somewhat small, rooms within walking distance of town and the golf course. The rooms are tasteful and modern, with comfortable beds. As a guest here you have access to the Sofitel Dalat's facilities. ✉ *7 Tran Phu St.,* ✆ *063/825–777,* 𝐅𝐀𝐗 *063/ 825–888,* 𝖶𝖤𝖡 *www.novotel.com. 156 rooms. Restaurant, café, cable TV, tennis court, mountain bikes, bar, playground, Internet, business services; no a/c. AE, MC, V.*

¢–$$ ☒ **Hang Nga Guesthouse.** Choose from 10 unique rooms, each with its own offbeat theme, at this small guest house close to the center of town. The Bear Room has a life-size bear with eyes that light up when you turn on the lights and a small fireplace in its belly. Funky, too, are the Ant and Tiger rooms; the latter has a tiger with red-lightbulb eyes that stare you down in the middle of the room. This wacky architectural monument is a cheerful alternative to the more traditional hotels in town, although the rooms are very small. ☒ *3 Huynh Thuc Khang St.,* ☎ *063/822–070,* ☒ *063/831–480. 10 rooms. Restaurant, travel services; no a/c. No credit cards.*

Nightlife and the Arts

Barring a few bohemian-type cafés, there isn't much to do at night unless you like karaoke, which you can find everywhere. **Café Tung** (☒ 6 Khu Hoa Binh St., ☎ no phone) is a tiny spot where you can get coffee in the evening and swap travel tales.

Outdoor Activities and Sports

BOATING

Paddleboats are available to rent from stands along Xuan Huong Lake for 20,000d an hour.

GOLF

The pristine **Dalat Pines Golf Club** (☒ Phu Dong Thien Vuong St., ☎ 063/821–201) has an 18-hole course overlooking Xuan Huong Lake. Fees are $25–$35 per day, less for Sofitel Dalat Palace guests.

HIKING

Dalat's hilly terrain makes it a great place for gentle hikes. The Lake of Sighs and the Valley of Love are ideal places to spend an afternoon wandering—it is possible to escape the cowboys and honeymooners. The **Dalat Tourist/Lamdong Tourist Company** (☒ 7/3 Thang 2 St., ☎ 063/822–125) can provide information on hiking in the Valley of Love and around the Lake of Sighs; it also arranges guided tours of these areas.

En Route   About 5 km (3 mi) southeast of Dalat toward Phan Rang along Highway 20, the Ngoan Muc Pass affords superb views of the surrounding lush countryside and the Pacific Ocean in the distance, some 55 km (34 mi) away. The drive to the top of the pass is windy and somewhat scary, but the view is definitely worth the trip.

The Southern Central Highlands

En route from Dalat to Ho Chi Minh City is the southernmost portion of the central highlands, an unspoiled landscape dotted with ethnic-minority villages and religious complexes. There are several Ede villages in the area; visits can be arranged through tourist agencies in Dalat and Nha Trang. In the matrilineal Ede society, families of women propose to men, who then live with the wife's family and take on the mother's name, as do any children from the union. Bright colors and chunky silver jewelry characterize the dress of the Ede, who live communally in longhouses built on stilts.

The lovely beaches of Phan Thiet and Mui Ne (☞ Side Trips from Ho Chi Minh City *in* Chapter 6) are here as well.

The Kingdom of Champa ruled this part of Vietnam from the 2nd to the 15th century, and today many Cham towers still dot the countryside around Phan Rang–Thap Cham, in the province of Ninh Thuan. Descendents of the Cham people still make their home in the area. The ★ ㉑ **Po Klong Garai and Po Re Me Cham Towers** are some of the best-preserved examples of Cham architecture in the country. The four Hindu temples of Po Klong Garai are remnants of a 13th-century complex built during the reign of the Cham king Jaya Simhavarman III. According to legend, King Simhavarman built these towers in honor of King Po Klong Garai, a figure revered by the Cham people for his efforts in leading the resistance against outside invaders. An intact carving of a dancing Shiva hangs over the entrance to the tallest tower; inside the entrance is a statue of the bull Nadin, a symbol of agricultural riches. Excavations around the towers by the French and later by the Vietnamese unearthed a number of gold and silver bowls and other artifacts. Vietnam's Cham community continues to use the towers for its religious and cultural celebrations. The towers are west of Dalat on Highway 20, just beyond the semiarid twin cities of Phan Rang–Thap Cham.

While the Po Klong Garai is the area's best-known sight, the **Po Ro Me Cham Towers,** about 15 km (9 mi) south of Phan Rang, also merit a visit. These 17th-century ruins, among the newest of Vietnam's Cham towers, take their name from the last ruler of an independent Champa, King Po Ro Me, who died as a prisoner of the Vietnamese in the mid-17th century. Note the intricately carved stone statues on the towers and the two guardian Nandin statues (Nandin, a bull, is a symbol of agriculture) flanking the entrance. Set on a hill accessed by a dirt trail, the towers are difficult to reach; you may want to have a guide take you there on the back of a motorbike rather than walking all the way up the path. The view from the top of the hill—semiarid plains flanked by mountains, and hazy blue water in the distance—is worth the effort. ⊠ *Po Klong Garai is off Hwy. 20; Po Ro Me is off Hwy. 1,* ☏ *no phone.* 🎫 *5,000d for each tower.* ☉ *Daily 8–5 (opening times may vary).*

Steep, slippery steps lead to excellent views of the 300-ft, thundering
㉒ Dambri Falls. The falls are about 75 km (47 mi) southwest of Dalat and 233 km (144 mi) northeast of Ho Chi Minh City. 🎫 *8,000d.* ☉ *Daily 7–5.*

㉓ Nam Cat Tien National Park shelters the endangered Javanese rhino, as well as monkeys, elephants, and several bird species. The park, which lies 250 km (155 mi) northwest of Ho Chi Minh City, is often inaccessible due to poor road conditions and flooding. *See* Side Trips from Ho Chi Minh City *in* Chapter 6 for more information.

㉔ Langa Lake supports several floating fishing villages, which are nothing more than groups of low-end houseboats. There may or may not be a roadside food stand open serving snacks. The lake lies approximately 100 km (62 mi) north of Ho Chi Minh City along Highway 20.

Central Highlands and Dalat A to Z

To research prices, get advice from other travelers, and book travel arrangements, visit www.fodors.com.

AIR TRAVEL
Vietnam Airlines has daily flights from Dalat's Lien Khuong Airport (30 km [19 mi] south of town) to Ho Chi Minh City (one hour, $30). Vietnam Airlines also flies from Dalat to Singapore. There are no direct flights from Hanoi, Nha Trang, or Danang to Dalat.
➤ CONTACT: **Vietnam Airlines** (San Bay Lien Khuong; ⊠ 5 Truong Cong Dinh St., Dalat, ☏ 063/822–895).

BUS TRAVEL
Dalat Tourist/Lamdong Tourist Company runs daily minibus service from Dalat to Ho Chi Minh City, 308 km (191 mi) south. The trip costs

$7 and takes six to seven hours. Try to go to the office one day in advance to reserve a seat.

Sinh Café Travel sells an open bus ticket that connects Dalat to Ho Chi Minh City heading south and Dalat to Nha Trang heading north. The open-ended ticket allows you to get on the bus any day of the week. The daily trip between Dalat and Ho Chi Minh City takes about seven hours and costs $7; for an open ticket from Ho Chi Minh City to Hanoi, you pay $38 (☞ Bus Travel *in* Smart Travel Tips for more information).

➤ CONTACTS: **Dalat Tourist/Lamdong Tourist Company** (✉ 7/3 Thang 2 St., Dalat, ☎ 063/822–125; ✉ 21 Nguyen An Ninh St., District 1, Ho Chi Minh City, ☎ 08/823–0485). **Sinh Café Travel** (✉ 246–248 De Tham St., District 1, Ho Chi Minh City, ☎ 08/836–9420).

CAR RENTAL
To travel around Dalat or visit the attractions of the region, you can hire a car and driver from Dalat Tourist/Lamdong Tourist Company.

➤ CONTACT: **Dalat Tourist/Lamdong Tourist Company** (✉ 7/3 Thang 2 St., ☎ 063/826–027, FAX 063/833–956).

CAR TRAVEL
The 200-km (124-mi) trip from Nha Trang to Dalat takes about seven to eight hours by car. Driving to Dalat from Ho Chi Minh City or Hanoi costs too much, takes too long, and is too complicated; you're better off taking either a plane, a bus, or a minibus.

Within Dalat itself, the best way to get around is by car with a hired driver and guide. Be prepared for narrow, hilly, and hazardous roads; along the roadside are small shrines to motorists who have been killed. Drivers, however, are usually good. You can also hire a motorbike for about $5 per day. Bear in mind, however, that helmets are rarely worn and you may not be able to get one when you rent a motorbike.

Langa Lake, on Highway 20, is hard to miss as you cross a bridge over it when traveling between Dalat and Ho Chi Minh City. Dambri Falls, 16 km (10 mi) off Highway 20, is just north of the town of Bao Loc. Look for signs on Highway 20. The Po Klong Garai and Po Re Me Cham Towers are also off Highway 20.

EMERGENCIES
Contact Sofitel Dalat Palace Hotel (☞ Dining and Lodging, *above*) if you need assistance.

MAIL AND SHIPPING
For stamps, go to the main post office branch or ask at your hotel.

➤ POST OFFICE: **Main Branch** (✉ 14 Tran Phu St., Dalat).

MONEY MATTERS
You can exchange money at the Agriculture Bank of Vietnam and at most hotels.

➤ MAJOR BANK: **Agriculture Bank of Vietnam** (✉ Nguyen Van Troi St., Dalat).

TRAVEL AGENCY
Dalat Tourist/Lamdong Tourist Company arranges cars with drivers and tours of the city. You can also arrange for trips to the hill-tribe villages in the area.

➤ CONTACT: **Dalat Tourist/Lamdong Tourist Company** (✉ 7/3 Thang 2 St., ☎ 063/826–027, FAX 063/833–956).

6 HO CHI MINH CITY

Ho Chi Minh City—Saigon to most—is a vibrant, bustling city that reflects Vietnam's past and its future. Its broad colonial boulevards leading to the Saigon River and its stucco villas are remnants of the French colonial presence. Cholon, the city's Chinatown, is a reminder of the Chinese influence on the country. And the office towers and international hotels that mark the skyline symbolize tomorrow's Vietnam.

By Andrew
Chilvers

Updated by
Craig Thomas

ARRIVING IN HO CHI MINH CITY can be a bewildering experience. At the airport the customs paperwork can be confusing, and the throngs of taxi drivers competing for business outside can be jarringly disorienting when you're jet-lagged. But don't be put off—confusion and chaos are at the very heart of the city. If at first you feel like you are on a breathtaking roller-coaster ride moving at breakneck speed, you soon get used to the feeling and may even grow to like it.

Once romantically referred to by the French as the Pearl of the Orient, Ho Chi Minh City is still called Saigon by almost everyone who lives here. The city has a more cosmopolitan feel than Hanoi—much of the old French colonial city is vanishing beneath the rapidly rising skyline and the sheer weight of recent history.

History, however, has bequeathed the city a kaleidoscopic melting pot of styles. Only in Saigon can you get a ride in a '50s French Citroën, a '60s Ford Mustang, a '70s Russian Volga, or a brand-new Toyota. For dinner you have your choice of not only Vietnamese food but also hamburgers, fine French cuisine, or black caviar at one of the city's Russian restaurants. Afterward you can head to one of the many sleek bars in the city.

The sidewalks here are crammed with noodle stands, cafés, and vendors selling fresh glasses of *bia hoi* (beer) for as little as 25¢. At the teeming markets, tropical fruits, king cobras, live chickens, and a hundred other such items are for sale. The roads are often gridlocked with motorbikes, scooters, bicycles, cyclos, buses, and an increasing number of cars. All kinds of people travel around by bicycle or motorbike: women dressed in traditional *ao dais* (straight-cut silk gowns worn over flowing pants), long gloves, and conical hats, and whole families all squeezed on one seat. Everyone seems to be going somewhere, no matter what time of day. And even if people have nowhere to go, they simply cruise around until it's time to go to sleep.

Meanwhile, far above the din of street life, a modern city is emerging amid the screech of jackhammers and pile drivers working on the newest Asian skyline. Since economic reforms—known as *doi moi*—were adopted in the mid-1980s, Ho Chi Minh City has witnessed on-and-off growth. In the early '90s, Ho Chi Minh City's economy expanded at the startling rate of 15% a year. Things slowed down briefly as a result of the regional economic crisis of the late 1990s, but the first years of the 21st century have seen high levels of growth return and future economic prospects again looking bright.

Unfortunately, many are being left behind in the struggle for self-enrichment. Homeless children roam the downtown streets, sometimes earning a living by shining shoes or by begging or pickpocketing. Limbless war veterans hobble behind wealthy tourists, badgering them for small change. Women desperate for tourist dollars carry seemingly comatose infants and endlessly shuffle through the streets like specters. And after twilight prostitutes cruise downtown on their Hondas, prowling for foreign customers.

Ho Chi Minh City encompasses a large region, stretching all the way north to Cu Chi, in Tay Ninh Province, and south to the upper reaches of the Mekong Delta. The part of the city known as Saigon is actually made up of only 2 of the 14 districts in Ho Chi Minh City: Districts 1 and 3. Bordered by the Thi Nghe Channel to the north, the Ben Nghe Channel to the south, and the Saigon River to the east, the city has served as a natural fortress and has been fought over by countless people during the past 2,000 years. The ancient empire of Funan used the area as a trading post, and the Khmer kingdom of Angkor transformed Prey Nokor, as Saigon was called, into a flourishing center of trade protected by a standing army. By the 14th century, while under Khmer rule, the city attracted Arab, Cham, Chinese, Malaysian, and Indian merchants. It was then known as the gateway to the Kingdom of Champa, the sister empire to Angkor.

In 1674 the lords of the Nguyen clan in Hue established a customs post at Prey Nokor to cash in on the region's growing commercial traffic. Saigon, as the Vietnamese called it, became an increasingly important administrative post. The building in 1772 of a 6-km (4-mi) trench on the western edge of old Saigon, in what is now District 5, marked the shift in control in the south from Khmer rule to Nguyen rule from Hue. Further Vietnamese consolidation came in 1778 with the development of Cholon, Saigon's Chinese city, as a second commercial hub in the area that is presently District 5.

In 1789 the Nguyen lords moved their power base from Hue to Saigon, following attacks by rebels from the village of Tay Son. Unhappy with the way the Nguyen lords had been running the country, the rebels massacred most of the Nguyen clan and took control of the government—briefly. In 1802, Prince Nguyen Anh, the last surviving heir of the Nguyen dynasty, defeated the Tay Son ruler—with French backing—regaining power and uniting Vietnam. He moved the capital back to Hue and declared himself Emperor Gia Long.

In quelling the Tay Son rebels, Gia Long's request for French assistance, which was readily provided, came at a price. In exchange for their help, Gia Long promised the French territorial concessions in Vietnam. Although the French Revolution and the Napoleonic Wars temporarily delayed any French claims, Gia Long's decision eventually cost Vietnam dearly. In 1859, the French, tired of waiting for the Vietnamese emperor to give them what they felt they deserved, seized Saigon and made it the capital of their new colony, Cochin China. This marked the beginning of an epoch of colonial-style feudalism and indentured servitude for many Vietnamese in the highlands.

The catastrophe that was to overtake Saigon and the rest of Vietnam during the latter half of the 20th century was a direct result of French colonial interference. Despite France's role, however, to this day the Vietnamese people, both north and south, maintain deep sentimental ties with French culture and art, as is apparent across the country.

Today, without the threat of colonial interference or war, the Saigonese are living life to the fullest—and trying to make money. Saigon is the most Western of all the cities in Vietnam, with the greatest range of international cuisine and Western-style high-rises. But reminders of the past still poke through the headlong rush into capitalism. The Hotel Continental, immortalized in Graham Greene's *The Quiet American,* continues to stand on the corner of old Indochina's most famous thoroughfare, the rue Catinat (known to the American G.I.s as Tu Do Street and renamed Dong Khoi Street by the Communists). The city still has its central opera house and its old French City Hall, the Hôtel de Ville. You can still see the spires of Notre Dame Cathedral from the decks of the cruise liners sailing up the Saigon River. And the city is still dotted with the bunkers and watchtowers of its more recent violent past.

This is a modern city by Asian standards and has been under firm Vietnamese control for only a little more than 200 years. Consequently, there are few historic monuments or ancient sights to see. The city's character remains essentially French—with wide boulevards, colonial villas, and a café society—and resolutely Asian. Combined with a vivacious street life, the French influences have bred a charm all their own. But it is the people even more than the city that you may remember most. The Saigonese have a reputation for being friendlier than their more serious Hanoi counterparts and are generally eager to make the acquaintance of foreign visitors.

Pleasures and Pastimes

Art

Nowhere is the French cultural influence clearer than in the works of Vietnamese artists. Ho Chi Minh City has countless art galleries, with many new ones opening each month, showcasing a gamut of European-influenced art movements. The most common type of artwork you'll see throughout downtown Saigon is Impressionist knockoffs. Galleries are chock-full of copies of Monets and van Goghs, although some of the upscale galleries carry original works. Many of the tremendously talented artists represented in these galleries are French trained and are only now exhibiting their work to the world—and the world is beginning to take notice. So if you want to buy some art, now is the time, while the prices are still (relatively) low.

Cafés

In Ho Chi Minh City, life is at its most colorful on the street, and the city's café society is at the center of this vivid spectacle. It is from a seat at one of the city's small cafés that you can really observe urban life. Order a strong, slow-filtered coffee or hot green tea, and spend an hour simply watching the street. It's hypnotic: you'll see market-bound cyclos crammed with pigs; chickens and ducks piled five deep and draped over the handlebars of bicycles; women selling noodle soup from bamboo baskets balanced on poles over their shoulders, singing their own distinctive tunes to attract customers; and young women wearing white ao dais riding motorbikes to school. You may also find that people are most relaxed and most sociable at the cafés, so don't be surprised if someone asks to join you for a drink.

Dining

Ho Chi Minh City teems with Vietnamese and international restaurants, local cafés, and sidewalk noodle stalls. The French had a major influence on the city's cuisine, which means you can find many superb French-Vietnamese restaurants. You'll also find Italian restaurants, sushi bars, American burger joints, fast-food spots, and even tapas bars. But most Vietnamese simply eat at street stalls serving noodles, rice dishes, satays, kebabs, *pho* (noodle soups), and other foods that are often as delicious and varied as at any of the more upscale establishments—at a fraction of the price. Note that the farther from the road (literally!), the more hygienic the establishment is likely to be. Although the city's air-conditioned restaurants are not always the most authentic places to eat, they are usually the most pleasant places to escape the heat.

Meals are serious business, and between 11:30 AM and 2:30 PM the city shuts down to enjoy its collective repast and a postlunch siesta, a tradition rooted in the French presence here. It's considered the height of bad manners to interrupt one of these naps. If your guide suddenly decides to sleep for an hour, it's advisable to let him be. It could make the difference between a good and a bad trip. Dinner is generally served any time between 6 PM and 1 AM.

Lodging

More and more international joint-venture hotels open every year, providing an alternative to the grimmer state-run hotels. The addition of so many new properties has greatly reduced the once-inflated prices. Minihotels, family-run guest houses, are excellent alternatives to the bigger hotels. Often only a third of the price of larger establishments, they are generally in good condition, are more sensitive to guests' needs, and have their own restaurants. The minihotels, however, lack the facilities and services provided by international hotel chains.

A third option is to stay in one of the famous old colonial establishments that Saigon Tourist, the state tourism agency, has renovated. Although these old hotels certainly have their charms and some modern conveniences (IDD phones, fax machines), their renovations are often shoddy, and service is sometimes lacking. If you're looking for service and amenities, you're better off staying at one of the international hotels—although it will cost you. (But, as with everything else in Vietnam, you can get better deals if you are prepared to negotiate.) Keep in mind that despite the facilities and conveniences at these newer hotels—Internet access, business services, health clubs, cable TV, and marble bathrooms—the level of service will still probably not be what you've come to expect elsewhere. Vietnam's service industry is still in its infancy and often requires patience.

Find out if your hotel provides complimentary airport pickup—most hotels, including minihotels, can arrange a driver for you. Call ahead and arrange to have someone from the hotel meet you at the airport. If you've never been to Saigon, you may be overwhelmed by the general chaos of arriving and the crush of taxi drivers vying for your business. When you're jet-lagged, this is not a pleasant way to start your visit.

Museums

Several museums pepper the city, most housed in old colonial palaces. Many were set up primarily to promote Communist Party propaganda, and the displays are less than memorable. Nevertheless, most are worth a visit, particularly the harrowing War Remnants Museum.

Shopping

In Ho Chi Minh City you can purchase all kinds of souvenirs of Vietnam—wood carvings, lacquerware, paintings, ceramics, and T-shirts—as well as idiosyncratic items such as imitation GI cigarette lighters. This is also a good spot to pick up linens, silk clothing, handbags, and footwear. Be sure to spend an hour or two at the old colonial Ben Thanh Market in the city center and the Binh Tay Market in Cholon, where you can sample the city going about its daily business.

EXPLORING HO CHI MINH CITY

Ho Chi Minh City is not noted for its sightseeing attractions. Although there are several sights that shouldn't be missed, the particular appeal of the city lies in its street life. From early morning to late at night, the streets and sidewalks portray a startling range of activity—from street hawkers and barbers to noodle sellers and street artists. It's a kaleidoscopic maze, where Western-style commercial activity takes place alongside traditional practices.

The city has 14 districts, but most areas of interest are in either District 1 (downtown Saigon) or District 5 (Cholon). In District 1 major arteries such as Le Loi Boulevard, Ham Nghi Boulevard, and Pham Ngu Lao Street converge at the Ben Thanh Market, an important commercial and transportation hub. Northeast of the central market, at the intersection of Le Loi Boulevard with Nguyen Hue Boulevard and Dong Khoi Street, is a cluster of French colonial–style public buildings—the Hôtel de Ville (now the Ho Chi Minh City People's Committee), the Opera House, and hotels like the Rex, the Continental, and the Caravelle, built by the French and made famous during the Vietnam War.

Saigon's waterways have traditionally served as a means of commercial transport as well as a natural moat. District 1 is bounded on the east by the Saigon River and on the south by the Ben Nghe Channel. Not only do the rivers provide an alternative way of getting around, they also serve as convenient landmarks. The city's rather daunting layout and chaotic traffic tend to discourage leisurely walking. The intermittent taxi, cyclo, or motorbike ride, which ranges from 6,000d to 10,000d, is an unavoidable but enjoyable alternative. Any of the walks below could also be done as a cyclo ride, an option particularly recommended on hot days. And keep in mind that if you find a cyclo driver you like early in the trip, you should use him again.

Great Itineraries

IF YOU HAVE 1–2 DAYS

With one day you can see many of the city's major sights, although you will have to be selective, especially if you want to visit a museum. Hiring a cyclo or taxi will allow you to see the city more quickly. After you've seen the main sights on the first day, you'll have to go farther afield to find areas of interest.

IF YOU HAVE 4 DAYS

With four days you can see all the city's sights, go to one or two markets, and take a day trip—or even two—to surrounding areas including the Mekong Delta, the Cu Chi Tunnels, and the Caodai Holy See. Make arrangements for these excursions with one of the city's tourist agencies, or hire a car and driver (and maybe a guide) and go on your own.

When to Tour Ho Chi Minh City

The best time to visit the city is during the dry season, roughly between November and April, especially if you want to go down to the Mekong Delta. The rainy season runs from about May through October, during which time outlying areas can become very flooded.

Central Saigon (Districts 1 and 3)

District 1 is the center of old Saigon. The broad Nguyen Hue and Le Loi boulevards converge at the Hôtel de Ville (now the People's Committee building), the historic Opera House (now known as the Municipal Theater), and the Hotel Continental. Dong Khoi Street, toward the eastern edge of District 1, is the neighborhood's historic main thoroughfare; it runs down to the Saigon River from Notre Dame Cathedral and the Central Post Office. Known as rue Catinat during the French colonial era, Dong Khoi Street might be more easily recognized as Tu Do Street, its moniker when it was Saigon's red-light district in the 1960s and '70s. Since then, chic shops and restaurants have replaced the bars. Ben Thanh, an old colonial covered market, is on the western edge of District 1, and the former presidential palace (now called the Reunification Palace) is on the northern boundary of the area.

Numbers in the text correspond to numbers in the margin and on the Ho Chi Minh City map.

A Good Walk

Although slightly away from the center, the provocative **War Remnants Museum** ① makes a good starting point for this walk. From here head northeast on Vo Van Tan Street toward tree-lined Nam Ky Khoi Nghia Street. When you come to Nguyen Thi Minh Khai Street, you will see the grounds of the modern Reunification Palace. Directly behind it is the old French sports club, the Cercle Sportif, now known as **Cong Vien Van Hoa Park** ②. To enter the park, turn right onto Nguyen Thi Minh Khai Street and follow it for about 200 yards; the entrance will be on your left. Exit the park at the southeast corner onto Nguyen Du Street, which is a one-way road running alongside the palace. Head north along Nguyen Du Street and turn left onto Nam Ky Khoi Nghia Street, walking until you reach the entrance to the **Reunification Palace** ③. Exiting the palace, walk northeast on Le Duan Boulevard, the street that intersects Nam Ky Khoi Nghia Street at the palace entrance. After passing Pasteur Street, you'll see the back of **Notre Dame Cathedral** ④, with its pink spires. On Le Duan Boulevard, just a couple of blocks past Hai Ba Trung Boulevard, is the site of the former U.S. Embassy, now the **U.S. Consulate** ⑤, which is worth noting only for its historical associations. Proceed about 1,000 ft down Le Duan Boulevard to get to the sprawling grounds of the **Zoo and Botanical Garden** ⑥ and the **History Museum** ⑦.

With your back to the main entrance of the complex, retrace your steps and walk southwest on Le Duan Boulevard until you reach Ton Duc Thang Street. Turn left and then make a right onto Le Thanh Ton Street; follow this road southwest until it intersects with **Dong Khoi Street.** Make a left onto Dong Khoi; you'll see the main branch for Saigon Tourist. Just past Saigon Tourist stands the **Hotel Continental** ⑧. Although a shadow of its former self, it's still worth a visit. Next door, at the end of Le Loi Boulevard, is the **Municipal Theater** ⑨, recognizable by its inverted dome. Beyond the theater is the **Caravelle Hotel** ⑩, once a favorite haunt of war correspondents at cocktail hour.

Retrace your steps northwest along Dong Khoi Street toward Notre Dame Cathedral—the front of the church this time. The beautiful French colonial **Central Post Office** ⑪ is on the right side of the square that opens up in front of the cathedral.

With your back to the cathedral, walk toward Nguyen Du Street; make a right, and then take the first left onto Pasteur Street and the first right onto Ly Tu Trong Street to get to the neoclassic **Ho Chi Minh City Museum** ⑫, formerly known as the Museum of the Revolution. Return to Pasteur Street; then proceed down to Le Thanh Ton Street to get to the **Ho Chi Minh City People's Committee** ⑬, built by the French as the Hôtel de Ville (City Hall). Follow Le Thanh Ton Street southwest, away from the People's Committee, and make a right on Truong Dinh Street. In the middle of the block between Ly Tu Trong and Le Thanh Ton streets is the **Mariamman Hindu Temple** ⑭, the last functioning Hindu house of worship in the city. With your back to the temple, make a left on Le Thanh Ton Street where the busy **Ben Thanh Market** ⑮ spills out onto the surrounding street.

TIMING

The walk could take a day or more, depending on how much time you want to spend in the museums. Start in the morning and take lots of breaks in the small sidewalk cafés along the way. Consider splitting the walk into two parts, with a break after the History Museum. Be careful not to overexert yourself, and remember to drink a lot of bottled water: walking around Saigon can be hot and tiring.

Sights to See

★ ⑮ **Ben Thanh Market** (Cho Ben Thanh). Every imaginable product of the Vietnamese economy is sold here—look for a cheap meal, a hat, even

Ho Chi Minh City

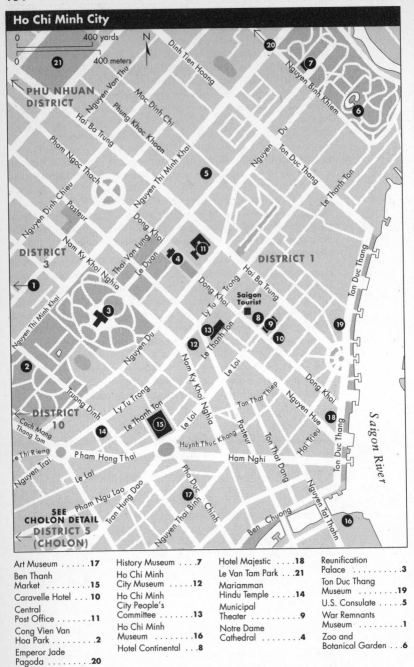

0 ____ 400 yards
0 ____ 400 meters

N

PHU NHUAN
DISTRICT

DISTRICT
3

DISTRICT 1

DISTRICT
10

Saigon Tourist

SEE
CHOLON DETAIL
DISTRICT 5
(CHOLON)

Saigon River

Street labels: Dinh Tien Hoang, Nguyen Binh Khiem, Nguyen Van Thu, Mac Dinh Chi, Du, Nguyen Ton Duc Thang, Le Thanh Ton, Phung Khac Khoan, Hai Ba Trung, Phan Ngoc Thach, Nguyen Thi Minh Khai, Nguyen Dinh Chieu, Pasteur, Nam Ky Khoi Nghia, Dong Khoi, Thai Van Lung, Le Duan, Dong Khoi, Ly Tu Trong, Hai Ba Trung, Nguyen Du, Le Thanh Ton, Ton Duc Thang, Le Loi, Ly Tu Trong, Truong Dinh, Nam Ky Khoi Nghia, Le Thanh Ton, Ton That Thiep, Nguyen Hue, Dong Khoi, Ham Nghi, Huynh Thuc Khang, Le Loi, Pasteur, Ton That Dang, Hai Trieu, Ton Duc Thang, Le Thi Rieng, Cach Mang Thang Tam, Nguyen Trai, Le Lai, Pham Hong Thai, Pho Duc Chinh, Pham Ngu Lao, Tran Hung Dao, Nguyen Thai Binh, Ben Chuong, Nguyen Tat Thanh live snakes. The building that houses most of the market was constructed in 1914 by the French, who called it Les Halles Centrales (the Central Market Halls). The best time to visit the market is first thing in the morning, when stocks of produce are piled high and vendors are hustling. ✉ *At circular intersection of Le Loi Blvd., Pham Ngu Lao St., and Ham Nghi Blvd., District 1,* ☎ *no phone.* ☼ *Daily 7–7.*

⑩ **Caravelle Hotel.** Most of the foreign correspondents stayed at this hotel during the Vietnam War. During the 1968 Tet Offensive, several U.S. Marines were killed here; journalists filmed the battle from the rooftop. ✉ *19 Lam Son Sq., District 1,* ☎ *08/234–4999.*

★ ⑪ **Central Post Office** (Buu Dien Trung Tam). Be sure to go inside to check out the huge map of old Indochina in this classic French colonial building, completed in 1891. Besides the usual mail services, there are phones and fax machines. To mail letters you need to use the entrance to the less romantic, Soviet-era expansion at 117 Hai Ba Trung Street. ✉ *At the top of Dong Khoi St. opposite Notre Dame Cathedral, District 1,* ☎ *no phone.* ☼ *Daily 7:30–7:30.*

🖰 ❷ **Cong Vien Van Hoa Park.** Huge tamarind trees line the road leading up to this park, which, with its lush flora teeming with deafening cicadas, resembles a botanical garden. Known as the Cercle Sportif to the French, this park was the elite sporting club of the French bourgeoisie in colonial times. Vietnamese people were actually barred from entering. Today there is still a sports club, with tennis courts, a swimming pool, a gym and weight room, and a colonial clubhouse. Use of the facilities will cost you no more than a dollar. These days the club is frequented mostly by young Vietnamese students eager to practice their English with any tourists who wander in. Midday, the park tends to be a base for siestas; you'll see plenty of people catching up on sleep. ✉ *Entrances on 115 Nguyen Du St. and 55C Nguyen Thi Minh Khai St., District 1.*

Dong Khoi Street. Once named rue Catinat, Dong Khoi Street was the 5th Avenue or Rodeo Drive of Saigon during the French colonial era. During the Vietnam War this road was the center of the infamous red-light district and was known as Tu Do Street. These days most of the old-time bars have been replaced by tony restaurants and shops. The street remains the center of the old city, but this is the new Dong Khoi: most shops are now geared toward tourists.

NEED A
BREAK?   The **Paris Deli** (✉ 31 Dong Khoi St., District 1, ☎ 08/829–7533), a European-style café, serves excellent cappuccinos and pastries. A sister café is at 65 Le Loi Street (08/821–6127).

❼ **History Museum** (Vien Bao Tang Lich Su). Although the front door leads you right to a statue of the ubiquitous "Uncle Ho" (as Ho Chi Minh is known), this museum is dedicated to Vietnamese history from the earliest inhabitants to 1930, when the Communist Party was established. Half the museum covers the history of the nation as a whole; the other half focuses on the art and artifacts of southern Vietnam. The ethnography section is particularly interesting. The neo-Vietnamese structure was built by the French in 1929, and much of the current collection was compiled by the French Far Eastern Institute. ✉ *2 Nguyen Binh Khiem, District 1,* ☎ *08/829–8146 or 08/829–0268.* ☐ *10,000d.* ☼ *Mon.–Sat. 8–11:30 and 1:30–4:30, Sun. 8:30–4:30.*

⑫ **Ho Chi Minh City Museum** (Bao Tang Thanh Pho). Constructed in 1886 as the residence for the French governor of Cochin China, the building is now a museum (formerly known as the Museum of the Revolution) dedicated to the Vietnamese struggle against the French and Americans. Displays focus on famous marches, military battles, and anti-French and anti-American activists. Exhibits include photos of historical events, uprisings, student demonstrations, and the self-immolation of the monk Thich Quang Duc as a protest against the war. The collection also has a lot of American G.I. paraphernalia—badges, lighters, helmets, and such—as well as a model of the Cu Chi Tunnels, the huge underground complex built by the Vietnamese Communists that allowed them to survive massive U.S. bombings and military sweeps. The displays are in Vietnamese, but you'll easily get the message. The building itself is as interesting as many of the exhibits inside: a neoclassic design, it has huge columns outside and high-ceiling, 19th-century ballrooms inside. Beneath the building are concrete bunkers and tunnels connecting to the Reunification Palace. It was here that President Ngo Dinh Diem (1901–63) and his notorious brother Ngo Dinh Nhu hid before being caught and eventually executed in 1963, three weeks before the assassination of President John F. Kennedy. Outside on the grounds are Soviet tanks, a U.S. helicopter, and antiaircraft guns. ⊠ *65 Ly Tu Trong St., District 1,* ☎ *08/829–9741.* 🎫 *10,000d.* ☉ *Daily 8–4.*

🔞 **Ho Chi Minh City People's Committee.** Built by the French between 1901 and 1908 to be Saigon's Hôtel de Ville (City Hall), this yellow-and-white colonial-style building now houses the city's main governing body. Unfortunately, the building is not open to the public, so you can't get a peek at its ornate interior. ⊠ *86 Le Thanh Ton St., at intersection with Nguyen Hue St., District 1.*

★ ⑧ **Hotel Continental.** In French colonial days, the Hotel Continental's open terrace (now simply a sidewalk), shaded by broad tamarind trees, was the town's most sought-after lunch spot. During the Vietnam War, journalists and diplomats met on the terrace to discuss the latest events. Graham Greene's *The Quiet American* was set here. ⊠ *132–134 Dong Khoi St., District 1,* ☎ *08/829–9201.*

⑭ **Mariamman Hindu Temple** (Chua Ba Mariamman). Vivid statues and colorful floral offerings at this temple, the last functioning Hindu house of worship in the city, create a microcosm of India in the streets of Saigon. Before the temple was returned in the early '90s to the Hindu community, the government used it as a factory for making joss sticks (incense) and processing dried fish. Today it serves a congregation of only 60 Tamil Hindus, but some Vietnamese and Chinese locals also revere it as a holy space. ⊠ *45 Truong Dinh St., District 1,* ☎ *no phone.* ☉ *Daily 7–7.*

⑨ **Municipal Theater** (Nha Hat Thanh Pho). This colonial-style theater was built by the French in 1899 as Saigon's opera house. Later it housed the National Assembly of South Vietnam, the congress of the South Vietnamese government. After 1975, when South Vietnam ceased to be, it became a theater again. ⊠ *7 Cong Truong Lam Son St., at intersection of Le Loi Blvd. and Dong Khoi St., District 1,* ☎ *08/829–9976.*

④ **Notre Dame Cathedral** (Nha Tho Duc Ba). The French built this neo-Romanesque cathedral, a prominent presence on the Saigon skyline, in 1880 on the site of an old fort. Spanish, Portuguese, and French missionaries introduced Catholicism to Vietnam as early as the 16th century. Today there are approximately 9 million Catholics in Vietnam, the largest Christian population in Asia after the Philippines. The Mass celebrated at 9:30 AM on Sunday is quite a sight, as hundreds of faithful converge on the church and stand in the surrounding square.

The service includes short sections in English and French. ⊠ *Top of Dong Khoi St., District 1,* ☎ *no phone.*

3 **Reunification Palace** (Hoi Truong Thong Nhat). This modern palace—the symbolic center of the South Vietnamese government—was the scene of the dramatic seizure of Saigon by the National Liberation Front in 1975, when tanks smashed down the gates and an NLF flag was draped over the building's balcony. On the grounds is said to be the actual tank that battered down the gates. (Another tank in Ban Me Thuat in the central highlands and a tank at the Army Museum in Hanoi lay the same claim to fame. For the victorious Communists, these relics are sometimes more symbols than the real McCoy, so don't take them too literally.)

Ngo Viet Thu, a European-influenced modernist architect, designed the classic '60s building when South Vietnamese president Diem decided he had an "image problem" after his own air force tried to assassinate him by bombing the old French palace. Another assassination attempt succeeded a year later, so Diem never saw the palace finished. The former building on the site was called Norodom Palace and was the home of the French governor-general of Cochin China. The present building still sits on large grounds, where there is a somewhat romanticized model of Ho Chi Minh's home.

There isn't much to see except the palace rooms: the cabinet room, the assembly room, the president's office, the war command room with maps and multicolor telephones, the dining rooms, the private quarters, and a bar-and-games room. You also get a look at the network of tunnels to which the government of South Vietnam would retreat in difficult times and the helicopter that bombed the building in 1975. It all sounds more interesting than it is, since there really isn't much in the rooms except some furniture. But the palace is worth a visit, if only to see a vestige of Vietnam's past. Be sure to stand out on the balcony for a view of the city down the long, tree-lined boulevard created by the French. Although tours are free to Vietnamese, foreigners must pay. ⊠ *Visitors' entrance on 106 Nguyen Du St., District 1.* 🖅 *15,000d includes English-language tour,* ☎ *no phone.* ☉ *Daily 7:30–10:30 and 1–4.*

5 **U.S. Consulate.** The consulate stands on the site of the former American Embassy, which was the scene of running battles during the 1968 Tet Offensive and was finally seized by the Vietnamese with the capture of Saigon in April 1975. The U.S. Embassy was the site of one of the most memorable images of the war: the U.S. ambassador, an American flag clutched to his chest, rushing into a helicopter waiting on the roof, while marine guards pushed back mobs of South Vietnamese who had been assured evacuation. The original building remained untouched after its evacuation in 1975; it was finally demolished in 1998 to make way for the consulate. A plaque in front of the building commemorates the sacrifice of the Vietcong sappers who died in an attack during the Tet Offensive. ⊠ *Intersection of Le Duan Blvd. and Mac Din Chi St., District 1,* ☎ *08/822–9433.*

1 **War Remnants Museum** (Nha Trung Bay Toi Ac Chien Tranh Xam). You may instinctively shy away from this museum, which is dedicated to publicizing the horrors perpetrated by U.S. armed forces during the Vietnam War. You'll probably come away with mixed feelings about the one-sided propaganda—ashamed of the U.S. actions, angry about the Vietnamese inaccuracies in depicting them, or both. Nevertheless, it's worth a visit.

Photographs, the majority of the items on display, depict the horrors and details of the war; their presentations range from poignant to dull to obviously slanted. Along with these photos are gruesome displays documenting the effects of Agent Orange, napalm, and other weapons of mass destruction as well as a mannequin of a rather dissolute-looking American soldier (smoking Marlboros, of course) and a replica of a Con Dao prison cell.

Although the museum has toned down slightly by changing its name from the Museum of American War Crimes to the War Crimes Museum and finally to the War Remnants Museum, its coverage continues to be skewed. Conspicuous in its absence, for instance, is any mention of the division of the country into South Vietnam and North Vietnam throughout the Vietnam War. (The Communist government tends to overlook this division; instead it claims a puppet government backed by American imperialists illegally ruled in the South against the will of the people.) There are, however, photos of captured spies who attempted to infiltrate and overthrow the Communist regime.

Also missing is information about some of the horrors perpetrated by the National Liberation Front, particularly the thousands of people believed to have been massacred in Hue during the 1968 Tet Offensive. There is little information about civilian protests in Vietnam and in America against U.S. military actions, except for a few photos of antiwar demonstrators. ⊠ *28 Vo Van Tan St., District 3,* ☏ *08/930–5587.* ᗧ *10,000d.* ⊙ *Daily 7:30–11:45 and 1:30–5:15.*

☝ **❻** **Zoo and Botanical Garden** (Thao Cam Vien). The fauna here does relatively well, and the flora thrives in its natural subtropical niche. In addition to seeing the lackluster live animals, you may want to visit the eerie "taxidermy-go-round," where you can ride stuffed animals. As if this were not enough, the gardens have been filled with additional carnival-like attractions—a rather unfortunate addition, as the gardens were one of the first French building projects in Vietnam and once one of the finest such parks in all of Asia. ⊠ *2 Nguyen Binh Khiem St., at Le Duan Blvd., District 1,* ☏ *08/829–3728.* ᗧ *8,000d.* ⊙ *Daily 7 AM–8 PM.*

Circling Old Saigon

Several interesting sights lie around the periphery of Old Saigon. South of District 1, on the broad waterfront along the Saigon River, is a less palatial section of the old city where the old docks and customs houses used to be. This was also the old banking district, and you can still see the colonial-era Hong Kong and Shanghai Banking Corporation, and Banque d'Indochine buildings. Most museums in this area are housed in the former customs houses and colonial buildings and predominantly contain collections dedicated to famous figures and moments in Vietnamese history. You'll need to hire a cyclo to take you to some of the sights in this area; otherwise you're in for a long walk, without sidewalks in some sections.

Numbers in the text correspond to numbers in the margin and on the Ho Chi Minh City map.

A Good Tour

Start at the **Ho Chi Minh Museum** ⑯, in a converted French customs house on Saigon Port. From the museum follow Nguyen Tat Thanh Street across the bridge over the Ben Nghe Channel. Take your first left after the bridge, following the channel along Ben Chuong Street until you get to Pho Duc Chinh Street. Make a right to get to the **Art Museum** ⑰, in a grand old colonial building. After you've seen it, return to Ben Chuong Street and continue back the way you came until you reach Ton Duc Thang Street, which curves along the Saigon River. At the intersection with Dong Khoi Street stands the late-19th-century **Hotel Majestic** ⑱. The hotel's rooftop bar provides magnificent views of the Saigon River and semirural Thu Thiem district opposite. If you're interested in a detour you can turn left at Nguyen Hue Boulevard and make the first left onto Hai Trieu Street, also known as Whiskey Row. Take a right on Ham Nghi Boulevard, where several international food stores (No. 64 is a good one) are jam-packed with Western specialties. Make a right onto Ton That Dang Street, where you can find everything from live eels to laundry detergent at the market that continues along intersecting Huynh Thuc Khang Street, a kind of electronics arcade. Continuing a block past Huynh Thuc Khang Street, you come to Ton That Thiep Street, in what has historically been the Indian quarter.

Back on Ton Duc Thang Street, head north until you reach the **Ton Duc Thang Museum** ⑲, dedicated to the first president of North Vietnam and later united Vietnam. From the museum take a cyclo along Ton Duc Thang Street, which turns into Dinh Tien Hoang Street. Follow Dinh Tien Hoang for about half a mile. After you cross the intersection with Dien Bien Phu Street, make a right onto Nguyen Van Giai Street. Proceed up Nguyen Van Giai until the first intersection, Mai Thi Luu Street. Turn right onto Mai Thi Luu Street; at No. 73 is the lovely **Emperor Jade Pagoda** ⑳. After checking out the pagoda, head back out to Dien Tinh Hoang and make a left onto Vo Thi Sau Street. Approximately 200 yards ahead before the intersection with Hai Ba Trung Street is **Le Van Tam Park** ㉑, once a French cemetery and now a popular recreation and gathering spot. After visiting the park, continue along Vo Thi Sau Street through the intersection with Hai Ba Trung Street until you reach Pham Ngoc Thach Street on your left. Pham Ngoc Thach eventually turns into Dong Khoi Street. Here you can either walk down the street toward the river or continue in your cyclo.

TIMING

Exploring this part of Saigon will probably take a day, including visiting the museums and the pagoda and browsing along Dong Khoi Street. All museums are open daily except Monday.

Sights to See

⑰ **Art Museum** (Bao Tang My Thuat). Incorporating European-type stucco and Asian designs, the Art Museum was designed in the classic French-Vietnamese architectural style once common to those edifices built for wealthy French and Vietnamese families and officials. But considering its grand colonial setting, this museum is something of a disappointment. The best reason to visit is the third floor, with its antique statues and other relics of the pre-Vietnamese south. Also here are objects from the ancient Funan and Khmer civilizations as well as some of the best examples of Cham art outside the central highlands. The collection on the first and second floors covers propaganda art of the Soviet socialist-realist variety—soldiers and peasants marching arm in arm to battle. At first it's interesting, but after a while you may start to feel bombarded by the number of images of war, Uncle Ho, and defeated foreign armies. ⊠ *97A Pho Duc Chinh St., District 1,* ☎ *08/822–2441 or 08/822–2577.* ⊐ *10,000d.* ⊙ *Tues.–Sun. 7:30–11:30 and 1:30–4.*

★ ⑳ **Emperor Jade Pagoda** (Chua Ngoc Hoang or Phuoc Hai Tu). The Cantonese community built this structure—the finest Chinese pagoda in Saigon—in 1909. It's also known as the Tortoise Pagoda. A mixture of Taoist, Buddhist, and ethnic myths provides the sources for the pagoda's multitude of statues and carvings—everything from the *King of Hell* to a *Buddha of the Future*. Slowly strolling around the interior to view them may be preferable to attempting to decipher the significance of each of the numerous, distinct deities. Take a moment to note the main altar, the side panel's depiction of hell, and in the side room, the miniature female figures who represent the range of human qualities. ✉ *73 Mai Thi Luu St., District 3,* ☎ *no phone.* ✍ *Free.* ☉ *Daily 7–6.*

⑯ **Ho Chi Minh Museum** (Khu Luu Niem Bac Ho). A mix of Vietnamese and French styles, this structure, nicknamed the Dragon House (Nha Rong) for its architectural design, is actually far more interesting than most of the displays within. It was constructed in 1863 as the original French customs house; any individuals coming to colonial Saigon would have had to pass through the building once they docked at the port. Ho Chi Minh (1890–1969) passed through here in 1911 on the way to his 30-year sojourn around Europe and America. Inside are some of his personal belongings, including his journals, fragments of his clothing, and his rubber sandals. Ho Chi Minh was an ascetic type of guy, known for wearing sandals made only from tires; these are now scattered at museums around the country. ✉ *On Saigon Port at 1 Nguyen Tat Thanh St., by quayside on Ben Nghe Channel at far end of Ham Nghi Blvd., District 4,* ☎ *08/940–1053.* ✍ *10,000d.* ☉ *Tues.–Sun. 7:30–11:30 and 1:30–5.*

★ ⑱ **Hotel Majestic.** Built in the late 19th century, the Majestic was one of the first French colonial hotels, and it still has the elegant decor to show for it. Head to the rooftop bar for an excellent view of the Saigon River. ✉ *1 Dong Khoi St., District 1,* ☎ *08/829–5514.*

㉑ **Le Van Tam Park.** Because, perhaps, this area was used as a cemetery by the French, the Saigonese have only recently embraced it as a park. It's not green and leafy, but it's still popular with morning joggers and people playing badminton. There are small rides for children, and benches that seem to invite cuddling couples. Like all parks in Vietnam, this one is best avoided after nightfall. ✉ *Bounded by Hai Ba Trung, Vo Thi Sau, Hai Ba Trung, and Dien Bien Phu Sts.* ☉ *Daily 5 AM–sunset.*

⑲ **Ton Duc Thang Museum** (Bao Tang Ton Duc Thang). This unremarkable museum celebrates the life and times of President Ton Duc Thang (1888–1980), who succeeded Ho Chi Minh as head of North and later unified Vietnam after Ho Chi Minh's death in 1969. Inside are artifacts that Ton Duc Thang used in everyday life as well as photos of him taken during his incarceration by the French on Paulo Condor (now Con Dao Island) and propaganda pictures of him exhorting the people of Vietnam to fight the French and Americans. A characterless Soviet-era building, on the waterfront by the Vietnamese navy barracks, houses the museum. ✉ *5 Ton Duc Thang St., District 1,* ☎ *08/829–7542.* ✍ *Free.* ☉ *Tues.–Sun. 7:30–11:30 and 1:30–5.*

Cholon (District 5)

Southwest of central Saigon is Cholon, a Chinese sister city, otherwise known as District 5. Cholon was and still is the heart of Chinese culture in Vietnam and a commercial center. The French supported the Chinese in Vietnam because of their success in commerce and their apolitical outlook—the Chinese seldom supported Vietnamese Nationalist struggles. The Communists, on the other hand, saw Cholon as a bastion of capitalism, and the area suffered greatly after 1975. Later, in 1979, during the war between Vietnam and China, Cholon was again targeted, since it was considered a potential center of fifth columnists (pro-Chinese agitators). Many of the first boat people to flee Vietnam were Chinese-Vietnamese from Cholon. Now, after having made money in Australia, Canada, and the United States, many have returned to Saigon and are among the city's wealthiest residents.

Stroll about on your own or negotiate a price of about 55,000d with a cyclo driver for a tour of the pagodas concentrated around Nguyen Trai Street and Tran Hung Dao Boulevard. Bright blue, yellow, red, orange, and gold cover the pagodas in a dazzling display that would put mating peacocks to shame. Pagodas are seldom shut to the public, and most monks begin their prayers early in the morning, so you are generally welcome to enter a pagoda at any time of day. There are no admission fees, but it is traditional to put a donation of about 10,000d or so in the box at the altar in front of Buddha. Monks never hassle you for money, but they do look a little upset if you don't donate. When you've seen enough (the pagodas may start to look the same after a while), alert your guide or cyclo driver so you won't have to see every single one in the area.

Spend the rest of the day exploring Cholon's streets, markets, shop-houses (stores that double as the owners' homes), and restaurants, with their distinctive Chinese appeal. Walk down the hundreds of small side streets, where the neighborhood is at its most colorful. And be sure to enter one of the many traditional medicine shops, which sell everything from herbal remedies being packaged for export to animals' hoofs, antlers, and tails to sea horses and snake wine.

Numbers in the text correspond to numbers in the margin and on the Cholon map.

A Good Tour

Begin at the bustling **Binh Tay Market** ㉒, on Phan Van Khoe Street. Make a left out of the market and walk along Phan Van Khoe Street until you get to Phung Hung Street; take a left and follow it until you reach the **Ong Bon Pagoda** ㉓, where you can pay your respects to the guardian of happiness and virtue. Exiting the pagoda, take Hai Thuong Lan Ong Boulevard east until you reach the French colonial–era **Post Office** ㉔, across from the statue of Phan Dinh Phung in the middle of the roundabout. Head north on Chau Van Liem Boulevard to Tran Hung Dao Boulevard, the center of Cholon, with its street markets and old, small shop-houses (and some newer, taller ones).

Keep walking straight ahead until you reach Nguyen Trai Street; Cholon's pagoda district is to your right. Continue on Chau Van Liem Boulevard until you come to small Lao Tu Street, on your right, and the **Quan Am Pagoda** ㉕, which is known for its elaborately decorated scenes. Walk south down Luong Nhu Hoc Street to the **Ha Chuong Hoi Quan Pagoda** ㉖, at No. 802, one of the many temples devoted to the goddess of the sea. Take a left on Nguyen Trai Street and walk along until you come to the **Thien Hau Pagoda** ㉗, at No. 710, where sailors would come before venturing out to sea. Farther along, past the intersection of Trieu Quang Phu Street, on the left at No. 678 is the **Nghia An Hoi Quan Pagoda** ㉘, famous for its detailed woodwork. On the other side of the street, at No. 118, is the **Tam Son Hoi Quan Pagoda** ㉙, dedicated to the goddess of fertility. Keep going straight on Nguyen Trai Street, past the intersection of Ly Thuong Kiet Boulevard, until you reach the **Cholon Mosque** ㉚. Go back to Ly Thuong Kiet Boulevard and turn right onto Tran Hung Dao Boulevard. Take this to Luong Nhu Hoc Street, turn left, and you'll be back at the post office.

TIMING

Depending on how interested you are in pagodas, this tour could take up to three or four hours. Portions of the tour—notably the beginning

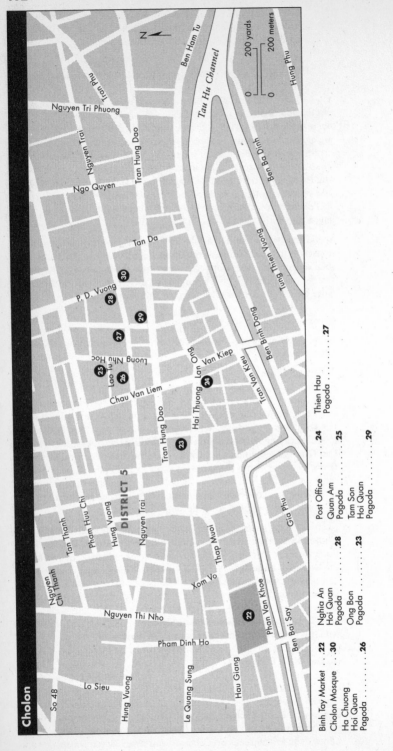

Cholon

DISTRICT 5

Tau Hu Channel

Ben Ham Tu
Ben Ba Dinh
Hung Phu
Tung Thien Vuong
Ben Binh Dong
Tran Van Kieu

200 yards
200 meters
0
0

Tran Phu
Nguyen Tri Phuong
Nguyen Trai
Tran Hung Dao
Ngo Quyen
Tan Da
P. D. Vuong
Luong Nhu Hoc
Lao Tu
Chau Van Liem
Tran Hung Dao
Hai Thuong Lan Ong
Van Kiep
Nguyen Chi Thanh
Tan Thanh
Pham Huu Chi
Hung Vuong
Nguyen Trai
Thap Muoi
Xom Vo
Gia Phu
So 48
Lo Sieu
Hung Vuong
Nguyen Thi Nho
Pham Dinh Ho
Le Quang Sung
Hau Giang
Phan Van Khoe
Ben Bai Say

and particularly Binh Tay Market—can be a bit hectic with street activity. The latter portion of the tour should be more relaxed. Consider bringing a guide to steer you and keep overly aggressive cyclo drivers at bay. Also bring bottled water and avoid the hotter hours of the day. If you have an interest in Chinese medicine, be sure to take time to explore the many stores along the small backstreets surrounding the Binh Tay Market.

Sights to See

㉒ Binh Tay Market (Cho Binh Tay). Cholon's main market is in a colonial-era Chinese-style building. The street outside is a frenzy of activity; inside can be a little calmer, although you have to wend your way through very narrow aisles. Lots of different items are sold, including dried shrimp and fruit, aluminum kitchenware, baskets, plastic goods, barrettes, straw hats, and food. ☒ *On Hau Giang Blvd., District 6,* ☏ *no phone.* ☉ *Daily 5 AM–8 PM; hrs may vary.*

㉚ Cholon Mosque. Built in 1932 by Tamil Muslims, the Cholon Mosque now serves Saigon's Indonesian and Malaysian Muslim community. Notice how much simpler the mosque is than the pagodas in the area, which are characterized by exuberant ornamentation and bright colors. ☒ *641 Nguyen Trai St., at Ly Thuong Kiet Blvd., District 5,* ☏ *no phone.*

㉖ Ha Chuong Hoi Quan Pagoda. Like many other pagodas built by Fujian congregations, this one is dedicated to Thien Hau, goddess of the sea and protector of fisherfolk and sailors. It has four stone pillars encircled by painted dragons; these were brought from China when the pagoda was constructed in the 19th century. Also note the scenes in ceramic relief on the roof and the murals next to the main altar. ☒ *802 Nguyen Trai St., District 5,* ☏ *no phone.*

㉘ Nghia An Hoi Quan Pagoda. This pagoda, built by the Chaozhou Chinese congregation in 1872, is worth seeing for its elaborate woodwork. There are intricately carved wooden boats and a large figure of the deified Chinese general Quan Cong's sacred red horse, as well as representations of Quan Cong himself with two guardians. A festival dedicated to Quan Cong takes place here every year on the 13th of the first lunar month. ☒ *678 Nguyen Trai St., District 5,* ☏ *no phone.*

★ **㉓ Ong Bon Pagoda** (Chua Ong Bon or Nhi Phu Hoi Quan). Many deities are represented at this pagoda, but the main attraction is Ong Bon himself, the guardian of happiness and virtue. Ong Bong is also responsible for wealth, so people bring fake paper money to burn in the pagoda's furnace in his honor, hoping the year ahead will bring financial rewards to their families. The centerpiece of the pagoda is an elaborately carved wood and gold altar and a finely crafted statue of Ong Bon. Look for the intricately painted murals of lions, tigers, and dragons. ☒ *264 Hai Thuong Lan Ong Blvd. (parallel to Tran Hung Dao Blvd.), at Phung Hung St., District 5,* ☏ *no phone.*

㉔ Post Office. This modernist building was constructed by the French in the 1920s. ☒ *Intersection of Hai Thuong Lan Ong Blvd. and Chau Van Liem Blvd., District 5,* ☏ *no phone.* ☉ *Daily 7:30–7:30.*

㉕ Quan Am Pagoda. Busy scenes in lacquer, ceramic, gold, and wood illustrate traditional Chinese stories at this pagoda, built in 1816 by a congregation of Fujian refugees from China. Many legendary and divine beings, some dressed in elaborately embroidered robes, are portrayed, as are some simple rural scenes representing the birthplaces of the original members of the congregation. Be prepared for a stifling cloud of incense when you enter—this is still one of Cholon's most active pagodas. ⊠ *12 Lao Tu St. (parallel to Hung Vuong Blvd. and Nguyen Trai St.), District 5,* ☎ *no phone.*

㉙ **Tam Son Hoi Quan Pagoda** (Chua Ba Chua). The Chinese Fujian congregation built this lavishly decorated pagoda dedicated to Me Sanh, the goddess of fertility, in the 19th century. Women—and some men—pray to the goddess to bring them children. Many other deities are represented here as well: Thien Hau, the goddess of the sea and protector of fisherfolk and sailors; Ong Bon, the guardian of happiness and virtue; and Quan Cong, the deified general, depicted with a long beard and his sacred red horse. ⊠ *118 Trieu Quang Phuc St., District 5,* ☎ *no phone.*

㉗ **Thien Hau Pagoda** (Chua Ba). Sailors used to come to be blessed at this pagoda dedicated to Thien Hau, the goddess of the sea and protector of fisherfolk and mariners. On the main dais are three statues of the goddess, each flanked by two guardians. Note also the figure of Long Mau, guardian of mothers and babies. The turtles living on the grounds are considered sacred animals and are a symbol of longevity. The Cantonese congregation built this pagoda at the beginning of the 19th century. ⊠ *710 Nguyen Trai St., District 5,* ☎ *no phone.*

DINING

Many international restaurants are in and around Districts 1 and 3, although there are several fine international restaurants in the city's suburbs. You can also find some good, inexpensive cafés serving Vietnamese and international cuisine along Pham Ngu Lao and De Tham streets in District 1. Most places are open for lunch and dinner but close in between, except cafés, which stay open all day and into the night. Most menus list English translations.

CATEGORY	COST*
$$$$	over 270,000 dong
$$$	170,000 dong–270,000 dong
$$	70,000 dong–170,000 dong
$	30,000 dong–70,000 dong
¢	under 30,000 dong

per person for a main course at dinner, including 10% tax and 5% service

Central Saigon (Districts 1 and 3)

American/Casual

$$ ✕ **Underground.** Modeled in theory on a London Tube station, this basement bar actually bears little resemblance to its namesake. Nonetheless, it's hugely popular with Saigon expatriates who come here for their American-food fix: cheeseburgers, Tex-Mex dishes, and pizza. The Underground also doubles as a popular nightspot and is one of the few places that do not play techno music (you're more likely to hear R&B and mellow dance music). Outdoor seating provides peace and quiet. ⊠ *Basement, Lucky Plaza, 69 Dong Khoi St., District 1,* ☎ *08/829-9079. AE, MC, V.*

Chinese

$$ ✕ **Ritz.** The name "Ritz" may not conjure up images of Chinese food, but this is indeed a favorite of Saigon's Chinese community and the place to come for authentic Taiwanese cooking. Try the spicy tofu, bok choy with garlic, or the sweet-potato porridge. The staff speaks little English, but the menu has pictures. ⊠ *333 Tran Hung Dao St., District 1,* ☎ *08/920-0003. MC, V.*

Ho Chi Minh City Dining

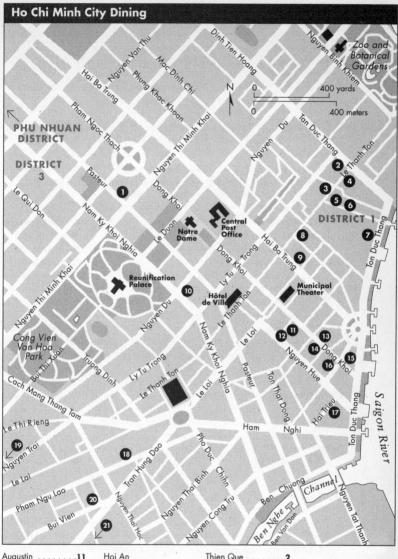

Augustin **11**	Hoi An	Thien Que **2**
Bi Bi **6**	Restaurant **4**	Thi Sac Street
Bodhi Tree II **18**	La Fourchette **16**	Cafés **8**
Le Camargue **9**	Lemongrass **12**	Underground **13**
Le Caprice **7**	Pho Hoa **1**	Urvashi **17**
Chao Thai **5**	Quan An Ngon . . .**10**	Vietnam House . . .**14**
Dai Dong	Restaurant 13 . . .**15**	Zen **3**
Restaurant **19**	Ritz **21**	
Good Morning		
Vietnam **20**		

French

$$$–$$$$ ✕ **Le Caprice.** Stodgy but run like a Swiss timepiece, this landmark provides Saigon's expat elite with unoriginal but fine French cuisine, passé but well-maintained hotel decor, snappy service, and a beautiful view of the Saigon River. Try the panfried salmon or beef tenderloin. If you don't actually get around to eating here, it's worth stopping by just to have a drink and take in the view at the small open-air bar upstairs. ⊠ *Landmark Bldg., 15th.floor, 5B Ton Duc Thang St., District 1,* ☎ *08/822–8337. AE, MC, V.*

$$–$$$$ ✕ **Bi Bi.** This is the type of intimate establishment you'd expect to find on a Parisian backstreet, and it's probably the best-value French restaurant in town. Bi Bi is more than just a restaurant or café: people come here to eat, gossip, play cards, and drink pastis. The steak, served with french fries, is a popular dish, as are the foie gras and escargots. ⊠ *8A/8D2 Thai Van Lung St., District 1,* ☎ *08/829–5783. MC, V.*

$$–$$$$ ✕ **La Fourchette.** A small and extremely intimate affair, La Fourchette, with only six tables, is more a café than a restaurant. The cuisine is good, not great, but the friendly atmosphere more than compensates. ⊠ *9 Ngo Duc Ke St., District 1,* ☎ *08/829–8143. MC, V.*

$$$ ✕ **Le Camargue.** One of the most romantic and tasteful restaurants in ★ Saigon, French-influenced Le Camargue is an exciting culinary forum in a handsome restored villa. The excellent cuisine fuses East and West, and there's a good wine list to go along with the menu. Roasted tiger shrimp is served with ratatouille and citrus-butter sauce, and slightly spicy ravioli is stuffed with baby octopus and topped with a light saffron sauce. Dining is on the elegant, plant-filled terrace or indoors in the warmly lighted dining rooms. A small, popular bar and a nightclub are also on the premises. ⊠ *16 Cao Ba Quat St., District 1,* ☎ *08/824–3148. Reservations essential. AE, MC, V. No lunch.*

$$ ✕ **Augustin.** Comfortably solo expats, often reading the newspaper at the bar, fill this small, intimate restaurant. Augustin serves tasty French-bistro food to a predominantly international crowd. Popular dishes include duck fillet in a mushroom sauce and beef carpaccio with mozzarella and basil. ⊠ *10 Nguyen Thiep St., District 1,* ☎ *08/829–2941. MC, V. No lunch Sun.*

Indian

$ ✕ **Urvashi.** Some of Saigon's best Indian fare is prepared at this small tucked-away and never-crowded restaurant. The service is good and the Indian owner always on hand, but prepare yourself for the nonstop Bollywood films that provide the atmosphere. Try the *rogan josh* (lamb masala with saffron and yogurt) or *murgh makhanwalla* (chicken in a butter sauce with spices and cream). ⊠ *27 Hai Trieu St., District 1,* ☎ *08/821–3102. No credit cards.*

Italian

$–$$ ✕ **Good Morning Vietnam.** This Saigon favorite serves the city's best Italian food at shockingly low prices. The thin-crust pizzas and pasta are exceptional, and the salads—particularly the Greek salad—are always fresh and tasty. The restaurant, which is in the backpacker district, is casual, with simple rattan tables and red tablecloths. ⊠ *197 De Tham St., District 1,* ☎ *08/837–1894. No credit cards.*

Japanese

$$ ✕ **Thien Que.** Japanese businesspeople who know a good thing when they taste it pack this popular sushi bar serving some of the freshest raw fish in town. The restaurant is less crowded on the upper floors, where you sit on tatami mats with low tables. ⊠ *2 Le Thanh Ton St., District 1,* ☎ *08/824–4491. MC, V.*

$–$$ ✗ **Zen.** One of Saigon's newest Japanese restaurants, Zen has also proven to be one of the best in the area known as "Little Tokyo." Sushi, yak-itori, and other Japanese dishes are available. In addition to the dining area, there is a comfortable bar-lounge with soft lighting and deep sofas where you can sip sake and dine. ☒ *20 Le Thanh Ton St., District 1,* ☎ *08/825–0782. AE, MC, V.*

Thai

$–$$ ✗ **Chao Thai.** This sensational restaurant serves the finest Thai food in the city. The cuisine is equal to the setting: a mock Thai longhouse decorated with *apsara* dancers and wood carvings. If you love spicy Thai food you won't be disappointed, and if you don't, you can request milder dishes. ☒ *16 Thai Van Lung St., District 1,* ☎ *08/824–1457. AE, MC, V.*

Vegetarian

¢ ✗ **Bodhi Tree II.** Bodhi serves delectable vegetarian delights in a quaint alley just off Pham Ngu Lao Street, next door to another unrelated vegetarian restaurant. The eggplant sautéed with garlic, the vegetable curry, and the braised tofu in a clay pot are superb. Don't miss out on the fresh-fruit shakes, which are like meals in themselves. ☒ *175/5–175/6 Pham Ngu Lao St., District 1,* ☎ *08/836–9545. No credit cards.*

Vietnamese

$$–$$$ ✗ **Hoi An Restaurant.** The best way to enjoy this upscale restaurant serv-★ ing delicious Vietnamese food is to go in a group so you can share and sample the many outstanding dishes. Dark-wood furnishings fill the dining room. The Hoi An's sister restaurant, the Mandarin, serves slightly less impressive and less expensive Vietnamese food just around the corner. ☒ *11 Le Thanh Ton St., District 1,* ☎ *08/823–7694. AE, MC, V.*

$$ ✗ **Lemongrass.** An expat and tourist favorite, Lemongrass serves ex-★ cellent Vietnamese food in a French-bistro atmosphere. Almost everything on the short menu is delicious, but the spicy mixed-seafood soup deserves special praise. ☒ *4 Nguyen Thiep St., District 1,* ☎ *08/822–0496. AE, MC, V.*

$$ ✗ **Vietnam House.** Travelers and expats flock to Vietnam House for its wide selection of hearty noodle dishes and other Vietnamese standards, all served in a glossy Eurasian-style dining room. Performances of live traditional music are held every night upstairs. ☒ *93 Dong Khoi St., District 1,* ☎ *08/829–1623. AE, MC, V.*

$–$$ ✗ **Restaurant 13.** This local and expat hangout, on a small road just off Dong Khoi Street, serves delicious, inexpensive traditional food in a no-nonsense setting. Popular dishes include the seafood hot pot and sweet-and-sour soup with mullett. ☒ *13 Ngo Duc Ke St., District 1,* ☎ *08/823–9314. No credit cards.*

$ ✗ **Thi Sac Street Cafés.** Thi Sac Street is a must if you love seafood: here you can get great freshwater and saltwater fish. From 5 PM onward the top part of Thi Sac Street where it borders Le Thanh Ton Street is almost impassable with street restaurants. Best bets are the steamboat (boiling broth in which seafood is cooked at your table), freshwater crabs, and colossal shrimp. On a balmy Saigon evening, with the cacophony of street life carrying on all around, dining here is a memorable experience. ☒ *Thi Sac St., District 1. No credit cards. No lunch.*

¢ ✗ **Pho Hoa.** If you're not quite game for the sidewalk-food-stall eating experience, this open-air noodle kitchen is the next best thing. The homemade noodles and the vegetable and meat stocks are fresh and delicious. Just say "chicken," "beef," or "pork," or point to whatever looks good at the next table. ☒ *260C Pasteur St., District 3,* ☎ *08/829–7943. No credit cards.*

¢ ✕ **Quan An Ngon.** The hordes of locals that descend upon this restaurant at meal time testify to the aptness of its name, which translates into "delicious." In an open-air dining area, Quan An Ngon serves traditional dishes from three regions of the country, including *bun cha* (charcoal-grilled meat and peanuts served over rice noodles) from Hanoi, *bun bo Hue* (spicy soup with beef and pork) from Hue, and *hu tieu* (sweet soup with wheat noodles and pork) from Saigon. ✉ *138 Nam Ky Khoi Nghia St., District 1,* ☎ *08/825–7179. No credit cards.*

Cholon (District 5)

Chinese

$–$$ ✕ **Dai Dong Restaurant.** Excellent Peking duck, shark's-fin soup, and a huge selection of other Chinese favorites round out the selection at this restaurant convenient to Cholon's "pagoda alley." The menu is in English and the prices are reasonable. The waiters whiz around, slapping down food with little fanfare. ✉ *121–127 Nguyen Tri Phuong St., District 5,* ☎ *08/855–1651. No credit cards.*

LODGING

You may want to stay in Districts 1 and 3—the center of old Saigon—where most of the museums, galleries, restaurants, bars, and nightclubs are found. Most old colonial hotels are in Districts 1 and 3, as are many newer international hotels, although some are also in District 5 and in the Phu Nhuan District near the airport. Lower-price accommodations are clustered around Pham Ngu Lao, De Tham, and Bui Vien streets in District 1.

Assume guest rooms in hotels listed below have private bathrooms unless otherwise noted. Note that all hotels charging more than $10 a night have air-conditioning. Most hotels and guest houses listed also have IDD phones and satellite TVs.

CATEGORY	COST*
$$$$	over 2.5 million dong
$$$	1 million dong–2.5 million dong
$$	750,000 dong–1 million dong
$	400,000 dong–750,000 dong
¢	under 400,000 dong

All prices are for a standard double room, including 10% tax and 5% service.

Central Saigon (Districts 1 and 3)

$$$–$$$$ 🏨 **Caravelle Hotel.** The restored and expanded Caravelle, where many
★ foreign correspondents stayed during the Vietnam War, may offer the best value of all the upscale hotels in town. In the bustling heart of the city, it has luxurious, well-appointed rooms with spectacular city views. The ninth-floor Saigon Saigon bar is a great place to unwind, and the Port Orient Restaurant serves an excellent buffet of Asian and Western food for lunch and dinner. ✉ *19 Lam Son Sq., District 1,* ☎ *08/ 823–4999,* 🆅 *08/824–3999,* 🌐 *www.caravellehotel.com. 335 rooms. 2 restaurants, café, in-room data ports, in-room safes, minibars, cable TV, in-room VCRs, pool, gym, massage, sauna, bar, concierge, Internet, business services, meeting rooms. AE, DC, MC, V.*

$$$–$$$$ 🏨 **Saigon Prince–A Duxton Hotel.** When the Duxton Hotels chain took
★ over the Saigon in 2002, it brought more than a name change: a refurbishment added facilities and more of a Vietnamese flavor, all to the hotel's advantage. Rooms are more spacious and have higher ceil-

Ho Chi Minh City Lodging

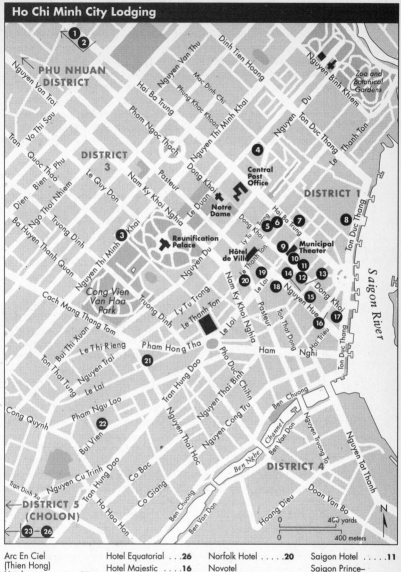

Arc En Ciel (Thien Hong) Hotel **25**

Asian Hotel **5**

Cam Minihotel **22**

Caravelle Hotel . . . **10**

Dong Khanh Hotel **24**

Grand Hotel **13**

Hotel Continental **9**

Hotel Equatorial . . .**26**

Hotel Majestic **16**

Kimdo Royal City Hotel **18**

Legend **8**

Mogambo Guest House **7**

Mondial Hotel **12**

New World Hotel Saigon **21**

Norfolk Hotel **20**

Novotel Garden Plaza Hotel **1**

Omni Saigon Hotel **2**

Palace Hotel **14**

Prince Hotel **23**

Rex Hotel **19**

Riverside Renaissance **17**

Saigon Hotel **11**

Saigon Prince– A Duxton Hotel **15**

Sofitel Plaza **4**

Sol Chancery Saigon **3**

Spring Hotel **6**

ings as well as finer finishing touches than many other hotels in the city. The hotel has an excellent location, in the center of District 1, and great city views from rooms on the seventh floor and higher. The staff is competent and pleasant, and the lobby bar is a nice spot for a calm mid-afternoon break. ✉ *63 Nguyen Hue St., District 1,* ☎ *08/822–2999,* ⒻⒶⓍ *08/824–1888,* ⓌⒺⒷ *www.duxton.com. 203 rooms. Dining room, room service, in-room safes, minibars, refrigerators, cable TV, gym, hot tub, massage, sauna, steam room, lobby lounge, nightclub, dry cleaning, laundry service, concierge, Internet, business services, meeting rooms, travel services, no-smoking rooms. AE, DC, MC, V.*

$$$ 🏨 **Hotel Majestic.** The Majestic, on the waterfront overlooking the Saigon
★   River, is one of Vietnam's truly great colonial hotels. The hotel lacks the service expertise of the international chains, but its charm and location more than make up for that. Rooms, with high ceilings and the original wooden trim, strike a delicate balance between airy and intimate. Be sure to sip a drink at the rooftop breeze bar overlooking the river. ✉ *1 Dong Khoi St., District 1,* ☎ *08/829–5514,* ⒻⒶⓍ *08/829–5510,* ⓌⒺⒷ *www.majestic-saigon.com. 122 rooms. 2 restaurants, café, room service, in-room safes, minibars, refrigerators, cable TV, pool, gym, massage, sauna, 2 bars, lobby lounge, piano, dry cleaning, laundry service, concierge, Internet, business services, meeting rooms, travel services, no-smoking rooms. AE, DC, MC, V.*

$$$ 🏨 **Legend.** Saigon's newest upscale hotel, the central Legend has all the amenities you'd expect in a hotel of this caliber. Rooms overlook either the river or the city and are decorated in beiges and greens and wooden furniture. The oversize lobby atrium is luxurious, with a stained-glass ceiling, marble from top to bottom, and two huge bronze horse statues. The ground-floor pool is one of Saigon's largest. Still working through its growing pains, the Legend is set to be one of Saigon's premier hotels. ✉ *2A–4A Ton Duc Thang St., District 1,* ☎ *08/823–3333,* ⒻⒶⓍ *08/823–2333,* ⓌⒺⒷ *www.legendhotelsaigon.com. 283 rooms. Restaurant, room service, in-room safes, minibars, refrigerators, cable TV, massage, gym, bar, lobby lounge, dry cleaning, laundry service, concierge, Internet, business services, meeting rooms, travel services, no-smoking rooms. AE, DC, MC, V.*

$$$ 🏨 **New World Hotel Saigon.** The New World's central location— across the street from the Ben Thanh Market—makes it very popular, particularly with tour groups and businesspeople. A park right in front of the hotel is a good place to sit back and relax and watch Saigon life pass by. The front foyer may look somewhat sterile, but if you're jet-lagged or just back from an exhausting day out at Cu Chi, it can seem like heaven. The Chinese and Japanese restaurants are excellent, but the Western buffet is lackluster. ✉ *76 Le Lai St., District 1,* ☎ *08/822–8888,* ⒻⒶⓍ *08/823–0710,* ⓌⒺⒷ *www.newworldvietnam.com. 541 rooms. 3 restaurants, room service, in-room safes, minibars, refrigerators, cable TV, driving range, tennis court, pool, gym, massage, sauna, bar, lobby lounge, nightclub, piano, baby-sitting, dry cleaning, laundry service, concierge, Internet, business services, meeting rooms, airport shuttle, car rental, travel services, no-smoking floor. AE, DC, MC, V.*

$$$ 🏨 **Norfolk Hotel.** This convenient superslick establishment stands between the Ben Thanh Market and the Hôtel de Ville (Ho Chi Minh City People's Committee) in central Saigon. White and chrome dominate, making the hotel resemble a cross between a cruise ship and a spaceship. Rooms are impeccable and comfortable, if small and simple. Facilities are oriented primarily to businesspeople—there is even a resident interpreter. ✉ *117 Le Thanh Ton St., District 1,* ☎ *08/829–5368,* ⒻⒶⓍ *08/829–3415. 109 rooms. Restaurant, in-room safes, minibars, cable TV, health club, massage, sauna, bar, baby-sitting, dry*

cleaning, laundry service, Internet, business services, meeting rooms, travel services. AE, MC, V.

$$$ ★ 🏨 **Riverside Renaissance.** This modern chain hotel has a lovely location overlooking the river. After a hard day of sightseeing, it's a lovely spot to sit back, relax, and drink a cocktail while watching the bustle of the waterfront. The Riverside Renaissance has all the comforts you'd expect of an international hotel, but it lacks the colonial flair of some of the older hotels in the city. ✉ *8–15 Ton Duc Thang St., District 1,* ☎ *08/822–0033,* FAX *08/823–5666,* WEB *www.renaissancehotels.com/sgnbr. 349 rooms. 2 restaurants, room service, in-room data ports, in-room safes, minibars, refrigerators, cable TV, gym, massage, sauna, bar, lobby lounge, dry cleaning, concierge, Internet, business services, meeting rooms, travel services, no-smoking rooms. AE, MC, V.*

$$$ ★ 🏨 **Sofitel Plaza.** Pine furniture and relaxing, subdued shades of deep green and blue decorate the very comfortable rooms of the Sofitel Plaza. A high-ceilinged, spacious lobby leads to the first floor and the Aromasia, a restaurant serving Western and Asian cuisine. The Sunday brunches are the best value in the city. The views of the city from the pool on the 18th floor are spectacular, and the hotel's fitness center is one of the city's best. ✉ *17 Le Duan Blvd., District 1,* ☎ *08/824–1555,* FAX *08/824–1666,* WEB *www.accorhotels-asia.com. 292 rooms. 3 restaurants, pool, health club, massage, sauna, laundry service, 2 bars, Internet, business services, meeting rooms. AE, MC, V.*

$$–$$$ ★ 🏨 **Hotel Continental.** If it's history you're after, stay at the French colonial–style Continental. Graham Greene's classic *The Quiet American* was set here; it was also once the most sought-after lunch spot in colonial Saigon and the meeting place of journalists and diplomats during the Vietnam War. The hotel has a unique outdoor courtyard garden and dining area that dates from the late 19th century; it's a superb place to relax with a drink below the frangipani trees. However, the Continental is only a shadow of its former self—the decor and finishing lack the finesse of the hotel's international counterparts. Rooms facing the street are noisy; ask for one overlooking the inner courtyard. ✉ *132–134 Dong Khoi St., District 1,* ☎ *08/829–9201,* FAX *08/829–0936,* WEB *www.continentalvietnam.com. 83 rooms. 2 restaurants, room service, in-room safes, minibars, refrigerators, cable TV, lobby lounge, dry cleaning, laundry service, concierge, Internet, business services, meeting rooms, travel services, no-smoking rooms. AE, MC, V.*

$$–$$$ 🏨 **Kimdo Royal City Hotel.** The spacious rooms at the elegant Kimdo have high ceilings and exquisite French and Chinese antique reproductions that provide a warmth lacking in many modern luxury hotels. An added plus is Kimdo's central location, in the heart of the city and convenient to shopping areas. ✉ *133 Nguyen Hue St., District 1,* ☎ *08/822–5914,* FAX *08/822–5913,* WEB *www.kimdohotel.com. 135 rooms. Dining room, café, room service, in-room safes, minibars, refrigerators, cable TV, gym, massage, lobby lounge, nightclub, dry cleaning, laundry service, concierge, Internet, business services, meeting rooms, travel services, no-smoking rooms. AE, DC, MC, V.*

$$–$$$ 🏨 **Sol Chancery Saigon.** This all-suites hotel run by Grupo Sol of Spain has a kind of nouveau-French facade and many amenities. Rooms, although comfortable and neat, are afflicted with low ceilings and pastel, no-wood, antiseptic decor. It's not too far from the War Remnants Museum and other points of interest. ✉ *196 Nguyen Thi Minh Khai St., District 3,* ☎ *08/930–4088,* FAX *08/930–3988,* WEB *www.chancerysaigonhotel.com. 96 suites. 2 restaurants, room service, in-room safes, minibars, refrigerators, cable TV, gym, massage, sauna, lobby lounge, dry cleaning, laundry service, concierge, Internet, business services, meeting rooms, travel services, no-smoking rooms. AE, DC, MC, V.*

$$ 🔳 **Grand Hotel.** Although more modest than the Majestic or the Continental hotels, this pleasant old colonial establishment evokes a bygone era of Francophone Saigon in the heart of the old rue Catinat. Unfortunately, like the other colonial-era hotels here, the Grand is state owned and suffers accordingly compared to some of the international chains. The rooms are light and airy, with real character. But the service is indifferent, and the restaurants should be avoided. Still, as locations go, this is as central as you can get. ⊠ *8 Dong Khoi St., District 1,* ☎ *08/823–0163,* FAX *08/823–5781. 107 rooms. 2 restaurants, in-room safes, health club, massage, sauna, bar, laundry service, business services. AE, DC, MC, V.*

$$ 🔳 **Rex Hotel.** The Rex stands as a monument to Saigon's recent history. Originally a French garage, it later became a hotel and then the base for American operations during the Vietnam War. Its conference room was the scene of the "five o'clock follies"—daily press briefings to journalists. In 1976 the unification of North Vietnam with South Vietnam was announced in the same room. Today the hotel is filled with kitsch: stuffed animals and statues. Even if you don't stay here, stop by for a drink at the rooftop bar, with its view of downtown and its songbirds, topiary animals, and decorative lights. Avoid the restaurants. ⊠ *141 Nguyen Hue St., District 1,* ☎ *08/829–2185,* FAX *08/829–6536,* WEB *www.rexhotelvietnam.com. 227 rooms. 2 restaurants, room service, in-room safes, minibars, refrigerators, cable TV, pool, hair salon, massage, sauna, steam room, lobby lounge, nightclub, dry cleaning, laundry service, concierge, Internet, business services, travel services, no-smoking rooms. AE, DC, MC, V.*

$–$$ 🔳 **Asian Hotel.** In the midst of the Dong Khoi shopping district, this no-frills hotel has small but tidy rooms. ⊠ *146–150 Dong Khoi St., District 1,* ☎ *08/829–6979,* FAX *08/829–7433,* WEB *www.webpro.au/asianhotel. 47 rooms. Restaurant, room service, in-room safes, minibars, bar, lobby lounge, dry cleaning, laundry service, business services, travel services. AE, DC, MC, V.*

$–$$ 🔳 **Palace Hotel.** The views of central Saigon are excellent from this pleasant but standard no-frills Vietnamese hotel in the center of town. One drawback is the slightly unfriendly front-desk staff, but a plus is the breakfast included in the room rate. ⊠ *56–66 Nguyen Hue St., District 1,* ☎ *08/829–2860,* FAX *08/824–4230,* WEB *www.palacesaigon.com. 130 rooms. 2 restaurants, café, room service, in-room safes, minibars, cable TV, pool, hair salon, massage, sauna, steam room, bar, lobby lounge, nightclub, dry cleaning, laundry service, business services, meeting rooms, airport shuttle, travel services. AE, MC, V.*

¢–$$ 🔳 **Mondial Hotel.** The renovated Mondial has small, tidy standard rooms. Large bas-relief wooden sculptures of dragons and mythical Vietnamese warriors decorate the lobby. The hotel's Skyview restaurant hosts traditional Vietnamese dancing and music nightly. ⊠ *109 Dong Khoi St., District 1,* ☎ *08/829–6291,* FAX *08/829–6273. 40 rooms. Restaurant, room service, in-room safes, lobby lounge, dry cleaning, laundry service, travel services. AE, MC, V.*

$ 🔳 **Saigon Hotel.** At the Saigon you can get a clean room overlooking the center of the city. The hotel betrays a '60s aesthetic despite modern black-lacquer furniture accents. ⊠ *41–47 Dong Du St., District 1,* ☎ *08/824–4982,* FAX *08/829–1466. 101 rooms. Restaurant, café, room service, in-room safes, minibars, lobby lounge, nightclub, dry cleaning, laundry service, business services, meeting rooms, airport shuttle. AE, MC, V.*

¢–$ 🔳 **Mogambo Guest House.** This minihotel above the restaurant of the same name is run by an American and is very popular with—guess who?—Americans. Like most of these small establishments, the

Mogambo is unexceptional looking but has clean rooms that are suitable for a good night's sleep. ⊠ *20bis Thi Sach St., District 1,* ☎ *08/ 825–1311,* FAX *08/822–6031. 10 rooms. Restaurant, cable TV, bar. AE, MC, V.*

¢–$ 🏨 **Spring Hotel.** The squeaky-clean rooms have new moldings and fixtures made to look old at this cozy, family-run minihotel in the hub of a major dining and nightlife area in District 1. Some rooms afford nice views of the street below, but the standard ones have no windows at all and are a lot less expensive. ⊠ *44–46 Le Thanh Ton St., District 1,* ☎ *08/829–7362,* FAX *08/821–1383,* WEB *www.vietnamonline.com/spring. 45 rooms. Dining room, room service, in-room safes, cable TV, bar, lobby lounge, travel services. AE, MC, V.*

¢ 🏨 **Cam Minihotel.** In a cluster of family-run minihotels in an alley be-
★ tween Pham Ngu Lao and Bui Vien streets, this place stands out because it's run with more care than other budget hotels. It has a 24-hour gate post, mandatory shoe removal at the door, and simple, spotless, well-maintained rooms. The extended family and friends who run the hotel are very friendly and helpful and speak English. ⊠ *40/31 Bui Vien St., District 1,* ☎ *08/837–2502. 12 rooms. Fans, refrigerators, cable TV. No credit cards.*

Cholon (District 5)

$$$$ 🏨 **Hotel Equatorial.** This is one of the best hotels in town, despite its somewhat out-of-the-way location on the edge of Cholon, about 15 minutes from the downtown area. Inside is one of Vietnam's nicest health clubs, with Jacuzzis, saunas, a very good gym, and a half-Olympic-size swimming pool with a poolside lounge area. In addition, the hotel has three fine restaurants, one serving Japanese, another Chinese, and a third an international buffet. ⊠ *242 Tran Binh Trong St., District 5,* ☎ *08/839–7777,* FAX *08/839–0011,* WEB *www.equatorial.com. 333 rooms. 3 restaurants, café, room service, minibars, refrigerators, pool, health club, bar, lobby lounge, nightclub, piano, dry cleaning, laundry service, business services, meeting rooms, car rental, travel services. AE, DC, MC, V.*

$$ 🏨 **Dong Khanh Hotel.** The Chinese theme at this hotel—wooden furniture with characteristic inlaid lacquerware and wall hangings depicting dragons and landscapes—is bold but elegant. Most of the guests here are businesspeople from Hong Kong and Taiwan. Although staff members speak little English, they know enough of the language to help you get by. ⊠ *2B Tran Hung Dao Blvd., District 5,* ☎ *08/923–4410,* FAX *08/923–6427,* WEB *www.saigon-tourist.com. 76 rooms. 2 restaurants, room service, in-room safes, minibars, refrigerators, cable TV, gym, massage, bar, lobby lounge, nightclub, dry cleaning, laundry service, business services, meeting rooms, travel services, no-smoking rooms. AE, DC, MC, V.*

$ 🏨 **Arc En Ciel (Thien Hong) Hotel.** This neon-clad hotel is done up in a mishmash of modern, '60s, and Chinese interior style, with accommodations on the higher end of utilitarian. But overall it's a good deal— if you're interested in staying in Cholon. The rooftop garden café is pleasant. ⊠ *52–56 Tan Da St., District 5,* ☎ *08/855–2869,* FAX *08/855– 2424,* WEB *www.saigon-tourist.com. 91 rooms. Restaurant, café, room service, cable TV, hair salon, massage, sauna, lobby lounge, dry cleaning, laundry service, concierge, business services, meeting rooms, travel services. AE, DC, MC, V.*

¢ 🏨 **Prince Hotel.** This small-time lodging in the middle of Cholon provides charm and efficiency at inexpensive rates. Unlike many hotel restaurants, the Prince's dining room actually serves good food. ⊠ *29 Chau Van Liem St., District 5,* ☎ *08/855–6765,* FAX *08/856–1578. 24 rooms.*

Restaurant, room service, refrigerators, cable TV, lobby lounge, travel services. MC, V.

Phu Nhuan District

$$$–$$$$ 🏨 **Omni Saigon Hotel.** One of the city's finest hotels was built in the shell of the former CIA headquarters in Saigon, with walls so thick cellular phones don't work. The Omni combines French elegance with a hint of glitz and a touch of '60s bunker architecture. More importantly, it's one of the few international hotels to have sent its staff abroad for training, and the service here is some of the best in town. The restaurants serve first-class Japanese, Chinese, and international cuisine. Even if you don't stay here, come for the Sunday brunch, a bacchanalian frenzy of Belgian waffles and omelets. ✉ *251 Nguyen Van Troi St., Phu Nhuan District,* ☎ *08/844–9222,* 𝗙𝗔𝗫 *08/844–9198,* 𝖶𝖤𝖡 *www. marcopolohotels.com/saigon. 248 rooms. 3 restaurants, room service, in-room safes, minibars, refrigerators, cable TV, pool, gym, hair salon, massage, sauna, lobby lounge, pub, nightclub, piano, baby-sitting, dry cleaning, laundry service, concierge, Internet, business services, meeting rooms, airport shuttle, car rental, travel services, no-smoking rooms. AE, DC, MC, V.*

$$$ 🏨 **Novotel Garden Plaza Hotel.** This international establishment is one of the city's best. Its sunken lobby and accompanying swimming pool are a departure from the hotel architecture usually seen in Vietnam. In fact, the hotel's style is more Thai or Balinese than Vietnamese. Its location could be a drawback for you (a good 15–20 minutes from downtown Saigon, though it's just 10 minutes from the airport), but it's a boon if you're a businessperson eager to settle into town quickly. ✉ *309B-311 Nguyen Van Troi St., Phu Nhuan District,* ☎ *08/842–1111,* 𝗙𝗔𝗫 *08/842–4370,* 𝖶𝖤𝖡 *www.asiatravel.com/vietnam/gardenplaza. 157 rooms. Restaurant, room service, in-room data ports, in-room safes, minibars, refrigerators, cable TV, pool, gym, massage, sauna, shop, lobby lounge, pub, dry cleaning, laundry service, concierge, business services, meeting rooms, airport shuttle, car rental, travel services, no-smoking rooms. AE, DC, MC, V.*

NIGHTLIFE AND THE ARTS

Saigon's thriving nightlife is a constant headache to the city's Communist leaders because most of it revolves around the kind of decadence they once promised to stamp out. In an effort to crack down on such "social evils" the authorities have instituted a policy of requiring the city's bars and discos to close around midnight. Enforcement is inconsistent, however, and Saigon is still a city that stays open, and parties, late.

Although Saigon's first Western-style cinema opened in early 2002, the city still lacks the sort of entertainment that you might take for granted in other large cities. Aside from the new movie theater, there are no other multiplex cinemas, for instance: for ideological reasons, authorities tend to view contemporary films as containing polluted materials. Pirated videos are now widely sold, however, and the newest films are often being viewed in the homes of Saigonese only days after their release in the West. Live theater is also making a dramatic comeback with new theaters opening up all over the city.

Rock music, too, is still very much in its infancy. Any rock band—local or international—wishing to perform in Vietnam has to go through endless red tape and must even submit lyrics to the Ministry of Culture for approval. Over the last decade Sting, Air Supply, and an obscure but incredibly popular Danish group, Michael Learns to Rock, performed in Vietnam to lackluster receptions (probably because tickets were far too expensive for the average Vietnamese). Incidentally, Sting's song "Russians" was rejected by the Ministry of Culture for ideological reasons. Classical concerts are more common but still infrequent.

For the most part, the city's nightlife revolves around drinking at one of the many bars and discos. Depending on the venue, the crowd may be predominately local, expat, or a mix of both. This may still be Communist Saigon, but many of these bars are as raucous as their counterparts in Hong Kong, Manila, and Jakarta. Nightclub owners take the authorities' hostile attitude in stride and get on with their business. Most expatriate bars are open throughout the night and only close their doors when everyone has left. Check in the weekly English-language supplement "Time Out" in the *Vietnam Investment Review* for information about what's going on around town.

The Arts

Film

The multiplex cinema at the department store complex **Diamond Plaza** (✉ 34 Le Duan St., District 1, ☎ 08/822–7897) screens English-language films.

Music and Theater

The **Conservatory of Music** (Nhac Vien Thanh Pho Ho Chi Minh; ✉ 112 Nguyen Du St., District 1, ☎ 08/822–5841) is the only regular venue in town for classical music performances. The theater's main season is from September through June; it's generally closed in summer except when there are special concerts of visiting orchestras. Look in the daily *Vietnam News* for information on upcoming events.

Hoa Binh Theater (Nha Hat Hoa Binh; ✉ 14 3 Thang 2 Blvd., District 10, ☎ 08/865–5760), an ugly Soviet-era palace, is mostly used for local Vietnamese dramas, circus acts, and the occasional fashion show.

Municipal Theater (Nha Hat Thanh Pho; ✉ intersection of Le Loi Blvd. and Dong Khoi St., District 1, ☎ 08/829–9976), built in 1899 by the French as an opera house, was later used as the home of the National Assembly of South Vietnam. It became a theater again in 1975. Most performances now are family shows with Vietnamese singers and dancers, although occasionally an international opera singer performs here.

Nightlife

Bars and Clubs

Apocalypse Now (✉ 2C Thi Sach St., District 1, ☎ 08/825–6124), one of the oldest clubs in Saigon, is loud, fun, and always packed with a cross section of expatriates and foreign tourists. It's the after-hours place to go in the city. Amiable pimps and local prostitutes shoot pool while hordes of foreigners drink tequila and vodka and dance until dawn. But keep in mind these words of warning: always take a taxi, not a cyclo, back to your hotel (cabs line up outside); cyclo drivers have been known to steal from inebriated foreigners. Also, you should leave any jewelry, including watches, at your hotel; there are pickpockets at this nightspot.

Café Latin (✉ 25 Dong Du St., District 1, ☎ 08/822–6363) is a multilevel tapas bar with constructivist decor that looks like something out of *The Jetsons* and fine Australian and French wines.

Café Mogambo (⊠ 20bis Thi Sach St., District 1, ☎ 08/825–1311), run by an American expat and his Vietnamese wife, is a kind of self-parodying Reno-style roadside stop where you can get good draft beer in a kitschy environment all dressed up with African statues, headdresses, and wall hangings.

Le Camargue (⊠ 16 Cao Ba Quat St., District 1, ☎ 08/824–3148), although really more of a French-influenced restaurant, also has an excellent terrace bar where you can sip a drink outside among tropical palms and creepers. It's an ideal first stop on your way to a night on the town. Vasco's, a small bar and nightspot here, is the city's most popular place to wind down after a hectic day. Fridays are particularly popular, when a live band performs.

Globo (⊠ 6 Nguyen Thiep St., District 1, ☎ 08/822–8855) was designed by the same people who did the Café Latin, thus the constructivist decor made out of metal—iron stairwells, relief art, and even a burnished metallic toilet. The small place looks like it could be in Paris, and it's very popular with the city's fashionable French set. Good French food is served, and there's often live music on Friday nights.

Long Phi (⊠ 163 Pham Ngu Lao St., District 1, ☎ 08/836–9319) is one of the few bars in town to attract expats, Vietnamese, *and* backpackers. It's a rattan affair—wicker armchairs and wicker tables—that spills out onto the street, with music blaring until dawn. There's also a pool table. As always, be sure to look after your valuables if you're sitting out on the street. The upstairs restaurant sells good, cheap French-country food. Recommended dishes include the steak with french fries and the chocolate mousse.

Number 5 Bar (⊠ 5 Ly Tu Trong St., District 1, ☎ 08/825–6300), on the edge of the downtown area, is popular with expats and tourists. In an old French bungalow, it's partly open to the outside and is a good place to start the night on balmy tropical evenings. You can also shoot pool and munch on snacks here.

Q Bar (⊠ 7 Cong Truong Lam Son St., District 1, ☎ 08/823–3479) is Saigon's trendiest nightspot, built into the side of the Opera House. Sit outside by the fountain or on one of the couches in the dark, candlelighted interior.

Sheridan's Irish House (⊠ 17/13 Le Thanh Ton St., District 1, ☎ 08/823–0793), in the downtown area, is a traditional Irish pub serving Guinness and, oddly, dim sum. It's often busy and is a nice retreat from the heat and dust of the city streets in the hot season.

Concerts

Tieng To Dong (⊠ 104 Nguyen Hue St., District 1, ☎ 08/822–1422), a converted theater across the street from the entrance to the Rex Hotel, hosts Vietnam's biggest pop stars nightly. The best acts normally don't begin until around 9:30, but come early if you want a seat up front.

Dance Clubs and Karaoke

Catwalk (⊠ 76 Le Lai St., District 1, ☎ 08/822–8888), in the New World Hotel Saigon, has private karaoke dens where you can sing to your heart's delight and a dance floor where dry ice sets the mood.

Gossip (⊠ 79 Tran Hung Dao St., District 1, ☎ 08/821–2716), a trendy Singaporean-run nightspot, is always packed. The crowd is decidedly young and Vietnamese, and the music loud and pulsating with a slant toward techno and house.

Metropolis (✉ 30 Nguyen Cu Trinh, District 1, ☎ 08/837–4838) is Saigon's largest dance club and one of its most popular. A young Vietnamese crowd gathers here to dance to the mostly techno and house music.

Hotel Bars

A more civilized alternative to Saigon's bar scene is one of the many rooftop establishments at the city's hotels. Although drinks are more expensive than those at other places, you often get a panoramic view of the city for your money. The following hotel bars are particularly good. **Caprice Hotel** (✉ Landmark Bldg., 5B Ton Duc Thang St., District 1, ☎ 08/822–8337). **Hotel Majestic** (✉ 1 Dong Khoi St., District 1, ☎ 08/829–5514). **Rex Hotel** (✉ 5th-floor veranda, 141 Nguyen Hue St., District 1, ☎ 08/829–2185). **Saigon Prince** (✉ Piano bar, 63 Nguyen Hue St., District 1, ☎ 08/822–2999). **Saigon Saigon** (✉ Caravelle Hotel, 19 Lam Son Sq., District 1, ☎ 08/234–4999).

OUTDOOR ACTIVITIES AND SPORTS

Participant Sports

Bowling

Saigon Superbowl (✉ A43 Truong Son St., Tan Binh District, ☎ 08/848–8888) is the biggest entertainment complex ever to hit Vietnam. Not only does it have state-of-the-art bowling facilities and an electronic games arcade—which is occasionally shut down for being a social evil—it also has a mall (with overpriced clothes from the West) and a Kentucky Fried Chicken. If you intend to go bowling here, you'll have to be patient: all the alleys are in constant use, and you often have to wait some time before getting to play. When you do get to play, be prepared for the crowds that may swarm around you—analyzing your bowling style and technique. The place opens at 7:30 AM and only closes when the last person leaves. Foreigners pay 55,000d per game, which is not cheap.

Diving

Indochine Divers (✉ 79 Truong Dinh St., District 3, ☎ 08/930–4612, WEB www.indochinedivers.com) offers diving courses and arranges diving excursions to Nha Trang.

Golf

There are three 18-hole golf courses outside Saigon. **Bo Chang Dong Nai Resort** (✉ Trung Tam Thi Tran Chang Bon, ☎ 061/864–407), about 50 km (30 mi) outside of the city, is the most scenic course in the area, with hills and lots of water. The cost is 1,110,000d on a weekday, 1,370,000d on Saturday or Sunday. **Song Be Golf Resort** (✉ Thai Thieu township, Thuan An District, Binh Duong Province, ☎ 0650/756–660) lies 20 km (12 mi) outside the city. The club's facilities include swimming pools, tennis courts, restaurants, and television rooms where family members can hang out while they wait for their links-playing relatives. The cost for a day is $50. **Vietnam Golf and Country Club** (✉ Ap Gian Dan, Long Thanh Mi Ward, District 9, ☎ 08/825–2951), in the outlying district of Thu Duc, 10 km (6 mi) north of Saigon, costs about $50 a day for a game.

Health Clubs and Swimming Pools

If it's fitness you're after you can use the city's health clubs, many of which are quite good and are usually based in the newer hotels. It simply depends on how much you're willing to pay.

Caravelle Hotel (⊠ 19 Lam Son Sq., District 1, ☎ 08/823–4999) has a gym, an outdoor swimming pool, sauna and steam rooms, and massage. The cost is $18 per day.

Hotel Equatorial (⊠ 242 Tran Binh Trong St., District 5, ☎ 08/839–7777) has the best gym in town, with a half-Olympic-size pool, stationary bikes, a rowing machine, a step machine, a treadmill machine, and weights. The cost is $15 for the day.

Hotel Majestic (⊠ 1 Dong Khoi St., District 1, ☎ 08/829–5514) has a small pool and gym, both available for use even if you're not a guest, as long as you order something from the bar.

New World Hotel Saigon (⊠ 76 Le Lai St., District 1, ☎ 08/822–8888) charges $12 for use of its small pool and standard gym.

Rex Hotel (⊠ 141 Nguyen Hue St., District 1, ☎ 08/829–2185) has a small rooftop pool, which you can use for just $2.

Sofitel Plaza (⊠ 17 Le Duan Blvd., District 1, ☎ 08/824–1555) has excellent fitness facilities and a swimming pool with a panoramic view of the city on the 18th floor. The cost is $11 per day.

Hiking

In and around Ho Chi Minh City's urban bustle there are very few spots where you can find green, open spaces and enjoy the outdoors. One nice place in the city for a stroll, however, is **Cong Vien Van Hoa Park,** near the Reunification Palace. You can wander among the subtropical foliage at the **Zoo and Botanical Garden** (⊠ 2 Nguyen Binh Khiem St., at Le Duan Blvd., District 1).

JOGGING

Saigon isn't really a good city for jogging; it's generally too hot, too crowded, and too polluted, even in the parks. Some Vietnamese do, however, go out jogging in the streets in the very early morning (around 5) before the traffic begins. They also head for the parks and squares in the wee hours of the morning to do stretching exercises and play badminton. If you're set on running during your visit, contact the **Hash House Harriers running club,** which meets every Sunday afternoon at 2:30 outside the Caravelle Hotel (⊠ 19 Lam Son Sq., District 1, ☎ 08/823–4999 information).

Spectator Sports

Horse Racing

Phu Tho Racetrack (⊠ 2 Le Dai Hanh St., District 11, ☎ 08/962–8205), built in 1900, was once an exclusive center of French colonial life. The track was shut down the day Saigon fell, on April 30, 1975—gambling was deemed a frivolous capitalist social evil by Hanoi—and wasn't reopened until 1989. The building and track are in fairly poor condition, but this place can still be a lot of fun. People go crazy when the racing starts: to get a grandstand view, they climb onto everything, including tops of buildings, telegraph poles, and even each other's shoulders. Most of the ponies racing are about half the size of racehorses you're probably used to seeing. They are a special type introduced by the French in the 19th century and are still being bred in villages outside Saigon. Notice how small the jockeys are, even compared to those in the West—that's because their average age is 9 or 10 years old. Occasionally motorbike racing is also held at the track. It's open weekends from 1 PM on, and there's no admission. Check in the daily *Vietnam News* for more detailed schedule information.

SHOPPING

Ho Chi Minh City is a good place to have casual clothes made or to have designer apparel copied. In addition, the city is famous for its lacquerware—boxes, trays, bowls—and its wood carvings of all kinds.

Continuing a tradition dating to the time when it was French Saigon's main shopping thoroughfare, Dong Khoi Street (formerly Tu Do Street and before that rue Catinat), between Le Loi Boulevard and the river, is lined with art galleries and shops selling jewelry, clothing, antique watches (or look-alikes), lacquerware, wood carvings, and other souvenirs mostly to tourists—which doesn't mean there aren't good finds. The galleries carry some works by fine local artists, although you may end up paying more than you expected for something you love.

Ready-to-wear Western-style clothes and shoes are available near the central Ben Thanh Market, on Le Thanh Ton and Ly Tu Trong streets in District 1. Both the Ben Thanh Market in the center of the city and the Binh Tay Market in Cholon sell all kinds of goods—clothes, wood carvings, shoes, plastic items, kitchenware, food, and more. No matter where you shop, even if a place says it has fixed prices but you are purchasing a large number of items, be sure to bargain—it's part of the shopping experience in Vietnam. But be polite: the debate over prices is expected to be a very civil and friendly process. Also, as is the case all over the country, most shops will either take dollars or dong and will often list prices in dollars only.

Department Stores

Diamond Plaza (✉ 34 Le Duan St., District 1, ☎ 08/822–7897), a shiny, modern department store complex, has three floors of shopping as well as restaurants, a bowling alley, and Saigon's first Western-style cinema.

On the ground floor of the huge **Tax Department Store** (Cua Hang Back Hoa; ✉ intersection of Nguyen Hue St. and Le Loi Blvd., District 1, ☎ no phone) you can find all kinds of souvenirs as well as a place to change traveler's checks. On the two upper floors are the best bargains in Vietnam. Many designer clothes and sneakers, made in China but redirected to Vietnam on the black market, end up here at unbeatable prices. There are also nice and very inexpensive bags made of Chinese, Vietnamese, and Cham fabrics, as well as tailors who can make you clothes in 24 hours. Curiously, a lot of the clothing here is for cold weather, so if you need to pick up a Gore-Tex anorak or a ski suit at absurdly cheap prices, this is the place to come. It's also good for electronic items. The latest video equipment, digital cameras, and minidisk players are on sale here.

Markets

The markets in Ho Chi Minh City are generally open from sunrise until sunset, although some vendors just outside the markets stay open later.

Clothing, shoes, bags, wood carvings, lacquerware, food, and more are available at the large **Ben Thanh Market** (Cho Ben Thanh), at the intersection of Tran Hung Dao, Le Loi, and Ham Nghi boulevards in the heart of District 1. Keep careful watch of your belongings; pickpockets have been known to strike in the narrow aisles here. But don't let this stop you from exploring this busy market.

Cholon's **Binh Tay Market** (Cho Binh Tay), on Hau Giang Boulevard in District 6 (near District 5), carries all kinds of wholesale items that can be purchased in small amounts by anyone: kitchenware, baskets, plastic goods (barrettes, magnets, toys, shopping bags, wigs, you name it), hats (traditional conical, straw, baseball caps), shoes, and food. This market is more authentic than the spruced-up, touristy Ben Thanh Market.

The charming open-air market on **Ton That Dam Street,** between Huynh Thuc Khang Street and Ham Nghi Boulevard in District 1, sells everything from fish and produce to plastic toys and cleaning products.

On the north side of **Ham Nghi Boulevard,** between Ho Tung Mau and Ton That Dam streets in District 1, you can purchase imported cheese, olive oil, and just about any international food at the tiny, jam-packed European-style specialty food shops.

Specialty Shops

Antique Replicas

Unless you have permission from the Ministry of Culture (☞ Shopping *in* Smart Travel Tips A to Z), it's against the law for you to take antiques out of Vietnam, and anyone found carrying antiques at the airport must hand them over to the authorities. This policy is unevenly enforced, however, and there's a vast gray area of what is and isn't an antique; often it's up to the whims of individual customs officers to decide. If you buy a fake article that looks like an antique, be sure to get a receipt in Vietnamese with the shop owner's signature guaranteeing the object is not genuine. Without it, you'll run into big trouble at customs. If you do decide to spend big bucks on the real thing (genuine antiques don't come cheaply in Vietnam), be sure you know what you're buying. It's very difficult to distinguish between genuine and fake items, especially on Dong Khoi Street, where both sell at comparable prices. In particular, beware of restored antique timepieces, which often have a 1950s Rolex face, for example, covering the much cheaper hardware of a 1970s Seiko.

Nguyen Freres (✉ 2A Le Duan Blvd., District 1, ☎ 08/822–9654) sells antique replicas, including prints of old colonial Saigon.

Art

Taking fine art out of the country isn't as problematic as taking antiques out, but have a receipt for your purchase to show customs just in case. Many art galleries are on Dong Khoi Street and the surrounding area. Paintings and lacquerware by master artists Do Xuan Doan, Bui Xuan Phau, Quach Dong Phuong, and Truong Dinh Hao are available at many galleries. Many of these artists base their art on French postimpressionist styles, and their work is generally apolitical (still lifes and pastoral scenes, for instance). Canvases fetch as little as $30 and as much as $15,000. Following is a list of suggested galleries.

ATC (Art Tourist Services; ✉ 55 Dong Khoi St., District 1, ☎ 08/829–2695) is a national art organization.

Dong Phuong Gallery (✉ 135 Nam Ky Khoi Nghia St., District 1, ☎ 08/930–9716).

Fine Arts Museum (✉ 97A Pho Duc Chinh St., District 1, ☎ 08/822–2441).

Hong Hac Art Gallery (✉ 9A Vo Van Tan St., District 3, ☎ 08/930–4160).

Particular Gallery (✉ Level 3, 123 Le Loi Blvd., District 1, ☎ 08/848–8213).

Phuong Anh (✉ 135 Nguyen Hue St., District 1, ☎ 08/821–3115) sells ethnic folk art and material.

Saigon Art Gallery (✉ 77 Mac Thi Buoi St., District 1, ☎ 08/822–6048).

Clothing

Creation (✉ 105 Dong Khoi St., District 1, ☎ 08/829–5429) sells ready-to-wear clothing for adults in imported and domestic cottons and silks. The staff speaks excellent English and is very helpful. The next-door Khai Silk is also worth a look.

Tropic (✉ 73A Le Thanh Ton St., District 1, ☎ 08/829–7452) carries contemporary and traditional clothing as well as some home-furnishing items.

Tuyet Lan (✉ 83 Nguyen Hue St., District 1, ☎ 08/832–6259), known for its quick turnaround and high-quality work, custom-designs clothes and other items, working from a collection of design books. The store specializes in clothing for children and adults, sandals, pillows, and bed-covers.

Housewares

Home Zone (✉ 41 Dinh Tien Hoang St., District 1, ☎ 08/822–8022) sells stylish silverware, furnishings, and other housewares.

Mai Huong (✉ 73 Le Thanh Ton St., District 1, ☎ 08/829–6233) is the place to go for beautifully embroidered tablecloths, napkins, and bedspreads, all made in Saigon.

Q Home (✉ 65 Le Loi Blvd., 2nd floor, District 1, ☎ 08/821–8268) carries brightly colored Western-style ceramics made in Vietnam.

Lacquerware

There are several galleries that sell lacquerware on Dong Khoi Street (from No. 137 to No. 145) and in the Phu Nhuan District on Nguyen Van Troi Street (and on its continuation, Cong Hoa Street).

Tay Son (✉ 198 Vo Thi Sau St., District 3, ☎ 08/932–5708 or 08/932–5525) is a large lacquerware distributor with a wide selection and good prices.

Musical Instruments

On the north side of Ham Nghi Boulevard between the circular intersection to the west and Nam Ky Khoi Nghia Street to the east are shops selling fake Fender Stratocasters and other cheap acoustic guitars that are actually not all that bad.

Shoes

Tran Van My (✉ 95 Le Thanh Ton St., District 1, ☎ 08/822–3041) sells ready-made, custom-made, embroidered, and leather shoes and sandals. The cobblers are quite adept at copying other shoes, but some of their own designs are also very nice. The quality of workmanship is very high, and the prices are low.

Wood Carvings

Not too far from the airport, in the Phu Nhuan District on Nguyen Van Troi Street and on its continuation, Cong Hoa Street (between Nos. 72 and 306), there are a number of shops where you can buy wood carvings—as well as lacquerware and rattan—and see the craftspeople at work.

SIDE TRIPS FROM HO CHI MINH CITY

When you find yourself ready to escape Ho Chi Minh City—or when you just want to see some of the countryside—make a short excursion outside the city. Some of the destinations around Ho Chi Minh City can be visited as day trips; others may take a few days. Some excursions are more rugged, adventurous trips through forests and islands; others will take you to sandy beaches and seaside resorts. Ho Chi Minh City even serves as a good departure point for trips to the Mekong Delta (☞ Chapter 7) or Cambodia (☞ Chapter 8). The easiest way to plan a trip outside Ho Chi Minh City is to use a travel agency or one of the tourist cafés that organize tours; almost all arrange trips to various points in the region.

Numbers in the margin correspond to points of interest on the Ho Chi Minh City Environs map.

Cu Chi Tunnels

❶ *65 km (40 mi) northwest of Ho Chi Minh City via Hwy. 22.*

A 250-km (155-mi) underground network of field hospitals, command posts, living quarters, eating quarters, and trapdoors, the Cu Chi Tunnels testify to the Vietcong's ingenuity in the face of overwhelming odds. (A note about the use of the term Vietcong: Vietcong is used throughout this book to refer to the opposition movement in the South because it is the term that is probably most familiar. However, Vietcong—which means, loosely, Vietnamese "Commies"—was the name given by the Americans and the Republic of South Vietnam to this opposition movement. The National Liberation Front [NLF] was the official name of the group fighting the southern government. For more history on these terms, *see* Chronology *in* Chapter 9.) First used in the late '40s to combat the French, the tunnels made it possible for the Vietcong in the '60s not only to withstand massive bombings and to communicate with other distant Vietcong enclaves but to command a sizable rural area that was in dangerous proximity (a mere 35 km [22 mi]) to Saigon.

After the Diem regime's ill-fated "strategic hamlet program" of 1963, disenchanted peasants who refused to move fled to Cu Chi to avoid the aerial bombardments. In fact, the stunning Tet Offensive of 1968 was masterminded and launched from the Cu Chi Tunnels nerve center, with weapons crafted by an enthusiastic assembly line of Vietcong-controlled Cu Chi villagers. Despite extensive ground operations and sophisticated chemical warfare—and even after declaring the area a free-fire zone—American troops were incapable of controlling the area. In the late '60s B-52 bombing reduced the area to a wasteland, but the Vietnamese Communists and the National Liberation Front managed to hang on.

The guided tour of the Cu Chi Tunnels includes a film that documents the handiwork of "American monsters" (with no mention of South Vietnamese involvement) and numerous booby traps demonstrated by former Vietcong soldiers. If you are prone to claustrophobia, you might consider skipping the crawl through the hot, stuffy, and tight tunnels (although sections have been expanded to allow room for tourists' bigger bodies). Amazingly, in these very same tunnels many Vietnamese survived for months and even years.

Arriving and Departing

The easiest and best way to visit is on a tour arranged through one of the travel agencies or tourist cafés, since every agency—state-run and private—does the identical trip. A day trip, which costs about $40 per person, generally combines the tunnels with a visit to the Caodai Holy See, in neighboring Tay Ninh.

Tay Ninh

❷ *95 km (59 mi) northwest of Ho Chi Minh City via Hwy. 22.*

★ The town of Tay Ninh is home to Caodaism, an indigenous hybrid religion founded in 1926 by a mystic named Ngo Minh Chieu, and its impressive and brightly colored temple, the **Caodai Holy See** (Thanh Thuc Cao Dai). Caodaism incorporates elements of the major Eastern and Western religions—Buddhism, Confucianism, Taoism, Vietnamese spiritualism, Christianity, and Islam. The religion fuses a Mahayana Buddhist code of ethics with Taoist and Confucian components. Sprinkled into the mix are elements of Roman Catholicism, the cult of ancestors, Vietnamese superstition, and over-the-top interior decoration that encompasses a fantastic blend of Asian and European architectural styles.

Caodaism has grown from its original 26,000 members to a present-day membership of 3 million. Meditation and communicating with spiritual worlds via earthly mediums or seances are among its primary practices. Despite its no-holds-barred decorative tendencies, Caodaism emphasizes abstinence from luxury and sensuality as well as vegetarianism as a means of escaping the reincarnation cycle. Although the priesthood is strictly nonprofessional, clergy must remain celibate.

Perhaps most important, the Caodaists believe the divine revelation has undergone three iterations: God's word presented itself first through Lao-tzu and other Buddhist, Confucianist, and Taoist players; then through a second set of channelers such as Jesus, Muhammad, Moses, Confucius, and Buddha. Whether because of the fallibility of these human agents or because of the changing set of human needs, the Caodaists believe the divine transmission was botched. They see themselves as the third and final expression—the "third alliance between God and man." Since anyone can take part in this alliance, even Westerners like Joan of Arc, Victor Hugo, and William Shakespeare have been added to the Caodai roster.

Caodaism's presence wasn't always so tolerated. Although it quickly gained a large following after its founding, including Vietnamese officials in the French administration, it soon became too powerful. By the 1930s the Caodaists had begun consolidating their strength in the region and recruiting their own army. Eventually the area became a mini-kingdom under the domain of the Caodaists. Needless to say, this didn't make the government very happy, and government officials did all they could to take away power from the region.

During World War II, the Caodaists were armed and financed by the Japanese, whom the sect saw as also fighting the government. After the war, the Caodaists gained the backing of the French in return for their support against the Vietminh. This collusion with the French, however, was not always so peaceful, and skirmishes often occurred between the Caodaists and the French. After the French left in the late '50s, the South Vietnamese government made a point to destroy the Caodaists as a military force, which caused many members of the sect to turn to the Communists, and the area became an anti–South Vietnamese stronghold. But when the Communists came to power in 1975, they repossessed the sect's land, and Caodaism lost most of its remaining power. Today the religion is tolerated but is not involved in politics as it once was.

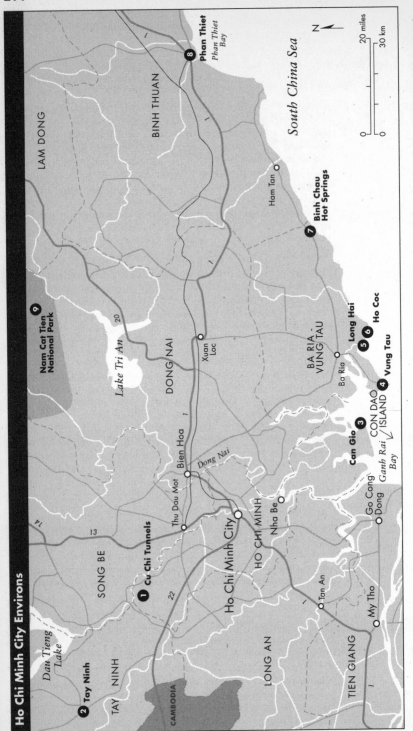

Ho Chi Minh City Environs

South China Sea

N

20 miles
30 km

Phan Thiet 8
Phan Thiet Bay

BINH THUAN

LAM DONG

Binh Chau Hot Springs 7

Ham Tan

Nam Cat Tien National Park 9

Lake Tri An

20

DONG NAI

Xuan Loc

Long Hai

Ho Coc
5 6

BA RIA - VUNG TAU

Ba Ria

Vung Tau 4

Bien Hoa

Can Gio 3

Dong Nai

CON DAO ISLAND

Ganh Rai Bay

Thu Dau Mot

1

Cu Chi Tunnels 1

13

HO CHI MINH CITY

HO CHI MINH

Nha Be

Go Cong Dong

SONG BE

22

Dau Tieng Lake

Tay Ninh 2

TAY NINH

CAMBODIA

LONG AN

Tan An

TIEN GIANG

My Tho

1

The noon ceremony (others are held at 6 AM, 6 PM, and midnight) at the Caodai Holy See is a fascinating and colorful religious vignette. A finely tuned hierarchical procession of men and women of all ages parades through the temple's great hall, where great painted columns twined with carved dragons support sky-blue arched vaults. Panels of stained glass with a cosmic-eye motif punctuate the walls. You are permitted to watch and take snapshots from the mezzanine. Ignore any feeling of complicity in what appears to be a collective voyeuristic sacrilege; the ceremony goes on as though you were not there.

Arriving and Departing
Generally a visit to Tay Ninh is part of a day trip to the Cu Chi Tunnels arranged through one of the travel agencies in Saigon. A guide will accompany you, explain the history of the Caodai sect, and take you through the temple.

Can Gio

❸ *60 km (37 mi) southeast of Ho Chi Minh City.*

Can Gio is a maze of channels, inlets, and tiny fishing hamlets hidden among swamp and forest. This young 30-ft-high mangrove forest, officially a district of Ho Chi Minh City and only one hour from the city proper by car, covers an area the size of Singapore. The old forest was destroyed by aerial bombing and defoliants—primarily Agent Orange—during the Vietnam War. The forest had been a regular hiding place for the Vietcong, who would fire mortars at the supply ships on the Saigon River. Residents of the area were forced to leave, and it wasn't until 1978 that surviving Can Gio families returned, replanted the forest, and gradually resettled. Surprisingly, the area's wild animals also returned, and today there are monkeys, wild boars, deer, leopards, and even the odd crocodile.

Arriving and Departing
The easiest way to reach Can Gio is by hiring a car and driver. It's best also to hire a guide through a tourist café in Ho Chi Minh City to lead you on hikes.

Vung Tau

❹ *130 km (81 mi) southeast of Ho Chi Minh City.*

Known as Cap St-Jacques during colonial times, Vung Tau was a popular beach resort for the French; some run-down colonial-era buildings still stand. During the Vietnam War it became a major U.S. and Australian army base. The area was later taken over by the Soviet Union as a concession for helping Hanoi win the war. The Soviets used the Vung Tau port as a navy base and drilled for oil off the coast. Many of the Stalinist-style concrete monstrosities dotting the town are a reminder of those postwar years. Following the collapse of the Soviet Union, many Russians left, although Vung Tau is still home to 2,000—a fairly large amount compared to the 200 remaining Russians in Ho Chi Minh City.

Vung Tau's beaches are the closest to Ho Chi Minh City, although they are not some of the country's nicest. But this is beginning to change—for better and worse—as the area is cleaned up for tourism and new hotels are built.

There are several beaches in the town. The most popular, Back Beach (Bai Sau) is a nice-enough beach that stretches for miles up the coast. The beach is at its best during the week when it is quieter; on weekends it gets very crowded. Be prepared to encounter beggars here.

Bai Dau is a cramped beach below the huge Ha Long Street. It's certainly not a place you would travel miles to see—it's fairly rocky and not ideal for swimming—but it is an acceptable tropical beach and the most secluded one in Vung Tau. Avoid Front Beach (Bai Truoc), the worst of them all; it's a dirty little beach strewn with fishing tackle and oil flotsam from the nearby rigs.

Other sites of interest here are the two small mountains crowned with pagodas and a giant statue of Jesus that overlooks the town on a headland above. Interestingly, this hill is currently the site of a club of Japanese hang gliders, based in Saigon, who come here every weekend to fly the local skies. You can get a guide to take you along the mountain circuit around Vung Tau; the trip takes about four hours.

At different times throughout its history the **White Villa** (Bach Dinh) served as the French governor's residence, the home of Emperor Bao Dai (1913–97), and the South Vietnam presidential summer house. The villa, now a museum showing the opulence of the old regime, is a beautiful example of French colonial architecture, with classical columns, busts, and stucco decorations. ✉ *12 Tran Phu St.,* ☎ *064/810–124 or 064/852–605.* 🎟 *5,000d.* ☉ *Daily 7–5.*

Lodging

$$$$ 🏨 **Binh An Village.** Perched on the side of a hill overlooking the ocean, Binh An Village serves up romance and luxury in heavy doses, making it an ideal getaway from the hectic activity of Saigon. The complex is set away from the water, but it does have a black-marble freshwater swimming pool and a saltwater pool. Terraced gardens and just six Balinese-style villas complete the intimate setting. ✉ *01 Tran Phu St.,* ☎ *064/510–016,* ℻ *064/810–264. 6 villas. Restaurant, minibars, cable TV, 2 pools. AE, MC, V.*

$ 🏨 **Petro House Hotel.** Surprisingly, this hotel is not bad at all, considering so few foreign tourists go to Vung Tau. It's a modern building, but it has an elegant, colonial feel to it. ✉ *63 Tran Hung Dao Blvd.,* ☎ *064/852–014,* ℻ *064/852–015,* 🌐 *www.viethotel.com. 75 rooms. Restaurant, minibars, cable TV, pool, bar, lobby lounge, laundry service, business services, meeting rooms. AE, MC, V.*

Arriving and Departing

It's possible to drive to Vung Tau, but the easiest way to get here is by hydrofoil (☞ Boat Travel *in* Ho Chi Minh City A to Z, *below*).

Long Hai

❺ *170 km (105 mi) southeast of Ho Chi Minh City, 30 km (19 mi) northeast of Vung Tau.*

This beach is about a two-hour drive from Ho Chi Minh City and 40 km (25 mi) up the coast from Vung Tau, but it feels like it's worlds away. Small kiosks and restaurants dot the bright, sandy beach, which runs for miles up the coast. Sit on the beach, which is equipped with deck chairs and umbrellas, and a waiter will take your order for fresh seafood. You may not want to overnight in Long Hai, but it does make a nice day trip from the frenzy of Saigon.

Lodging

$$$ 🏨 **Anoasis Beach Resort.** With its wonderful views of the coast, Long Hai's first international-style hotel makes a nice getaway from Saigon. A bamboo beach bar serves snacks and hosts barbecues on the beach. The swimming pool is great for doing laps or for just relaxing in the sun. The weekend seafood buffet is also a winner. ✉ *Domain Ky Van, Long Hai, Ba Ria-Vung Tau,* ☎ *064/868–227,* ℻ *064/868–229,* 🌐

www.anoasisresort.com.vn. 30 rooms. Restaurant, cable TV, pool, tennis court, beach, laundry service, Internet, business services, meeting rooms. AE, MC, V.

Arriving and Departing

To get here you can hire a car and driver in Ho Chi Minh City or take the hydrofoil to Vung Tau, from which you'd need to hire a taxi for the 30-minute ride to Long Hai.

Ho Coc

6 *190 km (118 mi) southeast of Ho Chi Minh City, 36 km (22 mi) east of Long Hai.*

Three hours from Ho Chi Minh City and farther up the coast from Long Hai is Ho Coc, the most beautiful beach in the area. It's a splendid, secluded retreat for anyone desperate to get away from the chaos of the city. The area is largely undeveloped. There are a few small sidewalk cafés, but you're best off bringing your own food from Ho Chi Minh City.

Lodging

¢ **Ho Coc Guest House.** This bare-bones but clean guest house has only five rooms, each sleeping two people. The bathrooms are basic—just a shower with cold water only and a toilet. But remember: you're not coming here for luxury but for the beautiful, secluded beach. ⊠ *Ask for directions in town,* ☎ *no phone. 5 rooms. No credit cards.*

Arriving and Departing

The area is very remote, and consequently no public transportation reaches it. To get here, you need to hire a car and driver in Ho Chi Minh City.

Binh Chau Hot Springs

7 *150 km (93 mi) southeast of Ho Chi Minh City, 50 km (31 mi) north of Long Hai.*

About half an hour's drive from Ho Coc are the Binh Chau Hot Springs (Suoi Nuoc Nong Binh Chau), famous among the Vietnamese for their therapeutic properties. People suffering from rheumatism or backaches come here to take the water. A veritable industry of acupuncture, massage, and other healing methods has developed around the springs. The springs are okay to use, although they can get very crowded on weekends and holidays. There are a few pho stands and some small cafés serving Vietnamese food.

Lodging

¢ **Binh Chau Hotel.** The only worthwhile accommodation in town is this very basic hotel. This may change in the next few years, but with few hotels now being built, this is probably it for the time being. ⊠ *Ask for directions in town,* ☎ *064/871–131,* FAX *064/871–130 or 08/ 997–0699. 64 rooms. No credit cards.*

Arriving and Departing

To get here, hire a car and driver or make arrangements with a travel agency in Ho Chi Minh City.

Phan Thiet

★ **8** *192 km (119 mi) northeast of Ho Chi Minh City.*

At lovely Phan Thiet, lush, tropical palm forest surrounds miles of empty sandy beaches interrupted only by the odd lone fisherman. **Mui Ne Beach** is a particularly beautiful and pristine spot. The town itself has a large fishing industry and is known for its *nuoc mam,* the ubiquitous fish sauce served with most Vietnamese food. Dividing the town is the Phan Thiet River; small, colorful fishing boats fill the harbor. In the colonial era the French built homes on the north bank of the river, and everyone else lived on the south bank. Until 1692 the area was controlled by the Cham, and some members of the present-day population are their descendants.

Dining and Lodging

$$$ ✕▥ **Co Co Beach.** A Swiss-run venture, Co Co Beach is one of the most popular destinations for Saigon's expats. It's regularly booked up weeks in advance, so call ahead to make reservations. The resort consists of 20 bungalows on stilts, each with a bathroom and a sitting room. The restaurant serves steaks, freshly caught seafood, and more. ⊠ *Hai Duong Resort Ham Tien, Phan Thiet,* ☎ *062/847–111/2/3,* FAX *062/ 847–115,* WEB *www.cocobeach.net. 20 bungalows. Restaurant, pool, meeting room. AE, DC, MC, V.*

$$$ ✕▥ **Novotel Ocean Dunes Resort.** A private beach and an adjoining golf course are two of the attractions of this chain hotel, 11 km (7 mi) outside of Phan Thiet City. The restaurant serves international cuisine with a focus on French food. ⊠ *1 Ton Duc Thang St., Phan Thiet,* ☎ *062/822–393,* FAX *062/825–682,* WEB *ww.accorhotels-asia.com. 123 rooms. Restaurant, minibars, cable TV, 18-hole golf course, tennis court, pool, massage, gym, beach, bar, laundry service, Internet, meeting room. AE, MC, V.*

$$$ ✕▥ **Victoria Resort.** This very popular place, about 5 km (3 mi) down the beach from Co Co Beach, consists of 50 thatch-covered bungalows on stilts, built in Thai style. Bungalows have views of the sea or a garden. The swimming pool and tennis courts are additional pluses. Beware, though: the staff has had little contact with foreign visitors, so patience is required. But the resort itself is worth it. It's always a good idea to book in advance, especially during Christmas and Tet. ⊠ *Victoria Phan Thiet Resort, Phan Thiet, Binh Thuan,* ☎ *062/847–170, 062/847–171, or 062/847– 172,* FAX *062/847–174,* WEB *www.victoriahotel-vietnam. com/english/pthiet.htm. 50 bungalows. Restaurant, room service, in-room safes, minibars, cable TV, tennis court, pool, bar, baby-sitting, laundry service, Internet, business center, meeting rooms, travel services. AE, MC, V.*

$$ ▥ **Mui Ne Sailing Club.** Thatched-roof bungalows stand right on the beach at the Mui Ne Sailing Club, which is operated by the same people who run the Nha Trang Sailing Club. This is great for people who enjoy outdoor sports: windsurfing, sailing, quadbiking, and more are all on offer along with training for beginners. ⊠ *24 Nguyen Dinh Chieu St., Mui Ne,* ☎ *062/847–440 or 062/847–441,* FAX *062/847–442. 32 bungalows. Restaurant, windsurfing, boating, bar. AE MC, V.*

Golf

The Nick Faldo–designed course at the **Ocean Dunes Golf Club** (⊠ Novotel Ocean Dunes Resort, ☎ 062/822–393) has a magnificent setting on the edge of the South China Sea, which is peppered with small boats and fishing junks. Games start at $60.

Arriving and Departing

Make arrangements to get to Phan Thiet through one of the travel agencies in Ho Chi Minh City.

Nam Cat Tien National Park

9 *250 km (155 mi) northwest of Ho Chi Minh City.*

Often inaccessible due to poor road conditions and flooding, Nam Cat Tien National Park, northwest of Ho Chi Minh City and close to the Cambodian border, shelters the endangered Javanese rhino, as well as monkeys, elephants, tigers, and several rare bird species. The park also has one of Vietnam's few banyan forests. Thanks to the encouragement of the regional tourist agency, Dong Nai Tourism, this national park has fast become the most popular adventure-travel location in the country. From Ho Chi Minh City, you may be able to arrange a two- to four-day jungle trip through one of the tourist agencies such as Vidotours (☞ Travel Agencies *in* Ho Chi Minh City A to Z, *below*). Dinner comes in your backpack, and accommodations are on a hammock—so this is only for you if you're a hardy traveler.

Con Dao Island

100 km (62 mi) off southern tip of Vietnam, about 40 mins by plane from Ho Chi Minh City.

One of the most fascinating areas in Vietnam but also one of the most isolated, Con Dao Island (or Poulo Condore, as the French called it) is actually an archipelago of 14 islands. The archipelago is a dream, with its beautiful but empty beaches, glistening coral in the water, and forests teeming with wildlife.

The largest of the islands, known as Con Dao or Con Son, was the Devil's Island of the South China Sea: it was used as a penal settlement by the French for more than 100 years. You can still see the solid French prison, with its infamous open "tiger cages"—where the guards would stand above the cells watching the prisoners pacing (if there was enough room) below—and the communal cells where sometimes more than 100 prisoners were manacled to the walls. Creeping jungle now surrounds most of the prison.

The South Vietnamese took over the prison in 1954, incarcerating their own political prisoners. The Americans, with the South Vietnamese, built a prison camp here during the Vietnam War. Today there is only a rotting reminder of the camp next to the old French prison, with its iron watchtowers corroding with age. All told, thousands of people died miserable deaths on Con Dao—Nationalist and Communist prisoners as well as revolutionary insurgents and criminals from all over the French empire. Only one of Con Dao's cemeteries still exists; it alone has 20,000 graves, victims of the struggles from the 1940s to the 1970s. The population of the island currently stands at about 1,000—including many local fishermen and their families.

The attractive French town of Con Dao has been left intact, with the prison officers' quarters now occupied by Vietnamese fishing families. The prison governor's mansion is now a museum. Hours depend on when you show up—they'll open it especially for you if no one else is around. Along the rotting seafront boulevard are the remains of old, crumbling French villas where Saigon's wealthy used to fly in for weekend visits in the shadow of the gulag.

Lodging

$ ⬛ **ATC Guest House.** This is the best of the few accommodation options on Con Dao. The guest house consists of four small "villas," all of which have air-conditioning, and four thatched-roof bungalows, which have only fans. ✉ *16B Ton Duc Thang St., Huyen Con Dao,* ☎ *064/*

830–111. 4 villas, 4 bungalows. Some fans; no a/c in bungalows. No credit cards.

Arriving and Departing

At present the only feasible means of transportation to the island is an expensive (Russian-made) helicopter charter from VASCO (☞ Air Travel *in* Ho Chi Minh City A to Z, *below*), the domestic arm of Vietnam Airline. The only other transportation option to the island is by boat, a 14-hour ride from Vung Tau, with departures just twice a week. But this is not advised, as the boats are generally in bad shape and the trip is extremely unpleasant, especially during the rainy season.

HO CHI MINH CITY A TO Z

To research prices, get advice from other travelers, and book travel arrangements, visit www.fodors.com.

AIR TRAVEL

Many international airlines, including British Airways and United, fly to Ho Chi Minh City. Vietnam Airlines, the Vietnamese national carrier, has international flights from Ho Chi Minh City as well as domestic flights to the following destinations: Buon Ma Thuot, Can Tho, Dalat, Danang, Haiphong, Hanoi, Hue, Nha Trang, Phu Quoc, Pleiku, and Qui Nhon. Prices for domestic flights range from $60 to $150. It's best to book several days in advance and to reconfirm your flight; you can always change your reservation at branch offices all over the city.

For information about helicopters run by VASCO, the domestic arm of Vietnam Airlines, inquire at the Vietnam Airlines office or at Vidotours (☞ Travel Agencies, *below*).

➤ CARRIERS: **Air France** (✉ 130 Dong Khoi St., District 1, ☎ 08/829–0981, www.airfrance.com). **All Nippon Airways** (✉ 114A Nguyen Hue St., District 1, ☎ 08/822–4141, svc.ana.co.jp/eng). **Asiana Airlines** (✉ Room 707, Diamond Plaza, 34 Le Duan St., District 1, ☎ 08/822–2622, WEB us.flyasiana.com). **British Airways** (✉ 114A Nguyen Hue St., District 1, ☎ 08/829–2262, WEB www.britishairways.com). **Cathay Pacific Airways** (✉ Jardine House, 58 Dong Khoi St., District 1, ☎ 08/822–3203, WEB www.cathaypacific.com). **China Airlines** (✉ 132–134 Dong Khoi St., District 1, ☎ 08/825–1388, WEB www.china-airlines.com). **China Southern Airlines** (✉ 21-23 Nguyen Thi Minh Khai St., District 1, ☎ 08/823–5588, WEB www.cs-air.com/en). **Emirates Airlines** (✉ 114A Nguyen Hue St., District 1, ☎ 08/825–6576, WEB www.emirates.com). **EVA Air** (✉ 32 Ngo Duc Ke St., District 1, ☎ 08/822–4488, WEB www.evaair.com). **Japan Airlines** (✉ Sun Wah Tower, 17th floor, 115 Nguyen Hue St., District 1, ☎ 08/821–9099, WEB www.japanair.com). **KLM Royal Dutch Airlines** (✉ 2A–4A Ton Duc Thang G/F St., District 1, ☎ 08/823–1990 or 08/823–1991, WEB www.klm.com). **Korean Air** (✉ 34 Le Duan St., District 1, ☎ 08/824–2878/9, WEB www.koreanair.com). **Lao Aviation** (✉ 181 Hai Ba Trung St., District 1, ☎ 08/822–6990, WEB www.lao-aviation.com). **Lauda Air** (✉ 9 Dong Khoi St., District 1, ☎ 08/829–7117, WEB www.aua.com). **Lufthansa** (✉ 132–134 Dong Khoi St., District 1, ☎ 08/829–8529, WEB www.lufthansa.com). **Malaysian Airlines** (✉ 132–134 Dong Khoi St., District 1, ☎ 08/829–2529, WEB www.malaysiaairlines.com.my). **Philippine Airlines** (✉ 229 Dong Khoi St., District 1, ☎ 08/827–2105, WEB www.philippineair.com). **Qantas Airways** (✉ 114A Nguyen Hue St., District 1, ☎ 08/823–8844, WEB www.qantas.com). **Siem Reap Airways International** (✉ 132–134 Dong Khoi St., District 1, ☎ 08/823–9288, WEB www.siemreapairways.com). **Sin-**

gapore Airlines (✉ Saigon Tower, Suite 101, 29 Le Duan Blvd., District 1, ☎ 08/231–1588, WEB www.singaporeair.com). **Thai Airways** (✉ 65 Nguyen Du St., District 1, ☎ 08/822–3365, WEB www.thaiairways. com). **United Airlines** (✉ Jardine House, 58 Dong Khoi St., District 1, ☎ 08/823–4755, WEB www.ual.com). **Vietnam Airlines** (✉ 116 Nguyen Hue St., District 1, ☎ 08/829–2118, WEB www.vietnamair.com.vn).

AIRPORT

Tan Son Nhat Airport, 7 km (4 mi) outside of central Saigon, is small and navigable. Depending on the officer behind the counter, getting through passport control is intermittently hassle-free. Be sure you have completed your immigration and customs forms correctly and completely to avoid being sent to the back of what can at times be a long line. The airport tax on a domestic flight is 20,000d or about $1.50 (you can pay in either currency); internationally it's 140,000d or $12.
➤ AIRPORT INFORMATION: **Tan Son Nhat Airport** (✉ Hoang Van Thu Blvd., Tan Binh District, ☎ 08/844–3179).

TRANSFERS

Take advantage of the complimentary hotel shuttle service provided by many of the middle to high-end hotels. Otherwise you'll have to deal with the throngs of taxi drivers outside the city airport, all vying for your business. But don't be put off if you do have to take a taxi: just choose an official-looking one and be on your way. From Ho Chi Minh City's airport, fixed-price and metered taxis are the best ways to get into the city center. It should not be necessary to negotiate a price if you choose a reputable-looking taxi. Just make sure the meter is turned on when the trip begins and that it is clear where you are going. The ride takes 10 to 20 minutes depending on traffic.

BIKE TRAVEL

Smog and heavy traffic make bicycling in Ho Chi Minh City quite challenging and unpleasant. Having said that, it is possible to rent bicycles in the city. Many of the tourist cafés on De Tham Street, District 1, in Ho Chi Minh City rent bicycles and scooters. Hotels also often rent out bicycles or can at least suggest where to rent decent ones. Those available from shops on the street are generally unreliable.

BOAT TRAVEL

Greenline and Vina Express run hydrofoil service to Vung Tau and the Mekong Delta. The hydrofoil to Vung Tau departs frequently from the waterfront opposite Nguyen Hue Boulevard. The returning hydrofoil from Vung Tau to Ho Chi Minh City also has several daily departures. Although schedules are relatively fixed, they are subject to change depending on demand, so check with a travel agency. If you are traveling on a weekend, be sure to book your ticket a day or so in advance. On Friday and Saturday the hydrofoil is usually filled with people headed to Vung Tau's resorts. The hydrofoil also travels down to the Mekong Delta. One-way fare to Mytho is $12, to Cantho $14, to Vinh Long $16, to Chau Doc $28, and to Vung Tau $10.
➤ CONTACT: **Greenline** (✉ 34 Ton Duc Thang St., District 1, ☎ 08/ 821–5609). **Vina Express** (✉ 2 Nguyen Hue St., District 1, ☎ 08/829–7892).

BUS TRAVEL

Traveling by bus around Vietnam is not recommended. Buses are usually overcrowded, hot, and uncomfortable, and they often break down. Schedules, too, are arbitrary. You're better off taking one of the minibuses that leave from the bus stations, and even preferable is going on a bus organized by one of the travel agencies or tourist cafés.

That said, Ho Chi Minh City has a number of bus stations. Cholon Station serves routes to the Mekong Delta. Mien Dong Station serves points north of Ho Chi Minh City. Mien Tay Station also serves towns in the Mekong Delta. Tay Ninh Station, near the airport, is where you catch buses to Tay Ninh and Cu Chi. Van Thanh Station serves Dalat and Vung Tau.

➤ Bus Stations: **Cholon Station** (✉ close to the Binh Tay Market on Tran Hung Dao B Blvd., District 5). **Mien Dong Station** (✉ National Hwy. 13, Binh Thanh District). **Mien Tay Station** (✉ Off Hung Vuong St., Binh Chanh District). **Tay Ninh Station** (✉ Le Dai Hanh St., Tan Binh Station, Tan Binh District). **Van Thanh Station** (✉ 72 Dien Bien Phu St., Binh Thanh District).

BUS TRAVEL WITHIN HO CHI MINH CITY

Public buses are the cheapest way to get around town, although not the fastest, most convenient, or most pleasant way to travel. Service is often erratic and painfully slow, and the buses generally have no air-conditioning and are crammed full of people at busy times. You're better off taking a cyclo or a taxi, either of which is faster, more efficient, and not too expensive. If you do decide to take a bus, it is important to know about the Saigon–Cholon line, which you are most likely to use; it starts in Me Linh Square at the Tran Hung Dao intersection and ends up at Cholon's Binh Tay Market. Tickets, available on board, cost 2,000d. The Mien Dong–Mien Tay line offers transportation between these two bus stations for 4,000d. The Van Thanh–Mien Tay line travels between the Van Thanh eastern bus station and the Mien Tay western bus station. You can pick up all these buses at Me Linh Square or at stops marked XE BUYT (bus stop).

CAR TRAVEL

One of the best ways to travel around Vietnam is by a car with a driver. Most hotels and high-end travel agencies such as Saigon Tourist and Vietnam Tourism (☞ Travel Agencies, *below*) rent private air-conditioned cars (Mercedes-Benzes, Mazdas, Renaults) with a driver for about $35 a day (less than 100 km [62 mi]; extra kilometers cost more). At budget agencies like Ann's Tourist and Sinh Café (☞ Travel Agencies, *below*), you can hire a car and driver for about $20–$30, depending on the season.

For Ho Chi Minh City itself, a car is necessary mainly for excursions outside the city. Taxis and cyclos are more useful for visiting sights within the city.

CONSULATES

For passport problems, contact your consulate.
➤ Consulates: **Australia** (✉ 5B Ton Duc Thang St., District 1, ☎ 08/829–6035, WEB www.ausinvn.com). **Canada** (✉ 235 Dong Khoi St., District 1, ☎ 08/824–5025). **New Zealand** (✉ 41 Nguyen Thi Minh Khai St., 15th floor, District 1, ☎ 08/822–6907). **United Kingdom** (✉ 25 Le Duan Blvd., District 1, ☎ 08/823–2604, WEB www.uk-vietnam.org). **United States** (✉ 4 Le Duan Blvd., District 1, ☎ 08/822–9433, WEB www.uscongenhcmc.org).

CYCLO TRAVEL

Although cyclos, or pedicabs, are slower than taxis, they are an excellent way to experience Saigon's street life. Cyclos are supposed to charge only 2,000d per kilometer, but 5,000d–10,000d is a decent rate (this includes the tip) for just about any destination within the same district. Going to districts in the outer suburbs will cost you more. Cyclo drivers, often former South Vietnamese soldiers, frequently speak English very well and can provide informative city tours for a small price (a generous half-day rate is about 30,000d–55,000d)—bargaining is advised. Drivers will wait for you when you visit sights; just don't leave any valuables in the cyclo. If you are happy with your cyclo driver, you can make arrangements to have him pick you up the next day; he will certainly ask if you would like him to do so.

EMERGENCIES

Round-the-clock medical treatment is available at SOS International Assistance, a clinic run by Western doctors who treat minor illnesses and injuries, do dental work, and take care of emergency evacuations. Cho Ray Hospital has regular and 24-hour emergency treatment. Emergency Centre can help you with emergency medical care.

My Chau Pharmacy comes recommended by the Travel Medical Consultancy. The pharmacy is open daily 7:30 AM–10 PM.
➤ DOCTORS, DENTISTS, AND HOSPITALS: **Cho Ray Hospital** (✉ 201B Nguyen Chi Thanh St., District 5, ☎ 08/855–8074). **Emergency Centre** (✉ 125 Le Loi Blvd., District 1, ☎ 08/829–1711). **SOS International Assistance** (✉ Han Nam Bldg., 65 Nguyen Du St., District 1, ☎ 08/829–8520).
➤ EMERGENCY SERVICES: **Ambulance** (☎ 115). **Police** (☎ 113).
➤ LATE-NIGHT PHARMACY: **My Chau Pharmacy** (✉ 389 Hai Ba Trung St., District 1, ☎ 08/822–2266).

ENGLISH-LANGUAGE MEDIA

There are a few bookstores in Ho Chi Minh City that sell English-language books. Many traveling street vendors are also well equipped with English-Vietnamese phrase books and dictionaries, as well as travel guides, Graham Greene's *The Quiet American,* and other books on Vietnamese culture and history.

Quoc Su, occupying a tiny space off Dong Khoi Street, not too far from the river, is jam-packed with lots of photocopied bootleg political literature. It also sells guides to Southeast Asian cities dating from the '20s and '30s. French translations abound, but English-language literature is scarcer.

Xuan Thu, Ho Chi Minh City's first foreign-language bookstore, is definitely lacking in the English-literature department, but it sells quite a few international newspapers and periodicals. You can also find Vietnamese-English phrase books and dictionaries here.

Xunhasaba, the largest foreign magazine and newspaper distributor in town, doubles as a tailor shop. Nice, cheap art books and some novels (mostly classics) in English are also available.
➤ BOOKSTORES: **Quoc Su** (✉ 20 Ho Huan Nghiep St., District 1, ☎ 08/824–5992). **Xuan Thu** (✉ 185 Dong Khoi St., District 1, ☎ 08/822–4670). **Xunhasaba** (✉ 76E Le Thanh Ton St., District 1, ☎ 08/824–2491).

MAIL AND SHIPPING

The Central Post Office, next to Notre Dame Cathedral, is open daily 7:30–5:30. Here you can buy stamps, send faxes, and use the phones.
➤ POST OFFICE: **Central Post Office** (✉ 2 Cong Xa Paris St., District 1).

MINIBUS TRAVEL

You should make reservations for minibus trips in or out of the city a day in advance through your hotel concierge, a travel agent, or a travel café.

MONEY MATTERS

Although they don't always offer the best exchange rate, hotels are usually the easiest places to change money; they can also change traveler's checks. Banks usually have better rates.

Major banks in Ho Chi Minh City include ANZ Bank, Citibank, Standard Chartered Bank, and Vietcom Bank. ATMs can be found at ANZ Bank and Hong Kong Bank.

If you have lost your credit cards, contact Vietcom Bank, which is affiliated with Western banks.

➤ MAJOR BANKS: **ANZ Bank** (Australia New Zealand Bank; ✉ 11 Me Linh Sq., District 1, ☎ 08/829–9319). **Citibank** (✉ 115 Nguyen Hue St. 15th floor, District 1, ☎ 08/824–2118). **Hong Kong Bank** (✉ Metropolitan Building, 235 Dong Khoi St., District 1, ☎ 08/829–2288). **Standard Chartered Bank** (✉ Unit 13/02, Me Linh Point Tower, 2 Ngo Duc Ke St., District 1, ☎ 08/829–8335). **Vietcom Bank** (✉ 29 Chuong Duong St., District 1, ☎ 08/823–0310; 08/829–3068 or 08/822–5413 for lost credit cards).

MOTORBIKE TRAVEL

You can rent your own motorbike from any number of cafés, restaurants, and travel agencies, especially Sinh Café and Ann's Tourist (☞ Travel Agencies, *below*). Daily rates usually start at about $4–$5. But beware: don't part with your deposit until you are convinced the place is legitimate. Legitimate establishments usually have a line of motorbikes for rent and a standard ticket they give to all customers. Some places may request that you leave a passport or other important piece of identification when renting a motorbike; it's best to leave instead a photocopy of your passport.

SAFETY

As with other major cities, you must be aware of what's going on around you in Ho Chi Minh City. While violent crime against foreigners is rare, theft is a frequent occurrence. Don't wear flashy jewelry, and keep a firm grip on your bag. Not only are there pickpockets, but robbers on motorbikes have been known to drive by and grab bags from people walking down the street. Be particularly careful to keep cameras and other valuables hidden when riding a motorbike, as a number of people have been pulled down by thieves and seriously hurt. It's relatively safe to walk around the city at night—even for groups of women— but even so, you should stay on guard and avoid walking down dark, deserted streets.

SIGHTSEEING TOURS

Boats touring the Saigon River start at 50,000d an hour and are available at the riverside on Ton Duc Thang Street, between Ham Nghi Boulevard and Me Linh Square. Choose any of the boats lining the river; almost all are family owned; you must negotiate an exact price with the owners before boarding the boat. They will take both individuals and groups. Ask at travel agencies for advice about the best trips.

Guided tours that cover only Ho Chi Minh City itself are virtually nonexistent, which is just as well. Since no one travels to Ho Chi Minh City just for its sights, but rather for the whole cultural experience, the few half-day major-sight tours, which cost around $35–$50, are ultimately not that worthwhile. Furthermore, although advertised as "English speaking," guides are often unintelligible in that language. You're better off exploring the city on your own or hiring an English-speaking cyclo driver—just make sure you can understand *his* English first.

On the other hand, do take advantage of the guided tours outside the city. For excellent tours to the Mekong Delta and the Cu Chi Tunnels and for various customized trips, check itineraries and schedules at the Saigon Tourist budget office or at any number of cafés and small travel agencies on Pham Ngu Lao Street (☞ Travel Agencies, *below*). Tours can cost as little as $4 for the Cu Chi Tunnels and $7 for one-day or $15 for two-day tours of the Mekong Delta.

TAXIS AND MOTORBIKE TAXIS

One of the quickest ways around the city is riding on the back of a motorbike taxi, known as a *Honda om* or a *xe om*. This service usually costs about 20,000d. Motorbike drivers are everywhere—they'll just drive up alongside you and ask where you're going and if you're interested in a ride. It's relatively safe to travel on motorbikes; unfortunately, the same can't be said for the roads, especially at rush hour. It's also wise to pay attention when choosing your xe om driver to ensure that he hasn't been imbibing Saigon's famous bia hoi moments before picking you up.

Taxis are available in front of all major hotels. Many cluster around the Hotel Continental; at the intersection of Le Loi Boulevard and Nguyen Hue Street, near the Rex Hotel and Caravelle Hotel; along Pham Ngu Lao Street; and outside the New World Hotel, near the Ben Thanh Market intersection. Most taxis have meters, and most drivers speak a little English. An average journey across town starts at 30,000d–60,000d. The best taxi companies are Saigon Taxi and Vina Taxi, which is run by a British company with a French manager; it's a good idea to book their taxis in advance. Other recommended taxi companies include Airport Taxi, Giadinh Taxi, Saigon Tourist, and V-Taxi.

➤ TAXI COMPANIES: **Airport Taxi** (☎ 08/844–6666). **Giadinh Taxi** (☎ 08/898–9898). **Saigon Taxi** (☎ 08/823–2323). **Saigon Tourist** (☎ 08/846–4646). **V-Taxi** (☎ 08/820–2020). **Vina Taxi** (☎ 08/811–1111).

TRAIN TRAVEL

Local train service connects Ho Chi Minh City to Nha Trang, Qui Nhon, and Hue. The faster train (if only by a little), the Reunification Express, goes to many of the larger coastal towns north of Ho Chi Minh City, from Phan Rang–Thap Cham all the way north to Hanoi (☞ Train Travel *in* Smart Travel Tips A to Z). This is not the fastest way to go or always the most comfortable, but it certainly is one of the most interesting modes of getting around the country.

Trains connecting Ho Chi Minh City with coastal towns to the north arrive and depart from the Saigon Railway Station (Ga Saigon). It's best to ask a travel agent to call for ticketing and information, although you could try contacting the Saigon Railway ticketing office yourself instead of having an intermediary do it; it's open daily 7:15–11 and 1–3. Note that Saigon Tourist does not provide any train service information.
➤ TRAIN STATION: **Saigon Railway Station** (✉ 1 Nguyen Thong St., District 3, ☎ 08/846–8704).
➤ TRAIN TICKETS: **Saigon Railway ticketing office** (✉ 275C Pham Ngu Lao St., District 1, ☎ 08/836–7640 or 08/837–7660).

TRAVEL AGENCIES

LOCAL AGENCIES

All the agencies listed below can help you organize tours of Ho Chi Minh City as well as trips to sights such as the Cu Chi Tunnels, the Caodai Holy See, and the Mekong Delta, a few hours from the city.

Ann's Tourist could very well be your only tourist-information stop. The company arranges tours both around Ho Chin Minh City and throughout the entire country, rents cars, makes flight arrangements, handles visa extensions, and provides all the historical, cultural, and orientation material you could ever possibly need. Ann's also has a great story behind it: after the fall of Saigon in 1975, Tony and his brother were separated from their mother, Ann, and removed to the United States. Ann founded Ho Chi Minh City's first privately run travel agency with the intention of finding her sons. Reunited as a family, they became a professional unit; Tony now runs the company full time. It's open Monday–Saturday 8–6 and Sunday 9–11.

Exotissimo is an upscale, international tour operator headquartered in Hanoi but with an office in Saigon. It's run by a helpful Frenchman.

Saigon Tourist, a government-run travel service, owns an enormous number of luxury hotels, restaurants, and tourist attractions in and around Ho Chi Minh City. It can arrange tours and accommodations in the city and throughout the country; provide maps, brochures, and basic tourist information; book domestic and international flights on Vietnam Airlines; and arrange car rental. The company basically operates as two separate agencies—one for budget travel and the other for standard or first-class excursions. Besides the price, the only difference seems to be the size of the bus; the main office arranges for large groups to cruise on colossal buses for five times the cost. Although many budget touring companies will cancel a trip if they haven't filled their bus, Saigon Tourist's budget division has a no-cancellation policy (just on their end—you are permitted to cancel), so a minibus will depart on schedule even if you are the only passenger. It's open daily 7:30–6:30.

Vidotours, a successful, privately run Vietnamese tour company, specializes in package and individual trips all over the country. It's one of the most upscale of the Vietnamese tour operators and consequently one of the most expensive. But Vidotours provides excellent personal service and English-speaking guides with an intimate knowledge of Vietnam.

➤ CONTACTS: **Ann's Tourist** (✉ 58 Ton That Tung St., District 1, ☎ 08/833–4356, FAX 08/832–3866, WEB www.anntours.com). **Exotissimo** (✉ 37 Ton Duc Thang St., District 1, ☎ 08/825–1723, FAX 08/829–5800, WEB www.exotissimo.com). **Getra Tour Company** (✉ 177 Nguyen Thai Hoc St., District 1, ☎ 08/837–6641, FAX 08/837–6695). **Saigon Tourist** (main office: ✉ 49 Le Thanh Ton St., District 1, ☎ 08/823–0100, FAX 08/822–4987; budget office in Café Apricot: ✉ 187A Pham Ngu Lao St., District 1, ☎ 08/835–4539, WEB www.saigon-tourist. com). **Tan Thanh Thanh Travel Agency** (✉ 205 Pham Ngu Lao St., District 1, ☎ 08/837–3595, FAX 08/837–1238). **Thanh Thanh Travel Agency** (✉ 212B Pasteur St., District 3, ☎ 08/829–2150, FAX 08/825–1550). **Vidotours** (✉ 145 Nam Ky Khoi Nghia St., District 1, ☎ 08/933–0466, FAX 08/933–0470, WEB www.vidotourtravel.com). **Vietnam Tourism** (✉ 234 Nam Ky Khoi Nghia St., District 3, ☎ 08/932–6276, FAX 08/932–6775, WEB www.vn-tourism.com).

TOURIST CAFÉS

These (mainly) private companies offer many of the services of large travel agencies but usually at lower prices. Many double as hotels and restaurants, and some have computers where you can check e-mail or surf the Internet. If you don't see a sign for bicycle and motorbike rentals, in most cases they can still be arranged.

Kim's Café organizes inexpensive trips to regions such as the Mekong Delta. Sinh Café Travel, specializing in budget travel, is by far the best tourist café in Saigon. This agency has Vietnam's greatest travel deal: a $33–$38 open-ended ticket good for bus travel the length of the country (☞ Bus Travel *in* Smart Travel Tips A to Z). The café is open daily 7 AM–11 PM. It also serves food, although you're better off eating at Kim's Café nearby.

➤ CONTACTS: **Kim's Café** (✉ 268 De Tham St., District 1, ☎ 08/836–8122). **Sinh Café Travel** (✉ 246–248 De Tham St., District 1, ☎ 08/836–7338, WEB www.sinhcafevn.com).

7 THE MEKONG DELTA

The Mekong Delta comprises a patchwork of waterways, tropical fruit orchards, mangrove swamps, and brilliant green rice-paddy fields that run their way into the emerald-color South China Sea. It's a land touched by ancient and modern cultures, from the Funanese to the Khmer, Cham, and Vietnamese. If you're looking for wild frontiers, head south to the farthest reaches of the Mekong Delta—it doesn't get much more isolated than this.

By Andrew
Chilvers

Updated by
Lisa Bjorksten

L USH, BEAUTIFUL, AND FLAT, the Mekong Delta (Cuu Long), Vietnam's southernmost region, is just 6 to 20 ft above sea level, which means the region is often flooded during the rainy season. Rivers and canals crisscross the land, functioning as waterways that transport people and goods.

In the northern part of the delta region, fruit grows in abundance: mangoes, jackfruit, lemons, custard fruit, dragon fruit, pineapples, durians, and papayas. The climate, which is hot and humid year-round, is ideal for cultivating these tropical fruits. Rice also grows throughout the region. In the Mekong's southern section, steamy mangrove swamps and thick palm forests thrive on the flat, flooded delta, making the area difficult to navigate.

Slicing through the heart of the delta is the Mekong River, also known as Song Cuu Long, or River of the Nine Dragons. Descending from the Tibetan plateau, the Mekong River runs through China, separates Burma (Myanmar) from Laos, skirts Thailand, passes through Cambodia, and flows through Vietnam into the South China Sea. Every second the river carries with it from 2,500 to 50,000 cubic yards of fertile soil deposits; this flow of soil created the delta and continues to extend it out into the South China Sea. As it enters Vietnam, the river divides into two arteries: the Tien Giang (Upper River), which splinters at My Tho and Vinh Long into several seaward tributaries, and the Hau Giang (Lower River), which passes through Chau Doc, Long Xuyen, and Can Tho to the sea. The river is filled with islands that are particularly famous for their beautiful fruit gardens and orchards.

Fifteen million people live in the Mekong Delta's 11 provinces. Most subsist by fishing or rice farming. Many people live on or at the edge of the region's rivers and canals in structures built from whatever materials are at hand—including pieced-together remnants of Coca-Cola cans. The more enterprising families construct cagelike structures of bamboo—makeshift fish farms—beneath their homes on these waterways and then feed the fish daily through a large hole in the floor.

Dotting the endless fields of rice paddies, poor farmers, shadowed by their limpet-shape hats, evoke the classic image of Vietnam. These days enough rice is produced to feed the country *and* to export abroad. Vietnam is now one of the world's largest rice exporters—a remarkable feat considering that as recently as the early '90s the country was importing rice.

Centered on Can Tho and My Tho is the northern delta, with its fruit farms and rice fields, which is far more accessible than the remote southern delta. Encompassing the Ca Mau Peninsula that juts into the sea from Soc Trang, the lower delta is wild country. Isolated fishing communities exist along the tributaries running through the area. The people here are friendly and welcoming, though they rarely see foreigners. In the southernmost province of Minh Hai, the ancient mangrove forests shelter monkeys, wildcats, boars, and even crocodiles. Around U Minh, on the Ca Mau Peninsula, is Vietnam's only large cajeput forest, which can only be seen by boat.

Over the centuries the Mekong Delta has provided refuge to people fleeing wars and chaos farther north. The region was first mentioned in Chinese scholarly works as a part of the ancient kingdom of Funan, or the Oc Eo civilization, which had its capital near the modern-day city of My Tho. The Funan civilization was influenced by Hindu and Buddhist cultures and flourished between the 1st and 5th centuries AD. It was well known by Malay, Arab, and Chinese traders and was even large enough to warrant Chinese ambassadorial status. However, in the 6th century the Funan kingdom inexplicably disappeared. The Mekong Delta was settled by the Cham and the Khmer in the 7th century and was annexed by the Khmer civilization based at Angkor between the 9th and 10th centuries. Some Vietnamese settlers lived in the area even under Khmer rule, but with the defeat of the Cham in the late 15th century, more Vietnamese moved south. In the 17th century some of the Chinese fleeing one of the many northern dynastic autocrats appeared in the Mekong Delta. The Tay Son Rebellion and the Lords of Hue retributions in the late 18th century brought even more Vietnamese into the region.

The Mekong Delta's modern borders were drawn up by the French in 1954. Under the French, Indochina was a fairly loosely administered region comprising Laos, Cambodia, Cochin China, Annam, and Tonkin (now northern Vietnam) under one governor-general based in Hanoi. Allegiances were based on ethnicity—Cham, Khmer, Vietnamese, and so on—rather than on nationality. And there was feuding: the Khmer believed that over the centuries the Vietnamese had taken away their land, and they wanted it back.

French colonialism briefly put a stop to the disputes—and later contributed to them. The French encouraged the Vietnamese and the Chinese, who were much more commercially driven than the Khmer, to continue settling here. As more Vietnamese moved south, more Khmer left. Uncertainty over who would have sovereignty over the Mekong Delta lasted until 1954, when the French bequeathed the area to the new country of South Vietnam. Under Pol Pot's rule in Cambodia, the Khmer again laid claim to the delta as their ancestral land, and there were frequent skirmishes between Khmer Rouge and Vietnamese soldiers along the border.

Other social upheavals over the last 50-some years have also contributed to the region's further settlement. During the Japanese occupation of Vietnam in the 1940s, colonial French and Vietnamese families fled from towns and villages farther north to avoid the fighting. But the fighting eventually spread to the Mekong Delta, and these refugees were forced to fan out into the previously uninhabited mangrove swamps, hacking them down as they went.

Today the Mekong Delta is still populated by several cultures. The majority of people living in the area are Vietnamese, with the Khmer comprising the second-largest ethnic group. Nearly 2 million Khmer people live in the vicinity of the city of Soc Trang and on the Cambodian border, and the Mekong Delta is still often referred to as Khmer Krom by Cambodians. A small number of Cham also live close to the Cambodian border, but these Cham, unlike their counterparts in the central highlands, are not Hindu but Muslim. The southern Cham were converted to Islam by Malay and Javanese traders who skirted the coast several hundred years ago. The northern Cham contemptuously call the southern Cham the "New Cham," and the groups don't really mix with each other. The cultural diversity of the region accounts for the variety of religions practiced: Buddhism, Catholicism, Caodaism, and Islam. Your travels throughout the delta will take you past examples of their remarkable coexistence.

Pleasures and Pastimes

Dining

For a region that produces so much fruit, which you can sample at one of the area's many orchards, the Mekong Delta has the least varied cuisine in Vietnam. Not surprisingly, rice is the diet staple and is usually accompanied by fairly bland boiled or grilled chicken, pork, or beef. Stick to a diet of plain boiled rice and grilled chicken or pork, or French bread and pâté, which you can bring with you from Ho Chi Minh City or buy in larger towns in the delta. The best places to eat throughout the Mekong Delta are restaurants in hotels or guest houses—the seafood there should be fine (at least in the northern delta). You can also get some satisfactory meals in bigger towns such as My Tho and Can Tho.

If in doubt, ensure that vegetables are properly boiled before eating them; many local vegetables are sprayed with toxic insecticides and are often washed only in local tap water. Watch your food being prepared, if necessary. In addition, avoid some of the local fish, particularly catfish and shrimp, especially in the far reaches of the southern delta—they tend to be raised on human and other excrement in small trenches below farmers' houses.

Be sure to try the elephant-ear fish, a specialty of the region. It's best to eat this fish in the northern delta. Stick to a busy spot, where the fish is likely to be fresh, and you'll be fine. Caught and cooked fresh, the fish is combined with herbs and vermicelli to make some of the best spring rolls in the country. If you're adventurous, try more exotic dishes—snake (usually cobra or python), turtle, deer, monkey, and even rat, more readily available in the southern delta. Cobras are often soaked with herbs in large flasks of whisky that can be bought in any of the Mekong markets or the snake market in Phung Hiep. This potent drink is said to cure all sorts of illnesses and jump-start the libido. You may also come across live snakes for sale in the market: as well as being a local delicacy—think snake gallbladder tonic and curry snake stir-fry—snakes are often exported to other Asian countries to be used as food and medicine.

CATEGORY	COST*
$$$$	over 225,000 dong
$$$	105,000 dong–225,000 dong
$$	45,000 dong–105,000 dong
$	15,000 dong–45,000 dong
¢	under 15,000 dong

*per person for a main course at dinner, including 10% tax and 5% service

Floating Markets
The Mekong Delta is renowned for its lively morning floating markets, where people buy and sell fruits and other products from boats all jostling each other. Phung Hiep market, near Can Tho, at the intersection of seven major canals, is one of the biggest. Cai Rang and Phong Dien are two other notable floating markets, although you'll find these centers of bustling trading in varying forms and size throughout the delta.

Lodging
Much of the Mekong Delta is a remote, undeveloped region, which means it has some of the most primitive accommodations in Vietnam. It's possible to find cheap rooms in most towns, but they're often so basic that you may want to pay more for the best hotel in the area or go to the nearest town with better hotels.

The lodging scene has improved slightly with the addition of a few international-standard hotels. For example, the Victoria chain has beautiful waterside hotels in Can Tho and Chau Doc that are much more expensive than but also far superior to other accommodations in the region. Around Can Tho, hotel standards are improving in general because of the growing number of tourists, although this doesn't mean accommodations are as nice as they are elsewhere in Vietnam. Keep in mind that the least expensive rooms probably won't have air-conditioning or adequate fans—and you'll definitely want a cool room after a scorching day outside. Most hotels and guest houses in the delta are state owned, which means prices are fixed and generally overpriced for what you get. But for $20 or more per night, you can usually get an adequate room with air-conditioning and a private bathroom. Rooms vary in grade from standard (which often have a fan and a communal bathroom) to deluxe (which generally have air-conditioning and a private bathroom), so be sure to make your request known when you book your room. Check the different options around town—new hotels and guest houses are opening all the time—before you make a decision.

Some accommodations have Internet access, although this is likely to be substantially more expensive, especially in the better hotels, than the going rate of 300d–500d in the few Internet cafés in the region.

CATEGORY	COST*
$$$$	over 1.5 million dong
$$$	900,000 dong–1.5 million dong
$$	600,000–900,000 dong
$	300,000 dong–600,000 dong
¢	under 300,000 dong

All prices are for a standard double room, including 10% tax and 5% service.

Exploring the Mekong Delta

The Mekong Delta stretches from the Plain of Reeds in the northern reaches to the wet mangrove forests of Ca Mau at the southernmost tip. A sprawling region, much of it isolated and totally undeveloped, the Mekong Delta can be somewhat difficult to travel around. Can Tho is the capital of the region and the best base for visiting the northern part of the delta. Southeast of Can Tho is Soc Trang, the center of Khmer culture, and northwest is Long Xuyen, famous for its relics from the Funan kingdom. Farther north is the Plain of Reeds, marshlands controlled throughout the French-Indochina War and the Vietnam War by the Vietminh and the Vietcong and by the Hoa Hao religious sect. (A note on the term Vietcong: Vietcong is used throughout this book to refer to the opposition movement in the South because it is the one that is probably the most familiar. However, the history of this term is a complex one; *see* Vietnam at a Glance: A Chronology *in* Chapter 9 for further explanation.) Close to Ho Chi Minh City, My Tho makes a good day trip. This area is very touristy, however, and state-owned tourist companies ensure prices are high. If time permits, head farther into the delta.

On the Cambodian border is the center of Cham culture, Chau Doc. The highest peak in the Sam mountain range is also just a few miles from the border. Farther down the coast is the Mekong's only resort town, Ha Tien, although you would be hard pressed to call it a real resort. Off the coast near Ha Tien is one of Vietnam's unexploited gems, Phu Quoc Island. Still largely undeveloped, the remote island has powder-white sand beaches and simple resort accommodations devoid of tourists. Along the southernmost tip of the delta are remote fishing villages, which, often cut off from the main roads and rivers much of the year because of flooding, are difficult to visit. Few tourists venture this far into the lower delta, but if you do, the journey can be rewarding. Most likely you will visit the region with a tour arranged through a travel agency in Ho Chi Minh City; many of these include prepaid boat trips.

*Numbers in the text correspond to numbers in the margin and on the
Mekong Delta map.*

Great Itineraries

You can spend anywhere from 1 to 10 days in the Mekong Delta. For
example, it's possible just to take a day trip from Ho Chi Minh City
to My Tho, in the Tien Giang Province, and go on a boat trip to an island orchard. Or, if you want to spend more time in the region, you
can find enough to see and occupy you for days.

IF YOU HAVE 2–3 DAYS

My Tho ① is only two hours from Ho Chi Minh City, so it's possible
to make a day trip of it or to visit as part of a longer tour. While in
My Tho, visit both the Island of the Coconut Monk, where the island's
namesake set up a religious sanctuary, and Tan Long Island, to see some
of the area's orchards. Just outside My Tho, on the road back to
Saigon, is the Dong Tam Snake Farm, which probably won't take you
more than a half hour to see. That evening, head to 🏨 **Can Tho** ③. Go
to the Floating Market at Phung Hiep at the crack of dawn; then take
a ride through the channels surrounding the city. Stop in at the Munirangsyaram Pagoda, a Khmer temple. The next day, make an excursion
to **Vinh Long** ②, a river island with abundant fruit gardens and orchards
and the large Chinese Van Thanh Mieu Pagoda.

IF YOU HAVE 4–6 DAYS

After covering the upper and lower Mekong River areas around **My
Tho** ① and 🏨 **Can Tho** ③, head west to 🏨 **Long Xuyen** ④, once a center of Funanese civilization. The Long Xuyen Catholic Cathedral, one
of the largest churches in the Mekong Delta, is worth seeing. From Long
Xuyen travel up through Dong Thap Province to the Plain of Reeds
and explore the area by boat. On the fourth day, head down to 🏨 **Chau
Doc** ⑤, one of the more cosmopolitan towns in the Mekong Delta. Spend
a morning visiting the Chau Giang Mosque, the religious center of the
local Cham community, and go to shrine-covered Sam Mountain. You
can see Cambodia from its peak when the weather is good. From
Chau Doc drive down to the coastal city of 🏨 **Ha Tien** ⑥ to relax on
the beach.

IF YOU HAVE 10 DAYS OR MORE

A visit to the lower delta—Minh Hai and U Minh—takes more time.
You could visit this area on a separate journey or tack it on to a trip
to the upper and western delta regions around 🏨 **Can Tho** ③. About
an hour and a half southeast of Can Tho is the Khmer city of **Soc Trang** ⑧,
with its many beautiful pagodas, a museum of Khmer culture, and a
large Catholic church. Spend a day in Soc Trang; then travel to 🏨 **Ca
Mau** ⑨, the last big town on the southernmost tip of Vietnam. Use Ca
Mau as a base for getting to the bird sanctuaries in Dan Dai, where
you can see exotic feathered creatures, and for exploring the large U
Minh Cajeput Forest and the Minh Hai Mangrove Forest. On the second day in Ca Mau, take a boat down the Ngang River to 🏨 **Nam
Can** ⑩, the last town in Vietnam before the sea. Traveling the Mekong
is fairly rough going, so if you're keen to work in some relaxation time,
set aside a couple of extra days to visit 🏨 **Phu Quoc Island** ⑦. You can
either take the one-hour flight from Ho Chi Minh City or travel overland through the delta, take a local ferry to the island from Rach Gia,
and fly back to Ho Chi Minh City.

When to Tour the Mekong Delta

The best time to tour the Mekong Delta is during the dry season, from
October to May. During the rainy season, from May to September, a
large portion of the region is under water and inaccessible.

The Mekong Delta

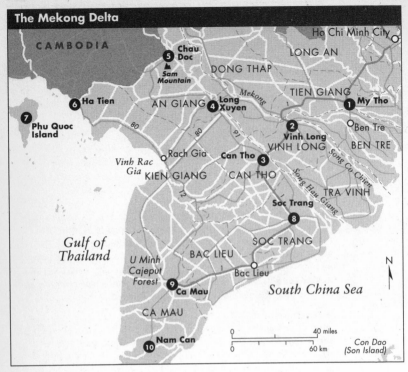

My Tho

❶ *70 km (43 mi) south of Ho Chi Minh City.*

My Tho is a good place to stop for lunch if you're coming from Ho Chi Minh City for a day of touring along one of the Mekong River's tributaries by boat (with a stop at one of the tropical fruit orchards on the river islands). This is the only port city along the upper Mekong River and the first ferry stop in the Mekong Delta. With a population of about 150,000, My Tho is one of the largest cities in the delta and one of the least attractive. Houses here are of the modern, concrete variety found throughout Vietnam—long, thin, and without windows on the side, they're often called tube houses. To find quaint wooden longhouses and cottages on stilts you have to travel farther south.

My Tho was the center of the ancient civilization of Funan from the 1st to 5th centuries AD, before the culture disappeared—no one really knows what happened. Today Funan relics are still being unearthed. The modern-day city was established by Chinese refugees fleeing Taiwan (then known as Formosa) in the 17th century. During the Vietnam War, My Tho was one of the centers of operations for American and Australian troops. The largest battle in the Mekong Delta was fought in 1972 at Cai Lai, only 20 km (12 mi) outside the city. My Tho is now known for its fruit and fish markets, a major food source for Ho Chi Minh City.

About 2 km (1 mi) from My Tho, on the Mekong River, is Phung Island (Con Phung), better known as the **Island of the Coconut Monk** (Ong Dau Dua). A religious sanctuary before the war, the island once had a garish, eclectic complex in a style similar to the Caodai Holy See in Tay Ninh. It was built in the 1940s by a monk named Nguyen Thanh

Nam, who was nicknamed the Coconut Monk by locals because he was reputed to have once lived for years on nothing but coconuts. The monk presided over a small community of followers, teaching a religion that combined elements of Buddhism and Christianity. He was imprisoned repeatedly, first by the Saigon regime and later by the Communists for antigovernment activities; he died in 1990. All that is left of the monk's utopian dreams are some dragons and gargoyles and columns with mythical creatures wrapped around them. ⊠ *Take boat from Trung Trac St., next to Mekong tributary.*

Like many of the islands in the Mekong River and its tributaries, **Tan Long Island** is covered with fruit gardens and large orchards. A pretty island with little paths and walkways, it's a patch of peace and tranquillity only a few minutes from the bustle of My Tho's docks. You're likely to be invited into someone's house for refreshments. The island is usually a stop on tour itineraries. ⊠ *Take boat from Trung Trac St., next to Mekong tributary.*

The **Dong Tam Snake Farm,** 10 km (6 mi) northwest of My Tho, is on an old U.S. military compound that lay deserted for years until a northern Vietnamese general decided to take over the land and develop it into a for-profit snake farm and research site for medicinal uses of reptile venom. The farm specializes in cobras, which are prodded and poked for reactions by delighted Vietnamese youths. The most dangerous are the king cobras, which, according to the farm, still have their venom sacs—hard to believe, but if in doubt, keep your distance. There's also a bunch of relatively docile pythons and a selection of rather miserable animals—many of them rare—such as monkeys, bears, wildcats, and pangolins, locked in tiny cages. These animals, too, suffer from the prodding of visiting children. Animal lovers will definitely want to stay away. The restaurant on the farm, which not surprisingly mostly serves snake dishes, is extremely popular with Vietnamese families on weekend day trips from My Tho. ⊠ *On road between My Tho and Vinh Long,* ☎ *no phone.* ▦ *15,000d.* ☉ *Daily 8–5.*

Vinh Long

❷ *74 km (46 mi) southwest of My Tho, 170 km (105 mi) southwest of Ho Chi Minh City.*

Lushly draped with thick palm forest and fruit orchards, Vinh Long, the best known of all the river islands in Can Tho Province, is a beautiful place to explore by boat along its canals and tributaries. On much of the island's coast are crumbling and renovated French villas, which were abandoned in the late 1940s as the Vietminh overran the territory south of Saigon. The locals are so hospitable that almost everyone will offer you tea and fruit at no expense if you happen to dock near their home. The most popular stop on tours of the island is at the **Binh Thuan hamlet,** where you eat lunch among the bonsai trees and fruit orchards of an eccentric old Francophone artist named Nguyen Thanh Gia. The fruit orchards and gardens are the island's main attraction. **Vinh Long** is also the name of the island's main town, but the town is not attractive enough to warrant a special visit.

About 5 km (3 mi) outside of the town of Vinh Long is the **Van Thanh Mieu Pagoda,** a large Chinese Confucian temple built in the mid-19th century. It's decorated with multicolor dragons and statues of Confucius, which is odd because the monks here practice Buddhism. Added to the original structure is a different style of hall built in honor of a local fighter against colonialism, Phan Tanh Gian, who committed suicide in the 1930s rather than submit to French rule. Often the locals refer to the temple by his name, so try both names if the boat guide seems confused.

Lodging

A home stay in one of the longhouses of the residents of the Vinh Long region can be an unforgettable experience. Arrange a visit with tourist agencies in Ho Chi Minh City or Cuu Long Tourist in Vinh Long (☞ Travel Agencies *in* The Mekong Delta A to Z, *below*). The houses are very basic, and the food is authentic for the region.

Can Tho

❸ *34 km (21 mi) southwest of Vinh Long, 108 km (105 mi) southwest of Ho Chi Minh City, 108 km (67 mi) southwest of My Tho.*

The meeting point of various waterways, Can Tho is the capital of the Mekong Delta and the region's gateway. This bustling hub of activity is connected to other centers in the Mekong Delta by a system of waterways—in order to get here you'll have to cross the river by car ferry, quite a daunting experience. Approximately 220,000 inhabitants make their home in this industrial city, with its big bottling companies and fish-sauce factories, but the town still manages to maintain a relaxed pace. Can Tho retains a French cosmopolitan feel—it was once one of the largest French colonial trading ports. Elegant villas can still be found throughout the city and along the shores of the surrounding river islands. Many have been renovated and are now occupied by rich Vietnamese merchants; others are falling to pieces. During the Vietnam War, Can Tho was almost constantly surrounded by hostile Vietcong forces, but the city itself stayed loyal to the Saigon regime and many U.S. and South Vietnamese troops were based here. It was the last city to fall to the North Vietnamese army, on May 1, 1975, a day after the fall of Saigon, as North Vietnamese forces moved south.

Consider hiring a bicycle from your hotel (about 15,000d per day) to explore the town—it's hard to get lost here. Escape the main streets and your journey will take you along tiny canal-side paths, through small communities, and past many local houses and friendly Can Tho inhabitants.

For a great daylong excursion from Can Tho, take a boat trip around the tiny islands in the river and canals surrounding the city. You can rent boats of various sizes from the quay along Hai Ba Trung Street; all come with a captain and a guide. Negotiate the price yourself, or let your tour guide do it for you. Expect to pay between $8 and $16 for three to five hours, less for small boats. Some of the finer hotels, such as the Victoria Can Tho, also rent their own small boats, although you'll be charged a higher fee.

Markets in the port and on the nearby rivers sell produce from the delta—mainly for markets in Ho Chi Minh City and for export. Can Tho has several floating markets, where people buy and sell from boats all jostling each other, but the **Floating Market at Phung Hiep,** 7 km (4 mi) southeast of the city by boat, is the largest and most picturesque. A bridge overlooking the market gives you a good view of the whole scene and a glimpse of delta life the way it has been conducted for centuries. Trading begins at dawn and carries on for much of the day. Goods are tied to poles to indicate what's for sale. A mango seller, for instance, will attach a mango to the top of his pole; others put grapes, pineapples, and other fruits on their poles. Be sure to rise very early to catch the frenetic trading as it takes off for the morning. It's the most pleasant time of day on the river.

One of Can Tho's highlights is the **Munirangsyaram Pagoda,** a Khmer temple built in the 1940s to serve and provide spiritual well-being to Can Tho's dwindling Khmer community. The pagoda is an emblem of one of the numerous ethnic groups that live side by side in the Mekong Delta. Unlike many of the elaborately decorated Vietnamese pagodas, this temple reflects the more spare Khmer sensibility. ☒ *36 Hoa Binh St.,* ☏ *no phone.* ☒ *Free.*

Dining and Lodging

$ ✗ **Quan Co Ba.** For cheap *bia hoi* (fresh, watery draft beer), try this simple eatery popular with locals, who sit around on plastic chairs, chatting and drinking the brew. There are plenty of good rice and *pho* (noodle soup) dishes. ☒ *9 Ly Thoung Kiet St.,* ☏ *no phone. No credit cards.*

$$$$ ✗▦ **Victoria Can Tho Hotel.** Without a doubt, the Victoria is the best hotel in the Mekong Delta. This beautiful 1930s colonial-style hotel is an ideal starting point for a trip around the islands of the Mekong River. It's also a great place to simply relax, take a tai chi class, swim in the great pool, and enjoy the picturesque Hau River (some rooms afford panoramic views of the bustling activity of the river). The elegant, airy rooms have wooden floors and furniture and spacious balconies. Spices restaurant serves fantastic Vietnamese food and seafood. Room rates include a large international buffet breakfast spread by the river. ☒ *Phuong Khe Tourist Center,* ☏ *071/810–111,* ℻ *071/829–259,* WEB *www.victoriahotel-vietnam.com. 92 rooms. Restaurant, cable TV with movies, pool, massage, bar, Internet, business services, meeting rooms, travel services. MC, V.*

$$ ▦ **Saigon-Can Tho Hotel.** Clean, good-size rooms and an elevator are the highlights of this otherwise ordinary hotel with a good location next to the main market and downtown shopping area. A state-run affair, the Saigon is nothing spectacular, but it's certainly one of the better hotels in the delta. Rooms have the usual borderline-tacky Formica furnishings and IDD phones; many have a rather unappealing view of the street. The restaurant serves an evening buffet of acceptable Vietnamese food, as well as burgers and fries. There's also karaoke nightly. Ask about ongoing special offers, such as tours and shopping trips, when you book. ☒ *55 Phan Dinh Phung St.,* ☏ *071/825–831 or 071/822–318,* ℻ *071/823–288. 46 rooms. Restaurant, cable TV with movies, gym, Internet, business center, meeting rooms, travel services. MC, V. CP.*

$–$$ ▦ **Quoc Te (International) Hotel.** The Quoc Te, close to the city market and Ninh Kieu pier, is one of the best of the many hotels along the waterfront. It touts itself as an international hotel, which it definitely is not, but it's clean and has good river views. Top and middle-range rooms have private bathrooms. The restaurant serves good Vietnamese food. ☒ *12 Hai Ba Trung St.,* ☏ *071/822–079 or 071/822–080,* ℻ *071/821–039. 42 rooms, 18 with bath. 2 restaurants, massage, cable TV, bar, nightclub, meeting room, travel services. No credit cards. CP.*

$ ▦ **Ninh Kieu Hotel.** This hotel on the corner of a street overlooking a small boat jetty has great river views. To get the best views of the bustling waterfront, try to book ahead and be sure to ask for a room overlooking the river. These come with balconies, which are a great place to unwind after a long day. Rooms vary from standard to deluxe, as in most hotels in the area; only those in the upper ranges have private baths. The hotel does not have Internet access, but there's an Internet café just 500 yards away. ☒ *2 Hai Ba Trung St.,* ☏ *071/821–171 or 071/825–285,* ℻ *071/821–104. 40 rooms, 30 with bath. Restaurant, cable TV, travel services. No credit cards. CP.*

¢–$ ▦ **Cuu Long Hotel.** Just off the waterfront and overlooking the main street is this basic state-run hotel, with nylon bedspreads and curtains, gaudy furnishings, pictures of castles and landscapes in the lobby, and the pervasive smell of dampness. Service is terrible, as it is in most state-run places. Nonetheless, this hotel is clean and one of the few options in Can Tho. Prices include a very basic Western breakfast. ⊠ *52 Quang Trung St.,* ☎ *071/820–300,* 𝔽𝔸𝕏 *071/826–157. 100 rooms. Restaurant, cable TV, massage, Internet, business services, meeting rooms, travel services. MC, V.*

¢–$ 🏨 **Hau Giang Hotel.** Basic but comfortable, the Hau Giang is popular with budget travelers, although there are cheaper rooms in town. Only the superior and deluxe rooms have private bathrooms, and only the deluxe rooms have air-conditioning. The more expensive rooms come with breakfast. Stay here only if every other place in town is booked. In the evenings there's karaoke. ⊠ *34 Nam Ky Khoi Ngia St.,* ☎ *071/ 821–851 or 071/821–139,* 𝔽𝔸𝕏 *071/821–806. 34 rooms, 4 with bath. Restaurant, travel services; no a/c in some rooms. No credit cards.*

Long Xuyen

❹ *190 km (118 mi) southwest of Ho Chi Minh City, 62 km (38 mi) northwest of Can Tho.*

Long Xuyen, like My Tho, was founded by the ancient Funanese, or Oc Eo, civilization. Until 1975 it was also the center of the Hoa Hao Buddhist sect, which, like the Caodai, had its own standing army to protect its interests against other sects and armies of the time. The Hoa Hao Buddhists often refer to themselves as Vietnamese Buddhists—that is, practicing a version of Buddhism distinct to Vietnam. Hoa Hao are proud and fiercely independent; during the 1950s and '60s they fought both the Saigon regime and the Vietcong with their own army. They were disarmed after the reunification of Vietnam. Their faith lives on, however, in communities like Long Xuyen.

The city is noteworthy for another reason: as Communists here will eagerly remind you, Long Xuyen was the birthplace of Ton Duc Thang (1888–1980), North Vietnam's president after Ho Chi Minh's death and the first president of the unified country after 1975.

Long Xuyen has one of the largest cathedrals in the Mekong Delta. The **Long Xuyen Catholic Cathedral** is newer than many other churches in Vietnam—it was completed only in 1973. Its most distinguishing feature is its huge bell. ⊠ *2 Nguyen Hue St., at Tran Hung Dao and Huong Vuong Sts.,* ☎ *no phone.*

The **Plain of Reeds** (Rung Tram) is the main reason to come to Long Xuyen. Swamp and marshlands interspersed with clumps of mangrove forest—much of which is impassable—cover the region on either side of the Dong Thap and Long An provinces. Also here is the **Tam Nong Nature Reserve,** famous for its rare wild birds. It's a great place to visit if you're an avid bird-watcher. If you want to see the rare herons, note that many migrate out of the region for much of the rainy season. The Plain of Reeds and the reserve lie 45 km (28 mi) from Long Xuyen and Cao Lanh (east of Long Xuyen), an utterly forgettable modern town, and are accessible from either. Tours of the area include the nature reserve and the Plain of Reeds; have the guide who has accompanied you from Ho Chi Minh City or from your hotel in the Mekong region organize the trip for you. Be aware that there are mosquitoes carrying many types of dangerous diseases, including dengue fever, malaria, and Japanese encephalitis; take precautions such as using mosquito repellent and wearing long-sleeve shirts and pants.

Lodging

¢   🏨 **Long Xuyen Hotel.** At this state-tourist-authority-operated hotel, rooms are comfortable but no-frills. There are few hotels in this very rural region, so this is the best lodging available. The lower-end rooms are extremely cheap and come only with a fan and the use of communal toilets. Ask for one of the deluxe rooms—these come with private toilet and shower and air-conditioning. ✉ *19 Nguyen Van Cung St.,* ☎ *076/841–927,* ℻ *076/842–483. 35 rooms. Restaurant, some fans, cable TV, Internet, business services, meeting room, travel services; no a/c in some rooms. MC, V. CP.*

Chau Doc

❺ *245 km (152 mi) west of Ho Chi Minh City, 119 km (74 mi) northwest of Can Tho.*

Chau Doc is a port town on the Hau Giang River only a few miles from the Cambodian border. Large populations of Hoa Hao, Catholics, Buddhists, and Muslims all coexist peacefully here, and the town is also well known for its ethnically mixed population, made up of Chinese, Cham, and Khmer minority groups, as well as Vietnamese. Each ethnic group has built its own distinctive temples—Khmer wats, Cham mosques, and Vietnamese and Chinese pagodas. In the late 1970s the town was notorious as a target of brutal border raids by the Khmer Rouge under the guise of seeking to reclaim land.

The border between Vietnam and Cambodia at Chau Doc was impassable for many years because of skirmishes between the two countries, but today it is safe and permissible to travel into Cambodia by river. The incredible journey evokes all the nostalgia of a bygone era of river travel in this remote part of Asia. It's best to prearrange your river trip with tourist agencies in Ho Chi Minh City; you'll be dropped off in Phnom Penh. The Victoria hotel chain also operates a daily service for $60 per person. The trip, on motorized sampan, takes about four hours, including border checks on both sides. Note that Cambodian visas are not issued on arrival at the border; you will have to prearrange this trip with a travel agency in Ho Chi Minh City.

The religious center for the local Cham community is the **Chau Giang Mosque.** As with other mosques in Vietnam, this one is starkly simple, with only some minarets and colonnaded entrances as embellishment. It provides a strong contrast to the many brightly decorated Buddhist pagodas and temples. The mosque stands on the riverbank opposite Chau Doc, so you have to take a ferry to get here (from the ferry terminal on Tran Hung Dao Street).

South of Chau Doc is shrine-covered **Sam Mountain** (Nui Sam), which is touted as the region's highlight. In fact, visiting is somewhat anticlimactic: this is more like a hill than a mountain. Nonetheless, it's worth seeing as long as you understand it will be a little less magical and a little tackier than claimed. At the base of the mountain are cafés and food stalls as well as street children begging for money. The walk up to the summit skirts several pagodas and a park with—oddly—plastic scale models of dinosaurs. The **Tomb of Thoai Ngoc Hau** is the most interesting shrine on Sam Mountain. Built in the early 19th century for Thoai Ngoc, an official of the Nguyen dynasty, the tomb is one of the few still-existing precolonial structures put up by the Vietnamese in the Mekong Delta. The tomb also served as the resting place of various other lesser functionaries of the time. When you reach the top of the mountain, you'll see splendid views into Cambodia. Let your guide organize an excursion to Sam Mountain.

Dining and Lodging

$ ✗ **Bay Bong.** Good restaurants are fairly hard to come by in the Mekong Delta, but this friendly, family-owned eatery is a nice option for delicious local fare and people-watching. The hot pots are the best dishes on the menu. ⊠ *22 Thuong Dang Le St.,* ☏ *076/867–271. No credit cards.*

$$$–$$$$ ✕⊞ **Victoria Chau Doc Hotel.** By far the best hotel in Chau Doc, the colonial-style Victoria has a degree of quality not found elsewhere in this part of the delta. Traditional Vietnamese handicrafts and nice touches such as jasmine flower rings in tiny bowls fill the rooms, and windows open out onto the bustling river. A cocktail at the Tam Giang Sky Bar overlooking Sam Mountain is the best way to relax after a hot, busy day touring the southern delta. Bassac Restaurant serves fine Vietnamese food. ⊠ *32 Le Loi St.,* ☏ *076/865–010,* FAX *076/865–020,* WEB *www.victoriahotels-asia.com. 93 rooms. Restaurant, cable TV with movies, pool, gym, massage, sauna, 2 bars, Internet, business services, meeting rooms, travel services. AE, MC, V.*

¢   ⊞ **Chau Doc Hotel.** Consider this no-frills, cheap backpacker hotel a place to stay and no more. There isn't much difference in price between the nicest and the shabbiest rooms, although the least expensive ones don't have private bathrooms or air-conditioning; be sure to ask for the most expensive. All, however, come with standard-issue nylon bedspreads and curtains. Make sure the hotel staff supplies you with a mosquito net if your room doesn't have one. ⊠ *17 Doc Phu Thu St.,* ☏ *076/868–666. 34 rooms, 6 with bath. Restaurant, fans, travel services; no a/c in some rooms, no room phones. No credit cards.*

Ha Tien

❻   *206 km (128 mi) northwest of Can Tho, 306 km (190 mi) west of Ho Chi Minh City.*

This resort town, just 8 km (5 mi) from the Cambodian border, has untouched stretches of beach and limestone formations, including a network of caves that have been converted into makeshift temples with Buddha images and psychedelic background lights. The coastal area is a pleasant diversion from the flatness of the rest of the delta and is a good place to spend a day or two just relaxing. The water is crystal clear, and the beaches are a brilliant sandy white. You can go snorkeling, diving, and fishing here, although you have to bring your own gear. **Mui Nai Beach,** 8 km (5 mi) west of Ha Tien, has beautiful sand beaches on either side of the peninsula. Nearby coconut-tree-lined **Bo Beach** is also nice.

Crumbling French colonial villas and a busy waterfront make the town itself quite charming. Today fishing is the main enterprise, and the area is known for its great seafood. Under Khmer rule the town was a thriving port; in the 17th century the Nguyen lords gave it to a Chinese lord, Mac Cuu, as a private, protected fiefdom. For the next 40 years the Khmer, Siamese, and Vietnamese all struggled for control of the port and the trade that would come with it. Ha Tien finally became an outpost of the Vietnamese Lords of Hue in 1780. The town's most famous site is the grave of the original Chinese lord, Mac Cuu, and his ancestors.

Lodging

¢   ⊞ **Dong Ho Hotel.** This no-frills establishment, run by the local state tourist agency, is a typically adequate and clean state-run hotel, with nylon bedspreads, pictures of European castles, and small rooms that smell damp. Only the more expensive rooms have air-conditioning, cable TV, refrigerators, and private bathrooms, so you probably want to request one of these. ⊠ *2 Tran Hau St.,* ☏ *077/852–141,* FAX *077/852–141. 19 rooms, 7 with bath. Some refrigerators, some cable TV; no a/c in some rooms. No credit cards.*

¢ 🏨 **Hon Trem Hotel.** Very basic but comfortable and clean, this small state-owned minihotel is good enough for an overnight stay. Only the higher-price rooms come with air-conditioning. ⊠ *Nga Ba Hon St., Binh An,* ☎ *077/845–331,* 🖷 *077/854–331. 15 rooms, 3 with bath. Restaurant; no a/c in some rooms, no room phones. No credit cards.*

Phu Quoc Island

❼ *45 km (28 mi) west of Ha Tien in the Gulf of Thailand.*

Phu Quoc Island (Dao Phu Quoc) is a relatively undiscovered gem, with white-sand beaches, hot springs, swaying palms, waterfalls, dusty red earth, and a laid-back local community that subsists on fishing, farming, and, increasingly, tourism. Mountains, forests, and some of the best beaches in Vietnam cover the 48-km-long (30-mi-long) island in the Gulf of Thailand.

To Cambodians, Phu Quoc is still known by its Khmer name, Koh Tral. While the island has never had a Khmer administration, it has—much to Vietnam's chagrin—long been claimed by Cambodia. To this end, Vietnam had designated much of the island as a military zone, with gun emplacements pointing out to the Gulf of Thailand. And naval ships are docked in An Thoi port. The guns and ships remain, but military and diplomatic disputes are in the past, though the rich fishing grounds in the area are still cause for discontent. Despite this, Phu Quoc Island is safe for travelers, and the Vietnamese government, which seems intent on developing tourism here, is in the process of upgrading basic Phu Quoc Airport and developing the port at An Thoi.

Hire a motorbike (or car and driver, though these aren't as readily available) from any of the hotels on the island and head north to the beautiful beaches of **Bai Dai** and **Bai Thom.** As these are in military zones, you must leave your passport with officials to access the beaches; inquire at your hotel before you visit. **Long Beach** stretches from the main port town of Duong Duong almost to An Thoi in the south. Lined with palm trees, Vietnamese fishing boats, basket boats, and a smattering of shacks, it's ideal for strolling. The eastern beaches, with their powdery white sand, are the best on the island, however. Wild and unsheltered **Bai Sao,** for example, is difficult to reach, but its deserted, unspoiled beach is worth the effort. By exploring sandy, winding paths you will also discover other little beaches on the east side of the island, all completely undeveloped and practically deserted.

Other than relaxing on the beach, there's not a whole lot to do on Phu Quoc. Some tour guides have set up snorkeling trips with local fisherfolk in the area. Ask at your hotel about treks to waterfalls and visits to pepper plantations—the island is know for its black-pepper production. Another local product is high-quality fish sauce, and you can also visit the fish-sauce factory Nuoc Mam Hung Thanh, a short stroll from the markets in Duong Duong; you'll probably be able to smell it on the approach.

Dining and Lodging

When making lodging reservations, consult with your hotel about traveling around the island; most hotels arrange boat trips and transportation, including motorbike rentals.

¢–$ ✕🏨 **Tropicana Resort.** Simple, down-to-earth, and relaxed, this charming resort on the beach is one of the best places to stay on the island. You can be unlucky with your room (the hot water is sketchy, but you can always ask to change rooms), but in general it's a great, basic resort. The restaurant serves fresh seafood on an outdoor terrace on the sand. It's a good idea to bring your own wine and spirits, although beer is available. The resort can arrange boat trips, snorkeling and scuba-diving tours, and other water activities. Motorbikes are available to rent for 50,000d per day. ⊠ *Long Beach, Duong Duong,* ☎ *077/847–127,* FAX *077/847–128. 6 rooms, 12 bungalows. Restaurant, snorkeling, boating, Internet, airport shuttle, travel services. AE, MC, V.*

$ 🏨 **Saigon Phu Quoc Resort.** If you seek the creature comforts of home, Phu Quoc's most modern resort may be for you. The large swimming pool is nice, though perhaps superfluous given that the resort sits right on Long Beach. A pool bar, massage, sauna, and steam room make this a great spot for pampering. The resort touts its villas as being colonial, but the modern sandstone structures look somewhat out of place on remote Phu Quoc Island. The large restaurant is pleasant, but you're better off wandering up the road to the basic Tropicana Resort for a tastier meal. ⊠ *1 Tran Hung Dao St., Thi Tran, Duong Duong,* ☎ *077/846–510,* FAX *077/847–163,* WEB *www.sgphuquocresort.com.vn. 95 rooms. Restaurant, cable TV, pool, massage, sauna, steam room, bar, nightclub, airport shuttle. MC, V.*

¢   🏨 **Thang Loi Resort.** Three German guys loved Phu Quoc so much they decided to set up a resort. Basic wooden bungalows with private bathrooms front Ong Lang Beach, on the western side of the island. The fresh seafood, which you can eat on a terrace watching the sun set, is superb. The resort also arranges motorbike rental and boat trips. ⊠ *Box 73, Ong Lang Beach,* ☎ *091/807–3494,* FAX *077/846–144,* WEB *www.phu-quoc. de. 20 rooms. Restaurant, boating, travel services; no a/c. MC, V.*

Soc Trang

❽   *63 km (39 mi) southeast of Can Tho.*

Soc Trang is the center of Khmer culture in Vietnam. Many inhabitants are either Buddhist monks or, oddly enough, Catholic nuns. It was once a provincial capital of the Angkor Empire, which covered much of Indochina from the 9th to the 15th century. Vietnamese settlers did not appear here until the 17th century; later, in colonial times, they were encouraged to come by the French, who sought to develop agricultural production in the region. Even though there is a fairly large Vietnamese population, Khmer culture is still very much present. Soc Trang's architecture mixes French colonial and Khmer styles. Many buildings are dilapidated but still impressive. Note that many roads in the town have no names, and inquiring about them only produces puzzled stares from passersby. However, the town is so small that finding your way around is not a problem.

On November 15 the town's Khmer community takes to the water to race traditional Khmer boats—long, slim rowing vessels, often with a half-man, half-bird figurehead—during the Ghe Ngo Water Festival, a fertility celebration. In April the Khmer New Year is celebrated with another water festival.

One of the most beautiful Khmer structures in Vietnam is the **Kleang Pagoda.** The pagoda and nearby communal longhouse and meditation center are off the road behind graceful palm groves and huge banana trees. The richly worked interior of the pagoda houses extensive gilded wood carvings. Originally constructed in the 16th century, the pagoda was rebuilt in the French-Khmer style at the turn of the 20th century. It's an almost ethereal photo opportunity if you can persuade monks to pose in the foreground. Watch out for their enthusiasm, though: local Khmer monks are often so delighted to see you that they may drag you to the nearby monastic school to introduce you to their friends and have you teach them a little English. ⊠ *Nguyen Chi Thanh St.,* ☎ *no phone.*

The **Khmer Museum** is housed in a large stucco French-Khmer colonial-style building with classical colonnades, Khmer flutes and eaves around the roof and half-man, half-beast Khmer figures on the walls and stairways leading to the entrance. The structure was originally built as a Khmer school in the 19th century. During the French-Indochina War the building served as the headquarters for the local French militia; during the Vietnam War it was a headquarters for American troops. The museum's collection includes Khmer statues and clothing, antique pots and utensils, and two long racing boats painted in vivid greens and reds. Across the street from the museum are Khmer religious schools. ⊠ *Nguyen Chi Thanh St.,* ☎ *no phone.* ☲ *Free.* ☉ *Tues.– Sun. 8–4:30.*

Built early in the 20th century, the large, active **Catholic church** and nearby convent are classic examples of French colonial neoclassical architecture. The church is the largest structure in town and can be seen from everywhere. ⊠ *Hai Ba Trung St.,* ☎ *no phone.*

The **Clay Pagoda** (Dat Set Pagoda) is a vibrantly decorated Vietnamese temple built entirely out of clay. Even the statues, dragons, and gargoyles inside are fashioned from clay and painted bright colors. This is the most popular temple with the town's Vietnamese population. Inside are candles so big and so broad—each about 40 ft high and so wide that two people extending their arms around it can barely reach each other—that they can burn continuously for 30 to 40 years. ⊠ *Hai Ba Trung St.,* ☎ *no phone.*

The **Matoc Pagoda** (Bat Pagoda), 6 km (4 mi) from Soc Trang, is the most interesting of the hundreds of Khmer temples and wats in the countryside around the town. Legend has it that about 400 years ago Khmer monks constructed the pagoda to honor the big bats that live in the mango trees surrounding it. In the Buddhist religion bats are considered sacred and, above all, lucky. Strangely, the bats don't eat the fruit of the trees on which they live but feed on fruit from forests several miles away. Many Chinese from the Cholon district of Ho Chi Minh City make two-day pilgrimages to the pagoda to gather good fortune from the bats. The best time to see these nocturnal creatures is dawn or dusk. After visiting the pagoda, take a walk through the surrounding Khmer villages. The first village is about 55 yards from the pagoda, hidden by a small copse of fruit trees. The next village is nearby. People in the villages live isolated lives but are friendly, and they may invite you to drink a cup of tea with them. ⊠ *Hai Ba Trung St.,* ☎ *no phone.*

Twelve kilometers (7 miles) outside town, in the village of Dai Tan, is the **China Bowl Pagoda** (Xa Lon), the largest Khmer pagoda and religious school (for novice monks) in the area. The original pagoda was destroyed during the Vietnam War and was rebuilt using China clay ceramic tiles—hence the name.

Lodging

¢–$ 🏨 **Khanh Hung Hotel.** The Khanh Hung is a basic, relatively comfortable place to spend a night or two. Don't be put off by the overly lighted and rather bleak-looking lobby—the better rooms are large, bright, and airy. Be sure to ask for one of the eight rooms with shower and private bathroom; the cheapest ones share a toilet down the hall, though they do have their own showers. Only the more expensive rooms have air-conditioning, and while the hotel claims to have cable TV, it doesn't seem to pick up any recognized cable channels. ⊠ *15 Tran Hung Dao St.,* ☎ *079/821–026 or 079/820–099,* FAX *079/820–099,* WEB *www. songmay.com/khanhhunghotel.htm. 55 rooms, 8 with bath. Restaurant; no a/c in some rooms. No credit cards. CP.*

¢   🏨 **Phuong Lan Hotel.** In the center of town and fairly comfortable, this hotel is Soc Trang's best. Rooms are large and have the standard uninspired state-run-hotel-style nylon curtains and bedspreads. The hotel also has karaoke rooms. ⊠ *124 Dong Khoi St.,* ☎ *079/821–619 or 079/821–993,* 🆎 *079/823–817. 20 rooms. Restaurant, some fans, massage; no a/c in some rooms. MC, V.*

En Route   After leaving Soc Trang, on the way to Ca Mau, you will pass through the village of **Vinh Loi,** 20 km (12 mi) away, where incense is made. It's easy to spot the village from the road—you'll see thousands of incense sticks drying along its sides.

Ca Mau

❾   *179 km (111 mi) southwest of Can Tho, 350 km (217 mi) southwest of Ho Chi Minh City.*

On the Dai Dong River at the Phung Hiep Canal, some 50 km (31 mi) from the South China Sea, Ca Mau is the heart of Vietnam's version of the Wild West. An isolated, rough-and-tumble kind of territory, it evokes what the American West must have been like long ago. The people here are very friendly, even if they do unabashedly stare at you. Most of the population of about 40,000 subsists on fishing. Tourists seldom come to Ca Mau because it's not very easy to reach. The town is inaccessible for much of the year because of the monsoons. Set amid Vietnam's largest swamp, Ca Mau is known for its large mosquito population. Protective clothing, repellent, and mosquito nets are a must in these parts.

Despite all this, it's worth trying to get here, whether by boat, by car, or bus from Can Tho or all the way from Ho Chi Minh City (a 13-hour trip). The town has an almost medieval atmosphere, with its chaotic collection of wooden houses leaning over the Dai Dong River, 20 ft below. Also running through the town are tributaries and canals that feed off the river. Ca Mau is great for nature- and bird-watching. Along the riverbanks are lush mangrove forests and palm groves with a fascinating panoply of river life: people fishing, sleeping, working, washing, and drinking. Boat trips from Ca Mau's waterfront cost about $70 a day on a private boat and $100 a day on a state-owned boat. Have your guide—either the person you've brought from Ho Chi Minh City or someone from a local hotel—ask around about boats. They range in size from small ones for a few people to larger ones for up to 20.

One of the highlights of a trip to Ca Mau is the **U Minh Cajeput Forest,** 35 km (22 mi) from town and reachable only by boat. This forest of pearl-white cajeput trees is in a swamp, so the boat has to wind its way through the sometimes thick undergrowth. The journey through the forest is quite breathtaking and eerily quiet. But beware of mosquitoes. The U Minh Forest can be approached from Ca Mau or Nam Can, to the south; let your guide or hotel make boat arrangements.

A daylong boat trip from Ca Mau will take you to the **Minh Hai Mangrove Forest,** one of the largest mangrove forests in the world and a truly primeval experience. The growth is so dense that it's almost unnavigable, but the boats manage to weave their way around the outskirts of the forest or to take wide channels through it. Often the most accessible areas are bordered by lone military outposts on the rivers and estuaries flowing to the sea. Most local soldiers live on their own or with their families in wooden houses above the wash on the muddy banks. Arriving tourist boats combat boredom, and often for no fee these soldiers will take you along the edge of the forest and, if possible, into the interior. Watch out for marauding monkeys and the odd crocodile.

Forty kilometers (25 miles) west of Ca Mau by boat is a series of riverine settlements called **Dan Dai.** The area is well known for its privately owned bird sanctuaries on 2 to 120 acres of small mangrove reserves. Not only can you see rare birds, but you can also find wildcats, monkeys, and deer. Beware: the owners of the reserves often ask for money *after* the fact, sometimes as much as $100, so be sure to negotiate a fee before you enter (you should pay no more than $2 per person). To get to the sanctuaries, take a small boat from Ca Mau.

Lodging

¢–$ 🏨 **Phuong Nam Hotel.** A pleasant surprise in Ca Mau, the Phuong is a large and rather busy hotel filled with Vietnamese tourists. It has a small ornamental rock pool and spacious rooms with balconies. Request one of the deluxe rooms, which are of a much higher standard than the several cheaper and more basic accommodations. ⊠ *91 Phan Dinh Phung St.,* ☎ *078/831–752,* 🆑 *078/834–402. 31 rooms. Restaurant, cable TV, travel services. MC, V.*

¢ 🏨 **Ca Mau Hotel.** Considering the town's frontierlike atmosphere, the quality of this hotel is surprising. In fact, it's actually one of the better hotels in the Mekong Delta. Rooms have many amenities, including IDD phones, private showers, and satellite TVs. There's also karaoke. ⊠ *20 Phan Ngoc Hien St.,* ☎ *0780/831–165,* 🆑 *0780/835–075. 30 rooms. Restaurant, cable TV, travel services. MC, V.*

Side Trip to Nam Can

🔟 The best part of a trip to **Nam Can,** 45 km (28 mi) south of Ca Mau by boat along the Dan Dai River, is actually the return journey to Ca Mau up the Ngang Canal, which is without doubt one of the most beautiful and exotic stretches anywhere in the delta region. Thick palm and mangrove forests line the water's edge, and tiny fishing and fruit hamlets sell goods from boats along the route.

Nam Can is the last settlement of any size in Vietnam before the sea. About 5,000 people live in the town, which consists of a series of lean-tos and old, abandoned boats used as homes. Although there is some fishing here, the town exists mainly to smuggle in commodities from all over, including consumer goods, fish, and rice. Many of the Vietnamese boat people, who left the country between 1975 and 1979, departed from Nam Can, and they bought many of the wretched vessels they used for their escape right here in town. The locals are very friendly.

There isn't much to do in town aside from visiting a fascinating daily market on the riverfront, with caged rats, as well as chickens, dogs, and cats, for sale as food; shellfish; vegetables; household goods; and clothing.

THE MEKONG DELTA A TO Z

To research prices, get advice from other travelers, and book travel arrangements, visit www.fodors.com.

There are several ways to get to the Mekong Delta, all of which must be arranged from Ho Chi Minh City: you can participate in an organized tour, use the hydrofoil service, fly to Phu Quoc Island, or hire a private car with driver and guide through a travel agency. All guides speak English. Guides can make all necessary travel arrangements, including boat trips. Vidotours (☞ Travel Agencies, *below*) organizes trips for individuals, and many of its tours and treks can take you to the most far-flung places.

AIR TRAVEL

In the dry season, October–May, Vietnam Airlines flies Wednesday–Thursday and Saturday–Monday between Ho Chi Minh City and Phu Quoc Island, although the timetable is notorious for its unreliability. Flights take one hour and cost about $50 one-way. It's a good idea to book in advance, as Phu Quoc is growing increasingly popular and seats are often sold out. You can also take the short flight from Rach Gia, near Ha Tien, to Phu Quoc for $35.

BOAT TRAVEL

The most scenic parts of the Mekong Delta are accessible only by boat. Boat trips can be prearranged by your tour company, hired by your guide, or arranged through your hotel for as little as $2 an hour at every dock in every town. Be sure to keep an eye on your bags and valuables during your trip. Can Tho is the departure point for riverboat trips to the river islands.

If you're traveling to Phu Quoc Island and are feeling adventurous, it's possible to head overland through the delta to Rach Gia, near Ha Tien, to catch a local ferry for the eight-hour trip to the island. Be warned that the ferries are somewhat old and are often overpacked. The cost ranges from $4.25 to $5.

Green Lines Company runs daily round-trip hydrofoil services between Ho Chi Minh City, My Tho, and Can Tho. It also operates a ferry Tuesday, Thursday, and Saturday between Ho Chi Minh City, Vinh Long, and Chau Doc. The cost ranges from $12 to $28.
➤ BOAT AND FERRY LINES: **Green Lines Company** (☎ 08/821–5609 in Ho Chi Minh City;071/829–372 in Can Tho; 076/865–568 in Chau Doc). **Rach Gia ferry** (☎ 077/863–242).

CAR TRAVEL

Private cars with drivers and tours can be arranged only in Ho Chi Minh City. A car can be expensive ($300–$500), but it enables you to plan your own trip and go farther into the Mekong Delta than you might be able to on a tour.

HEALTH

If you're planning to travel in the Mekong Delta for 10 or more days, make sure you're adequately prepared. There are malaria-carrying mosquitoes all over the delta and in some of the forests. Other mosquitoes carry diseases such as Japanese encephalitis (or Japanese B). Typhus, which is waterborne, is also a major health problem. However, it's almost unheard of for a tourist to contract any of these diseases; nevertheless, take precautions. Bring along mosquito coils and mosquito repellent for longer stays, and consider using malaria pills. Hotels usually provide mosquito netting. Try to cover your body at all times by wearing long-sleeve shirts and pants—day and night—and never drink anything but bottled or boiled water. *See* Health *in* Smart Travel Tips A to Z for more information on health precautions.

MONEY MATTERS

It's a good idea to bring cash, although if you need to change dollars or traveler's checks your hotel can probably do so.

MOTORCYCLE TRAVEL

If you want to see the Mekong Delta by motorbike, rent one from the Sinh Café (☞ Travel Agencies, *below*) in Ho Chi Minh City; there are special discount rates if you rent one for longer periods. Be sure to ask for the motorbike's documents, and try to get a newer Honda. Many of the scooters rented here—such as older Lambrettas from the '50s and '60s—break down almost immediately. Take your motorbike for a test drive before you venture on your way with it.

TOURS

Group tours that travel via tour bus and boat are available through the Sinh Café or Kim's Café, as well as through more upscale (although not necessarily better) state-run agencies such as Saigon Tourist. Vidotours is the best agency for tours of the region.

TRAVEL AGENCIES

Many agencies in Ho Chi Minh City arrange private and group tours to the Mekong Delta.

➤ IN HO CHI MINH CITY: **Kim's Café** (✉ 268 De Tham St., District 1, ☎ 08/836–8122). **Saigon Tourist** (main office, ✉ 49 Le Thanh Ton St., District 1, ☎ 08/823–0100, FAX 08/822–4987; budget office in Café Apricot, ✉ 187A Pham Ngu Lao St., ☎ 08/835–4539). **Sinh Café Travel** (✉ 246–248 De Tham St., District 1, ☎ 08/836–7338). **Vidotours** (✉ 145 Nam Ky Khoi Nghia St., District 1, ☎ 08/933–0466, FAX 08/933–0470).

➤ IN THE MEKONG DELTA: **Can Tho Tourist** (Cong Ty Du Lich Can Tho; ✉ 20 Hai Ba Trung St., Can Tho, ☎ 071/821–853, FAX 071/822–719). **Cuu Long Tourist** (✉ 1 Thang 5 St., top floor, Vinh Long, ☎ 070/823–616). **Phu Quoc Tourist** (✉ Duong Duong, ☎ 077/846–318). **Tien Giang Tourism** (Cong Ty Dy Lich; ✉ On riverfront at intersection of Rach Gam and Trung Trac Sts., My Tho, ☎ 073/872–154 or 073/872–105).

8 SIDE TRIP TO CAMBODIA

Though Cambodia requires some fortitude from its visitors, it's well worth the effort—if only to gape at the remarkable Angkor Wat. Reminders of past violence are here to be reflected upon, but Cambodia's cities buzz with the energy of a country on the mend.

THE CAMBODIANS ARE AN ENERGETIC and friendly people, whose quick smiles belie the inordinate suffering their nation has endured. Though practically destroyed by the regional conflict and home-grown repression of the 1970s, Cambodia has risen from those disasters like a phoenix. The streets of Phnom Penh are abuzz with a youthful vibrancy, and the tourism boomtown of Siem Reap is littered with construction sites. All the while the ancient temples of nearby Angkor attest to the nation's immutable cultural heritage.

Updated by
David
Dudenhoefer

As the seat of the Khmer empire from the 9th to the 13th century, Cambodia developed a complex society based first on Hinduism and then on Buddhism. After the decline of the Khmers and the ascendancy of the Siamese, Cambodia was colonized by the French, who ruled from the mid-1860s until 1953. Shortly after the end of World War II, during which the Japanese had occupied Cambodia, independence became the rallying cry for all of Indochina. Cambodia became a sovereign power with a monarchy ruled by King Norodom Sihanouk.

In the early 1970s, the destabilizing consequences of the Vietnam War sparked a horrible chain of events. The U.S. government secretly bombed Cambodia, arranged a coup to oust King Sihanouk, and invaded parts of the country in an attempt to rout the Vietcong. Civil war ensued, and in 1975 the Khmer Rouge, led by French-educated Pol Pot, emerged as the victors. A regime of terror followed. Under a program of Mao Tse Tung–inspired reeducation centered on forced agricultural collectives, the cities were emptied, and hundreds of thousands of civilians were tortured and executed. Hundreds of thousands more succumbed to starvation and disease. During the four years of Khmer Rouge rule, somewhere between 1 and 2 million Cambodians—almost one third of the population—were killed.

Vietnam, unified under the Hanoi government, invaded the country in 1978, forcing the Khmer Rouge into the region bordering Thailand, where they remained entrenched until United Nations–brokered peace accords were signed in 1991. International mediation allowed the return of Norodom Sihanouk, the formation of a coalition government that included Khmer Rouge elements, and parliamentary elections in 1993. In 1997, Second Prime Minister Hun Sen toppled the first prime minister, but political pressure forced new elections in 1998. Hun Sen won a plurality, amid charges of election rigging, and formed a government. Pol Pot died in the mountains in 1998, and the remaining Khmer Rouge threat quickly subsided. Most of the other Khmer Rouge leaders are still free, but Hun Sen is reluctant to bring them to justice. Foreign investment and the development of tourism have been strong in recent years, but it remains to be seen whether domestic problems are solved and whether Hun Sen can maintain his hard-line rule.

Pleasures and Pastimes

Architecture
Cambodia's temples, colonial buildings, and Khmer cities provide plenty to admire. Every town has a *wat* (Buddhist temple). The best of them is Wat Phra Keo, in Phnom Penh's Royal Palace compound, with its silver floor and emerald Buddha. Phnom Penh has plenty of colonial architecture, which melds Khmer and French influence to varying degrees—notable buildings include the National Museum and Hotel Le Royal. The country's most impressive structures, however, are the Angkor temples, whose abundant sculptures, massive towers, and intricate bas-relief murals are simply spectacular.

Dining

As might be expected from a country once ruled by the French, Cambodia has plenty of food to please epicureans. Phnom Penh isn't Paris, not by a long shot, nor is it Bangkok, but there are a few restaurants among the plethora that serve excellent meals. In Siem Reap, some of the best food is found in the restaurants of a few hotels. The cuisine choice is usually either Continental or Khmer, which is similar to Thai, but a few restaurants meld the two culinary traditions with laudable results.

CATEGORY	COST*
$$$$	over $20
$$$	$10–$20
$$	$5–$10
$	under $5

*per person for a main course at dinner

Lodging

Both Phnom Penh and Siem Reap have an abundance of hotel rooms, and the range of rates is remarkably wide. Travelers prepared to spend the money can enjoy colonial elegance at prices comparable to those of any major city, but visitors on a budget will be pleased to find comfortable accommodations at a mere fraction of those prices. All hotels expect payment in U.S. dollars.

CATEGORY	COST*
$$$$	over $200
$$$	$100–$200
$$	$50–$100
$	$30–$50
¢	under $30

*All prices are for a standard double room, excluding tax and service.

Exploring Cambodia

Cambodia is neatly sandwiched between Laos and Thailand in the north and west, and Vietnam to the east. It has a small, undeveloped coastline fronting the Gulf of Thailand, which is isolated by a low mountain range. Much of the country is a low-lying plain dominated by the region's largest lake, Tonle Sap, and a network of waterways forming the start of the Mekong Delta. Its northern border with Thailand is a remarkable escarpment, rising directly from the plains to heights of up to 1,800 ft—a natural defensive border and also the site of many ancient Khmer fortresses. The country is easily accessible from Vietnam, with regular air and bus services connecting the capital, Phnom Penh, with Ho Chi Minh City. Bus services between Phnom Penh and outlying towns and cities are frequent, cheap, and fairly reliable. For distances of less than 50 km (30 mi), taxis or *songthaews* (pickup trucks with benches in the back) are recommended.

Great Itinerary

The lively city of **Phnom Penh** is easily reached from Ho Chi Minh City and deserves at least two days. After you've acquainted yourself with the capital, fly to **Siem Reap;** three days here allow for a leisurely appreciation of the Angkor temples, though you could get the job done in one or two.

When to Tour Cambodia

The dry, cool season runs from November through February, with temperatures between 65°F (18°C) and 80°F (27°C). It heats up to around 92°F (33°C) from March through May. The monsoon season, with downpours for an hour or two most days, runs from June through October; during this time, temperatures range from 80°F (27°C) to 95°F (35°C).

Phnom Penh

As the capital of the Kingdom of Cambodia, Phnom Penh is strategically positioned at the confluence of four branches of the Mekong River. Though it was founded in 1434, Phnom Penh is a small city, with little more than 1 million inhabitants. During the Pol Pot regime's forced emigration of people from the cities, Phnom Penh had fewer than 1,000 residents. Buildings and roads deteriorated, and today most side streets are still a mess. The main routes are now well paved, however, and the city's wats sport fresh paint, as do many homes. Phnom Penh is clearly a city on the rebound, and its vibrance is in part due to the abundance of young people, many of whom were born after those dark years. Its wide streets are filled with motorcycles, which weave about in a complex ballet that only the dancers seem to understand, making it a thrilling achievement merely to cross the street. There are several wats and museums worth visiting, and the old city has plenty of attractive colonial buildings scattered about. The wide park that lines the waterfront between the Royal Palace and Wat Phnom—a great place for a sunset stroll—is about as lovely a spot as you will find anywhere.

According to legend, a wealthy woman named Penh found four statues of Buddha washed up on the banks of the Mekong, and in 1372 she commissioned a sanctuary to house them. That temple, **Wat Phnom,** is perched atop the 90-ft knoll—covered with lush vegetation—for which the city was named: Phnom Penh means "Hill of Penh." ⊠ *Preah 96, at Blvd. Norodom,* ☎ *no phone.* 🖅 *$1.* ☉ *Daily 7–6:30.*

The **Royal Palace** (Wayan), official residence of King Sihanouk, lies within a walled complex that covers several blocks near the river. The palace itself, a 1913 reconstruction of the one built in 1886, is closed to the public. Within the palace grounds is Phnom Penh's greatest attraction: the **Temple of the Emerald Buddha** (Wat Phrah Keo). The temple is often referred to as the Silver Pagoda because of the 5,000 silver blocks (6 tons of pure silver) that make up the floor. At the back of the temple is the venerated **Emerald Buddha**—some say it's carved from jade, while others hold that it's Baccarat crystal. Nearby is a 200-pound, solid-gold Buddha studded with 10,000 diamonds. Along the wall of the courtyard enclosing the temple complex are murals depicting scenes from the Hindu epic the *Ramayana.* Guides, who can be hired at the entrance for $5, may be able to take you to areas otherwise off limits, such as the throne room. ⊠ *Samdach Sothearos,* ☎ *no phone.* 🖅 *$3, camera fee $2.* ☉ *Daily 8–11 and 2–5.*

If the Silver Pagoda is a tribute to Cambodian civilization, the **Toul Sleng Museum** (Sarak Monty Toul Sleng) is a horrific reminder of the cruelty of which humans are capable. Once a neighborhood school, the building was seized in 1975 by Pol Pot's Khmer Rouge and turned into a prison and interrogation center. During its four years of operation, some 20,000 Cambodians were tortured here; many of them died and were dumped into mass graves in back, but most were taken to the Killing Fields for execution. Many of the soldiers who did the torturing were children, some as young as 10, and it is unsettling to think that those who survived may be walking the streets of Phnom Penh today. ⊠ *Preah 113 (Boeng Keng Kang), at Preah 348,* ☎ *023/300698.* 🖅 *$2.* ☉ *Daily 8–11 and 2–5.*

Thousands of Khmer Rouge prisoners who had been tortured at Toul Sleng were taken to the extermination camp of **Choeung Ek,** also known as the Killing Fields, for execution. Today the camp—located well outside the city, at the end of a rough and dusty road—is a monument called the Choeung Ek Genocidal Center. The site consists of little more than a memorial stupa filled with 8,000 skulls, which were exhumed from mass graves nearby. It is an extremely disturbing sight: many of the skulls, which are grouped according to age and sex, bear the holes and slices from the blows that killed them. ⊠ *15 km (9 mi) southwest of downtown Phnom Penh,* ☎ *no phone.* ⚑ *$2.* ☉ *Daily 7–6.*

The **National Museum** (Sarak Monty Cheat), a splendid colonial building, constructed in 1917, contains archaeological treasures. Exhibits chronicle the various stages of Khmer cultural development, from the pre-Angkor periods of Funan and Chenia (5th–9th centuries) to the Indravarman period (9th–10th centuries), classical Angkor period (10th–13th centuries), and post-Angkor period. Guides, who are usually waiting just inside the entrance, can add a lot to a visit here. ⊠ *Preah 13 (Ang Eng), at Preah 184,* ☎ *no phone.* ⚑ *$3, camera fee $1.* ☉ *Daily 8–5.*

Dining and Lodging

$–$$ ✕ **Shiva Shakti.** This small Indian restaurant just east of the Independence Monument has indoor dining and a few tables on the sidewalk. A statue of the elephant-headed god Ganesh stands by the door, and reproductions of Mogul art line the walls, making for a very pleasant dining room. The food is even better, from the succulent samosas and vegetable pacoras to the spicy lamb masala, chicken korma, and prawn biryani. It's a popular spot with expats, Indian, English, and other. ⊠ *70E Sihanouk Blvd.,* ☎ *012/813817. AE, MC, V. Closed Mon.*

$ ✕ **River House Restaurant.** The River House evokes a French bistro, with sidewalk seating and a daily set menu. It stands on a corner across the street from the northern end of the waterfront park, with half the tables outside, behind a potted hedge, and half beneath the ceiling fans of the open-air dining room. The menu is eclectic, ranging from couscous to coq au vin to homemade pastas. The bar upstairs, with a balcony overlooking the street and river, is a great place for a drink or a game of pool. It's a good idea to reserve ahead. ⊠ *Sisowath Quay at Preah 110,* ☎ *023/212302. AE, MC, V.*

$$$$ ✕🏨 **Hotel Cambodiana.** Massive and modern, the Cambodiana towers over the Mekong riverbank a short walk from the Royal Palace. Spacious guest rooms are short on personality but have large baths and picture windows—be sure to get a river view. Rooms on the fifth-floor Mekong Club, which include such perks as a private lounge and free airport transfers, are worth the extra money. Four restaurants ($$–$$$) give diners a choice of French, pan-Asian, international, and Italian cuisine by the pool. Ask about promotional rates. ⊠ *313 Sisowath Quay,* ☎ *023/426288,* FAX *023/426392,* WEB *www.hotelcambodiana.com.kh. 300 rooms. 4 restaurants, patisserie, minibars, cable TV, tennis court, pool, exercise equipment, bar, shops, laundry service, concierge, business services, meeting rooms, travel services, no-smoking rooms. AE, MC, V. BP, MAP.*

$$$$ ✕🏨 **Hotel Le Royal.** Phnom Penh's best hotel first opened in 1929, was
★ practically destroyed during the Khmer Rouge years, and then was meticulously restored by the owners of Singapore's Raffles Hotel in 1996. A colonial landmark surrounded by gardens, Le Royal offers an elegant lobby, tranquil pool area shaded by massive trees, and various bars and restaurants that are a world apart from this slightly chaotic city—and so are the prices. Guest rooms combine art deco furniture with fine Cambodian handicrafts and overlook either the pool or gardens—older Landmark rooms are nicer. The Restaurant Le Royal ($$–$$$) serves Khmer haute cuisine in a sumptuous dining room. ⊠ *92*

Rukhak Vithei Daun Penh, ☎ *023/981888; 800/637–9477 in the U. S.; 800/6379–4771 in the U.K.;* FAX *023/981168;* WEB *www.raffles-hotelleroyal.com. 208 rooms. 3 restaurants, patisserie, in-room safes, minibars, cable TV, pool, health club, spa, bar, lobby lounge, shops, laundry service, concierge, business services, meeting rooms; no-smoking rooms. AE, MC, V. BP, MAP.*

$$$ 🏨 **Royal Phnom Penh.** This tranquil hotel on the southern end of
★ town has the good fortune to be set amid beautifully tended gardens. Guest rooms, in rows of one-story buildings, have sliding glass doors that overlook the abundant foliage. They are large, bright, and colorful, if not terribly Cambodian. The lobby, with its patisserie, wicker furniture, and live Khmer music, has much more charm. A large, modern restaurant serves a mix of Western and Asian cuisine. ✉ *Samdech Sothearoh Blvd., Sankat Tonle Bassac,* ☎ *023/982673,* FAX *023/982661,* WEB *www.royalphnompenhhotel.com.kh. 75 rooms. Restaurants, patisserie, minibars, cable TV, driving range, 2 tennis courts, pool, health club, spa, bar, shops, laundry service, concierge, business services, no-smoking rooms. AE, MC, V. BP.*

$ 🏨 **Renakse Hotel.** If this place were for sale, it would be advertised as a "fixer-upper." The lovely, Khmer-style building dates from the colonial era and has the perfect location, across the street from the Royal Palace. Rooms are timeworn but clean, with small windows, dark wood furniture, and Cambodian landscapes paintings. A few of them have small balconies overlooking the ample grounds, which are shaded by coconut palms and large trees but littered with rubble. A simple, complimentary breakfast is served in the foyer, which is the most pleasant spot in the place. ✉ *Samdach Sothearos,* ☎ *023/215701,* FAX *023/722457. 30 rooms. Fans, refrigerators, cable TV, laundry service; no a/c. MC, V.*

Shopping

The largest market in Phnom Penh is the **New Market** (Pṣah Thmay), an art deco–style structure in the center of the city that sells foodstuffs, household goods, fake antiques, and some silver and gold jewelry. It's at the intersection of Boulevard 128 (Kampuchea Krom) and Preah 76 and is most active in the morning. For serious shopping, go to **Psah Tuol Tom Pong,** near Wat Toul Tompong, which has real and fake antiques, carved-wood furniture, and small Buddha statues, among other collectibles.

Angkor Temple Complex

★ *322 km (201 mi) north of Phnom Penh.*

The temples of Angkor constitute one of the world's great ancient sites and Southeast Asia's most impressive archaeological treasure. The massive structures surrounded by rain forest are comparable to the Maya ruins of Mesoamerica, or Peru's Machu Picchu, whereas the abundant statues and extensive bas-relief murals are as beautiful as those in the great temples of India, or the art of the ancient Egyptians. Unfortunately, the temple's reputation precedes it, and the complex is overrun with tourists from several continents, who arrive by the busload to gawk, sigh, contribute to a babble of collective admiration, and wander into each other's snapshots.

The Khmer empire reached the zenith of its power, influence, and creativity from the 9th to the 13th century, when Angkor, the seat of the Khmer kings, was one of the largest capitals in Southeast Asia. In all there are some 300 monuments scattered through the jungle, but only the largest have been excavated and reconstructed. Most of those lie within a couple of miles of each other and can be visited in one day, though two or three days allow you to better appreciate them. Though once the haunt of Khmer Rouge troops, who buried mines in certain areas, the temple complex was scoured by mine-removal teams years ago and is quite safe. Nevertheless, here and throughout Cambodia, you should stick to well-trodden paths.

Admission to the complex, which opens from 5 AM to 6:30 PM, costs $20 for one day, $40 for three, and $60 for a week. You can get a slight discount if you arrive after 4 PM: if you purchase a ticket for the following day, you'll be allowed into the complex free for the remaining 2½ hours, which is just enough time to do a little exploring and to catch the sunset at Angkor Wat. Most people visit the temples of Bayon and Baphuon, which face east, in the morning—the earlier you arrive, the better the light and the smaller the crowd—and west-facing Angkor Wat in the late afternoon. Ta Prohm can be visited any time, though it is best photographed when cloudy, whereas distant Banteay Srei is prettiest in the late-afternoon light. Transport is a necessity, and most independent travelers hire a car and driver ($20–$25 per day) or motorcycle ($6–$8 per day), though bicycles ($3–$4 per day) are available for those who can stand the heat and effort. It's best to hire a guide in Siem Reap, either through your hotel, a tour operator, or at the tourist office next to the Grand Hotel d'Angkor.

Siem Reap, which means "Siam Defeated," is a small market town 8 km (5 mi) south of the temple complex that serves as the base for tourism. Largely destroyed and abandoned during the days of the Khmer Rouge, Siem Reap is currently a boomtown, with dozens of hotels and restaurants and more under construction. Aside from being a base for visiting Angkor, however, Siem Reap has little going for itself.

Angkor Thom

Angkor Thom, the last great Khmer city, was built by King Jayavarman VII, who reigned from 1181 to 1200. It is surrounded by a square wall and moat and is entered via a bridge lined with statues and a massive stone gate. At its center stands the **Bayon**, a large, ornate structure that rises into 37 small towers, most of which are topped with four huge, strangely smiling faces. On the outer walls of the central sanctuary, and on some of the inner walls, are marvelous bas-relief murals—1½ km (¾ mi) of them in all—that depict historic battles, scenes from daily life, and the gods doing legendary deeds.

Just to the north of the Bayon is the slightly older **Baphuon**, built in the 12th century by King Udayadityavarman II. A fine example of poor planning, it was erected on a hill without the proper supports, so that when the earth shifted, it collapsed. The French government is painstakingly reconstructing the building and correcting its original structural flaws. It is consequently closed to the public till the work is completed (in 2004), though the ruins themselves can be seen.

Ta Prohm

Ta Prohm has been kept more or less as it was when French explorers rediscovered Angkor at the end of the 19th century, with many buildings reduced to piles of stone blocks and giant tropical trees growing on top of walls. Built by the prolific king Jayavarman VII to honor his mother, the complex originally had 566 stone dwellings, among them 39 major sanctuaries, and was attended by 2,740 priests, 2,202 assistants, and 615 dancers. Today, you're likely to share it with a couple hundred camera-toting tourists. Still, it is a gorgeous, magical spot, with thick, knotted tree roots sprawled over half-tumbled walls and flocks of parrots squawking in the branches high above.

Angkor Wat

The most impressive and best preserved of the Khmer temples, Angkor Wat was built at the beginning of the 12th century by King Suryavarman II (reigned 1112–52), who dedicated it to the Hindu god Vishnu. The temple is centered on five towers that form a giant lotus bud (the emblem of the Cambodian flag). Like all the other major monuments at Angkor, the buildings form a complex representing the Hindu (and Buddhist) universe. The central shrines symbolize Mt. Meru (mythical home of the Hindu gods), and moats represent the seven oceans that surround Mt. Meru.

Angkor Wat is reached by an impressive stone causeway, an avenue lined with balustrades in the form of serpents. The complex itself rises in three concentric enclosures, with terraces decorated with images of Hindu deities, many of which have lost their heads to looters. More impressive than the statues, towers, and the sheer size of the temple is the extensive bas-relief work that covers its walls, especially the mural on its outer front wall, and the more than 2,000 apsaras—mythical female dancers—scattered throughout it.

OFF THE
BEATEN PATH

CITADEL OF WOMEN – If you have the time, visit the Citadel of Women (Banteay Srei), 38 km (23 mi) northeast of Siem Reap. A small but magnificent 10th-century temple, it is dedicated to Shiva and contains fine sculptures of pink sandstone that are surprisingly well preserved. Admission is included in the Angkor ticket, but a hired car will usually charge an extra $5, and a motorbike $2, to go there. There have been robberies on the road, so be sure to return before dark.

Dining and Lodging

Siem Reap has an overabundance of hotels and restaurants, but most are mediocre, or worse. Some of the best food in town is served at a few of its hotels.

$$$$ ✕🏨 **Grand Hotel d'Angkor.** This grande dame, built in 1928, was restored and reopened after nearly being destroyed by occuping Khmer Rouge guerillas. Combining French sensibilities and Cambodian art, with Oriental carpets, wicker furniture, and abundant staff in traditional dress, the Grand now ranks among the region's finest, and most expensive, hotels. Rooms are large and elegant, with balconies that overlook the extensive, Taj Mahal–inspired gardens and blue-tile pool. Buffet breakfast and dinner are included in the rates, though fine dining is available at an additional cost. The nightly cultural show is free. ✉ *1 Vithei Charles de Gaulle,* ☎ *063/963888,* FAX *063/963168,* WEB *www.raffles-grandhoteldangkor.com. 150 rooms. 3 restaurants, patisserie, in-room safes, minibars, cable TV, pool, health club, spa, bar, lobby lounge, shops, laundry service, concierge, business services, meeting rooms; no-smoking rooms. AE, MC, V. BP, MAP.*

$$$$ ✕🏨 **Pan Sea Angkor.** Packed into a central, walled compound, this
★   hotel's guest rooms are stunning and spacious. Sliding glass doors open onto narrow balconies, and a subtle mix of hardwoods, white walls and covers, colorful pillows, and Khmer art creates an elegant, Asian ambience. Sliding wooden doors enclose a long bathroom–dressing area with a large round tub at one end of the room. The narrow green-tile pool, gardens, statues, and open-air bar are equally attractive. The restaurant ($$$), which serves an inventive mix of Asian and Western dishes, is one of the town's best. ✉ *Vithei Achasvar,* ☎ *063/963390,* FAX *063/963391,* WEB *www.pansea.com. 55 rooms. Restaurant, in-room safes, minibars, cable TV, pool, bar, shops, laundry service, concierge. AE, MC, V.*

$ ✕🏨 **Bopha Angkor.** Across the street from the Siem Reap River's east bank, this small hotel offers quality Khmer cuisine and comfortable rooms at very competitive prices. The guest rooms have tile floors, wood ceilings, local handicrafts, and mosquito nets. They surround an attractive, open-air restaurant ($) set amid gardens and small pools, where dinner is accompanied by live Cambodian harp music. A delicious and affordable selection—from chicken sautéed with pumpkin to fried fish with ginger and lemongrass—makes this a good dinner option even if you stay elsewhere. ✉ *Vithei Achasvar,* ☎ *063/964928,* FAX *063/964446,* WEB *www.bopha-angkor.com. 23 rooms. Restaurant, minibars, cable TV, laundry service. No credit cards.*

$$ 🏨 **Angkor Village Resort.** On a dusty street downtown is this oasis of ★ wooden buildings, gardens, and pools filled with lotus blossoms. It's a warm and welcoming place, from the airy, teak lobby to the tasteful rooms. Standard rooms are small, so it's best to pay for superior rooms, which are bigger and brighter and overlook the water and verdure. All rooms have Khmer handicrafts. The open-air restaurant, set in the middle of a pool, serves French and Asian cuisine. The cultural show performed in the hotel's gorgeous theater is a must-see. ✉ *Sangkat Svay Dong Kum,* ☎ *063/963563,* FAX *063/963363,* WEB *www.angkorvillage.com. 49 rooms. Restaurant, in-room safes, minibars, pool, lobby lounge, theater, shop, laundry service, concierge, business services. AE, MC, V. BP.*

$ 🏨 **Borran.** The rooms are attractive and the rates low at this tranquil, ★ small hotel a couple of blocks east of the river. Khmer handicrafts and antiques fill the rooms, which have high ceilings and tile floors. Each one has a large porch or balcony overlooking a nicely planted yard, which holds a small pool and open-air thatched restaurant. Large bathrooms with stone floors have both a shower and the traditional Cambodian bathing option of scooping water out of giant ceramic urn. ✉ *1½ blocks east of river, 1 block north of Preah No. 6,* ☎ *063/964740,* WEB *www.borran.com. 20 rooms. Restaurant, pool, massage, lounge, laundry service. No credit cards.*

Cambodia A to Z

To research prices, get advice from other travelers, and book travel arrangements, visit www.fodors.com.

AIR TRAVEL

Vietnam Airlines has daily flights from Ho Chi Minh City to Phnom Penh, and several direct flights to Siem Reap per week. Siem Reap Airways has daily flights from Ho Chi Minh City.

Phnom Penh's modern Pochentong Airport is 10 km (6 mi) west of downtown, whereas the Siem Reap Airport—under construction at press time—is 6 km (4 mi) northwest of town. The international departure tax is $20, whereas the charge for domestic departures is $5. A taxi to downtown Phnom Penh costs $7; to a hotel in Siem Reap, $5.

➤ CARRIERS: **Siem Reap Airways** (☎ 023/720022 in Phnom Penh; 063/380191 in Siem Reap; 08/823–9288 in Ho Chi Minh City; WEB www.siemreapairways.com). **Vietnam Airlines** (☎ 023/363396 in Phnom Penh; 063/964488 in Siem Reap; 08/823–0320 in Ho Chi Minh City; WEB www.vietnamairlines.com).

BUS AND CAR TRAVEL

Road travel between Ho Chi Minh City and Phnom Penh takes six to eight hours on a rough road, longer during the rainy months. The trip is cheap—for as little as $10—and you can arrange it through travel agencies and tourist cafés in Ho Chi Minh City (☞ Ho Chi Minh City A to Z *in* Chapter 6). Several guest houses, such as Narin's Guest House, arrange direct minibuses going the other way, from Cambodia into Vietnam. Otherwise you can catch one of the frequent buses from the Psa Thmey to the border and grab a bus to Ho Chi Minh City on the other side. Neak Krorhorm Travel in Siem Reap can also help you arrange bus trips.

Fairly reliable, cheap, and frequent buses connect Phnom Penh with outlying towns and cities.
➤ CONTACT: **Narin's Guest House** (✉ 50 Preah 115, Phnom Penh, ☎ 023/982554). **Neak Krorhorm Travel** (✉ across from Old Market, Siem Reap, ☎ 063/964924).

BUSINESS HOURS
Business hours are 8–12 and 2–5:30 weekdays; banks are open 8–3 weekdays, post offices 7:30–5 weekdays. Some banks may have limited weekend hours for currency exchange.

CUSTOMS AND DUTIES
ON ARRIVAL
You are allowed to bring into Cambodia 200 cigarettes, 50 cigars, or ½ pound of tobacco, and 946 ml of alcoholic liquor.

ON DEPARTURE
You are not allowed to bring in or take out local currency. The export of antiques or religious objects requires a permit—contact your embassy for assistance in obtaining one.

ELECTRICITY
Electrical current is 220 volts AC, 50 Hz.

EMBASSIES AND CONSULATES
New Zealanders should contact the British embassy.
➤ AUSTRALIA: **Embassy** (✉ Villa II, Preah 254, Phnom Penh, ☎ 023/426001).
➤ CANADA: **Embassy** (✉ 9 Preah 245, Phnom Penh, ☎ 023/426000).
➤ UNITED KINGDOM: **Embassy** (✉ 29 Preah 275, Phnom Penh, ☎ 023/427124).
➤ UNITED STATES: **Embassy** (✉ 18 Preah 228, Phnom Penh, ☎ 023/216436).

EMERGENCIES
If you need assistance, contact your hotel receptionist. For medical emergencies, visit the International SOS Medical Clinic, or English-speaking Dr. Gavin Scott of the Tropical & Travellers Medical Clinic. If you're really sick, consider flying to Bangkok, which has much better hospitals. In the case of a lost passport, immediately notify your embassy.
➤ CONTACTS: **International SOS Medical Clinic** (✉ 161 Preah 51, Phnom Penh 3, ☎ 023/216911; 015/912100 mobile). **Tropical & Travellers Medical Clinic** (✉ 88 Preah 108, Phnom Penh, ☎ 023/366802; 015/912100 mobile).

ETIQUETTE AND BEHAVIOR
As elsewhere in Southeast Asia, confrontational behavior and displays of anger are considered bad manners, as is too much bare skin at a religious site. Remove your shoes and hat before entering a temple or home. Homosexuality is tolerated but not encouraged. Public displays of affection should be avoided by all couples, gay or straight—Cambodians take this so seriously, even newlyweds are forbidden to kiss at their wedding ceremony.

HEALTH
Always drink bottled water and avoid uncooked food. There is a threat of malaria in rural areas, including a strain that is resistant to

some antimalarials. Consult the Centers for Disease Control's Web site (www.cdc.gov/travel) before departing, and use insect repellent at all times.

HOLIDAYS
New Year's Day (Jan. 1); International Women's Day (Mar. 8); Cambodian New Year (mid Apr.); Labor Day (May 1); Visak Bochea (Buddha's Birthday; early May); International Children's Day (June 1); Last King's Birthday (late June), Constitution Promulgation Day (Sept. 24); Taing Tok Ceremony (Oct. 20–22); Paris Peace Agreement (Oct. 25); Current King's Birthday (Oct./Nov.); Independence Day (Nov. 9); Water Festival (Nov.); Human Rights Day (Dec. 10).

LANGUAGE
The Cambodian language is based on the Khmer phonetic alphabet and is tonal. Within the tourist industry, English is spoken and, to a lesser degree, French.

MAIL AND SHIPPING
Airmail takes 4–5 days to Europe and 7–10 days to the United States.
➤ POST OFFICES: **Main Post Office** (⊠ Preah 13, between Preahs 98 and 102, Phnom Penh).

MONEY MATTERS
COSTS
Hotel prices range from $300 and up at the exclusive Raffles properties to $15 for a basic room with a private bath and air-conditioning at abundant guest houses. Within that spread, there are business-class hotels that charge $90–$150, and many hotels with decent rooms complete with cable TV and minibars in the $20–$50 range. Dinner for two at a restaurant, without wine, will run $12–$35, though it can be twice that at a big hotel. A one-way flight from Phnom Penh to Siem Reap is $60–$70. Taxis charge less than $1 per kilometer (half mile), and you can hire a car with driver for $20 a day, if you don't travel far. A local beer costs $1 in most restaurants, but an imported beer at a big hotel can be $4.

CURRENCY
The monetary unit in Cambodia is the riel, but the U.S. dollar is nearly as widely accepted, and payment in dollars is required by hotels, airlines, tour operators, and many restaurants. At press time, the exchange rate was approximately 4,000 riels to the U.S. dollar, but you do better to pay bills in dollars, since vendors and hotels often use an inflated rate if you pay in riels.

CURRENCY EXCHANGE AND ATMS
Since the riel and U.S. dollar operate as almost dual currencies, it is possible to change dollars to riels just about anywhere. There are plenty of banks and money changers in Phnom Penh and Siem Reap that will also change other currencies, but they don't give very good rates, so you're better off converting those currencies to dollars before traveling to Cambodia. Banks and businesses usually charge 2% to cash U.S.-dollar traveler's checks. Cambodia lacks ATMs, but there are plenty of banks that give cash advances on Visa or MasterCard, charging commissions that range from 1% to 5%—shop around. The Mekong Bank has exchange windows that open on weekends.
➤ BANKS: **Mekong Bank** (⊠ 1 Preah Kramuon Star, Phnom Penh, ☎ 023/217112; ⊠ 43 Preah Sivutha, Siem Reap, ☎ 063/964417). **Cambodian Commercial Bank** (⊠ 26 Monivong, Phnom Penh, ☎ 023/426208; ⊠ 130 Preah Sivutha, Siem Reap, ☎ 063/964392).

PASSPORTS AND VISAS

All visitors are required to have a valid passport to enter Cambodia. One-month visas are given to tourists from most countries upon arrival at the airports in Phnom Penh and Siem Reap; you'll need two passport photos and $20. If you enter by land from Vietnam you need to get a visa at the consulate in Ho Chi Minh City; allow a few days for processing.

➤ CAMBODIAN EMBASSIES AND CONSULATES: **Cambodian Consulate** (✉ 41 D Phung Khac Khoan, District 1, Ho Chi Minh City, Vietnam, ☎ 08/829–2751). **Royal Cambodian Embassy** (✉ 5 Canterbury Crescent, Deakin, ACT 2600, Australia, ☎ 02/6273–1259). **Royal Cambodian Embassy** (✉ 4500 16th St. NW, Washington, DC 20001, United States, ☎ 202/726–7742).

SAFETY

Cambodia is safer than most people think, but you still need to exercise caution. There have been muggings on the streets of Phnom Penh, mostly at night, where tourists have also been robbed at gunpoint while riding on motos or trishaws. It is a good policy to keep most of your cash, valuables, and your passport in a hotel safe, and avoid walking on side streets after dark. If you do stay out late, return to your hotel in a taxi rather than on a moto or trishaw. Also, be careful of overly friendly strangers who want to take you someplace, for whatever reason, and be wary of accepting drinks from strangers unless you can keep an eye on them to avoid being drugged and robbed. Siem Reap has much less of a crime problem than the capital, but it is unwise to wander its streets late at night. The U.S. embassy reports holdups on the road between Siem Reap and Banteay Srei.

SIGHTSEEING TOURS

Various companies arrange day tours of Phnom Penh and nearby sites, but since guides can be hired at the Royal Palace and National Museum, they aren't essential. However, a guide can greatly enrich your appreciation of Angkor's temples, which are full of details you're likely to miss or misunderstand. Angkor guides can be hired through your hotel, a tour operator, or at the tourist information stand next to the Grand Hotel d'Angkor; they charge $20–$30 per day, a true bargain.

➤ CONTACTS: **Diethelm Travel** (✉ 65 Preah 240, Phnom Penh, ☎ 023/ 219151; ✉ 4 Preah 6, Siem Reap, ☎ 063/963524).

TELEPHONES

To call Cambodia from overseas, dial the country code, 855, and then the area code, omitting the first "0." The code for Phnom Penh is 023, 063 for Siem Reap. Unfortunately, Cambodia's international lines are usually jammed, which will give you a busy signal. Booking and requesting information through Web sites is consequently the best option. Calling overseas from Cambodia is very expensive, and you can't do it from public telephones. If you have to make a call, either go to the main post office or call from your hotel room, but ask how much it costs first. Few public phones work, but there are lots of stands that rent cell phones. For long-distance calls within the country, dial the "0" as part of the area code.

TIPPING

Bellhops and doormen are happy to receive anything from 2,000 riels (50¢) to a dollar. Guides and drivers expect a few dollars on top of their day rate. At tourist hotels, a 10% service charge is added to the bill, but if you consider that most of the staff earns between $1 and $2 per day, you'll probably want to give them something extra.

TOURS AND PACKAGES

Though you'll spend much less money making your own arrangements, you can simplify things by booking a full itinerary through an agency, such as Journeys International, in the United States.

➤ CONTACTS: **Journeys International** (✉ 107 April Dr., Ann Arbor, MI 48103, ☎ 734/665–4407 or 800/255–8735, WEB www.journeys-intl.com).

TRANSPORTATION AROUND CAMBODIA

The road to Siem Reap from Phnom Penh is very rough, so most travelers either fly, or take a boat. Siem Reap Airways, Royal Phnom Penh Airways, and President Airlines each have several flights per day between Phnom Penh and Siem Reap. Siem Reap Airways charges a bit more, but its planes are much newer.

Several high-speed ferries depart Phnom Penh from the municipal port on Sisowath Quay, at Preah 84, early in the morning. A one-way ticket that includes a hotel pickup and a transfer from the landing dock to Siem Reap costs $20–$30, according to the boat, and can be purchased at most hotels and travel agencies. Mekong Express has the quickest boats.

The most common form of transportation in the cities is the moto (motorcycle taxi), and they cruise the streets in abundance, as well as gathering outside hotels and restaurants—wherever you walk, you'll attract them. The standard fare for a short trip is 1,000 riels (25¢), though they often try to get more from foreigners. Less-abundant pedal trishaws charge the same. Cruising taxis are nonexistent, but there are usually a couple parked outside large hotels, and the receptionist at any hotel can call one. Few drivers speak much English. You can arrange to hire a car with driver through any hotel, and Siem Reap now has *tuk tuks* (three-wheeled taxis), which are cheaper than a car but more comfortable, and safer, than a moto. With such cheap moto and taxi transportation, Phnom Penh's hot, crowded buses aren't worth the time and discomfort.

➤ CONTACTS: **Mekong Express** (☎ 023/427518 in Phnom Penh; 063/963662 in Siem Reap). **President Airlines** (☎ 023/212887 in Phnom Penh; 063/964338 in Siem Reap). **Royal Phnom Penh Airways** (☎ 023/216487 in Phnom Penh; 063/964454 in Siem Reap; WEB www.royalpnhair.com). **Siem Reap Airways** (☎ 023/720022 in Phnom Penh; 063/380191 in Siem Reap; 08/823–9288 in Ho Chi Minh City; WEB www.siemreapairways.com). **Tuk Tuk Taxi Service** (☎ 063/935018 in Siem Reap).

VISITOR INFORMATION

The people at the information booth in the Phnom Penh airport are in the business of booking hotel rooms, but they may have maps to give away. There is a city tourism office across from Wat Ounalon that produces a brochure, though the map in it is horrible. It is open weekdays 8–noon and 2–5:30 but isn't terribly helpful. The tourist office in Siem Reap does little other than set visitors up with guides, but several free glossy magazines distributed all over town are packed with useful information and ads. Various Web sites provide tourist information and recent news and let you book hotel rooms: www.cambodia-travel.ws, www.cambodiajournal.com, www.visit-mekong.com/cambodia, www.cambodia-hotels.net.

➤ CONTACT: **Department of Phnom Penh Tourism** (✉ 313 Preah Sisowath Quay, ☎ 023/913483). **Siem Reap Tourism Office** (✉ Pokambor Ave., ☎ 063/964347).

9 BACKGROUND AND ESSENTIALS

Chronology

Portraits of Vietnam

Books and Movies

Vocabulary

Menu Guide

CHRONOLOGY

Early History

ca. 1300 BC   The Dong Son, the earliest recorded civilization in what is now Vietnam, emerges in the Red River delta in the region that would later become Hanoi. This far-reaching culture is known for its elaborate bronze kettledrums, which have been discovered as far away as Sumatra, Bali, and Australia.

208 BC   The Lac Viet, the loosely organized feudal lords of the Red River delta, are conquered by a renegade Chinese general who claims the title of Nam Viet (emperor of the Viet people in the south).

111 BC   The Han Chinese invade and conquer Tonkin and Annam (what is now northern Vietnam). Through about 100 BC, the Han dynasty pursues a policy of administrative and cultural incorporation of Tonkin and Annam into the Chinese empire.

AD 40   The Trung sisters lead a successful rebellion against the Chinese: after the Chinese execute a high-ranking Vietnamese feudal lord, the lord's widow and her sister mobilize the disorganized Vietnamese chieftains against the Chinese governor. After a quick victory the sisters are proclaimed queens of the newly independent Vietnamese state.

AD 43   Chinese forces reconquer the new Vietnamese state. The Trung sisters choose to commit suicide rather than accept defeat.

AD 100–500   The Funan Kingdom rules the southern part of Vietnam (later known as Cochin China). This Indianized kingdom has major trading centers in the region near what is today Kien Giang. Archaeologists have found evidence of trade links between Funan, China, Indonesia, India, and Persia. Discovery of a Roman medallion in Funan dating from AD 152 indicates the Funanese may have had trade networks extending as far as ancient Rome. Although not much is known about this kingdom, many believe it was either the progenitor of, or a sister state to, the later Khmer Empire.

ca. AD 100   The Champa Kingdom emerges near present-day Danang in southern Annam. Like the Funan Kingdom, the Kingdom of Champa was based on strong trade links with India. The Cham culture adopted Indianized art forms and architectural styles as well as written Sanskrit. The Cham ruins still standing in central Vietnam reflect these influences.

AD 166   The first documented direct contact between Vietnam and the West occurs when Roman travelers arrive in the Red River delta.

Early Dynasties

939–70   The Annamese Ngo dynasty, under Ngo Quyen, ousts the Chinese and establishes an independent state in the Red River delta.

967–80   Dinh dynasty: Emperor Dinh Bo Linh ascends the throne and renames the independent state Dai Co Viet.

980–1009   Early Le dynasty: The Dinh dynasty is overthrown by Le Dai Hanh.

1010–1225   Ly dynasty: Emperor Ly Thai To establishes this dynasty and sets up his capital at Thang Long, the City of the Ascending Dragon, later to be known as Hanoi. This dynasty is known for promoting a

Chinese-style mandarin education system, symbolized by the construction of Van Mieu, the Temple of Literature, in Hanoi. The dynasty is also known for promoting Mahayana Buddhism over Confucian values and for expanding the Vietnamese state's territory southward into Cham lands through the promotion of agricultural development and the creation of Vietnamese villages. The mandarin Ly Thuong Kiet maintains the dynasty's independence by defeating successive Khmer, Chinese, and Cham army incursions.

1225–1400 First Tran dynasty: This dynasty is known for increasing the nation's population and cultivated land. Its most celebrated single achievement is the repulsion of Kublai Khan's invading Mongol forces in the late 13th century. In a brilliant naval victory in the Bach Dang River, Tran Hung Dao lures a superior Mongol fleet into the mouth of the estuary. He patiently held the Mongols at bay, positioning them in a vulnerable area in which their ships were impaled on steel-tipped poles planted by Vietnamese forces and the crews massacred when low tide arrived.

1400–06 Ho dynasty: In 1400 Tonkinese leader Ho Quy Le overthrows the Tran. Tran loyalists and the Cham, who had been fighting their Tonkinese northern neighbors, encourage the Chinese to intervene and reinstate the Tran.

Later Dynasties

1407–13 Later Tran dynasty: After being reinstated with Chinese assistance, the Tran reign briefly.

1413–28 The Chinese Ming Empire reconquers Vietnam and occupies the country, forcing further taxes, servitude, and Chinese culture on the Vietnamese.

1428–1786 Later Le dynasty: The Chinese officially recognize Vietnam's independence following the Lam Son uprising, a revolt led by Emperor Le Loi, who establishes the Le dynasty. It lasts until 1786.

1460–98 Under the rule of Emperor Le Thanh Tong, a comprehensive legal code is introduced and Vietnamese domination extended farther southward into Cham territory. Laos and the Khmer region become a vassal territory of Vietnam.

1516 Portuguese traders land in the port of Danang and set up trading posts alongside their Japanese and Chinese predecessors in the port of Fiafo, the site of present-day Hoi An.

1527 Dominican missionaries from Portugal arrive in Danang to gain converts among the people living there.

1545 As Le rulers' authority weakens, civil strife splits the country for nearly two centuries. The Le dynasty continues its official rule, but warring lords who accept Le rule operate largely independent of the emperor. Much of the conflict is between the Trinh lords, who dominate the north from Tonkin, and the Nguyen lords, who rule from Hue to the south. Although neither achieves dominance, the Nguyen establish control over the Khmer areas of the Mekong Delta and populate the area with Vietnamese settlers.

1580 Franciscan missionaries from the Philippines begin proselytizing in central Vietnam.

1613 English attempts at establishing trade links with Vietnam are thwarted with the murder of an East India Company representative in Hanoi.

1615   French Jesuit missionaries expelled from Japan arrive in Vietnam.

1627   Alexandre de Rhodes, a French Jesuit missionary, adapts spoken Vietnamese to the Roman alphabet, leading to the current Vietnamese script. He creates a Vietnamese dictionary in 1651, six years after being expelled from Vietnam for entering without permission.

1637   Dutch trade is established in North Vietnam.

1700   The country splits into the Trinh dynasty north of Hue and the Nguyen dynasty, which includes Hue and lands to the south. During the mid-17th century, Cambodia becomes a vassal territory of Vietnam.

1771–1802   Tay Son Rebellion: After years of a weak central government and warring factions, a rebellion starts in the village of Tay Son, near present-day Qui Nhon in south-central Vietnam. Led by the three sons of a wealthy merchant, the Tay Son rebels capture central and southern Vietnam by 1783, sending the surviving Nguyen lord, Prince Nguyen Anh, into exile in Thailand. In retaliation, Prince Nguyen Anh asks the French for their assistance in his return to Vietnam to defeat the Tay Son rebels. Meanwhile, the Tay Son conquer the Trinh in the north and pledge allegiance to the weak Le dynasty. The Le emperor, however, asks the Chinese to help him control the Tay Son. Mobilizing popular support against the Chinese, one of the Tay Son brothers proclaims himself Emperor Quang Trung and leads the Vietnamese in an overwhelming defeat of the Chinese forces near Hanoi in 1789. But soon after, Prince Nguyen Anh, with support from French-trained forces, returns to southern Vietnam and moves north against the Tay Son.

French Influence

1802–1945   In 1802 Prince Nguyen Anh proclaims himself Emperor Gia Long, officially beginning the Nguyen dynasty, which lasts until 1945. When Gia Long captures Hanoi from the Tay Son rebels, it marks the first time in 200 years that Vietnam is united, with Hue as its capital. French missionary activity begins to spread as the Nguyen develop a mutually tolerant relationship with the French.

1847   The first clash occurs between Emperor Thieu Tri, successor to the Nguyen throne, and the French after the French attack Danang Harbor in retaliation for a Vietnamese crackdown on Catholic converts. Also in this year Nguyen emperor Tu Duc ascends the throne and continues the struggle against the French.

1861   French colonial forces win the battle of Ky Hoa and take Saigon. Defeated, Tu Duc's forces disband. But unhappy with the prospect of French rule, local elites continue resistance, using anti-French guerrilla tactics in the south.

1862   Emperor Tu Duc negotiates a treaty with the French, giving broad religious, economic, and political concessions: permission for missionaries to proselytize throughout the country, the opening of ports to French and Spanish trade, surrender of the three eastern provinces of Cochin China, and payment of a large indemnity to the French.

1863   The French expand into Cambodia.

1866   The ultimately unsuccessful Mekong Expedition is mounted to find the source of the Mekong River and explore the commercial viability of an inland route to China. After expedition leader Captain Doudart de Lagrée dies in Cambodia, Lieutenant Francis Garnier assumes the lead and presses on to the Yangtze River and Shanghai before returning to Saigon as a hero.

1867 The French name the southern part of the country Cochin China and take over its administration after a final French offensive breaks Vietnamese resistance. Admiral Pierre de La Grandiére occupies the three westernmost provinces of Cochin China.

1872 French gunrunner Jean Dupuis is held under siege in Hanoi after delivering munitions to Yunnanese warlords up the Red River. The French dispatch gunboats under the command of Francis Garnier to retrieve Dupuis and restore order. Garnier instead overtakes the Hanoi Citadel, establishes it as his garrison, and demands tribute from Vietnamese vanguards along the Red River. In response, the Co Den (Black Flag), made up of H'Mong, Chinese, and Vietnamese pirates, fight to retake the citadel. Garnier is eventually captured and beheaded at the Cao Gia Bridge. Dupuis escapes with the returning gunboats. The Co Den terrorize Red River villages, and the first systematic purging of missionaries begins.

1879 French prime minister Jules Ferry, elected on a platform of imperialism and "*mission civilisatrice*" (civilizing mission), appoints colonial administrator Charles Marie Le Myre de Vilers the first civilian governor of Cochin China.

1883 After Tu Duc's death, French forces take the Imperial City in Hue and impose the Treaty of Protectorate on the Imperial Court. The French give protectorate status—as an independent government subject to French policy—to the north, which they designate Tonkin, and central Vietnam, which they designate Annam. Cochin China remains a colony administered directly by France.

1887 The French create the Indochinese Union in order to end Vietnamese expansion into Cambodia and Laos, thereby officially ending a unified Vietnamese state. The Union includes Tonkin, Annam, Cochin China, Cambodia, and the Port of Qizhouwan in China.

1890 Ho Chi Minh is born as Nguyen Sinh Cung in Nghe An Province in north-central Vietnam.

1893 France further extends its colonial influence by moving into Laos.

1911 Ho Chi Minh leaves Vietnam and begins his world travels. Over the next 30 years he works in France and spends time in Moscow, becoming involved with the growing Communist movement.

1919 Ho Chi Minh petitions American president Woodrow Wilson, at the Versailles peace conference held at the end of World War I, for self-determination for Vietnam and is refused.

1920 Ho Chi Minh joins the French Communist Party.

1930 Ho Chi Minh and his colleagues form the Indochinese Communist Party in Hong Kong, where they are free from French repression.

1932 Bao Dai, the nominal emperor of Vietnam, returns from his education in France to take over the Nguyen dynasty throne under French guidance.

1940 Rather than risk a full-scale confrontation, the French Vichy government peacefully capitulates to Japanese troops' occupation of Vietnam. The Japanese leave the French administration in place as the most efficient way of controlling the region.

1941 Ho Chi Minh returns to Vietnam and forms the Vietnamese Independence League, commonly known as the Vietminh Nationalist movement, to resist both the Japanese and the French.

1944 General Vo Nguyen Giap forms the Vietminh army in the north with military funding and arms from the U.S. Office of Strategic Services (OSS) to fight the allied Japanese and French.

1945 In March, as a major Vietminh military offensive gets started, the Japanese take over by force the administration of Indochina from the French. Backed by Tokyo, Emperor Bao Dai proclaims Vietnam an independent state under Japanese auspices. In August, as Japan's war machine crumbles, the Vietminh takes over large portions of the country. During that month the Japanese also transfer control of Indochina to Vietminh forces under Ho Chi Minh and Vo Nguyen Giap. Bao Dai abdicates in an attempt to maintain some national unity. Ho proclaims the area north of the 18th parallel the Democratic Republic of Vietnam; south of the parallel is declared an associated state within the French union by the allies, with Bao Dai as supreme counselor. Japanese policies of planting industrial crops and requisitioning rice to feed the Japanese army as well as bad flooding combine to cause famine throughout the north, killing 2 million of the north's 10 million inhabitants.

The French-Indochina War and the Vietnam War

1946 In March the French and Vietminh reach a peace accord, determining that Vietnam will be a "free state" within the French Union. In June the French violate the agreement by proclaiming a separate government for Cochin China. In November, as tensions grow, the French navy bombs Haiphong. Vietminh forces withdraw from Hanoi in December after attacking the French garrison, retreating to build their movement in rural areas. The French-Indochina War begins. Bao Dai flees to France as hostilities increase.

1947 In France Bao Dai reaches an understanding with the French on recognizing limited Vietnamese independence.

1949 Bao Dai returns to Vietnam after three years of self-imposed exile in France to designate Vietnam as an "associated state" of France. France retains control of defense and finances but grants administrative authority to the Vietnamese.

1950 Ho declares that the Democratic Republic of Vietnam is the only legal government. The Democratic Republic of Vietnam is recognized by the Soviet Union and China. The United States and Britain join the French in recognizing Bao Dai's government as legitimate. The Chinese begin to supply weapons to the Vietminh. U.S. president Harry S. Truman authorizes $15 million in military aid to the French in Indochina to fight the Vietminh. U.S. military assistance to France escalates to more than $2 billion over the next four years.

1953 Laos and Cambodia gain greater independence from France. French forces occupy Dien Bien Phu. The Vietminh pushes into Laos. Ho says he is ready to discuss peace with the French.

1954 The Vietnamese defeat the French at Dien Bien Phu, marking the end of the French-Indochina War. Bao Dai selects Ngo Dinh Diem, who has strong ties to the American government, as prime minister. Agreement is reached among France, Britain, the United States, and the Soviet Union as part of the Geneva Accords to cease hostilities in Indochina and to divide Vietnam temporarily at the 17th parallel until national elections determine a single government (ultimately the United States and the Saigon regime never endorse this division). The country is divided into the Democratic Republic of Vietnam in the north and the Republic of Vietnam in the south. Seeing a threat to his power, Bao Dai denounces the agreement. As part of the arrangement, French forces leave Hanoi. The U.S. government affirms support of Prime Minister Diem with a pledge of $100 million in aid. Hundreds of thousands of refugees, mostly Vietnamese Catholics worried that religious tolerance will not be practiced in the Vietminh-controlled north, flee to the south with U.S. Navy assistance.

1955 The United States begins to provide direct aid to the Saigon government and to train the South Vietnamese army. Diem rejects the Geneva Accords and refuses to participate in nationwide elections. He becomes president of South Vietnam and begins cracking down on suspected Vietminh members in the south. The Vietminh begins to show Communist tendencies as it promotes social upheaval and radical land reforms in the north.

1957 The Soviet Union proposes the permanent division of Vietnam at the 17th parallel. Southern-based Vietminh Nationalists and northern Communists strengthen ties in their opposition to the southern regime.

1959 As the Vietminh Nationalists from the south and the Communists from the north continue to strengthen ties, Diem increases repression against suspected Communists and dissidents in the south.

1960 The remaining southern Vietminh members change the name of their movement to the National Liberation Front (NLF), known to the South Vietnam government and the Americans as, and popularly called, the Vietcong. (The term Vietcong—which means, loosely, Vietnamese Communists—is generally used throughout this book in reference to the opposition movement in the south because it is probably the most familiar term.) As Diem's public popularity wanes, southern army officers stage an unsuccessful coup against him.

1961 Close advisers to U.S. president John F. Kennedy visit Vietnam and recommend American military intervention disguised as flood relief on behalf of the weak southern regime. Kennedy rejects the idea but provides military "advisers" and more equipment. Indirect American military support increases over the next few years.

1962 As Diem grows more unpopular, two insurgent South Vietnamese air force pilots try to assassinate him by bombing his palace. Diem is unhurt, though his sister-in-law is injured.

1963 Thich Quang Duc, a Buddhist monk from Hue, is the first of many monks to commit suicide through self-immolation in Saigon, protesting Diem's repressive tactics. With American support, Saigon generals murder Diem. By this time American aid is up to approximately 15,000 military advisers and $500 million.

1964 American-backed general Nguyen Khanh seizes power in Saigon. North Vietnam increases support for the southern revolutionaries. An unconfirmed attack on U.S. destroyers in the Tonkin Gulf prompts passage of the Gulf of Tonkin resolution in Congress, permitting the Americans to respond by bombing North Vietnam for the first time. Years later it is determined that the incident may have been staged by the U.S. government.

1965 The first American combat troops arrive in Danang. Sustained bombing of North Vietnam by American planes begins. Nguyen Cao Ky takes over the weak southern government. By the end of the year, 200,000 American troops are in Vietnam.

1966 President Charles de Gaulle of France calls for U.S. withdrawal from Vietnam. U.S. president Lyndon B. Johnson escalates American involvement in Vietnam; the number of U.S. troops reaches 400,000.

1967 Nguyen Van Thieu is elected president of South Vietnam, and Nguyen Cao Ky becomes vice president. Americans begin to fortify Khe Sanh, a hamlet in the central highlands, in preparation for a major North Vietnamese assault. By the year's end American forces number 500,000.

1968 After heavy fighting at Khe Sanh, U.S. troops withdraw from the area, leaving the battle-scarred hillsides bare. Later the United States realizes that Khe Sanh was likely a ploy to divert U.S. forces from the Tet Offensive. During the Tet Offensive southern insurgents and northern forces orchestrate coordinated attacks on southern towns and cities. Although tactically a failure, the offensive proves that South Vietnam and U.S. strategists have seriously underestimated the strength of the NLF. American troops massacre South Vietnamese civilians in My Lai. In part because of the Tet Offensive and My Lai, opposition to the war in Vietnam by the American public and politicians increases. American forces number 540,000.

1969 Paris peace talks, which began in 1968, expand to include the Saigon government and NLF representatives. The U.S. government, under President Richard Nixon's administration, begins the secret bombing of Cambodia to root out suspected NLF bases there. In response to growing domestic opposition and military frustrations, the American government says it will "Vietnamize" the war and begins withdrawing troops. Ho Chi Minh dies of natural causes in Hanoi.

1970 U.S. national security adviser Henry Kissinger begins secret talks with Le Duc Tho, the acting North Vietnamese foreign minister. President Richard Nixon announces that U.S. forces have attacked NLF sanctuaries in Cambodia, provoking a major upsurge of antiwar action in the United States. American troops in Vietnam number 280,000 at year's end.

1971 South Vietnamese forces enter Laos in an attempt to cut off the Ho Chi Minh Trail. This network of supply roads stretching from North to South Vietnam, a critical lifeline for the NLF, winds through the mountainous areas on the border between Vietnam, Laos, and Cambodia and is very difficult for Saigon troops to control. The number of American troops is reduced to 140,000.

1972 Nixon announces that Kissinger has been in secret negotiations with North Vietnam. Northern forces cross the 17th parallel. Americans resume the bombing of the north and mine Haiphong Harbor. Kissinger and Le Duc Tho make progress on a peace agreement, but South Vietnamese president Thieu resists a cease-fire.

1973 Kissinger and Tho sign a cease-fire agreement in Paris in January. The last American troops leave Vietnam in March. The United States halts the bombing of Cambodia.

1974 Thieu declares a continuation of war. The NLF further builds up supplies and troops in the south.

1975 North Vietnamese and NLF forces each capture key strategic towns. Thieu flees Vietnam for Taiwan before settling in Britain. The remaining Americans and their key Vietnamese colleagues in Saigon are evacuated in April. Images of the last overpacked U.S. helicopters lifting from the American Embassy in Saigon are emblazoned in the public mind as the United States—after 30 years in Vietnam—makes a hasty retreat. Communist forces capture Saigon on April 30 and accept the surrender of the government of South Vietnam, thereby unifying the north and the south. The U.S. government does not recognize the legitimacy of a reunified Vietnam. The U.S.-led economic embargo of North Vietnam, in place since the '60s, is extended to the whole of reunified Vietnam. The Soviet Union increases support for the newly unified country.

The Post–Vietnam War Years to the Present

1977 U.S. president Jimmy Carter commences talks between the United States and Vietnam about official recognition of Vietnam by the U.S. government. Due to the increasing links between Hanoi and Moscow, these talks eventually grind to a halt until the early '90s.

1978 Vietnam joins COMECON (the Soviet-influenced Eastern European economic community). Relations among Vietnam, Cambodia, and its Chinese benefactor deteriorate as skirmishes along the Vietnamese-Cambodian border increase. Hanoi signs a friendship pact with the Soviet Union. Following Khmer Rouge border incursions at Chau Doc and the growing China-Cambodia alliance, Vietnam responds and is involved in armed conflict with Cambodia until 1989, effectively ending the "killing fields," the brutal murder of more than a million Cambodians by the Pol Pot regime.

1979 In partial retaliation for Vietnam's conflict in Cambodia, China invades Vietnam. The Chinese Red Army penetrates as far as Vinh Yen, only 60 km (37 mi) north of Hanoi, but is quickly repulsed within two weeks by the People's Army of Vietnam.

1986 Hanoi selects reform-minded Nguyen Van Linh as general secretary of the Communist Party of Vietnam, signaling a cautious opening to the West. Vietnam commits to *doi moi*, the reform of socialist economic policies into a more market-oriented system.

1989 Vietnamese forces withdraw from Cambodia, ending a 50-year period of almost continuous war between the two countries.

1991 Ailing general secretary Linh is replaced by Prime Minister Do Muoi, who vows to continue the economic reforms begun by Linh. The Politburo and the Central Committee of the Vietnamese Communist Party undergo a major shift; aging, conservative leaders are replaced by younger, more liberally oriented members. Prime Minister Vo Van Kiet and Do Muoi visit Beijing in an attempt to heal relations.

1992 Chinese prime minister Li Peng visits Hanoi to further improve strained relations between Vietnam and China.

1994 The United States ends its economic embargo on Vietnam, which helps the country begin to rebuild its economy and infrastructure through International Monetary Fund (IMF) and World Bank loans and greatly increased foreign investments.

1997 The beginning of normalization of relations between Vietnam and the United States occurs. The U.S. Embassy officially opens

Hanoi, a U.S. consulate opens in Ho Chi Minh City, and the Vietnamese Embassy officially opens in Washington.

1998 General Le Kha Phieu assumes the top position of the Vietnamese Communist Party from General Secretary Do Muoi. In an effort to further normalize trade relations between the United States and Vietnam, the U.S. Congress waives the Jackson-Vanik Treaty, which had effectively prohibited trade between the two countries.

1999 Vietnam signs U.S. trade agreement in principal in July. U.S. secretary of state Madeleine Albright visits Vietnam.

2000 Bill Clinton is the first U.S. president to visit the country since the end of the Vietnam War. The country celebrates the 25th anniversary of the "Fall of Saigon," which signaled the end of the Vietnam War. Fourteen years after committing to the doi moi reform process, Vietnam enters the 21st century with limited political and business reforms in place.

2001 The U.S.-Vietnam Bilateral Trade Agreement is passed by both Vietnam and U.S. Congress, thereby normalizing trade between the two countries. Nong Duc Manh is appointed Vietnamese Communist Party chairman. Russian president Vladimir Putin visits Vietnam as a sign of strengthening cultural and economic ties.

2002 National Assembly elections see no change in political structure. Chinese president Jiang Zemin visits Vietnam. More than 900 Vietnamese ethnic-minority refugees in Cambodia are granted political asylum in the United States; Vietnam claims that they are illegal emigrants and requests their repatriation. Russian naval forces, based in Cam Ranh Bay since 1979, withdraw two years before their lease arrangement expires.

— By Jim Spencer

— Updated by William Richardson

RIDING THE DREAM

THE FIRST THING about Vietnam that struck me was how familiar it seemed. The second was how unique it was. The third thing that struck me was a Honda Dream motorbike—carrying a family of four through the chaos of midday traffic. Vietnam is a little surprising like that.

You, too, may find Vietnam oddly familiar, perhaps because you spent years glued to TV images of U.S. helicopters skimming over rice paddies in the Mekong Delta, American soldiers creeping through the thick jungles of the central highlands, and Vietnamese refugees passing trucks bringing GIs to the front; or maybe because you saw Hollywood's version of these events in movies like *Apocalypse Now* and *Platoon*; or maybe you even went to Vietnam yourself. The images of a familiar past may come flooding back to you as you approach the airport in Hanoi over a landscape speckled with craters left by U.S. bombs or touch down at the airport in Saigon, where American-built tarmac and hangars are still in use.

The desire to come looking for remnants of the war is understandable, especially for those of us from countries whose histories are linked with Vietnam's. And as someone who grew up in New York with a Vietnamese mother educated in America and an American father, surrounded by Vietnamese culture, I had yet another reason for wanting to understand how and why the United States became involved with Vietnam. On my first trip to Vietnam in 1990, I went to discover all I could about what life was like during the Christmas bombing of Hanoi in 1972, and what it was like living in the Vinh Moc underground tunnels. I visited the rooftop bar at the Rex Hotel to see where wartime journalists gathered nightly to reflect on the day's events.

What I found were only a few visible remnants of the war and its aftermath: Soviet-style memorials and cemeteries; towns where famous battles were fought; airplanes, helicopters, and artifacts on display in museums; and underground tunnel systems like those at Cu Chi, which are now open to tourists. The bomb craters at the Hanoi airport have been made into fish ponds, and the hangars at Saigon's have become storage sheds.

I also discovered that although many people are willing to talk with foreigners about the war, they are more often interested in reviewing the finer points of the latest American music videos, price fluctuations of the Toyota Camry, or the semiautomatic clutch on their new Honda Dream motorbikes—the latest in Vietnamese conspicuous consumption—than they are in rehashing the Battle of Khe Sanh. Others are understandably reluctant to talk about this painful history.

Younger people especially have little time for reflections on what they increasingly see as Grandpa's old war stories. After years of strife and isolation, they are ready for greater economic and cultural opportunities. The economic reforms instituted in 1986, *doi moi,* have been one of the major factors in bringing Vietnam out of isolation and onto a global stage where it once danced with the world's most powerful nations.

Until the early '90s Vietnam was under the influence of the Soviet bloc and was severely crippled by the U.S.-led economic embargo. As a result, the country has only been able to chart an independent course for a very short time. And for better or worse, the Vietnamese have decided that the road ahead lies with a free-market economy. As the country progresses on its journey toward becoming the next Southeast Asian "tiger"—a status that former Vietnamese foreign minister Nguyen Co Thach cautioned had to be preceded by becoming a "small cat"—Vietnam is at a critical point in its history. To comprehend why, you must first understand something about its history of conflict and synthesis.

As a crossroad of global trading, Vietnam has for more than 2,000 years been an object of desire of the major European and Asian powers. From the early Chinese, Cham, and Khmer empires competing a piece of what is currently Vietn~ up to the French, Americans. vying for political and c~'

Vietnam has been a contested land. All who have come have left their mark on the country, resulting in a culture that is an amalgamation of many foreign elements yet one that is uniquely Vietnamese. There are markedly few places in the world where you can find Catholic church spires poking out of the tropical rain forest, indigenous hill-tribe leaders speaking French and English, and farmers piling their Japanese and East German motorcycles high with Chinese-made dishes on their way home from the market.

It would be a mistake, however, to say that Vietnam has compromised its identity by assimilating elements of these invading cultures. This paradox is best summed up by the comments of an aging revolutionary who graciously welcomed me into his home when I first visited the country. Once a high-ranking member of the diplomatic team that negotiated the peace agreement with the Americans in 1973, he had been without question a thorn in the side of both the French and American governments. Strangely, though, on numerous occasions, while sipping French Cognac after dinner, he looked me in the eye and—in impeccable French—made sure I understood one thing: "*Je ne suis pas un Francophile, mais je suis vraiment un Francophone*" (I am not a Francophile, but I am very much a Francophone). Although he felt no lost love for his former colonizers, he did celebrate that he was himself a product of French culture. This kind of cultural adoption predates the French and has come to define a Vietnamese culture of adaptation.

The Conquering Chinese, and the Cham and Khmer Empires

From about 200 BC to AD 1428, Vietnam was subject to heavy Chinese influence and consequently made a national pastime of kicking out invaders from the north. For centuries Hanoi and Beijing danced in a cycle of liberation and domination until the Chinese were finally kicked out for good in the early 15th century.

The Chinese invaders influenced every aspect of Vietnam, from agriculture and architecture to education and cuisine, ~~especially~~ in the north. In the 3rd century ~~Chinese~~ began to promote in~~tensive~~ ~~fa~~rming in the Red River delta, replacing nonintensive dry-land crops. Over the centuries this system spread throughout the country and eventually came to symbolize the Vietnamese way of life. The Chinese also established an educational system in Vietnam modeled on the Chinese mandarin system. The system was embraced by the Vietnamese and thrived in Vietnam long after the Chinese had abandoned it in their own country.

Other Chinese elements include temples replete with dragons, words in the Vietnamese language, and, more recently, a taste for monosodium glutamate, which rumor has it was imported during wartime from China to add flavor to spare diets. Mahayana Buddhism and Confucianism, too, came to Vietnam from the north, and you can readily see their influence in today's Vietnam. These influences, however, never overshadowed the most Vietnamese form of religious practice in the country: *ban tho*, the altar to family ancestors that graces almost every Vietnamese home from Saigon to Son La to San Jose.

The influence of the Chinese wasn't as strong in the south, where they had competition. Beginning around AD 100, the Funan Kingdom ruled what is now southern Vietnam, and the Kingdom of Champa controlled the central region. Both Indianized kingdoms have had a major impact on this part of Vietnam and contributed to some of the regional differences found there.

Although attempts have been made to claim only one history for Vietnam, many believe these regions have as much in common with Cambodia, Thailand, the Philippines, and Indonesia as they do with China. Many point to the stronger social and economic roles of women, a warmer disposition, and a less regimented way of life in the south and central regions as vestiges of this earlier period. Since the Cham and Khmer were not as meticulous at imposing and institutionalizing social norms, their influences have not survived as well as those imported from China. Instead, the Indianness of *Indo*-China is mostly felt in the old Cham towers that pepper the central coast with images of Vishnu and Shiva, the Khmer temples in the Mekong Delta, and names of places such as Sadec, Kontum, and Daklak, which hark back to non-Chinese origins.

The Paternalistic French

The Chinese, the Khmer, and the Cham were merely the first to come. Centuries later the French burst onto the scene with their French bread, espresso coffee, and *"mission civilisatrice"* (civilizing mission) in an effort to mold the Vietnamese after themselves. As with the Chinese before them, the French had their own policies of domination and integration, and they saw Vietnam as fertile ground for the expansion of French culture.

For better or worse, the French administration took quite seriously the task of making Vietnam an economically productive Southeast Asian province of France. In doing so, the French extended the tentacles of their complicated educational system into the tropics. Under this system, throughout the early part of the century elite young Vietnamese traveled to France and other French colonies, gaining exposure to Western ideas, culture, and people. In addition, the Vietnamese elite were educated at French lycées in Vietnam. Ironically, at the Marie Curie School in Saigon, for instance, young Vietnamese girls were taught Vietnamese as a foreign language. And although many were impressively knowledgeable about which French province produced the finest French wine, they were unable to say which Vietnamese province grew the best rice.

Both Ho Chi Minh, the Nationalist turned Communist revolutionary, and his monarchist-counterpart Bao Dai, the dilettante last emperor of Vietnam, spent many of their early years in France absorbing the culture that would later influence their politics. Perhaps because both ends of the political spectrum of this generation of leaders were educated under the French, elements of French culture have survived Vietnam's tumultuous past few decades: the mildewed colonial villas lining the boulevards of both Hanoi and Saigon, the beret gracefully sported by the occasional man over 50, the excellent French bread hawked on almost every street corner, and the cafés serving espresso-like coffee.

The Americans Arrive

Although most people associate U.S. involvement in Vietnam with the time the first marines landed in Danang in 1965, the American government had been interested in the country since the end of World War II. In 1945 the U.S. government sent agents from the Office of Strategic Services (OSS) to collaborate with the British Special Air Service (SAS) in order to gather information in northern Vietnam on the transfer of power following the withdrawal of the Japanese from Southeast Asia. During the mission, code-named Deer, OSS agents and SAS soldiers went to live in Ho Chi Minh's camp in the northern highlands. Finding Ho on death's door, plagued by malaria and dysentery, the Americans and British treated him and probably saved his life.

The OSS officers were so impressed with Ho that they supplied him with arms and other materials, ultimately recommending that the United States back his Nationalist forces against the French. Ho, in turn, also had respect for the Americans. This relationship, no doubt, prompted Ho to have OSS officers by his side when he signed the declaration of independence of the Democratic Republic of Vietnam in Hanoi's Ba Dinh Square on September 2, 1945.

For political reasons, however, Washington chose to back its long-standing allies, the French, instead of Ho. Rather than alienate Paris by siding with the Vietnamese Nationalists, President Truman supported President Charles de Gaulle's efforts to regain Vietnam. From 1945 to 1954 the U.S. government provided substantial military aid to the French and set the stage for a protracted American presence in Vietnam that would splatter across headlines for the next 20 years.

After the French were officially defeated in 1954, the U.S. government continued its anti-Communist efforts by contributing military advisors who trained and sometimes fought alongside South Vietnamese troops. But it wasn't until 1965 that Uncle Sam's troops landed in Vietnam, bringing billions of dollars in military hardware, thousands of American GIs, and a robust dose of '60s culture. This time, however, the Americans were not there to support the Nationalist forces but rather Ho Chi Minh's arch rival Ngo Dinh Diem, president of a struggling southern regime based in Saigon.

Remnants of the American presence survive today in many forms, even if these don't always inspire the same nostalgic enthusiasm from the Vietnamese as do French bread and espresso. In the south, Zippo lighters still spark cigarettes among the elite. Even more apparent today is the inundation of contemporary American culture, especially in Saigon: for instance, videos of American movies and compact discs of American bands are sold in shops, and American-style bars and restaurants have replaced some of the less competitive noodle shops.

But there is yet another side to America's relationship with Vietnam: throughout the war both Nationalist and Communist Vietnamese leaders always recognized that the United States comprised both a government and a people. To this day they often speak with great appreciation about the Americans who protested the war. Less controversial yet perhaps more telling is that during a 35-year-plus era of strained and nonexistent official relations, American and Vietnamese people-to-people organizations have had long, respectful relationships. These positive legacies of an American influence on Vietnam are what many Vietnamese appreciate and remember. Today, too, they are more than happy to put the past behind them and to begin a new relationship with America.

The Eastern-Bloc Years

After the last overloaded helicopter took off from the roof of the U.S. Embassy in Saigon in 1975, another superpower stepped in: the Soviet Union. For the next 15 years Vietnam was overrun with Volgas—the boxy Russian-made cars—and thousands of Soviet advisers, engineers, and tourists.

This Soviet influx was part of a multibillion-dollar aid package to build up Vietnam's infrastructure and provide education for Vietnamese in Eastern-bloc countries. But the Soviet Union's efforts to help develop Vietnam were largely negated by the drain of two more wars. In 1979 Vietnam invaded Cambodia in response to numerous Khmer Rouge border incursions, and the People's Army of Vietnam effectively ended Pol Pot's reign of terror and the cultural genocide that had claimed more than a million Cambodian lives. China, an ally to the Khmer Rouge, sent the Red Army into the north of Vietnam as a human wave; the People's Army of Vietnam quickly repulsed the Chinese. Tensions festered until Vietnamese forces pulled out of Cambodia in 1989. The pe-

riod of peace that ensued had lasted only two years when, in 1991, with the disintegration of the Soviet Union and the rest of the Eastern bloc nearly complete, Soviet aid dried up and the Vietnamese were left to rebuild their war-torn economy with no major benefactor. Despite this withdrawal and the financial vacuum it left, Hanoi's leaders can be relieved that doi moi, their version of perestroika, has not led to the kind of social upheaval that the Soviets faced.

The Soviets have left Vietnam, and Vietnamese children have stopped shouting "*Lien Xo*" (the Vietnamese word for Soviet person)—as they did with me when I first visited in 1990—at any passing Westerner. Nevertheless the Eastern bloc has left a legacy of its own. Thousands of Vietnamese—educated in everything from civil engineering to commercial banking in Moscow, Budapest, and Havana—speak Russian, Hungarian, and Spanish. Their expertise and international experience have been an important and undervalued tool for helping Vietnam rebuild its infrastructure, schools, and economy after 40 years of devastation. The most visible remnants of the Soviet contribution, however, are the dour, concrete-block apartment buildings in neighborhoods around Hanoi and Saigon. Although probably the least appreciated foreigners to visit Vietnam in the 20th century, the Soviets have also contributed to the current culture that is Vietnam.

The Vietnamese Melting Pot

With its history of invasions, perhaps it was inevitable that Vietnam would end up reflecting a mélange of cultural influences. But by incorporating these foreign elements without compromising its identity, the country has created a culture that is uniquely Vietnamese.

An excellent way to get a sense of this melting pot is simply to explore the country. Walk through the streets of Hanoi and Saigon past the French colonial villas, American- and Russian-built monoliths (most notably the Cultural Friendship Palace, formerly known as the Viet Xo Cultural Palace, in Hanoi), Chinese-style pagodas, and shiny glass-fronted high-rises. Take a trip to Hue to see the old Imperial City, the former home of the Vietnamese emperors. Although it was modeled on the Forbidden City in Beijing, it is actually relatively new: it was built in the early 19th century by the French architect Olivier de Puymanel, who was influenced by that greater builder of French forts, Vauban. Go to Dalat and wander through Emperor Bao Dai's French colonial–style summer palace. The last emperor of Vietnam, Bao Dai had a reputation for dilettantism matched only by his love of French culture—an attitude reflected in this Dalat retreat.

The most distinctive example of Vietnam's cultural syncretism is to be found at the temple of the Caodai sect, in Tay Ninh Province northwest of Saigon. The sect was founded in the Mekong Delta in the 1920s by Ngo Minh Chieu, a civil servant for the French, who claimed to receive revelations from God. Through the French, Chieu was exposed to a variety of Western philosophies. Caodaism was his attempt to create a universal religion based on the major Eastern and Western religions—a fusion of Buddhism, Confucianism, Taoism, Vietnamese spiritualism, Christianity, and Islam.

By the 1950s and '60s the sect had become so strong that it provided an alternative to both the National Liberation Front and the American-backed Saigon regime. As the Caodai strived to maintain its control over the western part of the Mekong Delta, it grew increasingly politically active and heavily armed. After the war, however, the Caodai took on a lower profile and declined in both numbers and firepower. Today the Caodai faithful are concentrated mainly at the home of their Holy See in Tay Ninh, although temples can be found throughout the Mekong Delta and even in the United States and France.

Decorated in a wild array of colors, the massive Holy See has towering ceilings like those found in a cathedral. But the tile floors, no-shoes policy, and monks in white robes give it a distinctly pagoda-like feel. The most telling sign of Caodai's syncretic nature, however, greets you in the bright, open main room: a mural of the Caodai pantheon, which includes such diverse notables as Buddha, Jesus Christ, Muhammad, Sun Yat-sen, Victor Hugo, Joan of Arc, and others. The Caodai believe these leaders have all made great contributions to world culture and that their religious, political, and literary traditions have all been unified in a religion that is neither contradictory nor faddish.

Another example of this mélange of cultures is reflected in the Vietnamese language itself. A history of foreign influences is revealed: wherever you go, look at the signs. For example, many inscriptions on buildings are written in Chinese, as are many of Vietnam's oldest history books. Vietnamese began as a distinct language, with its own indigenous vocabulary and sentence structure but no widespread written form. With the coming of the Chinese and the mandarin educational system, Chinese characters came to be the dominant written language. Throughout this period many Chinese words (known as *Han Viet*, or words derived from Chinese) were integrated into the Vietnamese language (known as *Nom Viet*, those words derived from indigenous Vietnamese roots).

In 1627 a French missionary named Alexandre de Rhodes adapted spoken Vietnamese to Roman script in order to facilitate the conversion of the Vietnamese to Catholicism. Rhodes's system took hold, so Vietnam, unlike most of its neighbors, uses a Roman-based alphabet. But don't be fooled: although the language is recognizable to Westerners, spoken Vietnamese is based on a tonal system not easily reflected in the Roman script. Tones are denoted by accents, which are placed above or below words and provide clues to pronunciation. Be careful: a recognizable script doesn't make learning to say words correctly any easier, and you still may end up insulting someone's mother. For example, the different tones applied to a seemingly simple word like "ba" can have many meanings: daddy, three or third, grandmother or lady, poisoned food, a lure or bait, waste or residue, an embrace or hug, a fold in one's arms, a panacea, tasteless or devoid of nutrition, and exhausted.

Today the language continues to change; most recently there have been efforts to "Vietnamize" Vietnamese. But the difficulty in doing so is manifest in the tenacity of such words as *tam biet*, the Han Viet word for *chao* in Nom Viet (good-bye in English); and *banh ga-to*, the Vietnamese word for Western-style cake, which is derived from the French words for bread and cake—*pain* and *gâteau*. These words reflect the unique synthesis now a part of the Vietnamese language.

One word that is universally understood, however is *ca phe*, from the French word, café, or coffee. Unlike in most other countries in Asia, good coffee is ever-present in Vietnam, served espresso-style in almost every café. A tradition adopted from the French, the café takes different forms in Vietnam—both the familiar French indoor-outdoor style and a Vietnamized version with tables on the sidewalk surrounded by small plastic stools.

Although Vietnamese coffee is reminiscent of the strong, dark brew found in Paris, its method of preparation is uniquely Vietnamese. Order a *ca phe den* (black coffee) and you'll get a filtration device perched on top of a small espresso cup. You must then patiently wait for the coffee to drip through the filter into your cup until you are left with a rich, dark brew. An even better choice is a *cafe sua*, the Vietnamese version of a cappuccino (although the iced version is more like a shake)—coffee mixed with sweet, condensed milk.

While you sip your coffee, watch people go by: elderly women heading to market weighed down by poles bearing baskets filled with fruit; old men on bicycles sporting green pith helmets, remnants of the North Vietnamese army uniform and originally introduced by the French colonialists; and young women on motorbikes wearing T-shirts and jeans, long gloves, and conical hats or traditional *ao dais* (pronounced "ow-*yai*" in the south and "ow *zai*" in the north), the elegant, straight-cut silk gowns worn over flowing pants.

A hybrid of the old and the new, this gown is the perfect emblem for Vietnamese culture. It is said that it was adapted from a Chinese dress called the *cheong sam,* which was modernized in the 1930s by two Vietnamese painters, Cat Tuong and Le Pho, who were influenced by French styles. Tailors took their paintings and produced this new style of gown. The gloves, too, are a Western influence: they came into style in the late 1950s after Madame Ngo Dinh Nhu, the sister-in-law of then President Diem, started wearing them.

It is this ability to synthesize what has been forced upon it that has made Vietnam so resilient. Now, after such a long history of conflict and hardship, the Vietnamese are welcoming the chance to chart their own course. This is why people fantasize about the future so readily and why, finally, they are more excited about driving their Honda Dreams than they are about revisiting a painful history. Although only time will tell, there is little doubt that they will be able to adapt this time around as well.

— Jim Spencer

An amateur anthropologist and international development consultant, Jim Spencer has researched the consequences of Agent Orange in Vietnam, looked at the effects of environmental policy in the Mekong Delta, and worked with NGOs in Vietnam, Cambodia, and Laos. His preferred research methods include slurping a bowl of soup at a street-side noodle stand, enjoying a post–soccer game beer with Vietnamese friends, and test-driving Honda Dream motorbikes.

VIETNAMESE ARCHITECTURE

VIETNAMESE ARCHITECTURE is as eclectic as its culture. Several invading and vanquished civilizations—the Cham, the Chinese, the French, the Americans, and the Russians—have left their marks on the nation in a hodgepodge of contrasting styles.

Historically, the Vietnamese themselves were not big builders. The oldest existing buildings in the country are temples built by the Cham, the Indianized Hindu culture occupying central and south-central Vietnam around the area of present-day Nha Trang from the 4th to the 15th century (many Vietnamese from this region are descendants of the Cham people). Temple sites such as the Po Ro Me Tower and the Ra Thap Towers outside Phan Rang on the central coast are still centers of annual Cham pilgrimages. Khmer influence (descendants of the Kingdom of Angkor, now Cambodia) can be seen in the Kleang and Matoc pagodas at Soc Trang in the Mekong Delta.

Most temples and pagodas around the country reflect the Chinese influence on Vietnamese culture. But because the Vietnamese mainly built using wood, many ancient pagodas and temples "still standing" have actually been rebuilt, often many times. The layout and foundations of the Temple of Literature in Hanoi, for example, may be 900 years old, but many of the wooden structures of the pagoda and entrance gate are recent renovations. In Hue, the citadel surrounding the impressive Imperial City, although modeled on its Chinese counterpart, the Forbidden City in Beijing, is actually relatively modern—it was constructed in the early 19th century by French architect Olivier de Puymanel. Sadly, much of this exquisite palace was destroyed during the 1968 Tet Offensive. Hue also has an incredible collection of tombs—vast and beautiful temples to emperors, constructed in an array of architectural styles reflecting the wealth of Vietnam's royal families. Some structures, such as the 10th-century capital of Hoa Lu, southeast of Hanoi, have been around for centuries.

French architecture has probably had the most pervasive foreign influence on Vietnamese building. In Hanoi you still find such classic French colonial architectural treasures as the Presidential Palace, the National Assembly, St. Joseph's Cathedral, and the exquisite Opera House, modeled on its counterpart in Paris. The city also possesses treasures of various styles that would excite any student of architecture; for example, beautiful art deco blocks seem to step straight out of 1920s Le Corbusier–influenced designs.

In the south much of the French architecture was bulldozed to make way for American-style urban planning, although some of it still exists. Many colonial villas were demolished in the 1960s for what has been irreverently described as "bunker architecture"—buildings reflecting a city under siege. The best example of this in Ho Chi Minh City is the Reunification Palace (formerly the Presidential Palace)—a model of '60s-style building design. However, classic colonial buildings such as the ornate and rather flamboyant Hôtel de Ville (now the People's Committee Building) and the Central Post Office are vivid reminders of the romance of what the French once called the "Paris of the East."

One of the last architectural influences to take hold in Vietnam was, unfortunately, that of the Soviet Union. Apart from an imposing monolith, the Ho Chi Minh Mausoleum in Hanoi, there is very little to commend about most Soviet-era structures, which generally dominate the suburbs of most towns and cities. They usually are residential tower blocks that would not be out of place in a Moscow suburb.

Both Hanoi and Ho Chi Minh City have an amalgam of this overwrought Communist bloc nostalgia, early 20th-century art deco, French colonialist chic, mandarin Chinese elegance, and modern high-rises, all sprinkled with a healthy dose of kitsch. In Hanoi's Old Quarter and Ho Chi Minh City's Cholon district, a certain rhythm and style are at least maintained. But as residents turn to remodeling or rebuilding their homes, chaos has come to rule in the once-uniform 36 Streets (Pho Co) that make up the Old Quarter and the old, Chinese-style houses of Cholon. Plastic and aluminum-framed house exteriors now abut 100-year-old wooden homes or pagodas. Those who don't have the cash to renovate add to their century-old storefronts a hideous blinking neon sign advertising pho or iron smelting or gas cookers.

The race for space and the astronomical rise in real estate values are forcing new builders to head skyward with the funkiest and not always most pleasant of plans. This is also true in the areas outside the old quarters of both cities, where newfound wealth (or, more accurately, newfound nonpoverty) is precipitating a residential construction boom that has even the most avid reformers worried about the new Hanoi and the new Ho Chi Minh City. The soothing ocher-color walls of the French villas are being replaced with cheap concrete, aluminum, and plate glass. The result is houses that look centuries old about three months after they're built. You'll also see these old-looking new houses along the highways throughout the country—just look for the date of construction on top of the house. Only time will tell what a new Vietnam will look like—but no one can deny that the architectural face of the country is rapidly changing.

BOOKS AND MOVIES

Books

Some of the most comprehensive histories of the Vietnam War are David Halberstam's *The Best and the Brightest,* Stanley Karnow's *Vietnam: A History,* Neil Sheehan's *A Bright Shining Lie,* and George C. Herring's *America's Longest War: The United States and Vietnam, 1950–1975.* Marilyn B. Young's *The Vietnam Wars: 1945–1990* and Frances FitzGerald's *Fire in the Lake* provide histories of the war from both the American and Vietnamese perspectives. Other insightful accounts of the war include Jonathan Schell's *The Real War* and Michael Herr's *Dispatches.* Nayan Chanda's *Brother Enemy: The War After the War* looks at the close of the Vietnam War and Vietnam's emerging conflicts with both Cambodia and China throughout the 1980s.

Several moving personal narratives (some fictionalized) have been written about the war, including *A Rumour of War* by Philip Caputo, *In Pharaoh's Army* by Tobias Wolff, *Nam* by Mark Baker, *Fields of Fire* by James Webb, *Chickenhawk* by Robert Mason, and *The Things They Carried* and *Going After Cacciato* by Tim O'Brien. A more recent account of the war is Robert McNamara's *In Retrospect: The Tragedy and Lessons of Vietnam. From Both Sides Now: The Poetry of the Vietnam War and Its Aftermath* includes poems by both Americans and Vietnamese. *The Vietnam Reader* is an anthology of fiction, nonfiction, and poetry relating to the Vietnam War. An in-depth treatise on how the Vietnam War uprooted the American psyche is found in *Apocalypse Then: American Intellectuals and the Vietnam War* by Robert Tomes. For images of the war look for *Requiem,* a moving collection of war pictures by photographers who died at work in Indochina between 1954 and 1989.

Tom Mangold's *The Tunnels of Cu Chi* describes the Vietcong movement based in the tunnels around Cu Chi. *PAVN: People's Army of Vietnam* by Pike Douglas is a history of the war from the North Vietnamese point of view. Michael Lanning's *Inside the VC and the NVA* examines the workings of the North Vietnamese army and the

Vietcong. *When Heaven and Earth Changed Places* is Le Ly Hayslip's story of her life before, during, and after the Vietnam War. Truong Nhu Tang's *A Vietcong Memoir* is a narrative of the war as told by a former member of the Vietnamese National Liberation Front. Bao Ninh's novel *The Sorrow of War* chronicles hardships endured by a North Vietnamese soldier. Diem Bui's *In the Jaws of History* offers insight into how the Vietnamese saw Americans. Kiem Do's *Counterpart* brings to light little-known events of the South Vietnamese role at the end of the Vietnam War.

For a history of the French role in Vietnam, read Bernard Fall's *Street Without Joy* and Jules Roy's *The Battle of Dienbienphu.* Graham Green's literary classic *The Quiet American* is a prophetic tale of America's involvement in Vietnam. *The Lover,* by Marguerite Duras, is a fictionalized autobiographical tale of a French girl coming of age in 1930s Indochina.

Joachim Schliesinger's *Hill Tribes of Vietnam* gives insight into Vietnam's hill tribes. *Among the Tribes of Southeast Vietnam and Laos* is an English translation of French explorer Captain P. Cupet's encounters with hill tribes at the end of the 19th century.

To learn more about contemporary Vietnam read Henry Kamm's *Dragon Ascending: Vietnam and the Vietnamese* and Neil Sheehan's *After the War Was Over: Hanoi and Saigon.* Robert Templer's *Shadows and Wind* examines Vietnam's cultural transition through the '90s into an emerging economy under doi moi. *The Sacred Willow,* by Duong Van Mai Elliot, follows four generations of the author's family, beginning with her great-grandfather, a mandarin in the Imperial Court. Andrew X. Pham's memoir *Catfish and Mandala: A Two-Wheeled Voyage Through the Landscape and Memory of Vietnam* traces his bicycle journey through the homeland he left as a boy when his family fled to America following the Vietnam War.

Look for an account of traveling through Vietnam by train in Paul Theroux's *The Great Railway Bazaar.* For a sense of Vietnam before you go, take a look at *Viet-*

nam: Portraits and Landscapes, featuring the stunning photography of Peter Steinhauer, or *Passage to Vietnam: Through the Eyes of Seventy Photographers,* which is also available on CD-ROM.

Two literary anthologies that address postwar Vietnam are *The Other Side of Heaven: Postwar Fiction by Vietnamese and American Writers* and *Aftermath: An Anthology of Post-Vietnam Fiction.* Robert Olen Butler's Pulitzer prize–winning *A Good Scent from a Strange Mountain* is a collection of short stories about Vietnamese living in America.

Cambodia: Report from a Stricken Land, by Henry Kamm, is a perceptive, angry account of the last 30 years—how the world betrayed Cambodia as its leaders picked it clean. A terrific guide to Angkor Wat, complete with full-color photographs, maps, timelines, and diagrams, is *Angkor: Heart of an Empire* by Bruno Dagens. *Swimming to Cambodia,* written by actor Spalding Grey about his experience filming *The Killing Fields,* captures the feel and flavor of the country.

Movies

Apocalypse Now (1979) is Francis Ford Coppola's powerful look at the Vietnam War based on Joseph Conrad's *Heart of Darkness*; it stars Martin Sheen, Marlon Brando, and Dennis Hopper. Oliver Stone's *Platoon* (1986), with Tom Berenger, Willem Dafoe, and Charlie Sheen, is a harrowing, first-person tale of a young soldier's experience in the war. Stone's *Born on the Fourth of July* (1989) tells the stirring story of Ron Kovic, played by Tom Cruise, a gung ho soldier who is paralyzed during the war and becomes an antiwar activist. Brian de Palma's *Casualties of War* (1989) focuses on two soldiers in the same platoon, Michael J. Fox and Sean Penn, who battle over moral issues. *The Deer Hunter* (1978) is a Michael Cimino film about three steelworkers from Pennsylvania who go off to fight in Vietnam; it stars Robert De Niro, John Savage, Meryl Streep, and Christopher Walken. Stanley Kubrick's *Full Metal Jacket* (1987) takes an unblinking look at the realities of the Vietnam War from the perspective of a U.S. army journalist. In Randall Wallace's *We Were Soldiers* (2002), Mel Gibson plays a colonel leading his soldiers in the first major, and ultimately bloody, battle of the Vietnam War. *The Green Berets* (1968)

is a clichéd but classic movie with John Wayne as a Green Beret. *Hamburger Hill* (1987), a John Irvin film, follows a group of infantrymen from training to combat.

Barry Levinson's *Good Morning, Vietnam* (1987) takes a more humorous look at the Vietnam War era, with Robin Williams as a U.S. Army radio DJ. *Heaven & Earth* (1993), another Oliver Stone film about Vietnam, portrays the odyssey of a young Vietnamese woman, Le Lyn, from 1953 through the war and after in America. Eric Weston's *The Iron Triangle* (1989), starring Beau Bridges, attempts to show the conflict from both the Vietnamese and American sides.

For an inside look at the making of *Apocalypse Now,* see the documentary *Hearts of Darkness: A Filmmaker's Apocalypse* (1991). Abill Couturie, in his documentary about the Vietnam War, *Dear America: Letters Home from Vietnam* (1987), uses newsreels, amateur footage, and letters read by Robert De Niro, Sean Penn, and others to portray soldiers' experiences. The *War at Home* (1979) is a documentary about the antiwar movement. Barbara Sonneborn's *Regret to Inform* (1998) documents the tragedy of war as seen from the viewpoint of Vietnamese and American women.

Martin Scorsese's disturbing *Taxi Driver* (1976) stars Robert De Niro as Travis Bickle, an alienated Vietnam veteran. *Birdy* (1984), a film by Alan Parker, stars Nicholas Cage and Matthew Modine as a Vietnam veteran suffering post-traumatic stress disorder. Emilio Estevez stars in his directorial debut, *The War at Home* (1996), as a son pitted against his father (real-life father Martin Sheen), a Vietnam veteran haunted by his memories. *Alamo Bay* (1985), a Louis Malle film starring Ed Harris, is a revealingly candid story of a Vietnam veteran whose livelihood is threatened by immigrant Vietnamese fishermen on the Texas Gulf Coast. In Hal Ashby's *Coming Home* (1978), Jane Fonda star as a career soldier's wife who falls in love with a wheelchair-bound veteran played by Jon Voight.

The Quiet American (1958), starring Audie Murphy, is Joseph L. Mankiewicz's cinematic portrayal of Graham Greene's classic and prophetic book; a 2002 remake of this movie by Phillip Noyce stars Michael Caine, Brendan Fraser, and Hai Yen. *The Lover* (1991), a Jean-Jacques Annaud film based on the Marguerite Duras book, is the tale of a young French woman coming of age in colonial Vietnam and her relationship with her Chinese lover. Régis Wargnier's *Indochine* (1992), starring Catherine Deneuve, is another film set in Vietnam during the French colonial era; it showcases the beautiful scenery of North Vietnam.

Postwar Vietnam and the story of people coping with the ruin at home is the focus of Michael Rubbo's *Sad Song of Yellow Skin* (1970). Le Manh Thich and Do Kanh Toan's *Returning to Ngo Thuy* (1998) pays tribute to the spirit of the women of Ngo Thuy 30 years after they fought in the war. Le Duc Tien's *A Quiet Town* (1986) pokes fun at hypocrisy and greed.

Contemporary French-Vietnamese filmmaker Tran Anh Hung's cinematographically beautiful *The Scent of Green Papaya* (1993) follows the life of a young female servant in Saigon. For a look at present-day Ho Chi Minh City and Hanoi, see Tran Anh Hung's *Cyclo* (1995), which por-

trays the rough and violent life of a cyclo driver, and *The Vertical Ray of the Sun* (2000), the story of three sisters' everyday lives. *Three Seasons* (1999) is American-Vietnamese writer-director Tony Bui's excellent debut film; it weaves together three different stories in modern-day Vietnam, including a war veteran's (Harvey Keitel) search for his daughter.

Cambodia's troubles and America's involvement in Southeast Asia are examined in *The Killing Fields* (1984), journalist Sydney Schanberg's tale of the search for his Cambodian aide, Dith Prahn, who was left behind when Pnomh Penh fell to the Khmer Rouge in 1975. As a follow-up to this movie, the film version of Spalding Gray's *Swimming to Cambodia* (1987) is a must-see. Gray weaves poetry, humor, political discussion, and personal confessions into an entertaining, insightful monologue about his small role in *The Killing Fields*, U.S. military aggression, and the situation in Cambodia.

VIETNAMESE VOCABULARY

In the mid-17th century, the Vietnamese language, which had been based on Chinese characters, was Romanized by the French Jesuit, Alexandre de Rhodes. This change made the tonal language easier for Westerners to read, but not much easier to pronounce. Vietnamese has six tones, which can significantly change the meaning of a word spelled the same way. Within a certain context, however, Vietnamese people will understand what you are trying to say even if you get the tones wrong. A bit of body language also helps get your point across.

Keep in mind that vocabulary and pronunciation vary from region to region. For example, a spoon in northern Vietnam is a *thìa* but it is a *muỗng* in the south. The soft "d" and soft "gi" are pronouced like a "z" in the north but change to "y" in the south.

Also remember that there is an "honorific" system of address, so what you call people depends on their relation to you. There are many specific titles of address, but the five listed below are all you need in a pinch. Use *ông* for an older man, *anh* for a younger man, and *em* for a boy. Use *bà* for an older woman, *cô* for a younger woman, and *em* for a girl.

Words and Phrases

	English	Vietnamese	Pronunciation
Basics			
	I	Tôi	doy
	We	Chúng tôi	choong doy
	Yes/No	Có/Không	caw/kawm
	Please	Làm ơn	lamb un
	Thank you	Cám ơn	cam un
	That's all right	Không có chi	kawm caw chee
	Excuse me, sorry	Xin lỗi	seen loy
	Hello	Xin chào	seen chow
	Goodbye	Tạm biệt	tom be-it
	Mr. (older man)	Ông	awm
	Mrs. (older woman)	Bà	bah
	Miss (younger woman)	Cô	co (like co-op)
	Mr. (young man)	Anh	ine / un(s)
	Young person	Em	em
	Pleased to meet you	Hân hạnh được gặp (ông)	haan hine dook gup (title)
	How are you?	(Ông) có khoẻ không?	(ông) caw Kway kawm?
	Very well, thanks	Khoẻ, cám ơn	kway, cam un
	And you?	Còn (ông)?	cawn (ông)?
Numbers			
	one	một	moat
	two	hai	hi
	three	ba	bah
	four	bốn	bown

five	năm	num
six	sáu	sow (like cow)
seven	bảy	by
eight	tám	tom
nine	chín	chin
ten	mười	moy
eleven	mười một	moy moat
twelve	mười hai	moy hi
thirteen	mười ba	moy bah
fourteen	mười bốn	moy bown
fifteen	mười năm	moy num
sixteen	mười sáu	moy sow
seventeen	mười bảy	muoi by
eighteen	mười tám	moy tom
nineteen	mười chín	moy chin
twenty	hai mươi	hi moy
twenty-one	hai mốt	hi moat
thirty	ba mươi	bah moy
forty	bốn mươi	bown moy
fifty	năm mươi	num moy
sixty	sáu mươi	sow moy
seventy	bảy mươi	by moy
eighty	tám mươi	tom moy
ninety	chín mươi	chin moy
one hundred	một trăm	moat chum
one thousand	một nghìn (n)	moat nyin
	một ngàn (s)	moat nyan
one million	một triệu	moat chew

Colors

black	đen	den
blue	xanh	sine
brown	nâu	no
green	xanh lá cây	sine la kay
orange	cam	cahm
pink	hồng	hawm
purple	tím	teem
red	đỏ	daw
white	trắng	chaang
yellow	vàng	vang

Days of the Week

Sunday	chủ nhật	chu nyat
Monday	thứ hai	two hi
Tuesday	thứ ba	two ba
Wednesday	thứ tư	two tu
Thursday	thứ năm	two num
Friday	thứ sáu	two sow
Saturday	thứ bảy	two by

Months

January	tháng một	tang moat
February	tháng hai	tang hi
March	tháng ba	tang ba

April	tháng tư	tang tu
May	tháng năm	tang num
June	tháng sáu	tang sow
July	tháng bảy	tang by
August	tháng tám	tang tom
September	tháng chín	tang chin
October	tháng mười	tang moy
November	tháng mười một	tang moy moat
December	tháng mười hai	tang moy hi

Useful Phrases

Do you speak English?	(Ông) có nói tiếng Anh không?	(ông) caw noy ting ine kawm?
I don't speak Vietnamese	Tôi không biết nói tiếng Việt	doy kawm byet noy teng Viet
I don't understand	Tôi không hiểu	doy kawm hue
I understand	Tôi hiểu	doy hue
I don't know	Tôi không biết	doy kawm byet
I'm American/British	Tôi là người Mỹ/Anh	doy la noy mee/ine
What's your name?	Tên (ông) là gì	ten (ong) la zee (southern=yee)
My name is . . .	Tôi tên là	doy ten la . . .
How old are you?	(Ông) bao nhiêu tuổi	bow nyoo toy
What time is it?	Mấy giò rồi?	may zuh zoy (n) may yuh roy (s)
How?	Bằng cách nào?	bong cack now?
When?	Bao giờ?	bow zuh? (n) bow yuh? (s)
Yesterday	Hôm qua	home kwa
Today	Hôm nay	home ny (like hi)
Tomorrow	Ngày mai	ny my
This morning/	Sáng nay/	sang nye
afternoon	trưa nay	chewa nye
Tonight	Đêm nay/tối ňay	dem nye/doy nye
Why?	Tại sao?	tie sow (like cow)
Who?	Ai?	eye
Where?	Ở đâu	uh doe
Where is	. . . ở đâu?	uh doe
Train station	Ga tàu / Ga xe lửa	gah tow (n) gah say luh-ah (s)
Bus station	Bến xe	ben say
Bus stop	Trạm xe buýt	chum say boot
Airport	Sân bay	sun bye
Post office	Bưu điện	boo dien
Bank	Ngân hàng	nun hang
Hotel	Khách sạn	kack san
Temple	Chùa	chew-a
Restaurant	Nhà hàng	nya hang

Store	Cửa hàng	kua hang
Market	Chợ	chuh
Museum	Bảo tàng	bow taang
Art museum	Bảo tàng mỹ thuật	bow taang me twut
Gallery	Phòng tranh	fowm chine
Theater	Nhà hát	nya hat
Movie theater	Rạp cine	zap see-nay
Beach	Bãi biển	bye be-in
Lake	Hồ	hoe
Park	Công viên	cowm vee-in
Street	Phố (n)/Đường (s)	foe/dooahng
Hospital	Bệnh viện	ben vee-in
Telephone	Điện thoại	dee-in twai
Restroom	Nhà vệ sinh/toilette	nya vay sing
Here/there	ở đây/đằng kia	uh day/dang kee-uh
Left/right	trái/phải	chy/fye (as in 'bye')
Is it far?	Có xa không	caw sah kowm
Go	Đi	dee
Stop	Dừng lại	zoong lie
Slow	Chậm chậm	chum chum
Straight ahead	Thẳng	tang
I'd like . . .	Tôi muốn . . .	doy mun . . .
a room	một phòng	moat fong
the key	chìa khóa	cheah kwa
a newspaper	tờ báo	tuh bow
magazine	tạp chí	tup chee
a stamp	con tem	cawn tem
I'd like to buy . . .	Tôi muốn mua . . .	doy mun moo-a . . .
cigarettes	thuốc lá	twook la
matches	diêm (n)	zee-im
	bật lửa (s)	but luh-ah
dictionary	từ điển	tuh dien
soap	xà phòng/xà bông (s)	sa fong/sa bowm
city map	bản đồ thành phố	ban doe tine foe
envelopes	phong bì	fawm bee
writing paper	giấy viết thơ	zay vee-it tuh
		yay vit tuh (s)
postcard	bưu thiếp	boo tip
How much is it?	Bao nhiêu?	bow nyew
Expensive/cheap	Đắt/rẻ	dut/zay /ray (s)
A little/lot	ít/nhiều	eat/nyew
More/less	Nhiều hơn/ít hơn	nyew huhn/eat huhn
Too much/enough	Nhiều quá/đủ rồi	nyew kwa/
		doo zoy
		doo roy (s)
Too expensive	Đắt quá	dut kwa
Change money	Đổi tiền	doy tee-in
I am ill	Tôi bị ốm	doy be awm

Call a doctor	Gọi bác sỹ	goy back see
Help!	Cứu tôi!	ku doy
Stop!	Dừng lại!	zoong lie
Fire!	Cháy nhà!	chay nyah
Caution!/look out!	Coi chừng!	coy chung

Dining Out

A bottle of	Chai	chye
A glass of	Cốc (n)/Ly (s)	cup/lee
Bill/Check please	Tính tiền	ting tee-in
Bowl	Bát (n)/Tô (s)	baht/toe
Bread	Bánh mỳ	bine mee
Breakfast	Ăn sáng	ahn sang
Butter	Bơ	buh
Chopsticks	Đũa	doo-a
Delicious	Ngon	nawn
Dinner	Bữa tối	booa doy
Eat	Ăn cơm	ahn come
Fork	Dĩa	zee-a
Hot/cold	Nóng/lạnh	nawm/line
Thirsty	Khát nước	cat nooc
Fish sauce	Nước mắm	nooc mum
Knife	Dao	zow
Lunch	Ăn trưa	ahn chewa
Menu	Thực đơn	took duhn
Napkin	Giấy ăn	zay ahn/yay ahn (s)
Pepper	Tiêu	tyew
Plate	Đĩa	dee-a
Please give me . . .	Cho xin . . .	chaw seen . . .
Rice	Cơm	come
Salt	Muối	moo-ee
Shrimp paste	Mắm tôm	mum tome
Spicy	Cay	kai (as in eye)
Too spicy!	Cay quá	kai (as in eye) kwa
Spoon	Thìa (n)/Muỗng (s)	tee-ah/moong
Sugar	Đường	dooahng
Sweet	Ngọt	naught
Bon appetit	Chúc ăn ngon	chook ahn nawn
Bottoms up!	Trăm phần trăm	chum fun chum
I am a vegetarian	Tôi ăn chay	doy ahn chai (as in eye)
I am hungry	Tôi đói	doy doy
I cannot eat . . .	Tôi không biết ăn . . .	doy cawn bee-it ahn . . .
To your health	Chúc sức khoẻ	chook soo kway

MENU GUIDE

	Vietnamese	English

Soups

	Vietnamese	English
	Canh	Soup, broth
	Canh chua	Sour soup
	Bún	Round rice noodles
	Bún Riêu	Freshwater crab soup
	Cháo	Congee, or rice porridge
	Cháo cá	Congee with fish
	Phở	Flat rice noodle soup
	Phở bò	Beef noodle soup
	Phở gà	Chicken noodle soup
	Phở xào	Fried rice noodles
	Miến	Vermicelli
	Miến lươn	Vermicelli eel soup
	Miến gà	Vermicelli chicken soup
	Mỳ ăn liền	Instant noodles

Salads/Các loại gỏi

Gỏi đu đủ xanh	Green papaya salad
Gỏi ngó sen	Lotus stem salad
Nộm hoa chuối	Banana flower salad

Fish and Seafood/Đồ biển

Cá	Fish
Cá chép	Carp
Cá thu	Cod
Cá trê	Catfish
Cua	Crab
Ếch	Frog
Lươn	Eel
Mực	Squid
Tôm	Shrimp
Tôm hùm	Lobster

Meat/Thịt

Bít tết	Beefsteak
Bò	Beef
Chả	Grilled meat patties
Chó	Dog
Dê	Goat
Giò	Processed meat roll
Heo(s)	Pork
Lợn (n)	Pork
Ốc	Snail
Rắn	Snake
Sóc	Squirrel
Sườn	Pork ribs

Poultry/Chim

Chim cút	Quail
Gà	Chicken
Trứng	Egg

ốp-la/rán	fried
ốp lếp	omelet
luộc	boiled
Vịt	Duck

Vegetables/Các loại rau

Bắp cải	Cabbage
Cà chua	Tomato
Cà pháo	Baby eggplant
Cà tím	Eggplant
Đậu đũa	String bean
Đậu phụ (n) Tàu hũ (s)	Tofu
Giá	Bean sprouts
Gừng	Ginger
Hành	Onion
Khoai	Potato
Lạc	Peanuts
Măng	Bamboo shoots
Nấm	Mushroom
Ớt	Chili pepper
Rau cải	Mustard greens
Rau dền	Amaranth
Rau muống	Water convolvulus
Su hào	Kohlrabi
Súp lơ	Cauliflower
Tỏi	Garlic
Xả	Lemongrass

Methods of preparation

Chiên	Fried
Hấp	Steamed
Kho	Braised, with caramelized sauce
Kho tộ	Claypot
Lẩu	Steamboat
Luộc	Boiled
Nhúng dấm	Dipped in hot vinegar
Nướng	Grilled
Quay	Roasted
Rút xương	Filleted
Sống	Raw
Xào	Sauteed
Xốt	Sauce

For example: Gà xào nấm = chicken sauteed with mushrooms
Cá hấp bia = fish steamed with beer
Đậu phụ xốt cà chua = tofu with tomato sauce

Fruit/Hoa Quả

Cam	Orange
Chanh	Lemon
Chôm chôm	Rambutan
Chuối	Banana
Đu Đủ	Papaya
Dưa hấu	Watermelon
Dừa	Coconut

Dứa	Pineapple
Khế	Starfruit
Măng cụt	Mangosteen
Mít	Jackfruit
Na	Custard apple
Nhãn	Longan
Sầu riêng	Durian
Táo	Apple
Thanh Long	Dragon Fruit
Vải	Lychee
Vú Sữa	Milkfruit
Xoài	Mango

Miscellaneous delicacies

Bánh chưng (n)/Bánh tét (s)	Stuffed sticky rice cake
Bánh cuốn	Rice noodle crepe
Bánh xèo	Meat & shrimp crepe
Gỏi cuốn	Summer rolls
Nem (n)/Chả giò (s)	Spring rolls
Xôi	Sticky rice

Drinks/Đồ uống

Bia	Beer
Có đá	With ice
Không đá	Without ice
Nước cam	Orange juice
Nước chanh	Lemonade
Nước dừa	Coconut milk
Nước khoáng	Mineral Water
Nước	Water
Rượu Vang	Wine
Rượu	Alcohol
Sinh tố	Smoothie
Sô-đa chanh	Soda-water lemonade
Sô-đa	Soda
Sữa tươi	Fresh milk
Chè/Trà (s)	Tea
Trà đá	Iced tea
Cà phê	Coffee
Cà phê đen	Black coffee
Cà phê sữa	Coffee with sweetened milk
Cà phê đá	Iced coffee

Dessert/Tráng Miêng

Bánh flan/kem caramen	Flan
Bánh ngọt	Sweet cakes
Chè đậu đen	Black-bean compote
Chè đậu xanh	Green-bean compote
Chè thập cẩm	Assorted compote
Kem	Ice cream
Kẹo	Candy
Sữa chua	Yogurt

INDEX

NOTES

Fodor's Key to the Guides

America's guidebook leader publishes guides for every kind of traveler.
Check out our many series and find your perfect match.

Fodor's Gold Guides
America's favorite travel-guide series offers the most detailed insider reviews of hotels, restaurants, and attractions in all price ranges, plus great background information, smart tips, and useful maps.

Fodor's Road Guide USA
Big guides for a big country—the most comprehensive guides to America's roads, packed with places to stay, eat, and play across the U.S.A. Just right for road warriors, family vacationers, and cross-country trekkers.

COMPASS AMERICAN GUIDES
Stunning guides from top local writers and photographers, with gorgeous photos, literary excerpts, and colorful anecdotes. A must-have for culture mavens, history buffs, and new residents.

Fodor's CITYPACKS
Concise city coverage with a foldout map. The right choice for urban travelers who want everything under one cover.

Fodor's EXPLORING GUIDES
Hundreds of color photos bring your destination to life. Lively stories lend insight into the culture, history, and people.

Fodor's POCKET GUIDES
For travelers who need only the essentials. The best of Fodor's in pocket-size packages for just $9.95.

Fodor's To Go
Credit-card–size, magnetized color microguides that fit in the palm of your hand—perfect for "stealth" travelers or as gifts.

Fodor's FLASHMAPS
Every resident's map guide. 60 easy-to-follow maps of public transit, parks, museums, zip codes, and more.

Fodor's CITYGUIDES
Sourcebooks for living in the city: Thousands of in-the-know listings for restaurants, shops, sports, nightlife, and other city resources.

Fodor's AROUND THE CITY WITH KIDS
68 great ideas for family days, recommended by resident parents. Perfect for exploring in your own backyard or on the road.

Fodor's ESCAPES
Fill your trip with once-in-a-lifetime experiences, from ballooning in Chianti to overnighting in the Moroccan desert. These full-color dream books point the way.

Fodor's FYI
Get tips from the pros on planning the perfect trip. Learn how to pack, fly hassle-free, plan a honeymoon or cruise, stay healthy on the road, and travel with your baby.

Fodor's Languages for Travelers
Practice the local language before hitting the road. Available in phrase books, cassette sets, and CD sets.

Karen Brown's Guides
Engaging guides to the most charming inns and B&Bs in the U.S.A. and Europe, with easy-to-follow inn-to-inn itineraries.

Baedeker's Guides
Comprehensive guides, trusted since 1829, packed with A–Z reviews and star ratings.

At bookstores everywhere.   www.fodors.com/books